DUBLIN
in
REBELLION

A DIRECTORY 1913–1923

To Pam

Gra anois agus go deo

DUBLIN

in

REBELLION

A DIRECTORY 1913—1923

JOSEPH E.A. CONNELL JNR

THE LILLIPUT PRESS • DUBLIN

First published in 2006 by
Dublin City Council in
Where's Where in Dublin
A Directory of Historic Locations 1913–1923
Dublin City Library & Archive

© Joseph Connell, 2006, 2009

This revised 2009 edition
Dublin in Rebellion
A Directory 1913-1923
is published by
The Lilliput Press, Arbour Hill, Dublin 7

All photographs from Dublin City Archive Postcard Collection
courtesy of Seámus Kearns
Map of Dublin (p. 32) in 1910 courtesy of National Library of Ireland

ISBN 978 1 84351 137 3

Design and origination: Anú Design, Tara

Printed in England by Athenaeum Press Ltd, Tyne and Wear

Contents

Acknowledgments

I must thank my parents for everything; without them I would have had no such love for Ireland. And, of course, my brothers and sister and their families have supported me at all times.

Mary Mackey of the Irish National Archives has been most helpful and has given me wonderful direction as well as being very generous with her time.

Lisa Dolan and Stephen MacEoin of the Military Archives at Cathal Brugha Barracks provided me with their assistance and I am very appreciative.

The superb illustrations are from the postcard collection of Seámus Kearns, and my sincere thanks go to him for his kindness in providing these.

I am extremely grateful to Anthony Tierney for his advice and encouragement.

Lorcan Collins kindly let me lead his 1916 Easter Rising Tour on occasion and I particularly thank him for the opportunity.

Antony Farrell and all at The Lilliput Press inspired and revitalized me on innumerable occasions. Lilliput's editor, Fiona Dunne, especially deserves my sincerest gratitude for her counsel and efforts.

As I am technologically and computer incompetent, I am most thankful to Lou Yovin for his kind assistance.

I have always been welcomed throughout Ireland with the greatest kindness and hospitality, and I thank everyone with whom I've spoken. I assure you that those feelings are returned with the deepest and most lasting affection.

Those souls who have helped and encouraged me are too numerous to mention and I thank them all; everyone I asked always gave me assistance and direction and all heartened me when I needed that most. At the risk of offending someone I omit I must especially mention Pam Boyd, Áine Broy, Dr Mary Clark, Bob Clarke, Finbar Collins, C.B. Connell, Revd Paul Connell, Thomas O. Duffy, Kerry Edwards, Bob Fuquea, Barbara Hollandsworth, Grainne Áine Hollandsworth, Peggy Keating, Desmond Long, D.R. O'Connor Lysaght, Peter McDermott, Revd Anthony Mulderry, Donal Ó hUallachain, Gregory O'Connor, Pól Ó Murchú and Seán Spellissy.

And, always, Pam Brewster for all things.

Preface

Oliver St John Gogarty was a brilliant poet, raconteur, surgeon and member of the Irish Seanad. A roommate of James Joyce, he lived through the early twentieth century, always keeping an eye out for the outlandish in Ireland. In 1937 he published *As I Was Going Down Sackville Street*, a delightful commentary on the lives and times that exemplified Dublin of the period.

Whenever I walked Sackville Street (O'Connell Street) or any of Dublin's streets I wondered just what secrets were held there and within the buildings, rooms and halls that line those streets. I found there the ghosts of men and women who lived in those momentous times of rebellion. That humanized those who participated in the 'revolutionary' years between 1913 and 1923.

Certainly there is hero-worship in such a compendium. I freely admit to beginning this work as a means of getting to better know the participants of that time. I wanted to know where they worked and dreamed, where they were successful and not, and where they lived and where many died. What began as a study of their surroundings evolved into a complete account of the locations of that epic time and as much as I could of the people. To paraphrase Theodore Mommsen: 'History is neither made nor written without passion.' I am no historian, but it was easy to see the passion of those who participated in the times.

Each section of the book is arranged alphabetically to allow the easiest access to the information. The Address section is alphabetized by street and then chronologically within an address. The Garrison Lists of participants in the Rising Appendix (V) are also arranged alphabetically so one can find a name and that person's location of participation in the Rising as easily as possible. One should freely use the Index to move from one location to another, and to place a participant in all the sites listed. Every effort has been made to place individuals in their most important positions, and any errors or omissions are mine alone. It is not intended that the book should be read from cover to cover. It was not written that way and I wish it to be an awakening for the reader as it has been for me. This makes for a book one can read for just a few minutes or into which one can delve for hours. Any time spent will allow the reader to begin a process of getting to know those whose dedication, industry and life's blood made modern Ireland.

The Rising and the War of Independence were, like all revolutionary endeavours, a gamble. Dedicated men and women who believed that any effort was better than none launched them, but their plans of operations had not been, and could not have been, fully worked out. All revolutionaries extemporize – it is only their determination to be revolutionaries that is fixed. The participants left few notes and still fewer 'minutes' of meetings. Only afterwards did they write down their thoughts and try to memorialize events. However, though there are many primary source documents, and they are readily available, the recollections of those who took part differ markedly.

A good illustration is found in the organizational meeting that led to the founding of the Irish Volunteers, the central military unit of the Rising, as noted in the description of that meeting held in Wynn's Hotel, 35–37 Abbey Street Lower, on 11 November 1913. Even those most instrumental in calling the meeting – Bulmer Hobson and The O'Rahilly – could not agree either on those who attended or those who were invited.

The history of the period is replete with stories such as that and this book is an attempt to give the reader the fullest information available by noting where such events took place, the circumstances, and the most comprehensive lists of parties involved. Use was made of as many primary sources as possible – particularly newspapers of the time, journal articles that appeared very shortly after the events, official records and correspondence of the participants. Contrasts are made between current accounts of events and those that appeared in later sources.

Because of his special prominence during the War of Independence and the Civil War, there is an Appendix (II) devoted to locations used by Michael Collins. His presence was ubiquitous from 1917 to 1923 and he often appears in the main body of addresses, but I believe his activities, offices and the locations of those who were particularly connected with him merit an Appendix of their own.

I also wanted to include all the women and their stories I could find. Prior to the Rising, women worked a ninety-hour week (men: seventy hours) and received an average of 5 shillings' pay (men: 14 shillings). Life was terribly hard for all in Dublin in those years, but especially so for women. James Connolly aptly described them as 'slaves to the slaves'. Because of the labour shortage caused by World War I, many women entered the salaried workforce for the first time, and this had a consciousness-raising effect – they became much more politicized.

The commitment of women before, during and after the Rising helped to bring the Irish nation to support the separatist movement. The widows of those executed in Kilmainham Gaol after the Rising did more to bring attention to the independence movement than any other group. The widows and female relatives of the captives filled the voids in leadership and ensured Irish independence did not die with their loved ones.

Discussion of the women of the period usually focuses on the influence and activities of Countess Markievicz, Hanna Sheehy-Skeffington as well as Kathleen

Clark and other widows of the executed Rising leaders. While these women were the most noted activists of the time, mothers and wives who did not achieve public or celebrity status played an enormous role in changing popular opinion – they irrevocably changed the role for Irishwomen, albeit a role that is still to be completely achieved. THEY converted the nation. THEY pushed their families toward nationalist beliefs.

During the War of Independence women were primarily responsible for the propaganda that helped mould opinion to respect the martyrdom of the 1916 leaders. Women created a revolutionary fervour throughout the countryside, yet they were far removed from the decision-making levels of the Dáil and other organizations. Women were not put forward for Cabinet or other high offices, though there were many qualified candidates (Countess Markievicz was the only exception). They became judges, educators, writers, social and labour activists, freedom fighters, spies, county council officials, but seldom major politicians. Leaders such as Áine Ceannt, Helena Molony, Marie Perolz, Winifred Carney and so many others were ignored or relegated to lesser political roles, or were appointed to the Seanad, bypassing election to the Dáil.

Women became increasingly important in the pursuit of Irish independence. They came from every walk of life, asserting their claim to be part of the shaping of the nation and determining a share in the future society. They joined the male-dominated organizations of the period – particularly the Home Rule Party, Sinn Féin and the Gaelic League – but also started their own organizations. Often they had to do so in order to have a role in their operation and influence in their policies. The Women's Social and Political Union, the Irish Women's Workers' Union, Charlotte Despard's Women's Freedom League, Cumann na mBan, the Irish Women's Franchise League, the League of Women Delegates, the Women's Prisoners' Defence League and many others all contributed greatly to the independence, labour and franchise movements of the time.

Though Michael Collins worked there, Kathleen Clarke, widow of Tom, and Sorcha MacMahon, who was in the GPO during the Rising, primarily ran the Irish National Aid and Volunteers' Dependents' Fund. Members of Cumann na mBan were its foremost activists, collecting and disbursing its funds. And its women operatives were the principal means used to contact men and to pass along messages from the IRB throughout the country.

In the Irish Civil War, Republican women had to use every means at their disposal to convey their message about the fate and conditions of Republican prisoners. Those imprisoned in Kilmainham Gaol or Mountjoy Prison or the other prisons throughout the country left a history of hunger strikes and escapes. Those who were not imprisoned led countless demonstrations that attacked the censorship of the press. As he was in addressing most things during the period, James Connolly was correct here, too: 'If none of the men turn out, I'll go with the women.'

The participants did not leave minutes, but they left some of the most forward-looking and socially conscious documents of the era. In addition, the statements of those who were executed following the Rising, as well as those who sat in judgment, are heart-rending and poignant. Many are listed in Appendix III.

I am greatly indebted to all the authors of the sources listed, to those who left any notes of the period, and especially all that have given me their time in interviews and conversations. Since the publication of *Where's Where in Dublin* I have been contacted by many people correcting mistakes, adding information and directing me to further sources. I thank them all. Hopefully, this book will bring to life all those persons and locations that have such wonderful and historic tales to tell.

I am particularly grateful to those whose reminiscences and information have allowed me to list what I now believe are all the participants in the Rising: not just individuals whose future exploits made their names well known among readers of the literature of the time, but also those men and women who answered their country's call during that most heroic week and for whom I could find no other biographical information other than they served. Every one of them merits recognition and I am most pleased that this book provides a definitive list in Appendix V. Each of these persons deserves to be remembered and honoured.

Heroes every one.

ABBREVIATIONS

Ancient Order of Hibernians	AOH
Baronet	Bt
Criminal Investigation Division	CID
Defence of the Realm Act	DORA
Dublin Metropolitan Police	DMP
Dublin United Tram Company	DUTC
Gaelic Athletic Association	GAA
General Post Office	GPO
Honourable	Hon.
Irish Citizen Army	ICA
Irish Republican Army	IRA

During the Rising, James Connolly declared an amalgam of the Volunteers and Irish Citizen Army the Army of the Irish Republic, and it was frequently called the Irish Republican Army thereafter.

After the Rising and during the War of Independence, 1919-1921, members were often designated as IRA/Volunteers. During the Civil War, anti-Treaty forces are noted as IRA/Republicans.

The terms IRA and Volunteers or IRA and Republicans were often used interchangeably during the respective periods. In Irish it is the 'Óglaigh na hÉireann'. An individual member was usually called a 'Volunteer'.

Irish Republican Brotherhood	IRB
Irish Socialist Republican Party	ISRP
Irish Trade Union Congress	ITUC
Irish Transport and General Workers' Union	ITGWU
Irish Women's Workers' Union	IWWU
King's Counsel	KC
Member of Parliament	MP
Monsignor	Msgr
Queen's Counsel	QC
Reverend	Revd
Royal Irish Constabulary	RIC
Services, Industrial, Professional, and Technical Union	SIPTU
Teachta Dála	TD
Trinity College Dublin	TCD
Ulster Volunteer Force	UVF
University College Dublin (formerly National University)	UCD

MILITARY / RANK ABBREVIATIONS

Adjutant	Adj.
Aide de Camp	ADC
Brigadier	Brig.
Captain	Cpt.
Chief of Staff	C/S
Colonel	Col.
Commandant	Cmdt
Corporal	Cpl
First Lieutenant	1Lt
General	Gen.
General Officer Commanding	GOC
General Headquarters	GHQ
Headquarters	HQ
His Majesty's Ship	HMS
Lieutenant	Lt
Lieutenant Colonel	Lt Col.
Major	Maj.
Non Commissioned Officer	NCO
Officer Commanding	O/C
Officer Training Corps	OTC
Private	Pvt.
Quartermaster	QM
Second Lieutenant	2Lt
Sergeant	Sgt

BRITISH AWARD/DECORATION ABBREVIATIONS

Companion of the Most Honourable Order of the Bath	CB
Companion of the Most Eminent Order of the Indian Empire	CIE
Companion of the Most Distinguished Order of St Michael and St George	CMG
Distinguished Service Order	DSO
Most Honourable Order of the Bath	GCB
Royal Victorian Order	GCVO
Knight Commander of the Most Excellent Order of the British Empire	KBE
Knight Commander of The Most Honourable Order of the Bath	KCB
Knight of the Most Noble Order of the Garter	KG
Knight Commander of the Most Distinguished Order of St Michael and St George	KCMG
Military Cross	MC
Order of Merit	OM
Privy Councillor	PC

NAME CHANGES / AREA ALTERATIONS

Following the Civil War, many streets, Barracks, Bridges and other areas were renamed, several in honour of those who had been leaders or served in the Rising, the War of Independence or the Civil War.

For street names containing 'Upper', 'Middle', or 'Lower', the name may be determined as follows: the 'Lower' part of a street is that part nearest to the mouth of the Liffey. The following is a list of street/area names in italics with their contemporary names in roman.

Albert Quay: Wolfe Tone Quay
Amiens Street: Eastern end of Seán MacDermott Street
Amiens Street Railway Station: Connolly Station
Ancient Order of Hibernians Meeting Rooms: Kevin Barry Memorial Hall
Barrack Street—Tighe Street: Benburb Street
Broadstone Railway Station: Constitution Hill, Phibsborough, now closed
Chancery Street: Pill Lane
Clarence Street (Great Clarence Street): Macken Street
Clarence Street South: Macken Street
Constabulary Barracks: Garda Siochana HQ in Phoenix Park
Corporation Street: James Joyce Street
Davy's Pub: Portobello Pub (at Portobello Bridge)
Densil or Denzille Street: Fenian Street
Drogheda Street: First name of the street that became Sackville then O'Connell Street
Drumcondra Lane: Dorset and Bolton Street
Ellis Quay: Sarsfield Quay
Findlater Place: Cathal Brugha Street (the first block off O'Connell Street)
Gloucester Street: Cathal Brugha Street (the continuation east from O'Connell Street)
Gloucester Street North: (See Great Martin's Lane) Now Upper Seán MacDermott - Lower Seán MacDermott Street
Grangegorman Mental Hospital: St Brendan's Hospital
Grangegorman Road Upper: Rathdown Road Upper
Great Britain Street: Parnell Street
Great Brunswick Street: (Originally Moss Lane) Now Pearse Street
Great Clarence Street: Macken Street
Great Martin's Lane (until 1733): Then Mecklenburgh Street (until 1887) then named Tyrone Street, until it was named Railway Street for its proximity to Amiens Street Station. Now Waterford Street
The Green Lanes: Greenlea Road
Gregg Lane (Street): Cathal Brugha Street
Harcourt Street Railway Station: Demolished, now housing

Islandbridge Barracks: Partially demolished, it was Peadar Clancy Barracks. Clancy
    Barracks was sold to developers in early 2004
King George V Hospital: St Bricin's Military Hospital
King's County: County Offaly
Kingsbridge Railway Station: Seán Heuston Station
Kingstown Harbour: Dun Laoghaire Harbour (seven miles south-east of Dublin)
Linen Hall Barracks: Yarnhall Street; demolished, now housing
Marlborough Barracks: McKee Barracks in Phoenix Park
Maryborough Gaol: Portlaoise Prison
Mecklenburgh Street (until 1887) (*see Great Martin's Lane*): Then named Tyrone
    Street, until it was named Railway Street for its proximity to Amiens Street
    Station, now Waterford Street
Montgomery Street: Foley Street
North Dublin Union: St Lawrence's Hospital
Pill Lane: Then Pill Street; now Chancery Street
Pitt Street: Balfe Street
Portobello Barracks: Cathal Brugha Barracks
Queen's County: County Laois
Queenstown: Cobh, County Cork
Richmond Barracks: Originally in Bulfin Road, Inchicore, it became Keogh
    Barracks, then was taken over by the Christian Brothers and became St
    Michael's Primary School, then Keogh Square
Rochelle Street: Back Street
Rotunda Picture House: The Ambassador Theatre
Royal Barracks: Collins Barracks
Royal University: National University. See Earlsfort Terrace
Rutland Square: Parnell Square. The surrounding streets were once known as
    Charlemont Row, Cavendish Row, Palace Row, and Great Britain Street
Sackville Place (Lane): O'Rahilly Parade
Sackville Street: O'Connell Street (before Sackville Street it was Drogheda Street)
Ship Street Barracks: Government Buildings next to Dublin Castle
South Dublin Union: St James's Hospital
Stafford Street: Wolfe Tone Street
Wellington Barracks: Griffith Barracks (now a college)
Westland Row Railway Station: Pearse Station

Overview

The years 1913–23 comprised the most tumultuous decade in Irish history. The events of the decade stem from the developments of the mid-nineteenth century. Though there had been Irish revolutions against the English since that of Niall Mór Ó Neill in 1383, all were unsuccessful and often led to despair among Irish nationalists. The Irish existed as a persecuted and oppressed nationality, but the unsuccessful revolutions combined with a history of repression to make nationalism an innate part of the Irish identity. While the majority of Irish people felt helpless to effect change, in each generation there were always a few who worked to bring about independence.

Centuries of grievances against the English had generated some success: repeal of the penal laws, the Emancipation of Catholics, minimal education and some limited land reform. But the 1800 Act of Union left Ireland subservient and most of its population impoverished. The Irish were regarded not as different to the English, but inferior. By the middle of the nineteenth century, nationalist movements were sweeping Europe, but the Irish turned their thoughts to survival. Between 1845 and 1850, Irish farmers suffered through successive crop failures due to potato blight – the fungus *Phytophthora infestans* – and the waves of emigration that followed led directly to the most convulsive decades in Irish history. During these five years the population of Ireland fell by more than two million through starvation, disease and emigration, primarily to Britain and North America. The potato blight permanently seared the psyche of those whom it affected, notably the million that survived by fleeing.

From 1850 forward, the United States was to be the principal source of money and succour for all native Irish nationalist movements. Some who immigrated founded revolutionary groups dedicated to the overthrow of British rule in Ireland. In March 1855 John O'Mahoney and Michael Doheny organized emigrants who previously belonged to the Young Irelanders, and called themselves the Emmet Monument Association. The group immediately sent funds back to Ireland and fuelled a new Irish patriotic movement. On St Patrick's Day 1858, with the support of those exiled Young Irelanders in America, James Stephens formally established the Irish Republican Brotherhood (IRB) in Dublin. Stephens maintained contact with the Irish-American nationalist groups, including a sister organization to the IRB that O'Mahoney called the Fenian Brotherhood. Following abortive raids on Canada by the Fenian Brotherhood in 1867, it was outlawed in the USA, prompting another Irish emigrant, John Devoy, to establish Clan na Gael, and it was this organization that provided much of the funding for further nationalist efforts in Ireland.

Many Irish Americans gained military experience during the American Civil War and following its conclusion they decided the time was ripe to break Ireland away from the British Empire by means of force. In 1867 militant leaders in Ireland led an uprising known as the Fenian Revolt, a reference to the ancient Irish legendary warrior band of the Fianna. Thereafter 'Fenianism' became synonymous with underground Irish republicanism. The transient eclipse of the movement began when this attempt to establish an independent Irish republic failed, but those members of the secret society known as the IRB continued to plan and foment a military separation from Britain, albeit with no success. Sometimes called 'Fenians' even in Ireland (particularly by the police and army), the IRB carried on throughout the late nineteenth century with little recognition, but much impact.

> Its victories were few, yet Fenianism remained a weapon of the Irish poor wherever they were; radical in outlook, fiercely non-sectarian, and because of the anathemas of the bishops – anti-clerical. Fenians shouted defiance from the dock, challenged their jailers and walked erect to the gallows. The rank-and-file, not the leaders, saved the Fenians.[1]

For the remainder of the nineteenth century most efforts at improving the lot of the Irish were constitutional, led by Charles Stewart Parnell, 'The Chief' of the Irish Party in Westminster. Parnell believed that solving the land question should be the first step on the road to Home Rule. In December 1882, when the Irish National League replaced the suppressed Land League, he ensured that the new organization was under the control of his party and that its primary objective was the winning of Home Rule. William Gladstone, several times Liberal prime minister in England in the latter half of the nineteenth century, convinced by Parnell's success, gave the Home Rule movement his support. (The original idea of Home Rule, in 1870, was not independence but a form of dominionhood akin to that of Canada, then the only dominion, and, while dominion status broadened over the next forty years, Home Rule as proposed for Ireland narrowed to a form of a provincial assembly, like that of Northern Ireland between 1921 and 1972 or Scotland today.)

Though the Home Rule Bill of 1886 met with fierce opposition, it was Parnell's affair with the married Katherine O'Shea that was fatal to his leadership and,

1 Cronin, Seán. *The McGarrity Papers*, 1972, p. 14.

ultimately to Home Rule in his time. His refusal to step down following Mrs O'Shea's sensational divorce case produced a bitter split in the party. Meetings of the Irish Parliamentary Party were held in December 1890, and after a long and acrimonious discussion whether the man (Parnell) was more important than the cause (Home Rule), the Party split in two, and Parnell lost his leadership. By the 1890s, though, Home Rule was at the forefront of national politics. The land question had not yet been solved but Parnell's involvement in it was a vital factor and he helped future reforms to get underway.

Religious restrictions, class immobility and a lack of Irish cultural recognition still characterized Ireland in the late nineteenth century, but the re-emerging pride of the Irish people capitalized on the energy and zeal of a younger generation of Irish nationalists. Concurrently, there was a revival of both Irish games and Irish cultural studies throughout the country. In the 1880s many, including Archbishop T.W. Croke, maintained that 'ball-playing, hurling, football kicking according to Irish rules ... may now be said to be not only dead and buried, but in several localities to be entirely forgotten. What the country needed was an Irish organization to bring order and unity to sport on a nation-wide basis.'[2]

In August 1884 Michael Cusack outlined to a group of local athletic enthusiasts his plans to establish a national organization for Irish athletes and to revive hurling. On 1 November 1884 the Gaelic Athletic Association (GAA) was founded.

Similarly, the Gaelic League was founded by Douglas Hyde, Fr Eugene O'Growney, Fr Michael Hickey and Eoin MacNeill on 31 July 1893 as a non-political, non-sectarian organization dedicated to the preservation and revival of the Irish language, and the 'celebration of, and if possible the resuscitation of, traditional dress, dances and customs'.[3][4]

The Gaelic League quickly had a major impact on the social life of Ireland. It was responsible for giving the Irish language a prominent position in the national school system, it revived Irish poetry, drama and literature, and after 1903 St Patrick's Day became a national holiday; and to the Gaelic League is due the credit of 'having established the first Irish national society that accepted women as members on the same terms as men'.[5] The Irish people began to recognize, and take pride in, their Irish culture. 'Celtic Dawn' was an accurate description of the changes in many levels of Irish society. As injustices were rectified and educational and economic opportunities created, some of the growth and cultural expansion that had been halted by the Act of Union[6] re-emerged.

This cultural renaissance, advanced by both the GAA and the Gaelic League,

---

2 O'Dubghaill, M. *Insurrection Fires at Eastertide*, 1966, p. 17. **3** Garvin, Tom. *Nationalist Revolutionaries of Ireland, 1858-1928*, 1987, p. 79. **4** A precursor to the Gaelic League was the Society for the Preservation of the Irish Language founded in 1877 by Archbishop John MacHale of Tuam, Archbishop Croke, and Dr William Walsh, President of St Patrick's Institute in Maynooth. **5** Jenny Wyse-Power. 'The Political Influence of Women in Modern Ireland', in Fitzgerald, William G. editor. *The Voice of Ireland*, 1924, p. 159. **6** Coogan, Tim Pat. *1916, The Easter Rising*, 2001, p. 29.

led to an increasing desire for Home Rule. Irish separatists at this time still primarily promoted a 'constitutional' solution to their aspirations, rather than the 'physical force' solution fostered by the IRB. The IRB, however, utilized meetings of the Gaelic League and the GAA as prime opportunities for recruitment – not the last time that the Brotherhood would exploit other organizations to further its separatist aims.

In 1899 Arthur Griffith established the first of his separatist newspapers, *The United Irishman*. Through the power of his writing, Griffith shaped and set in motion many of the forces that created the organizations and individuals of the following revolutionary years. As his ideas developed in *The United Irishman*, then in *Sinn Féin*, Peadar O hAnnrachain, a leading Irish writer of the time, commented:

> But for the writings of Arthur Griffith and the work of the Gaelic League I, too, I believe, might still be unaware and I, too, might be uttering abuse of the [1916] rebels. But for these two influences I have mentioned we might have no rebels to abuse.[7]

Griffith's ideas ran far ahead of the times and they influenced all segments of nationalist, and mainly separatist thought throughout Ireland. He was opposed to the 'physical force' aims of the IRB but was no pacifist – he carried his Howth rifle on manoeuvres as a member of the Volunteers and, later, at the funeral of the Bachelor's Walk victims. He simply believed that an armed Volunteer movement was no match for English military power.

(The 1916 Rising was immediately called the 'Sinn Féin Rebellion', though Griffith disapproved of it. The name stuck because the authorities of Dublin Castle and all the influential newspapers of the period wrongly identified it with separatist nationalism. The organization Griffith founded in 1905 was really a monarchist movement, in which he proposed a dual monarchy with the same king both of England and of Ireland. Following the Rising and the return of the prisoners, though, 'Sinn Féin' became the general term used by the British to denote all Irish nationalists. This misnomer did have the effect of uniting all the nationalists under a single political banner. Soon Griffith's political party of the same name successfully wedded itself to the growing popularity of the Rising, and by 1918 it was the dominant party in Ireland, usurping the Irish Parliamentary Party as the legitimate voice of the Irish people.)

Meanwhile, the new leader of the Irish Parliamentary Party, John Redmond, who supported Parnell in the later stages of the fallen leader's political career, was appointed leader of the Home Rule Party in 1900. Redmond realized that the Liberal victory

7 Ó Luing, Seán. 'Arthur Griffith and Sinn Féin', in Martin, F.X., OSA, *Leaders and Men of the Easter Rising*, 1967, p. 55.

of 1906 in Britain gave the Home Rule Party its chance. The Liberals had been supportive of Home Rule since Gladstone's time and the 1911 Parliament Act effectively ended the power of the House of Lords to veto legislation passed by the House of Commons: now the Lords could only delay it. After 1911 Redmond and his party expected Home Rule to be proposed, and in 1912 a third Home Rule Bill was introduced. Redmond assumed it would be approved, and the Commons passed this Third Home Rule Bill in the early summer of 1914. (In August 1914, however, at the onset of World War I, the British suspended enactment of Home Rule 'for the duration'.)

All of these movements in Ireland reflected other European social, economic and cultural revolutions of the nineteenth century. Europe was the crucible for many of the ideas and institutions that now shape life in Ireland, including the industrial revolution (particularly in Ulster at that time), capitalism, demands for more democratic governments, socialism, unions, bureaucracy and nationalism. Yet life was not changing for the average worker in Dublin even though new ways of life for the working classes brought change to many other European cities. Dublin's large popular press expanded a political awareness, and new values and ideas such as nationalism and socialism started to emerge. The tinder that lit the fire was an economy that left many of the poor starving. The city was a miserable place in the early 1900s, with overcrowded and dilapidated housing, acute poverty and tens of thousands unemployed.

In these circumstances the appearance of three men in Dublin provided the catalyst for the changes that were to come. James (Big Jim) Larkin arrived in Ireland in 1907 to begin work as an organizer for the English National Union of Dock Labourers. In 1908, that union suspended Larkin from his post because of his concentration on specifically Irish problems. But Larkin's personality immediately drew all working people to him and his particular devotion to Ireland induced him to invest the labour movement in Dublin with a nationalist character.[8]

Thereafter he founded his own union, the Irish Transport Workers' Union, and the first members were enrolled and union cards issued on 20 January 1909 under that name, though the Union was uniformly known as the Irish Transport and General Workers' Union (ITGWU).[9]

The philosophy of the Union was expanded under the influence of James Connolly who returned from the United States and began his syndicalist teaching in 1910, especially his 'One Big Union' concept and the promotion of his socialist

---

8 Wells, Warre B, and N. Marlowe. *A History of the Irish Rebellion of 1916*, 1916, 1918, p. 30. **9** Nevin, Donal, editor. *Tribute to James Larkin, Orator, Agitator, Revolutionary, Trade Union Leader on the 50th Anniversary of his death*. Services, Industrial, Professional, and Technical Union (SIPTU) publication, Dublin, 1997.

ideals. After leaving the British army in 1889,[10] Connolly became a wandering union agitator, pamphleteer, a voracious reader and self-taught intellectual. He wanted a union with 'one card, one badge, one executive, and one common enemy'.

Though Connolly always believed in the claims of Ireland as an independent nation, on his return to Ireland his immediate preoccupation was with social rather than national revolution.[11] His single greatest belief was in the inherent dignity that comes from work. Born on 5 June 1868, at 107 The Cowgate, Edinburgh,[12 13 14 15] he was, first and foremost, a militant workers' leader. He fought for the workers with an absolute single-mindedness. Connolly's nationalism and socialism were fused in outrage at the appalling slum conditions in Ireland. 'All over the world it is known that the poor of Dublin are housed under conditions worse than those of any civilized people on God's earth.'[16] He was one of the founders of the Irish Socialist Republican Party in 1896, and outlined his philosophy in its initial manifesto:

> The struggle for Irish freedom has two aspects: it is national and it is social. The national ideal can never be realized until Ireland stands forth before the world as a nation, free and independent. It is social and economic, because no matter what the form of government may be, as long as one class owns as private property the land and the instruments of labour from which mankind derive their substance, that class will always have it in their power to plunder and enslave the remainder of their fellow-creatures.

In Connolly's life there was always tension between his commitment to working-class struggle and national liberation. He struggled to find the missing link between Ireland's socialist agitators and the nationalist revolutionaries, notably in

---

10 Most sources indicate that Connolly was in the British army in his youth, though there is no direct evidence for this. The earliest biography of Connolly, Desmond Ryan's *James Connolly and His Life*, published in 1924, makes no mention of military service. However, Greaves notes Connolly joined the 1st Battalion of the King's Liverpool Regiment in 1882, and served in a garrison in Ireland until 1889. Greaves, C. Desmond. *Life and Times of James Connolly*, 1961, p. 16, 20, 21 ff. See also Cowell: 'He joined the Royal Scots' Regiment, serving at Spike Island Detention Centre in Cork Harbour, where he was detailed to guard an Irishman on the night before his execution. The experience awoke an anti-British wrath in [Connolly], something that was to last his lifetime.' Cowell, John. *Dublin's Famous People, and where they lived*, 1980, p. 47.   11 Boyle, J.W. 'Connolly, the Citizen Army and the Rising', in *The Making of 1916, Studies in the History of the Rising*, edited by Kevin B. Nowlan, 1969, p. 57.   12 MacLysaght, Edward, 'Larkin, Connolly, and the Labour Movement', in Martin, *Leaders and Men*, p. 124-5.   13 But see Irish Census of 1911, in which Connolly's birthplace is listed as 'Monaghan'. http://www.census.nationalarchives.ie/reels/nai000119513/   14 It is generally accepted that Connolly was born in Edinburgh, and both his parents were from Clones, County Monaghan. But see Coogan, Tim Pat. *The Easter Rising 1916*, p. 30. Coogan writes 'Connolly was born in County Monaghan in 1870.'   15 See also O'Higgins, Brian. *The Soldier's Story of Easter Week*, 1925, p. 56. 'Born in Co. Monaghan in 1876.'   16 *The Workers Republic*, 26 February 1916.

the IRB. His insight was explicitly outlined as he continued his vision for the Irish Socialist Republican Party:

> The man who is bubbling over with love and enthusiasm for Ireland and yet can pass unmoved through our streets and witness all the wrong and the suffering, the shame and the degradation wrought upon the people of Ireland ... without burning to end it is, in my opinion, a fraud.

From the very outset, there was little doubt of his twin goals of socialism and an independent Ireland. He eloquently stated, 'The cause of labour is the cause of Ireland; the cause of Ireland is the cause of labour. They cannot be disserved.' Only later did he move more toward nationalism as a means to the end for the workers.[17][18]

His final words to the court martial that condemned him put his view clearly:

> We went out to break the connection between this country and the British Empire, and to establish an Irish Republic ... We succeeded in proving that Irishmen are ready to die endeavouring to win for Ireland those national rights which the British Government has been asking them to die to win for Belgium. As long as that remains, the cause of Irish freedom is safe.

(On the night before he was executed, his wife Lillie and his daughter Nora visited him in the hospital in Dublin Castle. To them he said 'The Socialists will never understand why I am here. They will forget I am an Irishman.'[19])

In 1873 Thomas Clarke, a young man who had been born on the Isle of Wight on 11 March 1857 as the son of an English soldier, travelled to Dublin to be sworn into the IRB. After being sworn in, he returned north to Dungannon, but the police soon got on his track and he left for America in 1880. In the United States he was inculcated with Irish separatism as a member of Clan na Gael. Sent to England in 1883, he was arrested as a member of an Irish separatist bombing campaign there and spent the next fifteen years as a prisoner in various English jails. Upon his release he returned to the United States. There he married Kathleen Daly from Limerick, the niece of John Daly, one of his cellmates in Pentonville Prison, and the man who had sworn him into the IRB.

---

17 But see McKenna, Lambert. *Social Teachings of James Connolly*, 1991, p. 43-53. McKenna did not deny Connolly's commitment to socialism, but held that Connolly was primarily a Fenian inspired by love of Ireland, and did not hold with most of the central tenets of Marxism. **18** See also, Lynch, Diarmuid. *The IRB and the 1916 Rising*, 1957. 'That Connolly's ideas gradually developed beyond the purely socialistic and took on a more national turn (as the term was usually understood) is of course beyond question. I wonder to what extent this change was brought about by the fact that many of his colleagues in the Labour Movement were old members of the IRB – William O'Brien, P.T. Daly, Cathal Shannon, Seámus Hughes, etc?' Lynch, footnote, pp. 84-5. **19** MacManus, Seumas. *The Story of the Irish Race*, 1921, p. 696.

On his return to Ireland in 1907, Clarke set out to bring the IRB's 'physical force' ideals to a new generation of Irish patriots. He must be given credit for reviving the IRB, establishing its newspaper *Irish Freedom* (a militant anti-English paper), and bringing new blood into the IRB leadership, especially mentoring his protégé, Seán MacDermott. Clarke became the trusted link between the Clan na Gael in the US and the IRB in Ireland and his contribution to the national revival and the events of the time was crucial:

> If any one man could be said to be responsible for the inspiration of Easter Week, or for the carrying through of the resolution to revolt – credit for that must be given to Tom Clarke. Clarke can truthfully be described as the man, above all others, who made the Easter Rising. He, it was, who inspired it originally, and he, it was, who, in broad outline, laid the plans.[20]

With these three highly influential men in place – Larkin, Connolly and Clarke – as well as other leaders, the stage was set for both economic and nationalistic upheavals to begin.

On 25 August 1913, trams all over Dublin stopped in their tracks. Larkin's action was not only to shut down the tram system but to mobilize all Dublin's workers as well, and thus began the Great Lockout of 1913. Under the leadership of Larkin and Connolly, the Dublin workers made their first concerted effort to raise their living standards and improve their lives. (Larkin said the Dublin worker is not a 'natural revolutionary, but he is a natural soldier'.)

In 1915 Connolly wrote of the Lockout:

> When that story [of the Lockout] is written by a man or woman with an honest heart, and with a sympathetic insight into the travail of the poor, it will be a record of which Ireland may well be proud … And it will tell how that spectacle of the slave of the underworld looking his masters in the face without terror, and fearlessly proclaiming the kinship and unity of all with each and each with all, how that spectacle caught the imagination of all unselfish souls so that the artisan took his place also in the place of conflict and danger, and the men and women of genius, the artistic and the literati, hastened to honour and serve those humble workers whom all had hitherto despised and scorned.[21]

The importance of the Lockout of 1913 lies in that 'it was the great turning point in the history of the working class in Ireland, and helped to give the workers of

---

20 O'Kelly, Seán T. *An Phoblacht*, 30 April 1926. **21** Connolly, James. *The Reconquest of Ireland*, pamphlet, 1915.

Ireland their place in the front ranks of the world army of militant and insurgent labour'.[22]

Larkin subsequently left for the United States on a fundraising tour. He had planned to go earlier but was dissuaded by the members of the ITGWU who understood the loss he would be to the Union. By the end of October 1914, he decided the time was right to make his move. With no organized agenda, Larkin's future plans were, at best, hazy. William O'Brien of the ITGWU tried to get an intended return date, but again Larkin was non-committal and, in fact, remained away from his Union for over seven years.

Thus Connolly became the central figure in the workers' opposition to the Employers' Federation. He assumed leadership of the ITGWU and pressed forward with the Irish Citizen Army (ICA) following the Lockout. The ICA was created to protect the workers from any groups that might be used by the employers, including the Dublin Metropolitan Police, whose assaults on workers had killed three and injured hundreds during the Lockout. Connolly vowed that the workers would protect themselves in the future. He saw the ICA not only as a defence force, but also as a revolutionary army, dedicated to the overthrow of capitalism and imperialism. It was also at this time that he revived a newspaper called the *Worker's Republic*, one of his many labour and radical publications.

Later, Connolly wrote:

> In the great Dublin Lockout of 1913–1914, the manner in which the Dublin employers, overwhelmingly Unionist, received the enthusiastic and unscrupulous support of the entire Home Rule Press was a fore-taste of the possibilities of the new combinations with which Labour in Ireland will have to reckon … From this lesson … Labour must learn that the time has come for a new marshalling of forces to face the future.[23]

Connolly moved toward nationalism in order to radicalize the Volunteers. He did so partly because it was tactically necessary and partly because he believed otherwise the socialist revolution he wished for Ireland would never occur. Though he became a vigorous nationalist, he declared:

> If you could remove the English army tomorrow and hoist the green flag over Dublin Castle, unless you set about the organization of the Socialist Republic, your efforts would be in vain. England would still rule you; she would rule you through her capitalists, through her landlords, through her financiers, through her usurers, through the whole array of commercial

22 *Ireland at Berne.* Reports presented to the International Labour and Socialist Conference held at Berne, Switzerland, February 1919. Issued by authority of the Irish Labour Party and Trade Union Congress.
23 Connolly, James. *The Reconquest of Ireland*, op. cit.

and individualist institutions she has planted in this country and watered with the tears of our mothers and blood of our martyrs. England would rule you to your ruin even while your lips offered hypocritical homage to the shrine of that freedom whose cause you betrayed.[24]

In addition to the ICA, two other armed militias were also established in Ireland in 1913: the Ulster Volunteer Force (UVF) and Irish Volunteers. In a direct reaction to the possibility of Home Rule for Ireland, Edward Carson and James Craig founded the UVF. The intention was that Protestant Unionists in the north would prevent the enactment of Home Rule. Soon, the need for arms led the UVF to procure 20,000 rifles and two million rounds of ammunition from Spiro in Hamburg, acquire the transport steamers SS *Clydevalley* and SS *Fanny* and bring the weapons back to Ulster.[25] The gunrunning was planned secretly and meticulously accomplished under the command of Maj. Fred Crawford. On 24 April 1914 the port of Larne was taken over by the UVF while the *Clydevalley* docked there and unloaded. Arms were also landed at Bangor and Donaghadee.[26]

As so often happened during the period, the perception grew that with armed men in Ulster threatening force to counter Home Rule, a similar force would be prudent and necessary to pressure Britain in the other direction. To this end Eoin MacNeill published an article in *An Claidheamh Soluis* on 1 November 1913, 'The North Began', arguing for the necessity of such a force, and on 11 November 1913 prominent nationalists met in Dublin to plan the formation of the Irish Volunteers. Padraig Pearse summed up the feeling at the time: 'An Ulsterman with a gun is not as ridiculous as a Nationalist without one.'[27] 'Men have rights who maintain them,' wrote MacNeill. In this spirit the Irish Volunteers, too, armed.

Though the British government had prohibited the importation of arms, the landing of arms at Larne prompted the Irish Volunteers to purchase and bring ashore their own arms shipment. The O'Rahilly directed Darrell Figgis and Erskine Childers to a firm in Hamburg where they purchased 1500 rifles and 45,000 rounds of ammunition. Childers' yacht, the *Asgard*, landed 900 rifles and 26,000 rounds of ammunition in the small port of Howth, just north of Dublin on 26 July 1914, and the remainder were landed in Kilcoole. While the 'Howth Mausers' were obsolete, they were the basis of arms for the Irish Volunteers, and about 800 Volunteers mustered and marched from Dublin out to Howth on the day of the landing. The British sent contingents of the Dublin Metropolitan Police and the army to prevent the landing, and upon the soldiers' return to Dublin there was a confrontation with civilians at Bachelor's Walk. Four civilians were killed and more

24 Greaves. *The Life and Times of James Connolly*, p. 69. **25** But see Coogan, Tim Pat and George Morrison who name the vessel that carried the arms from Hamburg not the *SS Fanny* but rather the *SS Mountjoy*. *The Irish Civil War*, 1998, p. 84. **26** Jackson, Alvin. 'Larne Gun Running, 1914', *History Ireland*, Vol. I, No. 1, Spring, 1993. **27** Edwards, Ruth Dudley, *Patrick Pearse: The Triumph of Failure*, 1977, p. 179, from an article by Padraig Pearse in *An Cladheamh Soluis*, November 1913.

than thirty-five were seriously injured during firing by soldiers of the King's Own Scottish Borderers. Ironically, the nationalist Irish Volunteers were sworn to uphold an act of the British parliament – Home Rule – while the Unionist Ulster Volunteers were preparing to fight Home Rule.

Within a fortnight, Archduke Franz Ferdinand was assassinated in Sarajevo, World War I erupted across the continent, Home Rule was shelved and the time the IRB had been anticipating was at hand. Quickly thereafter, John Redmond, as leader of the Irish Parliamentary Party, made a political calculation that in time would backfire. He encouraged Irishmen to join the British army in the belief that, mindful of Irish solidarity, England would not renege on its Home Rule commitments. In September 1914 in Co. Wicklow he told the Irish: 'I say to you, therefore, your duty is twofold. I am glad to see such magnificent material for soldiers around me, and I say to you: Go on drilling and make yourself efficient for the Work, and then account yourselves as men, not only for Ireland itself, but wherever the fighting line extends, in defence of right, of freedom, and religion in this war.'[28]

Thereafter, Theobald Wolfe Tone's declaration in 1798 that 'England's difficulty is Ireland's opportunity' became the bywords of the IRB. The movement's Supreme Council determined that with England engaged in World War I, a Rising should be planned and undertaken in Ireland. While the overt purpose of the Volunteers was firstly defensive against conscription and partition, at least from September 1914 the covert purpose was to mount a Rising before the war ended.[29] Simply, some IRB leaders regarded the Irish Volunteers as the material for a revolutionary army to be employed at the most opportune moment.

This decision was made by a small group of determined and dedicated men who became the IRB's Military Council and planned to use the Volunteers in a way that would have surprised many of those who drilled in their ranks. This certainly was not distrust of the integrity or discretion of many Volunteers – after all, The O'Rahilly was not taken into their confidence – but rather the result of a policy of confining such information only to those committed unconditionally to a Rising. It applied to IRB members as well as non-members.

P.S. O'Hegarty, a chronicler of the times and a member of the IRB from 1903, wrote: 'The Insurrection of 1916 came because the Supreme Council of the Irish Republican Brotherhood decided that it would come ... It was the Supreme Council of the IRB which decided the Insurrection, planned it, organized it, led it and financed it.'[30]

Thomas Clarke, Padraig Pearse, Joseph Plunkett along with Éamonn Ceannt, Thomas MacDonagh, Seán MacDermott and, later James Connolly, all of whom became IRB members, comprised its Military Council. (Pearse, MacDonagh, and

28 *Freeman's Journal*, 21 September 1914. **29** Thornley, David. 'Patrick Pearse', *Studies, An Irish Quarterly Review*, Spring 1966, p. 15. **30** O'Hegarty, P.S. *The Victory of Sinn Féin*, 1924, 1998, p. 2.

Plunkett were well-known authors and poets, which led the Rising to be called 'The Poets' Rebellion'.) Without informing the Commandant of the Volunteers, Eoin MacNeill, they planned the Easter Rising to take advantage of 'England's difficulty'.

Pearse was the indispensable link between the IRB and the Volunteers. When he issued orders for manoeuvres, culminating in the order for the Rising at Easter 1916, he did so in the dual capacity as a member of the Supreme Council of the IRB, as well as Director of Organization of the Volunteers. No other IRB man held such a prominent dual rank as Pearse. Thus, the IRB Military Council also elected him as commander-in-chief of the Rising.[31] To the IRB men in the know, Pearse represented the IRB. To the Volunteers, he was the most familiar figure of the signatories to the *Proclamation*, whose name had appeared on so many Volunteer orders. The duality of the secret and open organizations propelled Pearse to the titular leadership.

The Rising had been scheduled for Easter Sunday, 23 April,[32][33][34] and Pearse issued an order on 8 April for a general mobilization on that day. This order was issued publicly and with the full authorization of the Volunteer Executive partly to deceive Dublin Castle authorities with whom the Military Council was then in a race against time. Though the leaders of the Rising were under immense pressure to forestall action against the Volunteers and the ICA by the British authorities, and all shared a common desire to free Ireland, a romanticized notion that the Rising was a cohesive effort does not bear true. The goal was a unified vision for freedom, but the means and the final shaping of Irish life were far from agreed. To a great degree, the Rising's leaders were 'feeling their way' toward their revolt.

On Holy Saturday, the Military Council knew their plans had been severely compromised by the loss of a ship from Germany, the *Aud*. It was loaded with weapons[35] but its arrival at Fenit and delivery of arms was foiled due to a failure in communications and confusion on the part of the Volunteers who were to contact it. Its German crew scuttled it in Queenstown (Cobh) harbour after being intercepted by the British navy.

When MacNeill found he had been deceived about a Rising and the loss of the arms ship he cancelled the manoeuvres scheduled for Easter. Despite the inevitable confusion which MacNeill's cancellation caused, the Rising leaders decided that to

---

31 Thornley. 'Patrick Pearse', *Studies*, p. 16. **32** There is evidence that the Rising was first scheduled for Good Friday, 21 April 1916, but was changed to Easter Sunday because 'a mobilization on Good Friday was a departure from the usual rule that mobilizations were ordered only for Sundays and Holidays when the majority of men were not at work, and any change would cause comment and might also be a dangerous signal to the British'. O'Brien, William. 'Was the Date Changed?', *Irish Press*, 25 January 1936. **33** See also Dillon, Geraldine Plunkett. 'Casement and Easter Week', *Irish Press*, 3 January 1936. **34** Also, Dillon, Geraldine Plunkett. 'How Much did the Castle Know?', *Irish Press*, 14 January 1936. **35** Chatterton, Edward Keble. *Danger Zone*, 1934, p. 242. Chatterton summarizes the British Admiralty's attempt to survey the *Aud*, and found the weapons were captured from the Russians. He wrote the rifles bore the 'butt stamp of the Orleans small arms factory, 1902. The barrels were marked with the Russian War Office and overstamped with the name "Deutschland"'.

delay further would be fatal for their plans. The Rising was rescheduled for Monday at noon. However, commandants throughout the country received a series of conflicting orders during the weekend, not all delivered everywhere, and not always received in the sequence in which they had been issued. The result was a state of confusion, uncertainty and frustration, particularly outside Dublin, which largely immobilized those commands in the country.

On Easter Monday, 24 April 1916, approximately 800 Volunteers and 200 ICA members stormed buildings in central Dublin and declared an independent Irish Republic. Under the command of Pearse and Connolly, the Volunteers and ICA members were combined into what Connolly termed the Irish Republican Army (IRA). Joseph Plunkett was the primary planner, and the objective was that the Volunteers and ICA would seize strategic buildings throughout Dublin in order to cordon off the city and resist the coming attacks by units of the British army.

The Volunteers' plan had two elements: first, to prevent British access to the city centre from the major British military barracks or from Kingstown; and second, to keep open a line of communication between Dublin and the country (especially toward the north) in order to have a line of retreat if it became necessary to fall back into guerrilla war. While there was little hope of defeating the British army, the planners of the Rising felt international opinion would soon force the British to come to terms with the Volunteers, and to give independence to the country. The Republic would be proclaimed as an inherent right, and Irish forces would stand to arms and defend it as long as their sources permitted. Mistakenly the leaders believed that, after all, one of the proclaimed purposes of the British in World War I was to provide self-determination for small nations, and therefore the British would make terms with the Irish rebels.[36] Utmost secrecy was maintained in planning – only three copies of the plan were drafted and no original is known to exist.[37] [38]

(Historians have always debated the concept of the Rising as a 'Blood Sacrifice' led by men who felt that a rising, even though precipitate, was necessary.

> It was the British decision to declare war on Germany that allowed the Irish Republican Brotherhood to think seriously in terms of a rising by getting enough guns to challenge superior British firepower. This would have been irrelevant if the sole purpose of the Rising was simply a blood sacrifice. That was a purpose of the Rising for several of the leaders, but it was not the sole purpose of any one of them.[39]

---

36 Seán MacDermott had said to P.S. O'Hegarty, 'We'll hold Dublin for a week and save Ireland.' O'Hegarty, P.S. *A History of Ireland under the Union*, 1952, p. 700. 37 O'Donoghue, Florence. 'Ceannt, Devoy, O Rahilly, and the Military Plan', in Martin, *Leaders and Men*, p. 192. 38 O'Donoghue, Florence. 'Plans for the 1916 Rising,' *University Review*, Vol. 3, March 1963. 39 Lee, J.J. '1916 as Virtual History', *History Ireland*, Vol. XIV, No. 2, March/April 2006.

There is little doubt, though, that for Pearse the Rising as a blood sacrifice was necessary to bring the Irish people to revolt. He stated as much in his writings and especially in his play *The Singer* and poem *Renunciation* in 1915.[40] Other leaders, too, indicated their acceptance and even their wish for such a sacrifice.[41 42 43 44 45 46 47 48 49 50 51 52 53 54 55 56 57] However, few of the 'rank and file' members of the Volunteers and the ICA knew that the manoeuvres scheduled for Easter Sunday were to precipitate an actual revolt, and there was no feeling of a need for a 'blood sacrifice' among them.

Certainly the military plan was doomed once the *Aud* was scuttled, and arguably was ill conceived from the outset. Many also questioned the tactic of sitting within a tightening ring in Dublin waiting for the English to attack.)

After capturing the General Post Office (GPO) on Sackville Street, Pearse read the *Proclamation of the Provisional Government of the Irish Republic* on the steps of that landmark building. However, the few people assembled were more wary and confused than enthusiastic. The insurgents then barricaded their posts and awaited the inevitable British assaults. The buildings were put in a state of defence; outposts were established in commanding positions, many in street-corner houses covering the approaches to the GPO and surrounding areas; street barricades were erected, and boring commenced through the walls of adjoining buildings, so as to make each block a defensive unit.

40 'I have turned my face, To this road before me, To the deed that I see, And the death I shall die.' *Renunciation*. Pearse, Padraig H. *Collected Works of Patrick H. Pearse, Plays, Stories, and Poems*. 5th edition, 1922. 41 'The insurrection of 1916 was a forlorn hope and a deliberate blood sacrifice. The men who planned it and led it did not expect to win. They knew they could not win…. But they counted upon being executed afterwards and they knew that *that* would save Ireland's soul' (italics added). O'Hegarty. *The Victory of Sinn Féin*, p. 3. 42 Terence MacSwiney wrote in 1914: 'We want to set Ireland on fire: and we think our personal sacrifice not too high a price to pay…. Let Irish blood be the first to fall on Irish earth – there will be kindled a crusade for the restoration of liberty that not all the fires of hell can defeat…. Our Volunteers are not as yet fully alert…. A sacrifice will do it: like a breath from Heaven it will blow upon their souls and kindle the divine fire; and they shall be purified, strengthened, and made constant, and the destiny of Ireland will be safe in their hands.' *Cork Weekly Fianna Fail*, 7 November 1914. 43 'There was no hope of military success.' Béaslaí, Piaras. *Michael Collins and the Making of the New Ireland*, 1926, p. 101. 44 'Those that planned the Rising knew full well that their efforts would go down in blood and smoke and that their portion would be the firing squad in the grey dawn. No wonder that these poets who were alive at the time and those who have grown up amongst us since found inspiration in the acts that were done Easter Week.' McManus, M.J. *Limerick Leader*, 30 March 1940. 45 Stephens, James. *Insurrection in Dublin*, 1916, 1978, p. 70. 46 Brennan-Whitmore, W.J. 'How Long Could They Hold Out?', *Irish Independent*, 11 April 1966. 47 Ryan, Desmond. *The Rising*, 1957, p. 98. 48 Ryan, James. 'The GPO', *Capuchin Annual*. 1942. 49 Ó Dubghaill, M. *Insurrection Fires at Eastertide*, pp. 308 ff. 50 MacManus, Seumas. op. cit., pp. 696, 702. 51 The belief and interpretation of a 'Blood Sacrifice' with no popular support and leading to a 're-awakening' of national spirit suits both revisionist opponents and republican supporters of the Rising. See Lee, Joseph. *Ireland 1912-1985, Politics and Society*, 1989, pp. 24-38. 52 Shaw, Revd Francis SJ. 'The Canon of Irish History: A Challenge', *Studies, The Irish Jesuit Quarterly Review*, Summer 1972, pp. 117, 125-6. 53 Martin, Francis X., OSA. 'Myth, Fact and Mystery', *Studia Hibernica*, Vol. VII, 1966. 54 Martin, Francis X., OSA. 'The 1916 Rising—A Coup d'Etat or a "Bloody Protest"?' *Studia Hibernica*, Vol. VIII, 1968. 55 O'Hegarty. A *History of Ireland under the Union*, pp. 696 and 700 ff. 56 Greaves, C. Desmond. *1916 as History: The Myth of the Blood Sacrifice*, Dublin, 1991. 57 Neeson, Eoin. *Myths From Easter 1916*, Aubane, 2007.

The British military reacted quickly.[58] They initiated actions to relieve Dublin Castle, made certain of the security of the barracks throughout Dublin as well as other positions on the perimeter of the rebellion, and summoned reinforcements from every barracks in Ireland and from Britain.[59] Then the British put their efforts into securing the approaches to their administrative headquarters at Dublin Castle and isolating the rebel headquarters at the GPO. Artillery was brought into Dublin from the British military establishment at Athlone and, along with a small gun-boat, HMS *Helga*, the British shelled large parts of the city and destroyed much of the centre of Dublin by fire.

The Crown forces greatly outnumbered the rebels, marshalling almost 20,000 troops by week's end in opposition to about 1875 rebels. The British plan was to outflank and isolate the rebel defences, and soon the shelling and fires left the rebels in untenable positions in virtually all the buildings that they held. On Saturday, 29 April, 'in order to prevent the further slaughter of Dublin citizens, and in the hope of saving the lives of our followers, now surrounded and hopelessly outnumbered', Pearse gave the order to surrender, and shortly afterwards all the rebel positions were turned over to the British.

There was very little public support for the rebels during the Rising.[60] For the most part, the Irish people greatly supported the British war effort. Moreover, many civilians had been killed or lost their property in the fires. When the rebels were marched off to boats bound for prisons in Britain, many were pelted with vegetables, bottles and even the contents of chamber pots. Nothing these men and women had done during the week led the public to take their side, though the bitterness of the people was tinged with a little admiration – they had fought well against the regular troops. Soon, however, that adverse opinion of the rebels would change and the public would increasingly support their position and objectives.

Britain, still engaged in World War I, determined that the Rising was an act of 'treason' and that the participants and leaders should suffer the fate of traitors in wartime. Further to that the rebels had enlisted German support, a move that prompted outright vilification. Gen. Sir John Maxwell, the British commanding officer, ordained that all seven signatories of the *Proclamation* should be executed in Kilmainham Gaol. Those men and several other prominent commanders of rebel positions were executed – a total of fourteen men in all in Dublin. James Connolly, so badly wounded that he lay in a hospital bed in Dublin Castle from

---

58 At the start of the Rising, British troops in Dublin consisted of the 6th Cavalry at Marlborough Barracks, the 3rd Royal Irish Regiment at Richmond Barracks, the 3rd Royal Irish Rifles at Portobello Barracks, the 10th Royal Dublin Fusiliers at Kingbridge. The assigned Dublin garrison strength was approximately 120 officers and 2260 other ranks. **59** Hayes-McCoy, G. A. 'A Military History of the 1916 Rising', in Nowlan, *The Making of 1916*, p. 275. **60** Ironically, Pearse's play, *The Singer*, written in autumn 1915, foretold this 'quietness' in the country: 'Cuimin: We've no one to lead us. Colm: Didn't you elect me your captain? Cuimin: We did; but not to bid us rise out when the whole country is quiet.' Pearse, Padraig H. *Collected Works of Patrick H. Pearse, Plays, Stories, and Poems*. 5th edition, 1922.

the time of his surrender, was taken from the hospital, seated on a rough wooden box, and shot. The executions created a wave of protest and outrage in Ireland.

The Rising had hardly been the work of a massive conspiracy, but the British acted as if it were. Over 3000 men and women were imprisoned following the rebellion, most in jails in England and Wales. Some were never charged, and there were certainly some that had not participated at all. These mass arrests and increased military presence demonstrated bluntly that Ireland was in the control of an oppressive and alien government that could only rule the country by force. Shortly, too, a lack of evidence dispelled the German connection to the Rising, and the stain of treason could not be maintained. It became clear that, in the words of the banner hung over Connolly's Liberty Hall before the Rising, the rebels supported 'Neither King nor Kaiser'.

Many in Ireland began to feel a communion with past fighting generations, and the words of James Fintan Lalor were often quoted: 'Somewhere, somehow, and by someone, a beginning must be made.' Pearse, the idealist, and Connolly, the Lalor disciple, had begun the rebellion in Lalor's words: 'even if [it was] called premature, imprudent or dangerous – if made so soon as tomorrow – even if offered by ten men only – even if offered by men armed with stones'.[61]

The Rising was not an intellectual landmark but an event of enormous political power. It was a culmination of centuries of grievances against British rule, and of the effort of generations of nationalists, planned by those who feared that, without a dramatic gesture of this kind, the sense of national identity that had survived all the hazards of the centuries would flicker out within their lifetimes. They saw the Rising as a last desperate attempt to save Irish nationalism from the oblivion that appeared to them to face it in those first years of World War I, and they acted as they saw necessary in order to call dramatically to Ireland's soul. The necessity of the Rising arose from the need to reawaken a spirit of nationalism that seemed to them to have died in the hearts of a majority of the Irish.[62] Before the Rising, even most of Ireland's nationalist population did not subscribe to the violent Fenian beliefs. Immediately following the Rising this view had not changed.

Throughout Ireland, the executions began to revive the Irish spirit, and alter the people's views, as the Rising had not done. In a letter to Maxwell on 17 May, Dr Thomas O'Dwyer, bishop of Limerick, challenged the tyranny of the British action:

> You took care that no pleas for mercy should interpose on behalf of the poor young fellows who surrendered to you in Dublin. The first word we got of their fate was the announcement that they had been shot in cold blood. Personally, I regard your action with horror and I believe it has outraged the conscience of the Country.[63]

61 Curran, C.P. 'Griffith, MacNeill and Pearse', *Studies, the Irish Quarterly Review,* Spring 1966, p. 26.
62 FitzGerald, Garret. 'The Significance of 1916', *Studies, the Irish Quarterly Review,* Spring 1966, p. 29.
63 Macardle, Dorothy. *The Irish Republic,* 1937, 1965. p. 190.

(O'Dwyer had long been a critic of the Irish Parliamentary Party, and in August 1915 had challenged Redmond by calling on him publicly to support Pope Benedict XV's efforts for a negotiated peace to end World War I. Further to that, in November 1915, O'Dwyer reiterated his position that it was in Ireland's interest to remain aloof from the war. In response to an attack on Irish emigrants passing through Liverpool, he wrote:

> This war may be just or unjust, but any fair-minded man will admit it is England's war, not Ireland's. When it is over, if England wins, she will hold a dominant power in this world, and her manufactures and her commerce will increase by leaps and bounds. Win or lose, Ireland will go on, in our old round of misgovernment, intensified by a grinding poverty which will make life intolerable.[64]

The letter made O'Dwyer a hero with the nationalists overnight, but it separated him further from the position of the majority of Catholic bishops who remained loyal to moderate and constitutional politics. Still, O'Dwyer had not been in favour of the Rising.)

While O'Dwyer's letter to Maxwell demonstrated at least a small change in his attitude toward the rebels, the Catholic Church as a whole was almost uniformly opposed to any physical force movement, including the Rising. Of the thirty-one bishops in Ireland at the time, only one (Fogarty) gave a hesitant condemnation, and one other (O'Dwyer) could be said to have issued a partial condonation of it. Moreover, the Church had been one of the staunchest opponents of Larkin, and Connolly's socialism was anathema to the Church hierarchy.

The Catholic Church held that there were five traditional conditions required for a lawful revolt:

1. A tyrannical government, without legitimacy in the country
2. The impossibility of removing that government except by force
3. A proportion between the evil caused and that to be removed by the revolt
4. Serious possibility of success
5. Approval of the community as a whole

The Church's hierarchy, under the leadership of Michael Cardinal Logue, Bishop of Armagh and Primate of All Ireland, held that the Rising was unjustified because none of the required conditions was met. Yet, another bishop who spoke on the Rising was Dr Michael Fogarty of Killaloe who, in a sermon on 14 May, said:

> [I] am not going to trouble you with a denunciation of the unhappy

64 Whyte, John H. '1916 – Revolution and Religion', in Martin. *Leaders and Men*, p. 219.

young men who were responsible for that awful tragedy. There are
enough and plenty in Ireland to do that. [I] bewail and lament their mad
adventure; but whatever their faults or responsibility may be – and let
God be their merciful judge in that – this much must be said to their
credit, that they died bravely and unselfishly for what they believed –
foolishly indeed – was the cause of Ireland.[65]

This 'condemnation' was hedged with so many qualifications that it gave comfort
rather than otherwise to the survivors of the Volunteers.

O'Dwyer, still very much a loner in his position, went even further in September
1916, when he said:

Was I to condemn them, even if their rebellion was not justifiable theo-
logically? Was I to join that other gang of renegades who were throwing
dirt on Pearse and MacDonagh and Colbert and the other brave fellows
whom Maxwell had mercilessly put to death?…The British Government
and their friends ring the changes on the hopelessness of the Rising and
the folly of a couple of thousand badly armed Volunteers attempting to
overthrow the British power in Ireland. There is something in it, and
even, from the point of view of our country's freedom, there is wisdom
in the admonition:

> Bide your time, your worst transgression
> Were to strike and strike in vain;
> He whose hand would smite oppression
> Must not need to strike again.

The Irish Volunteers were too few for the enterprise, but that is, perhaps,
the worst that can be said against them. Rebellion to be lawful must be
the act of a nation as a whole, but while that is true, see the case of the
Irish Volunteers against England. The very Government against which
they rose, and which dealt with them so mercilessly, had proclaimed its
own condemnation. What is that ghost of Home Rule which they keep
in lavender on the Statute Book but a confession of the wrong of
England's rule in Ireland?…Sinn Féin is, in my judgment, the true principle, and alliance with English politicians is like the alliance of the lamb
with the wolf.[66]

Further, the same influences that inspired many of the rebels – the GAA, the
Gaelic League and Irish nationalism/separatism – also appealed to the younger

65 Ibid, p. 221. 66 Ryan, Desmond. *The Rising*, p. 264.

members of the clergy. As the dying words of the executed leaders were reported in a religious vein, the attitudes of the clergy began a very slow change.[67] Later some support for the nationalist ideals appeared in the younger priests who came forward at nationalist rallies and on Sinn Féin platforms. The conversion of some priests into more outspoken nationalists was vital to the growth of the movement following the Rising.

The action of the British in executing the leaders and imprisoning so many had its adverse effects outside Ireland as well. Particularly in the United States, with its active and powerful Irish population, there were outcries and protests. The same Irish separatist organizations that contributed so heavily to the Rising brought pressure to bear on the US government to intervene on behalf of the thousands of Irish prisoners in English jails. By the end of 1916 the British authorities determined to release most of the rebels, and these were home in Ireland by Christmas. They returned to a riotous welcome, a complete turnaround from the send-off they had been given by the populace eight months earlier on the way to prison. The tide of public opinion had clearly changed.

The War of Independence would not have occurred without the conversion of the Irish people from supporters of Home Rule to advocates of an open and, shortly, a violent revolution. There was yet to come another imperious decision that would harden attitudes against the British. Though about 210,000 men from Ireland served in the British army during World War I, of whom some 35,000 died, not one was conscripted.[68] Most entered the army for financial reasons, because they were poverty-stricken and employment opportunities were so few in Ireland. Others followed the recruiting promises of the British and believed that enlisting 'to fight for small nations' would lead to Home Rule.

Throughout 1917 and early 1918, reinforcements became such an urgent necessity for the British army that the British government decided to apply military conscription to Ireland in the spring of 1918. In April 1918 Westminster passed a compulsory Conscription Act, a move that unified Irish public opinion against Britain. Though no Irishmen was in fact conscripted during the war, the threat of conscription was such that an Irish Conference was convened as a protest against its possibility. The Conference issued the following pronouncement: 'The attempt to enforce conscription will be unwarrantable aggression which we call upon all true Irishmen to resist by the most effective means at their disposal.'[69]

---

67 One prayer card for the executed leaders read: 'O Gentlest Heart of Jesus, have mercy on the souls of thy servants, our Irish heroes; bring them from the shadows of exile to the bright home of Heaven, where, we trust, Thou and Thy Blessed Mother have woven for them a crown of unending bliss.' Prayer cards for the repose of the souls of the following Irishmen who were executed by English law, 1916, TCDMS 2074.
68 There is no agreement on the total number of Irish soldiers who served in the British army and navy in the First World War. There appears to be a consensus on the figure of 210,000, of whom at least 35,000 died though the figure on the National War Memorial is 49,400. http://www.taoiseach.gov.ie/eng/index.asp?docID=2517
69 *Manchester Guardian*, 13 May 1918.

The Catholic hierarchy concurred at their annual meeting at Maynooth. By now even the opinion of the Church had shifted toward approving Irish nationalism. In this fashion the plan to introduce conscription in Ireland led to widespread support for independence and fuelled support for the Republican separatist movement and Sinn Féin.

A further heavy-handed attempt by the British Viceroy, Lord French, to quell this reaction to conscription claimed there was evidence of a treasonable 'German Plot' between Sinn Féin and the German military. The arrests that followed on 17-18 May 1918 included seventy-three Sinn Féin leaders, among them Arthur Griffith, Maud Gonne MacBride, Darrell Figgis and Éamon de Valera, and had severe unintended effects, as many of those arrested were among the most moderate of the nationalist leaders. Those left free included the most strident separatists, including Michael Collins, Cathal Brugha, Richard Mulcahy and Harry Boland.

The most tangible change that occurred in Ireland after the Rising was the power shift in Irish politics from the Irish Parliamentary Party to the newly unified Sinn Féin. Immediately following the Armistice in November 1918, the British government called for a general election, and Sinn Féin comprehensively defeated the Redmondite parliamentarians in the December 1918 general election. That led in turn to the formation of the first Dáil Éireann, which convened on 21 January 1919. The 1918 election determined the future course of Irish history: as one looks down the names of successful candidates, the governments of Ireland for the next thirty or forty years emerge.

This is what the Election of 1918 did:

> It declared to the British that they had no claim to Ireland that was not rendered null and void by the Irish people's repudiation of such claim, and that the only just and constitutional government in Ireland was the Government of Dáil Éireann, which was elected by the people and represented the people. There is no gesture in Irish history quite so magnificent, quite so proud as that; and nothing that has happened can take away from it ... It brought the people to the point that they gave their allegiance to Dáil Éireann, obeyed it and recognized it, and helped it, suffered British government but did not recognize it and did not help it.[70]

Within two years of the Rising, Ireland had abandoned the Irish Parliamentary Party and its goal of Home Rule, and was marching forward resolutely under what was then described as the Sinn Féin banner, but what in reality was the IRB standard. For the first time in Irish nationalist history, the advocates of physical force and those of political agitation would work together rather than against each other. One of the members of that first Dáil (a member was known as a Teachta Dála

---

70 O'Hegarty. *The Victory of Sinn Féin*, p. 23, 25.

or TD) was Michael Collins. Born in Co. Cork in 1890, he went to London at the age of fifteen to work in the British Post Office. In November 1909 he became a member of the IRB, and in 1914 enrolled in the Irish Volunteers. He returned to Ireland for the 1916 Rising, but did not make his mark on events until after his release from prison at the end of 1916.

In the early years of the War of Independence, he set about reorganizing the Volunteer movement as Director of Organisation. As the Volunteer Director of Intelligence from January 1920 to July 1921, Collins became the mastermind of an Irish intelligence network that successfully countered British intelligence in Ireland. Though he often walked and cycled throughout Dublin after the Dáil met in January 1919, he was never arrested despite the fact that the head of the British army in Ireland, Gen. Neville Macready, wrote in March 1921 recommending the British government offer £10,000 for his capture.[71] (The average worker's wage at the time was £2.2s per week – yet no one seriously thought of betraying Collins.)

The intelligence system established by Collins was a crucial asset in the Irish War of Independence. In all the important military centres throughout the country, on the railroads, and on the docks and ferries Collins succeeded in planting someone who kept him well supplied with information. However, he decried the need for it: 'This damn spying business plays hell with a man. It kills the soul and the heart in him. It leaves him without pity or mercy. I am fed up with the whole rotten business … Look how the poor girls are ruined by us. There is no softness in them anymore!'[72] Collins, though, did not know what was happening in the inner circles of power in Westminster. This was a serious flaw particularly since there is strong evidence to suggest the British had a fairly good idea of the thinking within the Dublin Cabinet, and it became a major defect as the later Treaty negotiations ensued.

Collins was also a brilliant Minister of Finance: he devised and oversaw the Dáil Loan that raised millions for the cause of Irish independence. The final loan total, subscribed by over 135,000 Irish people, was £378,858 in Ireland alone. A sum of $5,123,640 was raised separately in the United States. The natural intelligence, organizational capability and sheer drive of Collins galvanized those who came in contact with him.

The War of Independence was a guerrilla campaign mounted against the British government in Ireland by the IRA/Volunteers from January 1919 until the truce in July 1921, under the proclaimed legitimacy of the First Dáil. Military operations remained limited during 1919, although raids for arms became a regular occurrence. The violence was at first deeply unpopular with the broader Irish population, but attitudes changed gradually in the face of the terror of the British government's campaign of widespread brutality, destruction of property, random arrests, reprisals, and unprovoked shootings. The small groups of IRA/Volunteers on the run were extremely vulnerable. Their success could make or break the activity

---

71 Coogan, Tim Pat. *Michael Collins*, 1992, p. 209. 72 Twohig, Patrick J. *Blood on the Flag*, 1996, p. 155.

of the IRA in a particular district – losing them often meant the end of operations. The local populaces provided more than just moral support – in many cases they provided logistics, intelligence, and men and women for local actions. In September 1919 the Dáil was banned by the British, which served to make it easier for the IRA/Volunteers to carry out attacks, because their politicians no longer had a public platform from which to restrain them.

And so rebellion continued in Ireland, not with a great takeover of Dublin or with pitched battles, but with brutal city and country ambushes designed to demoralize representatives of the British government and the British people themselves.

Meanwhile, following his escape from Lincoln Prison in England on 3 February 1919, Éamon de Valera was elected president of the Dáil on 1 April. After his dramatic escape he left for the United States to highlight British injustices in Ireland and drum up support for an Irish Republic. He was most successful in raising funds for the Dáil Loan, but was unsuccessful in his attempts to get either of the US political parties to officially recognize the Republic in their 1920 election programmes.

The arrival of the Black and Tans (Tans) in March 1920 changed the entire complexion of the war. These 'irregulars' were established as a section of the Royal Irish Constabulary (RIC) and first appeared in the village of Upperchurch, Co. Tipperary. The British government needed more troops in Ireland to maintain its position, and turned to demobilized soldiers from World War I who were unemployed. The name came from their uniforms that were black tunics and dark tan or khaki trousers, some with civilian hats, but most with green caps and black leather belts of the RIC. The name was given to them by Christopher O'Sullivan, editor of the *Limerick Echo*[73], who wrote that they reminded him of a pack of hunting dogs in Limerick: 'Judging by the colour of their cap and trousers, they resembled something one would associate with the Scarteen Hunt.'[74] The Scarteen Black and Tans were well known for their savagery, as were the Tans.

The second British force to augment the regular armed forces was the 'Auxiliaries' (Auxies), who arrived September 1920. Auxiliary to the RIC, they were originally called the Temporary Cadets – they were ranked as 'cadets' but were 'graded as RIC sergeants for the purpose of discipline'. They were apparently intractable, even to their own authority. To the Irish they were feared and hated most of all. By the end of the War of Independence in 1921 there would be over 7000 Black and Tans and 1500 Auxiliaries in the country.

Gen. Neville MacGready, the General Officer Commanding the British army in Ireland, refused to take responsibility for the RIC, the Black and Tans or the

73 *Limerick Echo.* 74 'This day, 25 March, Feast of the Annunciation, 1920, marked the arrival of the first Black and Tan in Limerick, *en route* to Newcastle West. To the late Christopher O'Sullivan, a local journalist/editor/proprietor of the old *Limerick Echo*, goes the credit of having given the new police force their colourful name, due to their manner of dress: a black tunic, as worn by the Royal Irish Constabulary, and khaki or tan trousers of the British soldier.' *The Limerick Leader*, 25 March 1980.

Auxiliaries and openly condemned their acts of indiscipline. This friction between the military and the police was a major factor in Britain's failure to implement an effective security policy during 1920. By October 1920, the 'King's Writ' no longer ran in many parts of Dublin or the countryside. All British forces were now being concentrated in the towns, or, at least, in very strong barracks, obviously with a view to shortening the front. The IRA/Volunteer forces opposing them were becoming stronger and highly organized, albeit with little overall coordination from Dublin.

However, there was also little coordination between the Royal Irish Constabulary, the Black and Tans, the Auxiliaries and the regular British army. As a result there was widespread hostility caused by the lack of control over the Tans and the Auxies, and it was often directed at any British official. Consequently the military was torn between those who thought it best to ride out the storm, letting politicians negotiate a settlement, and those who advocated sterner measures to stamp out the Volunteers completely.

Neither the Tans nor the Auxies exhibited much in the way of military discipline and the levels of violence and reprisals mounted daily. Their arrival and the brutality of their tactics drove many to support the IRA/Volunteers. The Irish, ruled by the British for so long, now began to think of their resistance as patriotism. The revolution, which began as a mixture of individual Irish ideals, soon developed into something real and challenging to the British. The Dublin execution of an eighteen-year-old medical student, Kevin Barry, for killing a British soldier, the shooting of the Lord Mayor of Cork, Thomas MacCurtain, in front of his wife and children, and the arrest and death on hunger strike of the succeeding Lord Mayor of Cork, Terence MacSwiney were events that made the British position in Ireland ever more untenable.[75] Ireland went into mourning when MacSwiney died on the seventy-fourth day of his fast. He had become a symbol of a new nation – disciplined, hard, clear, unsentimental, uncompromising, a conscious using of vigour to build up strength.[76]

In response to the growing violence, the British government introduced the Restoration of Order in Ireland Act. This Act, passed in August 1920, allowed for the non-judicial internment and court martial of civilians and led to the arrest of a large number of IRA officers. The level of public support for the IRA/Volunteers, however, continued to rise – though the IRA had shot 182 policemen and 50 soldiers by the end of 1920. The British government initially asserted that it was dealing with civil disorder rather than with war, but by this stage it realized otherwise. The struggle was embittered by successive acts of violence and terror, and the reprisals and counter-reprisals that followed.[77]

---

75 Mac Eoin, Art. 'Terence MacSwiney', *An Phoblacht*, 25 October 2001. **76** O'Malley, Ernie. *On Another Man's Wound*, 1936, p. 203. **77** By 1 January 1921, the British government embarked on a policy of 'official reprisals' for nationalist activity. Gallagher, Frank, writing under the pseudonym of David Hogan. *The Four Glorious Years*, 1953, pp. 270-4 presents a vivid description of the raids and reprisals.

In an effort to placate those in the North who were still opposed to any movement in the direction of Home Rule in Ireland, the Government of Ireland Bill was passed in the House of Commons on 11 November 1920 and enacted on 23 December. It proposed separate home rule parliaments for Southern Ireland and for Northern Ireland. A Council of Ireland was to be set up with members from each parliament with a view to one day remove partition and potentially reunite the two entities. Both parliaments would be subject to Westminster.

(The Parliament of Northern Ireland came into being in 1921. At its inauguration in Belfast City Hall on 22 June 1921, King George V made a famous appeal for Anglo-Irish and north-south reconciliation. The speech, drafted by David Lloyd George's government on recommendations from Jan Smuts, Prime Minister of the Union of South Africa, with the enthusiastic backing of the King, opened the door for formal contact between the British government and the Republican administration of de Valera.

(The Parliament of Southern Ireland never became a reality. Both it and the Parliament of Northern Ireland were to be bicameral legislatures as part of 'Home Rule'. All 128 MPs elected to the House of Commons of Southern Ireland were returned unopposed, and 124 of them, representing Sinn Féin, declared themselves TDs and assembled as the Second Dáil of the Irish Republic. When only the Lord Lieutenant, the four Unionist MPs [all representing graduates of the Irish Universities] and fifteen appointed senators turned up for the state opening of the Southern Ireland Parliament in the Council Room of the Department of Agriculture and Technical Instruction in Dublin [now Government Buildings] in June 1921, the new southern House of Commons was suspended.

(The Senate of Southern Ireland was to consist of the Lord Chancellor of Ireland as its chairman; fifteen peers of the realm, resident in southern Ireland, elected by their peers; eight Privy Councillors, elected by the Privy Council; two representatives of the Church of Ireland; two representatives of the Catholic Church [which declined to nominate]; sixteen individuals nominated by the Lord Lieutenant, including two who were to be nominated after consultation with the Labour movement, [which declined to be involved]; and seventeen elected by the members of the county councils in different territorial constituencies. But by this point local government was completely under the control of Sinn Féin and no nominations were received for the seventeen places. After few attempts at meeting, neither southern House met again.)

Connolly predicted a partition, previously proposed in 1914 by British Prime Minister Asquith and agreed upon by John Redmond, leader of the Irish Parliamentary Party, would be a disaster for Ireland. In the *Irish Worker* he wrote of partition:

> It is the trusted leaders of Ireland that in secret conclave with the enemies of Ireland have agreed to see Ireland as a nation disrupted politically and her children divided under separate political governments ... Such a

scheme as that agreed by Redmond and Devlin – the betrayal of the national democracy of industrial Ulster – would mean a carnival of reaction both north and south, would set back the wheels of progress, would destroy the oncoming unity of the Irish Labour Movement and paralyse all advanced movements while it endured. To it Labour should give the bitterest opposition, against it Labour in Ulster should fight even to the death if necessary.[78]

This 1920 partition action again backfired on the British government because it infuriated the IRA/Volunteers, but it did establish the partition that exists to this day.

Later that month, the single most damaging event in relation to the British intelligence organization in Ireland occurred. On Sunday morning, 21 November 1920, the special 'Squad' controlled by Collins executed fourteen British intelligence agents, known as the 'Cairo Gang', who had been poised to eliminate him and other important leaders. In response, Auxiliaries, Black and Tans and RIC units drove in armoured cars to Croke Park during a football match, shooting into the crowd at random. Fourteen unarmed people were killed and sixty-five wounded. Later that day three republican prisoners were 'shot while trying to escape' in Dublin Castle. This day became known as Bloody Sunday.

Dave Neligan, a Collins spy in Dublin Castle, reported that the killing of the intelligence personnel 'caused complete panic in the Castle'. Later Collins, when asked how he felt about the episode, stated: 'For myself, my conscience is clear. There is no crime in detecting and destroying, in wartime, the spy and the informer. They have destroyed without trial. I have paid them back in their own coin.'[79]

The executions of the British agents had a shattering effect on the morale of the British in Ireland, as well as in England. The British public and government were shocked and stunned and could not believe that with all their mighty resources they could be so humiliated. Though Lloyd George fumed about 'murderers' in public, it was this event as much as any other that led him to begin sending emissaries to Ireland seeking peace.

By 1921 the IRA/Volunteers had become a force in Dublin and its 'flying columns' had become feared throughout the counties of Cork, Kerry and Clare. The flying columns were mobile units of from ten to one hundred men, who could strike in devastating ambushes and then melt into a hinterland that they knew far better than the British soldiers who were deployed to fight them. However, most IRA units were chronically short of both weapons and ammunition. By the end of spring 1921, though a formidable opponent, the IRA had not been able to dislodge the British forces, and it became clear that it could not defeat those forces in the field.

De Valera had returned to Ireland in December 1920, and the continued British references to the IRA/Volunteers as 'murderers' led him to press for a full-scale

78 *Irish Worker*, 14 March 1914. **79** Gleeson, James, *Bloody Sunday*. 1962, p. 191.

engagement with the British as opposed to the guerrilla tactics used by the IRA. In Dublin on 25 May 1921 the IRA burned down the Custom House, a centre of British administrative rule in Ireland. As a military operation it was a disaster for the IRA, with over eighty men captured and five killed. The venture into conventional warfare was a setback, and Collins knew it. As worldwide propaganda, though, it was a huge success, demonstrating to the wider world how strong the IRA was and how weak the British position now was in Ireland. That 'strength', however, was illusory, and most IRA leaders, especially Collins, recognized that the organization's desperate shortage of weapons and ammunition would soon allow the British to wear it down.

As British hopes faded, they began to wonder whether Ireland was worth the price. Ireland now cost more to defend and control than it was worth. Progressively throughout the first half of 1921 'peace' feelers were extended, and in July 1921 a truce was agreed. On 9 July terms were agreed upon and the truce went into effect at noon on 11 July 1921. Following the truce, de Valera and British Prime Minister Lloyd George engaged in meetings in London to determine how negotiations should proceed. Both were skilled negotiators, and probably possessed the shrewdest political minds in Europe at the time.

De Valera continually pressed his interpretation of the meetings in correspondence through the next few months. However, Lloyd George just as firmly made it clear that Britain would not enter negotiations on the basis that Ireland was 'an independent sovereign state'.[80]

On 18 September 1921 Lloyd George wrote: 'From the very outset of our conversation I told you that we looked to Ireland to own allegiance to the Throne, and to make her future as a member of the British Commonwealth. That was the basis of our proposals, and we cannot alter it. The status which you now claim for your delegates is, in effect, a repudiation of that status.' Finally after more correspondence between the two over the next two weeks, on 30 September de Valera was able to write: 'Our respective positions have been stated and are understood and we agree that conference, not correspondence, is the most practical and hopeful way to an understanding. We accept the invitation, and our Delegates will meet you in London on the date mentioned "to explore every possibility of settlement by personal discussion"'.[81][82]

---

80 Pakenham, Frank (Lord Longford). *Peace by Ordeal*, 1935, 1972, p. 77. 81 Pakenham details at length the correspondence between de Valera and Lloyd George leading up to the Treaty negotiations. He takes pains to note there were two separate 'debates' entangled in the correspondence: (1) whether England had any right to restrict Ireland's form of government and (2) on what basis could a Conference be held in light of the first issue. He opines discussion on the first issue favoured Ireland and that on the second issue favoured England. He further points out that in de Valera's eyes the position of a Republic 'had been preserved', but the British position was clearly that Ireland would remain a member of the Empire. He concludes: 'On abstract rights De Valera had secured an agreeable academic triumph. On the question of status at the Conference he had, formally at least, held his own. But in the race to secure opinion favourable to the settlements that they respectively contemplated, De Valera was still waiting for the pistol while Lloyd George was half-way home.' Ibid, pp. 77-9.

The 'date mentioned' was 11 October, and on that date treaty negotiations began in London. Arthur Griffith, Michael Collins, George Gavan-Duffy, Robert Barton and Éamonn Duggan represented the Irish, as plenipotentiaries.

One thing that was absolutely clear from the London meetings and correspondence between de Valera and Lloyd George was that there was no question of a Republic. Both the Cabinet in Dublin and the Cabinet in London were aware of that. De Valera clearly grasped what was on offer: an acceptance of partition, an Irish Free State with the same Dominion status as Canada or Australia, an oath of allegiance to the Crown, and the installation of a Governor General.[83] The Republic had been shelved before the final negotiations began and everyone concerned, particularly de Valera, recognized it.[84] In July 1921 he had told Prime Minister Smuts, 'If the status of a Dominion is offered to me, I will use all our machinery to get the Irish people to accept it.'[85] (When asked to lead the delegation, Arthur Griffith agreed, but told de Valera 'I know, and you know that I can't bring back a Republic.'[86] Later, Michael Collins was to say 'if we all stood on the recognition of the Irish Republic as a prelude to any conference we could very easily have said so, and there would have been no conference ... It was the acceptance of the invitation that formed the compromise.'[87])

On 6 December 1921 Articles of Agreement for a Treaty were signed by the plenipotentiaries and returned to Ireland for ratification. De Valera was much opposed to the Treaty, though it has been said that he was greatly affronted he had not been consulted on the final day before signature in disregard of his 'instructions'. At an acrimonious Cabinet meeting, the Treaty was approved by a four-to-three vote majority. It was then presented to the Dáil for ratification, where the divisions of ideology and personality that had always existed were put on public display.

The 'Treaty Debates' in the Dáil took place between 14 December 1921 and 7 January 1922, when the Dáil voted 64–57 in favour of the Treaty. The Treaty Debates were the most vituperative in Irish history. Invective was hurled at and by both sides, personality conflicts that had simmered for many years degenerated into name calling and ad hominem insults, and the vote was considered a 'betrayal

---

82 For a contrasting view to Pakenham's, see Fitzgerald, Desmond. 'Mr Pakenham on the Anglo-Irish Treaty', *Studies, The Irish Jesuit Quarterly Review*, Vol. XXIV, 1935. Fitzgerald contends that de Valera's correspondence with Lloyd George was coloured by his need to placate Cathal Brugha (and to a lesser extent Austin Stack), who was 'a convinced irreconcilable' to whom the truce was only a period to re-arm. As a result, in de Valera's correspondence 'it will be seen that the word "Republic" is never used, while nothing is said that directly implies a readiness to accept the Crown'. Fitzgerald asserts that 'Mr Pakenham has failed to understand the situation at the time. This is probably due to the fact that documents were not available to him. Indeed, there is no documentation of that time.' Fitzgerald concludes 'Mr Pakenham's book reveals much that was not known to the public, and it is a valuable contribution to the history of our time. But the author omits vital facts and wrongly interprets others. In the absence of documents this may have been more or less inevitable. There are questions to which no answer perhaps can be given....His narrative, however, is eminently readable.' 83 Coogan and Morrison. *The Irish Civil War*, p. 20. 84 O'Hegarty. *The Victory of Sinn Féin*, pp. 46-8. 85 Kee, Robert. *The Green Flag*, 1972, p. 721. 86 O'Hegarty. *The Victory of Sinn Féin*, p. 87. 87 Michael Collins. *Dail Éireann Treaty Debates*, Dail Reports, GSO, p. 32.

of the ideals of 1916' by those who felt the only acceptable Treaty would be one unequivocally recognizing an Irish Republic. Most importantly, the Treaty called for an oath of allegiance to the English Crown, and Republicans considered that traitorous. Finally, the Treaty called for partition of the North, and although partition was an established fact after 1920, the conflict in the South only served to further undermine any possibility of reunification.

On learning of the details of the Treaty de Valera announced it was a matter for the Cabinet, and when the Cabinet approved the agreement, he said it was a matter for the Dáil. That democratically elected body of Irishmen and women had spoken, but de Valera led the anti-Treaty contingent from the assembly. De Valera claimed to know 'in his heart' the wishes of his Irish countrymen, and refused to accept the Dáil vote as binding. So when the Dáil approved, he contended only the Irish people could ratify the Treaty. Following the Dáil vote, the Treaty was sent to the people for ratification and an election was scheduled for 16 June 1922, when it was approved by the people and the Irish Free State was established. There could no longer be any argument about which side spoke for the Irish people. Collins' words, 'in my opinion, it gives us freedom. Not the ultimate freedom that all nations desire and develop to, but the freedom to achieve it', resonated with the people.

The election did not represent a vote of confidence in the Provisional Government, and still less an expression of resistance to Republican ideals. It represented a popular realization of the need for stable government, and the acceptance of a realistic compromise with regard to Anglo-Irish relations. The desire for settled conditions was more important to the electorate than the endless debate over constitutional authority. Thus, the election had an important role in legitimizing the Treaty and the status of the Provisional Government. Although it did not prevent the Civil War that was shortly to follow, it greatly helped to facilitate the establishment of the Free State Government during and after the war.

The most 'Republican' members of the IRA, the Dáil and the public still refused to accept the Treaty or the establishment of the Free State, and initiated an insurrection against the new Free State Government, which they accused of betraying the Irish Republic. On 13 April 1922 Dublin's Four Courts were occupied by IRA/ Republican troops led by Rory O'Connor. Upon taking it over, they issued the following proclamation:

> Fellow citizens of the Irish Republic. The fateful hour has come. At the direction of the hereditary enemy our rightful cause is being treacherously assailed by recreant Irishmen. Gallant soldiers of the Irish Republic stand rigorously firm in its defence. The sacred spirits of the Illustrious Dead are with us in this great struggle. 'Death Before Dishonour'. We especially appeal to our former comrades of the Irish Republic to return to that allegiance and thus guard the Nation's honour.

At 3.40 am on 28 June 1922, the insurgents in the Four Courts were given an ultimatum to surrender by troops of the Free State under the command of Michael Collins, and when they refused firing commenced twenty minutes later and the Irish Civil War had begun.

The war lasted until mid-1923 and cost an estimated 3000 lives, including some of the leaders of the independence movement, notably Free State President Arthur Griffith and Michael Collins, as well as anti-Treaty Republicans Cathal Brugha, Harry Boland, Liam Mellowes, Liam Lynch, Joe McKelvey, Dick Barrett, Erskine Childers and Rory O'Connor. Intransigence and inflexibility were attributes of both sides, and these characteristics certainly impeded progress toward peace.

The Irish Civil War came to an end after the death in action of IRA/ Republicans chief of Staff Liam Lynch on 10 April. On 27 April the IRA received an order issued by Frank Aiken, their new Chief of Staff, announcing the suspension of all offensive operations as from noon on 30 April. Shortly afterwards, on 24 May 1923, Aiken issued an order to the IRA to 'dump arms'. Éamon de Valera supported this in his statement 'Soldiers of the Republic, Legion of the Rearguard':

> Soldiers of the Republic, Legion of the Rearguard … The Republic can no longer be defended successfully by your arms … Further sacrifice of life would now be vain and continuance of the struggle in arms unwise in the national interest and prejudicial to the future of our cause. Military victory must be allowed to rest for the moment with those who have destroyed the Republic. Other means must be sought to safeguard the nation's right … Much that you set out to accomplish has been achieved. You have saved the nation's honour and kept open the road to independence. You have demonstrated in a way there is no mistaking that we are not a nation of willing bondslaves. The sufferings you must now face unarmed you will bear in a manner worthy of men who are willing to give their lives for a cause. The thought that you still have to suffer for your devotion will lighten your present sorrow, and what you endure will keep you in communion with your dead comrades, who gave their lives and all those lives promised, for Ireland. May God guard every one of you and give to our country in times of need sons who will love her as dearly and devotedly as you. Seven years of intense effort have exhausted our people. Their sacrifices and their sorrows have been many. If they have turned aside and have not given you that active support which alone could have brought you victory in this last year, it is because they saw overwhelming forces against them and they are weary and need a rest … A little time and you will see them recover and rally again to the standard … When they are ready, you will be, and your place will be again as of old with the vanguard.[88]

88 Neeson, Eoin. *The Civil War in Ireland*, 1966, p. 75.

Although the fighting ceased, peace did not really return. Distrust, bitterness, and hatreds festered for years to come. Perhaps Desmond Williams encapsulated the national tragedy best:

> When friends fall out, the daggers stay sharp. Families devour each other; the nearer in blood the bloodier. The causes of civil, as of other types of war, lie to some extent in the immediate past, and responsibilities for action, or lack thereof, are seldom clear cut. The participants rarely acknowledge this. But it cannot be repeated too often that no one person or party is ever wholly to blame for anything. Here again the Irish Civil War was no exception.[89]

The Civil War was the lowest point in recent Irish history. Few wars are as bitter as civil wars. Few civil wars were as bitter as the Irish Civil War. Its brutality was horrifying, and the tactics of both sides did no justice to the cause for which they fought. Its divisions lasted for generations, and the lives and leadership that were lost would penalize Ireland forever.

89 Williams, T. Desmond. *The Irish Struggle, 1916–1926*, 1966, p. 118.

Baile Átha Cliath

Town of the Hurdle Ford

A DIRECTORY OF
HISTORIC LOCATIONS IN DUBLIN

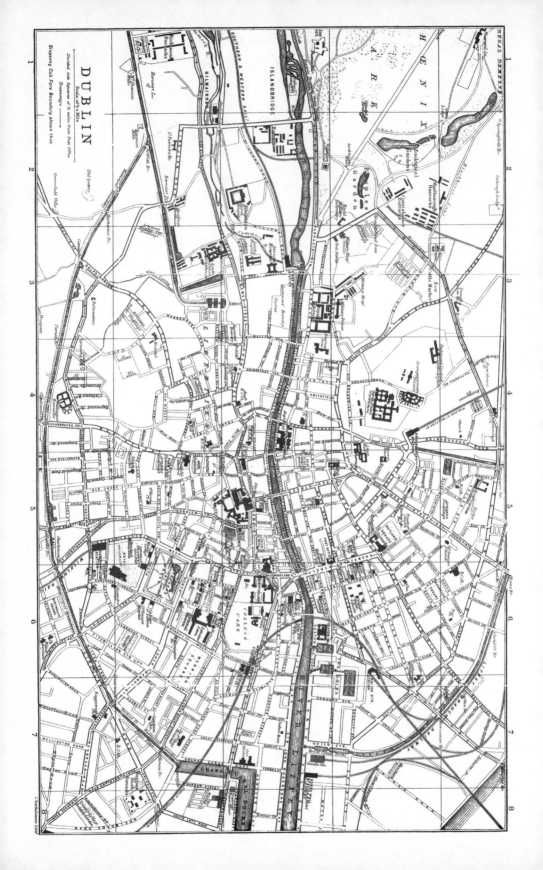

Abbey Street Lower Forty-five buildings were burned during the Rising, including Mooney's Pub, *Daily Express* office, Union Chapel, Methodist Chapel, Peacock Theatre.

3 Abbey Street Lower Keating's cycle shop; the bicycles were used for barricades during the Rising.

4 Abbey Street Lower Reserve printing offices of *The Irish Times*, a Unionist paper. During the Rising George Plunkett led the Volunteers who took newsprint rolls for barricades, which greatly contributed to fires started on Thursday afternoon. On the Tuesday morning of Easter Week, *The Irish Times* described the Rising:

> This newspaper has never been published in stranger circumstances than those that obtain today, an attempt to overthrow the government of Ireland…. At this critical moment our language must be moderate, unsensational, and free from any tendency to alarm. As soon as peace and order have been restored the responsibility for the intended revolution will be fixed in the right quarter….
>
> …During the last twenty-four hours an effort has been made to set up an independent Irish Republic in Dublin. It was well organised; a large number of armed men are taking part in it and to the general public, at any rate, the outbreak came as a complete surprise. An attempt was made to seize Dublin Castle but this failed. The Rebels then took possession of the City Hall and the *Dublin Daily Express* office. During these operations a soldier and policeman were shot dead. The General Post Office was seized and a green flag was raised over its roof. Several shops in this quarter of Sackville Street were smashed and looted…
>
> …In the very centre of the city a party of rebel Volunteers took possession of St Stephens Green where they are, as we write, still entrenched. Fierce fighting has taken place between the rebels and the soldiers and there is reason to fear many lives have been lost…
>
> Of course this desperate episode in Irish history can have only one outcome and the loyal public will await it as calmly and confidently as may be. Nothing in yesterday's remarkable scenes was more remarkable than the quietness and courage with which the people of Dublin accepted the sudden and widespread danger in the very neighbourhood of the fiercest fighting and the streets were full of cheerful and indifferent spectators. Such courage is excellent, but it may degenerate into recklessness.
>
> Perhaps the most useful thing we can do now is to remember that quietness and confidence shall be our strength and to trust firmly in the speedy triumph of the forces of law and order. Those loyal citizens of Dublin who cannot help their country's cause at this moment may help it indirectly by refusing to give way to panic and by maintaining in their household a healthy spirit of hope.

The ordeal is not over but it will be short.[90]

On 1 May in its first edition after the Rising, it opined:

The State has struck, but its work is not yet finished. The surgeon's knife has been put to the corruption in the body of Ireland and its course must not be stayed until the whole malignant growth has been removed. In the verdict of history weakness to-day would be even more criminal than the indifference of the last few months. Sedition must be rooted out of Ireland once for all. The rapine and bloodshed of the past week must be punished with a severity which will make any repetition of them impossible for generations to come. The loyal people of Ireland, Unionists and Nationalists call to-day with an imperious voice for the strength and firmness which have so long been strangers to the conduct of Irish affairs…

Where our politicians failed and failed badly, the British Army has filled the breach and won the day. The Dublin insurrection will pass into history with the equally unsuccessful insurrections of the past.[91]

A week later its editorial stated:

Much nonsense is likely to be written in newspapers and talked about in Parliament about the restrictions of Martial Law in Ireland. The fact is Martial Law has come as a blessing to us all…

For the first time in many months Dublin was 'enjoying real security of life and property'.

We have learned that the sword of the soldier is a far better guarantee of justice and liberty than the presence of politicians.[92]

5 Abbey Street Lower Ship Hotel and Tavern. Occupied by Frank Thornton's and George Plunkett's men during the Rising. It was a hangout of Oliver St John Gogarty when a medical student at Trinity.

26 Abbey Street Lower (at Marlborough Street): Abbey Theatre. On the site of the former Mechanics' Institute Building, and there was a Mechanics' Institute Theatre. The name was changed in 1904, and the first performance as the Abbey was on 27 December 1904.

15 October 1908: Thomas MacDonagh's play *When The Dawn Is Come* opened. This was his only full-length play.

25 October 1914: First Convention of the Irish Volunteers. This was the first 'Convention' of the Volunteers after John Redmond's Woodenbridge, Co. Wicklow,

---

90 *The Irish Times*, 25 April 1916. **91** Ibid, 1 May 1916. **92** Ibid, 8 May 1916.

speech (20 September 1914) pledging the 'Irish Volunteers' to fight for the English. This was the 'reconstitution' meeting. In his impromptu Woodenbridge speech to a group of East Wicklow Volunteers who were holding a Sunday parade, Redmond declared:

> The duty of the manhood of Ireland is twofold. Its duty is at all costs to defend the shores of Ireland against foreign invasion; it is the duty more than that of taking care that Irish valour proves itself on the field of war [as] it has always proved itself in the past. The interests of Ireland, of the whole of Ireland, are at stake in this war. This war is undertaken in the defence of the highest principles of religion and morality and right, and it would be a disgrace forever to our country, and a reproach to her manhood, and a denial of the lessons of our history, if young Ireland confined her efforts to remaining at home to defend the shores of Ireland from an unlikely invasion and to shrink from the duty of approval on the field of battle, that gallantry and courage which has distinguished our race through its history.[93]

(See also Woodenbridge, Co. Wicklow, Appendix I.)

Redmond genuinely believed that the war provided an opportunity to heal the divisions between Unionists and Nationalists, as both groups could cooperate to help Britain win the war. Significantly, the good relations that developed between Nationalists and Southern Unionists during the early phase of the war demonstrated that this was not mere wishful thinking. But Eoin MacNeill's Volunteers issued the following statement:

> Mr Redmond, addressing a body of Irish Volunteers last Sunday, has now announced for the Irish Volunteers a policy and programme fundamentally at variance with their own published and accepted aims and pledges, but with which his nominees are, of course, identified. He has declared it to be the duty of the Irish Volunteers to take foreign service under a Government which is not Irish. He has made his announcement without consulting the Provisional Committee, the Volunteers themselves or the people of Ireland to whose service alone they are devoted. Having thus disregarded the Irish Volunteers and their solemn engagement, Mr Redmond is no longer entitled, through his nominees, to any place in the administration and guidance of the Irish Volunteer organisation.[94]

Redmond's encouragement to support Britain's war effort was vigorously opposed by all the founding members of the Volunteers. Earlier that year Padraig

---

93 *Freeman's Journal*, 21 September 1914. **94** Macardle. *The Irish Republic*, p. 119.

Pearse had written:

> The leaders in Ireland have nearly always left the people at the critical
> moment; they have sometimes sold them. The former Volunteer movement
> was abandoned by its leader, hence its ultimate failure; Grattan 'led the
> van' of the Volunteers, but he also led the retreat of the leaders; O'Connell
> recoiled before the cannon at Clontarf; twice the hour of the Irish
> revolution struck during Young Ireland days and twice it struck in vain
> for Meagher hesitated in Waterford, Duffy and McGee hesitated in
> Dublin. Stephens refused to give the word in '65; he never came in '66
> or '67. I do not blame these men; you or I might have done the same. It
> is a terrible responsibility to be cast on a man, that of bidding the cannon
> speak and grapeshot pour ... Now my reading of Irish history is that
> however the leaders have failed, the instinct of the people has always
> been unerring.[95]

(Writing this eight months before the outbreak of World War I, Pearse wrote of a
rising as an event to take place at some vague time in the future. Following his
January article, Pearse continued to speak and write that the *people* of Ireland knew
what course to take and that the Volunteer leaders should listen to that 'instinct'.
This served as notice to all of the intent of the IRB 'leadership' of the Volunteers.[96])

Immediately after his speech, Redmond's supporters split into the 'Irish National
Volunteers' whereas a minority continued under Eoin MacNeill's leadership, reverted
to their former name, 'Irish Volunteers', and called for Irish neutrality in the war.
The 'National Volunteers' numbered about 175,000 at the time, while the 'Irish
Volunteers' were reduced to about 13,500 men and women. The split proved most
advantageous to the IRB, whose leaders were firmly in control of the Irish Volunteers.

The members of the original committee decided

> to declare that Ireland cannot with honour or safety take part in foreign
> quarrels otherwise than through the free action of a National Government
> of her own; and to repudiate the claim of any man to offer up the blood
> and lives of the sons of Irishmen and Irishwomen to the services of the
> British Empire while no National Government which could act and
> speak for the people of Ireland is allowed to exist.[97 98]

A new alliance with the ICA, resulting from the split with Redmond, was frustrated
by the refusal of the Volunteers to include two ICA members on the Provisional

---

95 Pearse, P.H. 'From a Hermitage', January 1914, in *Collected Works of P.H. Pearse: Political Writings and
Speeches*, p. 209. 96 Wall, Maureen. 'The Background to the Rising; from 1914 Until the Issue of the
Countermanding Order on Easter Saturday, 1916', in Nowlan. *The Making of the Rising*, p. 159. 97 Henry,
R.M. *The Evolution of Sinn Féin*, 1920, p. 196.

Committee or to affiliate with the ICA as a whole. The Provisional Committee consisted of: Eoin MacNeill (chairman), The O'Rahilly (joint treasurer), Padraig Pearse (press secretary), Seán MacDermott, Michael J. Judge, Thomas MacDonagh, Bulmer Hobson (general secretary), Piaras Béaslaí, Seán O'Connor (musketry training officer), Éamonn Martin, Padraig Ryan (publications secretary), Con Colbert, Joseph Plunkett (joint treasurer), Peadar Macken, Seán Fitzgibbon, Éamonn Ceannt (financial secretary), Colm Ó Lochlainn,[99] Peadar White, and Liam Mellowes. Joseph (J.J.) O'Connor and Eimer O'Duffy were appointed 'Volunteer Military Strategists'.

The convention formally adopted the following declaration of policy:

1. To maintain the right and duty of the Irish nation henceforth to provide for its own defence by means of a permanent armed and trained Volunteer Force.
2. To Unite the people of Ireland on the basis of Irish nationality and a common national interest; to maintain the integrity of the nation; and to resist with all our strength any measures tending to bring about or perpetuate disunion or the partition of our country.
3. To resist any attempt to force the men of Ireland into military service until a free National Government of Ireland is empowered by the Irish people themselves to deal with it.
4. To secure the abolition of the system of governing Ireland through Dublin Castle and the British Military power, and the establishment of a National Government in its place.

31 October 1915: Second Convention of the Irish Volunteers. This established a Declaration of Policy: 'To resist any attempt to force the men of Ireland into military service under any Government until a free National Government is empowered by the Irish people themselves to deal with it.'

Author St John Ervine was the manager of the Abbey in 1916. He was an anti-Nationalist and a 'revolt' by the theatre's actors on 29 April 1916 led to their dismissal. The play scheduled for the night of 24 April 1916 was *Cáitlín Ní hUallacháin*. Though very close to the fires of the Rising, the theatre suffered no damage – not even a window was broken. *The Spancel of Death* by Mayo Fenian T.H. Nally was

98 One of those most responsible for the founding of the Volunteers in 1913, Bulmer Hobson, voted to include Redmond's nominees and was severely criticized by others, particularly Tom Clarke and Seán MacDermott. As a result, Hobson resigned all his leadership positions in the IRB. However, he later wrote 'As I had anticipated, the Redmonite control proved completely illusory. The work was carried on by the officers and people who had started the movement. Except that the wrangling in the Provisional Committee was a waste of time and a nuisance, it had hardly any effect on the development of the movement.' Hobson, Bulmer. 'John Redmond and the Volunteers', in Martin, F.X. OSA, *The Irish Volunteers, 1913-1915*, 1963, p. 42.
99 Ó Lochlainn, Colm. Witness Statement 751.

to have starred Arthur Shields, and was scheduled to open on 25 April at the Abbey. Because of the Rising, it failed to open and because no script survived it was not produced.

32, 33 Abbey Street Lower Office of *The Leader*. D.P. Moran, editor, was founder of the 'Buy Irish' campaign – 'Irish Ireland'.

32 Abbey Street Lower On 12 April 1920 a general strike was called here for the next day by Thomas Farren, chairman, and Thomas Johnson[100], treasurer of the Irish Labour Party and Trades Union Council (a single body until 1930), and acting secretary of the National Executive of Trade Unions (in place of the interned William O'Brien).[101]

> To the Workers of Ireland. You are called upon to act swiftly to save a hundred dauntless men. These men, our comrades, have been forcibly taken from their homes, imprisoned without charge or trial for alleged offences of a political character in outrageous defiance of every canon of justice. They are suspected of loving Ireland and hating her oppressors – a heinous crime in the sight of tyrants but one which hundreds of thousands of Irish working men and women proudly acclaim as their birthright.[102][103]

In combination with the hunger strike that started about ten days earlier, this general strike resulted in the release of the prisoners at Mountjoy Prison.

32 Abbey Street Lower Meeting rooms of the Celtic Literary Society. Used by Maud Gonne MacBride for the founding meeting of Inghinidhe na hÉireann (Daughters of Ireland) in 1900. (See also Appendix IV.)

33, 34 Abbey Street Lower Royal Hibernian Academy. Burned during the Rising, and many great works of art were lost. At the time of the Rising Dermot O'Brien was the president.

35–37 Abbey Street Lower Wynn's Hotel (often written 'Wynne's' but photos clearly show the name without an 'e'). The Irish Volunteers first met here as a group on 11 November 1913. The following attended according to *both* The O'Rahilly and Bulmer Hobson: Piaras Béaslaí,* Joseph Campbell, Éamonn Ceannt,* James Deakin, Seán Fitzgibbon,* Bulmer Hobson, Eoin MacNeill,* Seán MacDermott,* The O'Rahilly,* Padraig Pearse,* W.J. Ryan. (*Became members of the Provisional Committee.) The O'Rahilly noted that D.P. Moran was invited but did not attend, but Hobson did not recall this. Hobson noted that Seámus O'Connor, Colm Ó Lochlainn and Robert Page *could* have attended. Others noted that Michael Judge, Éamonn Martin, and Col. Maurice Moore attended.[104]

100 Johnson, Thomas. Witness Statement 1755. **101** Gallagher/Hogan. *The Four Glorious Years*, p. 177 ff. **102** *Evening Telegraph*, 13 April 1920. **103** O'Brien, William. *Forth the Banners Go*, 1969, p. 191. **104** Ó Snodaigh, Aengus. 'The Irish Volunteers Founded', *An Phoblacht*, 26 November 1998.

Cumann na mBan (The League of Women) first met here in April 1914: Agnes O'Farrelly (Chairwoman), Áine Ceannt, Winifred Carney, Kathleen Clarke, Louise Gavan-Duffy, Mrs Thomas Kettle, Agnes MacNeill,[105] Countess Markievicz, Lily O'Brennan, Nannie O'Rahilly, Jennie Wyse-Power. (See also Appendix IV.) Members of the Irish Women's Franchise League also attended and strongly voiced their opinions that Cumann na mBan should not be subservient to the Volunteers. Hanna Sheehy-Skeffington vividly set forth their points, and a bitterly sarcastic account of their objections appeared in their newspaper later:

> The only question of interest at present was buying rifles for men, and that nothing else was of the slightest importance to the truly womanly – and the 'unwomanly' in the audience smiled to themselves and thought deep thoughts on the nature of men who cannot buy a rifle unless a woman collects the money – women, the ministering angel of the ambulance class, who provides the pyjamas and the lint, but who sinks below the human the moment she asks for a vote![106]

The time lag between the formation of the Irish Volunteers and the activation of its counterpart, Cumann na mBan, was at least partially due to disagreement whether the women would take a military part with the Volunteers, or whether they would be content to perform tasks like fundraising when requested by the men. Many men envisioned women's role to be totally subordinate to the needs of the Volunteers, and some women agreed.[107]

Heated exchanges over the role of women and the relationship between Cumann na mBan and the Volunteer movement continued for several months in the pages of the press. In April, *The Irish Volunteer* carried an article indicating that women were to follow in the footsteps of women in previous nationalist movements:

> We can form ambulance corps, learn first aid, make all the flags to be carried by the Volunteers, do all the embroidery required, such as badges on uniforms, etc…To a patriotic Irishwoman could there be any work of more intense delight than that?[108]

By September, the mood had changed to a more militant role for Cumann na mBan as Mary Colum, one of the original Privisional Committee, wrote 'Cumann na mBan members are not the auxiliaries or handmaidens or camp followers of the Volunteers … we are their allies.'[109]

---

105 MacNeill, Agnes. Witness Statement 213. **106** *Irish Citizen*, 9 May 1914. **107** Ward, Margaret. *In Their Own Voice*, 1995, p. 41 ff. **108** Caitlin de Brun. *Irish Volunteer*, 4 April 1914. **109** Mary Colum. *Irish Freedom*, September 1914.

In October, Countess Markievicz would advise in the *Irish Citizen*

If you want to walk around Ireland…dress suitably in short skirts and strong boots, leave your jewels and gold wands in the bank and buy a revolver… It would be well to aim at bringing out the masculine side of women's souls as well as the feminine side of men's souls. War is helping us to do this by shaking women out of old grooves and forcing responsibilities on them. We have got to get rid of the last vestige of the Harem before woman is free as our dream of the future would have her.[110]

One only has to look at the badge worn by Cumann na mBan members to know how militant they came to be: it was the initials C na mB superimposed over a rifle.

(Among the first women to declare for Cumann na mBan was Winifred Carney. 'Winnie' was born in Bangor, Co. Down, was educated at the Christian Brothers' School in Belfast and was for a time a junior teacher there. She worked as a clerk and became involved in the Gaelic League, in the suffragist movement and in socialist activities. In 1912 she met James Connolly and became secretary of the Textile Workers' Union, which was in practice the women's section of the Belfast branch of the Irish Transport and General Workers' Union, though officially part of the Irish Women Workers' Union. She typed Connolly's articles for publication and became a friend and confidant. In Cumann na mBan, she taught first aid and was the most proficient shot in rifle competitions. She was summoned to Dublin by Connolly on 4 April 1916 and typed the first round of mobilization orders; after the confusion caused by the cancellation by Eoin McNeill, she typed the second round of mobilisation orders on Easter Sunday. As Connolly's adjutant she joined the ICA in the GPO, and stayed with Connolly after he had been wounded. In 1917 she was the Belfast delegate to the Cumann na mBan convention and a year later stood as Sinn Féin candidate with the view to establishing a Workers' Republic. She lost the election, but continued to work for the Irish Transport and General Workers' Union until 1928. In 1924 she had joined the Labour Party. In 1928 she married George McBride in Wales, and they moved back to Belfast. She alienated people who could not understand why she would wish to spend her life with 'an Orangeman'. In the 1930s she joined the Belfast Socialist Party. The couple never had children and her grave in Milltown Cemetery remains unmarked.[111])

Abbey Street Middle In the early twentieth century William Rooney taught Irish in his school in this street. The Celtic Literary Society met in the same premises and was frequented by Arthur Griffith, Seán T. O'Kelly and John MacBride.

49 Abbey Street Middle Sinn Féin Company, publishers of *Sinn Féin*. Devereaux, Neuth & Co., printers; printed *Sinn Féin*, replaced by *Scissors and Paste* in late 1914

110 Countess Constance Markievicz. *Irish Citizen*, 23 October 1915. 111 The Dictionary of Ulster Biography.

after *Sinn Féin* was suppressed. Irish Industrial Printing & Publishing; printed *Fianna*.
55 Abbey Street Middle The *Irish Catholic* newspaper, owned by William Martin
Murphy. This newspaper was violently opposed to the ICA and the Volunteers, as
was Murphy's *Irish Independent*. In early May 1916, it wrote of the Rising and the
leaders:

> Pearse was a man of ill-balanced mind, if not actually insane, and the
> idea of selecting him as chief magistrate of the Irish Republic is quite
> enough to create serious doubts as to the sanity of those who approved
> of it ... Only the other day when the so-called Republic of Ireland was
> proclaimed ... no better President could be proposed ... than a crazy and
> insolent schoolmaster. This extraordinary combination of rogues and fools
> ... to find anything like a parallel for what has occurred it is necessary to
> have recourse to the bloodstained annals of the Paris Commune.

On 20 May it opined:

> What was attempted was an act of brigandage pure and simple, and there
> is no reason to lament that its perpetrators have met the fate which from
> the very dawn of history has been universally reserved for traitors ... We
> need say no more, but to say less would be traitorous to the highest and
> holiest interests of Ireland.

(See also 177 King Street North.)
64 Abbey Street Middle Harry Boland's tailor shop. Boland kept the shop open
during the early part of the War of Independence, but it was closed after he left for
America.
67 Abbey Street Middle Office of *Scissors and Paste*; Arthur Griffith, editor. It was
suppressed in March 1915. It attempted to get around Dublin Castle censorship by
printing only items that already had appeared in mainstream publications.

At the turn of the century, it was the headquarters of James Connolly's Irish
Socialist Republican Party (ISRP). It split in 1904 following months of internal
political rows. During its lifespan it only had one really active branch in Dublin.
The Party produced the first regular socialist paper in Ireland, the *Workers' Republic*,
ran candidates in local elections, represented Ireland at the Second International
and agitated over issues such as the Boer War and the 1798 commemorations.
Politically the ISRP was before its time, putting the call for an independent
'Republic' at the centre of its propaganda before Sinn Féin or others had done so.
Connolly left Ireland for the United States in 1903 following internal conflict. In
fact it seems to have been a combination of the petty infighting and his own poverty
that caused Connolly to go to the US. After a further split, where a small number
of members established an anti-Connolly organization called the Irish Socialist

Labour Party, the Party became inactive and wound up in March 1904. Other notable figures in the ISRP included Robert Dorman, Con Lehane, Tom Lyng, Thomas, Daniel and William O'Brien, and Edward Stewart. These seven and Connolly were the founding members, and the membership was always limited. That gave rise to the popular Dublin quip that it was the only Party with more syllables in its name than members! (See also Thomas Street.)

83 Abbey Street Middle *Evening Telegraph* office.

84 Abbey Street Middle The *Freeman's Journal* (main entrance) office. This was the most conservative, Catholic and anti-Parnellite of popular newspapers. It was said that the priests in the parishes read it to illiterates. Originally owned by William Freeman, it was the only newspaper that seemed to accept that the responsibility for the riots associated with the Lockout of 1913 could not be laid primarily on the shoulders of Dublin's hooligan element or its socialists. The *Freeman's Journal* was considered the voice of the decidedly non-revolutionary United Irish League.

At the time, the newspaper one read defined the Irish population. The Anglo-Irish establishment read the then Irish Unionist *The Irish Times*. With the split in the Irish Parliamentary Party over Parnell's relationship with Katherine O'Shea, its readership too split. While the *Freeman's Journal* went with the majority in opposing Parnell, a minority moved to read the *Irish Independent*.

The *Freeman's Journal* was also the voice of John Redmond's Nationalist Party. It had opposed true Irish independence, and accepted Home Rule as it was proposed in Parliament. Its circulation dropped greatly and it became a weekly after Redmond's recruiting speech to Parliament. Redmond's Party subsidized the paper at the time of the Rising. It continued to incur losses and was sold off in 1919.

The proprietor in 1920 was Martin Fitzgerald. He was arrested, imprisoned and the paper fined £3000 because of a report on ill treatment of a prisoner by the Black and Tans. On 29 March 1922, the IRA/Republicans wrecked the office in retaliation for publishing the names of the Executive chosen on 26 March. The greatest loss was the very large collection of photographic plates, as the *Journal* was the first Irish newspaper to use photographs extensively.

The building also housed the office of *Sport*.

85–89 Abbey Street Middle Alex Thom and Company. This published the leading street directory of the time.

96 Abbey Street Middle Maunsel & Co. Ltd, publishers; burned during the Rising.

111 Abbey Street Middle Situated in this street and at 3–4 Liffey Street stood Independent House, the offices of the *Irish Independent*, owned by William Martin Murphy. A major newspaper, very pro-English, pro-Unionist, anti-mainstream Irish Parliamentary Party, it tried to break up the ITGWU strike of 1913 and the Union itself, and its editorial stance advocated full dominion status for Ireland following the Rising.

On Friday, 15 August 1913, Martin informed his employees in the despatch department that they had to choose between membership in the Irish Transport and General Workers Union or their jobs. This action precipitated the Lockout of 1913 as it was an intentional confrontation with the Union. About forty employees refused to resign from the Union and were laid off. The following Tuesday, Martin gave the same ultimatum to his Dublin United Tram Company workers, and on Tuesday 26 August, the Union workers of the tram company walked off their jobs and the Lockout was underway. (See also Liberty Hall, Beresford Place.)

James Connolly suffered a serious leg/ankle wound emerging from the back entrance of this building while returning to the GPO late on Thursday afternoon of the Rising (he had been wounded in the arm earlier that afternoon). He crawled down Prince's Street and was carried into the GPO.

The *Irish Independent* called for the execution of the leaders of the Rising and was especially harsh on Connolly. The following appeared in its editorials:

4 May: No terms of denunciation that pen would indict would be too strong to apply to those responsible for the criminal and insane rising of last week.

10 May: It published a photo of Connolly with the caption: Still lies in Dublin Castle slowly recovering from his wounds.

10 May: If these men are treated with too great leniency they will take it as an indication of weakness on the part of the government and the consequences may not be satisfactory. They may be more truculent than ever, and it is therefore necessary that society should be protected against their activity. Let the worst of the ringleaders be singled out and dealt with as they deserve.

12 May: After Connolly was executed, but before it was known: Certain of the leaders remain undealt with, and the part they played was worse than that of some of those who have paid the extreme penalty …We think in a word that no special leniency should be extended to some of the worst of the leaders whose cases have not yet been disposed of.

The building previously housed the offices of Thomas Davis' *The Nation*, newspaper of the Young Irelanders. (See also Baggot Street Lower.)

111 Abbey Street Middle The *Sunday Independent*. The editor was Paddy J. Little. It was in this paper that Eoin MacNeill placed his notice 'cancelling' the Rising on Easter Saturday night. MacNeill gave the notice to Mr Cogley, the night editor, at midnight:

NO PARADES

Irish Volunteer Marches Cancelled

A SUDDEN ORDER

Owing to the very critical position, all orders given to the Irish Volunteers for tomorrow, Easter Sunday, are hereby rescinded, and no parades, marches or other movements of the Irish Volunteers will take place. Each individual Volunteer will obey this order strictly in every particular.[112]

The editor during the time of the War of Independence was Tim Harrington and the sports subeditor at the same time was George Gormby. The *Irish Independent*'s offices became overcrowded so some of the staff moved to Carlisle House on Westmoreland Street.

The building also housed offices for the *Evening Herald*.

10 Abbey Street Upper George Moreland, cabinetmakers. Bill Stapleton chose the name 'George Moreland' because he said it sounded 'Protestant and Jewish'.[113]

Meeting place for 'The Squad' after they moved from the Antient Concert Rooms. Some of the Squad were craftsmen and could answer callers' queries, but they always told callers that business was so good it would be many months before they could deal with their orders, whereupon 'customers' would take their business to other shops.

41 Abbey Street Upper and Liffey Street Bannon's Pub, where Michael Collins first met Dave Neligan in July 1902.

Adelaide Road Royal Victoria Eye and Ear Hospital.

36 Ailesbury Road Later home of Mrs Mary Ellen (Nell) Humphreys, sister of The O'Rahilly. (See also 54 Northumberland Road.)

The Cabinet and Army Council sometimes met here during the War of Independence. Ernie O'Malley stayed here and used it as an office from September to November 1922. O'Malley was captured here on 4 November 1922. At the outset of the raid he went to a hidden room built by Batt O'Connor during the War of Independence, but the Free State troops knew of it because O'Connor, who was a Treaty supporter, told them, and went right to it. O'Malley fled and was shot several times, but lived and was imprisoned in Mountjoy; sixteen bullets were removed from his body in hospital. Mrs Humphreys' children, Richard (Risteard MacAmblaoibh) and Sheila (Sighle), were arrested and imprisoned after O'Malley's capture.

37 Ailesbury Road Home of Denis Gwynn, editor of *New Ireland*.

16 Airfield Road, Rathgar Home of Julia Donovan, grandmother of Fionnuala

---

112 *Sunday Independent*, 23 April 1916. 113 Stapleton, William J. (Bill). 'A Volunteer's Story', *Irish Independent*, 1916 Golden Jubilee Supplement, April, 1966.

Donovan. This was one of Michael Collins' two main safe houses in Dublin. On the night of Bloody Sunday, Collins had dinner here. The famous wedding party photo, with Collins 'hiding' his face, was taken here after the wedding of Elizabeth Clancy and Michael J. O'Brien on 22 November 1920.[114]

13 Alphonsus Road, Drumcondra Áine Ceannt stayed here while Éamonn was in Richmond Barracks.

Amiens Street Amiens Street Railway Station. The terminus for the Drogheda and Dublin Railway, also known as the Great Northern Railway, built between 1844 and 1846. It was renamed Connolly Station in 1966.

Amiens Street Phil Sheerin's Coolevin Dairy. Located under the Loopline Bridge, it was a most important intelligence and weapons clearing house for Michael Collins' intelligence operations. Couriers from Belfast and other railway workers could drop messages unobtrusively and it was conveniently near the docks for sailors or dockers who were bringing in arms. Collins had an office of sorts in one of the back rooms.

26–30 Amiens Street North Star Hotel. Michael P. Colivet, commandant of the Limerick Brigade, met Padraig Pearse here on Spy Wednesday. The meeting took place in the restaurant and they 'disguised' their conversation by pretending to be a buyer (Pearse) and seller (Colivet) of farmers' goods. Colivet asked about the Rising and Pearse confirmed it was on for Sunday. This was to cause problems when the news got back to Eoin MacNeill.

41 Amiens Street J.M. Butler, newsagent. He was prosecuted and fined £20 in June 1916 for publishing a statement purporting to be that of Thomas MacDonagh in the dock. Four hundred and seventy copies of the publication were seized. (See also MacDonagh Statement to his Court Martial, Appendix III.)

55 Amiens Street Tom Clarke's first shop; in 1910 the family moved to 77 Amiens Street. Later this was the home of Seán Doyle, killed in the Custom House fire. (His brother, Paddy, had been executed in Mountjoy on 14 March 1921.)

77 Amiens Street Tom Clarke's second shop: the family lived in a flat above the shop until they moved to Richmond Street.

77a Amiens Street Houlihan's basketmakers shop. The Volunteer Military Council often met here prior to the Rising.

100–105 Amiens Street Parcels Office of GPO; Conor (Con) Collins was a clerk here.

26–27 Andrew Street and Church Lane Jammet's Restaurant was located here for some time. (See also Nassau Street.)

38 Anglesea Road, Ballsbridge Seán T. O'Kelly lived here with his family during the period before he was elected president in 1945.

Arbour Hill Arbour Hill Detention Centre; built in 1835 and redesigned in 1845, it was the smallest of Dublin's Victorian prisons. Its chapel has stained-glass windows

---

114 O'Donovan, Julia. Witness Statement 475.

by Earley Studios. The bodies of the executed 1916 leaders are buried here in a pit of quicklime; some DMP and British soldiers reported that they were buried in the order in which they were executed.[115]

During the War of Independence C.S. Andrews was a prisoner here, as was Éamon (Ned) Broy. Broy was imprisoned for four months, and was never allowed a change of clothes. When he was released after the Truce, Michael Collins came to collect him, carrying a suit he had had made for Broy at Callaghan & Son on Dame Street.[116] Maire Comerford was imprisoned here during the Civil War. She escaped and was recaptured and imprisoned in Kilmainham Gaol where she went on hunger strike.

8, 10, 11–12 and 22 Ardee Street Watkin's Brewery; Con Colbert's headquarters, from which the garrison moved to the South Dublin Union during Easter week.

Arran Quay St Paul's Church. Built in 1835, it was the first Catholic Church designed by Patrick Byrne (1783–1864), the most famous ecclesiastical architect of the time. He also designed St Audoen's (High Street), St John the Baptist (Blackrock), St James's (James Street), Our Lady of Visitation (Fairview Strand), St Pappin's (Ballymun), Our Lady of Refuge (Rathmines), SS Alphonsus and Columba (Ballybrack), St Assam's (Raheny), and the Three Patrons (Rathgar). Éamon and Sinead de Valera were married here on 8 January 1910.

Ashtown, County Dublin Ambush of Viceroy Lord French (formerly Field Marshal Sir John Denton Pinkstone French, GCB, OM, GCVO, KCMG, PC) on 19 December 1919. The IRA/Volunteers were Ben Barrett, Dan Breen[117], Vinnie Byrne[118], Paddy Daly (O/C of the operation and one section)[119], Seán (J.J.) Hogan, Tom Keogh, Tom Kilcoyne, Joe Leonard, Mick McDonnell (O/C of the other section)[120], Seámus Robinson, Seán Treacy, Jim Slattery[121] and Martin Savage. This was the latest of several attempts on French. Dan Breen calculated that in all twelve attempts were made. Tomás MacCurtain took part in one attempt and told Treacy and Robinson that the only good thing about it was he (MacCurtain) had been able to retain a revolver that he hadn't had before. The Volunteers were to mill about near 'Kelly's Inn' (the Halfway House) and to let the first car go by as their information was French would be in the second car. In fact, French was in the first car and escaped. The plan went awry, the road was not barricaded, Breen was wounded and Savage was killed.[122]

14–18 Aston Quay McBirney's General Retailers; had a reputation for the best linens. During the Rising British snipers fired from this location directly across the Liffey on Hopkins and Hopkins, jewellers, on Eden Quay.

27 Auburn Street (Phibsborough) Home of James Larkin in 1913. He lived here

115 Soughley, Michael T. Witness Statement 189. 116 Broy, Éamon. Witness Statement 1284. Author's personal interview with Áine Broy. 117 Breen, Daniel. Witness Statements 1739, 1763. 118 Byrne, Vincent. Witness Statement 423. 119 Leonard, Joseph. Witness Statement 547. 120 McDonnell, Michael. Witness Statement 225. 121 Slattery, Jim. Witness Statement 445. 122 Sugg, Wayne. 'Christmas Week Ambush', *An Phoblacht*, 16 December 1999.

with his wife and three sons, paying rent of nine shillings per week, out of his weekly salary of £2.2s.

Aungier Street Flanagan's Funeral Home; IRA/Volunteers often were buried from here.

Aungier Street St Peter's and St Kevin's Church. Robert Emmet was baptised here. Emmet's family resided in nearby St Stephen's Green, and attended services in the Church of Ireland St Peter's Church here. It has been the tradition of the Emmet family in America that Robert was finally laid to rest in the family vault in this church, as recorded by his grand nephew Dr Thomas Addis Emmet. (See also Kilmainham/Royal Hospital and Thomas Street.)

Aungier Street *An tÓglach* (The Youth/Volunteer/Soldier), conceived by Michael Collins in 1918 and edited by Piaras Béaslaí, was published from here. The first issue appeared on 15 August 1918. It was a 'secret' internal journal printed in Dublin and distributed to the Volunteers through the IRA. It was not only a 'military journal' but contained much of the Sinn Féin ideology, and had a great influence on the IRA/Volunteers and, later, the IRA/Republicans. Instead of preaching the politics of a party or of any particular leader, it always emphasized that the Volunteer's allegiance was to the Irish nation. The first leading article stated:

> Volunteers are not politicians; they were not created for the purposes of parades, demonstrations, or political activities; they follow no particular leader as such; their allegiance is to the Irish Nation. To their own chosen leaders they render the obedience that all soldiers render to their officers. Their obedience to their officers is not affected by personal considerations. It is the office, not the man, to whom deference is due.
>
> The Irish Volunteers have chosen in open Convention those leaders in whom they have confidence to control the public policy of the organisation. It is the duty of those leaders to conform that policy to the national will, by co-operating on the military side with those bodies and institutions which in other departments of the national life are striving to make our Irish Republic a tangible reality.[123]

77 Aungier Street A union office for the workers of Jacob's Biscuit Factory, locked out in the Lockout of 1913.

Bachelor's Walk On 26 July 1914 at 6.30 pm, following retrieval of the Howth Rifles, four civilians were killed and more than thirty-five were seriously injured when fired on by the King's Own Scottish Borderers (quickly nicknamed the 'King's Own Scottish Murderers' by Dubliners). About one hundred of the Borderers under the command of Cpt. Cobden had marched toward Howth to the Malahide Road where there was a confrontation with the Volunteers. Negotiations took

123 *An tÓglach*, 15 August 1918.

place between the Volunteers and William Vesey Harrel, the Assistant Commissioner of the Dublin Metropolitan Police (DMP), who had originally called in the military. The troops continued towards the city and were met along the way by a further sixty men under the command of Maj. Coke. They were harassed by civilians along the route and when they turned from Sackville Street onto Bachelor's Walk the command was turned over to a Maj. Haig.[124]

A British inquiry found that Harrell decided to illegally seize the arms from the Volunteers, and everything that happened afterwards was illegal.[125] Col. Sir Walter Edgeworth-Johnstone, the Chief Commissioner, and Sir Neville Chamberlain, the Inspector General of the DMP, were exonerated.[126 127] Those killed were James Brennan (eighteen), Mrs Mary Duffy (fifty, she was the mother of a soldier serving in the British army), Alice Brady (fifteen), and Patrick Quinn (forty-six).[128]

32 Bachelor's Walk Second office of the Irish National Aid and Volunteers' Dependents' Fund, primarily run by Kathleen Clarke and Sorcha MacMahon. Michael Collins went to work as secretary of the Fund on 19 February 1917, at a salary of £2.10s a week. Originally he worked in the 10 Exchequer Street office.

Collins, Tom Cullen, Bill Tobin and Frank Thornton used the office concurrently for intelligence work from 1917 to 1921.

Collins used another office in the building as a Finance Office. He was arrested here on 2 April 1918 and taken to the DMP's Brunswick Street Station accompanied by Detectives Smith and Thornton. From there he was taken to the Longford Assizes where he refused to recognize the court. Because it was not Volunteer policy to avail of bail he was then sent to prison in Sligo on 10 April 1918. Ultimately he was freed on bail from Sligo. (See also Ballinamuck, Co. Longford, Appendix II.)

56 Bachelor's Walk (corner of Lower Sackville Street): Kapp & Peterson's, pipes and tobacco; built on the site of 'Kelly's Fort' after it was demolished during the Rising. Later, the second floor housed the New Ireland Insurance Company, run by Michael Staines who was in the GPO during the Rising.

67 Baggot Street Lower Home of Thomas Davis, composer of the song 'A Nation Once Again'. Davis was born in 1814 and died in 1845. With John Blake Dillon and Charles Gavan-Duffy, he founded *The Nation* in 1841, the idea for which was conceived while the three men were walking in the Phoenix Park, and the first issue appeared in October 1842. Davis, Dillon and Gavan-Duffy had in *The Nation*, by means of theoretical essays and rousing ballads/poetry, re-established a sense of nationalism and patriotism. Its non-denominational stance and Trinity background reassured Protestant liberals. (See also Abbey Street Middle.)

92 Baggot Street Lower A Mrs Stack owned this house. On Bloody Sunday Bill

124 Figgis, Darrell. *Recollections of the Irish War*, 1925, pp. 49-58. **125** *Report of the Royal Commission on the circumstances connection with the landing of arms at Howth on 26th July 1914*, Parliamentary Papers, 1914-1916, xxiv, p. 805. **126** Ibid, pp. 824-89. **127** Townshend, Charles. *Easter 1916, The Irish Rebellion*, 2005, p. 57. **128** Ó Snodaigh, Aengus. 'Arming the Volunteers', *An Phoblacht*, 20 June 1997. **129** Stapleton, Wiliam J. Witness Statement 822.

Stapleton[129] and Joe Leonard[130] killed Cpt. W.F. Newbury, Royal West Surrey Regiment. He was killed in front of his wife who was eight months pregnant and she gave birth to a stillborn child two weeks later. (See also Bloody Sunday, Appendix II.)

119 Baggot Street Lower On Bloody Sunday Cpt. George T. Baggallay, a one-legged barrister and Courts Martial Officer, formerly the Army Judge Advocate, was killed here. He was known as a redoubtable prosecutor of the IRA, and was in charge of the detail that killed John Lynch, in the Royal Exchange Hotel on 23 September 1920. He had previously lived at 19 Eccles Street. One of 'The Squad' responsible for his death was Seán Lemass, future Taoiseach. Thomas Whelan and Patrick (Paddy) Moran were hanged in Mountjoy Prison on 14 March 1921 for this killing despite both having solid alibis placing them outside Dublin on Bloody Sunday. (See also Bloody Sunday, Appendix II.) (See also Paddy Moran: North Circular Road/Mountjoy Prison; South Circular Road/Kilmainham Gaol; Sackville Street Upper/Gresham Hotel.)

128 Baggot Street Lower Home of John and Henry Sheares. Members of the United Irishmen, they were beheaded outside Newgate Prison 14 July 1798. Their coffins can be seen in the vaults of St Michan's Church in Church Street.

134 Baggot Street Lower Ferguson's Garage. The Fergusons were a branch of a well-known Belfast firm. The garage was raided by a group of IRA/Republicans led by Leo Henderson who were intent on commandeering vehicles (valued at £9000) on 26 June 1922. The raid was in line with the so-called 'Belfast Boycott'. (Henderson was acting as director of the Belfast Boycott, though the Free State Government had abandoned the Boycott [officially] the previous March under an agreement between Collins, Griffith, and Sir James Craig. See also the Craig-Collins Pact, London, Appendix II.) The raiders were stopped by Free State troops led by Frank Thornton on the orders of Michael Collins, and Henderson and his men were taken prisoner.[131] Henderson was also a supporter of the minority, militant wing of anti-Treatyites garrisoned in the Four Courts (as opposed to Liam Lynch's majority of those less militantly republican). Accordingly, Henderson was seen by the Free State forces as a suitable target on which to make a gesture to placate the British after the assassination of Sir Henry Wilson in London on 22 June 1922. The capture of Henderson's group led to the retaliatory taking of Gen. J.J. 'Ginger' O'Connell (suggested by Ernie O'Malley) by the Republicans' Four Courts garrison, which led directly to the shelling of the Four Courts on 28–9 June.

139 Baggot Street Lower Toner's Pub; alleged to be the only one visited by W.B. Yeats (he was taken there by Oliver St John Gogarty).

16–18 Baggot Street Upper Royal City of Dublin Hospital; commonly called Baggot Street Hospital. Dr Alfred Parsons, Alfred Fannin's brother-in-law, worked here. He was singled out for his great service during the Rising. He was a leading

130 Leonard, Joseph. Witness Statement 547. **131** Thornton, Frank. Witness Statements 510, 615.

Dublin doctor and included J.M. Synge among his patients. He was taken to Dublin Castle to examine James Connolly, and was asked if Connolly was 'fit to be shot?' Parsons answered 'A man is never fit to be shot.' He also gave evidence that Cpt. J.C. Bowen-Colthurst, the officer who unlawfully shot Francis Sheehy-Skeffington during the Rising, 'was unbalanced'. (See also Rathmines Road/Portobello Barracks.)

George Jameson Johnston was a surgeon and lecturer in clinical surgery here, and was also professor of surgery at the Royal College of Surgeons in Ireland. Richard Atkinson Stoney was another famous surgeon who practised here.

Ballymun Road 'Jameson' (John Charles Byrne) was shot dead here on 2 March 1920. (See also Brendan Road, [Appendix II], Harcourt Street and Sackville Street Upper.)

Beechwood Avenue, Ranelagh Home of Seámus Moore and his sisters, Bridie and Mary, it was used as a safe house and meeting place by the IRA/Volunteers, and then by the IRA/Republicans during the Civil War. Josephine Ahern, Desmond Fitzgerald, Frank Gallagher, Maureen McGavock[132] and Ernie O'Malley stayed here.

54 Beechwood Avenue Upper, Ranelagh Briefly the home of James Larkin upon his return to Ireland in 1923, until he moved to live with his sister, Delia, at 17 Gardiner Place.

Belgrave Road, Rathmines Became known as 'Rebel Road' because of all the Fenians, TDs and Republicans living in close proximity to each other here.

3 Belgrave Road, Rathmines Home of the Count Plunkett family before they moved to Kimmage.

7 Belgrave Road, Rathmines Home of Thomas Kelly, Dublin Alderman. He read the 'Castle Document' allegedly 'forged' by Joseph Plunkett at the Dublin Corporation meeting on 19 April 1916. (See also under Kimmage, Dublin, Larkfield.)

7 Belgrave Road, Rathmines Home of Hanna Sheehy-Skeffington. Hanna lived here after Frank's murder and being evicted from 11 (now 21) Grosvenor Place, Rathmines, where she lived with Frank and their son Owen. She was a judge of the Dáil/Republican Courts and a member of the first Fianna Fáil Executive in 1926. Rosamund Jacob sometimes lodged here.

9 Belgrave Road, Rathmines Home of Dr Kathleen Lynn and Madeleine ffrench Mullen.

Educated in Dublin, England and Germany, Dr Lynn qualified as a doctor in 1899. Awarded degrees in surgery and medicine from the Royal University in 1899, having interned at Holles Street Hospital (1897–9), the Rotunda Hospital (1899), the Royal Victoria Eye and Ear Hospital (1899) and also the Richmond Lunatic Asylum, she became a Fellow of the Royal College of Surgeons in Ireland in 1909. She fought in the Rising, was imprisoned and deported, but was released in 1918 to fight the influenza epidemic of that year.[133]

---

132 Beaumont, Mrs Seán (Maureen McGavock). Witness Statement 385. **133** Lynn, Dr Kathleen. Witness Statement 357.

She died in September 1955, and was given a military funeral as she was a commanding officer during the Rising.

Ms ffrench Mullen was a member of the Irish Women's Franchise League, and a staunch supporter of James Connolly as a member of the Irish Citizen Army, serving in the Liberty Hall soup kitchens during the 1913 Lockout. A frequent contributor to *Bean na hÉireann*, she had a lifelong commitment to the causes of labour and women's rights and the emancipation of the working class. She invested a significant portion of her life in building the Irish Womens' Workers' Union, and was elected a vice-president in 1917 (as was Dr Lynn). During the Rising, she commanded the medical detachment at St Stephen's Green and was imprisoned in Richmond Penitentiary and Kilmainham Gaol.

Helena Molony often lodged here.[134]

(See also under Charlemont Street, St Ultan's Children's Hospital.)

10 Belgrave Road, Rathmines Home of Robert and Una Brennan. She is said to be one of only two women admitted into the IRB. (Her husband would not join without her.) (Some sources have Maud Gonne as the other woman, but others cite Kathleen Clarke. It is accepted Kathleen Clarke was given the duty to re-establish communications between surviving IRB members after the Rising, and Thomas gave her access to the IRB funds. She was actually told by the IRB *not* to take part in the Rising so that she would be able to help the families of the men who were killed or imprisoned after that.)

Belmont Ave, Donnybrook Home of Mrs Áine (Annie) Heron, a judge of the Dáil/Republican Courts. She had been in the Four Courts during the Rising.[135]

7 Belvedere Place Home of John Redmond in the early 1900s, by 1916 it had been let out into flats. Later home to William (Bill) O'Brien, a member of the IRB. James Connolly sent his son Rauri (Roddy) here for safety. Nora Connolly and Lily Connolly stayed here when James was in Dublin Castle. O'Brien succeeded James Connolly as head of the ITGWU.

43 Belvedere Place Home of Mrs O'Brien, a widow of a member of the Royal Irish Constabulary (RIC), and three of her four children. The two eldest, Daniel and Thomas (T.J.) and the youngest, William (Bill), had been early members of James Connolly's Irish Socialist Republican Party. Cecelia was active in Cumann na mBan. William was active in both Republican and Labour politics. In 1916 Daniel was mortally ill with tuberculosis, yet unlike his brother he was a member of the Volunteers, not the ICA. At that time T.J. was abroad as a foreign correspondent. By 1916, William was a member of the IRB, a former president of the Irish Trades Union Congress, and The Labour Party, as well as Connolly's closest associate (though not a member of the Irish Citizen Army.) He became treasurer of the ITGWU in 1919, and in 1924 he became the Union's general secretary.

In 1916, the Military Council of the IRB appointed William to a civilian

---

134 Molony, Helena. Witness Statement 391. **135** Heron, Áine. Witness Statement 293.

'Provisional Government', along with Arthur Griffith, Tom Kelly, Seán T. O'Kelly, and Hanna Sheehy-Skeffington for the purpose of maintaining food supplies during the fighting of the Rising. It was never able to function.

After the Rising, William tried to continue Connolly's strategy, joining the ITGWU to help rebuild it and entering Count Plunkett's Mansion House Committee that would be the centre around which would be built the new Sinn Féin. (See also the Mansion House, Dawson Street.) In this sphere, however, he had to resign after one month under pressure from other labour leaders who feared too close an association with the national struggle and felt that that might harm their organisation materially, as Connolly's participation led to the destruction of Liberty Hall.

Benburb Street Croppies' Acre; an area of untended grass left uncultivated because it is the grave of the United Irishmen killed in the eighteenth century. They were called 'croppies' because many of them cut their hair short in imitation of the revolutionary French.

18 Beresford Place (at Eden Quay): Liberty Hall. In the early nineteenth century the building had been a chophouse. Later in the century it was the site of the Northumberland Commercial and Family Hotel that had been the meeting place for members of the Young Ireland movement. Still later, the Northumberland became the meeting place for members of the Land League. By 1911 the hotel had become almost derelict.

In 1912 it became the headquarters of the Irish Transport and General Workers' Union (ITGWU). A decision to establish the Union was taken at a meeting in Dublin in December 1908. (James Larkin had arrived in Ireland in 1907 to begin his organizing work.) At that meeting a decision was made to revolt against the English National Union of Dock Labourers which suspended Larkin from his post as organizer because of his concentration on specifically Irish problems. The first members were enrolled, and union cards were issued, on 20 January 1909, as the Irish Transport Workers' Union. (The name was soon changed to the Irish Transport and General Workers' Union.[136]) The Union's first office was on Townsend Street, but soon it managed to rent a room at 10 Beresford Place. Later it secured affiliation to the Dublin Trades Council and, in May 1910, to the Irish Trade Union Congress. In March 1912 the rented room at 10 Beresford Place was vacated and the Northumberland Hotel was taken over in its entirety. Later, following the lead of James Connolly, who returned from the United States and began his syndicalist teaching, the role of the Union was expanded to include especially his 'One Big Union' concept and his socialist ideals.

In 1911 the ITGWU had about 4000 paid-up members, but this doubled to about 8000 by the end of 1912, and to 10,000 by the middle of 1913. Guinness workers remained outside of the Union because they were well treated by their employer, Lord Iveagh.

---

136 MacLysaght, Edward, 'Larkin, Connolly, and the Labour Movement', in Martin. *Leaders and Men,* p. 124.

On Monday 25 August 1913, at 9.40 am, tramcars all over Dublin stopped in their tracks. It was the first day of Horse Show Week. All the drivers and conductors affixed the Red Hand Union Badge on their clothes and ordered the passengers off because they were on strike. Though the trams were started again, Larkin's action was to shut down the tram system and instigate a general strike. Under the leadership of William Martin Murphy, the owners rushed up scab (strikebreaking) workers for many businesses and the Great Lockout of 1913 was underway.

On 28 August, during a speech, Larkin paused to say: 'Before I go any further, with your permission I am going to burn the Proclamation of the King. People make Kings and people can unmake them.' For this statement he was arrested for seditious libel. On Friday, 29 August, the government arrested P.T. Daly (full-time official of the ITGWU), William O'Brien[137] (vice-president of the Trades Council, and president of the Tailor's Society), Thomas Lawlor (Tailor's Society), William P. Partridge (ITGWU organizer and president of the Dublin district of the Amalgamated Society of Engineers [a British union]) and Larkin. After they were released on bail, Larkin promised a speech and, at a meeting outside Liberty Hall during the Lockout, he proclaimed:

> I would advise the friends and supporters of this cause to take Sir Edward Carson's advice to the men of Ulster. If he says it's right and legal for the men of Ulster to arm, why should it not be right and legal for the men of Dublin to arm themselves so as to protect themselves? If Carson has the right to arm his men in the North, then you men have a right to arm to protect yourselves from police attack. You will need it. I don't offer advice which I'm not prepared to adopt myself. You know me, and you know when I say a thing I will do it. So arm, and I'll arm. You will have to face hired assassins ...
>
> Now we will hold our next big meeting in O'Connell Street, come what may, and we will show them that we can use the property for which we pay.[138]

Larkin sneaked into the Imperial Hotel on Sackville Street on Sunday, 31 August, in order to deliver his speech to about 300–400 Union supporters gathered there. That speech was proscribed by an order of Magistrate Swifte. Larkin had just begun speaking when the DMP broke into the room and arrested him, and this caused a riot. Fighting erupted in Sackville Street, Great Brunswick Street, Abbey Street Lower, Eden Quay and Foley Street. John Byrne and James Nolan were seriously injured during these disturbances and died as a result. (See also Eden Quay and Foley Street.) Larkin was released on 12 September.

The employers required their workers to sign this pledge in order to return to

---

137 O'Brien, William. Witness Statement 1766. **138** *The Irish Times*, 30 August 1913.

work: 'I hereby undertake to carry out all instructions given to me by or on behalf of my employers and further I agree to immediately resign my membership of the Irish Transport and General Workers' Union (if a member) and I further undertake that I will not join or in any way support this union.' Four hundred Dublin employers subsequently decided to lock out all workers who were members of the Union or who would not sign the pledge. Magistrates were prevailed upon to prohibit public meetings called by the Union and to order their suppression. DMP policemen were posted on the trams driven by employees intimidated by dismissal.

The Irish Citizen Army (ICA) was proposed in October 1913, giving equal rights to men and women. The Starry Plough Banner made its first appearance at that time.

On 13 November, at a victory meeting to celebrate Larkin's release from prison, Connolly announced 'I am going to talk sedition. The next time we are out for a march I want to be accompanied by four battalions of trained men with their corporals and sergeants. Why should we not drill and train men as they are doing in Ulster?'[139]

In early 1914, Connolly announced the establishment of the Irish Citizen Army 'to protect workers' meetings' and 'to prevent the brutalities of armed thugs occurring in the future'. On 22 March 1914, Larkin presided at a meeting reconstituting the ICA. Primarily James Larkin, Seán O'Casey, Countess Markievicz, and other militarily minded members of the ITGWU drew up the new constitution. It provided for an Army Council, and included explicitly nationalist aims:

> Article One: The first and last principle of the Irish Citizen Army is the avowal that the ownership of Ireland, moral and material, is vested of right in the people of Ireland.

> Article Two: That its principal objects should be:
> a. To arm and train all Irishmen capable of bearing arms to enforce and defend its first principle.
> b. To sink all differences of birth, privilege and creed under the common name of the Irish people.

> Article Three: The Irish Citizen Army shall stand for the absolute unity of Irish nationhood, and recognition of the rights and liberties of the democracies of all nations.

> Article Four: That the Citizen Army shall be open to all who are prepared to accept the principles of equal rights and opportunities for the People of Ireland and to work in harmony with organised labour towards that end.

139 Greaves. *The Life and Times of James Connolly*, p. 263.

Article Five: Every enrolled member must be, if possible, a member of a Trade Union recognized by the Irish Trades Union Congress.

Cpt. Jack White, DSO, chaired the Army Council. (White originally proposed the name 'The Civic League' to Larkin and Connolly.) The vice-chairmen were Larkin, P.T. Daly, Countess Markievicz, William Partridge, Thomas Foran and Francis Sheehy-Skeffington. The secretary was Seán O'Casey and the treasurers were Countess Markievicz and Richard Brannigan. The Committee was: T. Blair, John Bohan, T. Burke, P. Coady, P. Fogarty, P.J. Fox, Thomas Healy, T. Kennedy, J. MacGowan, Michael Mallin, P. Morgan, F. Moss, P. O'Brien, Christopher Poole, and John (Seán) Shelly.[140] (At first the Council did not include Connolly who went back to Belfast to take care of the Union's affairs there, returning later in 1914.)

Ironically, though it had been formed as a force to protect the workers, the ICA was never called into action in any major way during the Lockout.

The Lockout lasted for about five months into early 1914 and directly involved some 20,000 workers. British trade unions sent over £100,000, an incredible sum at today's valuation, to support the locked-out workers, but their failure to call a 'sympathetic strike' in England was decisive in ending the Lockout.

Connolly clearly expressed his bitterness at the end of the Lockout: 'And so we Irish workers must go down into Hell, bow our backs to the lash of the slave driver, let our hearts be seared by the iron of his hatred, and instead of the sacramental wafer of brotherhood and common sacrifice, eat the dust of defeat and betrayal.'[141]

The IRB pressed many nationalists to join the Volunteers following their inception in 1913, but the Volunteers had not backed the ITGWU in the 1913 Lockout. As a result, there continued to be distrust and animosity between the ICA and the Volunteers. The ICA issued their recruiting handbill in 1914:

Why Irish Workers Should Not Join the National Volunteers
1. Because many members of the Executive are hostile to workers.
2. Because it is controlled by forces that have always controlled Labour.
3. Because many of its officials have locked out their employees for asserting their right to join the trades union of their choice.
4. Because they refuse to declare that they stand for the democratic principles of Wolfe Tone and John Mitchel.
5. Because they welcome in their organisation creatures that are proved renegades to their own class.

Reasons Why Irish Workers Should Join the Citizen Army
1. Because it is controlled by leaders of your own class.
2. Because it stands for Labour and the principles of Wolfe Tone, John Mitchel and Fintan Lalor.

---

140 O'Casey, Seán. *Story of the Irish Citizen Army*, pamphlet, 1919, Chapter II. **141** *Forward*, 9 February 1914.

3. Because it has the sympathy and support of the Dublin Trades Council.
4. Because it refuses to allow in its ranks those who have proved untrue to Labour.

Workers Do Not Be Misled: Trust Only Those Ye Know And Have Suffered For Your Class

Join The Irish Citizen Army Now![142]

Though their numbers were small, the equipment and training of the Irish Citizen Army were superior to that of most of the Irish Volunteers because the ICA had trades union money behind them and, consequently, full uniforms and a full-time, well-trained professional soldier to instruct them. Cpt. White was the son of Gen. Sir George White, the British commander of the defence of Ladysmith in the Boer War, and was, himself, a professional soldier.

(See also 70 Eccles Street for Seán O'Casey's and Jim Larkin's challenge to the Volunteers.)

(Connolly had a long history of collaboration with women's movements extending back to the 1890s. He had conventional attitudes to monogamy and marital morality, unlike many leaders of that era, and his positions on religion, marriage and morality were much more conservative than those of the Marxists of the time. However, he had an absolutely consistent record of co-operation with the militant feminist movements of the period and held steadfastly to his support for equal women's rights in all matters. The Citizen Army was another example of this – Connolly ensured women were treated exactly equally.[143])

The Dublin Trades Council approved the Citizen Army on 6 April 1914. Larkin sent a notice to all trades bodies indicating the ICA would begin recruiting.

MANIFESTO SENT TO IRISH TRADES BODIES.
IRISH CITIZEN ARMY HEADQUARTERS,
LIBERTY HALL, DUBLIN.
The Secretary...........Trades Union.
A Chara,
In view of the present situation it has been decided to reorganise and develop the scope of the Irish Citizen Army. No one knows what a day may bring forth. We have the Ulster Volunteers preparing for eventualities in the North, and the National Volunteers actively organising themselves in various parts of Ireland, while all the time the Labour Hercules leans foolishly and lazily on his club.

Would it not be a shame if the forces of Labour alone were content to believe all things, suffer all things, endure all things; to starve rather than take, to be stricken and not to strike back?

142 O'Casey. Op. cit., Chapter IV.   143 Hyland, J.L. *Life and Times of James Connolly*, 1997, p. 38.

Believing that Labour will shake itself to action, we have formed a Provisional Council to develop the power and influence of the Citizen Army in Labour circles, and we hope their efforts will receive the co-operation of your Trades Union. We propose to hold a meeting in your...................... shortly, and, in the meantime, we appeal to you to use your efforts to prevent the members of your Union from joining any organisation, how ever attractive its name or principles may seem, till we have the opportunity of fully explaining to them the principles, objects and aims of the Irish Citizen Army.

We enclose copies of Constitution, posters and handbills, and hope that these will show that the Irish Citizen Army is the only suitable organisation for the workers of Ireland.

Fraternally yours,
President, CAPTAIN WHITE, DSO,
Hon. Secretary, SEAN Ó CATHASAIGH,
Irish Citizen Army.[144]

White's goal was a well-trained ICA and he was intolerant of the conflicts between the ICA and the Volunteers. He resigned the ICA in May 1914 and gave his reasons:

Dear Sir

With reference to a paragraph which appeared in some of this morning's papers connecting my name with a challenge issued by the Citizen Army council to the provisional committee of the National Volunteers, I wish to state that I had nothing to do with it; in fact I resigned from the chairmanship of the said council a week ago, doubtful of my power to prevent, and determined not to become involved in such policy. In my opinion the all-important point is the speedy formation and requipment of a volunteer army implicitly or explicitly determined to achieve the independence and maintain the unity of Ireland…

For an 'army council' which has not yet created an appreciable 'army' to issue a challenge to the organisers of a strong and growing movement seems to me to be a little short of the absurd…[145]

In 1914 James Connolly spoke in commemoration of the workers killed in the 1913 Lockout:

---

144 O'Casey. Op. cit., Appendix. **145** *Evening Telegraph*, 5 May 1914.

The Irish workers hold themselves ready to bargain with whoever [sic] can make a bargain. If you are itching for a rifle, itching to fight, have a country of your own; better to fight for our country than for the robber empire. If you ever shoulder a rifle let it be for Ireland ... Our curse is our believe in our weakness. We are not weak, we are strong. Make up your mind to strike before the opportunity goes.[146] [147]

Just a month earlier Connolly wrote his hope for labour in the *Irish Worker*:

Let us not shrink from the consequences. This may mean more than armed battling in the streets to keep in this country the food for our people. But whatever it may mean it must not be shrunk from. It is the immediate feasible policy of the working-class democracy, the answer to all the weaklings who in this crisis in our country's history stand helpless and bewildered crying for guidance, when they are not hastening to betray her.

Starting thus, Ireland may yet set a torch to a European conflagration that will not burn out until the last throne and last capitalist bond and debenture will be shrivelled on the funeral pyre of the last warlord.[148]

On 24 October 1914 Larkin left for America and Connolly was in complete charge of the Union and the ICA. After 1914, Liberty Hall was the headquarters of the Irish Citizen Army, of which Connolly became O/C. Officers included: Maj. Michael Mallin (second in command), Cpt. Walter Carpenter, Cpt. Seán Connolly, Cpt. Richard MacCormick, Cpt. Seámus McGowan,[149] Cpt. John O'Neill, Countess Markievicz, Cpt. William Partridge, Cpt. Christopher Poole, Lt Michael Kelly, Sgt Joseph Doyle and Sgt Frank Robbins[150].

(Robbins was imprisoned after the Rising and upon his return felt that the spirit of the ICA had changed greatly. He wrote: 'There was a new atmosphere, a new outlook entirely from that which had been moulded by Connolly and Mallin. The kernel of the problem was that the majority of the new members, strange as it might seem, did not hold or advocate the social and political views that had motivated those who fought in 1916.'[151])

The *Irish Worker* was published here and was suppressed in 1914. *The Worker*, which James Connolly also edited, was subsequently founded and suppressed after six issues.

On 24 March 1916 the print shop attached to Liberty Hall was raided. Much of

146 *Irish Worker*, 5 September 1914, published Connolly's speech delivered at Liberty Hall on 30 August 1914. **147** Margaret Skinnider gave a complete account of Connolly's speech in the *Irish Press*, 9 April 1966. **148** James Connolly. *Irish Worker*, 8 August 1914. **149** McGowan, Seámus. Witness Statement 542. **150** Robbins, Frank. Witness Statement 585. **151** Robbins, Frank. *Under the Starry Plough*, 1978, p. 201.

the type was taken, so the printers had to 'borrow' type (from William H. West of Capel Street) to set the *Proclamation* later in April 1916. (It was printed in two parts – the first three paragraphs were set, then the type was broken down and 'reused' to set the final three paragraphs. This was because the printers at Liberty Hall could borrow only about half the type needed for the job.)

On 16 April 1916 the Irish Republic flag, with the harp but without the crown, was first raised over the Hall; Molly O'Reilly, aged fifteen, unfurled it. (She had been at Howth for the landing of the rifles, and had pushed a handcart load of them up to her home in Gardiner Street, where she hid them without her parents' knowledge. They were so opposed to her Republican activities that she finally left home.) Connolly handed the flag to her and said: 'I hand you this flag as the sacred emblem of Ireland's unconquered soul.'[152] Mary Shannon, a machinist at the Liberty Hall shirt-making cooperative, made the flag. Massed were the Irish Citizen Army, the ICA Women's Section, the ICA Boy Scouts under Cpt. Carpenter, and the Fintan Lalor Pipe Band. Cpt. Christopher Poole led a colour guard of sixteen that escorted the Colour Bearer who was also accompanied by three young girl-dancers known as the Liberty Trio.[153]

From 26 March to 16 April James Connolly's play, *Under Which Flag*, had its first performances at Liberty Hall, with Seán Connolly in the lead role. It was about an Irishman torn between serving Ireland in the ICA or in the British army.

On 19 April, Spy Wednesday, Connolly informed Citizen Army officers Richard MacCormick, Joseph Doyle and Frank Robbins that the Rising was scheduled for Easter Sunday – it would begin at 6.30 pm in Dublin and 7 pm in the provinces.

On 23 April, in his final lecture on tactics, Connolly warned: 'The odds against us are a thousand to one. If we win, we'll be great heroes; but if we lose we'll be the greatest scoundrels the country has ever produced. In the event of victory, hold onto your rifles because the Volunteers may have a different goal, and may stop before our goal is reached. Remember, we're out not only for political liberty, but for economic liberty as well. So hold onto your rifles.'[154] [155]

On 23 April *The Proclamation of the Irish Republic* was printed in the Liberty Hall print shop. Thomas MacDonagh gave the manuscript to three men and one woman to compose the type and print the sheets. Christopher Brady was the primary printer[156] (he worked in the printing department of the Bank of Ireland); Michael Molloy (a printer at the *Independent* newspaper)[157] and Liam F. O'Brien[158] (who worked at O'Reilly's Printing Works) assisted.[159] (When they presented themselves to Liberty Hall on Sunday, Connolly immediately had them 'arrested' so if they

152 *Workers' Republic*, 22 April 1916. **153** *Unfurling the Flag*, The Irish Republican Digest, Book 1, pamphlet, Cork, 1956, p. 31-32. **154** Caulfield, Max, *The Easter Rebellion, Dublin 1916*, 1963, 1995, p. 24. **155** Frank Robbins in *Irishman*, 19 May 1928, recorded his memory of Connolly's last speech at Liberty Hall, indicating that the 'Citizen Army would stand to arms until the Irish claim was heard'. **156** Brady, Christopher. Witness Statement 705. **157** Molloy, Michael. Witness Statement 716. **158** O'Brien, Liam. Witness Statement 3232. **159** O'Connor, John. *The 1916 Proclamation*, 1986, p. 27ff.

were questioned afterward they could honestly claim they had printed the *Proclamation* 'under duress'.[160]) The men previously had been printers for James Connolly's *Workers' Republic*. They knew that they did not have enough type for the *Proclamation*, so they borrowed type from William West, a printer in nearby Capel Street. Still, there was not enough type, so the *Proclamation* had to be printed in two 'halves'. Roseanne Hackett, a former Jacob's Factory worker who had not been re-employed after the 1913 Lockout, assisted the men.[161] [162] They finally finished late Sunday night, after borrowing the type and coping with problems with the press. They intended to print 2500 copies, but only about 1000 were completed. The machine used was a 'Wharfdale Double-Crown' of a very old pattern and in poor condition. The paper was of poor quality, similar to that used in the printing of the *Worker's Republic*, white with a greyish tinge to it and had been procured from the Saggart Paper Mills in Dublin. When the printing was completed, the *Proclamation* was given to Helena Molony, who supervised its distribution.[163] (See also 21 Henry Street.)

Because of the activities that issued forth from Liberty Hall, officials at Dublin Castle considered it the centre of nationalist sentiment, though it had little connection with the Volunteers. The newspapers described it as 'the centre of social anarchy in Ireland, the brain of every riot and disturbance'.[164]

William Oman was the bugler who sounded the 'fall in' for the ICA on Easter Monday, 24 April.[165] Originally the 2nd Battalion of Volunteers was to muster here and march to St Stephen's Green. Frank Thornton and Seámus McGowan[166] commanded the unit guarding the munitions that were transferred to the GPO on Monday afternoon in fifteen commandeered lorries and cabs.[167] Thereafter the Hall was deserted except for Peter Ennis, the caretaker.

On 26 April Liberty Hall was fired upon by HMS *Helga* – she fired twenty-four rounds. There are stories that the *Helga* 'lobbed shells' over the Loopline Bridge, but the flat trajectory of the *Helga*'s guns would have made this next to impossible. She fired under the bridge into Liberty Hall.[168]

Following Connolly's execution, the ITGWU's president, Thomas Foran, took over the acting general secretaryship. William O'Brien[169] and J.J. Hughes aided him.

Following the Rising, the Union leaders were uneasy about an 'Army'. Consequently, by December 1916 the Citizen Army was back in Liberty Hall, but under the name of the 'Connolly/Mallin Social and Athletic Club'.

On 10 June 1917 a protest meeting was held on behalf of the prisoners still in English jails. Cathal Brugha and Count Plunkett addressed it. Inspector Miles of the DMP was hit on the head with a hurley during the protest and later died. (The

160 Brady, Christopher. Witness Statement 705. **161** Hackett, Rose. Witness Statement 546. **162** Tallion, Ruth. *When History was Made: The Women of 1916*, 1996, p. 6. **163** Molony, Helena. Witness Statement 391. **164** *Weekly Irish Times*, 29 April 1916. **165** Oman, William. Witness Statement 421. **166** McGowan, Seámus. Witness Statement 542. **167** Thornton, Frank. Witness Statement 510. **168** Hayes-McCoy, G.A. 'A Military History of the Rising', in Nowlan. *The Making of 1916*, p. 325. **169** O'Brien, William. Witness Statement 1766.

Volunteers and ICA soldiers of the times used to refer to a hurley as a 'Tipperary rifle'.)

Standing at 195 feet the present-day Liberty Hall is the tallest building in Dublin and rises sixteen stories. Construction began in 1961 and finished in 1965. It is the headquarters of the Services, Industrial, Professional, and Technical Union (SIPTU).

Beresford Place Across from Liberty Hall stands the James Connolly statue. Sculpted by Éamonn O'Doherty, the work was unveiled by President Mary Robinson on 12 May 1996, the 80th anniversary of Connolly's execution. The flag that forms the background is the Starry Plough, the plough and the stars symbolising the present and the future of the working classes respectively.

10–13 Berkeley Road St Joseph's Church, noted for its Volunteer Commemorative Masses; an annual Mass is celebrated on 22 August for Michael Collins.

26–50 Bishop Street (corner of Peter Row, touching Wexford Street): Jacob's Biscuit Factory; the company's full name was W. & R. Jacob Co. Ltd. It employed approximately 3000 at the time of the Great Lockout of 1913. Its main gate was on Bishop Street, near Bride Street. About two hundred Volunteers, including about twelve members of Cumann na mBan, held it during the Rising. The occupying force commanded by Thomas MacDonagh mustered in St Stephen's Green and left just as the ICA contingent arrived to occupy that area. Fr McCabe, prior of the Carmelite Priory, attempted to dissuade the Volunteers from their course, declaring that the Rising was insane. The factory was a virtually immune stronghold during the Rising and didn't have to defend against frontal attack. Forty Volunteers were sent from here to reinforce the Portobello area and twenty more were sent back to St Stephen's Green.

The Dublin Institute of Technology now occupies most of the site, the remainder housing the National Archives.

5 Blackhall Street Gaelic League Hall; meeting place of the Gaelic League and of the Columcille Branch of Cumann na mBan. The Volunteers first 'paraded' here on 1 December 1913. The 1st Battalion of the Dublin Brigade (less D Company) mobilized here for the Rising under Cmdt. Ned Daly who declared: 'Today at noon, an Irish Republic will be declared, and the Flag of the Republic hoisted. I look to every man to do his duty with courage and discipline. The Irish Volunteers are now the Irish Republican Army…In less than an hour we may be in action.'[170]

Only about a third of the Volunteers appeared for the muster on Easter Monday, though some took their positions later. Piaras Béaslaí was second in command.

Blackrock, County Dublin Glenvar; Éamon de Valera's office from May 1921, raided by the Worchestershire Regiment on 22 June 1921. He was arrested and taken from Dublin Castle to Portobello Barracks, from where he was released after one night.[171]

Booterstown, County Dublin: Kevin O'Higgins' home after the Civil War. He

170 Ryan, Desmond. *The Rising*, p. 204. **171** Gallagher/Hogan. *The Four Glorious Years*, p. 301.

was the nephew of Timothy (T.M.) Healy. He was shot here on his way to Mass on 10 July 1927. Eoin MacNeill was the first to reach him. His killers were Archie Doyle, Timothy Coughlin and Bill Gannon. It was thought 'in part it was prompted by motives of revenge, in part by an impetus to reactivate the parent body [IRA]. The Civil War was five years away; the country was beginning to enjoy peace. It was time to stir things up again.'[172]

89 Botanic Road, Glasnevin Home of Seán (Johnny) Collins when he settled his brother Michael's estate. Michael died intestate, leaving an estate of £1,950.9s.11d. Nancy O'Brien, Michael's cousin, lived here while employed in Dublin Castle, and later married Johnny Collins.

1 Brendan Road, Donnybrook Home of Batt and Maire O'Connor. O'Connor was a builder and 'built' Brendan Road, naming it after the patron saint of his native Kerry. Michael Collins often stayed here.[173]

6 Brendan Road, Donnybrook House owned by the Dáil, frequently used by Michael Collins.

23 Brendan Road, Donnybrook Susan (Sinead) Mason, Michael Collins' secretary, lived here with her aunt. Collins often stayed here.

Bride Street and Ross Road Éamonn Ceannt and Thomas MacDonagh surrendered their garrisons to Maj. de Courcy Wheeler in this location.

9 Bridge Street Lower Limerick Clothing Factory; three hundred Irish Volunteer uniforms were ordered from here in 1914, to be made from material supplied by Morrogh Brothers at Douglas Woollen Mills in Cork.

20 Bridge Street Lower Brazen Head Pub and Hotel. The rebels of 1798 and 1803 met here to plan.

Bridgefort Street (at the corner of Usher's Quay): Location of 18-pounder guns, under the command of Emmet Dalton, used to shell the Four Courts at the start of the Civil War.

Brighton Square, Rathgar Home of Ewart Wilson, cousin of C.S. Andrews. Andrews often stayed here when 'on the run' during the War of Independence and the Civil War.

4 Brunswick Street North North Dublin Union. Occupied by Ned Daly's men during the Rising. Next door was the Convent of St John's of the Sisters of St Vincent de Paul. The nuns supported the Volunteers, prayed with them, and pleaded with God for their safe return. Daly's men knew the Sisters by name: Sisters Brigid, Agnes, Patrick, Monica, and Louise.[174]

The building was used as a barracks by the Black and Tans. During the Civil War, it was used as a women's prison.[175] [176] On 6 May 1923, Maire Comerford,

172 Coogan, Tim Pat. *Ireland Since the Rising*, 1966, p. 261 ff gives a personal account of the men involved. **173** O'Connor, Maire. Witness Statement 330. **174** Coady, Seán. 'Remembering St John's Convent', *Capuchin Annual*, (1966). **175** For the most detailed description of the conditions at the North Dublin Union see Buckeley, Margaret. *The Jangle of the Keys*, 1938, throughout, but especially pp. 59-61. **176** Macardle, Dorothy. 'Military Prison, North Dublin Union, 1 May 1923', *Éire-Ireland*, 26 May 1923.

Maura Deegan, and Aoife Taaffe escaped successfully. On the following night, 22 women escaped using the same route; however, most were recaptured.

Now St Lawrence's Hospital.

5–9 Brunswick Street and Red Cow Lane Richmond Hospital, a teaching hospital for surgery. Fifteen dead and two hundred wounded were received here during the Rising. Sir Thomas Myles, former president of the Royal College of Surgeons in Ireland, and A.A. McConnell, Ireland's first neurosurgeon, both practised here, as did Sir William Stoker, Sir William Thomson and Sir Conway Dwyer. Oliver St John Gogarty studied here and was a clinical clerk for Sir Thomas Myles.

About a week after the Rising, members of the DMP came looking for Volunteers Patrick (Paddy) Daly and Liam Archer,[177] but the house surgeon, Michael Bourke, informed them that they had been discharged. When the policemen then asked about Éamon Martin, Bourke told them Martin was dying.

12–13 Burgh Quay Tivoli Music Hall; occupied by British soldiers firing machine guns on Liberty Hall during the Rising.

Became the offices of the *Irish Press*, owned by the de Valera family; ceased publication in the late 1980s.

11 Bushy Park Road, Rathgar Home of Mrs Jackson; converted to an auxiliary hospital during the Rising.

12 Bushy Park Road, Rathgar The last Dublin home of Erskine Childers.

Cabra, County Dublin Home of Seán Harling. He witnessed de Valera's signing of the Letters Plenipotentiary and delivered the Letters to the Treaty Representatives. [178]

Cabra Park, County Dublin Home of Martin Conlon. Bulmer Hobson was held here from just before the Rising.[179] [180] [181] [182] Seán T. O'Kelly was sent from the GPO on the night of Easter Monday 1916 to have him released. Martin Conlon, Michael Lynch, Con O'Donovan, Maurice Collins,[183] and Seán Tobin held him. (See 65 Great Britain Street.)

5 Cabra Road Home of Michael Foley, where Michael Collins first met Éamon (Ned) Broy.

24 Cabra Road, Phibsborough Home of Louise Gavan-Duffy, member of the initial Provisional Committee of Cumann na mBan and its Hon. Secretary.

Sister of George Gavan-Duffy, later Minister for Foreign Affairs in the First Dáil, Louise Gavan-Duffy founded Scoil Bhríde, Ireland's first Gaelscoil for girls. She travelled through Dublin on Easter Monday, arriving finally at the GPO, where she asked to see Pearse: 'I said to him that I wanted to be in the field but that I felt that the Rebellion was a frightful mistake, that it could not possibly succeed, and that it was, therefore, wrong.' Pearse suggested that she help out in the kitchens,

177 Archer, Liam. Witness Statement 819. **178** Harling, Seán. Witness Statement 935. **179** Conlon, Martin. Witness Statement 798. **180** Conlon, Mrs Martin. Witness Statement 419. **181** Foy, Michael and Brian Barton. *The Easter Rising*, 1999, p. 131-132. **182** Townshend. *Easter 1916*, p. 137. **183** Collins, Maurice. Witness Statement 550.

and she agreed to this, since it was not active service. She stayed there until the GPO was evacuated on Friday, and next morning went to Jacob's Biscuit Factory 'to see what they were going to do there'.[184]

Camden Street Hartigan's Pub; gathering place for those with Republican sentiments during the War of Independence.

Camden Street The Bleeding Horse Pub, founded in 1648; often appeared in the works of Seán O'Casey written during the War of Independence.

1 Camden Street Upper Earley & Company, stained glass makers. Originally Earley and Powells, it opened in 1864. One of the largest and most prestigious ecclesiastical decorators, it secured its prominence through its versatility in being able to produce sculpture, painted decoration, glass and metal work, and through its well-established links with the Catholic hierarchy. The majority of its work was for stained glass windows and altars. The company was run by Thomas Earley (1819–93) and his nephews John Bishop Earley (1856–1935) and William Earley (1872–1956). The company also provided the windows for the chapel at Arbour Hill Prison.

Camden Street Lower The area comprising this street together with Wexford Street, Aungier Street and South Great George's Street was nicknamed 'The Dardanelles' during the War of Independence.

Camden Street Lower The location of Nora (Mrs Padraig) O'Keefe's restaurant. Michael Collins often lunched here. There was a room above the shop where Collins stayed for a few weeks in 1919 until he moved to 5 Mary Street.

5 Camden Street Lower Corrigan and Sons Mortuary; K Company (3rd Battalion) used the premises to make bombs. Michael Collins secreted some £20,000 (figures vary) in gold here, sealed in tobacco tins and buried under the floor, before it was all reinterred under Batt O'Connor's floorboards in Brendan Road, Donnybrook.[185]

34 Camden Street Lower Formerly housed the Irish National Theatre Society. The first meeting of Fianna na hÉireann in Dublin took place here on 16 August 1909: Bulmer Hobson (president), Countess Markievicz (vice-president), Padraig Ó Riain (secretary), Liam Mellowes (appointed National Organizer). On 21 August there was a report in *An Claidheamh Soluis* noting the meeting and stating that about one hundred boys attended. Seán Heuston was the leader of the Fianna on Dublin's Northside, while Con Colbert was the leader on the Southside.

The Volunteers used these premises as a drill hall. It was the fourth meeting place of K Company (3rd Battalion) after the Rising.[186] In 1919 all Volunteers of the Company took the Oath to the Dáil here. After its suppression in 1919, this was one of the private premises where the Dáil met.

67 Camden Street Lower Home of Councillor Richard O'Carroll who was shot by

184 Gavan-Duffy, Louise. Witness Statement 216. (Her statement is more reflective and politically aware than most of the others.) **185** O'Connor, Maire. Witness Statement 330. **186** Gallagher/Hogan. *The Four Glorious Years*, p. 230.

Cpt. J.C. Bowen Colthurst on Wednesday, 26 April, after his capture in an evacuated Volunteer post. He died nine days later in Portobello Hospital. He was the general secretary of the Brick and Stoneworkers' Union, and the leader of the Labour Party on the Dublin Corporation.

Capel Street Trade Council offices.

Capel Street Home of Harry O'Farrell, Captain of K Company (3rd Battalion) following Tom Cullen.

4 Capel Street Home of Seán and Noel Lemass. Seán fought for the IRA/Republicans in the Civil War. He was Taoiseach from June 1959 to 1966. Noel was captured in Glencullen but escaped and fled to the Isle of Man during the Civil War. He was suspected of tampering with Michael Collins' mail and of involvement in the Seán Hayes murder. He was recaptured on 3 July 1923. Allegedly kidnapped by the CID and murdered, his body was found in the Dublin mountains on 12 October 1923.

45A Capel Street Premises of William Henry West, printer; he provided the type for the *Proclamation*. He was prosecuted under The Defence of the Realm Act (DORA) in June 1916 for printing a statement purportedly made by Thomas MacDonagh in the dock; fined £5. (See MacDonagh Statement to his Court Martial, Appendix III.)

106 Capel Street Dublin Municipal Library; Thomas Gay was the librarian. Michael Collins and his men used the premises as a 'drop'. Gay was the one who gave the information to Harry Boland about the 17–18 May 1918 'German Plot' arrests. Boland passed the information along to Michael Collins, who told the Cabinet. Éamon de Valera, however, advised that they should all remain at home that night and many of the Cabinet members were arrested.[187] (See also Harcourt Street.)

Castle Street (8 Bristol Buildings): Home of Florence Williams. She received the Military Medal from the British for her heroic saving of men inside and outside Dublin Castle during the Rising.

16 Castle Street Dublin Municipal Buildings, where Éamonn Ceannt worked in the city Treasurer's Department.

11 Cathedral Street Dublin United Tramways Company, owned by William Martin Murphy.

6 Cavendish Row Home of John Gore, an elderly solicitor and first Hon. Treasurer of the Irish Volunteers. Bulmer Hobson said of him: 'He was not noted for his reticence.' Hobson purposefully misled him, telling him that the guns to be landed at Howth were to be landed into Wexford. Hobson felt that Gore would repeat this to all of his clients 'in confidence'. Whether he did or not, the English ship HMS *Panther*, which had been anchored in Dublin Bay, steamed south to Wexford. On Sunday, while the arms were brought ashore, the *Panther* was immobilized in Wicklow because the crew had been given shore leave.

187 Gay, Thomas B. Witness Statement 780.

Cecelia Street Catholic University of Medicine; accepted women beginning in 1896. Dr Kathleen Lynn received her degree here in 1899.

Charlemont Street James Connolly and family (his wife and three daughters) lived here in a one-roomed flat upon his arrival in Dublin in 1896. He had married the former Lily Reynolds, a Protestant woman from Co. Wicklow. Shortly afterwards, along with seven like-minded socialists, he formed the Irish Socialist Republican Party. (See also Middle Abbey Street, Beresford Place and Thomas Street.) Ultimately the Connollys had seven children, the firstborn of whom, Mona, died in a tragic fire in their home in 1904. Mona died on the very day she and the family were to depart for the US to join James who had moved to New York as a union organizer the year before.[188]

37 Charlemont Street: St Ultan's Children's Hospital; founded in 1919 (with £70 and two cots) by Dr Kathleen Lynn and Madeleine ffrench-Mullen. Appalled by the fact that 16% of Dublin infants in 1919 were dying from preventable diseases, Dr Lynn and her friend Ms ffrench-Mullen founded St. Ultan's, a hospital 'for the medical treatment of infants under one year of age'. With due reference to her treatment by her medical masters while training at the Adelaide Hospital, Dr Lynn was 'adamant that the staff of St Ultan's would be confined to women medical staff only'. (Though she was the first woman to be elected a resident doctor at the Adelaide Hospital, prejudice prevented her from going into residence there.) It became the front line in the battle against infant mortality, and provided the opportunity for Dr Dorothy Price to continue her research on childhood tuberculosis, leading to the establishing of the research unit at the hospital. They introduced a Montessori ward in the hospital and made a significant contribution to the eradication of tuberculosis in Ireland. Louie Bennett, Kathleen Clarke, Charlotte Despard, Maud Gonne MacBride, Countess Markievicz and Helena Molony all greatly contributed.

(Charlotte Despard, known as 'Madame Despard', spent a great deal of time in Ireland and in 1908 she joined with Hanna Sheehy-Skeffington and Margaret Cousins to form the Irish Women's Franchise League. [Ironically, her brother, General John French, was Chief of Staff of the British Army and commander of the British force sent to Europe in August 1914. He became Viceroy of Ireland in May 1918.] In 1920 Despard toured Ireland as a member of the British Labour Party Commission of Inquiry, and together with Maud Gonne she collected first-hand evidence of army and police atrocities in Cork and Kerry. Later, they also formed the Women's Prisoners' Defence League to support republican prisoners. Despard died in 1939.)

Louie Bennett fund-raised for the hospital on her trips to the US, as did Kathleen Clarke, who also sat on its board.

188 Collins, Lorcan, Conor Kostick and Shane MacThomais. 'Tragedy in the Connolly Family', *History Ireland*, Vol. XII, No. 3, 2004.

(Louie Bennett did not join any of the 'military'organisations of the time, but she was one of the most militant. She was educated in London at an academy for young ladies, where she and her sister were remembered for having formed an Irish League. Between 1910-1916 she was Hon. Secretary of the Irishwomen's Suffrage Federation; in 1915 she was also Organising Secretary of the Irish section, Union of Democratic Control (UDC). In 1913 she worked in the soup kitchens alongside Countess Markievicz, Delia Larkin, and Hannah Sheehy-Skeffington, but did so on humanitarian grounds rather than any republican or revolutionary sentiment. A key feature of her character was her desire for, and belief in, conciliation rather than conflict – she would have been very much in the consensus mode if in contemporary times. By 1916 she was also sub-editing The *Irish Citizen*, the organ of the Irish Suffragist movement, and in 1917 wrote in that paper on trade unions for women and the need for action rather than rhetoric. In 1918 she undertook, with Helen Chenevix, the re-organisation of the Irish Women Workers' Union, following the imprisonment, after 1916, of Helena Molony. In 1919 she was at the International Congress of Women, in Zurich; in 1920, she was in America to 'plead Ireland's cause against the Black and Tans'. On a brief return to Ireland, she had been clearly influenced by the American conviction of the importance of image and 'suggested' to her IWWU colleagues that 'a woman in public life could afford to be neither dowdy or eccentric'. Despite her own advice to others on this matter, she donned 'a pink feathered hat', and headed to Downing Street to persuade Lloyd George to 'take the Black and Tans out of Ireland'.[189])

Charles Street West Medical Mission. During the Rising the surviving Royal Lancers (two were killed), under the command of Col. Hammond, took the building on Monday afternoon and held it until relieved on Thursday evening. These Lancers had been escorting an ammunition delivery from the North Wall to Phoenix Park. Volunteers in the Four Courts attacked them as the Lancers passed by, and the surviving Lancers took shelter here. These were *not* the Lancers who had been sent from Marlborough Barracks to investigate the fighting and who trotted down Lower Sackville Street and were attacked in front of the GPO.

Charleston Road Home of Margaret Foley. Frank Gallagher (who wrote under the pseudonym of David Hogan) stayed here while on the run after the early summer of 1920.

Church Road, East Wall Home of Tommy Dorrins, killed in the Custom House fire.

Church Street, Howth 'Foil-tra'; Michael Collins' relations named Butterley lived here in 1914. Collins often stayed here, and some say he was here during the landing of the Howth guns.[190]

Church Street Church of St Mary of the Angels; opened in 1868 and completed

189 *Biography of Louie Bennett*, Irish Labour History Museum. **190** Osborne, Chrissy. *Michael Collins, Himself*, 2003, p. 101.

in 1881; the main altar was designed by James Pearse, father of Padraig and Willie. Later in 1916 Masses were said for those who died for Ireland in the Rising. The inscriptions on the Stations of the Cross are in Irish.

Church Street St Michan the Martyr's Church, named after an eleventh-century Viking martyr-bishop. Hundreds of almost perfectly preserved bodies dating back to the twelfth century lie in the vaults, including those of Henry and John Sheares, Jackson and Bond, the United Irishmen who were hanged in 1798. Charles Stewart Parnell's Requiem Mass was said here, then his body lay in state at the City Hall before being buried in Glasnevin Cemetery. There was a Volunteer garrison in the nearby Four Courts during the Rising, and British firing on that garrison greatly damaged the church.

Church Street (and North King Street) Reilly's Pub (known as 'Reilly's Fort'); Jack Shouldice commanded a unit here during the Rising.[191]

Church Street Home and shop of Alice and Kate Ryan; their niece was May Quigley, to whom Seán Treacy became engaged.

5 Church Street Home of Volunteer Michael Lennon. A group of Volunteers from the Four Courts, led by Peadar Clancy, converted the house to a canteen and first-aid post. Brigid Lyons (Thornton) hid here following the Rising.[192]

66, 67 Church Street These two tenement houses collapsed on 2 September 1913. Seven people were killed, including two children (aged four and five); another eight tenants were seriously injured. These tenants were representative of the workers involved in the Lockout of 1913 and the outcry among workers was immediate. One of those killed, Eugene Salmon, had been laid off by Jacob's Biscuit Factory the day before and died unsuccessfully trying to save his four-year-old sister.

79–80 Church Street Monks' Bakery; during the Rising, Commandant Daly oversaw the distribution of bread from here to the local residents who depended upon the bakery for their food.

Kevin Barry was captured here after an ambush on 20 September 1920 in which three British soldiers were killed. He stopped to reload his .38 caliber Luger (which the IRA always referred to as a 'Parabellum') and hid under a lorry. When it was about to be driven off a bystander innocently shouted, 'There's a man under the lorry' and Barry was arrested. The British troops engaged in this incident were from the 2nd Battalion of the Duke of Wellington's Regiment, commanded by Sgt Banks. The unit was on a thrice-weekly scheduled collection of the detachment's bread ration.

The IRA/Volunteers mustered at the O'Flanagan Sinn Féin Club on Ryder's Row. 2Lt Tommy McGrane, John Joe Carroll, James Douglas, Dave McDonagh and Frank O'Flanagan had entered the bakery through the side entrance at 38 North King Street and were waiting for the British troops. Jim Moran and Paddy Young were to wait at the Brunswick Street corner. Maurice Higgins and Tom

---

191 Shouldice, Jack (John F.). Witness Statement 162. **192** Thornton, Brigid Lyons. Witness Statement 259.

Kissane were to wait at the North King Street corner. Kevin Barry together with 2Lt Bob O'Flanagan and Seán O'Neill were to follow the lorry into Church Street and hold up the troops for their weapons. Harry Murphy, Thomas (Tucker) Reilly and Christy Boy Robinson were to close on the lorry from the Brunswick Street side. Seámus Kavanagh (the O/C), Frank Flood, Tommy O'Brien and Mick Robinson were to close on the lorry from a pub directly opposite. Eugene Fox, John Kenny, John O'Dwyer and Tom Staunton were to cover the withdrawal up Constitution Hill, where an escape lorry was waiting on Coleraine Street with drivers Davy Golden and Jimmy Carrigan.

Barry's .38 Parabellum jammed and he knelt down beside the lorry to clear it. He rose and it jammed again (on the fifth round) and he knelt under the lorry a second time. That's when the rest of the Volunteers withdrew due to the returned fire and he was left isolated, hiding under the lorry.

Privates Harold Washington, Thomas Humphries and Marshall Whitehead were killed. Barry was tried for the murder of Marshall Whitehead, though Whitehead was killed with .45 caliber bullets. It is thought Barry shot Pvt. Washington, but he was not charged with this killing. Kevin Barry was the first Volunteer captured in action since 1916 and he was the first person executed during the War of Independence.[193] [194] [195] [196] (See also North King Street, North Circular Road/Mountjoy Prison, and 28 South Circular Road.)

138–142 Church Street Capuchin Franciscan Friary and **131–137 Church Street** Fr Mathew Hall, also known as Capuchin Hall. Named after Fr Theobald Mathew (1790–1861), who preached against alcohol abuse throughout Ireland and the US. He was *very* successful in getting the Irish to take the teetotal 'pledge'. It is estimated that by 1842 out of a population of just over eight million, some five million had taken the pledge. He was born on 10 October 1790 in Rathclogheen, near Thomastown, Co. Tipperary, in the same house used as a hiding place by Dan Breen, Seán Hogan and Seán Treacy on the night of 21 January 1919, after the Soloheadbeg ambush. (See also Soloheadbeg, Appendix I.)

The building was used as a hospital in 1916. There is a plaque on the wall commemorating its importance during the Rising. It was the headquarters under Ned Daly of the 1st Battalion before the Battalion moved on Friday to the Four Courts. The Friars who attended those executed in Kilmainham Gaol lived here, and they were instrumental in bringing the British and the Battalion O/Cs together at the end of the Rising (Fathers Albert Bibby, Aloysius,[197] Augustine,[198] Columbus and Sebastian).

North Circular Road Conor (Con) Collins' home; he was sent to Tralee to take charge of the wireless arrangements at the Wireless College at Caherciveen on the

193 Cronin, Seán, *Kevin Barry*, pamphlet, 1965. **194** *Irish Independent*, 13, 15 October 2001. **195** *The Irish Times*, 7 September 2001, 15 October 2001. **196** *An Phoblacht*, 17 October 2001. **197** Aloysius, Revd. Witness Statements 200, 207. **198** Augustine, Revd. Witness Statement 920.

Ring of Kerry, which were forestalled when the car bringing others went off the Ballykissane Pier on the way to Cahersiveen.[199] (See Ballykissane Pier, Appendix I.) Collins and Austin Stack heard Sir Roger Casement had landed from a submarine and had been captured, and they went in search of him, but were taken into a police barracks at Causeway where Stack pulled his revolver. Collins and Stack escaped this barracks but were later re-arrested and imprisoned after the Rising. Collins was TD for Limerick West from 1919–23. From 1922 he abstained from attendance as an opponent of the Treaty.

North Circular Road (near Jones Road): MacDermott Sinn Féin Club.

North Circular Road, Cowley Place Mountjoy Prison ('The Joy').

Seán Treacy was imprisoned here in September 1917, and was one of the prisoners who demanded political status, which led to the hunger strike. The three leaders of the hunger strike were Austin Stack, Fionan Lynch and Thomas Ashe. Ashe was force-fed here during that strike; a lung was pierced during feeding by Dr Lowe on 23 September and he was taken to the Mater Hospital where he died on 25 September 1917 of 'heart failure and congestion of the lungs'. Ashe had been arrested on 20 August, just before he was to travel to Skibbereen with Michael Collins. Upon hearing of his arrest, Collins wrote to his sister Hannie: 'Tom Ashe has been arrested so that fixes him.' In Mountjoy, as Ashe was carried away to be force-fed, Fionan Lynch cried out, 'Stick it, Tom.' Ashe replied, 'I'll stick it, Fin.'[200]

The verdict of the Jury in the inquest held:

> We find that the deceased, Thomas Ashe … died from heart failure and congestion of the lungs on the 25th September, 1917; that his death was caused by the punishment of taking away from the cell bed, bedding and boots, and allowing him to be on the cold floor for 50 hours, and then subjecting him to forcible feeding in his weak condition after hunger striking for five or six days.
>
> We censure the Castle Authorities for not acting more promptly, especially when the grave condition of the deceased and other prisoners was brought to their notice …
>
> That the hunger strike was adopted against the inhuman punishment inflicted and a refusal to their demand to be treated as political prisoners … [201] [202]

At Ashe's funeral in Glasnevin on 31 September, after the IRA/Volunteers fired three volleys over his grave, Collins (in Volunteer uniform) said: 'Nothing additional remains to be said. That volley which we have just heard is the only speech

199 Collins, Con (Conor, Cornelius). Witness Statement 90. **200** Lynch, Fionan. Witness Statement 192. **201** *Irish Independent*. 28 September 1917. **202** Macardle. *The Irish Republic*, p. 228.

it is proper to make above the grave of a dead Fenian.'[203]

Collins arranged Robert Barton's escape on 16 March 1919.[204]

Another hunger strike for 'prisoner of war' status began on 5 April 1920 and continued until 15 April 1920. The prisoners had served the following demand on the governor on 1 April: 'The undersigned, acting on behalf of all untried and uncharged prisoners, hereby demand that on or before the morning of April 5th all such prisoners be released or given prisoner-of-war treatment.'[205] Among those on strike were Frank Gallagher and Peter Starkey.

Kevin Barry was hanged in Mountjoy Prison on Monday, 1 November 1920. The hangman was John Ellis, brought over from England for the execution. Barry was hanged one day after Terence MacSwiney was buried in St Finbarr's Cemetery in Cork (he died on 25 October in Brixton Prison). Barry was attended and accompanied onto the scaffold by Canon Waters[206] and Fr MacMahon from Clonliffe College. Acting Judge Myles Keogh signed Barry's death warrant, and it was in this warrant that the details on Barry's torture were outlined. Later Fr Waters would write to Barry's mother; 'You are the mother, my dear Mrs Barry, of one of the bravest and best boys I have ever known. His death was one of the most holy, and your dear boy is waiting for you now, beyond the reach of sorrow or trial.' On the eve of Barry's execution a large crowd gathered outside Mountjoy. People held lighted candles and recited the Rosary right through the hours of darkness. Barry's mother was in the crowd outside the prison; she was invited inside but refused and remained with the crowd, although in a very distressed state. Those gathered continued to pray that he would be shot as a patriot, rather than hanged, as he had been arrested in uniform. Barry was buried in Mountjoy in a plain, roughly painted coffin at 1.30 pm on 1 November, All Saints Day. (Either through indifference or ignorance, the British chose 1 November as the date of execution. All Saints Day was a Holy Day of Obligation for all Catholics, and thus Catholic Churches throughout Ireland were filled with those who prayed for Barry's soul.) The grave was in a small laurel plot near the women's prison. In April 2002, Barry's body was reinterred in the Republican Plot in Glasnevin. There was a huge funeral parade through the streets of Dublin and he was buried with the honours he so richly deserved.

Also hanged in Mountjoy and then buried there during the War of Independence were Thomas Bryan, Edmond Foley, Patrick Maher, Thomas Traynor, Patrick

---

203 Joseph Lawless served under Ashe in the 5th Battalion at Ashbourne in the Rising and described Ashe thus: 'He was an artist, with an artist's love of the beautiful, and a poetic outlook on life. I would say that his mind was free from any special inhibitions or complexes; his fervent patriotism and deeply religious feelings combining in his love of God and his fellow man. He thought deeply and would only pursue a course when he was satisfied of its righteousness, but, having once decided his course of action, he threw his whole heart into the pursuit.' Lawless, Joseph. Witness Statement 1043. **204** Barton, Robert. Witness Statement 979. **205** Gallagher, Frank. *Days of Fear, A Diary of Hunger Strike*, 1967, p. 88. **206** Laurence, Revd. Witness Statement 899.

Doyle, Frank Flood, Patrick (Paddy) Moran, Bernard Ryan and Thomas Whelan. Moran and Whelan were hanged on 14 March 1921 for their 'participation' in the Bloody Sunday killings, though both had clear alibis placing them outside Dublin at the time. However, the Volunteers at the Gresham Hotel on Bloody Sunday were actually under the command of Paddy Moran.[207] John Ellis was employed as the hangman in these cases as well.

(Paddy Moran was imprisoned in Kilmainham Gaol when the escape of Simon Donnelly, Ernie O'Malley and Frank Teeling was planned. Moran was one of those Michael Collins wanted to 'break out'. However, Moran was so sure of acquittal due to his alibi that he absolutely refused to leave, saying that his trying to get away would be interpreted as guilt if he were captured. He paid for his reliance on British justice with his life.) Moran and Thomas Bryan, Edmond Foley, Patrick Maher, Thomas Traynor, Patrick Doyle, Frank Flood, Bernard Ryan and Thomas Whelan have since been reinterred with full honours in their 'home' cemeteries, many in Glasnevin.[208]

While imprisoned here in December 1920, Arthur Griffith and Michael Staines met with Archbishop Patrick Joseph Clune. (See also 5 Merrion Square, Dr Robert Farnan).

Seán MacEoin was imprisoned here in March 1921 and thereafter Collins devised several attempts to free him. All failed, however, and he was finally released when the Truce was signed. The most ambitious of these attempts took place on 14 May when a commandeered armoured car, commanded by Emmet Dalton, and with a 'crew' of Joe Leonard,[209] Pat McCrea,[210] Tom Keogh, Bill Stapleton[211] and Paddy McCaffrey attempted to break MacEoin out. The 'schedule' at Mountjoy had MacEoin in the warden's office at the appointed time on a daily basis, but on that day the schedule was changed and he was in the infirmary.

Women arrested and imprisoned here during the War of Independence included May Burke, Eithne Coyle, Moya Llewelyn Davies, Patricia Hoey, Linda Kearns, Aileen Keogh and Eileen McGrane.[212] On 31 October 1921, Oliver St John Gogarty aided Eithne (Ni Chumhaill) Coyle,[213] Linda Kearns (MacWhinney), May Burke and Aileen Keogh to escape. They scaled a 25-foot wall with a rope ladder, then escaped in Gogarty's motorcar to Co. Wexford then to Co. Kildare.[214]

During the Civil War, the governor of the prison was Patrick (Padraig) O'Keefe.[215]

Among the IRA/Republicans captured in the Four Courts at the start of the Civil War were Dick Barrett, Joe McKelvey, Liam Mellowes and Rory O'Connor. They were executed in Mountjoy on 8 December 1922 in reprisal for the shooting of Seán Hales and wounding of Padraic Ó Maille on 7 December. This was such

207 Dwyer, T. Ryle. *The Squad*, 2005, p. 211-12. 208 http://www.taoiseach.gov.ie/index.asp?IocID=383&docID-511 209 Leonard, Joseph. Witness Statement 547. 210 McCrea, Patrick. Witness Statement 413. 211 Stapleton, William. Witness Statement 822. 212 For a complete list see McCoole, Sinead, *No Ordinary Women*, 2003, p. 218 ff. 213 O'Donnell, Mrs Bernard. Witness Statement 750. 214 Kearns, Linda. Edited by Annie P. Smithson. *In Times of Peril*, 1922, p. 54-57. 215 O'Keefe, Patrick. Witness Statement 1725.

an infamous event during the Civil War that it has long been questioned as to whom was 'responsible'. It appears Richard Mulcahy took the initiative and Kevin O'Higgins and Joseph McGrath were the last Cabinet members to give their consent. (Rory O'Connor was best man at O'Higgins' wedding in late 1921.) Terence de Vere White notes: 'O'Higgins was appalled, and argued against it in Cabinet at great length, only agreeing after Eoin MacNeill, whom he greatly respected, acquiesced. Kevin was the second to last to agree, followed by Joseph McGrath, who was utterly opposed and gave in for the sake of unanimity.'[216] Ernest Blythe thought O'Higgins had been 'over-sensitive about the executions'.[217]

Tim Pat Coogan has written 'a certain awfulness hung about his [O'Higgins] name'.[218] Besides being members of the IRA Executive, the four were from all of Ireland's four provinces: O'Connor – Leinster; Barrett – Munster; McKelvey – Ulster; Mellowes – Connaught. The executions of these four was officially expressed: 'As a reprisal for the assassination of Brigadier Seán Hales, TD, as a solemn warning to those associated with them who are engaged in the conspiracy of assassination against the Representatives of the Irish People.'[219] [220]

(The execution of Erskine Childers was another case that caused great hatred among the anti-Treatyites. The executions of these four, coming so soon after that of Childers, made it certain that a campaign of authoritative terror had begun. Following the death of Collins in August 1922, there was a hardening of the Cabinet's attitudes toward the IRA/Republicans. Collins had helped to moderate this attitude, but without his restraint a more severe attitude was to come about, mostly through the influence of Mulcahy and O'Higgins.[221] A total of seventy-seven men were executed by Free State forces during the Civil War. These embittered the anti-Treatyites even more than the outrages of the Black and Tans. The measures did not achieve their intended effects, probably extended the duration of the fighting as attitudes were hardened on both sides, and left the people of Ireland divided for generations. See also Beggars Bush Barracks, Shelbourne Road.)

During the Civil War Maire Comerford was imprisoned here after being arrested for attempting to kidnap William T. Cosgrave. She was wounded in the leg in an escape attempt, and was taken to the North Dublin Union from where she escaped. She was rearrested and imprisoned in Kilmainham, where she went on hunger strike, and was finally released. Among other women imprisoned in Mountjoy during the Civil War were Rita Bermingham, Moira Broderick, Margaret Buckley, Gretta Coffey, May Coghlan, Kathleen Devaney, Lily Dunn, Peg Flanagan, Cecelia Gallagher, Bridie Halpin, Sheila Hartnett, Mary Ellen (Nell) Humphreys, Sheila (Sighle) Humphreys, Maud Gonne MacBride, Annie MacSwiney, Mary MacSwiney,

216 White, Terence deVere, *Kevin O'Higgins*, 1948, 1986, p. 131. **217** Hopkinson, Michael, *Green Against Green: a History of the Irish Civil War*, 1988, p. 191. **218** Coogan. *Ireland Since the Rising*, p. 52. **219** Coogan and Morrison. *The Irish Civil War*, p. 237. **220** *The Irish Times*, 9 December 1922. **221** Coogan and Morrison. *Op. Cit.*, p. 234. **222** O'Brien, Nora Connolly. Witness Statement 286.

Florence McDermott, Annie McKeown, Lily McClean, Dorothy Macardle, Countess Markievicz, Kathleen Molony, Nora Connolly O'Brien,[222] Lily O'Brennan, Kathleen O'Carroll, Teresa O'Connell, Lena O'Doherty, Kathleen O'Farrell, Annie O'Farrelly, Rita O'Farrelly, Bridie O'Mullane, Áine (Anna) O'Rahilly, May O'Toole, Melina Phelin, Grace Gifford Plunkett, Roisin Ryan.[223]

147 North Circular Road Home of Patrick and Margaret (Collins) O'Driscoll, Michael's eldest sister. Michael often visited here. Margaret was elected to the Dáil, and served as a TD from 1923 until 1933.

422 North Circular Road Last Dublin home of Seán O'Casey.

South Circular Road Home of Professor Michael Hayes, raided on 10 November 1920.[224] Richard Mulcahy was almost captured in this raid, but escaped. The raid did generate some crucial files for the British, which included almost two hundred names and addresses of Volunteers.

South Circular Road Kilmainham Gaol. There has been a prison on this site dating back to the twelfth century; originally it was known as the Dismal House of Little Ease. There had been a gaol in the area since 1210, but by the eighteenth century the extant building was in deplorable condition and had to be replaced. The current gaol was opened in 1796 on a site known as Gallows Hill, altered in 1857, and reopened in 1863. Over the main door is a bronze-relief of five entangled snakes. These were known as the 'Demons of Crime' and were twisted and chained together to represent a warning to all whom passed through its gates. Henry Joy McCracken was a prisoner here after the 1798 Rebellion, as was Robert Emmet in 1803. The Invincibles were held and executed here in 1882. John J. O'Leary, John Devoy, Jeremiah O'Donovan Rossa and Charles Stewart Parnell were imprisoned here.

Brigadier J. Young was in charge here and laid down the procedures for the executions after the Rising; the first prisoner to be executed was paraded at 3.30 am to face a firing squad of twelve men. The commander of the firing squad was Maj. H. Heathcote. All those executed in Dublin were executed in the Stonebreaker's Yard in the gaol.

The marriage of Grace Gifford and Joseph Plunkett, presided over by Fr McCarthy, took place at 11.30 pm on 3 May. Two soldiers of the Royal Irish Regiment, John Smith and John Lockerby, signed the register as witnesses. Following their wedding Fr McCarthy took Grace to Mr Byrne's home on James's Street after the ceremony.[225]

On 14 February 1921, Simon Donnelly, Ernie O'Malley and Frank Teeling escaped from here. A sympathetic British soldier provided the bolt cutters and weapons. Patrick (Paddy) Moran, Frank Flood, Thomas Bryan, Pat Doyle, Thomas Whelan and Bernard Ryan were also prisoners at the time and did not escape. They were all hanged in Mountjoy Prison. (The Volunteers at the Gresham Hotel on Bloody Sunday were under the command of Paddy Moran. The others pleaded for

223 For a complete list see McCoole, Sinead. *No Ordinary Women*, p. 218 ff.   **224** Hayes, Michael. Witness Statement 215.   **225** Plunkett, Grace Gifford. Witness Statement 257.

him to escape, but he said he would not because he would not betray those who placed him in Blackrock at his home or at Mass that morning.[226] [227] Moran was hanged on 14 March 1921 in Mountjoy Prison for participation in the Bloody Sunday executions at Upper Baggot Street. See also North Circular Road/Mountjoy Prison, Sackville Street Upper/Gresham Hotel.)

The gaol was occupied by IRA/Republican troops on 13 April 1922, but quickly retaken by the Free State.

During the Civil War Kathleen Clarke, Maire Comerford, Mary Coyle (Mrs Todd Andrews), Sheila (Sighle) Humphreys, Dr Kathleen Lynn, Maud Gonne MacBride[228], Dorothy Macardle[229], Annie MacSwiney, Mary MacSwiney, Nora Connolly O'Brien, Lily O'Brennan, Kate O'Callaghan,[230] [231] Áine (Anna) O'Rahilly, Grace Gifford Plunkett and Nell Ryan (among other women) were held prisoner here.[232]

(Dorothy Macardle wrote the best-known history of the period, *The Irish Republic*. During the Civil War Macardle sided with Éamon de Valera, was very anti-Treaty, was imprisoned by the Free State in 1922, and served time in the North Dublin Union, Mountjoy and Kilmainham. Macardle recounted her Civil War experiences in *Earthbound: Nine Stories of Ireland* [1924], and also wrote a pamphlet *The Tragedies of Kerry* [1924]. She also meticulously researched her book *The Irish Republic* which was first published in 1937. Her political opponents considered her to be a hagiographer for Éamon de Valera and an apologist for her extreme political views. She died in 1958. Though she was somewhat disillusioned with the new Irish State [in particular, regarding its treatment of women], she left the royalties from *The Irish Republic* to her close friend de Valera who wrote the foreword to the book.)

The first executions of the Civil War were on 17 November 1922. Peter Cassidy, James Fisher, John Gaffney and Richard Twohig were all executed here for illegally possessing arms.

During the Civil War, the mail censor was Peadar Kearney.

The gaol was closed in 1924. Éamon de Valera was the last prisoner.

28 South Circular Road Home of Patrick Dowling, Kevin Barry's uncle, his mother Mary's brother. Barry often stayed here, and had been staying here for several nights before the raid on Monks' Bakery. After the raid the home was itself raided and pulled asunder.

1, 2 Clanwilliam Place Clanwilliam House, corner of Clanwilliam Place and Mount Street Lower. The home of Ms Wilson, it was occupied during the Rising by elements

226 Dwyer. *The Squad*, p. 211-212. **227** O'Malley. *On Another Man's Wound*, pp. 252 ff, 272. **228** MacBride, Maud Gonne. Witness Statement 317. **229** Macardle, Dorothy. Witness Statement 457. **230** Kate O'Callaghan was the widow of the Lord Mayor of Limerick, Michael, who was murdered by the Black and Tans, and who died in her arms in their home on 22 February 1921. She movingly tells her story in 'A Curfew Night in Limerick', in Fitzgerald, William G. *The Voice of Ireland*, 1924, pp. 147-50. **231** O'Callaghan, Cait. Witness Statement 688. **232** For a complete list see McCoole. *No Ordinary Women*, p. 218 ff.

of Éamon de Valera's Boland Mills Garrison. (See also 25 Northumberland Road.)

This became known as the battle of the Mount Street Bridge, as the British troops were halted trying to cross the bridge into the city.[233]

Clanwilliam House was on the city side, east side of the intersection; St Stephen's Parochial Hall was on the opposite side (the south-east side) of the Grand Canal on the east side of the street; 25 Northumberland Road was on the same side of the canal but further towards the south-east, towards Kingstown (Dun Laoghaire). There was a total of thirteen men in the three outposts.

Patrick J. Doyle was the O/C in Parochial Hall; he and Joe Clarke, William Christian and P.B. McGrath held off the Sherwood Foresters from their position as long as they could, then fled to Percy Place where they were captured.

George Reynolds was O/C in Clanwilliam House; he was killed as were Richard Murphy and Patrick Doyle (company musketry instructor); Willie Ronan, James Doyle,[234] Thomas Walsh and James Walsh survived.[235] [236] James Doyle (seventeen) had his rifle shot out of his hands. Richard Murphy was killed as he fired from the middle windows, partially reclining on a chair. He was to be married a week later. The Walsh brothers were using Howth Mausers. At one point Patrick Doyle suddenly stopped firing and spoke no more; he was an inveterate talker and when one of the Walshes shook him he fell over dead. A soda siphon was used to dowse a fire and it was shot out of Jim Walsh's hand. The survivors abandoned the burning house only when they had no more ammunition. In this engagement the Sherwood Foresters' casualties were four officers killed, fourteen wounded, and 216 other ranks killed or wounded.

18 Claremont Road, Sandymount Éamon de Valera's home after his release from prison in 1924.

Clarendon Street St Teresa's Church and Hall, and Carmelite Priory. The first church was built here between 1793 and 1797, and was one of the first city centre churches built after the end of the Penal Laws. On 2 April 1902 *Cáitlín Ní hUallacháin* was first performed in the Hall. W.B. Yeats had written it for Maud Gonne, and she 'lived' the part.

28 Claude Road, Drumcondra Home of Sara and Molly Allgood, two of the most renowned Abbey Theatre actresses of the twentieth century. Both were in Cumann na mBan.

Molly changed her name to Maire O'Neill, and was engaged to John Millington Synge when he died.

Both actresses moved to the US following the 1920s where they enjoyed successful careers. Sara passed away in the US in 1950, and Molly died after a tragic accident in London in 1952.

233 Donnelly, Simon. 'Thou Shalt Not Pass—Ireland's Challenge to the British Forces at Mount Street Bridge, Easter 1916', IMA CD 62/3/7, (pamphlet). **234** Doyle, Seámus (James). Witness Statement 166. **235** Walsh, Tom. 'The Epic of Mount Street Bridge', *Irish Press Supplement*, April 1966. **236** Walsh, James and Thomas. Witness Statement 198.

Clonskeagh, County Dublin Roebuck House; home of Seán MacBride, son of John and Maud Gonne MacBride. He fought for the IRA/Republicans during the Civil War, and became IRA C/S succeeding Moss Twomey in 1936. After leaving the IRA, he worked as a lawyer and, later, a journalist for the *Irish Press*. In 1946 he founded the political party Clann na Poblachta and became minister of external affairs 1948–51 (this was the first coalition government). In 1957 he left politics. He was one of the founders of Amnesty International. He received the Nobel Peace Prize in 1974, the Lenin Prize in 1977, was awarded the American Medal of Justice by President Carter in 1978 and the Dag Hammarskjoeld Prize for International Solidarity in 1981. He was the author of the MacBride Principles, an anti-discrimination code, which was adopted by many states in America. The MacBride Principles were aimed at forcing American companies operating in Northern Ireland to ensure equal employment opportunities for all, including Catholics, who were denied equal rights by the English.

A republican in her own right, Catalina (Mary) Bulfin MacBride married Seán on 26 January 1926. Born in Buenos Aires, she was the sister of Éamon Bulfin. Catalina Bulfin was secretary to Austin Stack while he was minister of home affairs during the War of Independence and continued to work for him after the Treaty. She, too, opposed the Treaty, and was arrested on 6 April 1923, to be imprisoned in Kilmainham Gaol and the North Dublin Union. She passed away in 1976.

Clontarf Town Hall frequent meeting place for the Volunteer Military Council prior to the Rising. Michael McGinn, its curator, was a friend of Padraig Pearse and was an old IRB man himself.

Clontarf (Marino) Marino Casino. There was a disused, wide, dry tunnel in which Michael Collins, Harry Boland, Gearoid O'Sullivan, Tom Barry and others fired and practised with the Thompson machine guns Clan na Gael purchased in America for the Volunteers.[237]

Clontarf (Marino): Croydon Park. The Park had been taken over by the ITGWU several years before the Rising, and used by Cpt. Jack White for drilling the Irish Citizen Army. In October 1913 about 500 workers travelled there to enlist in the army that was being discussed. Their names were taken, but they heard no more until Cpt. White took up James Connolly's announcement of the ICA the next month. After the 1913 Lockout, White offered Countess Markievicz £50 to buy shoes for the workers so they could drill and form a real army, and it was their primary training area for the ICA in 1914. There were three acres of park area and a house on the grounds. After James Larkin left for America, the ITGWU sold the estate.

Coleraine Street John Beirnes was killed here by South Staffordshire Regiment troops during the Rising.

College Green Bank of Ireland; former Irish Parliament Building. The Bank took

237 Bell, J. Bowyer. 'The Thompson Submachine Gun in Ireland', *Irish Sword*, Vol. VIII, No. 31, 1967.

possession on 24 August 1803 following the Act of Union. The Upper Chamber remains as it was when the building housed the Irish Parliament. Designed by Sir Edward Lovett Pearce in 1728, and with later contributions by James Gandon.

The original buildings on the site were at various times a hospital (1603), a mansion (1612), House of Commons (1730), House of Lords (1787), and finally the bank (1808).

The reviewing stand for the Volunteers' Parade on St Patrick's Day 1916 was here.

On 20 April 1922 Michael Collins spoke to a massive crowd here. He gave his view of the Treaty and said it granted the 'freedom to achieve freedom'. He also assured them that the boundary commission would give large parts of Northern Ireland to the Free State on the basis of demographics.

College Green Statue of Thomas Davis, composer of 'A Nation Once Again'.

College Green Trinity College Dublin (TCD). Founded in 1592 by Queen Elizabeth, it was built on land confiscated from the Priory of All Hallows. The College's complete name is the College of the Holy and Undivided Trinity.

Brig. Gen. William Lowe made it his HQ during the Rising. The Provost at that time was J.P. Mahaffey.

An 'Irish Convention' sat in Trinity from 25 July 1917 to 5 April 1918 (there were some sessions in Cork and Belfast); Horace Plunkett was its chairman. Its ninety-five members included mayors and chairmen of public bodies, together with almost every prominent Irishman outside politics, but its weakness was on the political side; Sinn Féin had five seats, but declined to take part; William O'Brien's All for Ireland Party declined.[238] It reaffirmed the measure of disagreement between the North and South. The Membership was comprised of: fifty-two Nationalists; twenty-six Ulster Unionists, headed by Hugh Barrie and George Clarke; nine Southern Unionists, headed by Lord Midleton; six Labour representatives; two Liberals.[239]

It was not until 1972, upon the death of Archbishop John Charles McQuaid, that it was no longer a 'mortal sin' for a Catholic to attend Trinity without written permission.

College Green (1 Grafton Street): Regent House, Trinity College.

College Green Thomas Ashe Memorial Hall; James Larkin lay in state here prior to his funeral in January 1947.

College Green: Seán Treacy shot G-Division Detective Sergeant John Barton here on 29 November 1919.

1 College Green *Fianna* publishing office.

1 College Green (College Street): office of John R. Reynolds. Also the first office used by Kathleen Clarke for the Irish Volunteers' Dependents' Fund, prior to its amalgamation with the Irish National Aid Association. Michael Collins worked here for her. The Fund combined with the Irish National Aid Association and

238 O'Brien, William. Witness Statement 1766. **239** Rees, Russell. *Ireland, 1905-1925, Volume I*, 1998, p. 231.

moved to 10 Exchequer Street. Clarke originally submitted the name 'Irish Republican Prisoners' Dependents' Fund' but that was not accepted by the censors and so no funds could be solicited in periodicals. The name was changed to the 'Irish Volunteers' Dependents' Fund' and was accepted by censors for publication in newspapers. Joseph McGrath was the first secretary of the combined Fund. Reynolds was ordered by the English military officials to deport himself to Coventry, England, and remained there until 1917.

7 College Green The O'Connell Press printed *The Eye Opener*, a strongly nationalist paper. Thomas Dickson was the editor, and he was shot in the same tragic incident during the Rising as Francis Sheehy-Skeffington and Patrick MacIntyre. C.S. Andrews called *The Eye Opener* 'a scandal sheet which was non-political but directed at exposing the sex life of British officers'.[240] Others noted that *The Eye Opener* was 'rabidly loyalist'.

12–14 College Green Star Assurance Building; Committee for Compensation for Property Destroyed in the Rising.

12–14 College Green Also office of Michael Noyk, solicitor. He often appeared in Dáil/Republican Courts during the War of Independence, and gave advice to the Dáil.[241] He was the solicitor for Éamon (Ned) Broy when Broy was imprisoned at Arbour Hill.

16 College Green: Office of Walter Hume, Assessor of Property Destroyed in the Rising.

34 College Green The heroic group of figures crowding the façade of the National Bank Building was sculpted by James Pearse[242], father of Padraig and Willie. The elder Pearse was described as 'the pioneer of modern Gothic art, as applied to Church work, in this country'.[243]

3, 4 College Street Offices of the Committee in favour of the Treaty, under the direction of Dan McCarthy. Brigid Lyons worked here in early 1922.[244]

5b College Street: Police station near Trinity College. Dave Neligan was posted here in 1918.

Connaught Street, Drumcondra Home of Mr and Mrs Seámus Doherty. IRA/ Volunteers 'on the run' often stayed here. Seán Treacy was a frequent visitor.

67 Connaught Street, Phibsborough Home of Michael O'Hanrahan; he lived here with his mother, his brother, Henry (Harry), and his sisters, Áine (Ciss), Maire and Eily.[245] The O'Hanrahan family were from Co. Carlow and they lived there until Michael was a young man. Eily was in Jacob's Factory in the Rising; Thomas MacDonagh sent her back to the house for a time as there were arms hidden here, and directed her to give them out to the men he sent with her.

Constitution Hill, Phibsborough Broadstone Railway Station, the terminus of

---

240 Andrews, C.S., *Dublin Made Me*, 1979, 2001, p. 83. **241** Noyk, Michael. Witness Statement 707. **242** Thornley. 'Patrick Pearse', *Studies*, p. 10. **243** *Freeman's Journal*, 8 September 1900. **244** Thornton, Brigid Lyons. Witness Statement 259. **245** O'Reilly, Eily O'Hanrahan. Witness Statements 270, 415.

the Midland Great Western Railway. This was the most monumental of the five railway termini of Dublin and the only one not controlled during the Rising because it was retaken on Tuesday, 25 April. It was sited on a hill, and its most dramatic feature was a railway shed with a huge colonnade. Designed by Richard Turner, the shed proved too ambitious for the span and was replaced after it collapsed in the early 1850s. Closed as a railway station in 1932, it is now a bus station.

The Coombe The Coombe Maternity Hospital, founded in 1826, occupied the building used by the Meath Hospital before the Meath moved to Long Lane. The Coombe moved to Cork Street in 1967.

Cork Hill (at Dame Street): Dublin City Hall. The Church of St Mary del Dam was originally built here; it was demolished when the Royal Exchange building was built and completed in 1779. The building was taken over by Dublin Corporation as its City Hall in 1852. The city's motto is 'Obedienta Civium Urbis Felicitas', roughly translated as 'Happy the city whose citizens obey'.

The Dublin City Council of the Dublin Corporation met here.

On 31 July 1915, Jeremiah O'Donovan Rossa's body lay in state here after the requiem Mass at the Pro Cathedral until the funeral march to Glasnevin Cemetery on 1 August.

City Hall was held on Easter Monday 1916 by a garrison primarily from the Irish Citizen Army. Seán Connolly was the O/C of the Volunteer/ICA force and was the first casualty of the Rising. (See also City Hall, Appendix V.)[246]

On 9 June 1918, Cumann na mBan organized an 'Ireland Women's Day' (Lá na mBan) as part of the Anti-Conscription campaign. Over 40,000 women signed this anti-conscription pledge at City Hall alone:

A Solemn Pledge for the Women of Ireland
Inaugurated on St Columcille's Day
Because the enforcement of conscription on any people without their
consent is tyranny, we are resolved to resist the conscription of Irishmen;
We will not fill the places of men deprived of their work through enforced
military service; We will do all in our power to help the families of men who
suffer through refusing enforced military service.[247]

On 3 May 1920, Dublin Corporation acknowledged the authority of the Government of the Republic of Ireland, Dáil Éireann, as the duly elected government of Ireland, and undertook to give effect to all decrees promulgated by the same Dáil Éireann.

On 14 June 1921, Seán MacEoin was tried here in a special court martial,

---

247 Countess Markievicz wrote: 'It wasn't talk blocked conscription: it was the astounding fact that the whole male population left at home and most of the women and kids would have died rather than fight for England, and they simply did not dare exterminate a nation.' Countess Markievicz to Eva Gore-Booth, 14 February 1919. Roper, Esther, editor. *Prison Letters of Countess Markievicz*, 1987, pp 194-5.

condemned to death, and transported to Mountjoy Prison. (See also North Circular Road/Mountjoy Prison.)

In 1922, National Army HQ was set up here. Also that year, the first director of medical services, Dr 'Stetto' Ahearne, opened his offices here. As her first assignment after passing her exams, Dr Brigid Lyons went to work here.[248]

Cork Hill (and 1–3 Parliament Street): Henry & James, outfitters; outpost of 1916 City Hall garrison.

Cork Hill (and 30–40 Parliament Street): *Mail & Express* office (sometimes called *Daily Express*); outpost of 1916 City Hall garrison.

Cork Street (at Marrowbone Lane): 'The Fever Hospital'.

65 Cork Street Home of Philip Clarke, who was killed in action with the ICA in St Stephen's Green. He left a widow and eight children.

Coulson Ave Home of George Russell (Æ) in 1903.

26 Coulson Ave Maud Gonne MacBride lived here in 1903, and the house was raided in August at the time of King George's visit.[249]

Cross Avenue, Blackrock 'Dunamase', home of Kevin and Brigid Cole O'Higgins and their daughter after the Civil War.

Cross Avenue, Blackrock 'Bellvue', formerly the home of the Bewley family. De Valera moved his family here in 1933.

Cross Avenue, Blackrock 'Heberton'. Éamon de Valera moved his family here in 1940 and renamed the house 'Teach Chuilinn'.

Cross Kevin Street Fintan Murphy arranged for a shoemaker here to make special shoes for Harry Boland when he went to America, into which were placed copies of the Irish Declaration of Independence and a copy of the prospectus for the Dáil Loan. The copy of the Declaration bore the signatures of the Speaker of the Dáil and the holders of the ministries.

3 Crow Street Department of Intelligence Office, 2nd Floor, above J.F. Fowler, printers; technically the office of Michael Collins but he infrequently came here. Under the name of Irish Products Company, Liam Tobin, Collins' chief of intelligence, had his office here,[250] and was assisted by Tom Cullen and Frank Thornton. The principal staff were: Charley Byrne, Paddy Caldwell, Charlie Dalton, Joe Dolan, Joe Guilfoyle, Ned Kelleher, Pat (Paddy) Kennedy, Dan McDonnell, Peter Magee and Frank Saurin.

6 Crown Alley Telephone Exchange in 1916. Michael King was in command of the ICA contingent that was supposed to capture it. It could have been occupied by the ICA early in the Rising, but they were deterred by a 'shawlie' who yelled, 'Go back, boys, the place is crammed with military'. It was taken over by the British about five hours later.

Custom House Quay The Custom House; designed by James Gandon and

---

248 Thornton, Brigid Lyons. Witness Statement 259. **249** MacBride, Maud Gonne. Witness Statement 317. **250** Tobin, Liam. Witness Statement 1753.

completed in 1791. Seat of nine British administrative departments including two taxing departments and the Local Government Board.[251]

Destroyed with the approval of the Dáil on 25 May 1921.[252] [253] [254] (It was once said of Gandon's buildings: 'Poor Gandon, all his sumptious structures were either burned, bombed, or blasted in the cause of Irish freedom.') The fire burned for five days. Tom Ennis was appointed O/C of the party ordered to seize the building, and was wounded. The operation was carried out by some 120 Volunteers, five of whom were killed: Tommy Dorrins, Seán Doyle, Dan Head, Cpt. Paddy O'Reilly and nineteen-year-old Lt Stephen O'Reilly (brothers). (There is a sculpture by Yann Renard-Goulet in the back yard of the Custom House commemorating the death of these five Volunteers, and all in the 2nd Battalion of the Dublin Brigade who gave their lives in the cause of freedom.) Two civilians were killed: Francis Davis, caretaker of the building, who resisted the Volunteers, and Mahon Lawless, who was mistaken for a Volunteer by the Tans. About eighty IRA/Volunteers were arrested. Jimmy Slattery lost his arm in the attack. Piaras Béaslaí wrote in *An tÓglach*: 'The burning of the Custom House symbolised the final collapse of English civil administration in this country.'

6 Dalymount Terrace, Phibsborough Harry Boland's family's home. James and Catherine Boland moved here from Phibsborough Road. Birthplace of Harry Boland in 1887. Nellie was the oldest, then Gerald, Harry, Kathleen, and Ned.

Dame Court Stag's Head Pub, one of Dublin's most lavish Victorian pubs. Often used as a meeting place in the War of Independence.

Dame Street Canon O'Leary gave Irish classes here attended by Padraig Pearse.

Dame Street The office of Countess Markievicz after she was released from Aylesbury Gaol in England in 1917. She wrote very unfavourably of her time in the English gaols: 'All they did was to teach you how to steal.'[255] [256] [257]

13 Dame Street Callaghan & Son, military tailor and gunsmith. Many British officers were outfitted here; after 1922, Free Staters used this establishment for outfitting as well. Michael Collins bought his uniforms here.

41 Dame Street Craig, Gardner & Co., Chartered Accountants. Michael Collins worked here before the Rising.

72 Dame Street Olympia Theatre, formerly Dan Lowrey's Star of Erin Music Hall; first 'cinema' show seen in Ireland in 1896.

Dawson Street P.S. O'Hegarty's bookshop; used as a 'drop' for Michael Collins.[258]

Dawson Street The Mansion House, the official residence of the Lord Mayor of Dublin since 1713. Lord Mayor James Gallagher in 1916 called Dublin 'Louvain by the Liffey' after the destruction of the Rising.

251 McAleese, Daniel. Witness Statement 1411. **252** Ó Mahoney, Seán. *The Burning of the Custom House in Dublin*, 1921. (pamphlet, Dublin, 2000). **253** McCann, John. 'Burning of the Custom House', *The Kerryman*, 17 March 1938. **254** Traynor, Oscar. 'The Burning of the Custom House — Dublin's Fighting Story', *The Kerryman*, 1939. **255** *Freeman's Journal*, 19 June 1917. **256** *The Voice of Labour*, 1 May 1919. **257** *New Ireland*, 8, 15 April 1922. **258** O'Hegarty, P.S. Witness Statement 26.

On 19 April 1917 Count Plunkett convened an 'Irish Assembly'. Over 1200 delegates attended, with sixty-eight public bodies represented, as well as forty-one of Arthur Griffith's Sinn Féin Clubs. Also in attendance were the Irish Nation League, Cumann na mBan and the National Aid Association. The dominant note was to get Ireland's position submitted to the Peace Conference following the end of the war in Europe. There was an affirmation proclaiming Ireland an independent nation and her freedom from all foreign control. The 'Organizing Committee' was composed of Seán Brown, Dr Thomas Dillon, Arthur Griffith, Alderman Thomas Kelly, Helena Molony, Seán Milroy, William O'Brien, Fr Michael O'Flanagan, Stephen O'Meara, Count and Countess Plunkett and George Plunkett. Four women were elected to the Executive: Kathleen Clarke, Dr Kathleen Lynn, Grace Gifford Plunkett and Countess Markievicz. In fact not much came of the conference.[259] [260]

On 20 April 1917 an auction was held here for the benefit of the Irish National Aid and Volunteers' Dependents' Fund; items of those executed after the Rising as well as articles of survivors/imprisoned were auctioned.

The Tenth Sinn Féin Ard-Fheis was held here on 25–6 October 1917. About 1700 delegates attended, including members from 1009 Sinn Féin Clubs.[261] The secretary stated that the total number of Clubs was about 1200, with a membership of almost 250,000.[262] [263] De Valera was elected president of Sinn Féin and the Irish Volunteers. Vice-presidents: Arthur Griffith and Fr Michael O'Flanagan. Secretaries: Darrell Figgis (later Harry Boland) and Austin Stack (he remained Hon. Secretary until his death in 1929). Treasurers: Laurence Ginnell and William Cosgrave. Eoin MacNeill was elected to the twenty-four member Sinn Féin Executive Council (there was controversy when MacNeill was proposed for the Executive – Éamon de Valera, Arthur Griffith and Seán Milroy voted for him, however Kathleen Clarke, Helena Molony[264] and Countess Markievicz opposed him – but he received an outstanding majority of votes). The other members of the Executive were: Piaras Béaslaí, Ernest Blythe,[265] Harry Boland, Cathal Brugha, Kathleen Clarke, Michael Collins, Dr Thomas Dillon, Dr Richard Hayes, David Kent, Diarmuid Lynch, Fionan Lynch, Dr Kathleen Lynn, Seán MacEntee, Countess Markievicz, Joseph McDonagh, Joseph McGuinness, Seán Milroy, Seán T. O'Kelly, Count Plunkett, Grace Gifford Plunkett, Fr Matt Ryan, Fr Thomas Wall and James J. Walsh.

Cathal Brugha proposed the Constitution, and Seán Milroy seconded it on 25 October 1917.

259 Lynn, Dr Kathleen. Witness Statement 357. **260** Ó Snodaigh, Aengus. 'The Mansion House "Irish Assembly"', *An Phoblacht*, 8 July 1999. **261** Gallagher/Hogan. *The Four Glorious Years*, pp. 22-23. **262** Dawson, Richard. *Red Terror and Green*, 1920, 1972, p. 118. **263** *Hansard*, 24 October 1917. Henry Edward Duke, Chief Secretary for Ireland 1916-1918, estimated that Sinn Féin's membership numbered about 200,000 in October 1917. **264** Molony, Helena. Witness Statement 391. **265** Blythe, Ernest. Witness Statement 939.

The Constitution stated:

Whereas the people of Ireland never relinquished the claim to separate Nationhood; and Whereas the Provisional Government of the Irish Republic, Easter 1916, in the name of the Irish people, and continuing the fight made by previous generations, reasserted the inalienable right of the Irish nation to Sovereign independence, and reaffirmed the determination of the Irish people to achieve it; and Whereas the Proclamation of an Irish Republic, Easter 1916, and the supreme courage and glorious sacrifices of the men who gave their lives to maintain it, have united the people of Ireland under the flag of the Irish Republic, be it resolved that we, the delegated representatives of the Irish People, in convention assembled, hereby declare the following to be the Constitution of Sinn Féin.

1. The name of the organisation shall be Sinn Féin.
2. Sinn Féin aims at securing the international recognition of Ireland as an independent Irish Republic. Having achieved that status, the Irish people may by referendum freely choose their own form of government.
3. This object shall be attained through the Sinn Féin Organisation which shall, in the name of the Irish People
   (a) Deny the right and oppose the will of the British Parliament and British Crown or any other foreign government to legislate for Ireland;
   (b) Make use of any and every means available to render impotent the power of England to hold Ireland in subjection by military force or otherwise.[266]

The meeting began with Brugha barely consenting to sit in the same room with Griffith and with Michael Collins and Rory O'Connor walking out and being brought back by de Valera. Early cracks in 'Republicanism' were apparent even then and would widen until the Treaty split.

De Valera devised the following formula to open the Ard-Fheis: 'Sinn Féin aims at securing the international recognition of Ireland as an independent Irish Republic. Having achieved that status the Irish people may by referendum freely

266 Macardle. *The Irish Republic*, p. 915.

choose their own form of government.' He subsequently closed the Ard-Fheis by declaring, 'We are not doctrinaire Republicans.'[267]

On 18 April 1918 a national conference was convened in the Mansion House by the Hon. Laurence O'Neill, Lord Mayor of Dublin. All sections of 'nationalist' opinion were to form the 'National Cabinet'. The Irish Parliamentary Party was represented by Joe Devlin and John Dillon, Sinn Féin by de Valera and Griffith, the dissident element of the old Home Rule Party by F.J. Healy and William O'Brien, the Irish Labour Party by Michael J. Egan (Cork), Thomas Johnson (Belfast)[268] and William O'Brien (Dublin)[269], and the Independents by T.M. Healy.[270] The conference was convened primarily as a protest against conscription measures which were passed by the British Parliament on 16 April 1918:

> Taking our stand on Ireland's separate and distinct nationhood and affirming the principle of liberty that the Governments of nations derive their just powers from the consent of the governed, we deny the right of the British Government or any external authority to impose compulsory military service in Ireland against the clearly expressed will of the Irish people. The passing of the Conscription Bill by the British House of Commons must be regarded as a declaration of war on the Irish nation. The alternative to accepting it as such is to surrender our liberties and to acknowledge ourselves slaves. It is in direct violation of the rights of small nationalities to self-determination, which even the Prime Minister of England – now preparing to employ naked militarism and force his Act upon Ireland – himself officially announced as an essential condition for peace at the Peace Congress. The attempt to enforce it will be an unwarranted aggression, which we call upon all Irishmen to resist by the most effective means at their disposal.[271]

The Catholic hierarchy concurred with this declaration at their annual meeting at Maynooth and declared in their own manifesto:

> An attempt is being made to force Conscription on Ireland against the will of the Irish nation and in defiance of the protests of its leaders. In view especially of the historic relations between the two countries from the very beginning up to this moment, we consider that Conscription forced in this way upon Ireland is an oppressive and inhuman law, which the Irish people have a right to resist by every means that are constant with God.[272]

267 Ibid, p. 232-233. **268** Johnson, Thomas. Witness Statement 1755. **269** O'Brien, William. Witness Statement 1766. **270** Gallagher/Hogan. *The Four Glorious Years*, pp. 24-28. **271** Kee. Op. cit., p. 619. **272** Ibid, p. 620.

An anti-Conscription pledge was set forth: 'Denying the right of the British Government to enforce compulsory service in this country, we pledge ourselves solemnly to one another to resist Conscription by the most effective means at our disposal'.

On 17 May the British authorities decided not to implement conscription in Ireland, but by then the reaction had solidified support for Sinn Féin. (See 'The German Plot' arrests, which took place on the night of 17-18 May 1918, their effect on the British effort to enforce conscription, and the people's embracement of Sinn Féin throughout the country. 'The German Plot', Harcourt Street.)

On 7 January 1919 twenty-six Sinn Féin representatives met and made arrangements to convene the First Dáil Éireann.[273]

On 21 January 1919 the First Dáil met in the Mansion House. At 3.30 pm, in the Round Room, Count Plunkett called the meeting to order and nominated Cathal Brugha to be Ceann Comhairle (speaker/chairperson) for Dáil Éireann. Padraig Ó Maille seconded this. Brugha presided thereafter and following the reading of the Declaration of Independence, Brugha told the cheering assembly: 'Deputies, you understand from what is asserted in this Declaration that we are now done with England. Let the world know it and those who are concerned bear it in mind.' Fr Michael O' Flanagan read opening prayers. (See also Harcourt Street for a complete list of TDs elected. See also Appendix III for the Declaration of Independence, the Constitution, Message to Free Nations, and the Democratic Programme.)

The Declaration of Independence was passed unanimously. Brugha read it in Irish, Éamonn Duggan in English, and George Gavan-Duffy in French. (The Provisional Constitution and Declaration of Independence were drafted by Piaras Béaslaí, Conor Collins, George Gavan-Duffy, Seán T. O'Kelly, James O'Mara and James J. Walsh). The 'Message to Free Nations' was read by Robert Barton in English and by J.J. O'Kelly in Irish.[274] [275] [276] [277] [278]

A Democratic Programme of Dáil Éireann was read and unanimously adopted, founded on the 1916 *Proclamation*. Thomas Johnson[279], secretary of the Irish Labour Party, and William O'Brien[280], at the request of the Dáil, prepared and submitted a draft for a social and democratic programme. About half of their draft was included in the programme as finally written and submitted by Seán T. O'Kelly. (See also Appendix III.)[281]

Twenty-eight TDs attended.[282] The answer to the roll call for thirty-four absent

273 Gallagher/Hogan. *The Four Glorious Years*, pp. 56-62. **274** Ó Snodaigh, Aengus. 'The Declaration of Independence', *An Phoblacht*, 13 January 2000. **275** Ó Snodaigh, Aengus. 'An Chead Dáil Éireann Opens', *An Phoblacht*, 20 January 2000. **276** Ó Snodaigh, Aengus. 'Ireland's Independence Declared', *An Phoblacht*, 27 January 2000. **277** Ó Snodaigh, Aengus. 'The Democratic Programme', *An Phoblacht*, 9 March 2000. **278** Ó Snodaigh, Aengus. 'An Address to Free Nations', *An Phoblacht*, 3 February 2000. **279** Johnson, Thomas. Witness Statement 1755. **280** O'Brien, William. Witness Statement 1766. **281** Macardle. *The Irish Republic*, p. 275-277. **282** *An Phoblacht*, 20 January 2000. Holt claims there were twenty-seven. Holt, Edgar. *Protest in Arms*, 1960, p. 171.

Deputies was 'imprisoned by the foreign enemy', and for three absent Deputies 'deported by the foreign enemy'. Answering 'present' were twenty-eight Sinn Féin TDs out of a total of 104 names called, including all other parties. Even Ulster's Edward Carson received an invitation – in Irish. Some TDs were elected for two constituencies, so there were only sixty-nine persons elected. Two were ill, others had been deported, five were on missions abroad, but the preponderance were in gaol in England. (Michael Collins and Harry Boland were in England working on de Valera's escape from prison but were marked present to keep others from asking where they were.)

Thirty-three per cent of Dáil members were under thirty-five years and another forty per cent were between thirty-five and forty. There were only two Protestant members: Ernest Blythe and Robert Barton.

The officers elected were: president, Éamon de Valera; vice-presidents, Arthur Griffith and Fr O'Flanagan; secretaries, Austin Stack and Darrell Figgis; treasurers, William T. Cosgrave and Laurence Ginnell. The Executive elected was Harry Boland, Michael Collins, Seán T. O'Kelly[283], Seán MacEntee, James J. Walsh and Kathleen Clarke. Clerks appointed were Risteard Ó Fogladha (chief clerk), Seán Nunan[284], Diarmuid O'Hegarty and Patrick Sheehan.[285] The photo taken that day showed twenty-four attendees.

No oath was administered to the Deputies on 21 January. The elected Deputies present had signed a Republican pledge at their meeting on 7 January: 'I hereby pledge myself to work for the establishment of an independent Irish Republic; that I will accept nothing less than complete separation from England in settlement of Ireland's claims; and that I will abstain from attending the English Parliament.'[286]

On 4 April 1919 a private session of the First Dáil was held. The Ceann Comhairle was Seán T. O'Kelly. Éamon de Valera presided and named the Cabinet as follows.

> Minister for Home Affairs: Arthur Griffith (arrested); succeeded by Austin Stack
>
> Minister for Defence: Cathal Brugha; Deputy: William Considine (Richard Mulcahy was Minister from January to April, when he became Assistant Minister under Brugha; he was the Volunteers' chief of staff)
>
> Minister for Fine Arts and of Foreign Affairs: Count George Noble Plunkett; Under-Secretary for Foreign Affairs: Robert Brennan
>
> Minister for Labour: Countess Markievicz (first European female minister; when she was appointed, she was in Holloway Prison in England)
>
> Minister for Industries: Eoin MacNeill

283 O'Kelly, Seán T. Witness Statements 611, 1765. **284** Nunan, Seán. Witness Statement 1744. **285** Ó Snodaigh, Aengus. 'The First Cabinet', *An Phoblacht*, 16 March 2000. **286** Murphy, Brian. 'The First Dáil Éireann', *History Ireland*, Vol. II, No. 1, 1994.

Minister for Finance: Michael Collins
Minister for Trade and Commerce: Ernest Blythe
Minister for Local Government: William T. Cosgrave; succeeded by Kevin
    O'Higgins, assisted by Rory O'Connor
Minister for Propaganda: Laurence Ginnell; succeeded by Desmond
    Fitzgerald (arrested in February 1921); succeeded by Erskine Childers
Minister for Agriculture: Robert Barton; succeeded by Art O'Connor.

On 10 April 1919 the second public session of the First Dáil was held. The photo taken on this day is the one most usually seen of the members of the First Dáil.

On 17 June 1919 the third public session of the First Dáil was convened. This established the consular service and the National Arbitration Courts. The trustees of the Dáil Loan were appointed as follows: Éamon de Valera, Most Revd Dr Michael Fogarty[287] (bishop of Killaloe) and James O'Mara.

The fourth public session of the First Dáil was held on 19 August 1919. It established the 'Dail/Republican Courts'.[288] [289] They were set up under Austin Stack, minister for justice, and had civil and criminal jurisdiction.[290] [291] [292] [293] [294] [295] Young barristers from the Law Library in Dublin's Four Courts drew up the Rules of Court, under the direction of King's Counsel James Creed Meredith, a Protestant, who served as the president of the Dáil/Republican Supreme Court from 1920 to 1922.

(The Dáil/Republican Supreme Court had three members who could sit as high court judges as well. Beneath this category were County/District and Parish Courts. Parish Courts corresponded to the British Petty Sessions Courts. The County Court Judges were primarily women, and corresponded to the British County Courts. There were five County/District Judges, elected by those who presided at the Parish Courts. Within four days the Parish Court could appeal to the District. The court decrees were enforced by the IRA/Volunteers and later by 'Republican Police' attached to companies. The mass of people long deprived of tribunals with which they could identify flocked to the Dáil/Republican Courts. Attempts at suppression by the British were futile. Within a short while the courts were operating in twenty-seven counties. In these courts, the amateur judges endeavoured to give a good and fair decision, which may not always have been

287 Fogarty, Most Revd Dr Michael. Witness Statement 271. **288** These courts were variously known as 'Dáil Courts', 'Republican Courts', and 'Sinn Féin/Republican Courts' in different sources. For consistency, they will be referred to as 'Dáil/Republican Courts'. **289** Gallagher/Hogan. *The Four Glorious Years*, pp. 70-82. **290** Casey, J. 'Republican Courts in Ireland, 1919-1922', *Irish Jurist*, Vol. V, 1970. **291** Casey, J. 'The Genesis of the Dáil Courts', *Irish Jurist*, Vol. IX, 1974. **292** Costello, Francis, 'The Republican Courts and the Decline of British Rule in Ireland', *Éire-Ireland*, Vol. XXV, No. 3, 1990. **293** Maguire, C.A. 'The Republican Courts', *Capuchin Annual*, 1984. **294** Kotsonouris, Mary. 'Revolutionary Justice: The Dáil Éireann Courts', *History Ireland*, Vol. II, No. 3, 1994. **295** O'Duffy, Seán M. Witness Statements 313, 618, 619.

according to the letter of the law so much as according to the conscience and private knowledge of the judges themselves.[296])

On 20 August 1919 in private session certain Volunteers took an oath of allegiance to the Dáil. The oath, moved by Cathal Brugha and seconded by Terence MacSwiney, was:

> I _____ do solemnly swear (or affirm) that I do not, and shall not, yield a voluntary support to any pretended Government, Authority, or Power inside Ireland hostile or inimical thereto; and I do further swear (or affirm) that to the best of my knowledge and ability I shall support and defend the Irish Republic, which is Dáil Éireann, against all enemies foreign and domestic, and that I will bear true faith and allegiance to the same and that I take this obligation freely without any mental reservation or purpose of evasion. So help me God.

The oath was to be taken by all Dáil Deputies, all Volunteers, all officials and clerks of the Dáil, and 'any other body or individual who, in the opinion of the Dáil, should take the same oath'. It was only in 1921 that Oscar Traynor, O/C of the Dublin Brigade, told his Volunteers that their 'activities will be directed by General Headquarters (GHQ), and the Government of the Republic will accept full responsibility for your operations against the enemy and for your future welfare'.[297]

On 12 September 1919 the Dáil was officially suppressed as a 'Dangerous Association':

> Whereas, as by special proclamation dated July 3, 1918, in pursuance and by date thereof certain associations in Ireland known by the names of Sinn Féin organisation, Sinn Féin clubs, Irish Volunteers, Cumann na mBan and Gaelic League to be dangerous.
>
> And whereas the association known by the name of Dáil Éireann appears to us to be a dangerous association and to have been after the date of said special proclamation employed for all purposes of the association known by the names of Sinn Féin organisation, Sinn Féin clubs, Irish Volunteers, and Cumann na mBan, now we, the Lord-Lieutenant General and General Governor of Ireland, by and with the advice of the Privy Council in Ireland, by virtue of the Criminal Law and Procedure Act of Ireland of 1887, and of every power and authority in this behalf, do hereby, by this our order, prohibit and suppress within the several districts specified and named in the schedule the association known as Dáil Éireann.[298]

296 O'Connor, Ulick. *A Terrible Beauty is Born*, (Panther Books edition) 1981, p. 150. **297** Traynor, Oscar. Witness Statement 340. **298** *The Irish Times*, 13 September 1919.

In spite of this suppression, on 27 October 1919 the fifth public session of the First Dáil was held in the Oak Room. By October 1919 all Deputies and officials had taken the Oath of Allegiance.

On 29 June 1920 the Dáil established Courts of Justice and Equity,[299] appointing James Creed Meredith as president of the Dáil/Republican Supreme Court, with Arthur Clery and Diarmuid Crowley as the other members of that Court. It appointed Cahir Davitt (son of agrarian agitator and nationalist Michael Davitt) as a High Court Justice.[300] These served as appellate courts for the Dáil/Republican Courts previously established.

On 11 March 1921, the Dáil agreed to the acceptance of a state of war with England, and that it should take full responsibility for the military operations of the Volunteers as the Army of the Republic.[301]

The Second Dáil was elected on 19 May 1921 in the Twenty-Six Counties and on 24 May in the Six Counties. This election became known as the 'Partition Election' because it was the first time in which an election in the Six Counties was held at a different time to that for the Twenty-Six Counties. All 'nationalist' parties agreed not to run against Sinn Féin; the Six Counties were to elect thirteen representatives to the English parliament and the Twenty-Six Counties were to send thirty-three. This was also the election in which proportional representation was introduced to Ireland on a national level. (It had been used on 15 January 1920 in urban and borough elections and on 15 June for county council elections.) In the Twenty-Six Counties, no elections were needed. All of the 124 seats filled by the popular election and the four seats allocated to the National University were given to men and women pledged to the Irish Republic. The entire elected opposition consisted of the four men returned by TCD unopposed. Winston Churchill remarked that: 'From that moment, the position of Ulster became unassailable'.[302]

On 8 July 1921 de Valera convened a consultation preparatory to a truce; Lord Mayor Laurence (Larry) O'Neill, Gen. Sir Neville Macready, Lord Midleton (representing Southern Unionists), Arthur Griffith and Robert Barton attended it. James Craig from Ulster refused to attend. The following day the terms of the truce were agreed upon and settled at a 3 pm meeting between Gen. Macready, Col. J. Brind and Alfred W. Cope for the British, and Robert C. Barton and Éamonn J. Duggan for the IRA/Volunteers. The terms went into effect at noon on 11 July 1921.

The First Session of the Second Dáil was held on 16 August 1921 in the Round Room. There were 130 Republican TDs, 6 Nationalist TDs and 44 Unionist TDs (who absented themselves as usual). All TDs took the oath to the Dáil.

On 17 August the Dáil's Foreign Representatives were named as follows: John Chartres (Germany), Harry Boland (USA), Seán T. O'Kelly (Paris)[303], George

299 Kotsonouris. 'Revolutionary Justice', Op. cit. **300** Davitt, Cahir. Witness Statements 993, 1751. **301** Martin. *The Irish Volunteers*, p. x. **302** Macardle. *The Irish Republic*, p. 456. **303** O'Kelly, Seán T. Witness Statements 611, 1765.

Gavan-Duffy (Rome)[304], Art O'Brien (London), Dr Patrick McCartan (Russia)[305], Éamon Bulfin (Argentina)[306], Frank W. Egan (Chile).

On 26 August the Cabinet and ministers were elected as follows:

Minister for Foreign Affairs: Arthur Griffith
Minister for Home Affairs: Austin Stack
Minister for Defence: Cathal Brugha
Minister for Finance: Michael Collins
Minister for Local Government: William T. Cosgrave
Minister for Economic Affairs: Robert Barton

The following were elected ministers outside the Cabinet:

Minister for Fine Arts: Count Plunkett
Minister for Propaganda: Desmond Fitzgerald
Minister for Education: J.J. O'Kelly
Minister for Labour: Countess Markievicz
Minister for Trade and Commerce: Ernest Blythe
Minister for Agriculture: Art O'Connor
Minister for Fisheries: Seán Etchingham
Kevin O'Higgins was elected as a Minister to assist William T. Cosgrave in Local Government
Director for Publicity: Desmond Fitzgerald

On 14 September 1921 the plenipotentiaries were chosen for the treaty negotiations: Arthur Griffith, Robert Barton, Michael Collins, George Gavan-Duffy, and Éamonn Duggan.

On 15 September de Valera proposed that the army (IRA/Volunteers) 'be put on a regular basis'. The Cabinet, in late November, affirmed: 'The supreme body directing the Army is the Cabinet. The immediate executive representative of the Government is the Minister for Defence who is, therefore, Administrative Head of the Army. The Minister for Defence is a civilian. All Army appointments are to be sanctioned by the Minister for Defence, who is to have the power of nomination and veto.'

On 30 September 1921 de Valera issued a final 'acceptance' of the Treaty Conference 'Terms':

We have received your letter of invitation to a Conference in London on October 11th 'with a view to ascertaining how the association of Ireland

---

304 Gavan-Duffy, George. Witness Statement 381. **305** McCartan, Patrick. Witness Statements 99, 100, 766. **306** Bulfin, Éamon. Witness Statement 497.

with the community of nations known as the British Empire may best be reconciled with Irish national aspirations'.

Our respective positions have been stated and are understood and we agree that conference, not correspondence, is the most practical and hopeful way to an understanding. We accept the invitation, and our Delegates will meet you in London on the date mentioned 'to explore every possibility of settlement by personal discussion'.[307]

On 7 October letters were issued to the plenipotentiaries.

TO ALL WHOM THESE PRESENTS COME, GREETING:
In virtue of the authority vested in me by Dáil Éireann, I hereby appoint
Arthur Griffith, TD, Minister for Foreign Affairs, Chairm.
Michael Collins, TD, Minister for Finance
Robert C. Barton, TD, Minister for Economic Affairs
Edmund J. Duggan, TD
George Gavan-Duffy, TD

As Envoys Plenipotentiary from the Elected Government of the REPUBLIC OF IRELAND to negotiate and conclude on behalf of Ireland with the representatives of his Britannic Majesty, GEORGE V, a Treaty or Treaties of Settlement, Association, and Accommodation between Ireland and the community of nations known as the British Commonwealth.
IN WITNESS WHEREOF I hereunto subscribe my name as President.
    [signed] Éamon de Valera
Done in the City of Dublin this 7th day of October in the year of our Lord 1921 in five identical originals.

While de Valera was not prepared to lead the delegation in London, this did not stop his attempt to direct events from Dublin. Accordingly, he drew up the following document of *instructions* that he circulated to the plenipotentiaries:

(1) The Plenipotentiaries have full powers as defined in their credentials.

(2) It is understood before decisions are finally reached on a main question, that a dispatch notifying the intention to make these decisions will be sent to members of the Cabinet in Dublin, and that a reply will be awaited by the Plenipotentiaries before final decision is made.

(3) It is also understood that the complete text of the draft treaty about

307 Gallagher/Hogan. *The Four Glorious Years*, p. 321.

to be signed will be similarly submitted to Dublin and a reply awaited.

(4) In case of a break the text of final proposals from our side will be similarly submitted.

(5) It is understood that the Cabinet in Dublin will be kept regularly informed of the progress of the negotiations.[308]

De Valera clearly intended that these instructions, particularly clauses 2 and 3, would enable him to veto any draft document that he considered unacceptable. It is also believed that these 'instructions' were formulated in order to placate Cathal Brugha and Austin Stack, much more doctrinaire and ideological than the Irish people, who were desperately anxious for a settlement. However, Griffith and Collins, for their part, were unhappy with the limitations, and they chose to ignore these further instructions, which had not been approved by the Cabinet, considering them only as guiding principles, not mandatory. There are contrasting views of these 'instructions'. A rigid interpretation is not reconcilable with the plenipotentiary credentials. Since the Dáil had already conferred full plenipotentiary powers, the instructions from the Cabinet, an inferior body, were not legally binding in any instance in which they limited the powers of the delegation. Brugha and Stack, however, viewed the 'instructions' as requiring the delegation in London to keep the Cabinet in Dublin duly informed at every step and not to sign the final draft without submitting it to the Cabinet and awaiting a reply.[309]

On 6 December 1921 *Articles of Agreement for a Treaty*[310] were signed in London and two days later the Cabinet met. Those in attendance at the Cabinet meeting were Robert Barton, Cathal Brugha, Michael Collins, William T. Cosgrave, Éamon de Valera, Arthur Griffith, Austin Stack, Erskine Childers and George Gavan-Duffy. Brugha, de Valera and Stack voted against the Treaty. Barton (reluctantly), Collins, Cosgrave[311] and Griffith voted for it. De Valera denounced the delegates for their breach of faith in failing to consult him before signing, but Barton countered by insisting that the real problem had been caused by de Valera's refusal to attend the conference.[312] [313] (Later, de Valera told the Dáil 'now I would like everybody clearly to understand that the plenipotentiaries went over to negotiate a Treaty, that they could differ from the Cabinet if they wanted to, and

308 Ibid, p. 322. **309** Fitzgerald, Desmond. 'Mr Pakenham on the Anglo-Irish Treaty', Op. cit. **310** Though all discussion in the Dáil, the newspapers and most books refer to a 'Treaty', the English and Irish Delegates did not sign a Treaty. They signed a document entitled 'Articles for Agreement'. The words 'For a Treaty' were added to the English copy, but by that time the Irish copy was being delivered to Ireland. Pakenham. *Peace by Ordeal*, p. 246. For convenience and to conform to other sources, the discussion here and in all other sites will refer to the 'Treaty'. (See also Appendix III for complete Articles.) **311** Cosgrave, William. Witness Statements 268, 449. **312** Barton, Robert. Witness Statement 979. **313** Rees. *Ireland*, p. 289.

that in anything of consequence they could take their decision against the decision of the Cabinet'.[314])

That evening de Valera issued a press statement he called a 'Proclamation to the Irish People' indicating he could not recommend acceptance of the Treaty:

> The terms of this agreement are in violent conflict with the wishes of the majority of this nation, as expressed freely in successive elections during the past three years. I feel it my duty to inform you immediately that I cannot recommend the acceptance of this treaty either to Dáil Éireann or to the country. In this attitude I am supported by the Ministers of Home Affairs and Defence. The greatest test of our people has come. Let us face it worthily without bitterness, and above all, without recrimination. There is a definite constitutional way of resolving our political differences – let us not depart from it, and let the conduct of the Cabinet in this matter be an example to the whole nation.[315]

On 14 December 1921 the Dáil assembled but there was no 'debate' on the Treaty, just a discussion of the actions of the plenipotentiaries in signing the Treaty without 'permission' from the Cabinet. Immediately upon mention of the 'Treaty', Collins pointed out that no 'Treaty' was signed, but rather an 'Articles of Agreement', and that the signing implied referral to their respective legislatures, not acceptance. Both the Dáil and the English House of Commons had to ratify the Articles before they would take effect.[316] The English wasted no time in ratification as the Articles were approved quickly by both the House of Commons and the House of Lords and received the assent of the King on 31 March 1922.

The next day the Dáil assembled in private session and de Valera proposed his 'External Association'/Document Number Two. It was rejected and he 'withdrew' it asking that it be held as confidential. On 19 December the debates continued, but on 22 December the Dáil adjourned on the motion of Collins to reassemble on 3 January 1922. At adjournment, de Valera said to the Dáil, 'There is a definite constitutional way of resolving our differences.'[317] Thereafter the debates were continued in the Convocation Hall of the National University in Earlsfort Terrace. (See also Earlsfort Terrace for the progress of the Treaty debates from 3 January to 8 January 1922, including the vote of the TDs on 7 January 1922.)

On 12 January 1922 the Dáil delegates again assembled in the Oak Room of the Mansion House following the Treaty debates and vote at Earlsfort Terrace. On 14 January officers and ministers of the Provisional Government were elected as follows:

---

314 Dwyer, T. Ryle. *De Valera, The Man and the Myths*, 1991, p. 85. **315** *Irish Independent*, 9 December 1921. **316** Pakenham. *Peace by Ordeal*, p. 266. **317** Dwyer, T. Ryle. *Michael Collins and the Treaty: His Differences with de Valera*, 1988, p. 114.

Arthur Griffith: President
Michael Collins: Minister for Finance
William Cosgrave: Minister for Local Government
Éamonn Duggan: Minister for Home Affairs
Kevin O'Higgins: Minister for Economic Affairs
Patrick J. Hogan: Minister for Fisheries and Agriculture (replaced Art
    O'Connor)
Joseph McGrath: Minister for Labour (replaced Countess Markievicz)
Michael Hayes: Minister for Education (replaced J.J. O'Kelly)
Desmond Fitzgerald: Minister for Publicity
Ernest Blythe: Minister for Trade and Commerce
Fionan Lynch and Eoin MacNeill were added to the Provisional Government
The Ministers of the Dáil became Ministers of the Provisional Government.

On 22 January the Belfast Boycott was initiated.

On 21 February the Civic Guard, An Garda Síochána, was established.

The draft Constitution was ready to be examined by T.H. Healy and George O'Brien by 15 March 1922. Michael Collins chaired the committee that was established to draft the Constitution, but Darrell Figgis wrote most of it. (Figgis was the deputy chairman of the committee and the greatest contributor to it.[318]) The committee members were: Collins, James Douglas, Figgis, C.P. France, Hugh Kennedy, James Murnahan, John O'Byrne, James O'Neill, Alfred O'Reilly and Kevin O' Shiel.[319] [320]

On 26 March 1922 an IRA Convention was convened in the Mansion House.[321] Over 230 delegates attended, representing forty-nine brigades of the IRA and claiming to represent approximately 95,000 members of the organization (about 80 per cent of its membership). The meeting went forward despite the fact that Richard Mulcahy, as Minister for Defence, tried to avoid convening a body that was clearly anti-Treaty. Only anti-Treaty men attended the Convention. It was adjourned until 9 April when Liam Lynch was elected chairman. The control of the IRA was turned over to a sixteen-man 'Executive' and Liam Lynch was named chief of staff. The Executive also included: Frank Barrett, Liam Deasy, Tom Hales,[322] Michael Kilroy, Joe McKelvey, Liam Mellowes, Seán Moylan, Joseph O'Connor, Rory O'Connor, Peadar O'Donnell, Florence O'Donoghue, Seán O'Hegarty, Ernie O'Malley, Seámus Robinson, and P.J. Ruttledge. Working closely with the Executive were Stan Dardise, Tom McGuire and Liam Pilkington. (Twelve members of the Executive were in the Four Courts when it was attacked – Liam Lynch and Liam Deasy left the building shortly before the attack and were

318 Figgis, Darrell. *The Irish Constitution Explained*, Dublin, 1922. **319** Akenson, D.H. and J.F. Fallon. 'The Irish Civil War and the Drafting of the Free State Constitution', *Éire-Ireland*, Vol. V, 1970. **320** O'Sheil, Kevin. Witness Statement 1242. **321** 'The IRA and the Treaty', *An Phoblacht*, 17 April 1997. **322** Hales, Tom. Witness Statement 20.

arrested but then released because Mulcahy hoped they would be an influence for peace.) The Convention demanded the recruitment for the Civic Guard and the Beggar's Bush Army of the Republic cease immediately. On 9 April this Convention of the IRA narrowly rejected a proposal for a Republican military dictatorship. This Executive appointed an Army Council: Liam Lynch (chief of staff), Joseph McKelvey (deputy chief of staff), Florence O'Donoghue (adjutant general), Ernie O'Malley (director of organization), Joseph Griffin (director of intelligence), Liam Mellowes (quartermaster general), Rory O'Connor (director of engineering), Seámus O'Donovan (director of chemicals) and Seán Russell (director of ammunition).

On 26 April a Labour Party conference was held, convened by Dr Edward Joseph Byrne, Archbishop of Dublin, Lord Mayor O'Neill and Stephen O'Mara of Limerick. William O'Brien[323], Tom Johnson[324] and Cathal O'Shannon were among those who attended. The Conference made proposals to all parties for a return to the Dáil's sovereignty; the unification of the Army; the establishment of a police force under civilian control; a revised electoral register. It proposed a meeting between Arthur Griffith and Michael Collins, Éamon de Valera and Cathal Brugha and the Republican Army Executive, but Griffith and Collins refused to attend.

On 4 May 1922 a conference was held between the Free State Army leaders and the IRA/Republicans. The two factions declared a truce to last while the conference continued, then an open truce was agreed upon. The objective was to try to reunify the army and avert a civil war. Michael Collins, Seán MacEoin, Richard Mulcahy, Eoin O'Duffy, Diarmuid O'Hegarty and Gearóid O'Sullivan represented the Free State Army. Liam Lynch, Liam Mellowes[325], Seán Moylan, Rory O'Connor and Seámus Robinson represented the IRA. The parties presented conflicting reports to the Dáil on 16 May.

On 23 May 1922 the Collins/de Valera Election Pact was agreed, ratified by the Dáil and provided:

(1) That a National Coalition panel for this Third Dáil, representing both parties in the Dáil and in the Sinn Féin Organization, be sent forward, on the ground that the national position requires the entrusting of the Government of the country into the joint hands of those who have been the strength of the national situation during the last few years, without prejudice to their present respective positions.
(2) That this Coalition panel be sent forward as from the Sinn Féin Organization, the number for each party being their present strength in the Dáil.
(3) That the candidates be nominated through each of the existing party executives.

323 O'Brien, William. Witness Statement 1766. 323 O'Brien, William. Witness Statement 1766. 325 Daly, Una. Witness Statement 610.

(4) That every and any interest is free to go up and contest the election equally with the National Sinn Féin panel.

(5) That the constituencies where an election is not held shall continue to be represented by their present Deputies.

(6) That after the election the Executive shall consist of the President, elected as formerly; the Minister for Defence, representing the Army; and nine other Ministers – five from the majority party and four from the minority, each party to choose its own nominees. The allocation will be at the hands of the President.

(7) That in the event of the Coalition government finding it necessary to dissolve, a General Election will be held as soon as possible on adult suffrage.[326] [327]

On 14 June, in Cork, Collins repudiated the Pact, saying 'I am not hampered now by being on a platform where there are Coalitionists. I can make a straight appeal to you – to the citizens of Cork, vote for the candidates you think best. The country must have the representatives it wants. You understand fully what you have to do and I call on you to do it.'[328] The Pact was ripped apart by this statement, producing political turmoil just before polling day. Collins' clear breach of the Pact so enraged some anti-Treatyites in the crowd that they started shooting revolvers in the air.[329]

On 15 June 1922 the Constitution was published. The next day a general election was held. The turnout was just less than 60 per cent as 600,283 votes were cast and the results were announced on 24 June. The pro-Treaty party received 239,193 votes and fifty-eight of its members were elected to the Dáil as TDs. The anti-Treaty party (Cumann na Poblachta) received 133,864 votes and a representation of thirty-six TDs. Seventeen TDs were elected for the Labour Party, seven for the Farmers Party, six Independents and four TDs for Trinity College. Anti-Treatyites won only five of forty-four seats in Leinster and did poorly in Ulster and in Cork city. Connaught produced a small anti-Treaty majority and Munster a small pro-Treaty majority. A total of 466,419 electors voted for the Treaty and 133,864 voted against.[330] The anti-Treaty candidates would have done considerably worse had there not been an election panel, pursuant to the Collins/de Valera Pact. Undoubtedly, a more open election would have caused further losses to the anti-Treatyites. Yet, it would have hurt the Treaty candidates, as well – there is evidence that anti-Treatyites voted for the pact more consistently than Treaty supporters did.

The election was notable for the large anti-Sinn Féin vote. It did not, however, represent a vote of confidence in the Provisional Government, and still less an

326 Henry, R.M. *The Evolution of Sinn Féin*, p. 166. 327 Gallagher, Michael. 'The Pact Election of 1922', *Irish Historical Studies*, Vol. XXI, 1979. 328 *Irish Independent*, 15 June 1922. 329 The *Daily Mail* commented in its editorial: 'After such a speech the Pact can only be described as breaking up.' *Daily Mail*, 16 June 1922. 330 Macardle. *The Irish Republic*, p. 982.

expression of resistance to Republican ideals. It represented a popular realization of the need for stable government, and the acceptance of realistic compromise with regard to Anglo-Irish relations. Settled conditions were more important to the electorate than the endless debate over constitutional authority. The election had an important role in legitimizing the Treaty and the status of the Provisional Government. Although it did not prevent the Civil War, it greatly helped to facilitate the establishment of the Free State Government during and afterwards.

Prominent anti-Treaty TDs who were defeated included Constance Markievicz, Seán Etchingham, Art O'Connor, Erskine Childers, Liam Mellowes, Seámus Robinson, Kathleen Clarke, Margaret Pearse, Domhnall Ó Buachalla[331] (later last Governor General [Seánaschal] of the Irish Free State) and Dr James Ryan.

On 18 June 1922 an Extraordinary Convention of the Irish Republican Army was held. Tom Barry suggested there should be an immediate attack on the British.[332] A majority of the executive was in favour of this. Cathal Brugha opposed the suggestion, as did Liam Lynch, Liam Deasy, Frank Barrett and Seán Moylan. The twelve who favoured the action were subsequently in the Four Courts as the Civil War began, repudiated the authority of Liam Lynch, and appointed Joe McKelvey chief of staff.

On 12 July Michael Collins resigned as Head of the Provisional Government, and thereafter acted as Army O/C.

The first session of the Third Dáil was convened on 9 September 1922. It met in Leinster House in Kildare Street, where the Dáil meets to this day. The Third Dáil was never 'accepted' by the Republicans, and the Second Dáil remains the 'Provisional Government' of Ireland, according to strict Republican doctrine.

Dawson Street (at Nassau Street) Morrison's Hotel: Charles Stewart Parnell was arrested here on 13 October 1881.

2 Dawson Street Briefly Irish Volunteer HQ in 1914, but prior to the Rising HQ moved to Great Brunswick Street. (See also 206 Great Brunswick Street).

The Volunteers had to reorganize after the split with John Redmond's National Volunteers in September 1914. This formal reorganization took place at their convention on 25 October 1914. (See also Abbey Street Lower, Abbey Theatre.)

The *Irish Volunteer* was printed here, edited by Eoin MacNeill. In an early issue Padraig Pearse wrote: 'We want recruits because we are absolutely determined to take action, the moment action becomes a duty ...'[333] P.S. O'Hegarty was a member of the Supreme Council of the IRB from 1908 until he was deported to Wales in August 1914. He wrote: 'The Insurrection of 1916 came because the Supreme Council of the Irish Republican Brotherhood decided that it would come ... It was the Supreme Council of the I.R.B. which decided the Insurrection, planned it, organized it, led it and financed it.'[334] The paper was suppressed and

331 Ó Buachalla, Domhnall. Witness Statement 194. 332 Barry, Tom. Witness Statement 1743. 333 *Irish Volunteer*, 15 May 1915. 334 O'Hegarty. *The Victory of Sinn Féin*, p. 2.

subsequently reissued by a pro-Unionist printer in Belfast. The last issue was dated 22 April 1916. (It was said that the Orangemen of Belfast were 'not loyal to the Crown so much as to the half-crown' and they would always print whatever was sent to them with payment.)

The Fianna also had an office here.

Michael O'Hanrahan worked here as a clerk before the Rising.

Claire Gregan, who later married him, was Bulmer Hobson's secretary and worked for him here.[335]

In April 1916, the last issue of the *Irish Volunteer* printed a notice that signalled to Dublin Castle an imminent manoeuvre by the Volunteers:

> Arrangements are now near completion in all the more important Brigade areas for the holding of a very interesting series of manoeuvres at Easter. In some instances the arrangements contemplate a one or two-day bivouac. As for Easter, the Dublin programme may well stand as a model for others.[336]

21 Dawson Street Home of Eileen McGrane; she was a lecturer at National University (now UCD). The house was raided on 31 December 1920. McGrane was imprisoned in Mountjoy Prison, then sent to England to Walton Prison in Liverpool, then returned to Mountjoy.

Éamon (Ned) Broy's documents were found here leading to his arrest.

It was a part-time office for Michael Collins and Ernie O'Malley.

48 Dawson Street Royal Hibernian Hotel; second Dublin home of the Arthur Hamilton Norway family.

Tom Barry stayed here in February 1923 when he met with Liam Lynch and tried to convince him to hold an IRA/Republican Executive meeting to determine how to put an end to the Civil War.[337]

56–58 Dawson Street Hodges & Figgis Books, associated with Darrell Figgis. Susan Killeen worked here; she was one of Michael Collins' most valuable couriers and 'The Bookshop' became a veritable post office for messages to Collins.

DeCourcy Square Home of Mr and Mrs John O'Mahony. IRA/Volunteers from the country often stayed here, and it was frequently raided. Liam Lynch stayed here when he came to Dublin.

Denzille Lane 'National' IRA/Republican munitions factory during the Civil War.[338]

12 D'Olier Street Office of *Nationality*; Bulmer Hobson was the first editor, then Arthur Griffith and Seán T. O'Kelly[339]. (Seámus O'Kelly immediately and briefly followed Griffith, but died of a heart attack on 11 November 1918 when there was

---

335 Gregan, Claire. Witness Statement 685. **336** *Irish Volunteer*, 22 April 1916. **337** Barry, Tom. Witness Statement 1743. **338** Leonard, Joseph. Witness Statement 547. **339** O'Kelly, Seán T. Witness Statement 611.

a riot outside the office in celebration of the Armistice ending World War I.) *Nationality* was suppressed after the Rising and printed in Belfast. John Chartres was a lead writer and contributor from 1917 onward, though not always under his own name. His first submission, on 6 October 1917, was an editorial on the death of Thomas Ashe. At the time he was still working in the Intelligence Section of the British Ministry of Munitions.

12 D'Olier Street Second office of *Irish Freedom–Saoirse* founded by Tom Clarke and managed by Seán MacDermott; it was suppressed in late 1914.

13 D'Olier Street Protestant Defence Association of the Church of Ireland; managed by a retired army officer, Cpt. Robert Wade Thompson, who was also secretary of the Reformed Priests Protection Society and one of Dublin's High Sheriffs.

Dolphin's Barn, Dublin James Connolly met with the Military Council of the Volunteers on 19 January 1916 and they stayed in a brickworks here until 22 January. An agreement was reached for the ICA and Volunteers to work together toward a Rising at Easter. Connolly agreed to abandon his openly declared intention to strike independently with the ICA.

Prior to this, the Military Council regarded Connolly as endangering the Volunteers' plans and he suspected them as 'would-be Wolfe Tones – legally seditious and peacefully revolutionary'. Week by week his writings in the *Worker's Republic* intensified the lack of understanding between the Volunteers and the ICA.

Some have said Connolly was not prepared to lead the ICA out alone, and he was merely trying to goad the English authorities into attacking him or the ICA and the Union. Others contend the Military Council simply preferred their own plans and timing for the Rising. However, it is unclear how far Connolly was really prepared to lead out the ICA alone, or how far he was trying to provoke the authorities into attacking him and the union. Certainly such a move would have given him far greater civilian support than an aggressive strategy on his part would have done, so it is also unclear if the Dublin Castle authorities would have taken such a 'bait' if that were Connolly's intention.

Some earlier writers opined that Connolly was 'kidnapped' on 19 January 1916 and 'held' here however, most now agree he met with the Council voluntarily. In September 1914, Connolly had attended a meeting at 25 Rutland Square with senior IRB officials, including Thomas Clarke, Seán MacDermott, Padraig Pearse, Joseph Plunkett, Éamonn Ceannt and Thomas MacDonagh, at which the prospect of a Rising was discussed. Connolly was enthusiastic, convinced that an Irish revolution would have to be a two-stage process in which the struggle to overthrow capitalism would have to be preceeded by a rebellion to gain independence from Britain.[340] (See also 25 Rutland Square.)

Later, Pearse and Eoin MacNeill met with Connolly in early January 1916 in an

340 Rees. Op cit, p. 201.

unsuccessful attempt to restrain him from any premature action. After this meeting, it is believed Pearse reported to the Military Council that Connolly should be brought into their confidence about the date when a Rising was planned.

There has always been this speculation about Connolly's disappearance, and recent authors have concluded that he met agreeably with the Military Council, and was not forcibly kidnapped and detained for the three days. Particularly so since even Michael Mallin of the ICA realized the English were not likely to 'take' Connolly and leave the other ICA and Volunteer leaders in place, and the Volunteers really didn't want to kidnap him.

The 'latest' theories seem to concur only that Connolly spent those three days in secret consultation, probably with Pearse, Clarke and Plunkett, and that he did so either on his own initiative and/or their invitation, without any question of coercion or military detention being involved.[341] In any case, from February 1916 onward, the 'War Parties' in the ICA, IRB and Volunteers formed a united block. Volunteers Frank Daly and Éamon Dore[342] were the ones who escorted him to Dolphin's Barn.[343] [344]

Upon his return he went to Countess Markievicz's home. When asked the next day by Bill O'Brien, he would not tell O'Brien where he had been. To Helena Malony he refused: 'That would be telling you', though his final word to her was that he 'had walked 40 miles that day'. To Markievicz he said he had been 'through hell'.[345]

2 Dolphin's Terrace, Dolphin's Barn/Rialto (off South Circular Road and Herberton Road): Éamonn and Áine Ceannt's home. Ceannt was quite tall at about six feet, and she was an excellent musician, playing the uilleann pipes before Pope Pius X in Rome in 1908. The family was originally from Co. Galway though they moved to Dublin when Éamonn was very young. His father was a member of the RIC, and Éamonn was born on 21 September 1881, reputedly in the RIC Barracks in Ballymoe, and christened Edmund Kent. He taught at St Enda's and was an official in the City Treasurer's Office of Dublin Corporation. As Commandant of the 4th Battalion, Ceant was a man of iron resolution, more naturally a physical-force man than any of the other leaders.

A native of Dublin, Áine was an avid member of the Gaelic League and met Éamonn at one of their meetings. They had one son, Ronan. Following the Rising, Áine (née Frances [Franny] O'Brennan) moved into a more public role and became an active member of Cumann na mBan, serving as vice-president from 1917 to 1925. She was a member of the Standing Committee of Sinn Féin from 1917 to 1925, and served on the District Council of Rathmines. From 1920-1921 she acted as a Judge for the Dáil/Republican Courts. She was a founder of the Irish

---

341 For a complete analysis and comparison of reports and theories see Ó Dubhghaill, M., *Insurrection Fires at Eastertide*, pp. 109-115, 'Connolly's "Three Days Incommunicado"'. **342** Dore, Éamon. Witness Statement 392. **343** However, J.L. Hyland claims Connolly was 'detained in Chapelizod'. Hyland. Op. cit., p. 48. **344** See, too, Ryan, Desmond. *The Rising*, p. 268. 'The house was near Chapelizod'. **345** Ibid. p. 61.

White Cross in 1920 which cared for so many orphans of the wars in Ireland, and later wrote a history of the White Cross after it closed in 1941. She was described by its Chairman James Webb: 'It would only be fair to say that SHE WAS the Association.'[346]

In the first week of February 1916, there was a meeting here of Ceannt, Tom Clarke, James Connolly, Seán MacDermott and Padraig Pearse (Thomas MacDonagh and Joseph Plunkett were absent). These men formed the entire Military Council. Connolly had agreed to abandon his openly declared intention to strike independently with the ICA, and he attended all Military Council meetings thereafter. Of all the members of the Council, Ceannt was closest to Connolly's social views, though Pearse was nearly so.

Dominick Street Lower St Saviour's Church; opened in 1861 by the Dominican Fathers. James Boland was buried from here.

13, 14 Dominick Street Lower During the Civil War IRA/Republican forces held these houses until driven out.

25 Dominick Street Lower St Mary's National School (since demolished); attended by Seán O'Casey.

4 Dominick Street Upper Arthur Griffith's birthplace on 31 March 1872, (since demolished); he became a printer by trade.

Donnybrook, County Dublin Dublin Metropolitan Police Station; Sgt Patrick Mannix, an undercover IRA/Volunteer agent, was stationed here.[347] He obtained the names and addresses of all the senior English secret service men sent from England, and gave them to Frank Thornton. This formed a great deal of the information Michael Collins used for the Squad's raids on Bloody Sunday.[348] [349] (See also Bloody Sunday, Appendix II.)

Donnybrook, County Dublin Home of Mary and Padraic Colum.

Mary Colum was one of the first organisers of Cumann na mBan, and sat on its Provisional Committee. It was she who wrote 'Cumann na mBan members are not the auxiliaries or handmaidens or camp followers of the Volunteers … we are their allies.'

Married in 1912, Mary and Padraic lived here until they moved to Howth, and then to the US where they spent the rest of their lives. (See Howth, County Dublin: Wentworth Cottage.)

68 Dorset Street Lower Birthplace of Peadar Kearney in 1883. A well-known poet and writer, he wrote the words to 'A Soldier's Song'. (See also Appendix IV.) His nephew was the writer Brendan Behan. Kearney was a house painter by trade, but preferred to work as a stagehand at the Abbey Theatre.

75 Dorset Street Lower Keogh Bros Ltd, photographers, who produced several

346 McCoole. *No Ordinary Women*, p. 146-7. **347** Mannix, Patrick. Witness Statement 502. **348** Thornton, Frank. Witness Statements 510, 615. **349** Sugg, Wayne. 'British Intelligence Wiped Out', *An Phoblacht*, 20 November 1997.

postcards showing ruined buildings and Dublin streetscapes after the 1916 Rising.

85 Dorset Street Upper Birthplace of Seán O'Casey on 30 March 1880, christened John Casey.

87 Dorset Street Upper Office of *Irish Fun* 'A Magazine for Boys and Girls', edited by Brian O'Higgins.

Drumcondra Archbishop Dr William Walsh's House. His feelings were always nationalist, but he thought the Rising 'madness'. Count Plunkett went to inform him of the Rising as the Pope had asked him to do. Walsh was ill and Plunkett was giving the message to Walsh's secretary, Fr Curran, when word came of the fighting at the GPO. Éamon de Valera stayed in the Gate Lodge here in 1919 prior to leaving for New York.

Drumcondra Home of Police Detective Captain Patrick Smyth. Known as 'Dog Smyth', he was killed here on 30 July 1919. He was the first member of the 'G-Division' to be killed. The members of the Squad were Tom Keogh, Tom Ennis, and Mick Kennedy.

82 Lower Drumcondra Road Home of Piaras Béaslaí.

Dublin Castle Construction began in 1204 under the orders of King John. The entrance used to be on Castle Street, now the main route is on Lord Edward Street. The Statue of 'Justice' is above the old Castle Gate; small holes are drilled in her scales to drain water so they don't become 'unbalanced' in the rain: 'The Statue of Justice/Mark well her station/Her face to the Castle/And her arse to the Nation.'

When the Rising began the Castle was quite empty of British troops; it was a bank holiday and many had gone to the Fairyhouse Races. (The Irish Grand National was run there on Easter Monday and won by All Sorts.) As the Rising continued, the Castle filled up with troops and was not attacked by the rebels.

There has never been consensus on the intent of the Volunteers in attacking Dublin Castle.[350] [351] [352] [353] Many have contended it was never the intent of the Volunteers and ICA to seize the Castle as they did not believe it would be easy to take it, and it would be very difficult if not impossible to hold.[354] *Irish War News* said 'the Castle was attacked'.[355] [356] Others felt the Castle could be taken, but not held, and it couldn't be destroyed, as there was a Red Cross Hospital there.[357] Others held that attempts to take the Castle were a designed part of the Rising, but were unsuccessful.[358] [359] Finally, still others conclude that the reduced strength as a result of the countermanding order precluded its capture.[360] [361] A sniper in the Bermingham Tower was responsible for fifty-three rebel casualties before he was killed on Saturday.

350 *The Irish Times Supplement*, 7-9 April 1966. **351** *Sunday Press*, 10 April 1966. **352** Foy and Barton. Op. cit., p. 54-5. **353** Townsend. Op. cit., p. 110, 162-164. **354** Ryan, Desmond. *The Rising*, pp. 116-118. **355** *Irish War News*, 25 April 1916. **356** Sinn Féin Rebellion Handbook, *The Irish Times*, 1916, p. 42. **357** Fox, R.M. *History of the Irish Citizen Army*, 1944, p. 146. **358** Béaslaí, Pieras. *Michael Collins and the Making of a New Ireland*, 1926, p. 97. **359** Peadar Kearney quoted in De Burca, Séamus. *The Soldier's Song*, 1958, p. 116. **360** Le Roux, L.N. *Patrick Pearse*, 1932, p. 384. **361** Macardle. *The Irish Republic*, p. 169 ff.

On the first day of the Rising, Baron Ivor Wimborne, the Lord Lieutenant, issued the following Proclamation:

> Whereas, an attempt, instigated and designed by the foreign enemies of our King and Country to incite rebellion in Ireland and thus endanger the safety of the United Kingdom, has been made by a reckless, though small, body of men, who have been guilty of insurrectionary acts in the City of Dublin:
>
> Now, we, Ivor Churchill, Baron Wimborne, Lord Lieutenant-General and Governor-General of Ireland, do hereby warn all His Majesty's subjects that the sternest measures are being, and will be, taken for the prompt suppression of the existing disturbances, and the restoration of order:
>
> And we do hereby enjoin all loyal and law-abiding citizens to abstain from any acts of conduct which might interfere with the action of the Executive Government, and, in particular, we warn all citizens of the danger of unnecessarily frequenting the streets or public places, and of assembling in crowds.
>
> Given under our seal, this 24th day of April, 1916.

The Church of the Most Holy Trinity in the Castle is a Catholic Church since 1943. It was the Viceroy's Chapel at the time of the Rising. *Hue and Cry* was the official police paper of Dublin Castle.

Sir James McMahon was director of the Posts and Telegraphs Office here. In 1918–19 he hired Nancy O'Brien, Michael Collins' second cousin, to decode messages in his office. Nancy married Johnny Collins (Michael's brother) after Johnny's first wife died leaving eight children.

Captains William King and Hardy led the intelligence officers in the Castle during the War of Independence.[362] They beat Christopher Carbury and made him drink his own blood. They beat Ernie O'Malley unconscious; he gave them the name Bernard Stewart, but yielded no other information. It was King and Hardy who interrogated Peadar Clancy, Dick McKee and Conor Clune on Bloody Sunday and murdered them while they were 'trying to escape'.[363] William Pearson, an ex-colonel in the British army and a doctor, went along with Edward McLysaght to the King George V Hospital to identify Clune's body. On examination of the wounds to Clune, Pearson believed that these wounds 'could not have been inflicted if Clune had been trying to escape'.

The Castle was formally handed over to Collins and the Free State Forces on 16 January 1922 by Edmund Bernard FitzAlan-Howard, 1st Viscount FitzAlan of

362 David Neligan described Hardy: 'McNamara and myself knew this man well. He was an Orangeman, with an artificial leg, on the Castle garrison and was an Intelligence Officer in the Auxiliaries and a very hostile killer', Witness Statement 380. 363 MacEoin, Art. 'Murder in the Castle', *An Phoblacht*, 22 November 2001.

Derwent, KG, PC, Lord Lieutenant of Ireland, who said, 'I am glad to see you, Mr Collins.' To which Collins replied, 'Like hell ye are!' The British O/C was Gen. Neville Macready. Collins arrived late for his meeting with him. To Macready's comment that he was 'seven minutes late', Collins replied, 'You've been here seven centuries, what bloody difference does seven minutes make now that you're leaving?'

Duke Street Cummiskey's Pub; after the Civil War, it became a Fianna Fáil/anti-Treaty meeting place.

2 Duke Street The Bailey Pub; upstairs was the smoking room where Parnell and his followers were wont to meet. A barrister/solicitor favourite for those from the Four Courts and surrounding area, it was a particular favourite of Oliver St John Gogarty.

It was also a meeting place for the IRA/Volunteers during the War of Independence. Arthur Griffith liked this pub, and in 1922, when the ministers of the Free State were virtual prisoners in the Castle, he had food imported from the Bailey. It was a very popular pub for writers, including Patrick Kavanagh, Brendan Behan, Gogarty, Padraic Colum, Brian O'Nolan, and James Joyce.

21 Duke Street Davy Byrne's Pub; frequented by Michael Collins and Arthur Griffith, as well as Brendan Behan and Padraic O'Connor later.

Earl Street Thirty-two buildings were burned here during the Rising, and many were looted.

29–31 North Earl Street Tyler's shoe shop, looted during the Rising. The Dáil Ministry of Lands had its office upstairs after 1920. Conor Maguire[364], Art O'Connor, and Kevin O'Shiel were in charge.[365]

1 Earlsfort Place Second home in Dublin of Douglas Hyde, after he moved here from Upper Mount Street; later demolished, but prior to that its address became 65 Adelaide Road.

Earlsfort Terrace During the Rising, 3rd Battalion A Company mustered here under Cpt. Joseph O'Connor, who led his men to Grand Canal Street, Upper Lotts Road and elsewhere.[366] Thirty-four men of 3rd Battalion C Company mustered here under Cpt. Simon Donnelly. Donnelly marched his men to Upper Mount Street, where they met Michael Malone and George Reynolds and proceeded on to Boland's Bakery.

Earlsfort Terrace (at corner of Hatch Street): University College, Dublin (UCD). Founded in 1851 as the Catholic University of Ireland on St Stephen's Green, it became a constituent college of the National University of Ireland. In 1879, the University Education (Ireland) Act provided for the formation of a new university in Ireland named Royal University. Previously, Queen's College was composed of the universities in Belfast, Cork and Galway. Following this 1879 Act, Queen's College (Cork and Galway branches) was granted a charter and renamed Royal

364 Maguire, Conor. Witness Statement 708. **365** O'Shiel, Kevin. Witness Statement 1770. **366** O'Connor, Joseph. Witness Statement 157.

University, and Queen's College was dissolved on 3 February 1882. In 1908, UCD was incorporated and, combined with the former Queen's Colleges of Cork and Galway, formed the National University of Ireland (NUI). It moved to these premises from St Stephen's Green at that time. The Universities Act of 1997 set down the legislative provisions which must be met for an educational institution or college to be established as a university in Ireland. The seven currently recognized universities are: University of Limerick; Trinity College, Dublin; University College, Dublin; University College, Cork; National University of Ireland, Galway; National University of Ireland, Maynooth; Dublin City University. UCD is now located at Belfield, Dublin 4.

Padraig Pearse attended Catholic University and took a BA in 1901. Pearse was soon called to the bar, but practised little as a barrister. (Later he described the lawyer's craft as 'the most ignoble ... the most wicked of all professions'.[367]) Oliver St John Gogarty and James Joyce attended UCD at the same time before moving together into the Martello Tower in Sandycove. (Joyce paid the rent, £8 annually, and Gogarty furnished the rooms.) Dr Denis Coffey was president of UCD in 1916. Thomas MacDonagh, Eoin MacNeill, and Tom Kettle were all professors here prior to the Rising. Kevin Barry enrolled in the autumn of 1919 to study medicine. He joined a UCD Volunteer contingent that included Frank Flood, Tom Kissane, and Mark Robinson. They were all on the Church Street ambush. Flood was hanged on 14 March 1921 for 'high treason'. (See also North Circular Road/Mountjoy Prison.)

The 'Treaty Debates' began in the Mansion House in Dawson Street on 19 December 1921. (See Dawson Street/Mansion House.) The Dáil assembled and Éamon de Valera's 'Document No. Two' was derided by Arthur Griffith and Seán Milroy. Griffith moved the Treaty to be ratified and Seán MacEoin seconded it. The next day the debate continued; de Valera remarked that 'Something else besides the Treaty came from Downing Street.'[368]

On 21 December 1921 the Dáil adjourned on the motion of Michael Collins to reassemble on 3 January 1922. The debates resumed on that date and continued for five days here in the Convocation Hall of the National University of Ireland.[369] [370]

On 4 January 1922 de Valera 'resigned,' but it was unclear whether he resigned as president or prime minister or both.

Though there was disagreement over the lack of a named 'Republic', Dominion status versus 'External Association', and Ulster partition, the primary disagreement was over the oath required in the Treaty:

> I...do solemnly swear true faith and allegiance to the Constitution of the Irish Free State as by law established and that I will be faithful to HM

---

367 Thornley. 'Patrick Pearse', *Studies*, p. 11. **368** De Burca, Padraig and John Boyle. *Free State or Republic?*, 1922, 2002, p. 18. **369** http://historical-debates.oireachtas.ie/en.toc.D.T.html **370** http://historical-debates. oireachtas.ie/D/DT/D.T.192112140001.html

George V, his heirs and successors by law, in virtue of the common citizenship of Ireland and Great Britain and her adherence to and membership of the group of nations forming the British Commonwealth of Nations.[371]

De Valera proposed an oath on the following lines:

I...swear to obey the Constitution of Ireland and to keep faith with his Britannic Majesty, HM George V, in respect of the treaty associating Ireland with the states of the British Commonwealth.[372]

('The chief mistake the Irish delegation made was to allow the two all-important issues of the Crown and Ulster to become confused. They did not sufficiently single out Ulster as the issue on which to challenge the British. This was largely because, though the unity of Ireland was more important than the issue of allegiance to most Irish citizens, the issue of allegiance was of equal importance to the minority of Republican dogmatists whom the delegates also represented.'[373])

On 7 January 1922 the Dáil voted 64–57 to ratify the Treaty. (A total of 122 TDs answered the roll for the day, but Eoin MacNeill [who would've voted in favour], as chairman, did not vote. Frank Drohan resigned as he was unwilling to vote for the Treaty, but did not want to flout the will of his constituents and vote against it. Tom Kelly [who would've voted in favour] was too ill to attend. Laurence Ginnell [who would've voted opposed] did not attend as he was in Argentina). It was an afternoon meeting, beginning at 4.00, and voting started at 8.35 with Diarmuid O'Hegarty calling the roll, continuing until 9.00. Five TDs represented more than one constituency (Collins, de Valera, Griffith, Liam Mellowes, Milroy). However, all such TDs cast only one ballot, even though Griffith objected strenuously to such multiple constituencies being 'disenfranchised'.

Those who voted for the Treaty were:

Robert Barton, Piaras Béaslaí, Ernest Blythe, Patrick Brennan, Éamon (Frank) Bulfin, Seámus Burke, C.M. Byrne, Thomas Carter, Michael Collins, Richard Corish, Philip B. Cosgrave, William T. Cosgrave, John Crowley, Liam De Roiste, James Derham, James N. Dolan, George Gavan-Duffy, Éamonn J. Duggan, Desmond Fitzgerald, Paul Galligan, Arthur Griffith, Seán Hales, Dr Richard Hayes, Michael Hayes, Seán Hayes, William Hayes, P.J. Hogan, Peadar Hughes, Andrew Lavin, Frank Lawless, Seán Leddy, Fionan Lynch, Joseph Lynch, Joseph MacBride, Seán MacEoin, Alex McCabe, Dr Patrick McCartan, Daniel McCarthy,

371 *Articles of Agrement for a Treaty between Great Britain and Ireland*, Article 4. **372** Macardle, Dorothy. *The Irish Republic*, p. 579. **373** Kee. Op. cit., p. 724.

Seán McGarry, Dr J.P. McGinley, P.J. McGoldrick, Joseph McGrath, Joseph McGuinness, Justin McKenna, Seán Milroy, Richard Mulcahy, James Murphy, George Nicolls, Thomas O'Donnell, Eoin O'Duffy, John O'Dwyer, Kevin O'Higgins, Padraig O'Keefe, Padraig Ó Maille, Daniel O'Rourke, Gearóid O'Sullivan, Lorcan Robbins, William Sears, Michael Staines, Joseph Sweeney, James J. Walsh, Peter Ward, J.B. Whelehan, Dr Vincent White.

Those who voted against the Treaty were:

E. Aylward, Harry Boland, Cathal Brugha, Daniel Buckley, Frank Carty, Erskine Childers, Kathleen Clarke, M.P. Colivet, Conor Collins, Daniel Corkery, Dr Seán Crowley, Dr Brian Cusack, Éamon Dee, Thomas Derrigg, Éamon de Valera, James Devins, Seámus Doyle, Dr Ada English, Seán Etchingham, Frank Fahy, Dr Frank Ferran, James Fitzgerald Jr, Thomas Hunter, David Kent, James Lennon, Joseph MacDonagh, Seán MacEntee, Mary MacSwiney, Seán MacSwiney, Countess Constance Markievicz, Thomas McGuire, Liam Mellowes, P.J. Moloney, Seán Moylan, Charles Murphy, Seán Nolan, Count P.J. O'Byrne, P.S. O'Cahill, Kate O'Callaghan, Daniel O'Callaghan, Art O'Connor, Joseph O'Doherty, Thomas O'Donoghue, Samuel O'Flaherty, Brian O'Higgins, J.J. O'Kelly ('Sceilg'), Seán T. O'Kelly, Seán O'Mahoney, Margaret Pearse, George Noble Count Plunkett, Seámus Robinson, Éamon Roche, P.J. Rutledge, Dr James Ryan, Philip Shanahan, Austin Stack, W.F.P. Stockley.[374]

There were six women TDs. All voted against the Treaty. Four* of the six (known as the 'Black Widows') had lost male relatives in the Rising or the War of Independence: Kathleen (Thomas) Clarke* (also the sister of the executed Ned Daly), Dr Ada English, Mary (elder sister of Terence) MacSwiney*, Countess Markievicz, Kate (Michael) O'Callaghan* (ex Lord Mayor of Limerick), Margaret (mother of Padraig and Willie) Pearse*.

The HQ staff of the IRA was split on the issue.

Those opposed to the Treaty were:

Cathal Brugha: Minister for Defence
Austin Stack: formerly Deputy Chief of Staff
Liam Mellowes: Director of Purchases
Rory O'Connor: Director of Engineering

374 http://historical-debates.oireachtas.ie/D/DT/D.T.192201070002.html

Seán Russell: Director of Munitions
Seámus O'Donovan: Director of Chemicals
Oscar Traynor: O/C of the Dublin Brigade.

Those in favour of the Treaty were:

Richard Mulcahy: Chief of Staff
. J.J. O'Connell: Assistant Chief of Staff
Eoin O'Duffy: Deputy Chief of Staff
Michael Collins: Director of Intelligence
Diarmuid O'Hegarty: Director of Organisation
Piaras Béaslaí: Director of Publicity.[375]

On 9 January de Valera resigned and put himself forward for re-election as president; he was defeated for president on 10 January (60 to 58 votes); Griffith was elected; de Valera did not vote. De Valera's expressed view was that 'The Republic must exist until the people disestablish it.'[376] He also said 'I hope that nobody will talk of fratricidal strife. That is all nonsense. We have a nation that knows how to conduct itself.'[377]

On 12 January the Dáil delegates again assembled in the Oak Room of the Mansion House.

3 Earlsfort Terrace Home of W.F. Bailey; John Dillon and Sir Matthew Nathan often met here before the Rising.

17 Earlsfort Terrace Oliver St John Gogarty's first home when he married and qualified as a doctor.

28 Earlsfort Terrace Cpt. John Fitzgerald was killed here on Bloody Sunday. He had previously been kidnapped and the IRA/Volunteers attempted to kill him in Co. Clare, but he escaped with a dislocated arm and was sent to Dublin for treatment. The 'Squad' asked for 'Lt Col. Fitzpatrick'. Could it have been mistaken identity? (See also Bloody Sunday, Appendix II.)

Eccles Street Lily O'Donnell's Private Nursing Home, owned by Geraldine O'Donnell; often used by the IRA/Volunteers and IRA/Republicans to care for the wounded.[378]

15–17 Eccles Street St Mary's College for Girls run by the Dominican order; Louise Gavan-Duffy had a teaching position here.

32–38 Eccles Street (and Berkeley Road): Mater Misericordiae Hospital. Originally established by Catherine McAuley's Congregation of Sisters of Mercy as the House of Mercy for Women on Baggot Street in the 1820s. Prior to and during the Rising, Dublin Castle believed many of the nuns at the Hospital were Volunteers or sympathizers.[379]

---

375 *Dáil Éireann, Parliamentary Debates*, Volume 3, 7 January 1922. **376** De Burca and Boyle. Op. cit., p. 78. **377** Ibid, p. 79. **378** O'Donnell, Geraldine. Witness Statement 861. **379** Reilly, Jerome. 'Mater Nuns Supported Rising, RIC Files Claim', *Irish Independent*, 2 April 2006.

Thomas Ashe died here on 25 September 1917, after being force fed while on hunger strike at Mountjoy Prison. (See also North Circular Road/Mountjoy Prison.) Dan Breen was taken here to recover from the wounds he suffered in the raid on Professor Carolan's home on 11 October 1920.

Cathal Brugha died here on 7 July 1922, at age forty-eight. Upon admission on 5 July, he had been operated on by Dr Patrick Smyth, Dr David Cotter and Dr Alexander Blayney, who tried to repair the damage to his left thigh, but his sciatic nerve and femoral artery were severed and he died from 'shock and haemorrhage'. Brugha died on a 'First Friday' and he received Communion from Fr Young, a hospital chaplain. Fr Francis Ryan administered the Last Rites. His body lay in the chapel here on 8 and 9 July, then was removed to St Joseph's Church on Berkeley Road on the evening of 9 July. There was a High Requiem Mass at 10 am on the following day and the body was then taken to Glasnevin. He died faithful to the Republic, and to him the Republic and Ireland were inseparable. Michael Collins said of him: 'I would forgive him anything. Because of his sincerity, I would forgive him anything. I number him among the very few who have given their all that this country – now torn by the Civil War – should have its freedom. When many of us are forgotten, Cathal Brugha will be remembered.'[380] Upon his death, his wife issued the following statement:

> Mrs Cathal Brugha requests that, apart from family relations and intimate friends, the chief mourners and the Guard of Honour should only include the women of the Republican Movement. She makes this request as a protest against the 'immediate and terrible' Civil War made by the so-called Provisional Government of the Irish Republican forces.
>
> She does not desire the presence of any of the representatives of the Free State or its officials at the funeral.
>
> NOTE – This does not exclude the general public from attending the funeral.[381]

From his role in the Rising onwards, Brugha gained a reputation for courage, single-mindedness, and incorruptibility, and remains one of the most admired men of the period.

70 Eccles Street Home of Helena Molony, 'owner' of the *Worker's Republic* on behalf of James Connolly and Countess Markievicz.[382]

An actress by profession, Helena Molony was also an active Irish woman before, during, and after the Rising. She was involved in the early years of Cumann

380 Taylor, Rex. *Michael Collins*, 1958, p. 236. **381** *Sinn Féin Publicity Department*, 9 July 1922, Sinn Féin Papers, National Library of Ireland. **382** Molony, Helena. Witness Statement 391.

na mBan and edited the women's newspaper *Bean na hÉireann*. She later served as an officer in the Irish Citizen Army and was part of the group that stormed the City Hall. She was imprisoned after the Rising, and attempted to escape using a spoon to dig a tunnel. She failed, and as a result the female prisoners were no longer allowed to eat with utensils. She remained a great friend of Constance Markievicz until the Countess' early death.

The *Worker's Republic* was the successor to *The Worker*, which had been suppressed after six issues and which was, itself, the successor to the *Irish Worker*, which had been suppressed in December 1914 and finally stopped in February 1915. In September 1914, Connolly wrote: 'A resurrection! Aye, out of the grave of the first Irishman murdered for protesting against Ireland's participation in this thrice-accursed war there will arise a new Spirit of Irish Revolution. We defy you! Do your worst!'

Seán O'Casey was secretary of the ICA and wrote the 'ICA Notes' in *The Worker* and the *Irish Worker*. He attacked the Volunteers week by week.

O'Casey continually argued that the workers of Ireland were not served by the intent of the Volunteers, and, in fact, the Volunteers were anti-labour and no working person should join the Volunteers or Cumann na mBan. In May 1914, at Jim Larkin's direction, O'Casey, as Secretary of the ICA, published a challenge to the Volunteers in The *Irish Worker*:

> To the Provisional Executive of the Irish National Volunteers:
> Whereas the Provisional Executive of the Irish National Volunteers have claimed from public platform and in the press the support of the Irish workers; and whereas the rank and file of the movement are almost wholly composed of members of the working class; and whereas the conviction is growing stronger in labour circles, owing to the ambiguous principles of the Volunteers' constitution and the class bias of the Provisional Executive, and the Ladies Auxiliary Committee [Cumann na mBan], and the strong element co-operating with the movement which have been consistently antagonistic to the lawful claims of labour.
> We, the members of the Council of the Irish Citizen Army, representative of organized labour, now challenge the Executive of the Irish National Volunteers to public debate in which to justify their appeal for the sympathy and support of the Irish working class.
> Details of the debate to be arranged by three members of the Volunteers' Executive and three members of the Council of the Irish Citizen Army.
> Signed: Seán Ó Cathasaigh
> Hon. Sec. ICA [383]

383 O'Casey. Op. cit., Chapter IV.

The following reply, written in Irish, was received from Eoin MacNeill:

19 Herbert Park, Dublin.
DEAR SIR,- I received your letter last night at the Volunteers' Headquarters, and I gather from its contents that you think that there is a distinction being made by the Volunteer Executive between the noble and the obscure, the rich and the poor, and that you wish to discuss the matter in public debate.

I am ignorant of the existence of such a distinction. I never heard much or little of it till I read your letter. It is impossible for me to enter into a discussion upon a matter about which I know nothing.
Sincerely yours,
EOIN MACNEILL.[384]

(O'Casey's history of the ICA appears biased. His personal dislike of James Connolly and Connolly's rise to power within the movement, in effect replacing not only James Larkin but also O'Casey, is O'Casey's dominant theme. He also distrusted nationalism, which Connolly fostered in the Irish labour movement. This ideological dispute prompted O'Casey's departure from the ICA. He attacked those who were drifting to nationalism:

A further indication of the singular change in Jim Connolly's ideas, and of his determined attachment to the principles enunciated by Sinn Féin and the Irish Volunteers, which were, in many instances, directly contrary to his life-long teaching of Socialism, was the fixing on the frontage of Liberty Hall a scroll on which was written the inscription: 'We serve neither King nor Kaiser – but Ireland.' His speeches and his writings had long indicated his new trend of thought, and his actions now proclaimed trumpet-tongued that the appeal of Caitlin Ni hUllachain - 'If anyone would give me help, he must give me himself, he must give me all' - was in his ears a louder cry than the appeal of the *Internationale*, which years of contemplative thought had almost written in letters of fire upon his broad and noble soul. Liberty Hall was now no longer the headquarters of the Irish Labour movement, but the centre of Irish National disaffection.[385])

O'Casey demanded that Countess Markievicz sever her ties with the Volunteers (some say just with Cumann na mBan). When she was vindicated by one vote of the ICA Army Council, his hostility was overruled and he resigned. Following his departure, the ICA and the Volunteers started to work more closely together.

384 Ibid, Chapter IV. **385** Ibid, Chapter IX.

Eden Quay Fourteen buildings were burned here during the Rising including Hopkins and Hopkins, jewellers and silversmiths, now Irish National Building Society (Eden Quay and Lower Sackville Street); Barry, O'Moore and Co, accountants and auditors (1, 2); Gerald Mooney, wine and spirit merchant (3); The London and NorthWestern Railway Co. (4); GR Mesias, military tailor (5); The Globe Parcel Express (8); J. Henry Smith, ironmongers (9); Joseph M'Greevy, wine and spirit merchant (10); Douglas Hotel and Restaurant (11); The Mission to Seamen Institute (13); and Moore's Pub (14).

Eden Quay A thirty-three year old labourer, James Nolan, was injured here during the Lockout riots on Saturday 30 August 1913; he died in Jervis Street Hospital on Sunday morning. (See also The Great Lockout, Liberty Hall, Beresford Place.)

Eden Quay Following his release from Frongoch, James Mallon opened a barber shop here as 'The Frongoch Barber'.

31 Eden Quay Offices of the Workers' Co-operative Society.

The offices were raided on 24 March 1916, as one premises of several in suppression of the nationalist journal *The Gael*. Upon hearing of the raids, James Connolly mobilised the Irish Citizen Army, and he personally came here, as he was also Manager of the Workers' Co-Operative Society. Connolly 'arrived on the scene just as one of the police got in behind the counter. Inquiring if the police had any warrant they answered that they had not. On hearing this, Mr Connolly turning to the policeman behind the counter as he had lifted up a bundle of papers, covered him with an automatic pistol and quietly said: "Then drop those papers, or I'll drop you". He dropped the papers. Then he was ordered out from behind the counter, and he cleared. His fellow burglar tried to be insolent and was quickly told that as they had no search warrant they were doing an illegal act, and the first one who ventured to touch a paper would be shot like a dog. After some more parley they slunk away vowing vengeance.'[386]

Elgin Road Home of Count and Countess Plunkett after 1916. Following the return of George and Jack Plunkett from internment camps after the Rising, they also lived here.[387] The Free State Government often raided the house during the Civil War.

15 Ely Place (now demolished): Home of Oliver St John Gogarty; the house was a Queen Anne house 'modernized' by Sir Thomas Dean, architect of the National Library and Museum. After the Treaty was signed, Michael Collins often came here. Senator Gogarty was kidnapped from here on 12 January 1923 by the IRA/ Republicans but escaped by diving into the Liffey.

Emerald Square, Dolphin's Barn (off Cork Street): The 4th Battalion of the Volunteers mustered here under Éamonn Ceannt.

33 Emorville Road (South Circular Road): First Dublin home of George Russell (Æ).

6 Essex Street West Home of Henry B. Knowles, killed during the Rising.

---

386 *Workers' Republic*, 1 April 1916. **387** Plunkett, John (Jack) . Witness Statements 488, 865.

Exchange Street Lower Church of Saints Michael and John; the sound of the Angelus Bell ringing over the River Liffey was heard by the ICA as they marched up Dame Street to seize City Hall.

10 Exchequer Street Irish National Aid Association, first under the direction of George Gavan-Duffy and Alderman Patrick Corrigan, combined with Kathleen Clarke's Irish Volunteers' Dependents' Fund to form the Irish National Aid and Volunteers' Dependents' Fund. This was the first 'real' office: Kathleen Clarke, president; Áine Ceannt, vice-president; Maire Nic Shiubhlaigh, treasurer; E. MacRaghaill, secretary, Margaret Pearse, Muriel MacDonagh, Eily O'Hanrahan,[388] Madge Daly[389] and Lila Colbert, directors. Clarke hired Michael Collins to work here after the Rising, starting on 19 February 1917 at a salary of £2.10s per week. (See also Bachelor's Walk.) The football match arranged at Croke Park on Bloody Sunday, 21 November 1920, was held as a benefit for this Fund; about £500 was raised.

Fairview Strand Gilbey's Wine Branch Depot; on the northwest side of the Tolka Bridge. Harry Boland fought here during the Rising with the Volunteers commanded by Frank Henderson, before going with them to the GPO.

Fairview Strand Lambe's Pub, on the north-east side of Tolka Bridge. There was a small garrison here under the command of Seán Russell, before it went to the GPO with the rest of Henderson's men.

Findlater Place (now Cathal Brugha Street) Findlater Building; directly across from Thomas's Lane which ran parallel to Lower Sackville Street and behind 'the Block'. The shot that killed Cathal Brugha was fired from this building, according to John Pinkman.[390]

5 Findlater Place (now Cathal Brugha Street) Office of *Irish Freedom-Saoirse*, 'official' publication of the IRB. The first 'Republican' newspaper was *Northern Star*, published 4 January 1792 by the Belfast Society of United Irishmen; the proprietor was John Rabb; its offices were raided in January 1793, again on 16 September 1796, and it finally closed on 19 May 1797. *The Press* followed it on 28 September 1797.

The establishment of this paper, *Irish Freedom-Saoirse*, is generally credited to Tom Clarke. As soon as he returned to Ireland in 1907 he recognized the need for a newspaper, but it took him some time to raise the funds. By 1910 he succeeded in getting sufficient funds to make a start. The committee of IRB men at the time was: Dr Pat McCartan,[391] John Daly, Bulmer Hobson, Seán MacDermott, Ernest Blythe,[392] Denis McCullough and Clarke. The paper was originally published as a monthly under the cover of the Dublin Wolfe Tone Clubs Committee. Seán MacDermott (MacDiarmada) was manager. Dr Pat McCartan was first editor, then MacDermott. Started in October 1910, its first issue appeared on 15 November 1910;

388 O'Reilly, Eily O'Hanrahan. Witness Statements 270, 415. **389** Daly, Madge. Witness Statements 209, 855. **390** Pinkman, John. *In the Legion of the Vanguard*, 1998, p. 140. **391** McCartan, Patrick. Witness Statement 99, 100, 766. **392** Blythe, Ernest. Witness Statement 939.

Bulmer Hobson and P.S. O'Hegarty did most of the writing. Contributors included: Piaras Béaslaí, Ernest Blythe, Roger Casement, Fred Cogley, Pat Devlin, Joe W. Good, P.S. O'Hegarty, Bulmer Hobson, Terence MacSwiney, Padraig Pearse and Seán O'Casey. The true purpose of its IRB sponsors was made clear in its first issue: 'We believe in and would work for the independence of Ireland ... and we use the term with no reservation, stated or implied; we stand for the complete and total separation of Ireland from England and the establishment of an Irish Republic ... Freedom can take but one form amongst us – a Republic.'

In an early issue, P.S. O'Hegarty concluded an article thus: 'Concessions be damned, England, we want our country!' (Repeating what the Young Irelander, John Mitchel, wrote. It was Mitchel who also said 'The Almighty, indeed, sent the potato blight, but the English created the Famine!') In December 1910, O'Hegarty wrote: 'History has a fashion of repeating itself, and we welcome with a shout this revival of public arming in Ulster. One hundred and thirty years ago it began also in Ulster, but it did not end there, it only ended where the four seas of Ireland stopped it.' In October 1913 Pearse wrote: 'There are only two ways of righting wrongs; reform and revolution. Reform is possible when those who inflict the wrong can be got to see things from the point of view of those who suffer the wrong.'

Finglas Road Glasnevin Cemetery; it is the largest cemetery in Ireland, officially opened in 1832 after a series of events prompted Daniel O'Connell to establish a burial place for the Catholic nation of Ireland. (The O'Connell Tower in the cemetery rises to a height of 164 feet). Often referred to by older Dubliners as 'Prospect Cemetery'. Monsignor Yore consecrated the land in September 1831 and the first person interred, Michael Casey, was buried in February 1832. All graves were dug by hand until 1972 when the first machine was used.

Among others, the following are buried in Glasnevin, many in 'The Republican Plot':

William Phillip Allen (Manchester Martyr)
Thomas Ashe
Kevin Barry
Piaras Béaslaí
Brendan Behan
Harry Boland
Christy Brown
Cathal Brugha (Charles William St John Burgess)
Lohn Keegan Casey (The Fenian poet 'Leo')
Roger Casement
Erskine Childers (Molly)
Peadar Clancy
J.J. Coade

Michael Collins
Kitty Kiernan Cronin
James Daley (Connaught Ranger Mutiny)
Charlotte Despard
Éamon de Valera (Sinead)
Anne Devlin (Robert Emmett's Housekeeper)
John Devoy
Thomas Dickson
Frank Duff
Charles Gavan-Duffy
Sheila (Julia) Grenan
Arthur Griffith
Timothy Healy
Revd Gerald Manley Hopkins, SJ
Peadar Kearney
Delia Larkin
James Larkin
Michael Larkin (Manchester Martyr)James Fintan Lalor
Maud Gonne MacBride
Seán MacBride
Muriel Gifford MacDonagh
Michael Malone
Countess Constance Gore Booth Markievicz
Dick McKee
Terence Bellew McManus (First Fenian Funeral)
Michael O'Brien (Manchester Martyr)
Daniel O'Connell–'My soul to heaven, my heart to Rome, my body to
    Ireland'
Batt O'Connor (Maire)
Eoin O'Duffy
Elizabeth More O'Farrell
Revd Michael O'Flanagan
Brian O'Higgins (Anna)
Kevin O'Higgins
Gearóid O'Sullivan
Grace Gifford Plunkett
The O'Rahilly (Michael Joseph) (Nancy)
Charles Stewart Parnell
John (Seán) A. Pinkman
Jeremiah O'Donovan Rossa
Frank Ryan
Francis Sheehy-Skeffington (Hanna)

James Stephens 'A day, an hour, of virtuous liberty is worth a whole eternity
in bondage.'
Oscar Traynor
Thomas Traynor
Bishop William Walsh
Monument to Hunger Strikers 1917, 1981

On 1 August 1915 Jeremiah O'Donovan Rossa was buried here after a great
Fenian funeral. He had been the founder of the Phoenix Society in 1856. Padraig
Pearse gave the graveside oration and William Oman of the Irish Citizen Army
played the Last Post.[393] Rossa was imprisoned in 1865, was released in 1871 and went
into exile in America. While in jail, he spent 123 days on a bread and water punishment diet, 231 days on a penal class diet in a darkened cell, 28 days in a completely dark cell and 34 days with his hands manacled behind his back. After this he was
occasionally punished for singing. At his trial, he had been accused of 'inciting the
lower classes to believe they might expect a redistribution of property'. Rossa died
in New York City on 29 June 1915, and the funeral was held in Glasnevin Cemetery
on 1 August. Kathleen McDonnell wrote that it was 'a chance for the Irish to prove
that a dead patriot is at once a challenge to British tyranny and an inspiration to
his own people'.[394] Seán McGarry approached James Connolly to write an article,
and was taken aback when Connolly replied: 'When are you fellows going to stop
blathering about *dead* Fenians? Why don't you get a few *live* ones for a change?
Rossa was prepared to fight England *at peace*. You fellows won't fight her *at
war*! Between the Molly Maguires and the Molly Coddles we'll [the ICA] be
landed in the soup!'[395] [396] Later Tom Clarke talked to Connolly, and Connolly wrote
an article in which he managed to turn a dead Fenian into a live incitement to
revolution:

> The Irish Citizen Army in its constitution pledges its members to fight
> for a Republican Freedom for Ireland. Its members are, therefore, of the
> number who believe that at the call of duty they may have to lay down
> their lives for Ireland, and have so trained themselves that at the worst
> the laying down of their lives shall constitute the starting point of another
> glorious tradition – a tradition that will keep alive the soul of the nation.
> We are, therefore, present to honour O'Donovan Rossa by right of our
> faith in the separate destiny of our country and our faith in the ability of
> the Irish Workers to achieve that destiny.[397]

393 Oman, William. Witness Statement 421. **394** McDonnell, Kathleen Keyes. *There is a Bridge at Bandon*, 1972,
p. 37. **395** Ryan, Desmond. *The Rising*, p. 57. **396** McGarry, Seán. Witness Statement 368. **397** *Diarmuid O
Donnabhain Rossa, 1831-1915: Souvenir of Public Funeral*, 1915.

It was at this funeral that Pearse made his most famous speech:

> They think that they have pacified Ireland. They think that they have
> pacified half of us and intimidated the other half. They think that they
> have foreseen everything, think that they have provided against every-
> thing; but the fools, the fools, the fools! – they have left us our Fenian
> dead, and while Ireland holds these graves, Ireland unfree shall never be
> at peace.[398]

(See Address of Padraig Pearse at the gravesite of Jeremiah O'Donovan Rossa,
Appendix III.)

(Pearse was the figurehead speaker pushed forward by Tom Clarke, in spite of
stiff opposition from many IRB men who disliked Pearse personally, and suspected
him of political opportunism. Yet Clarke saw in Pearse the qualitites necessary for
leadership. Not only was he a gifted writer and speaker, he was also an idealist and
romantic visionary whose clarity of purpose and air of nobility appealed to Clarke.
It was only after this oration that Pearse began to be taken seriously as a real IRB
leader.)

41 Fitzwilliam Place Home of Dr Brigid Lyons Thornton.[399] [400] She was commissioned in the Medical Services of the National Army in 1922, thus earning the
distinction of being the only woman to serve in the Army at the time.[401]

42 Fitzwilliam Place Home of James Stephens, author of *The Insurrection in
Dublin* (1916). He was Registrar of the National Gallery in 1916.

43 Fitzwilliam Place The O'Mara home; often used by Éamon de Valera for meeting
with British emissaries prior to the Truce.

Fitzwilliam Square Home of Harry MacCauley; used by Ernie O'Malley for
meetings during the Civil War.

20 Fitzwilliam Square: Home of Dr R. Travers Smith, visiting physician to Richmond
Hospital, where he treated casualties of the 1916 Rising.

29 Fitzwilliam Square City of Dublin Branch of the Red Cross.

32 Fitzwilliam Square Home of Ms Meade; converted to a field hospital during
the Rising.

35 Fitzwilliam Square Home of Ms Fletcher; converted to a field hospital during
the Rising.

64 Fitzwilliam Square Home of Tommy O'Shaughnessy; Dublin Recorder (judge),
often escorted by Dave Neligan.

69 Fitzwilliam Square Home of A.A. McConnell, Ireland's first neurosurgeon,
and surgeon at Richmond Hospital where he treated casualties of the 1916 Rising.

---

398 Many newspapers carried copies of the address, most completely in *The Irish Volunteer.* The original
handwritten script is on display in the Pearse Museum, St. Enda's, Rathfarnham, Dublin. **399** Cowell, John.
A Noontide Blazing. Brigid Lyons Thornton, Rebel, Soldier, Doctor, 2005. **400** See also Griffith, Kenneth and
Timothy O'Grady. *Ireland's Unfinished Revolution*, 1982. **401** Thornton, Brigid Lyons. Witness Statement 259.

3 Fitzwilliam Street Upper United Arts Club. Moved here from St Stephen's Green. (See also Lincoln Place and St Stephen's Green.)

15 Fitzwilliam Street Upper The 1890s home of John Redmond.

26 Fitzwilliam Street Upper First Dublin home of the Count Plunkett family, before they moved to 3 Belgrave Road in Rathmines. This was the address Joseph Mary Plunkett listed on his engagement announcement.

31 Fitzwilliam Street Upper House owned by Maeve MacGarry; used to 'shelter' a Dáil Department during the War of Independence; it was raided 13 April 1921.[402]

5 Fitzwilliam Terrace, Upper Rathmines (Darthy Road): Áine Ceannt stayed here while Éamonn was in Richmond Barracks.

Fleet Street at corner of D'Olier Street In 1920 Kathleen Clarke opened a tobacconist's shop here. Though frequently raided by the Black and Tans, it was often used to relay messages between IRA/Volunteers during the War of Independence, and later it was raided by Free State forces when it was used to relay messages between IRA/Republicans.

8 Fleet Street Home of Kevin Barry. He was born here on 20 January 1902, fourth of a family of two boys and five girls; Katherine, Mick, Monty, Kevin, Sheila, Elgin and Peggy. Katherine (known as Kathy) was a courier for the IRA/Republicans during the Civil War.[403] (See also Church Street and North Circular Road/ Mountjoy Prison.)

13 Fleet Street Wood Printing Works. *New Ireland* office, editor Denis Gwynn, then Patrick J. (Paddy) Little. Little later became Éamon de Valera's minister for posts and telegraphs. Prior to the Rising, *New Ireland* was the 'official' organ of the Redmondite National Volunteers under Little. Staff included: Austin Clarke, Mario Esposito, Frank Gallagher, Kathleen Goodfellow, Fred Higgins, Peadar Kearney, Stephen MacKenna, Seámus McManus, Andrew Malone, Jack Morrow, Liam Ó Briain, Padraic Ó Conaire, Rory O'Connor, Michael Scott, Liam Slattery and Jack B. Yeats.

New Ireland first published the 'Castle Document' just prior to the Rising. According to Little's account, Rory O'Connor first produced the document at a meeting at Dr Seámus O'Kelly's house in Rathgar. It was read by Alderman Thomas Kelly at a Dublin Corporation meeting on 19 April, and he indicated he had received it from Little. (See also Kimmage, Co. Dublin, Larkfield, 'The Castle Document'.)

Foley Street (Montgomery Street –'Monto'): Noted for prostitutes; renamed for Elizabeth Montgomery who married Lord Gardiner.

Foley Street During the Lockout on 30 August 1913, there was serious fighting here when a large police raid destroyed several workers' homes and left James Nolan (on Eden Quay) and John Byrne so badly injured that they both died. Nolan died in Jervis Street Hospital and, after being treated there, Byrne died a few days following

---

402 MacGarry, Maeve. Witness Statement 826. **403** Molony, Katherine Barry. Witness Statement 731.

discharge. Although 'The Great Lockout' began on 26 August when William Martin Murphy locked out workers from his businesses, this action really sparked the general Lockout. Most of those arrested during the riots were from an area bounded by Foley Street, Corporation Street, Gloucester Street and Buckingham Street. (See also Beresford Place, Liberty Hall.)

Foley Street Phil Shanahan's Pub. Shanahan was originally from Co. Tipperary and his pub was 'home' to Volunteers from 'the country'. He often advanced them money and gave shelter. This was a haunt of Dan Breen, Seán Hogan, Seámus Robinson, Seán Treacy and others while in Dublin. Dick McKee and Peadar Clancy were here before their capture on the night before Bloody Sunday. They left the pub and went to a 'safe house' on Lower Gloucester Street where they were captured.

James (Shanker) Ryan, the one who betrayed Clancy and McKee, was killed outside the pub on 5 February 1921. Ryan was the 'fancy man' of Becky Cooper, one of Dublin's most well known madams. Bill Stapleton[404] led the squad that killed him, which included Paddy Kennedy[405] and Eddie Byrne.

20 Fontenoy Street Home of Seán Heuston's mother; Seán lived here before the Rising.

1 Foster Place Wm. Montgomery & Son, assessors for property destroyed in the Rising.

2 Fownes Street Lawlor's. This was a money exchange that also sold guns and ammunition. Prior to the Rising, Volunteers 'thronged' Lawlor's buying bandoliers, canteens, belts, haversacks, swords, bayonets and all sorts of 'military' material.

17 Fownes Street Arthur Griffith's first office of the *United Irishman* (1899–1906) and then *Sinn Féin* (1906–14) newspapers. Griffith often wrote under the pseudonym of 'Cugaun' ('dove') from the language of the Kaffirs whom he oversaw when he worked in a mine in South Africa. Griffith first channelled his *The Resurrection of Hungary: A Parallel for Ireland* through the pages of *United Irishman*. It was first published as a series of twenty-seven articles in the paper in 1904, and issued in book form a year later. *Sinn Féin* moved to 9 Ormond Quay Upper.

21 Fownes Street Home of Patrick MacIntyre; he was thirty-eight when he was killed during the Rising in Portobello Barracks along with Francis Sheehy-Skeffington, and is buried in Mount Jerome Cemetery. Editor of *The Searchlight*, which was noted as a 'nationalist newspaper that was rabidly anti-German'. During the Lockout of 1913, he edited the anti-striker paper, *The Toiler*.

Francis Street Myra Hall. A children's play centre was established here by the first Lord Iveagh in 1909, and then transferred to Bull Alley/St Patrick's Park in 1909. (See Patrick Street/St Patrick's Park.) The 'bayno' for the children took its name from an 18th century word – 'beanfest', shortened to 'beano' – used to describe a party. In Dublin, the children pronounced this 'bayno', and characterised the area and the food as the 'bayno'.

404 Stapleton, William J. Witness Statement 822.   **405** Kennedy, Patrick (Paddy). Witness Statement 499.

Francis Street Church of St Nicholas of Myra; built on the site of the original Franciscan Church started in 1235, the present Church was erected between 1829 and 1845. There is stained glass from the Harry Clarke Studios dating from 1928 and statuary by John Smyth. Frank Duff founded the Legion of Mary here on 7 September 1921.

100 Francis Street Myra House. The Legion of Mary, worldwide lay apostolic organization, has its headquarters here.

Frankfort Avenue, Rathgar St Mary's – home of Count and Countess Markievicz, a wedding present to her from her mother.

16 Frankfort Avenue, Rathgar Home of Susan Mitchell, a poet and journalist who was a friend of W.B. and J.B. Yeats, George Russell (Æ), and Countess Markievicz, and an editor of *The Irish Homestead* for Horace Plunkett.

Frederick Street North Home of Martin Walton. A very close friend of Michael Collins, he became the Republic's largest music publisher with several outlets around Dublin.

Frederick Street North American Rifles Hall; IRA/Volunteers used to drill here after the Rising.

Frederick Street North An unemployed clerk, Peter Sheridan, attacked James Larkin here on Thursday, 21 August 1913. It was just before the Lockout and Larkin and Sheridan were summoned to appear in court on 23 August. Sheridan was a former socialist, briefly succeeding Connolly as secretary of the Irish Socialist Republican Party, but had consistently opposed Larkin's efforts to affiliate the ITGWU with the Irish Trade Union Congress. When Larkin won a seat on the Dublin City Council, Sheridan mounted a successful legal challenge to his election. Sheridan later joined the Irish National Workers' Union, and as it too was opposed to Larkin, Sheridan felt it was his membership that resulted in his firing from his position as a clerk on the North Wall.

Sheridan was the most vociferous of a group of Larkin opponents within the labour movement. (There is speculation that this group was financed by William Martin Murphy and the Employers' Federation.[406]) Larkin asked for leniency for Sheridan and he was 'bound over to keep the peace'.[407] [408]

14 Frederick Street North Office of Countess Markievicz's Dáil Department of Labour. RIC Constable Jeremiah Mee went to work for her here after he left the RIC in Listowel.[409] (See also Molesworth Street.)

15 Frederick Street North Home of Maire Tuohy, member of the Provisional Committee of Cumann na mBan.

18 Frederick Street North Keating Branch of the Gaelic League. Prior to the Rising, Michael Collins was active here. Cathal Brugha was branch president and members included Conor Collins, Richard Mulcahy, Diarmuid O'Hegarty, Gearóid O'Sullivan

406 Yeates, Padraig. *Lockout: Dublin 1913*, 2000, p. 10. **407** *Freeman's Journal*, 23 August 1913. **408** *The Irish Times*, 26 August 1913. **409** Mee, RIC Constable Jeremiah. Witness Statement 379.

and Rory O'Connor. At 8 pm on Easter Sunday night, Padraig Pearse arrived here with dispatches that couriers were to take throughout the country: 'We start operations at noon today, Monday. Carry out your instructions.'

28 Frederick Street North Office of Stephen Bollard, editor of *The Hibernian.*

33 Frederick Street North Studio of Joshua Clarke, father of Harry Clarke (1889–1931). Harry Clarke was acclaimed as a stained glass artist of genius. He worked and studied with another stained glass artist, A.E. Child. He designed the windows for the 'Stations of the Cross' in St Patrick's Cathedral on Lough Derg in 1928. He died in 1931 of tuberculosis at the age of forty-two.

18 Frederick Street South Office of the Volunteer Training Corps Fund for the Relief of Dependants: T.F. Moloney, chairman.

Fumbally Lane The 2nd Battalion of Volunteers assembled here under Thomas MacDonagh and occupied Barmacks Malthouse in New Row; Peadar Kearney was in the group.

Gale View, Athea Home of Con Colbert, leader of the Fianna, who was executed 8 May 1916.

17 Gardiner Place Home of Delia Larkin, sister of James. James stayed here after 1923 when he returned to Ireland from the US.

Delia Larkin was born in 1878 into their poor working family in Liverpool, and christened Bridget. She started work early to help her family so her education was cut short, though she had an interest in literature and social politics from an early age. Delia came to Ireland to help her brother Jim found the Irish Women's Workers' Union (IWWU) in 1911 and acted as its first secretary. She wrote a column in *The Irish Worker* summing up the aspirations of the new union: 'all we ask for is just shorter hours, better pay than the scandalous limit now existing and conditions of labour befitting a human being'. In 1912 the union affiliated independently from the ITGWU to the ITUC with its 1000 members. Delia represented her union at three annual conferences of the ITUC from 1912 to 1914. She also represented women on Ireland's first trades board, the joint industrial council formed to regulate pay within the poorly paid manufacturing sectors where women customarily worked.

Delia helped manage the soup kitchen at Liberty Hall during the 1913 Lockout, and when the Lockout ended in the early months of 1914 this provided little relief from the pressure of Delia's commitments in the coming year. Four hundred of her union members were not reinstated after the Lockout and in March she went on a tour with the dramatic group formed from the locked-out workers. In June she stood in the Poor Law elections in the North Dock ward of Dublin, the only woman of thirteen candidates nominated by the Dublin trade unions. She fell 561 votes short of being elected to a Poor Law guardian.

In 1915 with James Larkin away in America, James Connolly had taken charge at Liberty Hall as acting secretary of the ITGWU. Recollections by observers of that period say that relations between the two were poor. There is little known about Delia's activities from the summer of 1915 to 1918, though some reports say she worked as a nurse in military hospitals in London on humanitarian grounds rather than that of military service. She was back in Dublin in 1918 signing the anti-conscription pledge.[410]

On 8 February 1921, Delia married Patrick Colgan, a member of the Citizen Army, and they moved here.

Gardiner Row: Home of Linda Kearns; she was born in 1889 in Sligo.

A nurse, she opened a first aid station in an empty house in North Great George's Street and treated both Volunteers and British casualties during the Rising. While avoiding arrest after the Rising, she was imprisoned in 1920 when she was caught smuggling a large consignment of arms in Sligo.

Michael Collins used the house for meetings.

An opponent of the Treaty, Linda joined the garrison at Barry's Hotel at the start of the Civil War, and treated the wounded in various garrisons in O'Connell Street. She was in the ambulance that took the wounded Cathal Brugha to the Mater Hospital and applied compression to his left femoral artery.

Gardiner Row Fleming's Hotel; owned by Seán O'Mahoney, who lived here. Tom Clarke stayed with him on Holy Saturday night, thinking he might be captured otherwise. Next day, Clarke, Tom O'Connor and Seán McGarry[411] returned to the Clarke's home on Richmond Avenue where they stayed the night. In November 1916, Cathal Brugha organized a meeting here attended by about fifty Volunteers. Brugha presided, though still on crutches. This was the start of the 'reorganization' of the Volunteers. At this time they were known as 'Liberty Clubs' to avoid the Castle authorities.

4 Gardiner Row Plaza Hotel; used as a Volunteer HQ by 1920.

6 Gardiner Row HQ of the IRA/Volunteers during the War of Independence. In 1919, the HQ Staff of the Volunteers comprised:

> Chief of Staff: Richard Mulcahy
> Deputy Chief of Staff: Eoin O'Duffy
> Assistant Chief of Staff: J.J (Ginger) O'Connell
> Adjutant General: Gearóid O'Sullivan
> Quartermaster General: Seán McMahon
> Director of Chemicals: James (Seámus) L. O'Donovan
> Director of Engineering: Rory O'Connor (also O/C Britain)
> Director of Intelligence: Michael Collins
> Director of Munitions: Seán Russell
> Director of Organisation: Éamon Price
> Director of Purchases: Liam Mellowes
> Director of Training: Emmet Dalton
> Editor of *An tÓglach*: Piaras Béaslaí

---

410 *Biography of Delia Larkin*, Irish Labour History Museum. **411** McGarry, Seán. Witness Statement 368.

Diarmuid O'Hegarty and Michael Staines were also closely involved with the GHQ staff. On 21 May 1921 a meeting was held here to finalize the plans to burn the Custom House. In attendance were Collins, Seán Dowling, Mulcahy, O' Connell and Oscar Traynor.

Gardiner Street Second Dublin home of Kevin O'Higgins, known as 'Mr Wilson' here.

Gardiner Street Home of Dr John Ryan. A friend to the IRA/Volunteers, and later the IRA/Republicans, he often treated and 'patched them up' without notifying the police.

14 Gardiner Street Lower Home of Seán O'Reilly. Killed in action at City Hall, Dublin, 24 April 1916. Buried in the family plot, St Paul's, Glasnevin.

17 Gardiner Street Lower (and Talbot Street): Moran's Hotel. During Civil War hostilities in Dublin, Cumann na mBan used the basement as a large kitchen and several smaller rooms as an auxiliary hospital. Countess Markievicz took up sniper duty here during the Civil War.

35 Gardiner Street Lower Typographical Union Hall, HQ of Dublin Printers' Union. Many of Dublin's printers were members of the IRB and their premises were centres of Dublin Brigade activities. Michael Collins often attended meetings here. Dick McKee had his office as O/C of the Dublin Brigade here. On 20 November 1920 Collins met Cathal Brugha, Peadar Clancy, Paddy Daly, McKee, Richard Mulcahy and Seán Russell here to finalize plans for Bloody Sunday. Then Collins went to the bar at the Gaeity Theatre with Ned Broy, James MacNamara, Liam Tobin, Tom Cullen, Frank Thornton and Dave Neligan.[412] 'The Squad' used this as a meeting place; most members of 'The Squad' got their orders here for Bloody Sunday.[413] (See also Bloody Sunday, Appendix II.)

Gardiner Street Upper: St Francis Xavier's Jesuit Church; the foundation stone was laid in 1829, the year of Catholic Emancipation.

41 Gardiner Street Upper Home of Joe and Kate McGuinness. Joe spent many years in the United States where he worked with John Devoy and Joe McGarrity as a Clan na Gael organizer. On 9 May 1918 he was elected to the Dáil for South Longford, winning by thirty-seven votes. 'Put him IN to get him OUT' was the campaign slogan. He was in Lewes Gaol in England at the time of the election.[414] He was the uncle of Brigid Lyons and she often stayed with the couple when she was a student at University College Galway and visited Dublin. He caught pneumonia, took to his bed, and died here on 31 May 1922.

Glasnevin Bon Secour Hospital. Sister Angela from the Hospital smuggled food and comforts to Mountjoy Prison prisoners during the Civil War.

Gloucester Street (now Seán MacDermott Street) Tara Hall Printers' Union; HQ of C Company, 2nd Battalion, Dublin Brigade, under the command of Dick McKee from 1917. Joe Good was a member of C Company.

---

412 Neligan, David. Witness Statement 380. **413** Sugg, Wayne. 'Bloody Sunday', *An Phoblacht*, 27 November 1997. **414** Ó Snodaigh, Aengus. 'South Longford By-Election', *An Phoblacht*, 15 July 1999.

15 Gloucester Street (now Seán MacDermott Street) Painter's Hall. HQ of C Company, 3rd Battalion, Dublin Brigade.

35 Gloucester Street Lower (now Seán MacDermott Street) Home of Tom MacPartlin; on the upper floor of the HQ of the Builders' and Carpenters' Union. It was here that the National Executive agreed upon the General Strike of 13 April 1920, notice of which was sent out from offices at 32 Abbey Street Lower.

36 Gloucester Street Lower (now Seán MacDermott Street) Home of Seán Fitzpatrick, used as a safe house. Dick McKee and Peadar Clancy were captured here on the night of 20–21 November 1920. They were taken to Dublin Castle, and then tortured and killed by a squad led by Captains King and Hardy. Fitzpatrick was arrested with McKee and Clancy. (See Bloody Sunday, Appendix II.)

Grafton Street On 24 June 1921 Leonard Appleford and George Warnes were shot here by the Tans.

Grafton Street Cairo Café; Roberts' Café (this was the second one, opened after the one in Suffolk Street); both were often used as meeting places in the War of Independence.

Grafton Street Mitchell's Café. Known as one of the most fashionable in the street, it was often used as a meeting place in the War of Independence, especially by women of Cumann na mBan.

Grafton Street Kidd's Buffet (commonly known as 'Kidd's Back'). It was at the back of what was the Berni Inn in Nassau Street. A hangout for Castle 'touts' and Tom Cullen, Frank Thornton,[415] and Frank Saurin.[416]

Grafton Street: Office of Hon. Lord John Graham Hope de la Poer Beresford, The Baron Decies, censor-in-chief during the War of Independence.[417]

Grafton Street (Trinity College Dublin) Ponsonby and Gibbs, booksellers. Irish Volunteer companies bought the *English Infantry Manual, 1911* here, price one shilling. Other large sellers were the *King's Regulations* and *Small Wars: Their Principle and Practice*.

1 Grafton Street Home of the Provost of Trinity College. During the Rising Trinity's Provost was Dr J.P. Mahaffey, who memorably wrote on one occasion: 'In Ireland the inevitable never happens, the unexpected always.'

14 Grafton Street Trinity College Officers' Training Corps Commemorative Fund; secretary: Lewis Beatty.

22a Grafton Street D.A. Stoker, jewellers. Stoker was in the GPO buying stamps when it was overrun in the Rising. Grace Gifford bought her wedding ring here.

41 Grafton Street Fannin's surgical and medical supply. In 1916, this was a major company with a virtual monopoly on supply to all Dublin's hospitals; now named Fannin Healthcare, but no longer on Grafton Street.

---

415 Thornton, Frank. Witness Statements 510, 615. **416** Saurin, Frank. Witness Statement 715. **417** See Gallagher/Hogan. *The Four Glorious Years*, pp. 39-43 for methods used by nationalist publications to 'baffle' Beresford.

79 Grafton Street Bewley's Oriental Café; during the early twentieth century (as now) a popular meeting place for all. In the nineteenth century it was Samuel Whyte's School. The stained-glass windows are by Harry Clarke.

94–95 Grafton Street Edmund Johnson, jewellers; made the Liam McCarthy Cup, presented to the GAA in 1921. The Cup is presented to the All-Ireland hurling champions, and is named after Liam McCarthy, onetime chairman of the London GAA Board. In conjunction with his two sons, William and Eugene, McCarthy donated a sum of £50 for the purchase of ten Certificates in the Irish Loan set up by Michael Collins. When the loan was redeemed McCarthy used the money for the purchase of a silver cup based on the design of an ancient Gaelic Meither (Irish loving cup).[418] It is made from a 2.5-kilo single sheet of solid silver with only one seam, and was panelled into four sections before adding a celtic design to each, with the four handles soldered last. The whole process took four months. A replica replaced the original in 1988.

96 Grafton Street (and corner of Wicklow Street): Weir and Sons, jewellers. Michael Collins bought Kitty Kiernan a watch, her 'unofficial' engagement present, at this store.

Grafton Street (and Suffolk Street): Jeanne Rynhart statue of Molly Malone, erected to mark the Dublin millennium 1988.

Grand Canal Street: Sir Patrick Dun's Hospital. Sir Arthur Ball was a surgeon here in 1916. The official records indicate that seventy-nine military and sixty-nine rebels and civilians were treated here during the Rising; ten of the military and eleven of the civilians were either dead on arrival or died thereafter. Almost all of the casualties happened in the fighting around the Mount Street Bridge.

In June 1927 Countess Markievicz was admitted here to a ward filled with the poor. She had appendicitis and was operated on by Sir William Taylor. An infection set in following the operation and she developed peritonitis. She was very run down as a result of her many activities on behalf of the poor of Dublin and in support of Republicanism, and her health suffered badly. She was also heartsick, could not accept the Oath and could not enter the Dáil. At first she appeared to be getting better, but passed away on 15 July 1927. There was a huge outpouring of thousands in Dublin who followed her funeral to Glasnevin Cemetery.

Grand Canal Street Boland's Bakery. This was an important strategic stronghold because it covered the railway line out of the Westland Row terminus. Éamon de Valera's Rising HQ was actually in a small dispensary next door at the corner of Grand Canal Street and Great Clarence Street (now Macken Street). He knew every inch of the territory, and did not reduce his area of responsibility though Eoin MacNeill's order greatly reduced the men who mustered. De Valera has been depicted as one who scorned danger almost to recklessness. All his men believed that, as a leader, he was capable of the unexpected stroke that would extricate them

---

[418] http://www.rebelgaa.com/history/liammccarthy.asp

from danger. 'De Valera certainly knew every inch of the area under his command ... It was characteristic of de Valera to attempt the impossible and he made no reduction in the scale of his operations notwithstanding the fact that less than one-fifth of the men allotted to his command had responded to the mobilization order. He might have sat down in Boland's and waited to be dug out of it, but that was not his way.'[419]

On Thursday afternoon, shelling from a 1-pounder gun taken from HMS *Helga* began from the corner of Percy Lane.[420] De Valera had ordered Cpt. Michael Cullen to lead a party to raise a flag on the top of a tall disused distillery water tower of the abandoned Ringsend Distillery, just north of the railroad line, and this had attracted the shelling. (In fact the first shell from the 1-pounder on Percy Lane missed the tower and landed in the water near the *Helga*. Thinking she was under fire, the *Helga* fired back. That was soon sorted out.) The tower was hit, rupturing the water tank and almost drowning the defenders, but the British had been fooled and this saved Boland's.[421]

De Valera had not slept during the early days of the Rising and for two days prior to it. By Thursday/Friday he was exhausted: 'I can't trust the men – they'll leave their posts if I fall asleep, if I don't watch them.' When Lt James Fitzgerald assured his O/C he'd sit by him de Valera relented and fell asleep immediately. Soon he awoke screaming, 'Set fire to the railway!'[422] De Valera insisted that papers be dipped in whiskey and used to set fire to the waiting rooms and rolling stock, but another officer, Cpt. John McMahon, O/C of B Company, 'eventually persuaded de Valera to reason and the fires were put out. De Valera quickly regained his composure'.[423] Late on Friday, de Valera ordered the bakery to be evacuated, but there was no place for the Volunteers to go so they reoccupied it and remained in their positions until their surrender on Sunday.[424]

Following the garrison's surrender, de Valera was taken into captivity and held in the Weights and Measures Department of Ballsbridge Town Hall on Merrion Road. This was on the opposite side of the city to the main body of arrested Volunteers who were detained in Kilmainham Gaol or Richmond Barracks. He remained in Ballsbridge during the first of the executions, and was transferred to Richmond Barracks only on 8 May. (See also Richmond Barracks/Grangegorman Road Upper.)

Grangegorman Road Upper Richmond Barracks (now Richmond Female Penitentiary). The courts martial following the Rising were held here. (James

---

419 Lyons, George A. 'Occupation of Ringsend Area in 1916', *An tOglach*, 10-24 April 1926. **420** Later the *Helga* was one of the boats that went to the assistance of RMS *Leinster*, the Dublin–Holyhead mailboat that was torpedoed by a German submarine on 10 October 1918. Five hundred and one lives were lost in the sinking, the greatest loss of life ever due to a sinking in the Irish Sea. Following the Irish takeover of power after the Treaty, the *Helga* served in the Irish Fisheries Protection Service as the *LE Murchu*. **421** Lord Longford and T.P. O'Neill. 'De Valera in the Easter Rising', *Sunday Telegraph*, 27 March 1966. **422** Coogan. *1916, The Easter Rising*, p. 118. **423** Coogan. *Michael Collins*, p. 42. **424** Lyons. *An tÓglach*, 10-24 April 1926.

Connolly's was held in Dublin Castle because of his injuries.) They were directed by Brig. Gen. Charles Blackadder and three other military officers. The Brigadier said of Padraig Pearse: 'I have just done one of the hardest tasks I have ever had to do. I have had to condemn one of the finest characters I have ever come across. There must be something very wrong in the state of things, that makes a man like that a rebel.'[425] The prosecutor was William Wylie.[426] Although he fought against the rebels, he was strongly opposed to the speed and secrecy of the trials. He was rebuffed in his proposal to allow the defendants defence counsel, and only after MacDonagh's execution were they allowed to call witnesses. Alderman Laurence O'Neill, Lord Mayor of Dublin, refused to act as Crown Prosecutor, but acted as Counsel for the Defence.

They all faced the same basic charge that was handed to them only moments before the trial. It alleged that they 'did an act, to wit did take part in an armed rebellion and in the waging of war against His Majesty the King, such an act being of such a nature as to be calculated to be prejudicial to the defence of the realm, being done with the intention and purpose of assisting the enemy'. In some cases there was an additional charge that they 'did attempt to cause disaffection among the civil population of His Majesty'.[427] All the defendants except Willie Pearse pleaded not guilty. Daly attempted to plead guilty to just one part of the charge ('did take part in an armed rebellion') but he was told this was not permitted. Ned Daly was prisoner No. 21, Willie Pearse was prisoner No. 27 and Seán MacDermott was prisoner No. 91; James Connolly was designated prisoner No. 90 even though he was never actually a resident prisoner here.

De Valera was tried here on 8 May. There has always been confusion whether de Valera evaded execution because of his American citizenship. De Valera's view was that none of the American connection had the 'slightest influence' on his escaping execution. He said: 'What was decisive was that Tom Ashe, who was likely to be executed, and myself were court-martialled on the same day and just about the time when [English Prime Minister Herbert] Asquith made the public statement that no further executions would take place except those who had signed the *Proclamation*'.

The prosecutor, Judge William Wylie, gave this account of the ending of the executions:

> Maxwell: 'Who is next on the list?'
> Wylie: 'Connolly.'
> Maxwell: 'We can't let him off; who is next?'
> Wylie: 'De Valera.'
> Maxwell: 'Is he someone important?'

425 Countess of Fingal, *Seventy Years Young*, 1991, p. 376. 426 Wylie, W.E. Witness Statement 864. 427 *Reports of the court martial proceedings of rebel leaders*, PRO WO 71/344/58.

Wylie: 'No. He is a school-master who was taken at Boland's Mill.'
Maxwell: 'All right, we will go ahead with Connolly and stop with this fellow.'[428]

In reporting to Asquith regarding the executions, Maxwell wrote:

In view of the gravity of the Rebellion and its connection with German intrigue and propaganda and in view of the great loss of life and destruction of property resulting therefrom, the General Officer Commanding in Chief Irish Command [Maxwell] has found it imperative to inflict the most severe sentences on the organizers of this detestable Rising and on the Commanders who took an actual part in the actual fighting which occurred. It is hoped that these examples will be sufficient to act as a deterrent to intriguers and to bring home to them that the murder of Her [sic] Majesty's subjects or other acts calculated to imperil the safety of the realm will not be tolerated.[429]

13 Grantham Street Home of Mrs Malone, mother of Michael Malone (see also Northumberland Road), Brighid and Áine. Dan Breen was taken here to convalesce after the Ashtown raid of 19 December 1919. Breen married Brighid.[430]

Grattan Street Éamon de Valera surrendered the Boland's Volunteers here. He surrendered to Capt. E.J. Hitzen, O/C of the Fifth Lincolnshire Regiment.[431]

Great Britain Street (now Parnell Street) The Rotunda Hospital; its official name is The Dublin Lying-in Hospital. It was founded in 1745, and moved to its present location in 1748. The hospital was totally dependent on charity and for this reason the buildings and environs were created with an eye to fundraising. The 'social' rooms of the Rotunda existed to provide entertainment. The 'Round Room' became the 'Rotunda Picture House' and is now the Ambassador Cinema, the former 'Supper Rooms' became the Gate Theatre, and the 'Pillar Room' is used for concerts. The Roller Rink was in the basement.

On Tuesday, 28 November 1905, Arthur Griffith founded Sinn Féin at a meeting in the Round Room. (The first National Council was composed of Arthur Griffith, Henry Dixon, Alderman Thomas [Tom] Kelly, Maud Gonne MacBride[432], Seámus MacManus, and Edward Martyn.) The First Convention of the National Council of Sinn Féin proposed a Council of 300, composed of abstentionist MPs and local

---

428 Coogan, Tim Pat. *De Valera: Long Fellow, Long Shadow*, 1995, p. 78. **429** Coogan. *1916: The Easter Rising*, pp. 135-136. **430** Breen, Daniel. Witness Statements 1739, 1763. **431** But see Pinkman, John A., edited by Francis E. Maguire. *In the Legion of the Vanguard*, p. 201: 'Suffering from battle hysteria, Cmdt. de Valera had to be forcibly restrained by some of his men of the Boland's Mill garrison before the end of the Easter Week's fighting and removed to Sir Patrick Dun's Hospital. It was in a room of the hospital that de Valera made his formal surrender to Captain Hitzen of the 5th Lincolnshire Regiment at about 1 pm on Sunday, 30 April 1916.' **432** MacBride, Maud Gonne. Witness Statement 317. **433** De Bhuitleir, Maire. 'When the Sinn Féin Policy was Launched', in Fitzgerald, W.G., editor. *The Voice of Ireland*, 1924, pp. 105-109.

officials, to assume the powers of a de facto government. Maire de Bhuitleir (Mary Ellen Butler/Mrs O'Nuallain, cousin of Edward Carson) suggested the name 'Sinn Féin' at a meeting with Griffith in his earlier offices in Fownes Street. She was a language enthusiast and had used the name in her small news-sheet, published in Oldcastle, Co. Meath, in 1902–3.[433] It came from the early motto of the Gaelic League: 'Sinn Féin, sinn féin amháin' – Ourselves, ourselves alone.[434]

The meeting adopted the following resolutions:

> That the people of Ireland are a free people, and that no law made without their authority or consent is or ever can be binding on their consciences.
> That the General Council of County Councils presents the nucleus of a national authority and we urge upon it to extend the scope of its deliberations and action; to take within its purview every question of national interest; and to formulate lines of procedure for the nation.
> That national self-development through recognition of the duties and rights of citizenship on the part of the individual, and by the aid and support of all movements originating from within Ireland, instinct with National tradition, and not looking outside Ireland for the accomplishment of their aims, is vital to Ireland.

Griffith intended Sinn Féin to conduct its own affairs even while a national parliament was denied recognition by outside powers. This de facto 'Parliament' would call upon the people of Ireland to cooperate with it voluntarily in the administration of Ireland. Griffith envisioned establishing Harbour Boards, Arbitration Courts, National Insurance, National Banks, a National Mercantile Marine, and Irish Commercial Consuls sent to foreign trade centres.[435]

On 25 November 1913 Eoin MacNeill and Laurence Kettle (son of A.J. Kettle, aide to Charles Stewart Parnell) held the first meeting to enrol the Irish Volunteers. They intended the meeting to be held at the Mansion House but the then Lord Mayor, Lorcan Sherlock, refused to rent the Dawson Street premises to them. Sherlock later went on the Executive as one of John Redmond's 'forced' nominees. (See also 206 Great Brunswick Street.) The band that started off the night was the St James's Brass and Reed Band. The doors were opened shortly after 8 pm and Seán T. O'Kelly chaired the meeting. Eventually 4000 people managed to squeeze into the Rink while a remaining 3000 crammed the Concert Room and the adjacent gardens. Over 4000 people signed up that night. Padraig Pearse was one of the principal speakers. Others were Seán MacDermott, James McMahon, Michael Judge

---

433 De Bhuitleir, Maire. 'When the Sinn Féin Policy was Launched', in Fitzgerald, W.G., editor, *The Voice of Ireland*, 1924, pp. 105–109. 434 Ó Snodaigh, Aengus. 'Sinn Féin and Sinn Féin', *An Phoblacht*, 30 September 1999. 435 Henry. Op. cit., p. 90.

and Councillor Richard Carroll. Batt O'Connor and Bulmer Hobson addressed the crowd outside. The IRB pressed many nationalists to join the Volunteers, but the organization had not backed the ITGWU in the 1913 Lockout. Kettle was a well-known opponent of the Union. When he spoke, fights broke out between Union protestors but the disturbances were soon drowned out by the song 'God Save Ireland'. This marked the continuance of the disagreements between Union members and those who became Volunteers and led to Connolly's reluctance to join with the Volunteers. (See also Seán O'Casey, the *Worker's Republic*, 70 Eccles Street for public disagreements between the ICA and the Volunteers. See also Appendix III for Manifesto of the Irish Volunteers; also Kildare Street for the First Provisional Committee of the Irish Volunteers.)

MacNeill stated in his opening speech that the Volunteers meant no ill-will towards the Ulster Volunteer Force:

> We do not contemplate any hostility to the Volunteer movement that has already been initiated in parts of Ulster. The strength of that movement consists in men whose kinfolk were amongst the foremost and most resolute in winning freedom for the United States of America ...The more genuine and successful the local Volunteer movement in Ulster becomes, the more completely does it establish the principle that Irishmen have the right to decide and govern their own national affairs. We have nothing to fear from the existing Volunteers in Ulster nor they from us.[436]

On the Saturday night after the Rising the defeated Volunteers were marched here. In the early hours of Sunday morning, Cpt. Lea Wilson took charge. Of Seán MacDermott, who because of polio walked with a limp and only with of the aid of a cane, he said, 'So you've got cripples in your Army!' Wilson stripped Thomas Clarke and made him stand naked on the Rotunda steps in view of the nurses: 'That old bastard is Commander in Chief. He keeps a tobacco shop across the street. Nice general for your fucking Army.'[437] Michael Collins had Wilson killed in Gorey, Co. Wexford, on 15 June 1920.

After the Rising, the Royal Mail was sorted in the basement of the Rotunda while the GPO was being rebuilt. Michael Collins' intelligence agents often 'intercepted' the mail here, and the Dublin Brigade intercepted all the official correspondence for Dublin Castle on 15 July 1920. After it was opened and examined, it was delivered to the Castle marked 'Opened and censored by the Irish Republic'.

49 Great Britain Street (now Parnell Street) Jim (Seámus) Kirwan's Pub; Seán MacDermott's 'local'. Jim Kirwan was from Co. Tipperary and was a great friend of Dan Breen and Seán Treacy; when in Dublin they stayed here as often as once

---

436 Macardle. *The Irish Republic*, p. 96. **437** O'Higgins, Brian. Op. cit., p, 40.

a week while 'on the run'. Michael Collins hid some of the gold collected for the Dáil Loan in the basement here.

65 Great Britain Street (now Parnell Street) Home of Mr and Mrs Maurice Collins. *Who's Who* claims Bulmer Hobson was held here prior to the Rising.[438] Most commentators agree, however, that he was held at Martin Conlon's home at Cabra Park and that Maurice was one of those guarding him on Holy Saturday. (See also Cabra Park.) Maurice opened a tobacconist and confectioner's shop here after he was released from Frongoch prison. Raided on 31 January 1920.

68-69 Great Britain Street (now Parnell Street) (just off Rutland Square): Liam Devlin's Pub; 'Joint No 2', Michael Collins' 'unofficial HQ'. Collins waited here for Bloody Sunday reports.

69 Great Britain Street (now Parnell Street) Home of Paddy Daly, usually considered to be the O/C of 'The Squad'. (See also Ballyseedy Cross, Appendix I.)

70 Great Britain Street (now Parnell Street) (and Moore Lane): Now Patrick Conway's Pub. At 3.30 pm on Saturday, 29 April 1916, Padraig Pearse surrendered to Gen. William Lowe here. Lowe's son, John, who was also an officer in the British army, accompanied the general. Later John Lowe changed his name to 'John Loder' and became a successful film producer in Hollywood.

70, 71 Great Britain Street (now Parnell Street) Elizabeth O'Farrell met Col. Portal and Gen. William Lowe here before being taken to Tom Clarke's shop at 75A Great Britain Street.

74 Great Britain Street (now Parnell Street) Mooney's Pub; British hang-out during the War of Independence.

75A Great Britain Street (now Parnell Street) (corner of Sackville Street): Tom Clarke's tobacconist shop; opened in 1909. Clarke was arrested in London on 4 April 1883, and was imprisoned in Millbank, Portland, and Chatham prisons as Henry Hammond Wilson. He was finally released on 21 September 1898. He was prisoner number J464. Elizabeth O'Farrell was held here as a prisoner while waiting for Gen. Lowe.

165 Great Britain Street (now Parnell Street) (and Cavendish Row): National Bank; Elizabeth O'Farrell was subjected to a search here.

176 Great Britain Street (now Parnell Street) Home of Tom Clarke's mother.

204-206 Great Britain Street (now Parnell Street) Williams & Woods Soap and Sweet Manufacturers, 'jam factory'; formerly Simpson's Hospital. The factory was full of food and too close to their own lines for the British to shell it. The O'Rahilly was on his way here when killed and the Volunteers were also headed in this direction when they escaped from the GPO into Henry Street and then into Moore Street.

Great Brunswick Street (now Pearse Street) By the time of the Civil War, this was already called 'Pearse Street'. The Crampton ('Pineapple') Monument named after Philip Crampton, a wealthy bookseller and Lord Mayor of Dublin in 1758,

---

438 O'Farrell, Padraic. *Who's Who in the Irish War of Independence and Civil War*, 1997, p. 21.

stood at the junction of Townsend Street until it collapsed in the 1950s.

Great Brunswick Street (now Pearse Street) Home of Leo and Billy FitzGerald. The family's members were prominent Volunteers in the 3rd Battalion; raided for arms in February 1916. After the Rising, Seán McMahon, Quartermaster of the IRA/Volunteers, used their house as his HQ.

1–8 Great Brunswick Street (now Pearse Street) (corner of Townsend Street; see also Appendix II): Dublin Metropolitan Police (G-Division) HQ. In Dublin, the 'G' division of the DMP was a specially trained branch whose members thoroughly knew the city, its IRA/Volunteer officers and important separatists, and, guided by RIC information, followed all the marked men who came to Dublin from the country. Officers' caps and Bobbies' helmets over their respective doorways distinguished the entrances by class.

Éamon (Ned) Broy, a Michael Collins informant, let Collins and Seán Nunan in here on the night of 7 April 1919 to look over the G-division files on the Volunteers.[439] (Collins met Nunan on the way to meet Broy and took him along, so Nunan also saw the files.)[440] It was on this foray that Collins read his own file that indicated he 'belongs to a family of "brainy" people and of advanced Sinn Féin sympathies. They are of the farming class'. That gave Collins such a good and loud laugh that Broy heard him and was concerned Collins would be discovered. Upon leaving at 7 am the next morning, Collins gave Broy another scare when Collins realized he had left some papers behind and insisted on returning to retrieve them. Broy often gave copies of his typing to his cousin, Patrick Tracy, or to Thomas Gay for delivery to Collins.[441] James Kavanagh, another Collins informant, was also stationed here. Daniel Hoey was killed outside G-Division HQ on 13 September 1919.[442]

27 Great Brunswick Street (now Pearse Street) Pearse family home. The father, James, was a monument sculptor and produced many of the figures crowning Dublin buildings. He was a great believer in personal freedom, as well as national freedom from England, and wrote a pamphlet on it in 1886.[443] Emily Susanna Fox, his first wife whom he married in 1864, bore James three children: a daughter, Mary Emily, and later two others, of whom only James Vincent survived infancy. Margaret Brady was his second wife; he married her in October 1877. She bore him four children, two boys and two girls: Margaret, Patrick (Padraig), William (Willie), and Mary Bridget (Brigid). At the time of the birth of Padraig and William, baptismal records show the family name still spelled 'Pierce'. Padraig was born here on 10 November 1879, christened Patrick Henry Pierce after the American patriot.

---

439 Not into Dublin Castle as portrayed in the film *Michael Collins*. **440** Nunan, Seán. Witness Statement 1744. **441** Broy, Éamon. Witness Statements 1280, 1284. **442** MacAodh, Seán. 'IRA Wipe out "G" Division', *An Phoblacht*, 6 September 2001. **443** Pearse, James. *'England's Duty to Ireland as Plain to a Loyal Irish Roman Catholic'*, pamphlet, Dublin, 1886. This was written in response to the pamphlet written by Dr Thomas Maguire, professor of Moral Philosophy at Trinity College Dublin, which was an extreme piece of anti-home rule polemic.

He had a cast in his left eye, and was quite aware of it; he always had his profile photos taken from his right side.[444] William was born here in 1881.

It is now home to the Ireland Institute.

42e Great Brunswick Street (now Pearse Street) Antient Concert Rooms; home of the Dublin Orchestral Society.

On Saturday, 19 July 1913, William Martin Murphy arranged a meeting here to address his DUTC workers, and to counsel against any strike.[445] The meeting was held at midnight so it would not interfere with the workday. Six known ITGWU workers had been fired earlier, but Murphy laid on Bovril and sandwiches for all those who attended as well as giving each an extra half-day's pay. About seven hundred workers attended, and were told by Murphy that he had no objection to 'a legitimate union' but he wouldn't stand for them to 'ally themselves with disreputable organizations or become Larkin's tools'.[446] He first made his threat here, often repeated during the Lockout: 'The company's shareholders will have three meals a day whether the strike succeeds or not, but I don't know if the men who go out can count on this.'[447]

This was an IRA/Volunteer Department of Intelligence Office and was the first HQ of 'The Squad', but Michael Collins infrequently came here.

144 Great Brunswick Street (now Pearse Street) St Andrew's Club. The 3rd Battalion of Volunteers had been instructed to assemble here prior to the Rising. In 1921 it was the HQ of the IRA/Volunteers. Auxies surrounded it on 14 March 1921 when it was thought the Dáil was meeting here; a firefight ensued and there were casualties on both sides. The building is now part of Dublin City Library & Archive (138–144 Pearse Street).

178 Great Brunswick Street (now Pearse Street) Harrison's, monument sculptors; James Pearse joined this company as a journeyman.

180 Great Brunswick Street (now Pearse Street) 'Red Hand' division of the Ancient Order of Hibernians.

206 Great Brunswick Street (now Pearse Street) HQ of the Irish Volunteers at the time of the Rising. (See also 2 Dawson Street; Kildare Street.)

On 12 June 1914 Redmond issued his ultimatum demanding that his nominees be accepted onto the Provisional Committee, and on 16 June the Provisional Committee met here. The resolution was carried by a vote of eighteen to nine. Among those who voted for the resolution were Bulmer Hobson (IRB), Eoin MacNeill (unaffiliated), Joseph Plunkett (IRB), Roger Casement (unaffiliated) and Maurice Moore (United Irish League/Irish Parliamentary Party); those voting against included Padraig Pearse, Éamonn Ceannt, Con Colbert, Seán MacDermott, Piaras Béaslaí, Liam Mellowes and Éamonn Martin (all from the IRB), Michael Judge (AOH) and Seán Fitzgibbon (unaffiliated). Thomas MacDonagh was not present and did not vote. This vote effectively ended Hobson's influence in the IRB.

In 1914, the General Council of the Volunteers consisted of Eoin Mac Neill (president), Padraig Pearse, Joseph Plunkett, Thomas MacDonagh, Éamonn Ceannt, Seán MacDermott, Bulmer Hobson and a representative from each county. The Volunteer HQ Staff was:

Eoin MacNeill: Chief of Staff
Bulmer Hobson: Quartermaster General
*Padraig Pearse: Director of Organisation
*Joseph Plunkett: Director of Military Operations
*Éamonn Ceannt: Director of Communications
Thomas MacDonagh: Director of Training
The O'Rahilly: Director of Arms
Seán Fitzgibbon: Director of Recruiting (moderate, ally of MacNeill/Hobson)
J.J. O'Connell: Chief of Inspection (had the best military mind in the Volunteers; moderate, ally of MacNeill/Hobson)
(*As late as August 1915, these three were the only members of the HQ staff who knew what was really being planned for the Volunteers.)

On 19 April 1916, MacNeill drafted an order in response to the 'Castle Document' which included the following instructions:

Your object will be to preserve the arms and organisation of the Irish Volunteers, and the measures taken by you will be directed to that purpose.

In general you will arrange that your men defend themselves and each other in small groups so placed that they may be best able to hold out.

Each group must be provided with sufficient supplies of food, or be certain of access to such supplies.[448]

Great Charles Street Home of T.M. Healy before he became the first Governor General of the Irish Free State. Healy was married to an aunt of Kevin O'Higgins. He became the Governor General of Saorstat Éireann on 6 December 1922, one year to the day from the Treaty signing. As Governor General, he was representative to three entities: the British King, the British government, and the Irish government. Though Healy seemed to believe that he had been awarded the Governor Generalship for life, the decided in 1927 that the term of office of Governors General would be five years. As a result he retired from the office and public life in January 1928.
Great Clarence Street South (now Macken Street) Home of the James Pearse family before they moved to Great Brunswick Street.

Great Denmark Street Ossary Hotel. Seán Kavanagh, Michael Collins' primary agent in Kildare, stayed here the night before Bloody Sunday after he was told to vacate Vaughan's Hotel.

1–2 Great Denmark Street Barry's Hotel. Owned by Annie Farrington.[449]

The Tipperary football team stayed here before Bloody Sunday; still a popular residence of visiting football and hurling teams.

It was HQ of K Company, 2nd Battalion, during the War of Independence.

On 13–14 December 1920 a meeting of GHQ was held here to finalize plans to import arms from Italy; Cathal Brugha, Michael Collins, Liam Mellowes, Joe Vize, Liam Deasy and Florence O'Donoghue[450] attended. Michael Leahy, second-in-command of Cork No. 1 Brigade left Dublin on 2 January 1921 to go to Italy, but he soon returned to Dublin after the project failed.

This was also the first HQ of the Dublin Brigade of IRA/Republicans during the Civil War until 19 June 1922 when Oscar Traynor moved HQ to 'The Block', and particularly the Hammam and Gresham hotels on Sackville Street Upper.

6 Great Denmark Street Belvedere College; Dublin day-school run by the Jesuits; Attended by Kevin Barry when he joined the IRA/Volunteers in October 1917.

North Great George's Street Linda Kearns set up a Red Cross hospital here during the Rising. She nursed Volunteers and British army casualties alike, for which she was awarded the Red Cross Florence Nightingale Medal for Exceptional Services in 1951.

2 North Great George's Street The family town house of John Dillon. He spoke out in Parliament condemning the 1916 executions – 'Larne begat Dublin.' He was defeated by de Valera for the East Mayo seat in December 1918.

10 North Great George's Street At this address Marie Perolz 'owned' *The Spark* for James Connolly and Countess Markievicz.[451]

Marie Perolz was a member of the Irish Citizen Army and of Cumann na mBan and was recognised as one of the most faithful and devoted of the women who served Ireland's working women. In tandem with her membership the ICA, she mounted a further barricade in challenging the assumptions of the labour movement in relation to the rights of working women. As a delegate for the Irish Women's Workers' Union to the 22nd Annual Irish Trades Union Congress and Labour Party in 1916, she struggled with the machinery of the organised male working class to ensure that all resolutions addressing the concerns of working men were amended to include 'the working women' of the rank and file.

One of the advanced nationalist weeklies in the early part of the war, *The Spark* exerted the strongest influence against Irishmen enlisting in the British army in World War I.

Great Grand Street Christian Brothers' School which Arthur Griffith attended.

449 Farrington, Annie. Witness Statement 749. **450** O'Donoghue, Florence. Witness Statement 554. **451** Perolz, Marie. Witness Statement 246.

Green Lanes Home of Patsy O'Toole. The arms dump for E Company, 4th Battalion (Rathfarnham Battalion).

Gregg Lane (now Cathal Brugha Street) During the War of Independence, Volunteer John O'Carroll and his wife, May Gahan, opened a milk bar here, called the Republican Bar, and painted it green, white and orange. It was frequented by British soldiers, and May often used the opportunity to buy guns from them. Her greatest success was to buy a machine gun; she had it lowered over the wall of the Ship Street Barracks and took it away in a pram.

11 Grosvenor Place, **Rathmines** (now No 21): Home of Francis and Hanna Sheehy-Skeffington and their son, Owen; situated just on the other side of Portobello Bridge over the Grand Canal from Portobello Barracks.

Francis was the first lay registrar of University College, Dublin; he resigned after a dispute in which he favoured allowing academic status to women. He was thirty-seven when he was murdered during the Rising and is buried in Glasnevin Cemetery. Just after his death, Hanna and Owen were evicted and moved to 43 Moyne Road, Rathmines.

Born on 27 May 1877 in Kanturk, Co. Cork, Hanna was raised in Co. Tipperary. Hanna's father was an MP and she had an early memory of visiting her uncle, Fr Eugene Sheehy, in prison in Kilmainham for Land League activities. She attended the Dominican Convent School in Eccles Street, Dublin, being among the first generation of girls to benefit from the new educational reforms. She attended the Royal University, and received a BA in 1899 and an MA in 1902. She and fellow student Francis Skeffington were married on 27 June 1903. They combined their surnames on marriage and it was to her husband she gave credit for awakening her commitment to women's issues. They had one son, Owen.

The Sheehy-Skeffingtons, together with another couple, Margaret and James Cousins, founded the Irish Women's Franchise League (IWFL) in 1908 as a more militant and nationalist suffrage group than the existing Irish Women's Suffrage and Local Government Association (IWSLGA). Frank and James established and edited an influential suffrage paper, the *Irish Citizen*, which ran from 1912 until 1920. The Irish Parliamentary Party refused to support women's suffrage during the passage of the Home Rule Bill and the IWFL indulged in militant tactics. Hanna was arrested for breaking windows at Ship Street barracks and spent a month in Mountjoy Jail, including a week on hunger strike in protest at the treatment of two English women suffragettes, Mary Leigh and Gladys Evans. She was subsequently dismissed from her teaching post at Rathmines College of Commerce.

Hanna and Frank were friendly with James Connolly and supported the labour movement during the 1913 Lockout but took no active part in the 1916 Rising. As pacifists, they had been critical in the *Irish Citizen* of recruitment for the British Army and as feminists they denounced the subordination of Cumann na mBan to the Irish Volunteers. (Curiously, as a pacifist, Frank was on the first Council of the Irish Citizen Army and served as co-vice-chairman.)

(See also Grosvenor Place, Moyne Road, Rathmines Road [Portobello Barracks].)

Haddington Road St Mary's Church. British snipers climbed to the belfry here, overlooking the whole of 25 Northumberland Road and the Clanwilliam House area. The Curate here was Rev James Doyle.[452]

Haddington Road Home of the British Provost Marshal; raided by members of K Company, 3rd Battalion for its collection of weapons. Under the command of Tom Cullen, they were disguised as DMP constables.

Haddington Road Holy Faith Secondary School; founded in 1904 and run by the Holy Faith Sisters.

60 Haddington Road Home of Ben Dwyer and other IRA/Volunteers in 1920.

Haddon Road, Clontarf The house known as 'Craigmillar' was the home of John P. Twohig; Michael Collins often visited here. Twohig was said to be his uncle.

3 Halston Street O'Keefe's Printers: The *Irish War News* bulletins from the GPO were printed here in 1916.

The proprietor was Mr O'Keefe, and his shop was chosen by Joseph Stanley to print the bulletins. Assisting Stanley were M.S. MacSiubhlaigh (Walker), James O'Sullivan, Thomas Ryan, and Charles Walker (son of M.S.).[453]

Harbour Road, Howth (1 Island View House): Home of Mrs Quick. From 1914 to 1917, Nancy O'Brien, Susan Killeen and Dolly Brennan, among others, had lodgings here. Michael Collins often visited here.

Harcourt Street Volunteer Dan Carew was shot here in 1920.

Harcourt Street Elliot Hotel. In July 1923, the IRA held a two-day meeting here to draft a new constitution. It was decided to have nothing more to do with the IRB.

Harcourt Street (and corner of Cuffe Street): Little's Pub; one of the key defence points for St Stephen's Green during the Rising.

4 Harcourt Street Edward Carson's birthplace in 1854; his family moved to 25 Harcourt Street, 'the more fashionable end'.

6 Harcourt Street Home of John Cardinal Newman (1801–1890). Known as St Mary's University House, it was the residence for students of the Catholic University in St Stephen's Green.

In 1910 Arthur Griffith acquired permanent rooms here and thereafter it was the headquarters of Sinn Féin and the Inghnidhe na hÉireann branch of Cumann na mBan.

In April 1914 a Sinn Féin convention held here agreed to make Ulster, on behalf of Sinn Féin, the following proposals in order to secure Home Rule:

(1) Increased representation in the Irish Parliament on the basis partly of population, partly of ratable value and partly bulk trade, the Ulster representation to be increased by 15 members including one for the University of Belfast, and 2 members to be given to the Unionist constituency of Rathmines.

---

452 Doyle, Revd James. Witness Statement 311. **453** Walker, Charles. Witness Statements 241, 266.

(2) To fix all Ireland as the unit for the election of the Senate or Upper House and to secure representation of the Southern Unionist minority by Proportional Representation.

(3) To guarantee that no tax should be imposed on the linen trade without the consent of a majority of Ulster representatives.

(4) That the Chairman of the Joint Exchequer Board should always be chosen by the Ulster representatives.

(5) That all posts in the Civil Service should be filled by examination.

(6) That the Ulster Volunteer Force should be retained under its present leaders as a portion of an Irish Volunteer Force and should not, except in case of invasion, be called upon to serve outside Ulster.

(7) That the Irish Parliament should sit alternately in Dublin and Belfast.

(8) That the clauses in the Home Rule Bill restricting Irish trade and finance and prohibiting Ireland from collecting and receiving its own taxes, or otherwise conflicting with any of the above proposals, should be amended.

Though these proposals were accepted by the Belfast Trades Council, they were ignored by the Unionist leaders.[454]

On 8 August 1914, the following appeared as an editorial in the newspaper *Sinn Féin*:

Ireland is not at war with Germany. She has no quarrel with any Continental Power...

Our duty is in no doubt. We are Irish Nationalists and the only duty we can have is to stand for Ireland's interest, irrespective of the interests of England or Germany or any other foreign country...

(See also Ormond Quay.)

The Volunteers used it as a drill hall before and after the Rising.

It was the first meeting place of K Company, 3rd Battalion of IRA/Volunteers, after the Rising: Cpt. Tom Cullen, Adj. Lawrence (Larry) Nugent,[455] and Instructor Seán McClusky.

Michael Collins' Department of Finance office and some of his intelligence activities were situated here involving Gearóid O'Sullivan, Dairmuid O'Hegarty and Joe O'Reilly.

On 17–18 May 1918 Sinn Féin leaders and others were arrested because of the bogus 'German Plot', which put most of the Sinn Féin 'moderates' in prison.[456] [457] The pretext for this 'Plot' was the capture of Joseph Dowling, a member of Roger

---

454 Henry. Op. cit., p.167-8. **455** Nugent, Lawrence. Witness Statement 907. **456** Figgis. *Recollections of the Irish War*, pp. 195-221. **457** Gallagher/Hogan. *The Four Glorious Years*, pp. 29-33.

Casement's ill-fated 'Irish Brigade', on an island off the coast of Galway on 12 April. The Germans landed him from a submarine on their own initiative, but no one from Sinn Féin had ever contacted him, though Collins and some of the other GHQ staff were aware of the approach. On 15 May Éamon Broy secured a list of prominent Sinn Féin members who were to be arrested, and a series of raids on 17–18 May rounded up many. (These arrests were what brought Collins fully into the intelligence effort.) Seventy-three prisoners were deported to England immediately and others later. Those first arrested were S. Barry, Tadgh Barry, G. Behane, Joseph Berrilla, W.J. Brennan-Whitmore, John J. Clancy, Kathleen Clarke, Alderman Walter Cole, Dick Coleman (died of influenza in Usk Prison),[458] Christopher Collins, William T. Cosgrave,[459] Brian Cusack,[460] Richard Davys, J. Defors, Peter de Loughrey (Parliament Street, Kilkeel), Éamon de Valera (escaped from Lincoln Gaol), Thomas Dillon, Brian Doherty, J. Dolan, Frank Drohan, Seán Etchingham, Frank Fahy,[461][462] Bernard Failbar, Raymond Fallon, Darrell Figgis, Desmond Fitzgerald, Michael Fleming, Padraic Fleming, George Geraghty (escaped from Usk Prison), Arthur Griffith, R. Haskins, Dr Richard Hayes,[463] Peter Hughes, Thomas Hunter, Stephen Jordan, Frank Lawless, George Lyons,[464] Countess Markievicz, Joseph MacBride, Maud Gonne MacBride,[465] Seán MacEntee,[466] Pierce McCann (died in prison of Spanish Flu), Seán McGarry (escaped from Lincoln Gaol), Denis McCullough,[467] Joe McGrath (escaped from Usk Prison), Joseph McGuinness, Herbert (Barney) Mellowes (escaped from Usk Prison), J. Menahan, Seán Milroy (escaped from Lincoln Gaol), Philip Monaghan, Edward Moore (Moane), Charles Mullen, George Nichols, C. O'Connell, Jeremiah O'Connell, M.J. O'Connor, E. O'Driscoll, Coleman O'Gaoti, Brian O'Higgins, Peadar Ó Hourihane, John O'Hurley, Patrick (Padraig) O'Keefe,[468] G. O'Leary, John O'Mahoney, J.K. O'Reilly, P. O'Sullivan, Count Plunkett, G. Ready, T.M. Russell, Tom Ruane, Frank Shouldice (escaped from Usk Prison), Michael Spillane, Patrick Sugrue, V. Travers.[469][470]

Harry Boland worked here often, as did Frank Gallagher and Anna Fitzsimmons. It was raided on 20 November 1918, three weeks before the election. Robert Brennan, national Director of Elections and Publicity, was arrested and imprisoned in Gloucester Gaol.[471] James O'Mara took over this position.

The Election of 14 December 1918:[472] the count was postponed until 28 December. Sinn Féin won 73 seats but with four candidates elected to two seats

458 Ó Snodaigh, Aengus. 'Usk Jail Death, 1918', *An Phoblacht*, 2 December 1999. 459 Cosgrave, William. Witness Statements 268, 449. 460 Cusack, Dr Brian. Witness Statement 736. 461 Fahy, Frank. Witness Statement 442. 462 Fahy, Anna. Witness Statement 202. 463 Hayes, Dr Richard. Witness Statements 97, 876. 464 Lyons, George. Witness Statements 11, 104. 465 MacBride, Maud Gonne. Witness Statement 317. 466 MacEntee, Seán. Witness Statement 1052. 467 McCullough, Denis. Witness Statement 914. 468 O'Keefe, Patrick. Witness Statement 1725. 469 *Irish Independent*, 18, 19, 21 May 1918. 470 *The Irish Times*, 18, 19, 21 May 1918. 471 Brennan, Robert. Witness Statements 125, 779, 790. 472 Gallagher/Hogan. *The Four Glorious Years*, pp. 44-55.

(de Valera, Griffith, Eoin MacNeill and Liam Mellowes) the party returned 69 winning candidates. It should be noted that this was a 'first past the post' election. Sinn Féin polled 485,105 votes with the Irish Parliamentary Party getting 297,393 votes. No votes were counted in 24 constituencies where Sinn Féin candidates ran unopposed. Unionists took 26 seats: 315,394 votes.

The franchise for the election had been greatly expanded by the Representation of the People Act of 1918. In 1910, 701,475 were on the register; in 1918, there were 1,936,673. This increase in votes enabled the Irish Parliamentary Party to retain its following in most constituencies, but prevented it from securing its former seats.[473]

Harry Boland announced the Sinn Féin winners of the most notable contests from here.

The following are the Sinn Féin candidates who were elected to Parliament and sat as the First Dáil Éireann.

Robert Barton	Wicklow West
Piaras Béaslaí	Kerry East
Ernest Blythe	Monaghan North
Harry Boland	Roscommon South
Cathal Brugha; President Pro Tem, then Ceann Comhairle	Waterford County
Séamus Burke	Tipperary Mid
Michael Colivet	Limerick City
Conor (Con) Collins	Limerick West
Micheal Collins	Cork South
William T. Cosgrave	Kilkenny North
James Crowley	Kerry North
John Crowley	Mayo North
Brian Cusack	Galway North
Liam de Roiste	Cork City
Éamon de Valera	Clare East; won unopposed
	Mayo East; defeated John Dillon 8875 to 4514
	Lost in West Belfast to Joe Devlin 8438 to 3045
James Dolan	Leitrim
Éamonn Duggan	Meath South
Seán Etchingham	Wicklow East
Frank Fahy	Galway South
Desmond Fitzgerald	Dublin Pembroke
Peter Galligan	Cavan West
George Gavan-Duffy	Dublin County South

473 Murphy, Brian. 'The First Dáil Éireann', *History Ireland*, Vol. II, No. 1, 1994.

Laurence Ginnell;
He was one of two who had previously sat in
a 'parliament' previously.
James O'Mara was the other.   Westmeath
Arthur Griffith   Cavan East
                                                Tyrone North-West
Richard Hayes   Limerick East
Seán Hayes   Cork West
Thomas Hunter   Cork North-East
Thomas Kelly   Dublin St Stephen's Green
David Kent   Cork East
Frank Lawless   Dublin County North
James Lennon   Carlow
Diarmaid Lynch   Cork South-East
Fionan Lynch   Kerry South
Seán MacEntee   Monaghan South
Eoin MacNeill   Londonderry City
                                                National University of Ireland

Terence MacSwiney; when he was
sentenced to jail on 16 August 1920,
he declared; 'I will put a limit to
any term of imprisonment you may
impose. I have decided the terms of   Cork Mid
my detention whatever your
government may do. I shall be free,
alive or dead, within a month'.
He died on hunger strike in Brixton
Prison in London on 23 October
1920.
Joseph McBride   Mayo West
Alex McCabe   Sligo South
Pierce McCann; died 6 March 1919
in Gloucester Prison from influenza.
His death prompted the British to
release many other prisoners. The
other prisoners were released on   Tipperary East
the orders of the prison doctor,
Dr Bell. He was the brother of
Alan Bell, an Examining Magistrate
whom Collins later had executed in
Dublin. (See also 76 Harcourt
Street.)

Patrick McCartan	King's County (now County Offaly)
Joseph McDonagh	Tipperary North
Joseph McGrath	Dublin St James's
Joseph P. McGuinness	Longford
Countess Markievicz; first woman to be elected to Parliament. Her invitation to take her seat was sent to her at Holloway Prison.	Dublin St Patrick's
Liam Mellowes	Galway East Meath North
P.J. Moloney	Tipperary South
Richard Mulcahy	Dublin Clontarf
Domhnall Ó Buachalla	Kildare North
Seán T. Ó Ceallaigh (O' Kelly)	Dublin College Green
A. O'Connell	Kildare South
Joseph O'Doherty	Donegal North
Brian O'Higgins	Clare West
Kevin O'Higgins	Queen's County (now County Laois)
Patrick O'Keefe	Cork North
John O'Mahoney	Fermanagh South
Pádraig Ó Máille	Galway Connemara
John J. O'Malley	Louth
James O'Meara (O'Mara); He was he was one of two who had sat in a 'parliament' previously. Laurence Ginnell was the other.	Kilkenny South
Count Plunkett	Roscommon North
James Ryan	Wexford South
William Sears	Mayo South
Austin Stack	Kerry South
Michael Staines	Dublin St Michan's
Joseph Sweeney; youngest member	Donegal West
Roger Sweetman	Wexford North
James J. Walsh	Cork City
Peter Ward	Donegal South

The following were elected as MPs but refused to be seated as members of the First Dáil.

Party	Name	Constituency
Irish Unionist Party (22)	William Allen	Armagh North
	Hugh Anderson	Londonderry North
	E.M. Archdale	Fermanagh North
	T.W. Brown	Down North
	Edward Carson	Belfast Duncairn
	W. Coote	Tyrone South
	Charles Craig	Antrim South
	Sir James Craig, Bt	Down Mid
	Herbert Dixon	Belfast Pottinger
	Sir Maurice Dockrell	Dublin Rathmines
	Denis S. Henry	Londonderry South
	W.A. Lindsay	Belfast Cromac
	J.R. Lonsdale	Armagh Mid
	R.J. Lynn	Belfast Woodvale
	Robert McCalmont	Antrim East
	Thomas Moles	Belfast Ormeau
	Hon. R.W. Hugh O'Neill	Antrim Mid
	D.D. Reid	Down East
	Arthur Warren Samuels	Dublin University
	Maj. P. Kerr Smiley	Antrim North
	Sir William Whitla	Queen's University of Belfast
	Daniel M. Wilson	Down West
Irish Parliamentary Party (6)	J. Donnelly	Armagh South
	Joseph Devlin	Belfast Falls
	Thomas Harbison	Tyrone North-East
	E.J. Kelly	Donegal East
	Jeremiah McVeigh	Down South
	William Archer Redmond	Waterford City
Labour Unionist (3)	Thomas H. Burn	Belfast St Anne's
	T. Donald	Belfast Victoria
	S. McGuffin	Belfast Shankill
Independent Unionist (1)	Sir Robert Henry Woods	Dublin University

On 12 September 1919 the intelligence office of Michael Collins was raided. Det. Daniel Hoey led the raid. Patrick (Padraig) O'Keefe said to Hoey: 'You're for it tonight.' Hoey was killed that night outside Detective HQ. Ernest Blythe was also present during the raid.

On 16 October 1919 the Twelfth Sinn Féin Ard-Fheis met between midnight and 3 am.

On 25 November 1919 the Sinn Féin Party was officially suppressed.

On 21–23 February 1922 a special Sinn Féin Ard Feis was held to explore an attempted compromise with the Provisional Government. Its stated purpose was: 'To interpret the constitution of Sinn Féin with reference to the situation created by the signing at London of the Articles of Agreement for a Treaty, and the approval of Dáil Éireann by 64 votes to 57, and to decide the policy of Sinn Féin in view of possible forthcoming elections.' On the final day a draft agreement was prepared by Griffith and de Valera and passed without dissent.

> In order to avoid a division of the Sinn Féin Organisation, and to acquit an opportunity to the signatories of the London Agreement to draft a Constitution, so that when the people are asked to vote at elections to decide between the Republic and the Saorstát the Constitution of the latter may be definitely before them.
>
> It is hereby agreed: this Ard-Fheis shall stand adjourned for three months. In the meantime the Officer Board of the Organisation shall act as a Standing Committee. Dáil Éireann shall meet regularly and continue to function in all its departments as before the signing of the Articles of Agreement, and that no vote in Dáil Éireann shall be regarded as a Party vote requiring the resignation of the President and the Cabinet. That in the meantime no Parliamentary Election shall be held, and that when the Constitution of the Saorstát in its final form shall be presented at the same time as the Articles of Agreement. That this Agreement shall be submitted to the Ard-Fheis, and if approved, shall be binding.[474][475]

Dáil Éireann ratified this Agreement on 2 March. Griffith was strongly opposed to any compromise with anti-Treaty forces. He thought a Civil War was inevitable and the sooner it started the sooner it would be over. Four hundred and fifty-five votes were cast for eleven pro-Treaty candidates and one hundred and fifty-five votes for the remaining four.

On 15 March 1922, de Valera founded a new party, Cumann na Poblachta, and on 16 March he made an angry speech in Carrick-on-Suir saying 'They will have to march over the dead bodies of their own brothers. They will have to wade through Irish blood. There are rights which may be maintained by force by an

474 Macardle. *The Irish Republic*, p. 666. 475 Gallagher Frank. *An Phoblacht*, 28 February 1922.

armed minority even against a majority.'[476] In Dungarvan later on the 16th he said: 'The Treaty…barred the way to independence with the blood of fellow Irishmen. It was only by Civil War after this that they could get their independence…If you don't fight today, you will have to fight tomorrow; and I say, when you are in a good fighting position, then fight on'.[477] In Thurles, he repeated this imagery and added that if the IRA 'accepted the Treaty and if the Volunteers of the future tried to complete the work the Volunteers of the last four years had been attempting, they would have to complete it, not over the bodies of foreign soldiers, but over the dead bodies of their own countrymen. They would have to wade through, perhaps, the blood of some of the members of the Government, in order to get Irish freedom'.[478] In Killarney on the 18th he went on: 'In order to achieve freedom, if our Volunteers continue, and I hope they continue until the goal is reached, if we continue on that movement which was begun when the Volunteers were started and we suppose this Treaty is ratified by your votes, then these men, in order to achieve freedom, will have, I said yesterday, to march over the dead bodies of their own brothers. They will have to wade through Irish blood…The people never have a right to do wrong.'[479] (See also Appendix I: Carrick-on-Suir, Dungarvan, Killarney, Thurles. Later de Valera claimed he was misunderstood, that he was merely warning of war not encouraging it, and that the *Irish Independent* misinterpreted his words on each occasion.) In Dublin on 25 April he addressed a crowd: 'Young men and young women of Ireland, the goal is at last in sight. Steady; all together, forward. Ireland is yours for the taking. Take it.'[480]

(At the funeral of Liam Lynch in April 1923, de Valera said 'You have to fling yourselves across the stampede of a nation…It is better to die nobly as your Chief has died than like a slave.'[481])

Currently HQ of Connradh na Gaeilge (The Gaelic League).

8 Harcourt Street Ivanhoe Hotel; Michael Collins hid on the roof here when No 6 Harcourt Street was raided.

17 Harcourt Street Clonmel House, art gallery; John Lavery's pictures were often displayed here.

40 Harcourt Street Harcourt Street High School; Auxiliary hospital during the Rising.

74 Harcourt Street (at the corner of Clonmel Street): Standard Hotel (since demolished).

Michael Collins escaped a raid on 76 Harcourt Street by going along rooftops and swinging through the hotel skylight.

W.C. Forbes Redmond, Belfast RIC Assistant Commisioner of Police, stayed here before being killed on 21 Jan 1920. Paddy Daly shot him as he mounted the

---

476 *Irish Independent,* 17 March 1922. **477** *Irish Independent,* 18 March 1922. **478** *Ibid.* **479** *Irish Independent,* 20 March 1922. **480** Dwyer, T. Ryle. *Big Fellow, Long Fellow: A Joint Biography of Collins and de Valera,* 1998, p. 144-145. **481** Macardle. *The Irish Republic,* p. 976.

steps. The first shot shattered his jaw and he tried to draw a gun, but the second shot in the forehead killed him. The killing was carefully planned. Daly and Joe Dolan[482] stayed in the hotel two weeks previously to learn about Redmond's movements. The canteen manager of the King George V Military Hospital, a man named Houlihan, smuggled out the gun used in the killing.

Redmond led a raid on the Batt O'Connors' home on 17 January and assured Mrs Maire O'Connor he 'wouldn't bother her again'. Michael Collins made sure of it.

James McNamara was one of Redmond's 'confidants'. Redmond was involved with 'Jameson' (John Charles Byrne) in an attempt to capture Michael Collins. Redmond foolishly ridiculed G-Division detectives in front of McNamara, pointing out that he had made contact with a man who had met Collins, only a fortnight after arriving from London. Collins' agent at G-Division, David Neligan, informed Collins through Éamon Broy, and Redmond was killed a few days later.[483] 'Jameson' was killed on 2 March 1920. (See also Ballymun Road, Nutley Lane, Sackville Street Upper, Cork, Co. Cork, Winthrop Street [Appendix I], and Brendan Road [Appendix II].)

Lady Augusta Gregory stayed here when she was at the Abbey Theatre.

76 Harcourt Street Dáil Office from June 1919; raided in November 1919. In the raid, Seán Hayes, Frank Lawless, Michael Lynch, Dick McKee, Fintan Murphy, Dan O'Donovan, Diarmuid O'Hegarty, Seán O'Mahoney and Patrick Sheehan were arrested, and then spent two months in jail. Michael Collins escaped through the skylight to the Standard Hotel.

Collins purchased the house for the Dáil. It was used to house the Dáil Loan. Officially signed receipts in green, gold and black were issued in lieu of bonds; Colm Ó Lochlainn printed them.[484] There were constituency organizers for each province, paid £30 per week each: Leinster, E. Flemming; Ulster, E. Donnelly; Munster, P.C. O'Mahoney; Connaught, P. Ryan. By September 1920, the following had been subscribed: Leinster: £87,444; Ulster: £41,297; Munster: £171,177; Connaught: £57,797; England and France, £11,647; Cumann na mBan: £801. The final Loan total, subscribed by over 135,000 Irish people, was £378,858 in Ireland alone. $5,123,640 was raised separately in the US.[485] [486] The British attempted to confiscate the funds and on 1 March a secret commission was established which summoned bank managers to appear and identify the funds held in their institutions. When Collins heard of it, he had the signatory of the summons, Alan Bell, shot.

Batt O'Connor made hidden closets to hide people and documents here.

It currently houses the corporate services division of the Department of Foreign Affairs.

---

482 Dolan, Joe. Statements 663, 900. **483** Neligan, David. Witness Statement 380. **484** Ó Lochlainn, Colm. Witness Statement 751. **485** Hart, Peter. *Mick: The Real Michael Collins*, 2005, p. 194. **486** Macardle. *The Irish Republic*, p. 986.

Harcourt Street (and 103–104 St Stephen's Green): Russell Hotel; occupied by the British during the Rising. Margaret Skinnider, a mathematics teacher, was wounded on Wednesday of Easter Week when she was in a party sent to set fire to the Russell Hotel. William (Bill) Partridge carried her back to the College of Surgeons. She later wrote *Doing My Bit for Ireland*. Auxies stayed here after the Truce until rounded up by Dave Neligan. Count Sevigne's (the head of the British Secret Service in Ireland at the time) mother-in-law owned it.

Harcourt Street Station Terminus of the Dublin and Southeastern Railway, in use from its construction in 1859 until 1959. Taken early in the Rising by a detachment of the ICA under Cpt. Richard McCormack, it was almost immediately evacuated by the Volunteers because it was indefensible.

Hardwicke Street Hardwicke Street Theatre. Founded in 1914 by Edward Martyn, Thomas MacDonagh and Joseph Plunkett, it was intended to produce foreign and Irish plays ignored or rejected by the Abbey Theatre.

Hardwicke Street Fianna HQ; Seán Heuston was in charge of training and organization.

27 Hardwicke Street Home of Mrs Kissane. Seán MacDermott lived here until he moved to the Munster Hotel the week before the Rising, then on Holy Saturday he moved to the Fleming Hotel on Gardiner Street to stay with Tom Clarke at Seán Mahoney's home. Later it was used as a 'safe house' by the IRA/Volunteers.

43 Harrington Road Home of John Butler (Jack, J.B) Yeats.

12 Harrington Street Home of Thomas Dickson; killed with Francis Sheehy-Skeffington, he is buried in Glasnevin. (See also Rathmines Road/Portobello Barracks.)

7–8 Harry Street Mooney's Pub; a frequent haunt of Kevin O'Higgins when he was a student.

Hatch Street A detachment of the ICA under Sgt Frank Robbins was to defend this area and build barricades all around St Stephen's Green.[487]

20 Hatch Street Home of Dr Ella Webb, who had become a member of the St John's Ambulance Brigade of Ireland in 1914. She helped to set up an emergency hospital at the Brigade's headquarters at 14 Merrion Square during the Rising and cycled daily through the firing line to visit the hospital. Later Dr Webb was awarded an MBE for her work for the St John's Ambulance Brigade.

43 Lower Hatch Street Early home of Eoin MacNeill.

Henrietta Lane Messrs McMaster Hodgeson. A wholesale drug firm and purveyor of oils, it was burned during the Rising.

Henrietta Street On Constitution Hill, King's Inns. The Volunteers seized it and its arms were taken on 1 June 1920. One of the IRA/Volunteers was Kevin Barry.

Henry Place Volunteers escaping from the GPO rushed through here to get from Moore Street to Moore Lane.

---

487 Robbins, Frank. Witness Statement 585.

Henry Street An area with many retail outlets in 1916. Fifty-three buildings were burned on the street during the Rising.

9–15 Henry Street Arnott's Department Store. During the Rising, the Volunteers under Frank Henderson bored through the walls of Henry Street buildings from the GPO to here.[488]

The IRA/Republicans had a machine gun on the roof during the Civil War.

18, 19, 20 Henry Street Bewley's. This was the company's Dublin HQ and offices, though its most noted location was on Grafton Street. F.R. Ridgeway was the managing director at the time of the Rising.

21 Henry Street Home of Jennie and Charles Wyse-Power.

Charles had been a member of the IRB and Volunteers, but was told he would be more valuable as a lawyer, free from these associations, so he did not take part in the Rising.[489]

The *Proclamation* was agreed upon here and six signed it: Thomas Clarke, Padraig Pearse, James Connolly, Thomas MacDonagh, Seán MacDermott and Éamonn Ceannt, probably on Tuesday, 18 April. Joseph Plunkett signed on Easter Sunday morning. (There has always been confusion whether the 'signatories' actually affixed their signatures to the paper. However, Kathleen Clarke indicated Tom told her it was 'signed that night'.[490] Michael Molloy, one of the men who printed the *Proclamation*, said he carried with him the piece of paper signed by the signatories to the *Proclamation* until he found himself in Richmond Barracks after the surrender, when he chewed it up and spat it out to prevent its discovery.[491])

Jennie, (née O'Toole) grew up in Dublin in a nationalist family. She joined the Ladies' Land League in 1881, took an active part in its activities and became a member of its executive. She married John Wyse-Power, a journalist on the *Freeman's Journal*, and one of the founders of the Gaelic Athletic Association.

Jennie was an activist all her life. She was involved with the Dublin Women's Suffrage Association and the Gaelic League. She was a founder member and vice-president of Inghínidhe na hÉireann. She was a founder member of Sinn Féin, served on its executive from the beginning and was elected vice-president in 1911. She was elected first president of Cumann na mBan. She was elected Poor Law Guardian in 1903 and was one of five women elected to the Dublin Corporation in 1920. Jennie was a successful businesswoman and her restaurant in Henry Street was a well-known meeting place for nationalists.[492]

During the Rising the Wyse-Powers supplied food to the insurgents and, with their daughter, Nancy, later helped organize relief for prisoners' dependants.

Jenny supported the Treaty, and was appointed to the first Seanad of the Irish

488 Henderson, Frank. Witness Statement 821. **489** Wyse-Power, Charles. Witness Statement 420. **490** Clarke, Kathleen. Op. cit., p. 69. **491** Molloy, Michael. Witness Statement 716. **492** O'Neill, Máire. *From Parnell to de Valera, A Biography of Jennie Wyse Power, 1858-1941*, 1991.

Free State where she had an outstanding record as champion of women's rights from 1922 to 1936.

Their daughter, Dr Nancy Wyse-Power, was an emissary to Germany during the War of Independence and was a close associate of John Chartres. She was later appointed to the Free State Department of Industry and Commerce and was a strong advocate for women's rights.[493]

Irish Farm Produce Co. Michael Collins used space here as an office.

24 Henry Street (just opposite Moore Street): Coliseum Variety Theatre with 3000 seats. Ironically, it opened on Easter Monday 1915. Burned during the Rising, it was never rebuilt. Two British soldiers, Sgt Henry and Pvt. Doyle, let go in advance of The O'Rahilly's escape, hid in the basement and were not discovered until Wednesday, 3 May, unaware the Rising had ended.

45 Henry Street Under the name of Murray & Quirke, Solicitors, Austin Stack's first Ministry for Home Affairs office, as well as one of Michael Collins' Finance Ministry offices. Patrick (Paddy) Sheehan worked here for Collins.

47 Henry Street William's Stores, looted during the Rising.

14 Herbert Park, Ballsbridge Home of Fr Michael O'Flanagan, a member of the organizing committee of the Volunteers.

17 Herbert Park, Ballsbridge Home of F.H. Browning, who led one column of the Georgius Rex on Northumberland Road and was killed there.

18 Herbert Park, Ballsbridge Home of Mr and Mrs Arthur Mitchell; he was the director of Jameson's Distillery.

19 Herbert Park, Ballsbridge 1914 home of Eoin and Agnes MacNeill. He was professor of Early and Medieval History at UCD and chief of staff of the Irish Volunteers and she was on the Provisional Committee of Cumann na mBan.[494] By April 1916 they were living in Rathfarnham; their home there was known as Woodtown Park.

32 Herbert Park, Ballsbridge Home of Alfred and Violet Fannin, owner of Fannin medical and surgical supply on Grafton Street; it remained in the family until their son Eustace died in 1985, and is now an ambassadorial residence.

40 Herbert Park, Ballsbridge Home of The O'Rahilly; Michael Joseph O'Rahilly. His wife was Nancy Marie Browne O'Rahilly (usually known as 'Nannie'), originally from Philadelphia; she was on the Provisional Committee of Cumann na mBan. He was Eoin MacNeill's publisher. (See also Sackville Lane.)

On 2 March 1919 a meeting was held here about the establishment of Dáil/Republican Courts in the Pembroke and South City areas; Margaret Buckley, Áine Ceannt,[495] Kathleen Clarke, Áine Heron,[496] Helena Molony[497] and Hanna Sheehy-Skeffington were among those chosen to sit as judges.

---

493 Wyse-Power, Nancy. Witness Statements 541, 587, 732. **494** MacNeill, Agnes. Witness Statement 213. **495** Ceannt, Áine. Witness Statement 264. **496** Heron, Áine. Witness Statement 293. **497** Molony, Helena. Witness Statement 391.

(Margaret Buckley [née Goulding] was president of Sinn Féin from 1937 to 1950. Originally from Co. Cork she joined Inghinidhe na Éireann as a teenager. Arrested after the Rising she was released in the amnesty of June 1917 and played a prominent role in the reorganization of Sinn Féin. She opposed the Treaty and was interned in the North Dublin Union, Mountjoy and Kilmainham where she went on a hunger strike, and her book *Jangle of the Keys* is the classic history of the suffering of the imprisoned women.[498] During her imprisonment, she was elected OC of the prisoners in Mountjoy, QM in the North Dublin Union and OC of B-Wing in Kilmainham. She was an active member of the Womens' Prisoners' Defence League.)

Early in 1921 a meeting was held here to finalize plans for the taking of the Custom House. (Éamon de Valera's first choice was to capture Beggars' Bush Barracks, but Oscar Traynor deemed that impractical.[499] [500]) It included Piaras Béaslaí, Cathal Brugha, Michael Collins, de Valera, Seán MacMahon, Liam Mellowes, Richard Mulcahy, J.J. 'Ginger' O'Connell, Eoin O'Duffy, Diarmud O'Hegarty, Gearóid O'Sullivan, Seán Russell, Austin Stack and Traynor.

9 Herbert Place Edward Carson's first home as an adult.

Herbert Road at corner of Newbridge Avenue, Sandyford Fairfield House. Home of James Stephens, founder of the IRB.

71 Heytesbury Street Home of the Delaney family. Seán Treacy was a great friend and called here often, including the morning of the day he was killed. Ms Delaney was engaged to Seámus Robinson.

A meeting place for IRA/Republicans during the Civil War.

4 High Street Home of Freddie Ryan. A member of the St Stephen's Green garrison, he was killed (aged seventeen) trying to set the Russell Hotel on fire.

14–16 High Street St Audoen's Church, built in 1845 adjacent to the site of the original church that was one of Dublin's oldest, the original St Audoen's, built by the Normans in 1190. That church replaced one built and dedicated to St Columcille. Designed by Patrick Byrne. Repository of the 'Lucky Stone', an early Christian gravestone reputed to have mystical qualities. In the early 1900s the pastor was Canon Kavanagh. A group of Volunteers attended Mass in the nearby Catholic St Audoen's on 17 March 1916.

26 Highfield Road, Rathgar Home of Agnes O'Farrelly, member of the Provisional Committee of Cumann na mBan. Born in 1874, she was also known as Úna Ní Fhaircheallaigh, from Virginia, Co. Cavan. She graduated from the Royal University of Ireland with an MA and spent a year at the Sorbonne in Paris. She was co-founder with Mary Hayden of the Irish Association of Women Graduates in 1903. A devoted member of the Gaelic League, she studied Irish in the Aran Islands and was a close friend of its president Douglas Hyde. She was present at the first meeting

498 Buckeley, Margaret. *The Jangle of the Keys*, 1938. **499** Traynor, Oscar. Witness Statement 340. **500** Traynor, Oscar. 'The Burning of the Custom House — Dublin's Fighting Story', *The Kerryman*, 1939.

of Sinn Féin in 1906 and chaired the first meeting of Cumann na mBan in April 1914. She was not active in the 1916 Rising or in the War of Independence but took part in delegations attempting to prevent the Civil War. In 1932 she was appointed to the Senate and became professor of Modern Irish Poetry at University College, Dublin. With Mary Hayden, she led the National University Women Graduates' Association in their demand for the deletion of articles in the draft Constitution of 1937 which were seen as offensive to women.

Holles Street National Maternity Hospital, opened to all during the Rising. Known simply as Holles Street Hospital it opened in 1884.

Howth, County Dublin Arms were landed here on 26 July 1914. The event was planned by Roger Casement, Erskine Childers, Dermot Coffey, Darrell Figgis, Alice Stopford Green, Bulmer Hobson, Seán MacDermott, Eoin MacNeill, Conor O'Brien (grandson of William Smith O'Brien, leader of the 1848 Young Irelanders revolt), The O'Rahilly and Mary Spring-Rice. The O'Rahilly directed Figgis and Childers to the firm in Hamburg where they purchased 1500 rifles and 45,000 rounds of ammunition. The *Asgard* landed 900 rifles and 26,000 rounds of ammunition. On board the *Asgard* were Childers, his wife, Molly, Mary Spring Rice,[501] an English army officer named Gordon Shephard,[502] [503] and two Donegal fishermen, Patrick McGinley and Charles Duggan. (The yacht was a wedding present to the Childers and was designed and built in Norway in 1905. *Asgard* is the Norwegan word for 'Home of the Gods'.) George Fitz Hardinge Berkeley made the largest single contribution. The rifles were Mausers, Gewehr 98's, .31 caliber with a 5-shot magazine, and were captured from the Russians by German forces. About 800 Volunteers mustered and marched out to Howth that day. Seán Heuston was in charge of the transport, meaning the Fianna trek-cart. In spite of all the British efforts, the cart brought its entire cargo back to Dublin.[504] (See also Bachelor's Walk, Kilcoole [Appendix I], Merrion Square and 90 St Stephen's Green [south].)

Howth, County Dublin Wentworth Cottage, home of Mary M. Colum, member of the Provisional Committee of Cumann na mBan and its Hon. Secretary. She was a teacher at St Ita's school for girls, the sister school to Pearse's St Enda's school for boys. In *Irish Freedom* she explained the role of Cumann na mBan: 'Cumann na mBan members are not the auxiliaries or handmaidens or camp followers of the Volunteers – we are their allies.'[505] Mary (née Maguire) was born in Sligo in 1884, was a teacher and writer and was involved in many of the cultural movements of

---

501 Mary Spring Rice wrote the most detailed diary of the voyage, including from the time the arms were transferred to their landing. Spring Rice, Mary. *'Diary of the Asgard 1-26 July 1914'*, in Martin, F.X., OSA, editor, *The Howth Gun Running and the Kilcoole Gun Running*, 1964, pp. 79, 80, 95. **502** Bulmer Hobson notes 'a General Shepherd, [sic] who was later killed in France' was a member of Childers' crew. Hobson, Bulmer. *'Gun Running at Howth and Kilcoole, July-August 1914'*, in Martin, *The Irish Volunteers*, p. 42. **503** See Leslie, Shane, editor, *Memoirs of Brigadier-General Gordon Shephard*. (privately printed), 1924. **504** Figgis. *Recollections of the Irish War*, pp. 40-58. **505** *Irish Freedom*, September 1914.

the early years of the twentieth century in Dublin including the Irish Literary Revival. She married Padraic Colum, poet and playwright of the early years of the Abbey Theatre. They moved to America where they lived most of their lives and both continued to write. Later she wrote *Life and the Dream* telling her experiences during the period.

Hume Street Home of Anna Fitzsimons; known as 'Miss Fitz', she worked on the staff of the *Irish Bulletin*.

Hume Street (and Ely Place): Nora Connolly O'Brien had an office here during the Civil War.[506] She replaced Margaret Skinnider as assistant to Austin Stack. She was captured here in November 1922 and was imprisoned at Mountjoy Prison.

7 Hume Street Home of Fanny and Anna Parnell; they founded the Ladies' Land League in 1879. Anna and Fanny had lived in Paris and the USA where they gained experience of running organisations, fundraising and attracting publicity. When it seemed that the Land League men were likely to be arrested, it was suggested that a women's league in Ireland could take over the work in their absence. Public opinion at the time was against women in politics but Michael Davitt was positive and Anna Parnell, aged 28, returned to Ireland from the USA to help lead the Ladies' Land League. When Parnell and other leaders were imprisoned in 1881, as predicted, the Ladies' Land League took over their work. Offices were given to the ladies in Sackville Street, but very little help or detailed instructions. However, the women held public meetings and encouraged country women to be active in withholding rent, in boycotting and in resisting evictions. They raised funds for the League and for the support of prisoners and their families. They distributed Land League wooden huts to shelter evicted tenant families and by the beginning of 1882 they had 500 branches, thousands of women members and considerable publicity. Their meetings were frequently broken up by police and thirteen members were imprisoned – but as criminals and not as political prisoners like the men. Many people disagreed with the way they implemented their policies while others disapproved of women activists so they were highly controversial. Archbishop McCabe of Dublin publicly opposed them but Archbishop Croke of Cashel came to their defence. Archbishop McCabe and their brother, Charles Stewart, condemned them for 'outraging feminine modesty'. Anna felt that the efficiency of the Ladies' Land League was resented by many men. Fanny was a poet and her poem *Hold the Harvest* was described as the Marseillaise of the Irish tenants.

When Anna went to Ireland to help found the Ladies' Land League, Fanny did promotional and fundraising tours in America. Fanny's death in 1882 at the height of the Ladies' Land League controversy was a bitter blow to Anna, who became a recluse, living mostly in England. Anna drowned in 1911 at the age of sixty-nine. [507] [508]

Many always thought their League was a front for Fenian activity.

506 O'Brien, Nora Connolly. Witness Statement 286. **507** O'Regan, Danae. 'Anna and Fanny Parnell', *History Ireland*, Vol. VII, No. 1, Spring 1999. **508** Côté, Jane. *Fanny and Anna Parnell: Ireland's patriot sisters*, 1991.

Inchicore Islandbridge Barracks. Partially demolished, it was renamed Peadar Clancy Barracks. Clancy Barracks was sold to developers in early 2004.

Infirmary Road (Montpelier Gardens): King George V Hospital. (Now St Bricin's Military Hospital.) After he was wounded in Mullingar, Seán MacEoin was taken here and was visited by Brigid Lyons when she was studying at Mercer's Hospital. Seán Treacy's body was taken here and identified by Nora O'Keefe and Mollie Gleeson.

Inns Quay see King's Inns Quay.

Iona Road, Glasnevin Ernie O'Malley's family home.

9 Iona Road, Glasnevin Home of J.J. Farrell, former Lord Mayor of Dublin.

James's Street South Dublin Union Workhouse (now St James's Hospital). Formerly known as Queen Anne's Mansions, the building was begun in 1702.

Held by Cmdt. Éamonn Ceannt and the 4th Batallion Volunteers. The Volunteers occupied buildings here from Easter Monday until Maj. Sir Francis Vane took command of a column of British troops under Lt Col. W.C. Oates on Thursday. After that night Ceannt and the Volunteers were surrounded, but in comparative peace, until they surrendered on Sunday. (Ceannt had fewer than sixty Volunteers; he surrendered forty-two – Cathal Brugha was missing.)

There were several open fields surrounding the buildings, stretching southwards from the Volunteer HQ to the Grand Canal: the Master's Fields, McCaffrey Estate and the Orchard Fields. Nurse Margaretta Keogh, a nurse in the Union Hospital, was killed here, the first woman to die in the Rising. She was killed at Number 2 Hospital Building.

Cathal Brugha single-handedly saved the Volunteers here by his courage. For two hours he held the British at a courtyard, defending the Nurses' Home unaided. Alone he forced the British to retreat. He was propped against a wall singing 'God Save Ireland' when Ceannt and the Volunteers came to get him. He had been wounded twenty-five times and survived: '5 dangerous bullet wounds, 9 serious and 11 slight'. He never fully recovered the use of his legs. A Carmelite nun and a Red Cross worker took him to the Union Hospital on Friday morning, then to the hospital in Dublin Castle. The British ultimately released him because they did not think he could be of any future danger because he was hurt so badly. Afterward, it was said 'when he walked, one could hear the bullets rattlin'.

James's Street St James's Church. Fr Eugene McCarthy ministered here. He married Grace Gifford and Joseph Plunkett. On their wedding certificate, Plunkett was listed as a bachelor with an occupation of 'gentleman' and Grace was listed as a spinster with an occupation of artist. The two British soldiers who were 'witnesses' were John Smith and John Lockerby ('Sgt 3rd Battalion, The Royal Iniskillen Regiment'). At the Presbytery here, Fr McCarthy and Grace Gifford Plunkett were 'assaulted' by British troops after her wedding when they searched the premises and 'roughly handled them both'.[509]

---

509 Plunkett, Grace Gifford. Witness Statement 257.

Fr McCarthy also gave the Last Rites to James Connolly, and told that Connolly was first strapped to a chair but his wounds were so bad that the chair toppled over. The chair was put upright but again fell over. Finally, Fr McCarthy said 'a stretcher was brought out and Connolly was strapped to it in a slanting position against the wall and the volley rang out'.[510] [511] [512]

53 James's Street Home of Mr Byrne, bell-ringer at St James's. Grace Gifford Plunkett rested here after her wedding and was awakened at 2 am and taken to Kilmainham to see Joseph Plunkett for ten minutes before he was executed. Then Fr McCarthy escorted her to lodgings on Thomas Street where she spent the remainder of the night.

174 James's Street Early home of Phil and William Cosgrave.

Phil became Quartermaster of the Dublin Battalion during the War of Independence, and was later governor of Mountjoy Prison.

William succeeded Michael Collins as president of the Provisional Government (upon Collins' resignation) in July 1922 and then Griffith (on Griffith's death) as president of the Dáil Cabinet in August 1922, merging the two posts from September 1922 as president of the Executive Council of the Irish Free State.

Jervis Street (corner of York Street) The Swan Hotel; often used as meeting place in the War of Independence.

14-20 Jervis Street Jervis Street Hospital. Forty-five fatalities and 550 injured were treated here during the Rising. Seán Hales and Padraig Ó Maille were taken here after being shot on 7 December 1922. Hales was dead on arrival but Ó Maille survived.

Jones Road Croke Park. The grounds were originally acquired by the GAA in 1913 and were named after Archbishop Thomas Croke of Cashel, patron of the Association.

On 19 November 1917 the Third Convention of The Irish Volunteers was held here: President, Éamon de Valera; Chief of Staff, Cathal Brugha; Director of Organization, Michael Collins; Director of Communications, Diarmuid Lynch.[513]

The general secretary of the GAA at the time was Seán McGarry.

On 6 April 1919 Tipperary played Wexford in Gaelic football. The game was played to raise money for the Irish National Aid and Volunteers' Dependents' Fund. Collins and de Valera threw in the ball, and Harry Boland was the referee.

On 21 November 1920 Tipperary played Dublin in Gaelic football. The crowd was estimated to be 15,000. The Tans, Auxies and RIC attacked the grounds at

---

510 MacThomais, Éamonn. *Down Dublin Streets: 1916,* 1966, p. 43. **511** See also, MacLysaght, Edward. 'Larkin, Connolly and the Labour Movement', in Martin, *Leaders and Men,* p. 131. **512** But J.L. Hyland notes that Connolly 'was not strapped to a chair, but placed seated on a rough wooden box…and then executed'. Hyland. Op. cit., p. 54. **513** In March 1918 Lynch was deported to the US because he was an American citizen. He had 'intercepted' a load of pigs to be sent to England for the army, had them butchered in Dublin, and sent the proceeds to their owners – but the pigs never reached England, so the British deported him. He wanted to marry prior to deportation to help with his bride's citizenship, but the British wouldn't authorize it, so he was married in secret in Dundalk Gaol, and his bride accompanied him and his supporters to Amiens Street Station. The following March he was elected to the Dáil in his absence.

3.45 pm.[514] (See also Bloody Sunday, Appendix II.) Jack Shouldice was on the committee and was in charge of the gate and collections that day.[515] Others on the committee with whom Shouldice discussed the possibility of cancelling the game were Alderman James J. Nowlan, Luke O'Toole, Andy Harty and Dan McCarthy. They decided to go forward with the game despite warnings of British reprisals. The game was played for the benefit of the Irish National Aid and Volunteers' Dependents' Fund and about £500 raised. The referee was Mick Sammon from Kildare.

Tipperary player Mick Hogan was killed and is commemorated now by the 'Hogan Stand'. Thomas Ryan was killed as he held Hogan and whispered the Act of Contrition in his ear. Ryan was from Co. Wexford, and soon Dublin's children were singing:

> Croke Park, Bloody Sunday
> As the dying goalman lay on the ground
> And as the British bullets went flying round
> Brave Thomas Ryan from Wexford fair
> Knelt by his side in dying prayer
> And as he aided the dying man
> Was brutally shot by a Black and Tan.
> God grant that both their souls
> Find rest in Heaven among the blessed.

Fr Crotty gave Mick Hogan and Ryan the Last Rites. Jane Boyle (aged twenty-six), James Burke, Daniel Carroll, Michael Feery, Thomas Hogan, James Matthews, Patrick O'Dowd, Jerry O'Leary (aged ten), Willie Robinson (aged eleven), John Scott (aged fourteen), Joseph Traynor, and James Teehan were killed. The Black and Tans and Auxies injured sixty-two and a further twelve were injured in the stampede out of the grounds.[516] [517] [518]

The 'Nally Stand' is named after Pat Nally from Bally, Co. Mayo, an IRB and early GAA man.

Jones Road Home of Paddy and Stephen O'Reilly, both of whom were killed in the Custom House fire. Paddy was the Quartermaster of the 2nd Battalion. Stephen was only 18, and a volume of his poetry, *Spirit Flowers*, was published posthumously in 1923.

Jones Road Home of Denis Lynch, a chemist at the Dublin Whiskey Distillery (usually known as DWD). It was a frequent meeting place for IRA/Volunteers during the War of Independence, often including Michael Collins.

---

514 Leeson, David. 'Death in the Afternoon: The Croke Park Massacre, 21 November 1920', *Canadian Journal of History*, Vol. XXXVIII, No. 1, April 2003. **515** Shouldice, Jack. Witness Statement 162. **516** Gleeson, James. *Bloody Sunday*, 1962, p. 144 ff. **517** Carey, Tim and Marcus de Burca. 'Bloody Sunday 1920: New Evidence, *History Ireland*, Vol. XI, No. 2, Summer 2003. **518** 'The First Bloody Sunday', *An Phoblacht*, 25 February 2007.

53 Kenilworth Square, Rathgar Éamon de Valera's presidential office after Blackrock was raided. Later this was the Peterson home (of Kapp and Peterson), and was often used as a safe house during the War of Independence.

Kevin Street A major DMP barracks and training depot. At one time it was the palace of the Archbishop of Dublin. Michael Collins' spy, Dave Neligan, was first posted here. It was an 'A' Division post and was in the same yard as a detachment of mounted police. In 1917 it had Inspector Carey, Sgt Hurley and Constable Birmingham on its staff.

Kildare Street Busby's Hotel and Pub; after the Civil War, it became a Fine Gael/pro-Treaty haunt.

Kildare Street On 24 August 1918 a British recruiting rally address was delivered here by Col. Arthur Lynch MP, formerly of the Irish Brigade in the Boer War. He was asked during his speech: 'Why not stop in Ireland and share our dangers?' His reply, 'Stop in Ireland and share your cowardice', infuriated the Irish.[519]

Kildare Street Leinster House, where the Dáil now meets, and did so after 1922. Lord Edward Fitzgerald was born here on 15 October 1763. He did not like the house: 'It does not inspire the brightest ideas.' The First Session of the Third Dáil was held here on 9 September 1922. (The IRA/Republicans never recognized this Dáil. To this day, the strictest IRA supporters hold that the Second Dáil was never 'disestablished', is still in existence, and is the basis for their Republican claims, because it was the successor in interest to the 'Republic' established by the *Proclamation* of 1916.) Only the elderly Laurence Ginnell attended as a Republican and he was rapidly ejected for his repeated enquiries as to its constitutionality. Because of the Republican abstention, the only source of criticism came from the Labour Party, especially Thomas Johnson[520] and Cathal O'Shannon.

This Third Dáil ratified the Constitution of the Irish Free State on 18 September 1922. The document was drafted in the Shelbourne Hotel in the 'Constitution Room', which can now be seen by tourists. The committee appointed to draft the Constitution was chaired by Michael Collins, but Darrell Figgis, the vice-chairman, was responsible for most of its drafting.[521] William Cosgrave was elected president of the Executive Council of the Free State and minister for finance. Other Cabinet members included: Ernest Blythe, minister for local government; Desmond Fitzgerald, publicity director and minister for external affairs; Patrick Hogan, minister for agriculture; Eoin MacNeill, Ceann Comhairle of the Dáil until 9 September, minister without portfolio from January to August 1922 and minister for education from August to the following September; Joe McGrath, minister for industry and commerce and economic affairs (labour); Richard Mulcahy, minister for defence; Kevin O'Higgins, vice-president of the Executive Council and minister

---

519 Denman, Terence. '"The red livery of shame": the campaign against army recruitment in Ireland, *1899-1914*', *Irish Historical Studies*, Vol. XXIX, No. 114, November 1994. 520 Johnson, Thomas. Witness Statement 1755. 521 Figgis. *The Irish Constitution Explained*, Op. cit.

for home affairs; James J. Walsh, postmaster general; Éamonn J. Duggan, minister without portfolio; Fionan Lynch, minister without portfolio, then took over the ministry for fisheries. Michael Hayes was Ceann Comhairle of the Third Dáil, Padraic Ó Maille was Leas-Ceann Comhairle.

The Seanad na hÉireann (Senate) was established here and originally had 36 Catholic members and 24 non-Catholic members. In 1921 Arthur Griffith, as the leader of the Irish delegation at the Treaty negotiations, sought to ensure the status of the Unionist and Protestant minority in a new Irish Free State. The day the Treaty was signed, Griffith met with southern Unionist representatives and assured them of due representation in the Senate. Griffith did not live to realize his promise but W.T. Cosgrave, president of the Executive Council, fulfilled Griffith's legacy.[522] Thirty senators were appointed to the Senate by Cosgrave in December 1922 and a further 30 were elected by the Dáil. In all, seven peers, a dowager countess, five baronets and several knights were represented. The Senate consisted of 36 Catholics, 20 Protestants, three Quakers and one Jew. Cosgrave's nominees numbered 16 southern Unionists. Anti-Treaty forces believed, however, that the Senate was designed primarily for the purpose of upholding the interests of the pro-British element in the Irish Free State. The execution of Erskine Childers in November 1922 introduced a new dimension to the ongoing Civil War. Anti-Treaty forces gave notice that senators were legitimate targets unless they resigned their office, but this request was rejected by the new senators. By the end of March 1923, 37 senators' homes had been burnt to the ground.[523] The members included a number of representatives from the landed gentry as Griffith's policy had been to utilize all sections of the country and his offer to 'come and get the country under way' was well received by Protestant Unionists. The Earl of Dunraven and Mount-Earl, the Earl of Granard, the Earl of Mayo, the Earl of Wicklow, Sir Hutchinson Poe, Sir Thomas Esmonde, Sir Nugent Everard Bt, Sir John Purser Griffith, H.S. Guinness, Andrew Jameson, W.B. Yeats, and Oliver St John Gogarty were among those who became Free State Senators. The first Presiding Officer of the Seanad (Cathaoirleach Seanad na hÉireann) was Lord Glenavy, who had been an ally of Carson in 1912.[524]

On 27 September 1922 the Public Safety Bill was passed; it set up military courts, which were given powers, including that of execution, for various offences. This ushered in a harsher period of the Civil War. Ernest Blythe pointed out that the reluctance to take life had weakened their cause; Mulcahy was convinced that compromise was impossible. The Labour TDs were the only dissenters, pointing out the dangers of a military dictatorship.

In early October an amnesty for surrendering IRA/Republicans was agreed.

On 5 December T.M. Healy was appointed Governor General.

On 7 December Seán Hales was killed outside the Dáil and Padraic Ó Maille,

522 Cosgrave, William. Witness Statements 268, 449. **523** Byrne, Elaine. 'Hands that shaped Irish history', *The Irish Times*, 29 July 2008. **524** O'Connor, Ulick. *A Terrible Beauty is Born*, (Panther Books edition) 1981, p. 178.

Leas-Ceann Comhairle of the Dáil, was wounded. IRA/Republicans of the Dublin No 1 Brigade attacked them in reprisal for the passage of the Public Safety Bill. This was the only time the reprisal orders of Liam Lynch (called 'Orders of Frightfulness'), that were to kill any TD who voted for the Bill, were carried out. Dick Barrett, Joe McKelvey, Liam Mellowes and Rory O'Connor were executed in Mountjoy Prison on 8 December 1922 as a reprisal for the shooting. This is such an infamous event in the Civil War that it has long been questioned as to whom was 'responsible'. It appears Mulcahy took the initiative, and Kevin O'Higgins and Joe McGrath were the last Cabinet Members to give their consent. (See also North Circular Road/Mountjoy Prison.)

In the general election on 27 August 1923 Cumann na nGaedhael won sixty-three seats (415,000 votes for the former pro-Treatyites); Sinn Féin (abstentionists) won forty-four seats (286,000 for 'Republicans'); Independents won sixteen seats; the Farmers won fifteen seats; Labour won fourteen seats; Independent Labour won one seat.

1–3 Kildare Street Kildare Street Club (fronted the grounds of TCD and extended into Kildare Street); used as a major position by the IRA/Republicans in the Civil War.

41 Kildare Street first HQ of the Irish Volunteers, 1913–14; briefly moved to 2 Dawson Street from here in 1914, then to 206 Great Brunswick Street.

The First Provisional Committee of the Irish Volunteers operated from here. The formal executive was established after the Volunteer Convention of 1914. The affiliations noted below are those at the time of the inception of the Volunteers (November 1913), not as they became later. Those not formally affiliated with any party at that time are blank. Piaras Béaslaí (IRB); Roger Casement; Éamonn Ceannt (IRB); Con Colbert (IRB); James Deakin; Seán Fitzgibbon; Liam Gogan; John Gore (United Irish League, Irish Parliamentary Party); Bulmer Hobson (IRB); Michael Judge (Ancient Order of Hibernians); Laurence Kettle (United Irish League, Irish Parliamentary Party); Tom Kettle (United Irish League, Irish Parliamentary Party); James Lenehan (Ancient Order of Hibernians); Michael Lonergan (IRB); Thomas MacDonagh; Eoin MacNeill; Seán MacDermott (IRB); Peadar Macken (IRB); Éamon Martin (IRB); Liam Mellowes (IRB); Col. Maurice Moore (United Irish League, Irish Parliamentary Party); Seámus O'Connor (IRB); Colm Ó Lochlainn; The O'Rahilly; Peter O'Reilly (Ancient Order of Hibernians); Padraig Ó Riain (IRB); Robert Page (IRB); Padraig Pearse[525] [526] [527] [528], Joseph Plunkett; George Walsh (Ancient Order of Hibernians); Peadar White.

---

525 It has always been questioned exactly *when* Pearse joined the IRB. The most probable date is shortly *after* the foundation of the Volunteers. See Thornley. 'Patrick Pearse', *Studies*, p. 11. **526** Martin, F.X., OSA. 'McCullough, Hobson, and republican Ulster', Martin. *Leaders and Men*, p. 103: 'In December [1913], Hobson took a further decisive step – he swore Pearse into the IRB.' **527** However, see Ryan, Desmond. *The Rising*, p. 11. 'He joined the IRB in 1913, five months before the Irish Volunteers began.' **528** Pearse was also said to have been refused membership in a club in the ordinary way and was 'co-opted' into the IRB at the end of 1913. LeRoux, Louis N. *Tom Clarke and the Irish Freedom Movment*, 1936, p. 127.

Kilmainham Royal Hospital. After his execution on Thomas Street, Robert Emmet's remains were conveyed first to Newgate Prison and then back to Kilmainham Gaol, where the gaoler George Dunn was under instructions that if no one claimed the remains but they were to be buried in Bully's Acre, a nearby unofficial but popular burial place in the grounds of the Royal Hospital, Kilmainham. Some of Emmet's relatives and friends had also been arrested, including those not involved in the Rebellion, and all were too afraid to come forward. So Emmet's body was buried after some hours in Bully's Acre, 'near the right-hand corner of the burying ground, next the avenue of the Royal Hospital, close to the wall, and at no great distance from the former entrance, which is now built up'. His body was later 'allegedly' moved, and Emmet's final resting place is not now known with certainty. (See also Aungier Street and Thomas Street.)

This was the HQ of the British Military in Ireland at the time of the Rising.

Kimmage, Dublin, Larkfield Home of Count Plunkett.

The 4th Battalion, Dublin Brigade, trained and were billeted here before the Rising. Nearly all the men in the 'Kimmage Garrison' were born in, or came from England. Michael Collins and Joe Good worked here prior to the Rising.[529] There was a mill on the property where Volunteers manufactured most of the pikes, buckshot and bayonets used in the Rising.

There was a small hand press here on which it is said 'The Castle Document' was printed on 13 April 1916. This document alleged that the Castle authorities proposed to arrest many important and well-known public figures, and to raid the homes and residences of them and several other persons, including the residence of Dublin Archbishop William Walsh:

> The following precautionary measures have been sanctioned by the Irish Office on the recommendation of the General Officer Commanding the Forces in Ireland. All preparations will be made to put these measures in force immediately on receipt of an order issued from the Chief Secretary's Office, Dublin Castle, and signed by the under-secretary and the General Officer Commanding the Forces in Ireland.
>
> First, the following persons are to be placed under arrest – All members of the Sinn Féin National Council; the Central Executive Irish Sinn Féin Volunteers; General Council Irish Sinn Féin Volunteers; County Board Irish Sinn Féin Volunteers; Executive Committee National Volunteers; Coisde Gnotha Committee Gaelic League. See list (a) three and four and Supplemenatary List (a) two …
>
> … Dublin Metropolitan Police and Royal Irish Constabulary Forces in Dublin City will be confined to barracks under the direction of Competent Military Authority. An order will be issued to inhabitants of the city to remain in their houses until such time as Competent Military Authority

529 Good, Joe. Witness Statement 388.

may direct or otherwise permit; pickets chosen from units of Territorial Forces will be placed at all points marked on maps three and four. Accompanying mounted patrols will continuously visit all points and report every hour.

The following premises will be occupied by adequate forces and all necessary measures used without reference to headquarters – First, premises known as Liberty Hall, Beresford Place; number six Harcourt Street, Sinn Féin Building; number two Dawson Street, Headquarters Volunteers; number twelve D'Olier Street, Nationality Office; number twenty-five Rutland Square, Gaelic League Office; number forty-one Rutland Square, Foresters' Hall; Sinn Féin Volunteer premises in city; all National Volunteer premises in city; Trade Council premises, Capel Street; Surrey House, Leinster Road, Rathmines.

The following premises will be isolated and all communication to or from prevented – Premises known as Archbishop's House, Drumcondra; Mansion House, Dawson St; number forty Herbert Park; Larkfield, Kimmage Road; Woodtown Park, Ballyboden; Saint Enda's College, Hermitage, Rathfarnham; and in addition premises in List five (d). See Maps three and four.[530]

The general consensus today is that after Joseph Plunkett 'forged' the document he sent Rory O'Connor with it from Miss Quinn's Private Nursing Home in Mountjoy Square to Kimmage. O'Connor took it to George Plunkett and Colm Ó Lochlainn to print it.[531] However, its provenance has never been proven.

Thomas MacDonagh's son, Donagh, claimed that there really was a secret order from a file in Dublin Castle directing that 'immediately on receipt of an Order from the Chief Secretary's Office, Dublin Castle, and signed by the under-secretary and the General Officer Commanding the Forces in Ireland' all the leaders of the different separatist organizations should be arrested.[532]

This document was branded as bogus by the British authorities then and now, but Grace Gifford Plunkett stated she was present while Plunkett decoded part of it.[533 534 535 536 537 538 539 540 541 542] In addition, Eugene Smith, a telegrapher at the time in

530 Macardle. *The Irish Republic*, p. 912. **531** Ó Lochlainn, Colm. Witness Statement 751. **532** MacDonagh, Donagh. 'Plunkett and MacDonagh', in Martin, F.X., OSA, editor, *Leaders and Men*, p. 170-71. **533** Plunkett, Grace Gifford. Witness Statement 257. 'I remember the document that was published because I wrote it out myself for Joe, sitting on his bed in Larkfield House. Joe did not do it in the nursing home…It did come out from the Castle, I know who brought it out. Donagh MacDonagh was married to a girl named Smith. It was her father that brought it out.' **534** Sheehy-Skeffington, Hanna. *Irish Press*, 4 January 1937. **535** Plunkett, Geraldine. *Irish Press*, 8 January 1937. **536** O'Neill, Marie. *Grace Gifford Plunkett and Irish Freedom*, 2000, p. 34-5. **537** Ryan, Desmond. *The Rising*, p. 64-75. **538** O'Hegarty. *A History of Ireland under the Union*, p. 699-700. **539** Brennan, John. 'The Castle Document', *The Irish Times*, 28 March 1958. **540** Townsend. Op. cit., p. 125-136. **541** Foy and Barton. Op. cit., p. 34-45. **542** But see 'The "Not-So-Bogus" Castle Document', O'Dubhghaill, M., *Insurrection Fires at Eastertide*, p. 196-203.

Dublin Castle, gave Patrick J. Little a signed and witnessed statement that he recognized the document as genuine and abstracted from the Castle files.[543] [544] In Kilmainham, on the night before he was executed, Seán MacDermott swore to Msgr Patrick Browne that the Document was genuine.[545] [546] The document had several 'errors' which Joseph Plunkett was unlikely to have made. (For example listing 'number two Dawson Street' as 'Headquarters Volunteers' when by that time the Volunteer HQ had been moved to 206 Great Brunswick Street for some time. Further, in the 'original' of the document, the Archbishop's Palace was incorrectly designated as *Ara Coeli*, when that was the name of Cardinal Logue's home in Armagh. 'Jack Plunkett was immediately sent on his motor bike to the nursing home and returned with the message from his brother: "Make it Archbishop's House".')[547] [548] [549]

Alderman Thomas (Tom) Kelly read the Document at the Dublin Corporation meeting on 19 April. He was highly regarded by all parties, and thus the document was taken very seriously.

King Street South Gaiety Theatre. The manager in 1916 was Charles Hyland whose son, C. Hanchette Hyland (twenty-nine), was killed while looking out of the back door of 3 Percy Place (near Northumberland Road). The Carl Rosa Opera Company often played here. The D'Oyly Carte Opera Company opened on 24 April 1916. On Saturday night, 20 November 1920, Michael Collins went to the bar here for a further meeting after the 'final' Bloody Sunday meeting had been held. He often met people in this bar: 'It had a respectable air of legal and loyal comfort, no one would expect a Republican to pollute its atmosphere.'

King Street North (and Church Street): 'Reilly's Fort'. Held by the 1st Battalion. Jack Shouldice commanded a unit here during the Rising.[550] Patrick O'Flanagan was killed here.

Now the Tap Bar.

King Street North (See also King Street North Nos 27, 168, 170, 172, 174, 177, following, and 27 Little Britain Street, below.): Atrocities were committed here by the South Staffordshire Regiment (South Staffs), under the command of Lt Col. Henry Taylor, on Saturday, 29 April 1916.[551] Taylor refused to attend the inquest that followed the Rising. Five South Staffs officers were wounded and 42 men killed, mostly in this street. Perhaps the actions of the British troops can be traced

543 Little, P.J. 'A 1916 Document', *Capuchin Annual*, 1942. **544** Smith, Eugene. Witness Statement 334. **545** Martin, F.X., OSA. 1916-Myth, Fact, and Mystery, *Studia Hibernica*, 1967, p. 119-121. **546** Browne, Msgr Patrick. Witness Statement 729. **547** Plunkett, John (Jack). Witness Statements 488, 865. **548** Ryan, Desmond. *The Rising*, p. 73. **549** 'It [the Document] was not (as has usually been said) a forgery, but it was "sexed up" (by Joseph Plunkett) to make the plans appear imminent, to try to get MacNeill to support immediate action'. Townshend, Charles. 'Making Sense of Easter 1916', *History Ireland*, Vol. XIV, No. 2, March/April 2006. **550** Shouldice, Jack (John F.) Witness Statement 162. **551** On 1 January 2001, the British War Office in London released papers detailing the atrocities. *WO 141.21 and WO 141.27*, Public Records Office, Kew, London.

to Gen. William Lowe's orders which included the following: 'No hesitation should be shown in dealing with these rebels. By their action they had placed themselves outside the law. They must not be made prisoners.'[552]

In his written statement to the inquest, Lt Col. Taylor wrote:

> The operations in the portion of King St between Linenhall St and Church St were conducted under circumstances of the greatest difficulty and danger for the troops engaged, who were subject to severe fire, not only from behind several rebel barricades…but from practically every house in that portion of King St and other buildings overlooking it.
>
> Strong evidence of these difficulties and dangers is afforded by the fact that from 10 am on the 28th of April until 2 pm on the 29th to force their way along King St from Linenhall St to Church St, a distance of some 150 yards only; and that the casualties sustained by the regiment (the great majority of which occurred at this spot) included five officers (including two Captains) wounded, eleven NCOs and men killed and twenty-eight wounded.
>
> I am satisfied that during these operations the troops under my command showed great moderation and restraint under exceptionally difficult and trying circumstances.

The Court refused to accept Taylor's statement.[553]

Sir Edward Troup, the Investigating Law Officer of the Home Office told Prime Minister Herbert Asquith in regard to one of these incidents that he found: 'The source of the mischief was the military order to take no prisoners. This in itself may have been justifiable, but it should have been made clear that it did not mean that an unarmed rebel might be shot after he had been taken prisoner … I have no doubt that if the evidence were published, he [Sgt Flood, see No 177 below] should be tried for murder.' In his advice to Asquith, he admitted that if the events had occurred in England, 'the right course would be to refer the cases to the DPP [Director of Public Prosecutions]'.[554]

The verdict of the coroner, Dr Louis A. Byrne, held:

> We find the said Patrick Bealen [see No 177 below] died from shock and haemorrhage, resulting from bullet wounds inflicted by a soldier, or soldiers, in whose custody he was, an unarmed and inoffensive prisoner. We consider that the explanation given by the military authorities is very unsatisfactory, and we believe that if the military authorities had any inclination they could produce the officer in charge.[555]

552 *Irish Catholic*, 20 May 1916. **553** Coogan. *1916: The Easter Rising*, p. 147. **554** Ibid, p. 148. **555** *The Irish Times*, 1 January 2001.

On 18 May, Gen. Sir John Maxwell issued the following statement:

> Possibly unfortunate incidents, which we should regret now, may have occurred …. it is even possible that under the horrors of this particular attack some of them "saw red". That is the inevitable consequence of a rebellion of this kind. It was allowed to come into being among these people, and could not be suppressed by velvet-glove methods where our troops were so desperately opposed and attacked.[556]

He added in a letter to the *Daily Mail*: 'A revolt of this kind could not be suppressed with velvet-glove methods.'[557]

27 King Street North A large rebel barricade was first thrown across the street here.

27 King Street North Louth Dairy, kept by Mrs Lawless. It was here that Peadar Lawless (twenty-one), James McCartney (American citizen, thirty-six), James Finnegan Jr (forty) and Patrick Hoey (twenty-five) were murdered by the South Staffs.

38 King Street North Private entrance of Monks' bakery. Three Volunteers entered by this entrance to take over the office in the raid in which Kevin Barry was captured. (See also Church Street Upper.)

168 King Street North Mrs Hickey, shopkeeper, was in her shop when men were taken to from here to 170 North King Street and murdered. Kate Kelly, who did housework for the Hickeys, was a most colourful and damning witness at the inquest.[558]

170 King Street North Peter Connolly (thirty-nine, lived at 164 North King Street, a member of Redmond's Volunteers but did not participate in the Rising), Thomas (thirty-eight, the father) and Christopher Hickey (sixteen, the son) were murdered here by the South Staffs. They were removed from Hickey's victualler shop at 168 North King Street.

172 King Street North Michael Hughes (thirty-six) (Mick and Sally Hughes owned this house), and John Walsh (fifty-six) were murdered here by the South Staffs.

174 King Street North Michael Noonan (thirty-four), who owned a newsagency and tobacconist shop here, and George Ennis (fifty-one) were murdered here by the South Staffs.

Anne Fennel was a resident here and a witness.

177 King Street North A 'licensed public house' owned by Mrs Mary O'Rourke. Patrick Bealen (thirty) and James Healy (forty-four, labourer at Jameson's Distillery) were murdered here by South Staffs Sgt Flood and Cpl Bullock who were spirited away to England prior to the 'line-up' of the South Staffs for ID purposes.

On 20 May 1916, the *Irish Catholic* reported and opined:

556 Caulfield. Op. cit., p. 293. **557** *Daily Mail*, 20 May 1916. **558** Reynolds, John J. *A Fragment of 1916 History*, 1919, p. 11-12.

A Dublin Coroner's jury on Tuesday found that Patrick Bealen and James Healy, whose bodies were found buried in a cellar in North King Street, died from the result of bullet wounds inflicted by the military, in whose custody they were unarmed and unoffending prisoners. They considered the explanation given by the military authorities as very unsatisfactory and expressed the opinion that the latter could produce the officer in charge… Little as we approve the rebellion, we are not going to remain silent when unoffending fellow citizens are killed in cold blood and the responsible local military chiefs take no adequate steps to secure investigation.[559]

King's Inns Quay (between Richmond and Whitworth Bridges): The Four Courts. These were: Exchequer (presided over by the Chief Baron of the Exchequer); Chancellory (presided over by the Lord Chancellor); King's Bench (presided over by a Chief Justice); Common Pleas (presided over by a Chief Justice). The site was the Priory of the Frairs Preachers, a monastery confiscated after the proclamation of Henry VIII as King of Ireland and Head of the Church.

The King's Inns is the governing body of Irish barristers. The full title is The Benchers of the Honourable Society of the King's Inns.

Joseph McGuinness led the garrison that occupied the Four Courts during the Rising. They entered through the Chancellory gate. Much of the garrison was composed of the 'football teams' that had tried to blow up the Magazine Fort in Phoenix Park. Fianna members of the garrison included: Paddy Daly, Gerry Holohan, Patrick (Paddy) Holohan, L. Marie and Herbert (Barney) Mellows.

On 13 April 1922 the buildings were occupied by IRA/Republican troops, led by Rory O'Connor, although Joe McKelvey was chief of staff. Liam Mellowes, Seán Moylan and Ernie O'Malley were also present. Upon taking their positions, they issued this proclamation:

> Fellow citizens of the Irish Republic. The fateful hour has come. At the direction of the hereditary enemy our rightful cause is being treacherously assailed by recreant Irishmen. Gallant soldiers of the Irish Republic stand rigorously firm in its defence. The sacred spirits of the Illustrious Dead are with us in this great struggle. 'Death Before Dishonour'. We especially appeal to our former comrades of the Irish Republic to return to that allegiance and thus guard the Nation's honour.

Éamon de Valera quickly described the members of the Four Courts garrison as the 'best and bravest of our nation' and joined the IRA/Republicans as an unranked soldier after the bombardment of the Four Courts.

At 3.40 on the morning of 28 June 1922, the occupying force was given an ultimatum to surrender; firing commenced twenty minutes later. Joe Considine, Seán Cusack and Thomas Wall were killed in the Four Courts bombardment. One hundred prisoners were taken sent to Mountjoy Prison, among them Rory O'Connor, Liam Mellowes, Joe McKelvey and Dick Barrett. These four were executed in Mountjoy Prison on 8 December 1922 in reprisal for the shooting death of Seán Hales on 7 December (see North Circular Road/Mountjoy Prison; Kildare Street/ Leinster House). Ernie O'Malley was among a group who escaped on the way to Mountjoy.

32 King's Inn Street Home of Mrs O'Toole, probably a friend of a soldier to whom Tom Clarke gave a letter for Kathleen while he was in Kilmainham Gaol.

Kingsbridge Station (now Seán Heuston Station): Éamon (Ned) Broy's relation, Pat Treacy, worked here and was a major contact between Broy and Michael Collins. Treacy also collected messages from the trainmen who passed through the Station and forwarded them to Collins.

26 Landerdale Terrace Home of Tom Cullen before the Rising. Along with Liam Tobin, he became a leader of Michael Collins' Department of Intelligence.

10 Langrishe Place HQ of Irish National Foresters.

Lansdowne Road Home of William T. Cosgrave.

29 Lawson Terrace, Sandycove Road Roger Casement's birthplace on 1 September 1864.

Leeson Lane (on St Stephen's Green): St Vincent's Hospital (located in St Stephen's Green on Leeson Lane during the War of Independence and the Civil War. The hospital was established in St Stephen's Green in 1834 and was relocated to its present site in Elm Park in 1970.) Harry Boland died in St Vincent's and his body was removed to the Church of Our Lady of Mount Carmel in Whitefriar Street. Michael Collins was 'laid out' in the mortuary chapel before his body was removed to the Pro-Cathedral for burial. Oliver St John Gogarty and Desmond Fitzgerald supervised Collins' embalming. Gogarty sent Seán Kavanagh for sculptor Albert Power to fashion Michael Collins' death mask. Dr Richard Tobin was a surgeon in St Vincent's at the time.

Leeson Park Litton Hall; auxiliary hospital during the Rising.

Leeson Street Home of the MacGilligan family. IRA/Volunteers and IRA/Republicans often stayed here. Ernie O'Malley stayed here and often used the house for meetings during the War of Independence and the Civil War.

Leeson Street Home of Ken and Kay Brady. Ernie O'Malley often used the house for meetings during the War of Independence and the Civil War.

35 Leeson Street Lower Irish Jesuit Headquarters. The archives contain original material of the Jesuit Generalate dating back to 1540. Office of *Studies, the Irish Jesuit Quarterly Review.*

89–90 Leeson Street Lower Catholic University School, run by the Marist Community. Fr Watters was the president. He was killed at the Clanwilliam House fighting on Northumberland Road during the Rising.

96 Leeson Street Lower St Vincent's Private Hospital, run by the Sisters of Mercy.

(This was a private hospital, not to be confused with the St Vincent's Hospital in Leeson Lane.) Oliver St John Gogarty admitted Arthur Griffith here and Griffith died on 12 August 1922. Of Griffith, P.S. O'Hegarty wrote: 'He forced England to take her right hand from Ireland's throat and her left hand out of Ireland's pocket.'[560] William Cosgrave said: 'Though he was only 51, the worries and anxieties of the past two years had taken a terrible toll on him. The hard bargaining with the British and all the travelling back and forth during the Treaty negotiations had broken his health. Finally the eruption of the Civil War was a blow from which he never recovered.'[561] At the graveside, Michael Collins said 'In memory of Arthur Griffith let us resolve now to give fresh play to the impulse of unity, to join together one and all in continuing his constructive work, in building up the country which he loved.'[562]

38 Leeson Street Upper Home of The O'Rahilly and his family between 1909 and 1912.

97 Leeson Street Upper Early home of Arthur Griffith.

25 Leinster Road, **Rathmines** Susan Mitchell moved here late in 1917 and lived here until December 1920.

49B Leinster Road, **Rathmines** Surrey House; home of Countess Markievicz. She moved into the house in 1912. James Larkin hid here after he was arrested on 28 August 1913 and before he addressed the crowd from the Imperial Hotel on Sackville Street on 31 August. James Connolly and his family lived here between 1913 and 1916. Prior to the Rising it was a great meeting and gathering place for nationalists.

It was Connolly and Markievicz's office for *The Spark* and the *Workers' Republic,* which were also printed here. (See also 70 Eccles Street.) In the 22 January 1916 issue of the *Workers' Republic* the following appeared under the heading 'What is Our Programme?':

> Mark well, then, our programme. While the war lasts and Ireland is still a subject nation we shall continue to urge her to fight for her freedom. We shall continue, in season and out of season, to teach that 'the far-flung battle line' of England is weakest at the point closest to its heart; that Ireland is in a position of tactical advantage; that a defeat of England in India, Egypt, the Balkans, or Flanders would not be so dangerous to the British Empire as any conflict of armed forces in Ireland; that the time for Ireland's battle is NOW, the place for Ireland's battle is HERE; that a strong man may deal lusty blows with his fists against a host of surrounding foes, and conquer, but will succumb if a child sticks a pin in his heart ... We are neither rash nor cowardly. We know our opportunity when we see it, and we know when it is gone.

560 O'Hegarty. *The Victory of Sinn Féin*, p. 94-95. **561** Mackay. Op. cit., p. 275. **562** *The Irish Times*, 15 August 1922.

This was published the day after Connolly's return from his 'kidnapping' but was undoubtedly written before it. (See also Dolphin's Barn.)

143 Leinster Road, Rathmines Laurence Ginnell's home after 1917. Ginnell was the founder of the Land Distribution Society in Co. Westmeath, worked as a land agitator, was elected an MP and was a former Redmonite who broke with the Irish Parliamentary Party. After 1914, he denounced the Party's pro-war stance in the British Parliament and condemned those who cheered the Rising executions in Parliament as 'Huns'. He resigned his seat in 1917, joined Thomas Dillon's Irish Nation League that merged with Sinn Féin in 1917, and then became treasurer of Sinn Féin. Later Ginnell spent two and a half years in jail and while there wrote the book *The Brehon Laws*. Appointed Sinn Féin director of publicity in April 1919, he had to resign in June because of imprisonment and his subsequent illness. The Dáil made him Special Envoy to South American Republics. He opposed the Treaty, and challenged the credentials of the Third Dáil, but was taken bodily from the Dáil.

26 Lennox Street Harry Boland's family moved here in 1907.

Liffey Street O'Neills Pub; James Connolly was slightly wounded in the arm on returning from observing positions here on Thursday morning of the Rising.

30 Liffey Street Upper The *Gaelic Press* was printed here as well as all kinds of 'republican' publications and posters during the period. The proprietor was Joseph Stanley who was in the GPO in the Rising and was the printer in charge of the *Irish War News* bulletins issued from there. (See also Halston Street, and GPO [Appendix V].)

Lincoln Place (near Trinity College): On Bloody Sunday, Black and Tans shot seven civilians in the back here, and two died.

Lincoln Place Office of the *Irish Homestead*, founded by Horace Plunkett in 1894 as the official publication of his Irish Agricultural Organization Society. Harry Norman succeeded him as editor, followed by George Russell (Æ) in 1905. Susan Mitchell began work here as a sub-editor in 1899. It moved to Merrion Square in 1908.

Lincoln Place United Arts Club; founded in 1907 by Count Casimir Markievicz, Countess Markievicz and Ellen Duncan. Ms Duncan, curator of the Municipal Gallery, was the prime mover in establishing a non-sectarian, non-political social club for the cultivation and study of the arts.

Over the years, the Club circle included William Butler Yeats, J.B. (Jack) Yeats, Lady Gregory, William Orpen, Hugh Lane, Frank Cruise O'Brien, Thomas Bodkin, Susan Mitchell, Dermot O'Brien, Lennox Robinson, Oliver St John Gogarty, Joseph Plunkett, Mary Colum, Padraic Colum, James Stephens, Seámus O'Sullivan, Erskine Childers, Jim Duncan, Robert Barton, Darrell Figgis and Katherine Tynan Hinkson. In 1910, the Club moved to larger premises at 44 St Stephen's Green, and subsequently to its present location at 3 Fitzwilliam Street Upper.

Lindsay Road, Glasnevin Cuilleannach, home of Maureen MacDonagh O'Mahoney, member of the Provisional Committee of Cumann na mBan and Hon. Treasurer.

Linenhall Street Linen Hall; erected in 1728. Once the distribution centre for Irish linen before that trade moved to Belfast. A high protective wall surrounded the building when it eventually became a British military barracks, opened in 1873. During the Rising it was attacked by Volunteers of the 1st Battalion under the command of Cpt. Denis O'Callaghan and Gerry Holohan. The building was burned in the Rising and closed in 1928.

Linenhall Street Trueform Shoe Shop; looters during the Rising started fires here and the building was burned down.

6–8 Lisburn Street Linenhall Barracks. Held by forty members of the British Army Pay Corps, it was taken by Volunteers late on Wednesday of the Rising. The Volunteers set it alight and, though they subsequently tried to control the fire, it burned until Friday.

4 Little Britain Street Arthur Griffith's family moved here from his birthplace at 4 Dominick Street.

27 Little Britain Street During the Rising, soldiers of the South Staffs killed James Moore at his front door here. The inquiry by Sir Edward Troup found that 'he was probably a perfectly innocent person'.[563] (See also King Street North.)

Lombard Street Peter Lanigan's timber yard. On St Patrick's Day 1858, James Stephens established the Irish *Revolutionary* Brotherhood, but the name was soon changed to the Irish *Republican* Brotherhood (See also Appendix IV).

23 Longwood Avenue Home of Alderman Thomas Kelly in the early 1900s. He was a former independent nationalist member of the Dublin Corporation who became a founding member of Sinn Féin. In 1916 he was appointed as a member of the abortive 'Provisional Civilian Administration' by/under the IRB Military Council, along with Arthur Griffith, William O'Brien, Seán O'Kelly, and Hanna Sheehy-Skeffington. A member of the first three Dáils, he was elected Lord Mayor of Dublin in January 1920 (Dublin's only Sinn Féin Lord Mayor), but had to resign after three months due to illness caused by internment. (See also under Belgrave Road, Rathmines and Kimmage, County Dublin, Larkfield, 'The Castle Document'.)

23 Longwood Avenue Early home of Francis and Hanna Sheehy-Skeffington, as tenants of Thomas Kelly.

29 Longwood Avenue Home of James Grace who fought at 25 Northumberland Road in the Rising and survived.

40 Longwood Avenue Early home of Michael Hayes. Later he was minister for education in the Second Dáil; he became the first Ceann Comhairle of the post-Treaty Dáil and, later, a Senator. He was professor of Irish at UCD.

Lord Edward Street British 'Irish' Department of Labour; John Chartres, transferred here in 1920. He was an advisor to the Irish delegates, and particularly to Michael Collins, during the Treaty negotiations in London in 1921.

South Lotts Road, Ringsend Home of James Connolly and his family on his return to Ireland from the US in 1910.[564] He moved to Belfast before returning to Dublin in 1913, and then he lived at Countess Markievicz's home on Leinster Road, Rathmines.

---

563 Coogan. *1916: The Easter Rising*, p. 148. **564** See Irish Census of 1911.

39 Mabbott Street Birthplace of William Rooney in 1873. A great friend and advisor to Arthur Griffith, Rooney was a leader in the revival of the Irish language. He was one of the founders of the Celtic Literary Society, and often published in Griffith's *United Irishman*. He died in May 1901, aged twenty-eight.

Malahide Road O'Brien Institute. A school maintained by the Christian Brothers for the education of orphans or children of families in dire straits, attended by Gerald Boland.

167 Mangerton Road Home of Lily Mernin.[565]

24 Manor Place Home of (John) Joseph Byrne, who fought under Seán Heuston at the Mendicity Institution during the Rising. He worked as a messenger for the Great Southern & Western Railway. He was sentenced to three years' penal servitude after the Rising.[566]

3 Marino Crescent, Clontarf Home of Frank Shouldice, who was arrested here in the 'German Plot' arrests the night of 17-18 May 1918.

15 Marino Crescent, Clontarf Birthplace of Abraham (Bram) Stoker on 8 November 1847. He was the author of *Dracula*, though it was written after he left Dublin. The Boland family moved here about 1910. IRA/Volunteers from the country, including Seán Treacy, often stayed here.

Marlborough Road, Donnybrook Home of the James Pearse family in 1904.

Marlborough Street (at corner of Findlater Place): St Thomas' Church of Ireland, destroyed in 1922 during the Civil War.

Marlborough Street (at corner of Cathedral Street): Pro-Cathedral (St Mary's). Dublin's Catholic Cathedral, begun in 1815 and opened in 1825. The portico is a copy of the Temple of Theseus in Athens. The three statues on it are Mary the Mother of God in the centre, with the two diocesan patrons, St Kevin and St Laurence O'Toole, on either side. A British sharpshooter was positioned in the bell tower during the Rising. Fr O'Doherty, a priest here, was shot dead when he went to talk to the rebels, fully vested and with a cross in his hand. Seán Treacy was laid out here before being removed to Soloheadbeg for burial. Michael Collins sometimes served Mass here during the War of Independence years. Peadar Clancy, Dick McKee, Arthur Griffith and Collins were buried from here.

Marlborough Street Rabbiatti's Bar, a British intelligence officers' hangout. Tom Cullen and Frank Thornton, who drank here in order to pick up information, one day were asked by British spies how Cullen and Thornton learned the Irish brogue: 'we've been here for the last twelve months and can't get it'.[567]

Marlborough Street A Dublin United Tramways Co. office, owned by William Martin Murphy.

Marlborough Street Home of Paul Moore. The IRA/Volunteers met here during the War of Independence.

---

565 Mernin, Lily. Witness Statement 441. 566 Byrne, Joseph. Witness Statement 461. 567 Thornton, Frank. Witness Statement 510.

29 Marlborough Street Central Model School. George Bernard Shaw attended here. Brigid Lyons was medical officer here during Civil War fighting in July 1922.[568]

14–21 Marrowbone Lane Guinness buildings; James (Seámus) Murphy's HQ during the Rising; he put hats and jackets on brush handles and put them in windows to 'increase' the size of his 'garrison'.[569]

43–45 Marrowbone Lane Marrowbone Lane Distillery, usually known as Jameson's Distillery.

8 Mary Street Thomas Fallon & Co.; sold Volunteer uniforms, headdress, badges, etc. Haversacks cost 10d or 1s.6d; great coats were 25s; green Cronje hats (named after the Boer leader Gen. Peter A. 'Piet' Cronje) were 1s.8d; infantry swords in brown leather scabbards were five guineas.

47 Mary Street Todd, Burns & Co., tailors; Harry Boland worked here before the Rising.

Maunder's Terrace, **Ranalagh** Birthplace of Victor Herbert on 1 February 1859. He made a musical arrangement of 'A Soldier's Song' in New York and had the royalties forwarded to Peadar Kearney in Dublin.

78 Meath Street James (Jim) Larkin, fancy baker. No relation to the labour leader although in 1913 he advertised himself as 'The Worker's Baker'.

7 Mecklenburgh Street Home of James Gandon when he designed The Custom House.

101 Mecklenburgh Street Home of Paddy Heaney, Peadar's Kearney's childhood pal who collaborated with him in writing the music to 'A Soldier's Song'. (See also Appendix IV.)

Mercer Street Mercer's Hospital. The street and hospital were named after Mary Mercer who founded the hospital for the poor in 1734. The hospital was built on the site of the ancient St Stephen's Church and the even older leper hospital. Sixteen dead civilians and 278 injured non-combatants as well as four dead and five wounded soldiers were treated here during the Rising.

Merchant's Quay (opposite the Four Courts across the Liffey): Church of the Immaculate Conception; stands on the site where the Franciscan Friars ministered to the people since penal times. Popularly known as 'Adam and Eve's Church' because in penal times the congregation entered the Friar's house through a pub of that name.

Merrion Avenue 'South Hill'; first Dublin home of the Arthur Hamilton Norway family; he was the secretary of the GPO in 1916; his wife and son, Nevile, were in Dublin (another son, Fred, died near Armentieres). The family later moved to the Royal Hibernian Hotel on Dawson Street. (Nevile Shute Norway became known as Nevile Shute, the novelist.)

Merrion Road, Ballsbridge Pembroke Town Hall, Ballsbridge; C.P. O'Neill was the chairman of the Urban Council during the Rising; J.C. Manly was Town Clerk. The Town Hall was commandeered by the 177th Infantry Brigade (The Lincolnshire Regiment) of the 59th (North Midland) Division after the Rising.

---

568 Thornton, Brigid Lyons. Witness Statement 259. **569** Murphy, Seámus. Witness Statement 1756.

Merrion Road, Ballsbridge Royal Dublin Society. The first enrolment of An Garda Síochána (The Civic Guard) took place here on 21 February 1922; the first commandant was Michael Staines, former Quartermaster of the Dublin Brigade, IRA, and TD for Dublin (St Michans, 1918–21, North West, 1921–23).[570] Staines soon retired and was succeeded by Eoin O'Duffy.

9 Merrion Road, Sandymount Home of Maire Comerford. Born in Co. Wicklow in 1892, she was in Dublin during the Rising; she volunteered to aid Countess Markievicz in St Stephen's Green, but was turned away and carried dispatches for the GPO garrison. Later she worked for the Countess. She joined Cumann na mBan in 1918 and was an extremely valuable Michael Collins courier and source.

She was active in the Civil War fighting in Dublin, and carried dispatches between the Four Courts and O'Connell Street. The most 'energetic' of Cumann na mBan members in the Civil War, she was passionately republican. She was shot in the leg while imprisoned in Mountjoy Prison, but escaped. She was subsequently imprisoned in the North Dublin Union and Kilmainham after recapture, where she endured an hunger strike. She remained an avid republican her entire life – in 1976, aged eighty-three, she was arrested for participation in a banned march to commemorate the Rising. She remained a member of what was generally seen as a committed group of republicans that would not compromise in terms of everyday politics on constitutional matters. She never married and died in 1982.

Merrion Square Provisional Government's Departmental Offices during the War of Independence.

1 Merrion Square Home of Dr William Wilde; it was the boyhood home of his son, the playwright and wit Oscar Fingal O'Flahertie Wills Wilde.

5 Merrion Square Home of Dr Robert Farnan, a prominent gynecologist. Éamon de Valera stayed here on 26 March 1919 – his first night home from England after his escape from Lincoln Gaol on 3 February 1919 – and in December 1920 on his return from the US.

Michael Collins met Archbishop Patrick Joseph Clune of Perth, Western Australia, here on 7 December 1920, at Prime Minister David Lloyd George's behest, to discuss peace feelers.[571] Archbishop Clune, born on 6 January 1864 in Ruan, Co. Clare, was first asked to mediate on behalf of his native land by the Hon. Lord Morris, T.P. O'Connor MP and Joe Devlin MP at a luncheon in London on 30 November. That night there were severe Black and Tan reprisals at Lahinch, Co. Clare, with several people killed and many homes burned. Prime Minister Lloyd George condemned all reprisals, and asked the archbishop to go to Dublin, interview the Sinn Féin leaders, arrange a temporary truce, and prepare an atmosphere for negotiations. These negotiations were opposed by Gen. Neville Macready, but favoured by most of the British Cabinet and government.

However, Lloyd George could not guarantee the safety of the archbishop, and

---

570 Staines, Michael. Witness Statement 284. **571** McMahon, Revd J.T. Witness Statement 362.

would not consent to a safe conduct for the Sinn Féin leaders to meet the arch-bishop. In order to remain incognito, Archbishop Clune travelled to Ireland on the mailboat as 'Revd Dr Walsh'. On arrival in Dublin on 6 December, he first stayed at All Hallows College, Drumcondra. On 7 December, accompanied by Dr Michael Fogarty, bishop of Killaloe, he was driven here to meet Collins.[572] (Farnan was attending the wives of two Auxies at the time, and to this he attributed the fact that his house was never raided or searched.) Collins was 'on the run' but Arthur Griffith was in Mountjoy Prison at this time, and on 8 December, Dr Fogarty and Archbishop Clune met with Alfred W. Cope, the assistant under-secretary for Ireland, at Mountjoy, and then with Griffith. Griffith enthusiastically welcomed a truce. Then they met with Eoin MacNeill who was not so enthusiastic, but accepted it. The idea was presented to Michael Staines. Cope was told to present a draft of a truce to Dublin Castle, but this received a hostile reception by Sir Hamar Greenwood and the British Military.

Archbishop Clune returned to London and met Lloyd George on 10 December, had another meeting with him on 11 December, and returned to Dublin that night. Authorities in Dublin Castle agreed to meet with the Dáil, but Collins and Richard Mulcahy could not attend. Moreover, the IRA/Volunteers would have to surrender all their arms, and the Dáil could not meet publicly. Archbishop Clune returned to London on 18 December, and though meetings continued until 28 December, the negotiations were at an end. (See also St Stephen's Green, [north].) Archbishop Clune was an uncle of Conor Clune, who had just been tortured and killed on Bloody Sunday.

On 6 September 1922, Msgr Ryan from San Francisco arranged a meeting here between Éamon de Valera and Richard Mulcahy. Previously the Free State Cabinet had decided that further talks regarding the Civil War were futile, but Mulcahy, as leader of the army and minister for defence, agreed to meet and arranged a safe conduct for de Valera. Mulcahy felt that two things were imperative: one, that somebody should be allowed to 'work' the Treaty and, two, that if there was an Army in Ireland it should be subject to the Dáil. De Valera then stated: 'Some men are led by faith and some men by reason, but as long as there are men like Rory O'Connor taking the stand that he is taking, I am a humble soldier following after them.'[573] As a result, Mulcahy decided on the drastic course of reprisal executions.[574] (See also North Circular Road/Mountjoy Prison.)

14 Merrion Square HQ of the St John's Ambulance Brigade of Dublin.

The training and volunteer work of the St John's Ambulance Brigade stems from the Order of St John, which had its beginnings in an eleventh-century Jerusalem hospital built to care for pilgrims. The first division in Ireland was formed in 1903 at the Guinness Brewery by Dr (later Sir) John Lumsden. In his

---

572 Fogarty, Most Revd Dr Michael. Witness Statement 271. 573 Valiulis, Maryann. *General Richard Mulcahy*, 1992, p. 175-6. 574 Coogan and Morrison. Op. cit., p. 50.

post as Medical Officer for Guinness, Dr Lumsden was asked to provide first-aid classes for employees at the Brewery. The classes became so popular that they later became the first registered division of the St John's Ambulance Brigade of Ireland, and it became known as St James Gate division. In 1905 the City of Dublin Division was formed, the first unit open to the public for membership; in 1909, women were allowed to join the ranks with the formation of the first nursing division.

The Brigade was involved with many major events in Irish history, including treating casualties from the clashes during the Lockout of 1913. In 1914 many members served in World War I providing medical aid for those injured in combat. However, the Brigade became most prominent in Dublin during the Rising when it treated casualties on both sides and fed and cared for evacuees.

33 Merrion Square Home of Sir Thomas Myles; former president of the Royal College of Surgeons in Ireland. He was a lifelong nationalist, and took part in the running of guns to Ireland, picking up six hundred guns from Conor O'Brien's *Kelpie*, which delivered them from Germany to the Welsh coast, and sailed them in his vessel, *Chotah*, to Kilcoole, Co. Wicklow on 1 August 1914. James Creed Meredith, who became president of the Dáil/Republican Supreme Court, helped him. Myles disapproved of the Rising, which he considered rash. (See also Bachelor's Walk, Howth, Kilcoole [Appendix I] and 90 St Stephens Green [south].)

39 Merrion Square Home of Dr (Sir) Robert Henry Woods. Oliver St John Gogarty replaced him as the ENT specialist at the Richmond Hospital; Woods went to nearby Sir Patrick Dun's.

40 Merrion Square War Hospital Shipping Department, converted to an auxiliary hospital during the Rising.

58 Merrion Square Home of Daniel O'Connell (it was No. 30 in his time).

68 Merrion Square CID moved here from Oriel House on Westland Row in February 1923.

80 Merrion Square Edward Carson's home as he advanced as a solicitor; he moved here from Herbert Place. He was the first Irish QC to 'take silk' in England. He studied law at TCD and became assistant to the chief secretary of Ireland, Arthur Balfour, who appointed him Ireland's Solicitor General in 1892. He became an MP for Dublin University, and was the prosecutor in the famous Oscar Wilde trial. He became the leader of the Irish Unionist Party, including, as its cutting edge, the mass Ulster resistance to the third Home Rule Bill.

Of him, Piaras Béaslaí wrote:

> He, more than any other man, is responsible for the events which have created the Irish Free State. He defied law, appealed to force; he preached the doctrines which led to the founding of the Volunteers – and the amazed Irish people, with their pathetic faith in the infallibility of their Party leaders, and the honesty of the British Government, saw that Government recoil before the bluff of the 'Ulster Volunteers'. They found

threats of physical resistance by a minority accepted as a successful argument against justice to a majority. They found that the rifles and parading of the 'Ulster Volunteers' were jeopardising the long-expected Home Rule Act. Here was the opportunity of the IRB.[575]

(See also Craigavon and Curragh [Appendix I].)

82 Merrion Square Home of William Butler Yeats.

84 Merrion Square Became known as Plunkett House; Sir Horace Plunkett owned the building and had his office here as well. It was the second office of *The Irish Homestead*, in 1908. George Russell (Æ) was editor and Susan Mitchell was his assistant. Also the office of *The Irish Statesman*, founded by Plunkett in June 1919. The first editor was Warre B. Wells, who wrote *A History of the Irish Rebellion of 1916* with N. Marlowe (1916). *The Irish Statesman* was the organ of the Irish Dominion League, dedicated to dominion status, with an independent government, avoiding partition. Writers included George Birmingham, Erskine Childers, Stephen Gwynn, Susan Mitchell, Cruise O'Brien, George O'Brien, George Russell (Æ) and George Bernard Shaw. In 1923 it was revived and George Russell became the editor.

85 Merrion Square First HQ of the Free State Army Medical Services, under the command of Maj. Gen. (Dr) Maurice Hayes. In September 1922, Dr Brigid Lyons went to work here as a 1Lt earning 8 shillings per day.[576] Following Dr Hayes as directors were Col. Tom O'Higgins and Frank Morrin.

24 Upper Merrion Street Mornington House; birthplace of Arthur Wellesley, Duke of Wellington on 1 May 1769. He disclaimed his Irish heritage and remarked, 'Just because one is born in a stable, one doesn't have to be a horse.' Daniel O'Connell's riposte: 'One doesn't have to be an ass, either.'

Merrion View Avenue Home of Éamon de Valera after his time in Blackrock College.

77 Mespil Road Mrs Julia O'Donovan's dairy; The Pembroke Creamery. She was the aunt of Gearóid O' Sullivan. Michael Collins often used her home here and in Rathgar as shelters, particularly for those coming from Cork. Collins also used her accounts to 'hide' Dáil Loan funds.[577]

Military Road, Ballybrack Rose Lawn; home of Michael Davitt. Born in 1846, he lost his right arm in a cotton mill accident when he was eleven. He wrote: 'As long as I have tongue to speak, or head to plan, or hand to dare for Ireland, Irish land-lordism and English misgovernment in Ireland shall find me a sleepless and incessant opponent.' He joined the IRB in 1865, and was one of its leaders thereafter.

In 1882 Davitt was elected for Co. Meath but was disqualified because he was in prison. Upon his release later in 1882 he travelled to the United States with William Redmond to collect funds for the Land League, then campaigned for land national-ization and an alliance between the British working class, Irish labourers and tenant

575 Béaslaí, Piaras. *Michael Collins and the Making of a New Ireland*, 1926. **576** Thornton, Cmdt. Brigid Lyons. 'Women and the Army', *An Cosantoir*, November 1975. **577** O'Donovan, Julia. Witness Statement 475.

farmers. This alienated Parnell and even many of the tenants. Davitt was subsequently elected MP for North Meath in 1892, North-East Cork in 1893 and for South Mayo in 1895. Davitt's unceasing efforts were instrumental to future Land Acts.

Davitt died in Elphis Hospital, Dublin, on 30 May 1906, aged sixty, from septic poisoning. The fact that the Lord Lieutenant of Ireland attended the funeral was a public indication of the dramatic political journey this former Fenian prisoner had taken. A public funeral was not planned, and hence Davitt's body was brought quietly to the Carmelite Friary, Clarendon Street. However, the next day over 20,000 people filed past his coffin.

11 Molesworth Street *The Irish Bulletin*; Desmond Fitzgerald was the editor, succeeded by Erskine Childers. Piaras Béaslaí, a Dublin journalist, acted as liaison with IRA/Volunteer HQ.

An 'underground newspaper', it was the biggest newspaper bane to the British. The office, disguised as an Insurance Society, shared the building with the 'Church of Ireland Widows and Orphans Society'. Its journalists included Robert Brennan, Erskine Childers, Desmond Fitzgerald and Frank Gallagher (Gallagher wrote *The Four Glorious Years* under the pseudonym of David Hogan). Anna Fitzsimmons ('Miss Fitz') Kelly was the secretary, and the staff included Seámus Heaney, Seámus Hynes (messenger), Kathleen McGilligan, Kathleen McKenna[578], Honor Murphy, Sheila Murphy, and Michael Nunan. It was published daily (except on Sundays and Bank Holidays) from 11 November 1919 until the Truce.[579]

On 19 June 1920, it reported the words of Lt Col. Gerald Brice Ferguson Smyth DSO, King's Own Scottish Borderers, Divisional Commander for Munster, who addressed RIC members at their barracks in Listowel:

> Well, Men, I have something to tell you. Something I am sure you would not want your wives to hear. Sinn Féin has had all the sport up to the present, and we are going to have the sport now. The police have done splendid work, considering the odds against them. The police are not in sufficient strength to do anything but hold their barracks. This is not enough, for as long as we remain on the defensive, so long will Sinn Féin have the whip hand. We must take the offensive and beat Sinn Féin with its own tactics. Martial law, applying to all Ireland, is coming into operation shortly, and our scheme of amalgamation must be complete by June 21st. If a police barracks is burned or if the barracks already occupied is not suitable, then the best house in the locality is to be commandeered, the occupants thrown into the gutter. Let them die there, the more the better. Police and military will patrol the country at least five nights a week. They are not to confine themselves to the main roads, but make across the country, lie in ambush and, when civilians are seen approaching,

578 McKenna, Kathleen (née Napoli). Statement 643. **579** Gallagher/Hogan. *The Four Glorious Years*, p. 83 ff.

shout 'Hands up!' Should the order not be immediately obeyed, shoot and shoot with effect. If the persons approaching carry their hands in their pockets, or are in any way suspicious looking, shoot them down. You may make mistakes occasionally and innocent persons may be shot, but that cannot be helped, and you are bound to get the right parties sometime. The more you shoot, the better I will like you, and I assure you that no policeman will get into trouble for shooting any man. In the past, policemen have got into trouble for giving evidence at coroners' inquests. As a matter of fact coroners' inquests are to be made illegal so that in future no policeman will be asked to give evidence at inquests. We want your assistance in carrying out this scheme and wiping out Sinn Féin. Are you men prepared to cooperate?

(Smyth denied giving this speech in this form.)

A member of his audience, Constable Jeremiah Mee, replied: 'By your accent, I take it you are an Englishman, and in your ignorance you forget you are addressing Irishmen. These, too, are English [taking off his cap, belt, and arms]. Take them, too.'[580] [581] [582] Mee later worked in the Ministry of Labour for Countess Markievicz.[583]

In its 21 June 1920 issue it published lists of RIC men who had resigned.

On 17 July 1920 it reported that Col. Smyth was killed in the Cork City and County Club.

On 10 September 1920 it published its most memorable issue, in which it traced the story of the Dáil stationery stolen from 76 Harcourt Street in November 1919, through the letters to slain Dáil members, and traced/outlined the English knowledge of and action in their deaths.

On 26–7 March 1921 (Holy Saturday night) C Company of the Auxies raided it.

On Tuesday, 29 March, Issue No 56, Volume IV, was published from Maureen Power's front room in Harold's Cross; on the following day there were two issues – one dated No 56, Volume IV, was an 'official' forgery put out by Dublin Castle; the forgery collapsed after a month – it was often quoted by the 'real' *Bulletin*.

17–18 Molesworth Street Masonic Lodge. Daniel O'Connell's regalia is preserved here. Also known as the Freemasons' Hall. During the Rising, it was occupied by the Volunteers and surrounded by the British. The British withdrew and the Volunteers abandoned the Hall. There was Masonic influence on both sides.

19 Molesworth Street Royal Irish Academy, founded in 1785.

25–26 Molesworth Street Buswell's Hotel. In April and May 1914 Eoin MacNeill (representing the Volunteers) often met here with representatives of John Redmond's

Irish Parliamentary Party, although the Parliamentarians were furious when they discovered that MacNeill had no authority from the Volunteer authority to negotiate with them. Roger Casement, Erskine Childers and Bulmer Hobson met here at the end of June 1914 to plan the Howth landing of guns.

39–40 Molesworth Street Molesworth Hall. In 1914 Francis Sheehy-Skeffington wrote a feminist play produced here, *The Prodigal Daughter*, the benefits to go to the Women's Franchise League.

Montpelier Gardens (Infirmary Road): King George V Hospital. Seán Treacy's body was taken here and identified by Nora O'Keefe and Mollie Gleeson.

Moore Lane (corner of Henry Place): Cogan's Greengrocer. Volunteers from the GPO went through this shop to get to the home at 16 Moore Street, which was their last Rising HQ. 'The Provisional Government' spent Friday night here and ate breakfast here on Saturday morning served by Mrs Cogan.

6–8 Moore Lane The Flag Pub. The British killed Robert Dillon, the owner, and his wife and child who were fleeing the fire while running under a flag of truce. Upon seeing this, Padraig Pearse determined to surrender rather than have more civilian casualties. Dillon had carried on the business of The Flag for thirty-five years.

Moore Street An area with many food sellers in 1916 and now; eleven buildings were burned here during the Rising. Escapees from the GPO left there at 8 pm on Friday 28 April, went into Henry Street, through Moore Street and Henry Place and into Moore Lane. As the escapees burrowed through the walls of houses on Moore Street on Friday night, they stopped and sheltered in many homes and shops. They spent Friday night there.

Moore Street (at the corner of Henry Place, behind Cogan's Greengrocer's shop): Thomas McKane's family home. When breaking in, one of the Volunteers shot at the door, but the bullet went through the door, wounding Tom McKane and killing his daughter, Brigid. Fr McInerny annointed him and several other wounded Volunteers.

5 Moore Street Dunne's Butchers.

After their escape from the GPO on Friday night, 25 April 1916, the Volunteers entered this building and began tunneling between buildings.

15 Moore Street Home of the Gormans. Elizabeth O'Farrell went out their door at about 12.45 pm on Saturday, in order to find the British commander, Gen. William Lowe. She first met Col. H.S. Hodgkin, DSO, who told her to go back, then said, 'I suppose this will have to be reported.' He reported to Col. Portal who said, 'Take that Red Cross off her, she is a spy.' Gen. Lowe treated her in a more gentlemanly fashion.

16 Moore Street (corner of Henry Place): Plunket home and poultry shop.

The rebel forces fled the GPO on O'Connell Street for Moore Street on 28 April 1916, and spread themselves throughout the terrace.[584] The following day Padraig and Willie Pearse, Tom Clarke, Joseph Plunkett, and Seán MacDermott

---

584 http://www.ireland.com/focus/easterrising/saturday/

congregated alongside James Connolly's bedside in No 16,[585] the Plunkets' home (no relation to Joseph Plunkett) to determine the course of negotiation to undertake. (Connolly, with some other wounded, was taken to this house earlier.)[586][587] From here, Elizabeth O'Farrell and ultimately Pearse eventually approached British forces to declare the surrender.[588][589]

Séamus Devoy, nephew of the Fenian John Devoy, came to 16 Moore Street informing those inside that he had made the necessary arrangements to have the Parnell Street barricade opened to receive Connolly, and the rest of the men began to gather in the street. Filing up and forming ranks, with sloped arms, the first group marched off picking up any stragglers on the way. Next, Willie Pearse headed the main body waving his white flag. Close behind him walked Tom Clarke and towards the rear walked Seán Mac Diarmada and Joseph Plunkett, supported by Julia Grenan and Winifred Carney.[590]

A recent report recommending its preservation notes that the interior of No 16 is 'largely complete' in its eighteenth-century form, though in recent decades the buildings along the street have largely fallen into disrepair. In January 2007 14, 15, 16, and 17 Moore Street were granted a Preservation Order under the National Monuments Act.[591]

20–21 Moore Street O'Hanlon's Fish Shop. O'Hanlon's house was behind. Some GPO escapees, including some Volunteer leaders, stopped here on Friday night, 28 April.[592]

---

585 Ryan, Desmond. *The Rising*, p. 253. **586** Elizabeth O'Farrell always wrote of this as the building in which the leaders met after breakfast on 29 April, and that 'after breakfast, Mr Connolly and the other wounded men were carried through the holes and all the others followed. Mr Connolly was put to bed in a back room in 16 Moore Street. The members of the Provisional Government were in this room for a considerable length of time.' McHugh, Roger. *Dublin 1916*, The Account of Miss Elizabeth O'Farrell, 1966, p. 207. **587** O'Higgins. Op. cit., p. 84. **588** O'Dubhghaill, M. *Insurrection Fires at Eastertide*, p. 266. **589** Ms O'Farrell's account of the scene in 16 Moore Street and her role in the surrender negotiations with the British is most completely given in *An t-Éireannach*, Feabhra 12-29, 1936, in two chapters of 'Cu Uladh's' *Blaidhain na h-Aiserighe*, a complete history of the Rising in Irish based on the original statements of the participants, and translations of documents, and covering all the Volunteer positions throughout Dublin. **590** MacThomais, Shane. 'The Historical Significance of Moore Street, *An Phoblacht*, 1 September 2005. **591** 'Documents from this period now firmly established that Number 16 Moore Street and the adjacent buildings, at Nos. 14, 15 and 17 are indeed the buildings occupied by the leaders retreating from the GPO at the end of Easter Week. The historical significance of this building is mostly [sic] vividly captured in the moving written account of the surrender given by Nurse Elizabeth O'Farrell who was in 16 Moore Street with Padraig Pearse, the wounded James Connolly, Thomas Clarke, Joseph Plunkett and Seán Mac Dermott. Nurse O'Farrell's contemporaneous account included her witnessing Pearse, comforting a wounded British prisoner in the house, before she took the white flag to the Crown forces at the top of Moore Street. She was the person who brought out the surrender communication ending the Rising to General Lowe, who was in operational control of the British forces. From a historical, social and political standpoint 16 Moore Street, is of significant national importance. Last year, Dublin City Council [declared] that 16 Moore Street, the 1916 leaders' "last stand" headquarters, should be preserved and added to the Record of Protected Structures. It gives me great pleasure to announce today… to declare 16 Moore Street as a National Monument.' Taoiseach Bertie Ahern, at the Annual Liam Mellowes Commemoration, Castletown, Co. Wexford, 10 December 2006.

9 Morehampton Road House owned by Batt O'Connor. Mrs Andrew Woods lived here; Michael Collins often stayed here.

68 Morehampton Road Home of Charles Dalton.

117 Morehampton Road House owned by Thomas Herbert Smith. Cpt. Donald L. MacLean of the Rifle Brigade was killed here on Bloody Sunday (he was the British Chief Intelligence Officer). (See also Bloody Sunday, Appendix II.) John Caldow, McLean's brother-in-law and a former soldier with the Royal Scots Fusiliers, was wounded. The owner of the house, Thomas Smith, was a friend of McLean, but Smith, who was not in intelligence or the Army, was also killed.[593]

23 Morehampton Terrace, Donnybrook First home of Éamon and Sinead (Ni Fhlannagain) (née Jenny Flanagan) de Valera, 1910–16.

Mount Street Sinn Féin HQ after 6 Harcourt Street was raided on 20 November 1918.

Mount Street Bridge (over Grand Canal):   It was in Éamon de Valera's 3rd Battalion area during the Rising.[594] Some of the heaviest fighting during the Rising took place here on Wednesday 26 April 1916.[595] [596] (See 1, 2 Clanwilliam Place, Grand Canal Street, 25 Northumberland Road.)

15 Mount Street Lower Home of Countess Markievicz just prior to the Rising.

22 Mount Street Lower On Bloody Sunday Lt H.R. Angliss (generally known as, and referred to in most books as, 'Patrick McMahon') was killed here by Tom Keogh. Angliss was one of the men recalled from Russia to organize the intelligence group in Dublin. Lt 'Peel' escaped by piling all the furniture against the door. Jim Slattery, Billy McClean and Jim Dempsey were in the Volunteer team.[597] [598] [599] (See also Bloody Sunday, Appendix II.) Two Auxies were killed outside, Frank Garner and Cecil Morris. These were sent on foot to Beggars Bush Barracks, but were intercepted by IRA/Volunteer lookouts and killed. They were the first Auxiliaries killed in Ireland. Keogh made a date with the servant maid here who opened the door, and when he was escaping he told the others 'I've got to keep that date.' A military motorcyclist saw the fight and drove to Beggars Bush Barracks. Brig. Gen. Frank Crozier was inspecting the Auxies in the Barracks and drove to the scene. Crozier returned to Beggars Bush Barracks with the first accurate reports.

Frank Teeling was shot here by Auxies and was taken to hospital. Michael Collins arranged his escape from Kilmainham Gaol with Simon Donnelly and Ernie O'Malley. (See also South Circular Road/Kilmainham Gaol.)

---

592 McHugh, Roger. *Dublin 1916*, The Account of Miss Elizabeth O'Farrell, 1966, p. 206-219. 593 Vinnie Byrne and Seán Doyle were incorrectly identified as among the Volunteers involved according to *An Phoblacht* on 20 November 1997. They were at 38 Mount Street Upper. 594 Ó Snodaigh, Aengus. 'Remembering the Past: The Battle of Mount Street Bridge, *An Phoblacht*, 20 April 2000. 595 O'Connor, Joseph. Witness Statement 157. 596 O'Connor, Joseph. 'Boland's Mill Area', *Capuchin Annual*, 1966. 597 Dwyer correctly identifies the English and members of the Squad. Dwyer. *The Squad*, p. 211. 598 An example of the confusion regarding names can be found in Gleeson, James, *Bloody Sunday*, p. 129. 599 Slattery, Jim. Witness Statement 445.

101 Mount Street Lower *Honesty*, edited by Mary Walker.

Mount Street Upper 'Mrs K's' home; Austin Stack stayed here during the Civil War and met de Valera here.

22 Mount Street Upper Home of Mr and Mrs Larry Nugent; he was a Volunteer Adjutant. Prior to moving to Molesworth Street *The Irish Bulletin* was housed here. Early in 1920, the Nugents agreed to lease the Dáil Propaganda Department a flat on the upper floor of their home.[600]

38 Mount Street Upper On Bloody Sunday Lt Peter Ashmunt Ames, Grenadier Guards, and Lt (Brevet Cpt.) George Bennett, Royal Artillery, were killed here. Ames was the son of Mrs Eleanor Ames of Morristown, NJ. Bennett had been in British intelligence in World War I, and was asked to rejoin to work in Ireland. Vinnie Byrne was in charge of the detail, which walked here after Mass and included Tom Ennis, Tom Duffy, Seán Doyle, Herbie Conroy and Frank Saurin.[601][602] Katherine Farrell was the maid who let the IRA into the house. (See also Bloody Sunday, Appendix II.)

69 Mount Street Upper First Dublin home of Douglas Hyde and his wife, Lucy Kurtz.

Mount Brown Roe's Distillery; Thomas McCarthy's HQ. McCarthy and his entire garrison mysteriously disappeared on Tuesday morning of Easter week, weakening the entire South Dublin Union area's defences.

1 Mountjoy Square Home of T.M. Healy before he became the first Governor General of the Irish Free State.

3 Mountjoy Square Home of Alderman Walter Cole. The Dáil met here in 1919 and 1920. Michael Collins sometimes stayed here.

27–28 Mountjoy Square Joseph Plunkett left Miss Quinn's Private Nursing Home here on Good Friday or Holy Saturday, having had surgery on his neck three weeks prior to the Rising.

Mountjoy Street Home of Seán McGarry. He had been in charge of the security party on the pier at Howth. He was editor of the *Literary Souvenir* for the O'Donovan Rossa Funeral. (See also Finglas Road/Glasnevin Cemetery.)

McGarry accidentally shot Clarke in the elbow on 30 January 1916; the wound never completely healed. Michael Collins stayed here on the night the Volunteer Cabinet was arrested, after McGarry had been taken that night in the 'German Plot' arrests (17–18 May 1918). McGarry escaped from Lincoln Gaol with Éamon de Valera and Seán Milroy (Milroy was the prisoner who drew the cartoon Christmas card of a man with a key – the key was the shape of the one Collins and Harry Boland made to open the doors for the escape.) He was to become an Irish Free State TD.

IRA/Republicans burned the McGarry's home on 10 December 1922, and their

600 Nugent, Lawrence. Witness Statement 907. **601** Saurin, Frank. Witness Statement 715. **602** Byrne, Vincent. Witness Statement 423.

seven-year-old son died later from burns received. His electrical fittings shop was bombed the following month.

Later the family moved to 25 Booterstown Ave, Blackrock.

19 Mountjoy Street Susan Killeen, a 'girlfriend' of Michael Collins before Kitty Kiernan, lived here with the family of her uncle, Patrick.

30 Mountjoy Street (across from Aras na nGael): Home of Madeline 'Dilly' Dicker, a 'girlfriend' of Michael Collins before Kitty Kiernan. She lived here with her father, Edwin. Dilly was an ardent nationalist, and a member of Sinn Féin and Cumann na mBan. She undertook many risky tasks for Collins.

44 Mountjoy Street Munster Private Hotel, also known as Aras na nGael or Grianan na nGaedheal, owned by Myra T. McCarthy. She was a staunch republican from Kerry.

Seán MacDermott stayed here before the Rising. The week before the Rising MacDermott briefed the Volunteers here who were go to the Wireless College at Caherciveen on the Ring of Kerry to take equipment from there and to broadcast news of the Rising to the world. Present were Denis Daly (leader of the team), Charlie Monaghan, Donal Sheehan and Colm Ó Lochlainn[603] as well as two from Caherciveen: Denis Healy and Con Keating (a skilled wireless operator). Monaghan, Sheehan and Keating were killed when their car drove off the Ballykissane Pier on the way to Cahersiveen.

Michael Collins lived here in 1917, as did Fionan Lynch (who was arrested with Austin Stack and Thomas Ashe for violations of the DORA). Even after Collins went 'on the run,' he still left his laundry here and picked it up on Saturdays. During 1918, the English spy Timothy Quinlisk stayed here. (See also Ballymun Street, Cork, Co. Cork: Winthrop Street [Appendix I], Brendan Road [Appendix II].)

28 Mount Pleasant Avenue Upper Home of J.J. Coade; shot by Cpt. J.C. Bowen-Colthurst in Portobello Barracks, he is buried in Glasnevin. (See also Rathmines Road/Portobello Barracks.)[604]

43 Moyne Road, Rathmines Home of Hanna Sheehy-Skeffington and her son Owen after they were evicted from Grosvenor Place following the killing of Francis. They then moved to Belgrave Road. (See also Belgrave Road, Grosvenor Place, Rathmines Road [Portobello Barracks].)

34 Munster Street, Phibsborough Sinead de Valera stayed here after the Rising. This was her parents' home and she stayed here with them until her mother died in January 1917. Rauri de Valera was born in November 1916, and after her mother's death, Sinead's other children, Mairin and Vivion, joined her and the family remained here until Éamon was released from prison.

603 Ó Lochalinn, Colm. Witness Statement 751. **604** Sheehy-Skeffington, Hanna. *British Militarism As I Have Known It*, pamphlet, New York, 1917.

11 Nassau Street Home of Grace Gifford Plunkett for many years after the Civil War.

32 Nassau Street British Department of Munitions Office opened in 1917; it was opened to coordinate Ireland's World War I efforts. It was said John Chartres was connected with this office.

45 Nassau Street Frank Gallagher, cigar importer. Later the Berni Inn; at the back of this was Kidd's Buffet, known as 'Kidd's Back'. It was a very important meeting place for English touts. Tom Cullen, Frank Thornton[605], Liam Tobin[606] and Frank Saurin[607] met their 'contacts' here and passed themselves off as friends of the English officers in order to get information.

46 Nassau Street Jammet's Restaurant (David Hogan wrote of 'Kidd's, which has since become Jammet's'); for some time previously it was located at Andrew Street and Church Lane. It was the finest French restaurant in Dublin prior to and after the Rising. Yvonne Jammet, a sculptor and painter from Paris came to Dublin with her restaurateur husband Louis Jammet. Their restaurant was soon a meeting point for artists and writers.

Seán MacDermott took his closest friends here for a 'last meal' just prior the Rising. Often used by Michael Collins and Harry Boland, it was raided on 10 January 1921. Boland ate here with Collins' former secretary, Anna Fitzsimmons (later Mrs Kelly), on 30 July 1922, and told her 'not to worry'. Boland was shot on 31 July at the Grand Hotel, Skerries, and died on 2 August in St Vincent's Hospital.

It subsequently moved to Grafton Street in 1928.

North Quays Mooney's Bar; IRA/Volunteer meeting place during the War of Independence.

1–5 Northumberland Road St Stephen's Parochial Hall, opposite Clanwilliam House on Clanwilliam Street; the hall was also opposite 25 Northumberland Road, toward the Grand Canal. Patrick Doyle (leader), Joe Clarke, William Christian and P.B. McGrath held off the Sherwood Foresters from here as long as they could, then fled to Percy Place where they were captured. St Stephen's Parish School was across the road. Denis O'Donoghue and a couple of men occupied the school building.

25 Northumberland Road (corner of Haddington Road) (See also 1, 2 Clanwilliam Place): Clanwilliam House was on the city side, east side of the intersection; St Stephen's Parochial Hall was on the opposite side (the south-east side) of the Grand Canal on the east side of the street; 25 Northumberland Road was on the same side of the canal, but further toward the south-east, toward Kingstown (Dun Laoghaire). St Stephen's Parochial Hall was the most exposed of the three positions.

There were thirteen men in the three outposts. They opened fire on the 1st Dublin Battalion Associated Volunteer Corps, the Georgius Rex ('The George Royals')

605 Thornton, Frank. Witness Statements 510, 615. **606** Tobin, Liam. Witness Statement 1753. **607** Saurin, Frank. Witness Statement 715.

(also derisively known as 'God's Rejected', 'Gorgeous Wrecks', or 'Methusiliers') who were returning from manoeuveres at Tickmonock in the Dublin hills, wounding seven and killing five – F.H. Browning, Reginald Clery, John Gibbs, Thomas Harborne and James Nolan. G. Hosford was shot by a sniper while in Beggar's Bush Barracks, and died later. One column of the GRs was led by Sub-Cmdt. F.H. Browning, who later died. He was a graduate of TCD, an outstanding cricketer, president of the Irish Rugby Union, played for his university as well as for the Wanderers and founded the Irish Rugby Volunteer Corps. Known as 'Chicken' Browning, he was one of the best cricketers Ireland ever produced. The other column of GRs was larger and was under the command of Maj. G.A. Harris of TCD OTC Barracks, and, though coming under some fire, it managed to reach the Barracks with only one casualty.

The Sherwood Foresters were the 7th and 8th Battalions, part of the 178th Infantry Brigade. Sherwood officers Lt Col. W.C. Oates and Col. E.W.S.K. Maconchy, CB, CIE, DSO, were ordered to go straight to Beggar's Bush Barracks and through the Mount Street Bridge area, even though they had been warned of the casualties to the Georgius Rex reserves.

Cpt. Frederick C. Dietrichsen, marching into Dublin with his troops, saw his wife, Beatrice, and his two children on the street watching the troops arrive. Without his knowledge, his wife had brought them to Ireland for safekeeping from Zeppelin raids in England. He greeted and hugged them. He was later killed at Mount Street Bridge, and was buried in Dean's Grange Cemetery.

Brigid Grace warned her brother, James, and the other men in 25 Northumberland Road of the advance of the Sherwoods, though she was unable to get food through the blocked door. Lt Michael Malone was killed at the top of the house (he had been Éamon de Valera's ADC). James Grace (in the basement) survived but was captured.[608] (He had a revolver and four bullets left when he hid in the garden.). Malone sent Paddy Byrne and Michael Rowe, two youths, home because he didn't think anyone would survive – he had them leave their weapons and ammunition.

Holden Stoddart, Superintendent of the St John's Ambulance Brigade, was killed as he accompanied a stretcher party to aid a wounded soldier here.

Three bodies were buried in the grounds of the Parochial Hall, and one body was buried at 25 Northumberland Road. These bodies were not removed until 12 May 1916.

29, 31, 33 Northumberland Road Used as field hospitals by the Sherwood Foresters during the fighting at the bridge.

54 Northumberland Road Home of Mary Ellen (Nell) Humphreys at the time of the Rising; a sister of The O'Rahilly. She and her husband, David, an eye surgeon from Limerick, moved here in 1909, and she was involved in nationalist activities from her arrival in Dublin. She continued those activities after the Rising, and

608 Grace, Seumas. Witness Statement 310.

was very opposed to the Treaty. Always very interested in design, she was largely responsible for the family home on Ailesbury Road to which the family moved from here.

She was in the GPO several times during the Rising, but she was captured in the vicinity of her home here, and was imprisoned. (See also 36 Ailesbury Road.)

North Strand Creighton House, early home of James Larkin upon arrival in Dublin.

North Strand Road (see also Poplar Row): Wicklow Chemical Manure Company.

Nutley Lane At the corner of Simmonscourt Road – Elm Park Golf Club. Alan Bell was taken off a tram opposite here and shot on 27 March 1920. ('Come on, Mr Bell, your time has come.') Earlier that month he signed an order requiring banks to disclose all details of client's accounts. He had been working with Sir John Taylor, the undersecretary, and had recently seized £20,000 from accounts in the Munster and Leinster Bank believed to belong to Sinn Féin depositors. Previously he had been the English 'spymaster' handling 'Jameson', John C. Byrne. (See also Ballymun Road, Harcourt Street, Sackville Street Upper, Cork, Co. Cork, Winthrop Street [Appendix I], and Brendan Road [Appendix II].) Bill Stapleton[609] and Joe Dolan[610] were the members of the Squad.

21 Oakley Road, Cullenswood Ave, Ranelagh/Rathfarnham Cullenswood House.

Padraig Pearse's *Scoil Éanna,* St Enda's school. (See also Oakley Road, Ranelagh/Rathfarnham.)

This was the first site of St Enda's in 1908. It was originally conceived as St Lorcan's School, but took the name St Enda's from the patron saint of Pearse's Aran. Founded by Padraig Pearse and Thomas MacDonagh, and opened on 8 September 1908.

When St Enda's moved to another site on Oakley Road, this site became St Ita's. The first House Mistress was Gertrude Boomer. However, Pearse apparently allowed another candidate, Eleanor (Lena) Butler, to believe she would be appointed. Ms Butler subsequently became an assistant mistress along with the assistant resident mistress Mary Cotter, but the confusion was to be the continuing cause of acrimony at the school.

Louise Gavan-Duffy taught here, and after making a loan to the school she replaced Ms Bloomer. Kitty, Helen and Maud Kiernan attended St Ita's from 1910 until the school closed in 1912, and a daughter of D.P. Moran also attended, as did Catalina (Mary) Bulfin, who married Séan MacBride.

Mrs Pearse reopened St Enda's here after the Rising while The Hermitage was occupied by British troops, then moved back to the other Oakley Road site.

Cullenswood House is currently being refurbished to house Gaelscoil Lios na nÓg, an Irish-language primary school founded in 1996.

29 Oakley Road, Ranelagh/Rathfarnham The Grace House, Thomas MacDonagh's home. He moved here in 1910 in order to be closer to St Enda's. Muriel Gifford

---

609 Stapleton, William. Witness Statement 822. **610** Dolan, Joe. Witness Statements 663, 900.

(sister of Grace Gifford Plunkett) married Thomas MacDonagh on 3 January 1912. Grace Gifford stayed here at the time of the Rising.

44 Oakley Road, Ranelagh/Rathfarnham In April 1917 there was a 'Conference of Women Delegates' that met here to petition Sinn Féin for representation and demanded equality of status for women. The petition was for six members to represent women on the Sinn Féin Executive: Áine Ceannt,[611] Kathleen Clarke, Alice Ginnell,[612] Dr Kathleen Lynn, Helena Molony[613] and Jennie Wyse-Power.

The conference was to protest that only one delegate was assigned to women on the Sinn Féin Executive Council (Countess Plunkett). The conference noted that six members of the Irish Nation League had been seated on the Executive and that women should have no less representation. Alice Ginnell, writing as the Hon. Secretary noted 'The claim of women to be represented is based mainly on the Republication Proclamation of Easter Week, 1916, which of course you are determined to uphold.'[614]

The petition was presented to the Sinn Féin Convention of 1917, and was carried.[615]

Later in April 1917 the League of Women Delegates was founded. At a meeting on 16 October the name was Gaelicised to Cumann na dTeachaire. The primarily focus was to promote the representation and participation of women in the reorganisation of Sinn Féin. (See League of Women Delegates, Appendix IV.)

Oakley Road, Ranelagh/Rathfarnham 'The Hermitage', St Enda's (*Scoil Éanna*) was situated here from 1910 until it was occupied by the British army after the Rising. Named for St Enda of Aran, who abandoned the heroic life of a warrior to teach a devoted band of scholars in the remote seclusion of the Aran Islands. Formerly known as 'The Hermitage', it was an eighteenth-century house, set on fifty acres of woods and parklands, enhanced by a lake and river near its boundary. The motto of the school was 'Truth on our lips, strength in our hands, and purity in our hearts.' The school was known for liberal teaching methods and unyielding nationalism. Irish was the school language at St Enda's and only the sciences, in which an Irish vocabulary was lacking, were taught in English. Scoil Éanna was seen as a huge educational experiment at the time, with Pearse intent on providing a child-centred education to its pupils. Boys attending the school enjoyed a huge range of subjects, from tending the large gardens to Egyptology, and they had their own informal magazine, *An Scoláire* (The Scholar). Among its teachers (full or part time) were Frank Burke, Vincent Brien, William Carroll (physical education), Joseph Clarke, Con Colbert, Padraic Colum, Dr Patrick Doody (classics), John Henry, Owen Lloyd (music), Tomás MacDomhnaill (music), Thomas MacDonagh,

---

611 Ceannt, Áine. Witness Statement 264. **612** Ginnell, Alice. Witness Statement 982. **613** Molony, Helena. Witness Statement 391. **614** Minutes of Conference of Women Delegates, 1 August 1917, *Sheehy-Skeffington Papers*, MS 21,194, National Library of Ireland. **615** *Sinn Féin Convention Report*, MS 21,523, National Library of Ireland.

Joe MacDonagh, Michael MacRuaidhri (gardening classes), Standish O'Grady, Margaret Pearse, Michael Smidic, Michael Smithwick (mathematics). Guest lecturers included: Beatrice Elvery, Alice Stopford Green, Edward Martyn, Dr Douglas Hyde, Eoin MacNeill, Mary Hayden, Sarah Purser, and W.B. Yeats.

Among its students were James Larkin's sons Jim, Denis and Fintan, three sons and a nephew of Eoin MacNeill, two sons of Peter McGinley, a son of William Bulfin, and various relatives of Seán O'Casey, Padraic Colum, and Agnes O'Farrelly.

The enrollment went from 30 in 1908 to 130 in 1909–10, but shrank after that to 70 in 1910–11. After 1912 the numbers never reached 60, and in the final year before the Rising there were only 28 boys over fourteen who stayed for two terms.

In 1919, Michael Collins participated in a film made here encouraging people to sign up for the Dáil Loan. He read a supportive letter from Dr Thomas O'Dwyer, the bishop of Limerick,[616] and the film showed many Republican notables, including Cathal Brugha, Kathleen Clarke and Mrs Pearse, endorsing the scheme. John MacDonagh, brother of the executed Thomas, directed the film. The film showed Collins seated behind the block on which Robert Emmet was beheaded and the contributors to the Loan signed their names on this block. When the film was made no cinema owner would risk showing it so IRA/Volunteers were sent to theatres with copies and ordered to interrupt features and force projectionists to show it at gunpoint.

Mrs Pearse reopened The Hermitage in 1919, but it was always in financial trouble and closed in 1935. She willed a life estate to her daughter, Senator Margaret Pearse, and it passed to the Irish State upon her death in 1969. When it reopened after the Rising, Thomas MacDonagh's brother Joseph became headmaster, and Frank Burke and Brian Joyce returned as teachers after they were released from internment. Joseph MacDonagh was rearrested in 1917, and the ex-chemistry master, Peter Slattery, replaced him. Frank Burke replaced him later and stayed on as headmaster until the school finally closed.

The Hermitage is now the Pearse Museum and its grounds form St Enda's Park, both under the Office of Public Works.

Oakley Road, Rathfarnham 'The Mill House'; Bulmer Hobson's home. Hobson was the only Quaker among the Volunteer leaders.

Oakley Road, Rathfarnham 'The Priory': just across the road from St Enda's. Home of John Philpot Curran, Ireland's foremost legal scholar of the late 1700s and early 1800s. His daughter, Sarah, had a love affair with Robert Emmet, and it was she whom Emmet returned to Dublin to see, which led to his capture. Curran treated her abominably in regard to the affair, probably because it might have imperiled his promotion to the Bench. Though Curran defended all the other United Irishmen, he rejected Emmet's appeal for assistance. The 'Emmet Walk' can still be found at nearby St Enda's (The Hermitage).

616 Lavan, Revd Thomas J. Witness Statement 1407.

30 O'Connell Villas, Fairview Home of Michael W. O'Reilly. Quartermaster of the Volunteers prior to the Rising, he became O/C at Frongoch prison camp.

25 O'Donohoe Street, Inchicore Final home of Peadar Kearney; he died here in 1942.

Ormond Quay Office of *The Republic*; the editor was Darrell Figgis. It was suppressed in September 1919, following publication of an advertisement for the Dáil Loan.

Figgis was a novelist before the Rising, and helped raise money for the *Asgard's* gunrunning to Howth.[617] He was elected to the Third Dáil as an independent pro-Treaty TD. Figgis wrote *Recollections of the Irish War*, and later Figgis was the deputy chairman of the committee that wrote the Irish Constitution in 1922, and he was the greatest contributor to it. That same year he wrote a book, *The Irish Constitution Explained*. At the time Figgis was disliked by many; he was thought too vain.[618] He committed suicide in London in 1925, after his lover, Rita North, died following an abortion. His wife shot herself a year earlier.

7–11 Ormond Quay Ormond Hotel. Seán Hales stayed here the night before he was shot.

14 Ormond Quay Lower Lalor Ltd, ecclesiastical candlemakers. Cathal Brugha was the Managing Director.

9 Ormond Quay Upper Office of Arthur Griffith's *Sinn Féin* newspaper from 1906 until 1914. It moved here from Fownes Street. (It was preceeded in Fownes Street by his newspaper *United Irishman*.)

After World War I was declared, John Redmond spoke in the House of Commons on 3 August 1914. He assured the British government that they might with confidence withdraw all their troops from Ireland; that the Irish Volunteers would co-operate with the Ulster Volunteers in guarding Ireland's shores.[619] In response, Arthur Griffith wrote an editorial for *Sinn Féin* on 8 August:

> Ireland is not at war with Germany. She has no quarrel with any continental power. England is at war with Germany, and Mr Redmond has offered England the services of the National Volunteers to defend Ireland. What has Ireland to defend, and whom has she to defend it against? Has she a native Constitution or a National Government to defend? All know that she has not. All know that both were wrested from her by the power whom Mr Redmond offers the services of national Ireland. All know that Mr Redmond made his offer without receiving a quid pro quo. There is no European Power waging war against the people of Ireland. There are two European Powers at war with the people who dominate Ireland from Dublin Castle. The call to the Volunteers to 'defend Ireland' is a call to them to defend the bureaucracy entrenched in that ediface.

---

617 Figgis. *Recollections of the Irish War*, pp. 15-21. **618** O'Malley, Ernie. Op. cit., p. 71. **619** Macardle. *The Irish Republic*, p. 116.

Our duty is in no doubt. We are Irish Nationalists, and the only duty we can have is to stand for Ireland's interests, irrespective of the interests of England, or Germany, or any other foreign country. This week the British Government has passed measures through all stages – first reading, second reading, committee, third reading, and report – in the House of Commons in the space of six hours. Let it withdraw the present abortive Home Rule Bill, and pass in the same space of time a full measure of Home Rule, and all Irishmen will have some reason to mobilise in the defence of their institutions. At present, they have none. In the alternative, let a Provisional Government be set up in Dublin by Mr Redmond and Sir Edward Carson and we shall give it allegiance. But the confidence trick has been too often played upon us to deceive us again.

If the Irish Volunteers are to defend Ireland they must defend it for Ireland, under Ireland's flag, and under Irish officers. Otherwise they will only help to perpetuate the enslavement of their country.[620]

17 Ormond Quay Upper Whelan and Son, music and literary publishers. First published 'A Soldier's Song' in 1908. (See also Appendix IV.) Some military equipment was also on sale here before the Rising. Dublin Castle thought it a Sinn Féin HQ before the Rising.

Palmerston Road, Rathmines, 8 Temple Villas Home of Grace Gifford Plunkett. It was this address she listed on her wedding engagement announcement.[621] (They became engaged on 2 December 1915.)

Joseph Plunkett and Grace Gifford annouced their engagement on 11 February. Both Grace and her sister Muriel, wife of Thomas MacDonagh, were fervent nationalists and converts to Catholicism. It was said 'whenever those vivacious girls entered a gloomy Sinn Féin room, they turned it into a flower garden'. Grace was an artist with a special talent for caricatures, and left a lovely painting of the Madonna in her cell at Kilmainham Gaol, where she was imprisoned during the Civil War.

Parkgate Street Phoenix Park Works; in 1918, there was a British shell factory here. Joe Good[622] worked here as an electrician, along with Matt Furlong, Joe Leonard[623] and Sam Reilly.

Parkgate Street British Army Pay Corps HQ. At the end of the Rising, Padraig Pearse was taken here to meet Gen. Maxwell. Ironically, the office where Pearse was held captive after signing the surrender became the office of the Irish Minister for Defence.

During the War of Independence, dozens of civilian clerks were employed by the Pay Corps here, many of them IRA/Volunteers or IRB members. Martin

620 *Sinn Féin*, 8 August 1914. **621** Plunkett, Grace Gifford. Witness Statement 257. **622** Good, Joe. Witness Statement 388. **623** Leonard, Joseph. Witness Statement 547.

Hoare, a Volunteer, was arrested here while armed. Seán Tumbleton, a Volunteer, used to throw bombs at the British in 'The Dardenelles'. Finally he had to go 'on the run' when Hoare was arrested.

Fergus Brian Mulloy was stationed here. He worked for the Chief Intelligence Officer at Parkgate, Col. Hill Dillon. Through a Sinn Féin TD, Dr Frank Ferran (who voted against the Treaty in 1922 and died during the Civil War in the Curragh internment camp), Molloy was introduced to Batt O'Connor, and told O'Connor that his superiors wanted him to join the British Secret Service, but he'd do so only if he could pass information to Michael Collins. Thereafter Liam Tobin[624], Tom Cullen or Frank Thornton[625] would meet Molloy in the Café Cairo or Kidd's, but they never trusted him. His true identity was known almost from the start, having been revealed by Piaras Béaslaí's cousin, Lily Mernin, who was typist for Col. Dillon.[626] (Mernin was also 'identified' as one of Collins' most important sources, 'Lt G'.[627] In her statement, Ms Mernin indicates her activities and that Collins referred to her as the 'little gentleman'.) Molloy was killed on 25 March 1920 outside the Wicklow Hotel by a team led by Mick McDonnell.[628]

28 Parkgate Street Ryan's Pub; one of the finest Victorian pubs in Dublin, opened in 1896.

1–3 Parliament Street Henry & James' Outfitters; an outpost of the Irish Citizen Army garrison at City Hall during the Rising.

5–7 Parliament Street Royal Exchange Hotel; Cmdt. W.J. Brennan-Whitmore stayed here prior to the Rising. It was a favourite of IRA/Volunteers from the country. John Aloysius Lynch (a Dáil/Republican Court Judge and County Councillor from Killmallock, Co. Limerick) was mistakenly killed here on 23 September 1920 by a detail led by Cpt. G.T. Bagalley, who was subsequently killed on Bloody Sunday. Some feel John was mistaken for Liam Lynch, but probably not.[629] He had just delivered £23,000 to Collins for the Dáil Loan, so there was some connection to the Volunteers. (See also Bloody Sunday, Appendix II.)

12 Parliament Street Office of *The Irish People*, edited by James Stephens. Raided in 1865 on the word of an informer. Pierce Nagle was one of the few Fenians to escape.

22 Parliament Street Powell Press; printing works owned by Michael Branagan. It was Padraic Ó Conaire's publisher, including publishing his *Tír na n-Iongantas*, issued in 1916.

38–40 Parliament Street Office of the *Dublin Evening Mail*, an outpost of the Irish Citizen Army garrison at City Hall during the Rising.

Parnell Street See Great Britain Street.

Parnell Square See Rutland Square.

624 Tobin, Liam. Witness Statement 1753. **625** Thornton, Frank. Witness Statements 510, 615. **626** Mernin, Lily. Witness Statement 441. **627** Ryan, Meda. *Michael Collins and the Women in His Life*, 1996, p. 70. **628** McDonnell, Michael. Witness Statement 225. **629** Neligan, David. Witness Statement 380.

Patrick Street St Patrick's Park, next to St Patrick's Cathedral. The Guinness family provided some flats for working-class families, along with public baths and a cup of cocoa and a bun for the children every day (known popularly as 'The Bayno'). (See Francis Street.) Thomas MacDonagh came here with Gen. William Lowe to discuss surrender, and his surrender was made here at 3.15 pm on Sunday, 30 April, ending the Rising.

19 Pembroke Road Home of Maureen Power, and her sister Tess. IRA/Republican meeting place and safe house, 1922–23. C.S. Andrews, Fr Paddy Browne (of Maynooth and, later, president of University College Galway), Brendan Considine (became engaged to Maureen Power but she died before they could be married), John Dowling, Seán Lemass and Desmond Murphy all took part in evening 'teas'.

122-24 Pembroke Road (and Northumberland Road): Carrisbrook House, an outpost of de Valera's garrison at Boland's Bakery. The house was taken over early in the Rising, but it was abandoned as no safe escape route was available.

The Embassy of Israel now stands on the site.

5 Pembroke Street Lower James Hicks, manufacturer and restorer of fine furniture. The Irish Free State Government commissioned many of the furnishings in Leinster House from Hicks.

23 Pembroke Street Lower Home of Frank and Cecelia Gallagher. A journalist who was the principal writer of *The Irish Bulletin*, he wrote *The Four Glorious Years* under the pseudonym of David Hogan.

6 Pembroke Street Upper Home of Desmond Fitzgerald during the War of Independence.

28 Pembroke Road Upper Boarding house run by Mrs Grey. On Bloody Sunday, Maj. C.M.G. Dowling, Grenadier Guards, Col. Hugh F. Montgomery, Lancashire Fusiliers, and Cpt. Leonard Price MC, Middlesex Regiment, were killed here. Col. W. Woodcock DSO, Lancashire Fusiliers, Lt R.G. Murray, Royal Scots, and Cpt. B.C.H. Keenlyside, Lancashire Fusiliers, were all wounded. The IRA/Volunteer squad included Mick Flanagan (O/C), Martin Lavan[630], Albert Rutherford, George White, Charlie Dalton[631], Andy Cooney, Paddy Flanagan, Mick O'Hanlon, Leo Dunne, and Ned Kelliher. Cooney removed a great many documents and took them to Michael Collins. (See also Bloody Sunday, Appendix II.)

'Maudie' the maid said, 'Oh, why did you do that to them. I thought you would only kidnap them and send them away.' James Green was the porter.[632] [633]

3 Percy Place Home of C. Hanchette Hyland (twenty-nine). He was killed while looking out the back door of 3 Percy Place near Northumberland Road. He was a dentist, and when the fighting started he donned a white coat and went out to help

630 Lavan went on the run to the US in 1922 following his involvement in Civil War killings in Kiltimagh, Co. Mayo. He became a wealthy lawyer, was a colourful pillar of the community in Brighton, Michigan, and was a vocal Irish republican his entire life. **631** Dalton, Charles. Witness Statement 434. **632** Dwyer. *The Squad*, p. 173. **633** Gleeson, identifies them as 'Rosie' and 'Matt'. Gleeson. Op. cit., p. 129.

the wounded, and was unscathed. The next morning, he was merely looking out his door when he was shot dead.

Peter's Place Home of Mr and Mrs Ely O'Carroll; meetings of the National Aid Association were held here.

2, 7a, 10–15 Peter Street (corner of Bishop Street): W. & R. Jacob's Biscuit Factory. A principal garrison during the 1916 Rising under the command of Thomas MacDonagh. (See also 26–50 Bishop Street, corner of Peter Row, touching Wexford Street).

15 Peter Street Elizabeth O'Farrell met Thomas MacDonagh here bringing Padraig Pearse's order to surrender.

22–28 Peter Street Adelaide Hospital; it amalgamated in recent years with several other Dublin hospitals and moved to Tallaght. Kathleen Lynn trained here as a doctor.

Phibsborough Road (formerly Avenue): Home of Mrs Toomey; Dan Breen was first taken here after the attack on Gen. French on 19 December 1919. Dr James M. Ryan treated his wounds.[634] Breen then went to Mrs Malone's house on Grantham Street.[635]

Phibsborough Road (formerly Avenue): Early home of the James and Catherine Boland family.

Phibsborough Road (formerly Avenue): Dalymount Park, home of the Bohemians Football Club. Bohemians GAA team also played here. Also known as 'The Pisser's Field' because farmers travelling home from the nearby Cattle Market relieved themselves here.

Philipsburgh Avenue, Fairview (Fr Mathew Park): The 2nd Battalion companies paraded here during Easter Week, 1916. Fr Walter McDonnell, a Fairview Curate, came into the Park on Monday and heard Confessions and blessed the Volunteers.

Philipsburgh Avenue, Fairview National School. Irish classes were taught here by Thomas O'Neill Russell and attended by Frank Henderson.

Phoenix Park Fianna attacked the Magazine Fort here after their 'soccer' game. Paddy Daly and Gerry Holohan led the Fianna. Tim Roche commandeered a horse-drawn jaunting car as an 'escape vehicle'.

The Fort was under the command of a temporary officer who was at the Fairyhouse Races, with the keys to the ordnance sections in his pocket. The Fort's O/C was Col. Playfair who was serving with an Irish Regiment in France. His family still lived in the Fort. At first, Mrs Isabel Playfair and her two sons and a daughter were detained in their residence. When they were released and told to evacuate the area, her son, Gerald, ran first to a DMP constable, then headed toward Islandbridge Barracks. Holohan chased after him on a bicycle and when Plairfair would not stop, Holohan had to shoot him to prevent him from sounding the alarm.

54 Pimlico Street, The Liberties Home of James Connolly's family on his first stay in Dublin.

---

634 Ryan, Dr James M. Witness Statement 70. 635 Breen, Daniel. Witness Statements 1739, 1763.

Poplar Row (and North Strand Road): Wicklow Chemical Manure Company. A force of ICA, originally under the command of Thomas Craven, held this early in the Rising. Vincent Poole was second in command. Frank Henderson took charge of this force[636] and in it were Harry Boland and Harry Colley until they fled to the GPO.

Portland Place North Mrs O'Riordan's boarding house. John Pinkman stayed here after he came to Dublin in 1922.

Prince's Street North Fifteen buildings were burned here during the Rising.

4–8 Prince's Street North In 1916, this was an entrance to the offices of the *Freeman's Journal*. Prior to the Rising, the *Journal* was John Redmond's paper and a fierce opponent of the Irish Volunteers. (See also Abbey Street Middle.)

4–8 Prince's Street North La Scala Theatre; on 16 May 1926 Éamon de Valera founded the *Fianna Fáil* party here. His speech addressed 'more than republicanism in its different forms and practical manifestations'. He concentrated once again on the Oath of Allegiance and his strategy 'to remove it by means of a referendum', but he also spoke about the need 'to achieve full national independence and freedom, about the evil and injustice of partition and about the purposes of freedom'.[637]

29 Prince's Street North Capitol Cinema Theatre; destroyed in the Rising. It was rebuilt under this name, remaining so called for many years before becoming the Capitol, and being demolished in 1970. Éamon de Valera's republican party, Fianna Fail, held its founding conference here in May 1926.

Raheny: Belcamp Park. Countess Markievicz leased this as a training centre for Na Fianna Éireann.

Raheny: St Anne's Estate. Home of Arthur Edward Guinness III, Lord Ardilaun, great grandson of the founder of the brewery. Lady Ardilaun left St Anne's Estate to the City of Dublin. The Corporation's Housing Committee, chaired by James Larkin, divided it into park and housing estates. Later the road on its northeast side was named after him.

In 1877 Lord Ardilaun bought St Stephen's Green and reopened it to the public.

7 Ranelagh Road Cpt. Noble, a British intelligence agent, had rooms here. On Bloody Sunday, IRA/Volunteers led by Joe Dolan[638] and Dan McDonnell[639] were assigned to kill him, but he wasn't home. Also in the Volunteer team were C.S. (Todd) Andrews, Francis X. Coghlan, Hubert Earle, and James Kenny. (See also Bloody Sunday, Appendix II.)

19 Ranelagh Road The Ryan family home. Jim and his sisters lived here before the Rising.[640] Mary Kate (Kit, she married Seán T. O'Kelly, but the couple had no children), Ellen (Nell, who never married), Mary Josephine (Min, who became Mrs Richard Mulcahy and had six children),[641] and Phyllis (she became Seán

---

636 Henderson, Frank. Witness Statement 821. **637** Kee. Op. cit., p. 749. **638** Dolan, Joe. Witness Statements 663, 900. **639** McDonnell, Daniel. Witness Statement 486. **640** Ryan, Dr James. Witness Statement 70. **641** Mulcahy, Mary Josephine. Witness Statement 399.

T. O'Kelly's second wife two years after her sister's death, but they, too, had no children).

Although Kit and Nell had taken no part in the Rising they were both imprisoned. Phyllis and Min brought food and messages to the GPO. Min escaped arrest and was sent to the US to coordinate with John Devoy and Clan na Gael.

16 Rathdown Road The Belton family home. Seán Hurley found Michael Collins a room here on Collins' return from London in January 1916.

Rathfarnham, County Dublin Woodtown Park; Eoin MacNeill's home at the time of the Rising. In the foothills of the Dublin mountains, it was here that in the early hours of Good Friday, 21 April, MacNeill was informed the Rising was planned for Easter Sunday[642] Some people reported that when the Rising went ahead despite his notice calling it off, he wanted to fight, and on Monday said: 'I will go home for my Volunteer uniform, and go out and fight! My friends and comrades are fighting and dying, and I must join them.' Others were not so complimentary: 'MacNeill could not make up his mind whether to fight in his uniform or in civilian clothes, and he racked himself so much with speculations on these points that the Rising was over before he made up his mind.'[643] One of Tom Clarke's last comments to Kathleen was that MacNeill's role in the cancellation should never be forgotten or forgiven.

MacNeill was arrested on 26–7 November 1920 and imprisoned in Mountjoy Prison.

3A Rathgar Avenue 'Halcyon Cottage'; Susan Mitchell moved here in October 1923. She was a friend of the Yeats family and editor of George Russell (Æ)'s paper *The Irish Homestead*.

17 Rathgar Avenue Home of George Russell (Æ); one of his last addresses in Dublin, it was the most famous location of his Sunday evening 'at-homes'.

54 Rathgar Road Home of Dr Seámus O'Kelly. Arthur Griffith, Eoin MacNeill, The O'Rahilly, Seán Fitzgibbon, Liam Ó Briain[644], Joseph Plunkett and Seán MacDermott met here at various times on Holy Saturday (22 April) night. MacNeill determined that the 'Castle Document' was a fake, and the *Aud* had been captured/sunk and no German arms were forthcoming. Thereafter MacNeill dispatched messengers throughout the country with countermanding orders for the Sunday Rising: 'Volunteers completely deceived. All orders for special action are hereby cancelled, and on no account will action be taken.' (See also Kimmage, County Dublin, 'The Castle Document'.)

77 Rathgar Road Mrs Julia O'Donovan's dairy; she was the aunt of Gearóid O' Sullivan. Michael Collins often used her homes here and in Mespil Road as shelters, particularly for those coming from Cork. Collins also used her accounts to 'hide' Dáil Loan funds.[645]

642 O'Kelly, Dr Seámus. Witness Statement 471. **643** Ryan, Desmond. *The Rising*, p. 119. **644** Ó Briain, Liam. Witness Statement 6. **645** O'Donovan, Julia. Witness Statement 475.

Rathmines Road Portobello Barracks (now Cathal Brugha Barracks). The 3rd
Reserve Battalion of the Royal Irish Rifles was stationed here under the command
of Lt Col. McCammond, who was on sick leave, and command devolved on Maj.
J. Rosborough. Cpt. J.C. Bowen-Colthurst shot Francis Sheehy-Skeffington here.
Sheehy-Skeffington's intent was to establish a 'citizen's police force' to prevent looting.
His 'manifesto' read:

> When there are no regular police on the streets, it becomes the duty of
> the citizens to police the streets themselves – to prevent such spasmodic
> looting as has taken place in a few streets. Citizens (men and women)
> who are willing to this end are asked to attend at Westmoreland Church
> at five o'clock this Tuesday afternoon.

There were no takers for his force.[646]

Cpt. Bowen-Colthurst was a sixteen-year veteran of the Royal Irish Rifles, was
seriously wounded in France, and he often said this prayer there: 'O Lord God, if
it shall please Thee to take away the life of this man, forgive him for Christ's sake.
Amen.'[647] Then Bowen-Colthurst found the biblical quotation he was looking for
that evening in the Gospel of Luke: 'But those mine enemies, which would not
that I should reign over them, bring hither and slay them before me'.[648] [649] [650]

Hanna Sheehy-Skeffington's two sisters, Mrs Tom Kettle and Mrs Culhane,
went to Portobello Barracks and were arrested on a charge of 'talking to Sinn
Féiners'– meaning Hanna and Francis.[651] [652] [653] [654]

Shot with Sheehy-Skeffington were J.J. Coade (a young man aged about nineteen returning from a Sodality meeting and unaware of the curfew) as well as two
magazine editors, Patrick MacIntyre and Thomas Dickson. Councillor Richard
O'Carroll when asked if he was a Sinn Féiner answered: 'From the backbone out',
and he was immediately shot. He died nine days later in Portobello Hospital.

All the deceased were Catholic. Fr F. O'Loughlin administered last rites and
they were buried in Portobello Barracks. They were reinterred after the Rising. Fr
O'Loughlin was the Army chaplain who presided at the exhumation of Sheehy-
Skeffington, Dickson, and McIntyre and read the service at their reinterment. A
court martial found that Bowen-Colthurst was guilty but insane and he was confined
in the Broadmoor Criminal Lunatic Asylum, but was later released. A British inquiry
found there was 'no incriminating evidence' on any of the men shot.

646 Foy and Barton. Op. cit., p. 190. **647** Townsend. Op. cit., p. 193. **648** *Royal Commission on the Arrest
and Subsequent Treatment of Mr Francis Sheehy-Skeffington, Mr Thomas Dickson, and Mr Patrick James
McIntyre*, Cd. 8376, paras. 7, 11, 13, 16. **649** Sheehy-Skeffington, Hanna. *British Militarism As I Have Known
It*, 1917. **650** Gospel of Luke, Chapter 19, Verse 27. **651** Townsend. Op. cit., p. 194. **652** See 'A Pacifist Dies',
a lecture delivered by Hanna Sheehy-Skeffington in 1917, quoted by Roger McHugh in *Dublin 1916*, 1966,
p. 276-288. **653** Sheehy-Skeffington, Hanna. *British Militarism As I Have Known It*. **654** Hughes, Julia.
Witness Statement 880.

This barracks was Gen. Michael Collins' office during the Civil War. He left Dublin from here on his fatal journey 20 August 1922.

Portobello Barracks is now known as Cathal Brugha Barracks and houses the Irish Military Archives.

77 Rathmines Road Susan Mitchell moved here in December 1920.

10 Richmond Avenue, Fairview Tom and Kathleen Clarke's first home upon moving to Dublin from the US. They were married in 1901 in New York City, and John MacBride was best man at their wedding. Ned Daly, Kathleen's brother, lived here with them. (See also 75A Great Britain Street.)

31 Richmond Avenue, Fairview Tom and Kathleen Clarke's home at the time of the Rising; she lived there after the Rising with their sons. Though Clarke stayed at Fleming's Hotel on Holy Saturday night, he, Seán McGarry[655] and Tom O'Connor returned to stay here on Easter Sunday night.

Kathleen was one of the most well known women of the period and one of very few privy to the plans of the Rising. She served as a TD for the Dublin Mid constituency and was the first female Lord Mayor of Dublin. Born Kathleen Daly in Limerick she preferred to be known as Caitlín Bean Uí Chléirigh (Mrs Tom Clarke) and has this inscription on her headstone. Tom Clarke met her uncle, John Daly, while in prison, and married Kathleen, 21 years his junior, on his release in 1898. Kathleen was specifically given the responsibility to 'carry on' the IRB following the Rising, as Tom knew many of its leaders would be killed or imprisoned. For her role, it was said she was one of only two women (Una Brennan being the other) to be sworn into the IRB. 'On Holy Thursday, [she] was sent to Limerick with despatches. I took my three children with me to leave them with my mother, so that I could be free to take on the duty assigned to me in the Rising.'[656] After the Rising and her imprisonment, Kathleen was unwell and moved her sons to her uncle's home in Limerick until 1917. The house was let furnished to P.S. O'Hegarty during this time, and when she returned to Dublin she took a furnished house in Dundrum for a while. Following her imprisonment she headed the Irish National Aid and Volunteers' Dependents' Fund. She was elected unopposed as a Sinn Féin TD to the Second Dáil in May 1921. Always adamantly against the Treaty, she failed to be re-elected in 1922 but was re-elected to the short-lived Fifth Dáil in June 1927; however, she again lost her seat in September 1927 and did not regain it. She contested the 1948 election on behalf of Clann na Poblachta. Following her failure to be elected to the Dáil in 1927 she was elected to Seanad in 1928 and retained her seat in two subsequent elections until it was abolished in 1936. She was Lord Mayor of Dublin from 1939–1941. Following her death aged 94 in 1972 she received the rare honour of a state funeral.

3 Richmond Parade Home of Peadar Kearney at the time of the Rising. He was a member of the garrison at Jacob's Factory.

655 McGarry, Seán. Witness Statement 368. **656** Clarke, Kathleen. Op. cit., p. 71.

71 Richmond Road, Drumcondra Home of Richard Kent, brother of Éamonn Ceannt.

109 Richmond Road, Drumcondra Home of Michael Lynch. Michael Collins sometimes stayed here. Joe Good lived here from 1918 onwards.[657] IRA/Volunteers often stayed here. Opposite, and beyond the Walter House across the street, were the grounds of Croke Park.

Richmond Street South (and Charlemont Mall, overlooking Portobello Bridge): Portobello Hospital, across from Davy's Pub.

33 Richmond Street South (and Charlemont Mall): Overlooking Portobello Bridge, J. & T. Davy's Pub. The name was subsequently changed to Shearson's and now it is called the Portobello Pub.

Joe Doyle (a Sgt in the ICA) and James Joyce (an ICA member) were barmen here prior to the Rising. Doyle led sixteen men in the occupation of Davy's. Michael Kelly led another section of sixteen to a position on the railway bridge crossing of the Grand Canal in support of the Davy's men, and this section was to cover the Davy's retreat.

Richmond Street North Christian Brothers' School: 'A veritable Revolutionary Seminary'. It was said the students sold little flags on which were the words, 'Tá ár lá a' teacht' ('Our day is coming'). Founded in Co. Waterford by Ignatius Rice between 1803 and 1820, the Order was approved by Pope Pius VII as 'The Institute of the Brothers of the Christian Schools of Ireland'. The Christian Brothers' Schools were to become the renowned educators of the poor and downtrodden boys of Ireland, but with a reputation for severity in the classroom.

Attended by Éamonn Ceannt, Oliver St John Gogarty and Tom Kettle.

On the day World War I started and the Germans invaded Belgium, Kettle was in Belgium secretly buying rifles for the Volunteers. Subsequently he joined the Royal Dublin Fusiliers and was killed at Ginchy, during the Battle of the Somme in 1916. Previously, Kettle had been a Home Ruler and described it thus: 'Home Rule is the art of minding your own business well. Unionism is the art of minding someone else's business badly.' Shortly before his death he sent back to his wife a sonnet he wrote for their daughter, Barbara. Its lines expressed the disillusion of many Irish Nationalists fighting in the trenches:

> In wiser days, my darling rosebud, blown
> To beauty proud as was your Mother's prime.
> In that desired, delayed incredible time,
> You'll ask why I abandoned you, my own,
> And the dear heart that was your baby throne,
> To dice with death. And oh! they'll give you rhyme
> And reason: some will call it the thing sublime,

---

657 Good, Joe. Witness Statement 388.

And some decry it in a knowing tone.
So here, while the mad guns curse overhead,
And tired men sigh with mud for couch and floor,
Know that we fools now with the foolish dead,
Died not for Flag nor King nor Emperor,
But for a dream born in a herdsman's shed,
And for the secret scriptures of the poor.[658]

6 Riverdale Terrace, Inchicore Home of the Holland family, including sons Dan, Frank, Robert and Walter. All but Walter were members of the IRB. All were Volunteers and fought in the South Dublin Union in the Rising. Robert and his company set out to equip themselves by buying rifles from British soldiers.[659]

Ross Road (and Bride Street): Éamonn Ceannt and Thomas MacDonagh surrendered their garrisons to Maj. de Courcy Wheeler here.

15 Russell Place, North Circular Road Home of Seán MacDermott; in 1916 Dublin Castle recorded his address as 500 North Circular Road.

Rutland Square (now Parnell Square) The first of Dublin's Georgian Squares. Its four sides were originally known as Charlemont Row, Cavendish Row, Palace Row, and Great Britain Street. The central park was named after the 4th Duke of Rutland, who was Lord Lieutenant of Ireland, 1784–87. Now named for Home Rule leader Charles Stewart Parnell.

Rutland Square (now Parnell Square) Garden of Remembrance; it was in this location that the Rising prisoners were held in the open overnight on 29 April 1916. The current garden opened in 1966 on the fiftieth anniversary of the Rising, was designed by architect Daithi Hanly and features a sunken pool with mosaics depicting discarded weapons. The statue is by Oisin Kelly, and represents the *Children of Lir*, an ancient Irish legend of three children who were turned into swans and condemned to live for 900 years – a spell finally broken by St Patrick, who restored them to humanity and baptised them before they died.

Rutland Square (now Parnell Square) Geraghty's Hotel; Neary's Hotel; Meath Hotel; all were located a few doors from Vaughan's Hotel. IRA/Volunteers from the country during the War of Independence used all.

Rutland Square (now Parnell Square) Gate Theatre. Opened in 1928. It was actually on the corner of the Rotunda Hospital grounds.

Rutland Square, 8 Cavendish Row Grocery shop of Robert MacKenzie. He was a survivor of the RMS *Lusitania*'s sinking and was killed on 27 April 1916 as he was sitting in his shop.

3 Rutland Square (now Parnell Square) Home of Edward Fannin; a doctor with the Royal Medical Corps.

---

658 O'Connor, Ulick. *A Terrible Beauty is Born,* (Panther Books edition) 1981, p. 103. 659 Holland, Robert. Witness Statements 280, 371.

4 Rutland Square (now Parnell Square) One-time HQ of the Irish Volunteers.
5 Rutland Square (now Parnell Square) Birthplace of Oliver St John Gogarty on 17 August 1878.
10 Rutland Square (now Parnell Square) This Orange Hall was seized by IRA/Republicans in March 1922 and converted to a dormitory, while they used the Fowler Memorial Hall to the rear of the building as a Centre of Direction for the seizure of private property.
11 Rutland Square (now Parnell Square) Kevin O'Higgins' office. Also in this building were the offices of Dublin County Council, which were raided on 25 November 1920. The British were looking for some specific evidence in the County Council offices and though they 'lined up' O'Higgins and his staff, they ignored their offices. O'Higgins was an assistant minister for local government in the First and Second Dáil, and became minister after the Treaty.
17 Rutland Square (now Parnell Square) Abbey Presbyterian Church, known as Findlater's Church.
20 Rutland Square (now Parnell Square) Bamba Hall, a progressive trade union centre.
25 Rutland Square (now Parnell Square) Grocer's Hall/Gaelic League Building (Coisde Gnotha Branch).

This was the usual parade hall of C Company, 2nd Battalion, prior to the Rising.

It was also the Central Branch of Cumann na mBan (the original branch). There were forty-three affiliated branches before the Rising. The officers of the Central Branch at the time of the Rising were: Kathleen Clarke, president; Sorcha MacMahon, secretary; Branch members included: Áine Ceannt,[660] Louise Gavan-Duffy, Niamh Plunkett, and Jennie Wyse-Power.

Cumann na mBan played a larger role in the Civil War than in the Rising. It held its own convention on the Treaty on 5 February 1922, and voted 419 to 63 against the Treaty. Countess Markievicz was elected president at the time. Pro-Treaty members were asked to resign, and they formed their own group, called Cumann na Saoirse (Society of Freedom), which was not militarily active during the Civil War.

P.S. O'Hegarty wrote:

> As the war lengthened, it became more brutal and more savage and more hysterical and more unrelievedly black. But the worst effect was on the women. They were the first to be thrown off their base, and as the war lengthened they steadily deteriorated. They took to their hearts every catch-cry and every narrowness and every bitterness, and steadily eliminated from themselves every womanly feeling ... War, and the things war breeds –intolerance, swagger, unwomanness – captured the women, turned them into unlovely, destructive-minded, arid begetters of violence.[661]

660 Ceannt, Áine. Witness Statement 264. 661 O'Hegarty. *The Victory of Sinn Féin*, p. 38.

The 1st Battalion, Dublin Brigade, drilled here weekly after the Rising. The IRA/Republicans used it as HQ from March 1922.

25 Rutland Square (now Parnell Square) Offices in the Gaelic League Building of Seán T. O'Kelly, who was president of the Free State from 1945, and became the first president of the Republic of Ireland in 1949.[662]

On 9 September 1914 there was a meeting here of the Supreme Council of the IRB (albeit not exclusively of the IRB; non-IRB members were also present).[663] It was decided that 'England's difficulty is Ireland's opportunity' (Theobald Wolfe Tone) and there would be a Rising before the end of the war. Among those present were Éamonn Ceannt, Thomas Clarke, James Connolly, Arthur Griffith, John MacBride, Seán MacDermott, Seán McGarry, William O'Brien[664], Seán T. O'Kelly, Padraig Pearse, Joseph Plunkett, and James Tobin.[665] The Volunteer 'Advisory Committee' was formed; original members were Pearse and Plunkett and 'a considerable number of Volunteer Officers'. Pearse proposed two resolutions:

(1)   Volunteer action during the war should be confined to the defence of Ireland

(2)   Volunteers should announce their intention to occupy the ports, in the event of shortages, to prevent food from being exported.

By December 1914, with its attendant risks of leakage, the 'Volunteer Advisory Committee' was discontinued.

Early in the summer of 1915, the Executive of the IRB approved Ceannt, Pearse and Plunkett as a 'Military Committee'. Diarmuid Lynch asserts repeatedly that the 'Military Council' was instituted not by the Supreme Council, but by the IRB Executive Council.[666] P.S. O'Hegarty wrote that the Supreme Council, at its last meeting in January 1916, was not convinced an offensive insurrection was warranted.[667] Desmond Ryan contended that the resolution that 'we fight at the earliest date possible' apparently was adopted with some reservations on the part of some members of the Supreme Council.[668] [669] Yet Denis McCullough has said: 'The decision by the Supreme Council to call a Rising at the earliest possible date, after prolonged discussion under my chairmanship, was unanimous. I know my worth. I was there all the time, working and building up the IRB. But the actual Rising was the work mainly of four men – Pearse, MacDermott, Connolly and Clarke.'[670] [671]

Some months later when Seán MacDermott was released from prison, he and Thomas Clarke acted as ex-officio members of the Military Committee. After the

662 O'Kelly, Seán T. Witness Statements 611, 1765.   **663** Ó Ceallaigh, Seán T. 'The Irish Volunteers', *Capuchin Annual*, 1963.   **664** O'Brien, William. Witness Statement 1766.   **665** Lynch, Diarmuid. *The IRB and the 1916 Revolution*, 1957, p. 30, and footnotes on p. 131-132.   **666** Ibid, p. 150-151.   **667** O'Hegarty. *The Victory of Sinn Féin*, p. 3.   **668** Ryan, Desmond. *The Rising*, p. 9.   **669** Ryan, Desmond. Witness Statement 725.   **670** McCullough, Denis. Witness Statements 914, 915.   **671** Coogan. *Ireland Since the Rising*, p. 10.

last meeting of the Supreme Council on 16 January 1916, all additions to the renamed Military Council were at the discretion of the Executive. After James Connolly's 'disappearance and reappearance' in January 1916, he was co-opted onto the Council. In the second week of April, Thomas MacDonagh was co-opted onto the Council, and it thereafter consisted of the seven signatories to the *Proclamation*.

29–30 Rutland Square (now Parnell Square) Vaughan's Hotel; owned by Mrs Vaughan of Clare who sold it to Tom McGuire, formerly of Limerick. Michael Collins' 'Joint No 1'. After mid 1920 it was unsafe for the Volunteers.

Christy Harte was the usual night porter.[672] It was said he was offered many thousands of pounds by the British to turn in Collins and others; he'd be given the money, protection, transportation out of Ireland and a new name. Irish wags said he'd have to change his name to Christy 'Eleyison'.

Conor Clune was arrested here on 20 November 1920. He was an Irish scholar from the west who had nothing to do with the IRA/Volunteers but had to come to see Piaras Béaslaí about Irish language projects. Béaslaí and Seán O'Connell escaped out the back.

31 Rutland Square (now Parnell Square) Ancient Order of Hibernians Hall; the AOH was very much closer to the ICA than were the Volunteers. Joseph Scollan, from Derry, was the National Director after 1911; he bought thirty rifles from the ICA for £30 in 1915. The commander of the Hibernian Rifles in Dublin in 1916 was John J. Scollan.[673]

39 Rutland Square (now Parnell Square) Home of Dr Paddy Browne of Maynooth College (later president of University College Galway), from where Michael Collins watched the raid on Vaughan's on 20 November 1920 (during which Conor Clune was arrested). Earlier that evening, Collins had a meeting at the Gaiety Theatre bar.

41 Rutland Square (now Parnell Square) Irish National Forester's Hall. The GAA often met here. Padraig Ó Riain's father was the caretaker and let the Fianna and Volunteers use the hall. Watching the Ulster Volunteer Force arm, the IRB began drilling here in secret prior to the meeting in Wynn's Hotel, supervised by members of Na Fianna Éireann. (See also 35–37 Abbey Street Lower.) The Fianna 'teachers' were primarily Con Colbert, Michael Lonergan, Éamon Martin and Padraig Ó Riain. Irish Volunteers learned military drill here prior to the Rising.

On Easter Sunday night, 23 April 1916, Volunteers met here for a concert after the Rising was 'cancelled'. The 3rd Battalion officers and men met here under the command of Éamon de Valera. On Easter Monday, the 1st Battalion mustered here.

In 1922 the IRB held conferences here for the express purpose of endeavoring to save the IRB from disruption on the Treaty issue. Michael Collins and Liam Lynch were the principal protagonists of the opposing views. On 10 January 1922 those in favour of the Treaty argued that to accept would be in line with well-

---

672 Harte, Christopher. Witness Statement 2. **673** Scollan, John J. Witness Statements 318, 341.

accepted IRB policy, that it was a matter of expedience and not of principle. Those opposed to the Treaty argued that the Republic was 'established' and acceptance of the Treaty would disestablish it. On 18 March (postponed from 12 March) Collins determined to accept the Treaty and to do whatever was necessary to operate it and tried to convince all of the necessity for it. Lynch decided that even if the people voted for the Treaty the Army could not be committed to it. On 19 April once again Collins and Lynch squared off, but neither side was able to convince the other. Attendees included Collins, Harry Boland, Eoin O'Duffy, Diarmuid O'Hegarty, Michael Staines[674], Seán Ó Murthille, Gearóid O'Sullivan, Martin Conlon[675], Seán McKeown, Lynch, Humphrey Murphy, Pax Whelan, Florence O'Donoghue[676], Joe McKelvey, Seán Boylan[677], Michael Sheehan, Larry Brady, Patrick Mullaney and Tom Larkin.

Later, the Supreme Council of the IRB held a conference at which it was decided to endorse the Treaty. Liam Lynch cast the only dissenting vote, but stated, 'Thank God all parties can agree to differ.'[678]

44 Rutland Square (now Parnell Square) The Ancient Order of Hibernians Meeting Rooms. (Now Kevin Barry Memorial Hall). It became HQ of the Irish National Volunteers and was used as a Drill Hall. Dublin Castle had it under surveillance before the Rising because the Volunteers stored arms here. After the Rising it was the second meeting place of K Company, 3rd Battalion of IRA/ Volunteers. In August 1917, Col. Maurice Moore (a former member of the Connaught Rangers) presided over a Convention of 176 companies and called for the reunification of the National Volunteers with the Volunteers. It was raided at the end of August 1917.

It is currently the Dublin Sinn Féin HQ.

46 Rutland Square (now Parnell Square) Gaelic League HQ (Conradh na Gaeilge).

The League was founded here on 31 July 1893.

On Easter Sunday night the 2nd Battalion officers and men met here under the command of Thomas MacDonagh. Arms were hidden here and taken by The O'Rahilly to the GPO on Monday in his blue De Dion Bouton motorcar, which was later used as a part of a barricade and burned.

In August 1917 a meeting was held here to establish a National Executive of Óglaigh na hÉireann (IRA). It was decided to have the meeting at the same time as the Sinn Féin Ard-Fheis, which met on 27 October 1917. Present were Thomas Ashe, Cathal Brugha, Michael Collins, Éamon de Valera, Diarmuid Lynch[679], Richard Mulcahy, Diarmuid O'Hegarty, and Michael Staines[680].

Joe Good wrote that in April 1918 there was a meeting here chaired by Brugha

674 Staines, Michael. Witness Statements 284, 984.   **675** Conlon, Martin. Witness Statement 798.
676 O'Donoghue, Florence. Witness Statement 554.   **677** Boylan, Seán. Witness Statements 212, 1715.   **678** Dwyer. *Michael Collins and the Treaty*, p. 46.   **679** Lynch, Diarmuid. Witness Statement 4.   **680** Staines, Michael. Witness Statements 284, 984.

and Mulcahy[681]. At this meeting it was decided to send IRA/Volunteers to London possibly to assassinate the British Cabinet. Brugha led the team to London in May and it stayed there until August, but he never received approval for the assassinations. Those on the team included Tom Craven, Good, Matt Furlong, Martin Gleeson, James 'Ginger' McNamara, James Mooney, Peter Murtagh, Sam Reilly and William (Bill) Whelan.[682] 'The Squad' was initiated here on 19 September 1919. Collins and Mulcahy presided at a meeting at which 'The Squad' was officially formed. Its original meeting had been on 1 May 1919[683]. Ben Barrett, Paddy Daly, Seán Doyle, Tom Keogh, Joe Leonard, Mick McDonnell[684] and Jim Slattery[685] attended. Barrett, Daly, Doyle and Leonard were told to leave their jobs, as they would become fulltime employees. Daly was named the O/C[686] (See also 'The Squad', 46 Rutland Square, Appendix II.)

27 Rutland Street Upper (now Parnell Street) Home of Seán T. O'Kelly in 1916. Padraig and Willie Pearse stayed here for the two nights preceding the Rising.

29 Rutland Street Upper (now Parnell Street) Home of Oscar Traynor at the time of the Rising.

Rutledge Terrace The McGrath family lived here in 1916, and the two eldest sons, George and Joseph, were active in the Volunteers in the Rising and afterwards. George, the eldest son, became Controller-General of Finances in the Free State Government. Joe, the second eldest, was elected to the Dáil in 1918 and became substitute minister for labour in 1920-1921; after the Treaty, he became minister for labour, and, after September 1922, minister for industry and commerce, including the former ministry for labour. He left politics in 1924 and went into business, founding the Irish Sweepstakes.

Ryder's Row O'Flanagan Sinn Féin Club. This was where Volunteers, including Kevin Barry, mustered on the morning he was captured.

Sackville Lane (now O'Rahilly Parade) The O'Rahilly crawled up this lane after being wounded, and died here. He died slowly – at least four hours after he was shot he was heard calling for water. (It is noted that at the moment of surrender nineteen hours later a British ambulance came across him, barely alive, but that is probably incorrect. The ambulance driver, Albert Mitchell, made a statement that The O'Rahilly was alive the next day, and that a British officer was then said to remark: 'The more of them that die naturally, the fewer we'll have to shoot', but that seems quite unrealistic.[687] Elizabeth O'Farrell saw his body when she returned

---

681 Good, Joe. *Enchanted by Dreams: The Journal of a Revolutionary*, 1996, p. 130 ff. **682** Whelan, William. Witness Statement 369. **683** Leonard, Joseph. Witness Statement 547. **684** McDonnell, Michael. Witness Statement 225. **685** Slattery, James. Witness Statement 445. **686** Leonard, Joseph. Witness Statement 547. **687** Mitchell made the following statement: 'While driving through Moore St. to Jervis St. Hospital one afternoon towards the end of the week the sergeant drew my attention to the body of a man lying in the gutter in Moore Lane. He was dressed in a green uniform. I took the sergeant and two men with a stretcher and approached the body which appeared to be still alive. We were about to lift it up when a young English officer stepped out of a doorway and refused to allow us to touch it. I told him of my instructions from H.Q. but

from her first meeting with Gen. William Lowe in Tom Clarke's shop. More likely is her recollection. Ms O'Farrell related it was 2.30 pm on Saturday when she reached Moore Street, and as she passed Sackville Lane again, 'she saw O'Rahilly's corpse lying a few yards up the laneway, his feet against a stone stairway in front of a house, his head towards the street'.[688])

The O'Rahilly wrote this note to his wife: 'Written after I was shot, Darling Nancy I was shot leading a rush up Moore Street, took refuge in a doorway. While I was there I heard the men pointing out where I was & I made a bolt for the lane I am in now. I got more than one bullet I think. Tons & tons of love dearie to you & to the boys & to Nell & Anna. It was a good fight anyhow. Please deliver this to Nannie O'Rahilly, 40 Herbert Park, Dublin. Good bye darling.' A plaque replicating the note was placed in O'Rahilly Parade in 2005.

Sackville Place Six buildings were burned here during the Rising.

Sackville Street (formerly Drogheda Street, now O'Connell Street): Reputed to be Europe's widest street at 150 feet, with a 50-foot wide central mall and two 50-foot wide roadways. Designed in the 1700s by Henry Moore, the Earl of Drogheda, and named after his friend, Lionel Sackville. In the early years of the twentieth century, it was 'divided', with the west side being given over to the British military and their girls, and the east side to the Dublin civilians. Its name was officially changed in 1924. A previous attempt to change it in 1885 was prevented by Hedges Eyre Chatterton, the Vice-Chancellor of Ireland, who got an injunction preventing it. The citizens started using the O'Connell name, though, and the old street plates disintegrated without replacement.

Sackville Street Carlisle Bridge/Sackville Bridge/O'Connell Bridge; 154 feet wide, wider than it is long. In 1798, the captured United Irishmen were hung the middle of it. The present concrete structure was started in 1879 and completed in 1882.

Sackville Street (now O'Connell Street) On 31 March 1912, there was a monster meeting to welcome the Home Rule Bill. The first speaker was John Redmond: 'Trust the old party and Home Rule next year.'[689] The second speaker was Eoin MacNeill:

> There is no government so very bad that it would not be better for the
> Irish people to accept it if they themselves were in charge of it. If the

---

all to no avail. When back in the lorry I asked the sergeant what was the idea? His answer was – "he must be someone of importance and the bastards are leaving him there to die of his wounds. It's the easiest way to get rid of him." We came back again about 9 o'clock that night. The body was still there and an officer guarding it, but this time I fancied I knew the officer – he was not the one I met before. I asked why I was not allowed to take the body and who was it? He replied that his life and job depended on it being left there. He would not say who it was. I never saw the body again but I was told by different people that it was The O'Rahilly.' Mitchell began his recollections by reminding the questioner that it was more than thirty years after the event. Mitchell, Albert. Witness Statement Number 196. **688** Ryan, Desmond. *The Rising*, p. 253-4. **689** *Irish Independent*, 2 April 1912.

English people have sense, they will not endeavor to keep back from Ireland as much as one inch of her rights, especially in regard to the financial question and the question of taxation. We are not asking for charity but demanding our rights.[690]

Padraig Pearse appeared third. He, like MacNeill, spoke in Irish:

We have no wish to destroy the British, we only want our freedom. We differ among ourselves on small points, but we agree that we want freedom, in some shape or other. There are two sections of us – one that would be content to remain under the British Government in our own land, another that never paid, and never will pay, homage to the King. I am of the latter, and everyone knows it. But I should think myself a traitor to my country if I did not answer the summons of this gathering, for it is clear to me that the Bill we support today will be for the good of Ireland, and that we will be stronger with it than without it. Let us unite and win a good Act from the British: I think it can be done.

He concluded with the following words, however:

If we are tricked this time, there is a party in Ireland, and I am one of them, that will advise the Gael to have no counsel or dealing with the Gall but to answer henceforward, with the strong arm and the sword's edge ... If we are cheated once more there will be red war in Ireland.[691]

In the early years, Pearse's 'nationalism' was more cultural than political, but by this time he had come to the conclusion that force was needed in the face of Unionist opposition to Home Rule. With the passage of just four years he would read the *Proclamation* from about the same spot on the street.

Sackville Street Lower This ran from Henry Street on the west and Earl Street on the east to O'Connell Bridge. All buildings from 1 to 47 were burned during the Rising. Some were burned as a result of British artillery fire, and some from fires started by looters; both fireworks and lamp oil were set alight by the looters.

Sackville Street Lower James 'Big Jim' Larkin's Statue sculpted by Oisín Kelly in 1977. Larkin led the workers during the Lockout of 1913 and left in 1914 to go to America on a fundraising mission. He was in America during the Rising and returned in 1923. The words, 'The great appear great because we are on our knees: let us be free', are attributed to Larkin, but they were probably written by Camille Desmoulins during the French Revolution in 1789. On the west side of the plinth the following lines appear, written by Patrick Kavanagh:

690 Ibid. **691** Macardle. *The Irish Republic*, p. 82.

And tyranny trampled them in Dublin's gutter
Until Jim Larkin came along and cried
The call of Freedom and the call of Pride
And Slavery crept to its hands and knees
And Nineteen Thirteen cheered from out the utter
Degradation of their miseries.

On the east side of the plinth are the words of Seán O'Casey: 'He talked to the workers as only Jim Larkin could speak, not for an assignation with peace, dark obedience or placid resignation; but trumpet-tongued of resistance to wrong, discontent with leering poverty, and defiance of any power strutting out to stand in the way of their march onward.'

Sackville Street Lower Nelson's Pillar, between Henry Street and North Earl Street, distinguished Upper Sackville Street from Lower Sackville Street. The original stone was laid on 15 Feb 1808 and the monument was completed in 1809; it was the first such monument to Lord Nelson and cost £6858, raised by public subscription. William Watkins of Norwich designed the pillar, but Nelson's 13-foot tall statue was the work of an Irish sculptor, Thomas Kirk. The pillar stood 134 feet tall, carved out of white Portland stone, with 168 winding steps to the lookout balcony. It was blown up by the IRA at 1.32 am on Tuesday, 8 March 1966, by a team led by Joe Christie and Seán Treacey.

Sackville Street Lower The General Post Office (GPO); opened in 1818, it was 200 feet long and 150 feet wide, with a height of 50 feet in three storeys. Its architect was Francis Johnston. (The site had been suggested for the new Catholic Cathedral later opened on Marlborough Street, but the authorities did not think it appropriate for a Catholic Cathedral to be built in this prime location.) A major edifice of Dublin's eighteenth-century and nineteenth-century classical architecture, it was built from mountain granite with a portico of Portland stone. The portico is 50 feet long, Ionic, with six fluted columns, a pediment surmounted with statues by John Smyth of Hibernia – Fidelity and Mercury – and a tympanum decorated with the royal coat of arms. Pearse read *The Proclamation of the Irish Republic* on the steps at 12.45 pm on Monday, 24 April 1916 (some reports erroneously cite 12.04 pm). Florrie O'Donoghue said:

> It was considered essential that the Proclamation should be in such terms and issued in such circumstances that, no matter how the Rising ended, the event would take an authentic place in historic succession to earlier efforts to achieve freedom, and that it redefine in modern terms the unchanging aspiration of the Irish people for sovereign control over their own destinies. That aspiration had to be set on the highest moral plane and expressed publicly in a definite form.[692]

---

692 O'Donoghue, Florence. Witness Statement 554.

(For the text of the *Proclamation* see Appendix III.)

After the Rising, *The Irish Times* reported that 'his audience became progressively bored ... On a rumour that [Clery's was going to be breached for looting] his audience moved over to the shop windows, and left the speaker finishing his peroration with no one to listen to him but his guard. Like the revolution itself, the proclamation was a fiasco.'[693]

After the Rising, and before the GPO was reconstructed, a temporary 'GPO' was located at 14 Sackville Street. The GPO was reopened in 1929 after renovation.

In 1966 a plaque was placed in the building's alcove near where Pearse read the *Proclamation*. It displays the following message in both English and Irish: 'Here on Easter Monday 1916, Padraig Pearse read the Proclamation of the Irish Republic. From this building he commanded the forces that asserted in arms Ireland's right to freedom. It is they who keep the fire alive.' (The last sentence was NOT translated into English.) In the lobby there is a statue of Cúchulainn, sculpted by Oliver Sheppard, dedicated to the 1916 Rising.

Sackville Street Lower The Daniel O'Connell Monument; O'Connell lived between 1775 and 1847 and was known as 'The Liberator'. His monument was designed by John Henry Foley and unveiled in 1882. One of the higher female figures holds a copy of the 'Catholic Emancipation Act' of 1829. Thomas Brock completed the work eight years after Foley died. Brock designed the lower figures of angels around the base. They represent Patriotism, Fidelity, Courage, and Eloquence. There are many bullet holes in the statue, relics of the Rising and the Civil War.

1 Sackville Street Lower (and Eden Quay): Hopkins and Hopkins, jewellers and silversmiths. During the Rising, it was held by Seámus Robinson, Seámus Lundy and Cormac Turner alone until James Connolly sent ICA member Andy Conroy, a crack shot as a sniper.

Hopkins and Hopkins made the Sam Maguire Trophy for the GAA in 1928; fashioned to the design of the Ardagh Chalice. Maguire was a Protestant, originally from Dunmanway, and moved to London where he swore Michael Collins into the IRB. Maguire joined and captained the successful London Hibernians Gaelic football team to several All-Ireland finals between 1900 and 1904. In 1907 Maguire went into the administration of the London GAA becoming the Chairman of the London County Board. He later became a trustee of Croke Park.

6, 7 Sackville Street Lower Dublin Bread Co.; its glass roof was described by James Stephens as a 'Chinese-like pagoda'. A detail under the command of Fergus O'Kelly held it during the Rising. In 1917, the initials DBC were worn on the uniforms in the restaurant leading one waitress to tell a questioning English officer they represented: 'Death Before Conscription'.

---

693 *The Irish Times*, 6 May 1916.

10, 11 Sackville Street Lower (corner Abbey Street Lower): Reis & Co. Building. The Irish School of Wireless Telegraphy was situated here; it was closed in 1914 and all its apparatus was dismantled then. In the Rising Fergus O'Kelly led six men to take and restore the wireless equipment to get the 'story out to the world'. The first 'broadcast' was at 5.30 pm on Tuesday, but the receiver could not be repaired. Johnny 'Blimey' O'Connor was the telegrapher. The building was burned out on Wednesday.

15 Sackville Street Lower City and County of Dublin Permanent Building Society, burned during the Rising.

17 Sackville Street Lower Hoyte & Son, druggists and oilworks, 'The City of Dublin Drug Hall'. The premises housed a mixture of chemicals, methylated spirits, turpentine, oils etc. It burst into flames during the Rising and many oil drums exploded, giving extra fuel to the flames: 'The most wonderful fireworks show ever'.

20 Sackville Street Lower Clery's Department Store (first floor of the Imperial Hotel); founded by Limerick businessman Michael Clery in 1853.

21–27 Sackville Street Lower Imperial Hotel, owned by William Martin Murphy. On Sunday, 31 August 1913, James Larkin addressed the crowd in Sackville Street as he promised. He did so from a window of the Imperial Hotel. Following his appearance, police entered the room and arrested him. In Sackville Street there were riots and a police 'baton charge'. The majority of the police 'baton work' was at the Prince's Street corner, and was carried out by both RIC and DMP constables. Sgt Richardson was in charge of the DMP constables as well as the RIC members. Countess Markievicz was one of those injured and she named it 'Bloody Sunday'. From Sackville Street, the rioting spread to the Liberties, Clanbrassil Street, Aungier Street and the Quays. Thereafter, the Dublin Employer's Federation, headed by Murphy, locked out all the workers who would not sign the following pledge: 'I hereby undertake to carry out all instructions given to me by or on behalf of my employers, and, further, I agree to immediately resign my membership of the Irish Transport and General Workers' Union (if a member); and I further undertake that I will not join or in any way support this union.'[694] All those who refused to sign were locked out and the 1913 Lockout was underway. (See also Beresford Place/Liberty Hall.)

Michael W. O'Brien was in command of the unit that occupied this building during the Rising and the Plough and the Stars flag was raised over it. Volunteer Cpt. Thomas Weafer died in the fire here. Mrs Thomas Dillon (née Geraldine Plunkett) watched the storming of the GPO from here on Easter Monday. She had been married on Sunday in what was to be a double wedding with Grace Gifford and Joseph Plunkett.[695]

33 Sackville Street Lower Burned during the Rising. Situated at the corner of Talbot Street, the building housed the Pillar Café, restaurant and tea rooms. Ms McFarland

694 Yeates. Op. cit., p. 114. **695** Dillon, Geraldine Plunkett. Witness Statement 29.

was the manager. During the Rising Cmdt. W.J. Brennan-Whitmore was the O/C of the North King Street Volunteers. He was charged with taking this building and building barricades. He tried fruitlessly to stop the looting, until he shot into the air. It was his command that set up the 'string and can' communication system from the Imperial Hotel across Sackville Street to the GPO. When Brennan-Whitmore was captured he met the Australian sniper, stationed in Trinity, who hit one of his cans and tried to hit the string.[696]

35–39 Sackville Street Lower (corner of Prince's Street): Hotel Metropole, demolished during the Rising. Grace Gifford often attended the Nine Arts Balls held here. Michael Collins came here to escort Joseph Plunkett to the GPO. (Plunkett was moved here from a nursing home on Saturday, then moved back to the home when the Sunday attack was called off. He was taken to the Metropole to pick up his weapons on Monday morning.) Harry Boland came here from the GPO, under the command of Oscar Traynor, then returned to the GPO prior to the surrender.[697]

40 Sackville Street Lower Eason's bookshop. British army training manuals were on sale here; Volunteers bought and used them from before the Rising until the Truce.

55 Sackville Street Lower Chancellor and Son Photographic Studio, next to Kelly's; the slogan 'Photographer to the King' was painted on the Sackville Street wall.

56 Sackville Street Lower (corner of Bachelor's Walk): Kelly's gun and ammunition shop, 'Kelly's Fort'. The sign on building announced: 'Fishing Tackle and Gunpowder Office'. Peadar Bracken commanded the garrison here; Joe Good was a member.[698]

Sackville Street Upper Eight buildings were burned here during the Rising. Two of the 1916 garrisons were mustered here after their surrender: the Four Courts garrison and the GPO/Moore Street garrison.

Sackville Street Upper (at Great Britain Street): Charles Stewart Parnell Monument. The obelisk was commissioned and the foundation stone laid in 1899 and completed in 1910. Sculpted by Augustus Saint-Guadens. It bears Parnell's declaration, made in Cork City on 21 January 1885: 'No man shall have the right to fix the boundary to the march of a Nation.'

5, 6, 7 Sackville Street Upper (corner of Cathedral Street): William Lawrence's Bazaar, a photo, toy and stationery shop; it was looted and burned during the Rising. The shop contained fireworks that were set off, starting fires elsewhere in the street. This was the main photo studio of William Lawrence. Lawrence and his assistant, Robert French, were Ireland's most noted photographers of the time, and the foremost sellers of picture postcards. The fires destroyed hundreds of thousands of glass plate negatives, which were mostly family portraits. The majority of Lawrence's plates of views of Dublin and the countryside were in a warehouse in Rathmines.

---

696 Brennan-Whitmore, W.J. *Dublin Burning: The Easter Rising from Behind the Barricades*, 1996, p. 116 ff.
697 Traynor, Oscar. Witness Statement 340. **698** Good, Joe. Witness Statement 388.

9 Sackville Street Upper Dublin United Tramways Offices, destroyed during the Rising.

10 Sackville Street Upper Hibernian Bible Society, destroyed during the Rising.

11–22 Sackville Street Upper The so-called 'Block' was the location which included the Crown, Granville, Gresham, and Hammam Hotels. During the Civil War it was taken by IRA/Republicans in late June 1922 and held until 5 July.

11 Sackville Street Upper Gleeson & Co., tailors and outfitters. The company advertisement stated: 'Irish goods only'. During the War of Independence it ran an advert with a man in a trench coat (the 'usual' IRA 'uniform'): 'Don't Hesitate to Shoot – straight to Gleeson & Co.'.

12–13 Sackville Street Upper The Hammam Hotel. The Civil War IRA/ Republican HQ. It was noted for its Turkish Baths. Part of 'The Block' of buildings held by IRA/Republicans, it was taken on 29 June 1922 by IRA/Republicans under Oscar Traynor, and the garrison was then commanded by Cecil Malley, brother of Ernie O'Malley. (Only Ernie used the "O"' form.) Cecil was captured and imprisoned at Portlaoise and Mountjoy Prison. The billiard room became the IRA/ Republican hospital. Éamon de Valera, Oscar Traynor[699] and Austin Stack left on 3 July and went to a safe house, intending to start a guerrilla war; Seán M. Glynn led them to safety. Seventeen men held the Hammam Hotel finally, and three women to nurse the wounded remained.

17 Sackville Street Upper Granville Hotel

Cathal Brugha was fatally shot leaving here on 5 July 1922. Twice he had been ordered to surrender by Oscar Traynor, and he refused.[700] [701] On 5 July Brugha ordered the others out and after some reluctance they left under a flag of truce and surrendered to the Free State soldiers who had sealed off the rear laneway, Thomas's Lane. Linda Kearns and Dr Joseph P. Brennan, Dublin County Coroner, suspecting what Brugha was about to do, secured his permission to remain. Brennan and Dr Seán Geraghty treated him after he was shot. Brugha ran out and the Free State soldiers were ordered to 'fire low' but a bullet hit him in his left thigh.[702] The bullet severed his femoral artery, and he was driven to the Mater Hospital with Linda Kearns holding the artery's end in her fingers. Finally, he died of the effects of blood loss.

'Jameson,' a British spy whose real name was John Charles Byrne, stayed here

---

699 Ibid. **700** Ibid. **701** Lt Col. Andrew J. McCarthy, a member of the St John's Ambulance Brigade, went into the hotel to escort Brugha out, but Brugha refused, saying 'they'll never get me'. McCarthy quoted in the *Sunday Express*, 18 May, 1952. **702** See, though, Ernie O'Malley: 'They called on [Brugha] to surrender. He rushed on and fell gravely wounded; later he died. I knew what he must have thought before he rushed out. We had destroyed an effective resistance by the surrender of the Four Courts; the death of a prominent TD and former Minister of Defence was needed to compensate. He had preferred death rather than outlive the dishonour of his comrades. That, to me, was a policy of desperation, and it was unsoldierly. Dying to carry out orders in a job of work was one thing, seeking death was a different idea.' O'Malley, Ernie. *The Singing Flame*, 1978, p. 137-38.

during the War of Independence. (See also Ballymun Road, Harcourt Street, Nutley Lane, Cork, County Cork, Winthrop Street [Appendix I], and Brendan Road [Appendix II].)

21–22 Sackville Street Upper Gresham Hotel; surrender point for the Volunteers under Cmdt. Ned Daly's command during the Rising.

On 21 November 1920 (Bloody Sunday) Cpt. Patrick MacCormack in Room 22 (the IRA/Volunteers had asked for Room 24) was killed by mistake. Hugh Callaghan was the doorman who led the IRA to the rooms, and he mistakenly took them to Room 22 instead of Room 24. MacCormack was really a member of the Royal Medical (Veterinary) Corps. Also killed was L.E. Wilde (Room 14) who had no connection with the Army or Intelligence.[703] The Volunteers were under the command of Patrick (Paddy) Moran.[704] (He was hanged on 14 March 1921 in Mountjoy Prison for participation in the Bloody Sunday executions at Upper Baggot Street. He was not actually there, and while he was a prisoner at Kilmainham Gaol he had an opportunity to escape, but refused it knowing he was not guilty of the crime with which he was charged. See also Paddy Moran: North Circular Road/ Mountjoy Prison; South Circular Road/Kilmainham Gaol.) Also in the Volunteer team was Paddy Kennedy. (See also Bloody Sunday, Appendix II.)

On Christmas Eve, 1920, Michael Collins, Gearóid O'Sullivan, Rory O'Connor and Tom Cullen met here to celebrate (David Neligan was invited, but declined: Collins said, 'Dave's getting windy!'). The private dining room Collins had arranged was not available, so they took a table in the public dining room. A raid by Auxies took Collins to the cloakroom where he was 'compared' with his 'official' photo. It was his closest escape ever. After the raid, they were released; they got drunk and went up to Rutland Square to Vaughan's and then to Devlin's Pub. There Cullen and Piaras Béaslaí borrowed a car and drove them all to Julia O'Donovan's where they slept until Christmas morning.

In April 1921 Lord Derby stayed here, ineffectively disguised by horn-rimmed glasses and under the name 'Edwards'. He met with Éamon de Valera to begin negotiations for a truce. There was little progress at these meetings.

Almost as soon as the Truce came into effect, Collins moved his main office and residence here. It had been one of his regular stopping places earlier, but after the Truce, until well into 1922, it became his headquarters.

24 Sackville Street Upper Offices of the Catholic Truth Society. It was the Gaelic League premises at the turn of the century.

25 Sackville Street Upper Power's Irish Lace. Also the Dublin HQ of the St Vincent de Paul Society.

42 Sackville Street Upper The Catholic Commercial Club. In 1914 Cumann na mBan held a meeting here to determine what action to take on the Redmond/

703 Doyle, James. Witness Statement 771. **704** Dwyer. *The Squad,* p. 176 and 211-12.

Volunteer split after John Redmond's Woodenbridge speech. There was a large majority for the Redmond position, and this led to a split in Cumann na mBan too. The members of the Executive Committee who stayed with the original Volunteers included: Kathleen Clarke, Áine Ceannt[705], Lily O'Brennan, Sorcha MacMahon, Mrs Martin Conlon[706], Kate McGuinness, Maire Tuohy, Mrs Reddin, Maura McCarron, the two Misses O'Sullivan and the two Misses Elliott. Sorcha MacMahon subsequently acted as secretary.

43 Sackville Street Upper YMCA, opposite the Gresham Hotel, was burned during the Civil War.

50 Sackville Street Upper M.H. Gill & Son, Catholic publishing house. Dick McKee worked here, and had a firing range in the basement with a full-size figure of King George V as a target.

65, 66 Sackville Street Upper Northern Banking Co., burned during both the Rising and the Civil War.

68 Sackville Street Upper The GAA held meetings here, often attended by Harry Boland. Dublin Castle held this to be the 'Central Council of the GAA' prior to the Rising. On 20 July 1918, the GAA held a meeting here in response to the Dublin Castle edict banning GAA football and hurling matches without an official permit. After a short discussion, it was decided that 'no permits would be asked for under any conditions; and provisional councils, county committees, leagues and clubs were to be notified accordingly; and also that no member was to participate in any competition if any permit had already been obtained'. It was further decided 'to arrange for Sunday, 4 August, at 3 pm a series of matches throughout each county to be localised as much as possible'.[707] In response, on 4 August 1500 hurling or football matches were held throughout the country.

2 St Andrew's Street Office of A. Corrigan, solicitor for some of the Volunteers.

8 St Columba's Road Upper, Drumcondra Home of Emmet Dalton. During World War I he fought with the Royal Dublin Fusiliers, winning the Military Cross at Ginchy; at the time, he believed he was fighting for Ireland. He joined the Volunteers in 1914, and rejoined after his World War I service, in 1919.

9 St Edward's Terrace, Rathgar Countess Markievicz moved here in 1909.

82 St George's Avenue, Blackrock James Stephens (founder of the IRB) died here in 1901.

St George's Villa, Sandymount Early home of the Pearse Family. They moved here from Great Brunswick Street in 1884, but moved back to Great Brunswick Street in 1890.

15 St Helen's Road, Booterstown, County Dublin Home of David Neligan; his DMP badge was No. 46. He left the DMP on 11 May 1920, then at Michael Collins' request returned to become *The Spy in the Castle*.[708] He joined the English

705 Ceannt, Áine. Witness Statement 264. **706** Conlon, Mrs Martin. Witness Statement 419. **707** Deasy, Liam. *Towards Ireland Free*, 1973, p. 23. **708** Neligan, David. *The Spy in the Castle*, 1968, p. 68 ff.

Secret Service in May 1921 and became Agent No. 68 assigned to the district of Dalkey, Kingstown (Dun Laoghaire) and Blackrock. Count Sevigne (alias Major Geary) was the head of the Secret Service at the time.[709] The oath Neligan had to take upon being sworn into the Secret Service ended 'If I fail to keep this Oath in every particular I realize that vengeance will pursue me to the ends of the earth, so help me God.'

122 St Lawrence Road, Clontarf Home of Arthur Griffith; he moved here in 1910 after marrying the former Maud Sheehan. Raided on the evening of 26–7 November 1920, when Griffith was arrested and imprisoned at Mountjoy Prison. Griffith only occasionally stayed at his home at this time, but he was here that night because it was his wedding anniversary.[710]

St Mary's Place Christian Brothers' School. Arthur Griffith and Seán O'Kelly attended here.

6 St Mary's Road Home of Laurence J. Kettle (son of A.J. Kettle, an aide to Charles Stewart Parnell). He was the first Hon. Secretary of the Irish Volunteers and head of Dublin Corporation's electrical department.

St Mary's Terrace, Rathfarnham Home of Cpt. Seámus Murphy, who was in the GPO during the Rising.[711]

St Stephen's Green It covers about sixty acres and has eight gates; named after St Stephen's Church and Leper Hospital, sited from 1224 to 1639 in the vicinity of Mercer Street. In 1877 Sir Arthur Guinness paid for it to be refurbished; it was placed under the management of the Board of Works, and reopened in 1880.

During the Rising, both sides stopped firing twice a day so the park-keeper, Jack Kearney, could leave his cottage in one corner to feed the ducks. The cottage is still there, as are the ducks.

There are monuments here to Countess Markievicz, the Fianna, Robert Emmet, James Clarence Mangan, Tom Kettle, James Joyce, Jeremiah O'Donovan Rossa, Theobald Wolfe Tone, Oscar Wilde and W.B. Yeats; there is also a famine memorial. The Fusilier's Arch is at the Grafton Street entrance (a Boer War monument to the Dublin Fusiliers); older Dubliners often called that entrance the 'Traitor's Gate'.

8 St Stephen's Green (north, next to Shelbourne Hotel): Hibernian United Services Club.

After the Rising Molly O'Reilly was employed at the Club and became an invaluable intelligence source for Michael Collins.

11 St Stephen's Green (north) The Loreto Convent was originally here, then moved to 21 St Stephen's Green. Louise Gavan-Duffy ran the school here; she formerly ran St Ita's. Michael Collins used this school for meetings. Collins met Archbishop Patrick Joseph Clune of Perth, Western Australia, here on 4 December 1920, at Lloyd George's behest, to discuss peace feelers.[712] (See also Merrion Square.)

709 Neligan, David. Witness Statement 380. **710** Griffith, Maud. Witness Statement 205. **711** Murphy, Seámus. Witness Statement 1756. **712** McMahon, Revd J.T. Witness Statement 362.

17 St Stephen's Green (north) Dublin University Club (now Kildare Street and University Club). The pageboy, Walter McKay, aged seventeen, testified that he saw Countess Markievicz aim and fire through the windows at the members of the club. It was this testimony that was used by the court martial to convict her on the two charges: 'took part in an armed rebellion against His Majesty the King and did attempt to cause disaffection among the civilian population of His Majesty'. She always denied that she shot at the club.

27–32 St Stephen's Green (north, corner of Kildare Street): Shelbourne Hotel. Opened in 1824 by Martin Burke, originally of Co. Tipperary. The General Manager from 1904 to 1930 was G.R.F. Olden.

During the Rising, the English were under the command of Cpt. Carl Elliotson and Cpt. Andrews. There were over a hundred troops in the garrison. It was left undefended by the Volunteers not because they did not recognize its importance, but because 50 Volunteers and ICA men who were to have taken it simply were not there.[713] Paddy Kelly, a Shelbourne porter, made stealthy access to the roof at frequent intervals to signal with flags to the rebels in St Stephen's Green, as did Eileen Costello.

In May 1916, The Commission to Inquire into the Rising met here under the chairmanship of Lord Hardinge. The other members of the Commission were Mr Justice Montague Shearman and Sir Mackenzie Chalmers. Hardinge was Baron of Penshurst and had been Viceroy of India for 6 years. Chalmers was a KCB, and undersecretary of state, and had been on many royal commissions. Shearman seemed to have no qualifications at all and the papers of the time could only describe him as 'a jolly good sport who played rugby for Oxford'.[714]

A strike from April–June 1920 basically closed the hotel, and only the assistant manager, Mr Powell, remained in residence.

On Bloody Sunday, 21 November 1920, a squad entered and tried to kill some British officers but the officers all escaped. The squad climbed a staircase, turned a corner and fired at armed men, only to find they had fired at their reflection in a large mirror.

From February to May 1922, the drafting of the Constitution of the Free State took place in Room 112, renamed The Constitution Room. (By the time it was replaced in 1937, 41 of its 83 Articles had been amended.) The Drafting Committee was composed of Michael Collins (chairman), James Douglas, Darrell Figgis (vice-chairman, who actually did most of the drafting), C.P. France, James MacNeill, R.J.P. Mortished, James Murnaghan, John O'Byrne, Professor Alfred O'Rahilly, P.J. O'Toole, and E.M. Stephens.

St Stephen's Green (north) Office of H.C. Love, secretary of Rebellion Victims' Committee.

32 St Stephen's Green (north) Dr Oliver St John Gogarty's consulting rooms.

---

713 Ryan, Desmond. *The Rising*, p. 121.   **714** MacThomais, Éamonn. *Down Dublin Streets: 1916*, 1966, p. 37.

44 St Stephen's Green (east) The United Arts Club moved here from Lincoln Place; founded in 1907 by Count Casimir Markievicz, Countess Markievicz and Ellen Duncan. Subsequently moved to 3 Fitzwilliam Street Upper. (See also Lincoln Place and Fitzwilliam Street Upper.)

51 St Stephen's Green (east) Office of James V. Healy, Atlas Insurance Co.; insured many buildings destroyed in the Rising and the Civil War.

56 St Stephen's Green (east) Home of Henry Grattan, the eighteenth-century orator whose name is given to Grattan's Parliament. He declared in 1782:

> We hold the right of private judgment in matters of religion to be equally sacred in others as in ourselves ... as men and as Irishmen, as Christians and as Protestants, we rejoice in the relaxation of the Penal Laws against our Roman Catholic subjects, and we conceive the measure to be fraught with the happiest of consequences to the union and prosperity of the inhabitants of Ireland.[715]

73 St Stephen's Green (south) Home of Maud Gonne MacBride. At the time, she was universally described as 'the most beautiful woman in Ireland'. W.B. Yeats had written the play *Caitlin Ni Uallachain* for her, and it was said she 'lived' the part. Maire nic Shiubhlaigh, another renowned actress and activist of the time, said of Gonne's performance 'Watching her, one could readily understand the reputation she had as the most beautiful woman in Ireland, the inspiration of the whole revolutionary movement. She was the most exquisitely fashioned creature I have ever seen. Her beauty was startling...Yeats wrote *Kathleen Ni Houlihan* [sic] specially for her, and there were few in the audience who did not see why. In her the youth of Ireland saw all that is magnificent in Ireland...She was the very personification of the figure she portrayed on stage.'[716] Gonne founded Inghinidhe na hÉireann/Daughters of Ireland in 1900 and the Women's Prisoners' Defence League in 1922 and was always very active in Republican and feminist causes.[717] She published her autobiography in 1938, ironically titled *A Servant of the Queen*, a reference to a vision she had of the Irish queen of the play, *Caitlin Ní Uallachain*. She passed away 27 April 1953 at age 87.

Her son, Seán, was sent by IRA/Volunteer headquarters to Wicklow to organize during the War of Independence. He fought for the IRA/Republicans in the Civil War, and was sent to Donegal with C.S. Andrews. Much later he was awarded the Nobel Peace Prize as one of the founders of Amnesty International. (See also Clonskeagh, County Dublin, Roebuck House.)

78–81 St Stephen's Green (south) Inveagh House; originally two houses; donated to the state by the Guinness family in 1939. It is now the Department of Foreign Affairs.

715 Macardle. *The Irish Republic*, p. 38. **716** Nic Shiubhlaigh, Maire. *The Splendid Years*, pp. 14-19. **717** MacBride, Maud Gonne. Witness Statement 317.

86–87 St Stephen's Green (south) The Catholic University (now Newman House) was founded here in two superb Georgian houses, and opened in 1854 with John Henry Newman as the founding Rector. It is now part of University College, Dublin. (See Earlsfort Terrace.) University Church is not visible from the street, lying behind the door of the house at Number 87. James Grace (25 Northumberland Road) reported here at 11.00 on Easter Monday; the Company O/C was Simon Donnelly, but only about thirty-four members of the company's roster of over a hundred showed up.

90 St Stephen's Green (south) Home of Irish historian Alice Stopford Green, daughter of Sir Charles Gavan-Duffy, widow of the British historian John Richard Green. When she lived in London, she was responsible for raising most of the funds for the purchase of the Howth Rifles, which cost £1500. The largest single contributor was George Fitz Hardinge Berkeley, with Mrs Green the next largest subscriber – Roger Casement, and Erskine Childers and his wife subscribed the rest of the money.[718] Childers stayed here following his service in the British army during World War I. IRA/Volunteers often stayed here during the War of Independence, and the house was repeatedly raided.

Maire Comerford worked here as a secretary.[719]

93 St Stephen's Green (south) Centenary (Methodist) Church; Revd F.E. Harte was the minister, Alfred (Alfie) Deale was the choirmaster and Edwin Deale was the organist.

94 St Stephen's Green (south) Wesley College. Revd T.J. Irwin was the principal.

113 St Stephen's Green (west) Home of Michael Donnelly. He approved the occupation of his home during the Rising. A lieutenant in the ICA, he pressed for more involvement of the ICA in the War of Independence. In July 1920, Donnelly initiated a strike of railwaymen against the carrying of arms by the English soldiers. The strike lasted until December.[720]

123 St Stephen's Green (west) Royal College of Surgeons in Ireland. There are three statues atop the Royal Coat of Arms: Athena, Goddess of Wisdom and War; Asklepios, God of Medicine; and Hygeia, Goddess of Health. It was opened to women in 1885.

Countess Markievicz and Michael Mallin surrendered the St Stephen's Green/ College of Surgeons garrison to Maj. de Courcy Wheeler on nearby York Street. She removed her Mauser and kissed it before handing it over.[721]

George Jameson Johnston was leading professor of surgery in the Royal College.

124 St Stephen's Green (west) (since demolished),: Birthplace of Robert Emmet on 4 March 1778. He led the abortive revolt in 1803.

718 Figgis. *Recollections of the Irish War*, pp. 15-21. **719** Griffith and O'Grady. Op. cit., p. 156. **720** Townsend, Charles. The Irish Railway Strike of 1920 — Industrial Action and Civil Resistance in the Struggle for Independence', *Irish Historical Studies*, Vol. XXI, 1978-79. **721** This type of 7.63 mm Mauser pistol converted into a rifle with a removable stock and was nicknamed a 'Peter the Painter'. Peter Piaktow was a Latvian anarchist in London, a painter, and was sought but never caught following the 1911 London riots on Sidney Street. The weapon he used was nicknamed after him and it was as such that the Volunteers called it.

140 St Stephen's Green (west) Home of Thomas Henderson, grandfather of Frank and Leo Henderson; Frank wrote *Recollections of a Dublin Volunteer.*

Sallymount Avenue 'Brookville'; home of the Pearse family in 1907.

Sampson's Lane (and Moore Street): Where The O'Rahilly was fatally wounded in front of Kelly's Shop, shot by troops of the Sherwood Foresters. He died of blood loss. (See Sackville Lane.)

5 Sandford Terrace, Ranelagh Home of Mrs Augustine Henry. A wealthy lady, she kept a diary of all she observed during the Rising, and how it affected the citizenry of Dublin.[722]

Sandymount Avenue Home of W.B. Yeats.

Sandymount Lamb Doyle's; this well-known public house was used for Volunteer and IRA meetings.

Sandymount, Lisreaghan Terrace Early home of the James Pearse family.

Sarsfield Road, Inchicore (3 St Michaels): Home of Timothy Donovan. Michael Collins often visited here, and Donovan was said to be an uncle of Collins.

Schoolhouse Lane The Model School; attended by Peadar Kearney.

3 Seafield Road, Clontarf Home of Arthur Shields at the time of the Rising.

Seville Place Home of Dan Head, killed in the Custom House fire.

100 Seville Place Gaelic Football Club; raided by the Black and Tans and one man killed. After 1919, 'The Squad' met here daily.

Shelbourne Road Beggar's Bush Barracks. The Free State Army was officially established here on 31 January 1922. There was a chronic high level of unemployment at the time so the appeal for recruits met with a large number of men wishing to serve.

On 10 November, Erskine Childers, the Director of Publicity for the anti-Treaty IRA/Republicans, was captured in Co. Wicklow. In his possession was a .32 Spanish automatic pistol that had been given to him two years earlier by Michael Collins. As unauthorized possession of a pistol was now punishable by death, Childers was taken to prison, and tried by court martial in camera on 17 November. He was executed here on 24 November.[723]

Childers was executed although his case was still under appeal. Jurists in Ireland and England generally regard this particular execution as judicial murder, for Childers was executed before his legitimate appeal, which had been granted, could be heard.

As a result of this execution, the IRA/Republican Executive decided upon a policy of summary execution of prominent Free State figures, and Childers' death caused Liam Lynch to abandon all ideas of making peace.[724] It was immediately following this that Lynch issued his 'Orders of Frightfulness' that led to the shooting of Seán Hales. (See also Kildare Street.) After this, the Civil War entered an increasingly grim phase.

Sherrard Street Home of Frank Molony, brother of Helena Molony. In August

722 *Mrs Augustine Henry Diary*, National Library of Ireland. **723** Kee. Op. cit., p. 743. **724** Coogan and Morrison. Op. cit., p. 52.

1909, Bulmer Hobson, Helena Molony and Countess Markievicz met here and discussed the establishment of na Fianna hÉireann in Dublin. Hobson had earlier founded the Fianna in Belfast in 1902.[725]

Sir John Rogerson's Quay Birthplace of Elizabeth More O'Farrell in 1884. (See also Great Britain Street, Moore Street, and Sackville Lane.) In 2007 a monument to Elizabeth O'Farrell was unveiled here.

Sir John Rogerson's Quay Home of Julia Grenan. With Elizabeth More O'Farrell, she conveyed the instructions for the Rising surrender of the Volunteers who fled the GPO and were in buildings in Moore Street. Most commentators agree that the woman's name was Julia Grenan, although Brian O'Higgins has it spelled 'Grennan'.[726][727] *Last Words* by Piaras MacLochlainn, published by the Kilmainham Jail Restoration Society in 1971 names her as Julia Grenan.[728] *Who's Who* names her as 'Sheila Grennan'.[729] She also wrote articles under the name 'Julia Grenan' shortly after the Rising.[730][731]

However, it should be noted that she is buried in the same grave as her great friend Elizabeth O'Farrell in Glasnevin Cemetery, and the gravestone reads 'And her faithful comrade and lifelong friend — Sheila Grenan'.

Skerries, County Dublin Grand Hotel. Harry Boland, sharing a room with Joe Griffin, was shot here on 30 July 1922 and taken to St Vincent's Hospital, where he died after surgery.

13 Stafford Street (now Wolfe Tone Street) City Printing Works; it printed *The Irish Worker* for James Connolly as well as many ICA posters and handbills.

44 Stafford Street (now Wolfe Tone Street) (since demolished): Birthplace of Theobald Wolfe Tone on 20 June 1763. The street is now named in his honour.

Steevens' Lane Dr Steevens' Hospital; named for Dr Richard Steevens, a wealthy doctor who willed his estate to his sister on condition that a hospital was to be built for the poor in Dublin after her death – she built the hospital during her lifetime, however. It was built between 1721 and 1733, which made it the oldest public hospital in Ireland. It is now the HQ of the Eastern Health Board (Health Service Executive).

Store Street Dublin City Morgue.

165 Strand Road Loughnavale, Éamon de Valera's office from January until April 1921; owned by Maeve MacGarry.[732]

Strand Street Christian Brothers' School; Arthur Griffith attended here.

Strand Street Inghinidhe na hÉireann used an empty loft here as a classroom in the early 1900s.

15 Strandville Avenue Home of George Norgrove; he and his wife and daughters, Annie and Emily, were in Dublin's City Hall during the Rising.

725 Molony, Helena. Witness Statement 391.   **726** http://www.ireland.com/focus/easterrising/saturday/   **727** O'Higgins, Brian. Op. cit., p. 88.   **728** MacLochlainn, Pieras. *Last Words, Letters and Statements of the Leaders Executed after the Rising at Easter 1916*, 1971, p. 183.   **729** O'Farrell, Padraic. *Who's Who*, p. 39.   **730** Grenan, Julia. 'Events of Easter Week', *Catholic Bulletin*, June 1917.   **731** Grenan, Julia. 'After the Surrender', *Wolfe Tone Annual*, Special 1916 Edition.   **732** MacGarry, Maeve. Witness Statement 826.

Suffolk Street Quill's photoengraving shop; the family lived upstairs. It was close to Dublin Castle, and Michael Collins used to have documents brought here from The Castle and 'copied' overnight, then returned before they were missed.

Suffolk Street Robert's café; a second one was opened later on Grafton Street. An IRA/Volunteer meeting place during the War of Independence.

22–23 Suffolk Street IRA/Republican HQ, Sinn Féin Party HQ during the Civil War. Éamon de Valera often used this as an office during the period between the Treaty debates and the outbreak of the Civil War.

Joseph Clarke was the secretary of the post-Civil War Sinn Féin.

In June 1923, the Organizing Committee of Sinn Féin decided to contest seats in the general election and in August the party put up 87 candidates on an abstentionist policy. Their election manifesto stated: 'The Sinn Féin candidates in this election stand as they have stood in every election since 1917, for the unity and untrammelled independence of Ireland.' Of the 87 candidates, 64 were in prison or 'on the run'. Forty-three Sinn Féin candidates were elected, and two further seats were won in bye-elections in November 1924: Dublin (Seán Lemass) and Mayo (Dr Madden).

10 Summer Street, North Circular Road Home of Cpt. Jack White at the time of the Rising.

30 Summerhill Parade Home of Frank Flood, 1Lt of the Dublin Brigade during the War of Independence. A student at UCD with Kevin Barry, Flood led an abortive ambush in Drumcondra, and was hanged in Mountjoy Prison on 14 March 1921.

42 Summerhill Road Home of C.S. (Todd) Andrews, author of *Dublin Made Me*. He was sent by IRA/Volunteer HQ to Donegal to organize during the War of Independence, but spent most of the time in Dublin and was imprisoned in Mountjoy Prison, Arbour Hill and finally in the Rath Internment Camp in the Curragh (he was prisoner number 1569 in hut 32). He escaped from the camp after the Truce on 9 September 1921. He fought for the IRA/Republicans in the Civil War, and again was sent to Donegal to train the senior officers of the Donegal Brigade, then became an ADC to Liam Lynch before Lynch was killed. He was captured in Cork and imprisoned there, then transferred to Newbridge where he was again interned (he was prisoner number 2571 in Newbridge and was in army hut number 60 with many other Dubliners). In January 1924 he was transferred to an internment centre at the Curragh Camp, Tintown Number 2 (where he became prisoner number 876 and was with Jack Plunkett).[733] He was released in April 1924.

25 Sydney Parade Last home of Gen. Emmet Dalton; he died here on his eightieth birthday, 4 March 1978.

16–17 Synge Street Christian Brothers' School. Harry Boland attended here for a while but left after a clash with one of the brothers. C.S. Andrews attended, as did George Reynolds (Clanwilliam House garrison) and Gerald Keogh, who was killed

---

733 Plunkett, John (Jack). Witness Statements 488, 865.

in front of Trinity during the Rising. Michael Hayes was a teacher here; he was minister for education in the Second Dáil and became the first Ceann Comhairle of the post-treaty Third Dáil. He became a Senator later and was professor of Irish at UCD.

33 Synge Street Boyhood home of George Bernard Shaw (it was 3 Upper Synge Street when he lived here). He described the Rising as 'a collision between a pram and a Pickford's van'. It later became the home of a DMP police officer. Michael Collins arranged rooms here for Kevin O'Higgins, who stayed as 'Mr Casey'. O'Higgins moved to Gardiner Street from here.

The house is now the Shaw Museum.

Talbot Street Tara Hall; it was used by Cumann na mBan as an auxiliary hospital during the Civil War fighting in Dublin.

82 Talbot Street Home of Seán Milroy. He escaped from Lincoln Gaol with Éamon de Valera and Seán McGarry. Milroy was the prisoner who drew the cartoon Christmas Card of a man with a key – the key was the shape of the one Collins and Harry Boland made to open the doors for the escape.

92 Talbot Street Spiedel's pork shop, next door to Republican Outfitter's. It was directly in front of this shop that Treacy fell.

94 Talbot Street Republican Outfitter's owned by Peadar Clancy and Thomas Hunter. Seán Treacy (Seán Ó Treasaigh) was killed in front of this shop on 14 October 1920. Lt Price and G Division Sgt Francis Christian were also killed. Two civilians, Patrick Carroll and Joseph Carrington, were killed, and a DMP constable was wounded by indiscriminate Auxie firing.

Treacy was followed here by RIC Sgt Christian after he attended Professor Carolan's funeral. (See also Whitehall, 'Fernside', Drumcondra.) RIC Sgt Roche was brought up from Co. Tipperary to identify Treacy, and gloated over his body in the street. Treacy was the Vice-Brigadier of the Tipperary Brigade, and was on his way to a meeting with Dan Breen[734], Tom Cullen, Dick McKee, Joe Vize (a former British Naval officer who was the Volunteer Director of Purchases and was arrested after the raid; he was succeeded by Liam Mellowes), Frank and Leo Henderson, George and Jack Plunkett[735] and Liam Tobin[736]. Volunteer Seán Brunswick went to 'help' Treacy and emptied his pockets of all documents before the RIC and DMP could get to him.

Treacy was to have married May Quigley on 25 October 1920, within a fortnight of being killed.

Tara Street (corner of Townsend Street): Tower Fire Station opened in 1900. British machine guns and small artillery pieces were taken out of Trinity College, winched to the top of the tower, and fired across the Liffey at Liberty Hall.

9 Temple Bar Printer Robert Latchford was prosecuted and fined £5 under DORA

---

734 Breen, Daniel. Witness Statements 1739, 1763. **735** Plunkett, John (Jack) . Witness Statements 488, 865. **736** Tobin, Liam. Witness Statement 1753.

in June 1916 for printing a statement purportedly made by Thomas MacDonagh in the dock. (See Statement of Thomas MacDonagh at his Court Martial, Appendix III.)

12 Temple Lane: Printer Paul Curtis was similarly prosecuted and fined under DORA for printing the same statement.

Temple Street Temple Street Children's Hospital, where Dr Ada English worked; she was later a member of the Second Dáil, and voted against the Treaty.

Temple Street D Company of the 1st Battalion, Dublin Brigade, mustered here under Cpt. Séan Heuston for the Rising.

14 Temple Street Home of Charles Stewart Parnell.

Terenure, County Dublin First home of Mr and Mrs Kevin O'Higgins after their marriage. The IRA/Republicans attacked it during the Civil War, and Mrs O'Higgins moved into the safety of Government Buildings.

Thomas Street St Catherine's Church (Church of Ireland). The gibbet where Robert Emmet was executed on 20 September 1803 was in front of the church. The block on which he was beheaded is now at St Enda's.

Thomas Street The Church of Saints Augustine and John; erected by the Augustinian Fathers in the late 1800s on the site of one of the first hospitals in Europe, built by the Danes in the twelfth century. It has the tallest spire in Dublin, visible all over the city. James Pearse (father of Padraig) was responsible for some of the statues and stone work. It contains the Chapel of Our Lady of Good Counsel.

Thomas Street Fr Eugene McCarthy found lodgings here for Grace Gifford Plunkett on the morning of 4 May, after he presided at the wedding between Grace and Joseph Plunkett.

Thomas Street IRA/Volunteers used a home here to make 'Mills Bombs' during the War of Independence.

1 Thomas Street home of Arthur Guinness. He bought Rainsford's Brewery at James' Gate in 1759 with a lease for 9,000 years! His home is now part of the main gate of the Brewery. 'Porter' was so named because it was the favorite libation of London railway porters and from 1799 his brewery concentrated on this drink.

50 Thomas Street Formerly Pearse Ryan's public house in the snug of which James Connolly and others founded the Irish Socialist Republican Party in 1896. (Connolly gave the numbers present as six; Tom Lyng said there were eight present, but all agreed everyone drank lemonade.) Its aim was to establish an Irish workers' republic. (See also 76 Abbey Street Middle.) In 1916, it was a cinema.

Townsend Street (corner of Great Brunswick Street): This was the HQ of the detective division of the DMP. (See also Great Brunswick Street and Éamon [Ned] Broy.)

Townsend Street James Larkin founded the Irish Transport and General Workers Union (ITGWU) in a tenement here.

Townsend Street DMP Sgt Morris was seriously injured here during the 1913 Lockout riots on 21 September. He returned to work, but died on 1 February 1914 of pneumonia. He is the only DMP or RIC member to be listed as 'killed' as a result of the Lockout.

Townsend Street Mercy School. Both Julia Grenan and Elizabeth O'Farrell attended here.

Trinity Street Statue of King William stood here in 1916, it was subsequently destroyed.

Trinity Street Moira Restaurant, used as a Volunteer meeting place.

Usher's Island Mendicity Institution, directly across the Liffey from the Royal Barracks (now Collins Barracks). This was formerly the Moira House, home of Lord and Countess Moira. He was an opponent of the Union, and was a Governor General of India, and became Marquess of Hastings. He was a friend, supporter and protector of Robert Emmet and Theobald Wolfe Tone, Lord Edward and Lady Pamela Fitzgerald, and Michael Dwyer. They and other 'rebels' often dined here.

It was given to the citizens of Dublin as an 'Institution for the Suppression of Mendicancy in Dublin' in 1826. In the days of the Rising, and before, mendicants were not permitted to enter through the front door.

In the Rising it was held by D Company, 1st Battalion, Dublin Brigade, under Cpt. Seán Heuston. Approximately 30 Volunteers, all between the ages of eighteen and twenty-five, were in the garrison (thirteen Volunteers from Swords, under the command of Richard Coleman, and seventeen Fianna held out against approximately four hundred Royal Dublin Fusiliers). Heuston was only twenty-five years old. He was instructed to hold this position for two hours to delay British deployment – they held for three days. They started with two weapons and one box of ammunition. There were twenty-eight survivors and two killed. The Volunteers and Fianna only surrendered when they ran out of ammunition on Wednesday, infuriating the British that so few youngsters held them off for so long. A British sniper in Roe's Distillery killed Peter Wilson from Swords as the men were being formed up after the surrender. Dick Balfe and Liam Staines were badly wounded.

12 Vernon Avenue, Clontarf Childhood home of Arthur Shields and William Joseph Shields (Barry Fitzgerald), noted Abbey Theatre actors at this time and during the twenties. Arthur was in the GPO. He never changed his name, and was in John Ford's film *The Quiet Man* with his brother, who by then was known as Barry Fitzgerald. (See also 1 Walworth Road.)

8 Victoria Terrace, Rathgar Home owned by May Lanagan (later Mrs Kilbride); it was Erskine Childers' Ministry of Propaganda office. The staff included Lily O'Brennan and Moira O'Byrne.

9 Vincent Street Home of Gerald Boland.

12 Villiers Road, Rathmines Home of H.J. Tipping; he was the Controller of the GPO and was in charge of opening accounts and funding after the Rising.

1 Walworth Road, Portobello Birthplace of Arthur and William Joseph Shields. William Joseph became known as Barry Fitzgerald, born 10 March 1888. Educated to enter the banking business, he was bitten by the acting bug and joined Dublin's

Abbey Players. He famously starred in the Abbey Theatre production of Seán O'Casey's *Juno and the Paycock* and, many years later, in John Ford's film *The Quiet Man*. Barry Fitzgerald received an Oscar for his role in *Going My Way*. Arthur was born on 15 February 1896. He was in the GPO during the Rising, and was imprisoned at Frongoch. (see also 12 Vernon Avenue.)

Waterford Street: 'House' of Becky Cooper, a 'Monto' madam. British agents were alleged to use her as a front to pass on information.

Waterloo Road: Home of Erskine Childers. Michael Collins often came here.

Waverly Avenue: Home of Margaret Skinnider. This home was 'behind' the home of Kathleen Clarke, and it was to Ms Skinnider's home that Mrs Clarke sent Countess Markievicz when the Clarke home was raided in a search for Markievicz during the War of Independence. The Countess stayed here for several months before being captured.

Weaver Square Home of James Connolly and his family on his first stay in Dublin; his daughter Nora wrote that it was 'the first that we did not have to share with anyone'.[737]

Wellington Quay Ministry for Home Affairs under Austin Stack. Madge Clifford managed the office.

2–7 Wellington Quay Clarence Hotel. Dave Neligan stayed here when he returned to Dublin to rejoin the DMP.

Liam Lynch was sleeping here when the attack on the Four Courts commenced; he left to go to the south and was captured with Liam Deasy. They were taken for questioning by Eoin O'Duffy, who let them go. They subsequently went to Kingsbridge Station and caught a train south with Seámus Robinson. From southwest Ireland Lynch and Deasy became the leaders of the anti-Treaty forces during the Civil War.

Wellington Quay Dolphin Hotel. It was Emmet Dalton's forward HQ during the Civil War Four Courts bombardment.

Wellington Road Home of Louise Murphy. Frank Gallagher stayed in this safe house. (David Hogan was his pseudonym as the author of *Four Glorious Years*).

20 Wellington Road Erskine Childers lived here after he left the home of Mrs Green on St Stephen's Green and before he moved to 12 Bushy Park Road.

41 Wellington Road Home of Patrick Colgan and Delia Larkin Colgan. James Larkin joined them and lived out his last years in their flat here. In the final years of her life, Delia suffered from ill health which caused 'a very quiet life, quite against my inclination', as she said in a letter to R.M. Fox shortly after her brother's death. Delia Larkin died at her home on 26 October 1949 and was buried in Glasnevin Cemetery.

The last home of James Larkin, where he died in his sleep on 30 January 1947.

55 Wellington Road Home of Seán T. O'Kelly. On 5 January 1922 a committee of

737 O'Brien, Nora Connolly. Witness Statement 286.

five, from all sides of the Treaty question, met here. Proposals were made that if the Dáil voted in favour of the Treaty, Éamon de Valera should remain as president, the Dáil should retain ultimate authority, and that only members of the Provisional Government would be called upon to declare allegiance to the Treaty. Michael Collins and Arthur Griffith agreed, but de Valera turned them down, and the recommendations were never forwarded to the Dáil. Eoin MacNeill and Liam Mellowes dissented at the meeting.[738] Seán T. O'Kelly became president of the Free State in 1945 and of the Republic of Ireland in 1949.[739]

17 Wesley Road Susan Mitchell, an avid Republican and Cumann na mBan member, moved here on 7 June 1917.

Westland Row St Andrew's Church. Built with the assistance of Daniel O'Connell between 1832 and 1837, it was the first church built on a main road after Catholic Emancipation. Willie Pearse sculpted the Mater Dolorosa statue here.[740] Kevin Barry was baptised here.

20 Westland Row Office of Daniel Maher, solicitor. Pearse left letters with Maher 'to be opened in case of my death', including his will, and other documents/ instructions of a financial character.

21 Westland Row Birthplace of Oscar Wilde on 16 October 1854. This address is given in the register of his baptism in St Mark's Parish Church, in nearby Great Brunswick Street (now Pearse Street).

36 Westland Row Oriel House; HQ of Special Branch, a unit of the Irish Free State's detectives section. It was under the command of Liam Tobin in the early years[741]. Of a semi-military character, it was the nucleus of a special detection and intelligence unit, and reached a strength of about 125 by the end of the Civil War. In February 1923, all units of detectives and intelligence were merged under Joe McGrath with a complement of about 350. In that same month the unit moved to 68 Merrion Square. Dave Neligan[742], Éamon (Ned) Broy, James McNamara and Tom Cullen worked in the unit after the Civil War.

The building now houses the Royal Irish Academy of Music.

45–46 Westland Row Christian Brothers' School; Brother Maunsell, from Co. Kerry, and Brother Craven were noted teachers here. It was attended by Padraig and Willie Pearse (starting in 1891)[743] and by Desmond Ryan in 1907.

48–52 Westland Row Westland Row Railway Station, now Pearse Station. It was the terminus for the Dublin-Kingstown Railway.

Westmoreland Street The British placed 18-pound artillery pieces here to shell Lower Sackville Street during the Rising, and destroyed many buildings.

Westmoreland Street Carlisle House; *Irish Independent* offices.

---

738 Daly, Una. Witness Statement 610. 739 O'Kelly, Seán T. Witness Statement 611. 740 Thornley. 'Patrick Pearse', *Studies*, p. 11. 741 Tobin, Liam. Witness Statement 1753. 742 Neligan, David. Witness Statement 380. 743 'They were schoolboys – The Pearse Brothers at the "Row"', *Christian Brothers Westland Row Centenary Record, 1864-1964.*

31 Westmoreland Street Main office of *The Irish Times*.
38 Westmoreland Street James Duffy & Co. Ltd, publishers; it published many history books by 'revolutionary' authors.
28 Wexford Street Boland's tobacco shop; run by Harry's mother, Catherine, after his father died.
Whitefriar Street Church of Our Lady of Mount Carmel (Carmelite Church). Erected in 1825, this church occupies a site acquired by the Carmelites in 1280. It contains the statue of Our Lady of Dublin. Pope Gregory XVI gave St Valentine's remains in a wine cask to Fr Spratt in 1835, and they are held here. Fr McCabe was the prior in 1916.

Harry Boland was buried from here; his remains arrived at the Church from St Vincent's Hospital on 3 July 1922. Revd Michael Browne[744] of Maynooth (later bishop of Galway) was the principal celebrant of the Requiem Mass. As the cortege proceeded up O'Connell Street to Glasnevin Cemetery, a Lancia armoured car containing Free State troops stopped, the troops disembarked, laid down their arms in the street, removed their caps and stood at attention until the hearse had passed. The government had allowed the funeral to proceed without interruption. Many thought the armoured car incident was the only way Michael Collins could pay his last respects.

Éamon de Valera was buried from here in 1975. He was an 'honorary' member of the Carmelites and was buried in a Carmelite habit.
Whitehall, Drumcondra 'Fernside'; Professor Carolan's house. On 11 October 1920, the Cairo Gang surprised Dan Breen and Seán Treacy (Seán Ó Treasaigh) here.[745] Breen and Treacy escaped, but killed two, including Maj. George O.S. Smyth. Smyth was the brother of Lt Col. Gerald Brice Smyth, who had been killed for his address to the RIC at Listowel. Upon Lt Col. Smyth's death, Maj. Smyth requested a transfer from Egypt to Ireland and to go after Breen and Treacy who he mistakenly blamed for his brother's death. (See also Molesworth Street.) Breen was wounded several times and badly cut on a broken windowpane in making his escape.[746] Professor Carolan was put up against a wall and shot. Before he died, he was able to give a full account of what happened. (See also 94 Talbot Street.)
Wicklow Street Fergus Brian Mulloy was a British spy who offered to take Tom Cullen, Frank Thornton[747], and Liam Tobin[748] into Dublin Castle to obtain information, but they never took up the offer. His body was found here after Michael Collins had him killed on 25 March 1920. (See also Parkgate Street.)
1–3 Wicklow Street (corner of Grafton Street) Weir and Sons, jewellers. It was next door to the Wicklow Hotel. Michael Collins bought Kitty Kiernan's 'unofficial' engagement present, a watch, at this store.

744 Browne, Revd Michael. Witness Statement 538. 745 Ryan, Desmond. Seán Treacy, from 'The Active Service Unit', *Dublin Brigade Review*, p. 75. 746 Breen, Daniel. Witness Statements 1739, 1763. 747 Thornton, Frank. Witness Statements 510, 615. 748 Tobin, Liam. Witness Statement 1753.

4 Wicklow Street Wicklow Hotel, next to Weir's, one building away from Grafton Street. On Easter Monday John MacBride was on his way to have lunch here with his brother (who was to be married) when he unexpectedly met a Volunteer column led by Thomas MacDonagh at St Stephen's Green and was told the Rising was underway. He was 'invited' to participate and that is how he ended up at Jacob's. It was a complete accident, for which he was executed.

This was a usual meeting place for Tom Cullen, Dave Neligan, Liam Tobin and Michael Collins. Paddy O'Shea, from Kerry, was the waiter and often passed messages. William Doran, the porter, betrayed IRA/Volunteers and was killed outside the hotel on 29 January 1921 on Collins' order. Joe Dolan[749], a member of the Squad, arrived at the hotel in a taxi, and when Doran picked up the luggage he was shot. When Doran's wife put in a 'claim' on behalf of herself and her children, Collins arranged for her to be paid from Sinn Féin funds and they never knew the true circumstances of his betrayal.

William's Lane Rear of Independent House (the *Independent* newspaper owned by William Martin Murphy was very pro-English prior to the Rising, and became more strongly opposed to the Volunteers afterwards.) Also on the premises was the *Freeman's Journal*. James Connolly was seriously wounded in his ankle upon returning from here to the GPO late on Thursday afternoon.

William Street Sinn Féin Hall.

North William Street National School; attended by Seán Connolly

39 North William Street Home of Sgt, then Lt Frank Robbins of the ICA. He was in the Stephen's Green/College of Surgeons garrison.

South William Street Home of Richard Murphy, who was killed in the Rising in Clanwilliam House.

58 South William Street William Street Courthouse. Kathleen Clarke was president of the Children's Court and the Court of Conscience, which were held here. For many years the building housed the Dublin Civic Museum and the Old Dublin Society.

5 Windsor Villas, Clontarf Childhood home of the Henderson family. Some of the Howth rifles were hidden under the floorboards here. Frank[750] wrote *Narratives: Frank Henderson's Easter Rising*. He was in the GPO, and was later a captive at Frongoch. Leo was also in the GPO, became a leading IRA/Republican figure, led the raid on Ferguson's garage which was the prelude to the attack on the Four Courts in 1922, and spent the rest of the Civil War in Mountjoy Prison. (Leo was the Director of the Belfast Boycott, albeit without official status in the eyes of the Free State from April, 1922. He felt he was carrying out his duties.) Nora was a member of Cumann na mBan, and was in the IRA/Republican Four Courts garrison in 1922. Gertie married Maj. Leech of the British army and moved to England. Maurice was involved post-1916 and was interned by the Free State in 1923. Robert did not participate in the military struggle.

749 Dolan, Joe. Witness Statements 663, 900. **750** Henderson, Frank. Witness Statements 249, 821.

Winetavern Street and Merchant's Quay The first artillery fired on the Four Courts came from here at 4.29 am on 28 June 1922. These were the first shots of the Irish Civil War. Cpt. Johnny Doyle fired the first round. Single rounds were fired at fifteen-minute intervals and a total of 375 shells were fired before the garrison surrendered.

Wood Quay The British shelled the Four Courts from here during the Rising. Free State troops also placed 18-pounder guns here to shell the Four Courts in June 1922 at the start of the Civil War. The British did not trust the Irish with high explosive shells and issued only shrapnel rounds, which were mostly ineffective against the stone walls of the building.

Yarnhall Street Linenhall Barracks; burned down in 1916. Cmdt. Ned Daly's men retreating from the Four Courts lighted the fires. In 1916 and during the War of Independence it was the HQ of the British Army Pay Department. The site now contains housing.

3 Yarnhall Street Patrick Mahon, printer, printed *Irish Freedom* here.

York Street (and St Stephen's Green): Royal College of Surgeons in Ireland, garrisoned during the Rising under the command of Maj. Michael Mallin and Countess Markievicz. Maj. de Courcy Wheeler accepted the surrender of Mallin and Markievicz in York Street.

41 York Street Dublin Conservative Workingmen's Club. Many Protestant workers belonged to this club. The Southern Battalion of the Dublin Brigade met here before the Rising. It was the third meeting place of K Company, 3rd Battalion of Volunteers, after the Rising. Those speaking against conscription often used the hall here for rallies. David Hogan spoke here in 1918. It became the HQ of the Fianna after the Rising. It was a meeting place for anti-Treatyites, IRA/Republicans.

Bridges across the River Liffey

There are nineteen bridges presently. On 2 January 1922 and after, several were rechristened in honour of Irish National heroes.

Butt Bridge Named after Isaac Butt, it connects Beresford Place and Tara Street. A 'swivel' bridge opened in 1879, and in 1932 the present bridge was built.

East Link Bridge Takes East Wall Road over the Liffey; opened in 1984, it is both a lift bridge and a toll bridge.

Grattan Bridge Formerly *Essex Bridge*, it connects Capel Street and Parliament Street. Essex Bridge was originally built in 1676 with stones taken from St Mary's Abbey. The current bridge was built in 1755, with many alterations since then, and this one can be most firmly traced back to 1872.

Liffey Bridge Formerly *Wellington Bridge,* then *Ha'penny Bridge*. It connects Liffey Street Lower and Merchant's Arch. Toll of a halfpenny was charged from when it was built in 1816, until 1922. Its official name is still Liffey Bridge, but all call it the Ha'penny Bridge.

Seán Heuston Bridge Formerly *King's Bridge* and *Sarsfield Bridge*. It connects Wolfe Tone Quay and Victoria Quay. It was the first cast-iron bridge in Ireland, and was opened in 1828 to provide a direct route from the Royal Hospital in Kilmainham to Royal Barracks. It was renamed the *Sarsfield Bridge* in 1922, and in 1941 was renamed Seán Heuston Bridge.

Island Bridge Formerly *Sarah Bridge*. It takes South Circular Road across to Conyngham Road. Previously there had been a stone bridge built in 1577 at the site of one of the earliest fording points on the river. This bridge was completed in 1793, and named after the wife of the Lord Lieutenant Westmoreland. The name was changed in 1922.

James Joyce Bridge A road bridge spanning the the south quays to Blackhall Place on the north side.

The Liffey Viaduct A railroad bridge built in 1877, near Kingsbridge (now Heuston) railway station, the viaduct traverses the river and leads to a tunnel which goes under Conyngham Road and the Phoenix Park.

The Loopline Bridge A railroad bridge built between 1888 and 1890, there was so much opposition to its construction as it would obstruct the view of the Custom House that a wooden 'mock-up' was constructed. It was constructed even though there was still uniform opposition to its design.

Father Mathew Bridge Site of the first ford across the Liffey, records of the first one date it to 1210. It connects Church Street and Bridge Street. The current bridge was opened in 1818, and was formerly known as *Whitworth Bridge* and *Church Street Bridge*.

Liam Mellowes Bridge Oldest surviving bridge across the Liffey, it was originally built in 1683, rebuilt after it collapsed in 1763, then again in 1768. It connects Queen Street and Bridgefoot Street. Originally *Bridewell Bridge*, then, *Queen Street Bridge*, then *Queen Maeve Bridge*, then *Aran Bridge*.

The Millenium Bridge It connects Ormond Quay and Wellington Quay. A pedestrian bridge, it opened in 1999.

Seán O'Casey Bridge A bridge, joining Sir John Rogerson's Quay in the Grand Canal Docks area, to North Wall Quay and the International Financial Services Centre.

O'Connell Bridge Formerly *Carlisle Bridge*. It connects O'Connell Street and Westmoreland/D'Olier Streets. Originally constructed of rope in 1791 it could carry only one man and a donkey at a time, it opened to pedestrians in 1792 and carriages in 1795. James Gandon designed it. The original bridge had a hump and was much narrower at forty-three feet wide. It was replaced with a wooden structure in 1801, widened and the hump removed. The bridge as it is today was finished in 1880, and is 154 feet wide and 150 feet long.

O'Donovan Rossa Bridge Formerly *Richmond Bridge*. It connects Winetavern Street and Chancery Place. Begun in 1813 and opened in 1816, and renamed in 1922.

Frank Sherwin Bridge It connects Steeven's Lane across to Wolfe Tone Quay. Built in 1982, it was named after a popular Dublin City Councillor.

Matt Talbot Memorial Bridge It connects Memorial Road and Moss Street. Opened in 1978, it is named after Matt Talbot, an ordinary Dublin workingman who campaigned for temperance. He died in 1925 and was beatified in 1976. It also commemorates all the sailors from Dublin who died at sea.

Watling St. Bridge: Rory O'More Bridge It takes Watling Street across between Sarsfield Quay and Ellis Quay. Site of the second bridge to be built across the Liffey. A bridge was originally built here of wood in 1670, which came to be known as 'Bloody Bridge' because of the riots (in which four were killed) caused when ferry-owners thought a bridge would ruin their businesses, and was replaced by a stone bridge built in 1704. In turn the current cast-iron bridge replaced this with stone piers in 1861. Originally named the *Queen Victoria Bridge* (sometimes *Victoria and Albert Bridge*), it was completed in 1861 and renamed in 1922 after one of the leaders of the 1641 Rebellion, Rory O'More, but that name is little used today.

West Link Toll Bridge Opened in September 2003. There used to be another from 1682 to 1802. Called the **Ormonde Bridge**, it was located between the sites of the O'Donovan Rossa and Grattan Bridge. Although repaired many times, it finally collapsed in 1802, and was never replaced.

Appendix I

Historic locations outside Dublin, 1913-1923

Ballinasloe, Co. Galway *The Toiler*, Patrick MacIntyre was the editor. He opposed the ICA and the ITGWU, and was pro-employers in the Lockout of 1913: this newspaper was one of the most vociferous supporters of the Dublin employers. The Western News Company printed *The Toiler*, also at Ballinasloe, Co. Galway. Later he moved to Dublin, and lived at 21 Fownes Street. He was thirty-eight when he was killed during the Rising in the same tragic killing by Cpt. J.C Bowen-Colthurst as Francis Sheehy-Skeffington. MacIntyre is buried in Mount Jerome Cemetery. At the time he was shot, he was editor of *The Searchlight*, which was noted as a 'nationalist newspaper that was rabidly anti-German'.

Ballyseedy Cross, Co. Kerry On 6 March 1923 five Free State soldiers were killed by a bomb while clearing a road at the village of Knocknagoshel, Co. Kerry. The Free State explanation was that a mine was detonated in an attempt to kill a Free State officer, Lt Pat O' Connor, who was alleged to have tortured Republican prisoners.[751] The IRA/Republicans always claimed this explanation for the bombing was a fabrication and that they had not detonated any such bomb. In any event, Lt O'Connor, two captains and two privates were killed and that day the Dáil authorised the use of IRA/Republican prisoners to clear mined roads. Paddy Daly, the O/C of the Free State troops may have interpreted this as permission to take revenge on the anti-Treaty side and issued a statement saying from then forward Republican prisoners would be used to clear suspect mines. ('Nobody asked me to take any kid gloves to Kerry and I didn't take them.'[752])

On 7 March, nine Republican prisoners were taken from Ballymullen barracks in Tralee to Ballyseedy crossroads and tied to a landmine, which was exploded and the survivors machine-gunned. One of the prisoners, Stephen Fuller, who later became a TD, was blown to safety by the blast of the explosion and, although badly injured, escaped to tell of the event afterwards. The eight IRA/Republicans

751 *Enquiry into Ballyseedy killings*, National Library of Ireland, MS 22956.   **752** Macardle, Dorothy. *Tragedies of Kerry*, 1924, p. 16.

who were killed were: Patrick Buckley, James Connell, John Daly, Patrick Hartnett, John O'Connor, George Shea, Timothy Twomey, and James Walsh.[753]

The Free State troops in nearby Tralee had prepared nine coffins and were surprised to find only eight bodies on the scene.[754]

Bodenstown, Co. Kildare On 22 June 1913, at the annual Wolfe Tone memorial at Tone's grave, Padraig Pearse gave the commemorative oration:[755]

> We have come to the holiest place in Ireland; holier to us even than the place where Patrick sleeps in Down. Patrick brought us life, but this man died for us. And though many before him and some since have died in testimony of the truth of Ireland's claim to nationhood, Wolfe Tone was the greatest of all that have made that testimony, the greatest of all that have died for Ireland whether in old time or in new. He was the greatest of Irish Nationalists; I believe he was the greatest of Irish men.[756]

(See also Appendix III for the entire speech.)

It was this speech that put Pearse at the forefront of those who spoke for complete separation from Britain as opposed to those who supported Home Rule.[757]

Carrick-on-Suir, Co. Tipperary On 16 March 1922 Éamon de Valera spoke here saying 'If the Treaty was accepted, the fight for freedom would still go on; and the Irish people, instead of fighting foreign soldiers, would have to fight the Irish soldiers of an Irish government set up by Irish men. They will have to march over the dead bodies of their own brothers. They will have to wade through Irish blood. There are rights which may be maintained by force by an armed minority even against a majority.'[758] [759]

Carrigaholt, Co. Clare O'Curry College (Irish College); Brian O'Higgins was the Secretary from January 1917 until he was imprisoned (again) in May 1918 for the purported 'German Plot'.

Connemara, Co. Galway Renvyle House; this was Oliver St John Gogarty's house in the west. It was built by the Blakes, a Protestant family, in 1680. During the

---

753 *North Kerry and the Irish Civil War* http://www.rootsweb.com/~irlker/kercivwar.html 754 A monument sculpted by Yann Renard-Goullet was erected to commemorate those murdered by the Free State soldiers. 755 Even before Pearse joined the IRB, Thomas Clarke chose him for the Emmet and Tone orations. Wall, Maureen. 'The Background to the Rising', in Nowlan, Kevin. *The Making of the Rising*, p. 191. 756 Henry, R.M. *The Evolution of Sinn Féin*, 1920, p. 225-6. 757 Le Roux, Louis. *Tom Clarke*, 1936, p. 119-122. 758 Of his speeches quoted here, de Valera later claimed he was misunderstood, that he was merely warning of war not encouraging it, and that the *Irish Independent* misinterpreted his words on each occasion. On 23 March he wrote to the *Irish Independent* that attempts to characterise his utterances as incitements to Civil War were 'villainous'. *Irish Independent*, 23 March 1922. However, *The London Times* also quoted his speeches and editorialised: 'Mr de Valera's wild speeches in the South of Ireland have shocked the whole country. They indicate a rapid change in his attitude for some little time ago he was protesting that the will of the electors must be respected.' *The London Times*, 21 March 1922. 759 *Irish Independent*, 17 March 1922.

Land League wars of the late 1800's, the Blake widow who owned the house at the time converted it to a hotel. Gogarty bought it in the early 1900's. The IRA/Republicans burned it on 22 January 1923 during the Civil War. Gogarty received compensation for its burning from the Irish Free State government.[760]

Connemara, Co. Galway Rosmuc, near Roundstone. Padraig Pearse built this small cottage at Rosmuc as his summer cottage. It expressed two of his passions: his love of the Irish language and the spirit of the Gaeltacht and his sensitivity to the natural beauty of the Irish landscape.[761]

Craigavon, Co. Armagh Ancestral home of Sir James Craig.

On 19 September 1912, Sir Edward Carson read the Ulster Covenant from the steps of Craigavon.

> Being convinced in our consciences that Home Rule would be disastrous to the material well-being of Ulster as well as the whole of Ireland, subversive of our civil and religious freedom, destructive of our citizenship, and perilous to the unity of the Empire, we, whose names are underwritten, men of Ulster, loyal subjects of His Gracious Majesty King George V, humbly relying on the God whom our fathers in days of stress and trial confidently trusted, do hereby pledge ourselves in solemn covenant throughout this our time of threatened calamity to stand by one another in defending for ourselves and our children our cherished position of equal citizenship in the United Kingdom, and in using all means which may be found necessary to defeat the present conspiracy to set up a Home Rule Parliament in Ireland. And in the event such a Parliament being forced upon us we further solemnly and mutually pledge ourselves to refuse to recognise its authority. In sure confidence that God will defend the right we hereto subscribe our names. And further, we individually declare that we have not already signed this covenant.
> God Save the King.

Ultimately the Covenant was signed by a total of 471,414 including civil servants, soldiers, and police in uniform.

Crossbarry, Co. Cork On 19 March 1921, the English Army commenced a major attack on IRA/Volunteer units in Co. Cork, near Crossbarry, situated about twelve miles south-west of Cork city. The engagement began as a huge encircling operation by the British forces involving the Hampshire Regiment (from Cork), the Essex Regiment (Bandon and Kinsale), and Auxiliaries from Macroom; approximately 1120 seasoned troops facing about 100 IRA soldiers.[762]

IRA/Volunteer Cmdt Tom Barry, only becoming aware of the danger at the last

760 Gogarty, Oliver St John. Witness Statement 700. **761** *Sceal Scoil Eanna, The Story of an Educational Adventure*, Dublin, 1986, inside back cover. **762** Neeson, Eoin. *The Battle of Crossbarry*, 2008.

minute, resolved that his men would have to fight their way out of the encirclement.[763] Barry's calculation was that his men, who had only 40 rounds each, could not sustain the all day fight that they could expect if they retired before the British. However, Barry observed that one of the British columns advancing towards Crossbarry was well ahead of the other British units. If his men could break through this British force, roughly the same strength as his own, then they could break out of the British encirclement.[764]

Barry laid out an ambush for the British at Crossbarry crossroads — his men being in position by 5.30 am. When the first British lorries reached Crossbarry, about 12 vehicles according to Barry's account, they were caught by surprise and hit by a crossfire at very close range. The British took significant casualties and many of them fled the scene. Barry's men collected the British arms and ammunition before setting fire to the lorries. At this point, they were attacked again by another British column of about 200, coming from the south-west, but they retired after a stiff fire-fight. Two more British units converging on the area from the southeast tried to dislodge the IRA/Volunteers from their ambush position, but again without success and they, too, retired in disorder. Taking the chance that was offered by his quick victory to get away, Barry marched his men to safety in the Gurranereigh area, while the British were still disoriented by the ambush. There was another exchange of fire as the IRA column got away. The action lasted for under an hour.[765] [766]

From the beginning of the fighting Florence Begley, the brigade piper, played martial airs on his war pipes in Harold's farmyard and continued to play while the firing lasted.[767] Volunteers who fought at Crossbarry spoke later of the way the piper spurred them on to greater effort. Tom Kelleher often said 'that man's music was more effective than twenty rifles'. The piper also had an effect on the morale of the British troops. They would have associated a piper with a battalion in their army, and consequently would have thought that there were many more Volunteers present than there really were. Liam Deasy wrote that 'this was Begley's finest hour and he will always be remembered as "The Piper of Crossbarry" '.[768]

Curragh Army Camp, Co. Kildare By the early 20th century, this army barracks located just east of Kildare town, had become Britain's premier military base in Ireland.

The Ulster unionist movement's opposition to the passage of Home Rule in 1912 was heightened by the support it received from elsewhere in the United Kingdom. Not surprisingly, given its predominantly privileged background, the officer class in the British army also sympathised with the unionists.[769]

In March 1914, British government Ministers considered taking strong action

763 Barry, Tom. *Guerilla Days in Ireland*, 1981, p. 122 ff.   **764** Barry, Tom. Witness Statement 1743.   **765** *Daily Mail*, 21 March 1921.   **766** *The London Times*, 21 March 1921.   **767** Begley, Florence. Witness Statements 32, 1771.   **768** Deasy, Liam. *Towards Ireland Free*, 1973, p. 239.   **769** Ryan, A.P. *Mutiny at the Curragh*. London, 1956.

to crush unionist resistance. Intelligence reports had reached London suggesting 'evil-disposed persons' were plotting to raid stores of arms and ammunition in Ireland. Lt Gen. Sir Arthur Paget, Commander-in-Chief of troops in Ireland, was summoned to London and instructed to move 800 men into Ulster to reinforce depots and arms stores there, particularly in Armagh, Omagh, Enniskillen, and Carrickfergus.[770] On his return to the Curragh, Paget summoned his Brigadiers and informed them that active operations against Ulster were imminent. Officers whose homes were actually in the province of Ulster who wished to do so could apply for permission to be absent from duty during the period of operations, and would be allowed to 'disappear' from Ireland. Such officers would subsequently be reinstated, and would suffer no loss in their career. Any other officer who from conscientious or other motives was not prepared to carry out his duty as ordered, should say so at once. Such officers would at once be dismissed from the service, though strangely without compromising their 'reinstatement' and their careers.[771] The Brigadiers were to put these alternatives to their men and report back; 57 of the 70 officers consulted elected for dismissal. Brigadier Gen. Herbert Gough who, like many of them had Irish family connections, led them in their objections.[772]

English newspapers uniformly criticised the officers. The *Daily Chronicle* reported: 'For the first time in modern English history a military cabal seeks to dictate to Government the Bills it should carry or not carry into law. We are confronted with a desperate rally of reactionaries to defeat the democratic movement and repeal the Parliamentary Act. This move by a few aristocratic officers is the last throw in the game.'[773] The *Daily News* queried 'It is a question whether we govern ourselves or are governed by Gen. Gough. Speaking on the Irish Question, at a meeting held at Huddersfield on March 21st, Mr Lloyd George [British Chancellor of the Exchequer] said: "We are confronted with the greatest issue raised in this country since the days of the Stuarts. Representative government in this land is at stake. In those days our forefathers had to face a claim of the Divine Right of Kings to do what they pleased. Today it is the Divine Right of the aristocracy to do what its pleases. We are not fighting about Ulster. We are not fighting about Home Rule. We are fighting for all that is essential to civil liberty in this land".'[774]

The 57 officers technically were not guilty of 'mutiny'; they had not disobeyed direct orders of any kind. Nonetheless, news of their resignations caused the British government alarm. If orders had existed for the repression of the Ulster unionists and the arrest of their leaders, they were at once withdrawn. Prime Minister Herbert Asquith claimed publicly that no such action had been contemplated and that the

---

770 No written notes were allowed to be kept of Paget's meetings in London, and no written notes were permitted of his subsequent meetings with his commanders in Ireland. Later Paget, Brigadier Gough, and Major General Sir Charles Ferguson (GOC 5th Infantry Division) 'reconstructed' notes. Ferguson's were the most complete and form the basis of most histories of the orders given. 771 http:///www.curragh.info/articles/mutiny.htm 772 http://www.bbc.co.uk/history/british/easterrising/prelude/pr06.shtml 773 *Daily Chronicle*, 21 March 1914. 774 *Daily News*, 22 March 1914.

whole episode had resulted from an 'honest misunderstanding'. The War Office stated that Ministers had no future intention of using the army to enforce submission to the Home Rule Bill.

Overall, the episode greatly increased the confidence of Ulster unionists; they firmly believed that the government had intended to crush them but its plan had failed for lack of military support. For Irish nationalists, the events merely confirmed their increasing doubts about Asquith's real commitment to granting Home Rule.[775] As far as the nationalists were concerned, the die was cast. With all confidence now lost in parliamentary procedure, it followed that resorting to arms was unavoidable.

Thomas Davis Street, Cork, Co. Cork Cork Lord Mayor Thomas MacCurtain was shot by Black and Tans in his home, in front of his wife and children, on the night of 20 March 1920.[776]

After a week's trial in the Crown Court, the jury issued this verdict:

> We find that Alderman Thomas McCurtain [sic], Lord Mayor of Cork, died from shock and haemorrhage caused by bullet wounds and that he was wilfully murdered under circumstances of the most callous brutality and that the murder was carried out by the R. I. C., officially directed by the British Government. We return a verdict of murder against David Lloyd George, Prime Minister of England; Lord French, Lord Lieutenant of Ireland; Ian McPherson, late Chief Secretary of Ireland; Acting Inspector-General Smith of the R. I. C.; Divisional Inspector Clayton of the R. I. C.; and District Inspector Swanzy and some unknown members of the R. I. C.[777]

Dungarvan, Co. Waterford In Dungarvan on March 16 1922, Éamon de Valera said: 'The Treaty...barred the way to independence with the blood of fellow Irishmen. It was only by Civil War after this that they could get their independence.... If you don't fight today, you will have to fight tomorrow; and I say, when you are in a good fighting position, then fight on.'[778]

Falls Road, Belfast Catholic Boys' Hall. Bulmer Hobson founded Fianna na hÉireann here on 26 June 1902. In 1905, he and Denis McCullough founded the Dungannon Clubs (named after the meeting place of the Volunteers in 1778) and engaged Seán MacDermott as their full-time organiser.[779] (See also Appendix IV.)

Fenit Pier, Tralee, Co. Kerry The German arms ship *Aud* was supposed to land its arms here, to be taken by the Co. Clare Volunteers and distributed throughout Ireland.[780] (The *Aud* was the former Wilson Liner *Castro*; it was trapped in the Kiel

775 http://www.bbc.co.uk/history/british/easterrising/prelude/pr06.shtml **776** Feeley, Michael J. Witness Statement 68. **777** Macardle, Dorothy. *The Irish Republic*, 1937, 1965, p. 334. **778** *Irish Independent*, 18 March 1922. **779** McCullough, Denis. Witness Statement 914. **780** O'Leary, Mortimer. Witness Statement 107.

Canal at the start of World War I and captured by the Germans. It was re-named the *Libau*, then finally re-named the *Aud* for its voyage to Ireland).

15 Frederick Street, Limerick, Co. Limerick The Daly family home, where Kathleen Daly Clarke was born and raised.

Greystones, Co. Wicklow A fashionable resort about twenty miles south of Dublin. Éamon de Valera's family lived there while he was in the US.

Greystones, Co. Wicklow Grand Hotel; this was the hotel where Kitty Kiernan frequently stayed when she came to the Dublin area. She and Michael Collins often met here.

Kilcoole, Co. Wicklow Arms were landed here on 1 August 1914 for the Irish Volunteers. These were part of a shipment that had been purchased in Munich, the majority of which were landed at Howth, Co. Dublin. Sir Thomas Myles, a life-long nationalist, took part in the running of guns to Ireland, picking up 600 guns from Conor O'Brien's *Kelpie*, which had delivered them from Germany to the Welsh coast.[781] Myles sailed them in his vessel, *Chotah*, to Kilcoole. James Creed Meredith, a Protestant, who served as the President of the Dáil/Republican Supreme Court from 1920-22, helped him. The Chotah landed 600 rifles and 19,000 rounds of ammunition.[782]

Killarney, Co. Kerry In Killarney on 18 March 1922 Éamon de Valera was quoted: 'In order to achieve freedom, if our Volunteers continue, and I hope they continue until the goal is reached, if we continue on that movement which was begun when the Volunteers were started and we suppose this Treaty is ratified by your votes, then these men, in order to achieve freedom, will have, I said yesterday, to march over the dead bodies of their own brothers. They will have to wade through Irish blood…The people never have a right to do wrong.'[783]

Killorglin, Co. Kerry: Ballykissane Pier Con Keating, Charles Monaghan and Domhnall (Donal) Sheehan were killed here when their car went off the pier on Good Friday, 21 April, just prior to the Rising. Keating was a wireless expert who previously tried to set up a wireless at Count Plunkett's home in Kimmage. He was carrying a lamp he received from Éamonn Ceannt, which was to have been used to signal the *Aud*. They were in Kerry attempting to meet with Roger Casement. Michael McInerney was the surviving driver and was imprisoned at Frongoch.[784]

Kilmichael, Co. Cork The first engagement between IRA/Volunteers and Auxiliaries, remembered in the ballad 'The Boys of Kilmichael', took place on 28 November 1920.[785]

In the fall of 1920, about 150 Auxiliaries arrived in Macroom, Co. Cork, and commandeered Macroom Castle as their barracks.[786]

---

781 *An Poblacht*, 3 August 2000. **782** Rosney, Joseph. Witness Statement 112. **783** *Irish Independent*, 20 March 1922. **784** Perhaps the most interesting account of the accident can be found in the statement of the owner of the car, John Quilty. Quilty, John J. Witness Statement 516. **785** O'Rourke, Peter. 'The Kilmichael Ambush', *An Poblacht*, 30 November 2000. **786** Macardle. *The Irish Republic*, p. 384.

At 2 am that Sunday morning, a flying column of 36 heavily armed Volunteers led by Cmdt Tom Barry, assembled at Ahilina and marched ten miles through the night in the lashing rain, to engage the Auxiliaries on the road between Macroom and Dunmanway at Kilmichael Cross. By 9 am all the men were in position, and they waited all day for the Auxies.

At 4.30 pm, through the gathering dusk, two Crossley tenders carrying 17 Auxiliaries drove into Barry's carefully prepared ambush. In a fierce gun battle which lasted over 30 minutes and ended in hand-to-hand fighting, 16 Auxiliaries were killed and one mortally wounded.[787]

Having set fire to the tenders, the column marched off with the captured enemy equipment and at 11 pm, after an eleven-mile hike, reached Granure, where they camped overnight. After a three-day march south, zig-zagging to avoid enemy reinforcements, the column dispersed and the Volunteers returned to their various units.

During the days following the ambush, the British forces converged on Kilmichael and carried out large-scale reprisals against the local population. Martial law was proclaimed throughout Munster and a proclamation was issued by the Auxiliary division at Macroom, directing that all males passing through Macroom with their hands in their pockets would be shot on sight.[788] [789] [790] [791]

The Volunteers suffered three casualties, Pat Deasy (Kilmacsimon), Michael McCarthy (Dunmanway), and Jim O'Sullivan (Rossmore). All three were killed by a number of Auxiliaries who pretended to surrender during the battle.[792] [793] [794] [795] [796]

The British lost sixteen soldiers at the site of the ambush: Col. F.W. Craik, Maj. F. Hugo, Cpt. P.N. Graham, Cpt. W. Pallester, Cpt. C. Wainwright, Cadet W.T. Barnes, Cadet L.D. Bradshaw, Cadet J.C. Cleve, Cadet A.G. Jones, Cadet W. Hooper-Jones, Cadet E.W.H. Lucas, Cadet H.O. Pearson, Cadet F. Taylor, Cadet B. Webster, Temporary Cadet C.D.W. Bayley, and Temporary Constable A.F. Poole. There was a Memorial Service for them in the Macroom Church of Ireland on 1 December 1920.[797]

The seventeenth Auxiliary was Lt Cecil Guthrie who was wounded in the ambush[798] but apparently 'played dead' and escaped. He was captured by the Volunteers two days later, executed and buried in a nearby bog.

Knocklong Railway Station, Co. Limerick (Close to Tipperary Town, but in Co.

787 Barry. Op. cit., p. 36 ff. **788** Twohig, Patrick J. *Green Tears for Hercuba*, 1996, p. 144. **789** O'Neill, Stephen. 'The Ambush at Kilmichael', *Christmas Number*, December, 1937. **790** Deasy. Op. cit., p. 169 ff. **791** Kee, Robert. *The Green Flag*, 1972, p. 694-5. **792** Barry, Tom. Witness Statement 1743. **793** Hart, Peter. 'Peter Hart and His Enemies', *History Ireland*, Vol. XIII, No. 4, July/August 2005. **794** Ryan, Meda. 'Tom Barry and the Kilmichael Ambush', *History Ireland*, Vol. XIII, No. 5, September/October 2005. **795** Hart, Peter, P. O'Cuanachain, D.R. O'Connor Lysaght, B. Murphy and Meda Ryan. *Kilmichael: The False Surrender.* (Aubane, 1999). **796** *The Irish Times*, 25 January 1921, reported that the wounded had been bayoneted in the road by the IRA according to survivors of a later ambush. **797** Macroom Church of Ireland parish book, 1 December 1920. **798** Twohig. *Green Tears for Hercuba*, p. 145.

Limerick.) Following the Soloheadbeg ambush on 21 January 1919, Séamus Robinson, Seán Treacy, Seán Hogan and Dan Breen[799] went on the run.

On 11 May 1919, Hogan was captured and taken to Thurles. From there he would be moved to Cork. In order to rescue Hogan, the Volunteers boarded the train to Cork. Treacy was in the lead, followed by Ned O'Brien, Jimmy Scanlan, Seán Lynch, John Joe O'Brien[800] and Edward (Ned) Foley. Lynch, Scanlan and Foley were un-armed. Hogan was seated, with his back towards the engine, flanked by Sergeant Peter Wallace and Constable Enright. Facing them were Constables O'Reilly and Gerry Ring. Enright pressed his gun against Hogan's head and the Constable was shot dead by Treacy and Ned O'Brien. A fierce hand-to-hand fight followed: Ring escaped through the door; O'Reilly was knocked down by a blow to the head from Jimmy Scanlan; but it was only when the huge Sergeant Peter Wallace was fatally wounded that the struggle ended. By then Seán Treacy had been seriously wounded in the throat. Constable O'Reilly, who crawled out of the carriage carrying Ring's carbine with him, began shooting into the train from the platform and he wounded Ned O'Brien and Jimmy Scanlan. The arrival of Séamus Robinson and Dan Breen ended the rescue. Breen was hit in the arm and chest.[801] Hogan was taken away.

Afterwards five men living in the neighbourhood of Knocklong were arrested: Edward Foley, Patrick Maher, Michael Murphy, and Mick and Tom Shanahan. Foley and Maher were condemned to death and hanged. Maher had nothing to do with the Volunteers or the attack.[802]

Lisburn, Co. Antrim Detective Inspector Oswald Ross Swanzy was shot outside a church here on 22 August 1920. Swanzy was one of those responsible for the murder of Thomas MacCurtain, Lord Mayor of Cork, and one who was indicted for 'wilful murder' by the investigating jury. Michael Collins had him traced to Lisburn and sent a special team to kill him. The man who fired the shots was Seán Culhane, and Richard (Dick) Mulcahy was also present.

Soloheadbeg, Co. Tipperary Soloheadbeg is about two miles outside the town of Tipperary. On 21 January 1919 (the same day as the first meeting of the First Dáil in Dublin) Tipperary County Council workers Edward Godfrey and Patrick Flynn, guarded by two armed RIC Constables, James McDonnell and Patrick O'Connell, were carrying gelignite to the local quarry.[803] IRA/Volunteers led by Seán Treacy and Dan Breen lay in wait for the convoy, and shot dead both Constables who had attempted to ready their rifles. The rebels then rapidly withdrew, taking the gelignite.[804] Those involved on the day of the operation were four officers of the 3rd Tipperary Brigade IRA/Volunteers: Seán Treacy, Dan Breen, Seán Hogan (then only 17) and Seámus Robinson. Five other Volunteers joined them: Tadhg Crowe,

799 Breen, Daniel. Witness Statements 1739, 1763.　**800** O'Brien, John Joe. Witness Statement 1647.　**801** Kearney, Dr Joseph. Witness Statement 704.　**802** Twohig, Patrick J. *Blood on the Flag*, 1996, p. 88.　**804** Ó Snodaigh, Aengus. 'Gearing Up for War: Soloheadbeg 1919', *An Phoblacht*, 21 January 1999.

Paddy McCormack, Paddy O'Dwyer (Hollyford), and Michael Ryan (Donohill) and Seán O'Meara (Tipperary), both cycle scouts.[805] Treacy, Breen[806], Robinson and Hogan went on the run following the ambush.[807] As a result of this action, South Tipperary was placed under martial law and declared a Special Military Area under the Defence of the Realm Act.

Thurles, Co. Tipperary On 17 March 1922 Éamon de Valera repeated his earlier bloody imagery and added that if the IRA/Volunteers 'accepted the Treaty and if the Volunteers of the future tried to complete the work the Volunteers of the last four years had been attempting, they would have to complete it, not over the bodies of foreign soldiers, but over the dead bodies of their own countrymen. They would have to wade through, perhaps, the blood of some of the members of the Government, in order to get Irish freedom.'[808]

117 Victoria Street, Belfast Fianna Hall; it became the Belfast HQ of the Fianna.

Winthrop Street, Cork, Co. Cork Wren's Hotel. Sgt (Henry, H.H.) Timothy Quinlisk was a former member of the Casement Brigade in Germany before the Rising. While in Dublin, he stayed at the Munster Hotel in Mountjoy Street. Always known by Michael Collins and his men by the one name 'Quinlisk', he was a British double agent. As a ruse he was told Collins was here and when he subsequently gave the Cork RIC this information Quinlisk was killed on 19 February 1920.[809]

Woodenbridge, Co. Wicklow On 20 September 1914, John Redmond spoke to a meeting of Volunteers here. He encouraged members of the Irish Volunteers to join the British army and in this speech at Woodenbridge, he pledged his support to the Allied cause.

Wicklow Volunteers, in spite of the peaceful happiness and beauty of the scene in which we stand, remember this country at this moment is in a state of war, and your duty is twofold. The duty of the manhood of Ireland is twofold. Its duty is at all costs to defend the shores of Ireland against foreign invasion; it is the duty more than that of taking care that Irish valour proves itself on the field of war [as] it has always proved itself in the past. The interests of Ireland, of the whole of Ireland, are at stake in this war. This war is undertaken in the defence of the highest principles of religion and morality and right, and it would be a disgrace forever to our country, and a reproach to her manhood, and a denial of the lessons of our history, if young Ireland confined her efforts to remaining at

805 Kee. Op. cit., p. 632. **806** Breen, Dan. *My Fight for Irish Freedom*, 1924, p. 15-16. **807** Most sources consider the Soloheadbeg ambush the 'start' of the War of Independence, but it was not the first such ambush. On 7 July 1918 there was an ambush at Béal a' Ghleanna, near Ballingeary, Co. Cork, in which a policeman was wounded and some weapons were captured. The men had worn masks and simply went home afterwards. At Soloheadbeg, the ambushers did not wear masks and were easily identified, thus forcing them 'on the run'. **808** *Irish Independent*, 18 March 1922. **809** 'Quinlisk Killed', *Cork Examiner*, 24 February 1920.

home to defend the shores of Ireland from an unlikely invasion and to shrink from the duty of approval on the field of battle, that gallantry and courage which has distinguished our race through its history.

I say to you, therefore, your duty is twofold. I am glad to see such magnificent material for soldiers around me, and I say to you: Go on drilling and make yourself efficient for the Work, and then account yourselves as men, not only for Ireland itself, but wherever the fighting line extends, in defence of right, of freedom, and religion in this war.[810]

Following Redmond's speech at Woodenbridge, the Volunteer movement split. Those supporting Redmond's call to join up for the war were called the National Volunteers and comprised the majority of the Volunteers. Thirteen thousand, led by Eoin MacNeill, called themselves the Irish Volunteers, determined not to fight for the British. The Volunteers who fought in the Rising came predominately from these Irish Volunteers.

810 *Freeman's Journal*, 21 September 1914.

1916–1922

AN ICONOGRAPHY

IRISH REBELLION, MAY, 1916.

P. H. PEARSE,
(Commandant-General of the Army of the Irish Republic.)
Shot, by Order of Courtmartial, May 3rd, 1916.

City Printing Co., Limerick.

IRISH REBELLION, MAY 1916.

THOMAS MacDONAGH
(Commandant of Bishop Street Area),
Executed May 3rd, 1916.
One of the signatories of the "Irish Republic Proclamation."

IRISH REBELLION, MAY 1916.

THOMAS J. CLARKE,
Executed May 3rd, 1916.
One of the signatories of the "Irish Republic Proclamation."

IRISH REBELLION, MAY, 1916.

WILLIAM PEARSE
(Younger Brother of P. H. Pearse, also Executed).
Executed at Kilmainham Prison, May 4th, 1916.

IRISH REBELLION, MAY 1916.

JOSEPH PLUNKETT (son of Count Plunkett),
Commandant-General Irish Republican Army,
Executed May 4th, 1916.
Who was married a few hours before his execution.

IRISH REBELLION, MAY, 1916.

MRS. JOSEPH PLUNKETT
(MISS GRACE GIFFORD),
Who Married Joseph Plunkett in Kilmainham Prison a few hours
before his Execution on May 3rd, 1916.

EDWARD O'DALY,
Commandant, 1st Dublin Batt., Irish Republican Army.
Executed May 4th, 1916.

EAMONN CEANNT
(Commandant of the South Dublin Area),
Executed May 8th, 1916.
One of the signatories of the "Irish Republic Proclamation."

SEAN MAC DIARMADA,
Executed May 12th, 1916.
One of the signatories of the "Irish Republic Proclamation."

IRISH REBELLION, MAY 1916.

JAMES CONNOLLY,
(Commandant-General Dublin Division),
Executed May 9th, 1916.
One of the signatories of the "Irish Republic Proclamation."

IRISH REBELLION, MAY, 1916.

SEAN CONNOLLY,
(Irish Republican Army),
Killed in Action at City Hall, Dublin, Easter Monday, 1916.

IRISH REBELLION, MAY 1916.

Lieutenant THOMAS ALLEN
("C" Coy., 1st Battalion, Irish Volunteers).

Shot in Action at Four Courts,
April 28th, 1916.

Irish Rebellion — May 1916

Sackville Street in Flames — A Photograph taken by a "Daily Sketch" Photographer under fire.

The Insurrection in Dublin.—Armoured Motor Car in Bachelor's Walk.

Irish Rebellion, May, 1916.

*Soldiers bivouacking opposite Liberty Hall,
the Rebel Headquarters in Dublin.*

Irish Rebellion, May, 1916.

Holding a Dublin street against the Rebels.

Irish Rebellion, May, 1916.

Arrest of Edmund Kent. at 4 a.m.
He was subsequently shot.

Irish Rebellion _ May 1916.
A group of Officers with the captured rebel flag.

Irish Rebellion, May, 1916.
The wreck they made of Church Street. Dublin.

Henry Street, Dublin, showing side of G.P.O., Coliseum, and Arnott's.

Looking from Nelson Pillar down North Earl Street.

W. & G. BAIRD, LTD., BELFAST.

Liberty Hall, Dublin.

W. & G. BAIRD. LTL., BELFAST.

Irish Rebellion, May, 1916.
The General Post Office, Dublin (Rebel Headquarters), destroyed.

6719-10

THE SINN FEIN REVOLT IN DUBLIN.
GENERAL VIEW OF THE DEVASTATED CITY.

ROTARY PHOTO, E.C.

After the Insurrection.—Sackville Street from Eden Quay to Abbey Street.
Outer Walls of D·B·C· Restaurant still standing.

After the Insurrection.—Ruins of Eden Quay

Kilmainham Jail, Place of Execution

Exterior Kilmainham Jail, Dublin

IRISH PEACE CONFERENCE, JULY, 1921.   Gathering at the Mansion House.

Photo, Hogan, Dublin.

DAIL EIREANN IN SESSION, MANSION HOUSE, DUBLIN, AUGUST, 1921.

Military Operations, Dublin, June–July, 1922. [Photo, Hogan, Dublin.

NATIONAL TROOPS SEARCHING CIVILIANS.

THE FOUR COURTS, DUBLIN. JULY 1922.
LUMEX SERIES. N°1.

COMMANDANT H. BOLAND, T.D.
Killed in the Grand Hotel Skerries, July 30th 1922. R.I.P.

Michael Collins, T.D.

Photo by   COUNTESS MARKIEVICZ.   Keogh Bros.

Miss LILY WILLIAMS—Arthur Griffith

Comairle Catrac áta Cliat.
CORPORATION OF DUBLIN
(Municipal Gallery of Modern Art)

Appendix II

Addresses associated with Michael Collins (Micheal Ó Coileain)[811]

Abbey Street Middle (O'Connell Street corner): Dáil Secretariat; on the second floor there was an office, usually called 'The Dump'.

10 Abbey Street Upper George Moreland, cabinetmakers; the usual meeting place for 'The Squad'.

41 Abbey Street Upper Bannon Brothers' Pub; Collins first met Dave Neligan here.

16 Airfield Road, Rathgar Home of Julia O'Donovan; Collins often stayed here while 'on the run'. He ate dinner here on the night of Bloody Sunday.[812]

32 Bachelor's Walk Second office of the Irish National Aid and Volunteers' Dependents' Fund. Collins worked here as Secretary for the Fund from 19 February 1917 to 1918 at a salary of £2.10s per week.

The address was also an intelligence office from 1917 to 1921. Liam Tobin and Tom Cullen were in charge of intelligence directly under Collins.[813] Members included: Charlie Byrne, Paddy Caldwell, Charles Dalton, Joe Dolan, Joe Guilfoyle, Ned Kelliher, Patrick Kennedy, Dan McDonnell, Peter Magee, Frank Saurin, and Frank Thornton.

Another office here was Collins' Finance Office.

Collins was arrested outside this building on 2 April 1918, and he was taken to the DMP's Brunswick Street Station accompanied by Detectives Smith, Bruton, and O'Brien. Later he was taken to the Bridewell escorted by Detectives Smith, Thornton, and Wharton. From there he was taken to the Longford Assizes where he refused to recognise the court and since it was not Volunteer policy to accept bail he was then imprisoned in Sligo on 10 April 1918. Ultimately he was set free on bail from Sligo. (See also Ballinamuck, Co. Longford.)

Ballinamuck, Co. Longford (near Granard) Legga Chapel: on 3 March 1918

---

811 The addresses cover the period 16 October 1890 to 22 August 1922 (Collins' Glasnevin tombstone indicates his birthday as 12 October 1890). 812 O'Donovan, Julia. Witness Statement 475. 813 Tobin, Liam. Witness Statement 1753.

Collins made a speech here determined by the British as being 'calculated to cause disaffection':[814]

> You will not get anything from the British Government unless you approach them with a bullock's tail in one hand and a landlord's head in the other … Do not participate in raids for arms of useless old shotguns and old swords – go where you will find arms that will be of some use to you [a RIC Barracks], and we call on the Irish Volunteers to defend their arms until death.[815]

This speech led to a warrant for his arrest sworn on 11 March 1918 to return him 'to the locality pending his trial at assizes'. This warrant led to his arrest outside his Bachelor's Walk office on 2 April 1918, and he was taken to the DMP's Brunswick Street Station, and after he was transported to Longford he was brought before the magistrate, M. Johnson. Magistrate Johnson 'took depositions and returned the accused for trial at the next assizes for the county. The accused, who was very abusive and insulting, refused to recognise the court or give bail and was remanded to Sligo Gaol'. He was conveyed to Sligo Gaol on 10 April 1918, and released on 20 April. The magistrate granted the adjournment but required bail of £50 and two sureties of £25 each. Michael Doyle of Main Street, Longford, and Michael Cox (a cousin of Brigid Lyons) of Ballymahon Street, Longford, went as Collins' sureties.

The official charges, noted as the 'Outrage' on RIC forms were:

> Unlawfully incited to riot.
> Unlawfully incited the public to raid for arms.
> Unlawfully incited forcible entry.
> Unlawfully incited to assault on persons.
> Unlawfully incited to steal arms.[816]

A change of venue to the 'Londonderry' Assizes was issued on 28 June 1918, with his appearance scheduled for 17 July 1918, but Collins did not appear. A bench warrant was executed on that date. As a consequence of this warrant, his description was inserted in *Hue and Cry* and first appeared in the issue of 4 April 1919 under Co. Longford[817]. After that, Collins was officially 'on the run' and remained so until the Truce.
Barnesbury Hall, London In November 1909, Collins was sworn in here as a member of the IRB by his fellow post-office worker, Sam Maguire (a Protestant, originally from Dunmanway), and by Pat Bolton. Collins went on to become treasurer of the IRB in London.

---

814 Stewart, A.T.Q. *Michael Collins: The Secret File*, 1997, p. 82. **815** Notes taken by Sgt M. Casey, RIC files, Public Records Office, Kew, London. **816** Stewart, A.T.Q. Op. cit., p. 141. **817** *Michael Collins papers*, National Library of Ireland.

Béal na mBláth, Co. Cork (Usually translated as 'The Mouth of Flowers' or 'The Pass of the Flowers'.)

Collins' fatal itinerary, 20–22 August 1922:

Collins' convoy left Portobello Barracks, Dublin, at 5.15 am on Sunday, 20 August 1922, and made its first stop at Portlaoise Barracks where Collins discussed transferring some of the prisoners there to Gormanstown camp to relieve the overcrowded conditions. Then the convoy headed to Roscrea Barracks for an inspection and breakfast. At Limerick Barracks they were met by the O/C Southern Command, Gen. Eoin O'Duffy, and the two men discussed Collins' belief that the Civil War would soon be over and that Collins wanted to avoid any rancour. The convoy then headed through Mallow, and spent that night in Cork City, where he stayed at the military HQ in the Imperial Hotel. There Collins met his sister, Mary Collins-Powell, and his nephew Seán Collins-Powell who asked if he could accompany his uncle. Collins replied 'You have your job to do and I have mine.'[818] The rest of the evening was spent in consultation with the O/C of the area, Gen. Emmet Dalton. Most of the escort spent the evening in the Victoria Hotel.

On Monday, 21 August, Collins again visited his sister, then he and Gen. Dalton went to *The Cork Examiner* to discuss the general Free State position on publicity with the editor, Tom Crosbie. After lunch at the Imperial, they headed out to review the military in Cobh, and then returned to Cork in early evening.

Collins' party left the Imperial Hotel, Cork, at 6.16 am on Tuesday, 22 August. That day, the convoy included the following:

A motorcyclist, Lt John 'Jeersey' Smyth (from Enniscorthy). He was shot in the neck while helping to move Collins' body, but continued on his motorcycle.

A Crossley Tender under the command of Cmdt Seán (Paddy) O'Connell (he said the Act of Contrition in Collins' ear), Cpt. Joe Dolan, Sgt Cooney, John O'Connell[819] (the driver) and eight riflemen.

Collins and Emmet Dalton[820] in a yellow Leland Thomas touring car. The driver was Pvt. Michael Smith Corry (English born)[821] and the reserve driver was M. Quinn.

A Rolls Royce Whippet armoured car, named the *Slievenamon*. Jim Wolfe was the driver, Jimmy 'Wiggy' Fortune the co-driver. The Vickers' gunner on the armoured car was John (Jock) McPeake. (He deserted on

---

818 Maj. Gen. Collins-Powell vividly describes the meetings in *Hang Up Your Brightest Colors*, Video by Kenneth Griffith, 1966. **819** O'Connell's account provides the basis for the description of the day's travels of the convoy and the ambush as related in Taylor, Rex, *Michael Collins*, 1958, p. 242 ff. **820** Gen. Dalton's account was published in the *Freeman's Journal*, 27 August 1922, and reprinted as Appendix J in Taylor, ibid, p. 321. **821** Corry's account is Appendix I in Taylor, ibid, p. 320.

2 December 1922 with Pat and Mick O'Sullivan and took the armoured car to the IRA/Republicans; he said he did it for a woman. He was arrested in Glasgow in July 1923 and was imprisoned in Portlaoise where he endured an hunger strike). Cooney and Monks were the other members of the armoured car crew.

The convoy went through Macroom, where Collins met Florrie O'Donoghue[822], then to Crookstown and having passed through Béal na mBláth at 8 am it stopped to get directions. At Bandon Collins briefly met with Maj. Gen. Seán Hales. At Clonakilty the convoy stopped for lunch at Callinan's Pub. In the afternoon the convoy went to Roscarberry and Collins had a drink in the Four Alls Pub (owned by his cousin Jeremiah) at Sam's Cross where Collins declared: 'I'm going to put an end to this bloody war.'

(There was a sign over the pub door showing four pictures with the inscriptions:

> 'I rule all [King]
> I pray for all [Bishop]
> I fight for all [Croppy Boy]
> I pay for all [Farmer]')

The convoy left Skibbereen at 5 pm and headed back to Cork. Collins met his great friend John L. Sullivan on this journey.[823] The convoy detoured around Clonakilty on the way back because of a roadblock. It stopped at Lee's Hotel (Munster Arms) in Bandon for tea. Gen. Seán Hales was in command here. His brother, Tom Hales,[824] was the column leader on the other side and led the IRA/Republican ambush.

The ambush party met in Long's Pub (owned by Denis Long, who was the 'lookout' for Collins' party as it passed through Béal na mBláth in the morning).[825] Originally, the ambush party numbered between 25 and 30, including, according to varying sources, Dinny Brien, Pat Buttimer, John Callaghan, Dan Corcoran, Jim Crowley, Seán Culhane, Liam Deasy, Bill Desmond, Bobs Doherty, Mike (O') Donoghue, Sonny Donovan, Charley Foley, Tom Foley (he collected the gelignite which had been taken for the mine and was hidden in John Lordan's house),

822 *Florence O'Donoghue Papers*, Manuscript 31, p. 305, National Library of Ireland. Collins met O'Donoghue in Macroom, and the notes in O'Donoghue's papers include most of the names of those in the ambush 'party'. **823** See Griffith and O'Grady, *Ireland's Unfinished Revolution*, 1982, p. 293-4. **824** Hales, Tom. Witness Statement 20. **825** There is no consensus on who or even how many were in the ambush party during the day or at the time of shooting. Early in the day, the party set an ambush with a cart across the road, laid a mine, and waited all day for the column's return, but then dismantled the mine and was in the process of moving the cart when Collins' column came upon them. It has been said there were many more IRA/Republicans in the ambush party during the day, but by the time of the arrival of Collins it is thought there were only 4 members left in the ambush party with 3 other groups of 2–3 men 'passing through', including Liam Deasy and his Deputy Tom Crofts who walked through about 7.00 pm.

Shawno Galvin, Tom Hales, Daniel Holland (O/C 1st Battalion), Jim Hurley, Seán Hyde, Jim Kearney (an engineer, he helped set the mine), Pete Kearney (O/C 3rd Battalion), Tom Kelleher (Cmdt Gen. 1st Southern Division), John Lordan, Con Lucey, Jeremiah Mahoney, Con Murphy, Joe Murphy, John O'Callahan (he was the 1st Battalion Engineer and was in control of the mine which was buried in the road), C. O'Donoghue, Denis (Sonny) O'Neill (from Maryborough, Co. Cork, who was to provide covering fire to retreating IRA ambush members), Jim Ormond, Tadhg O'Sullivan, Bill Powell, Tim Sullivan (an engineer, he helped set the mine), and Paddy Walsh.[826] [827] [828] [829]

The ambush took place at Béal na mBláth (between Macroom and Bandon but closer to Crookstown than Bandon) just before sunset, at 7.30 pm.

Most agree Denis (Sonny) O'Neill fired the fatal shot, however he never publicly indicated he did so.[830] [831] [832] [833] [834] [835] [836]

On the way into Cork City, Dalton stopped the convoy at the Sacred Heart Mission at Victoria Cross. Here Fr O'Brien administered the Last Rites to Collins.

Then the convoy headed back to the Imperial Hotel, where Dalton, Cmdt O'Connell, Sgt Cooney and Lt Gough went into the Hotel to inform Dr Leo Ahern and asked him to take charge of the body.

Maj. Gen. Dr Leo Ahern first examined Collins' body when it was brought to the Imperial Hotel, and then at Shanakiel Hospital. He was the first doctor to examine the body and pronounced Collins dead. His examination found a large, gaping wound 'to the right of the poll. There was no other wound. There was definitely no wound in the forehead.'[837]

From the Hotel Collins' body was taken to Shanakiel Hospital in Cork, escorted by Cmdt O'Connell and Cmdt O'Friel.[838]

Dr Michael Riordan was detailed by Dr Ahern to examine and prepare the body, and they conducted the autopsy. Dr Christy Kelly was present during a thorough second examination later and confirmed a huge wound on the right side behind the ear, with no exit wound.[839] (In contrast, Dr Patrick Cagney, a British surgeon in the British army during the war who had a wide knowledge of gunshot wounds and who examined the body later confirmed there was an entry wound as well as a large exit wound.[840])

826 O'Donoghue, Florence. Witness Statement 554. **827** Ryan, Meda. *The Day Michael Collins Was Shot*, 1989, pp. 191-92. **828** Twohig, Patrick J. *The Dark Secret of Béal na mBláth*, 1991, p. 16. **829** Ó Cuinneagain, Michael. *On the Arm of Time: Ireland 1916-1922*. 1992, p. 79-105. **830** Ryan, Meda. Op. cit., p. 125, 145. Throughout her book she identifies him as Sonny 'Neill'. **831** Twohig. *The Dark Secret of Béal na mBláth*, p. 284. **832** Coogan, Tim Pat. *Michael Collins*, 1992, p. 418. **833** Mackay, James. *Michael Collins*, 1996, p. 289. **834** Ryan, Ray. 'The Man Who Stood Next to Collins' Killer', *The Cork Examiner*, 5 November 1985. **835** However, see also Twohig, Patrick J. *The Dark Secret of Béal na mBláth*, p. 106 and 158. **836** John Feehan writes 'It was certainly *not* Sonny O'Neill'. (Emphasis added). Feehan. *The Shooting of Michael Collins*, 1981, 1991, p. 129 ff, p. 133. He declines to name anyone in particular. **837** Ryan, Meda. Op cit., p. 138-9. **838** *Cork Examiner*, 24 August 1922. **839** Ryan, Meda. Op cit., p. 138-9. **840** Feehan. Op. cit., p. 95.

Collins' death was not officially registered.

Eleanor Gordon, Matron of Shanakiel Hospital, cleaned and attended to Collins' wounds and also later testified to the nature of the wounds. His body was first taken to room 201, then to room 121 after the autopsy where Free State soldiers guarded it until taken to the ship for transport to Dublin.

The steamship *SS Classic* (later known as the *SS Kilbarry*) left Penrose Quay in Cork and brought Collins' body from Cork to Dublin[841]. Gen. Dalton sent this handwritten telegram from the Cork GPO to The Dublin HQ:

CHIEF OF STAFF
DUBLIN
COMMANDER-IN-CHIEF SHOT DEAD IN AMBUSH AT
BEALNABLATH NEAR BANDON 6.30 [sic] TUESDAY EVENING
WITH ME, ALSO ONE MAN WOUNDED. REMAINS LEAVING
BY CLASSIC FOR DUBLIN TODAY WEDNESDAY NOON.
ARRANGE TO MEET. REPLY DALTON.[842 843 844 845]

As the vessel passed down channel from Cork it passed the assembled remaining British naval vessels, upon the decks of which the British sailors mustered, saluted, and 'The Last Post' played.[846]

Though he was within a few miles of Béal na mBláth on the day Collins was killed, Éamon de Valera had hoped to meet him, but no plan had been made. Moreover, de Valera had had no involvement in the ambush; he had little political influence on the IRA/Republicans at the time, and no military influence at all. The most reliable evidence indicates de Valera went to Long's Pub and tried to prevent the ambush, but was rebuffed by the IRA. Liam Lynch, O/C of the IRA, specifically had given orders that de Valera's efforts to cease hostilities should not be encouraged. Despite rumour and innuendo there is no evidence that de Valera was involved in the planning of the ambush being laid for Collins. Later de Valera was quoted: 'What a pity I didn't meet him.' And 'It would be bad if anything happens to Collins, his place will be taken by weaker men.'[847]

On the morning of 23 August Gen. Richard Mulcahy, as Free State Army Chief of Staff issued the following message to the Army;

841 Ryan, Meda. Op cit., p. 117, 195. **842** Taylor names the vessel the *SS Innisfallen*. Taylor, Rex,. *Michael Collins*, 1958, p. 255. **843** Younger also names it the *SS Innisfallen*. Younger, Calton. *Ireland's Civil War*, 1968, p. 444. **844** O'Farrell also identifies the vessel as the *SS Innisfallen*. O'Farrell, Padraic. *Who's Who*, 1997, p. 166. **845** Gen. Dalton wrote this telegram, and remembered the vessel as the *SS Classic*, but most sources report the vessel was the *SS Innisfallen*. However, the *SS Innisfallen* was torpedoed and sunk without warning by a German submarine, *U-64*, on 23 May 1918, 16 miles east of the Kish Light Vessel. She was on her way from Liverpool to Cork, and 10 died. **846** Linge, John. 'The Royal Navy and the Irish Civil War', *Irish Historical Studies*, Vol. XXXI, No. 121, May 1998. **847** Mackay. Op. cit., p. 286.

Stand calmly by your posts. Bend bravely and undaunted to your task. Let no cruel act of reprisal blemish your bright honour.

Every dark hour that Michael Collins met since 1916 seemed but to steel that bright strength of his and temper his brave gaity. You are left as inheritors of that strength and bravery.

To each of you falls his unfinished work. No darkness in the hour: loss of comrades will daunt you in it.

Ireland! The Army serves – strengthened by its sorrow.[848]

In Dublin, Collins' body was taken to St Vincent's Hospital where Dr Oliver St John Gogarty embalmed the body[849], and had Sir John Lavery paint Collins' portrait. Albert Power sculpted the death mask.

Collins' body was taken to the chapel in St Vincent's on Thursday, 24 August, then in late evening to Dublin City Hall for the public lying-in-state until Sunday evening. On Sunday evening his body was removed to the Pro-Cathedral where it remained under guard overnight.

His funeral Mass was said in the Pro-Cathedral on Monday, with several Bishops celebrating the Requiem High Mass.

The gun carriage on which the casket was transported to Glasnevin Cemetery had been borrowed from the British and used in the bombardment of the Four Courts in June. The Free State Government specially purchased four black artillery horses from the British to pull the caisson to Glasnevin.

At Collins' funeral in Glasnevin on Monday, 28 August, Richard Mulcahy, who would take Collins' place as Commander in Chief of the Army, delivered the oration:

> …Tom Ashe, Tomas MacCurtain, Traolach MacSuibhne, Dick McKee, Micheal Ó Coileain, and all you who lie buried here, disciples of our great chief, those of us you leave behind are all, too, grain from the same handfull, scattered by the hand of the Great Sower over the fruitful Soil of Ireland. We, too, will bring forth our own fruit. Men and women of Ireland, we are all mariners on the deep, bound for a port still seen only through storm and spray, sailing still on a sea full 'of dangers and hardships, and bitter toil'. But the Great Sleeper lies smiling in the stern of the boat, and we shall be filled with that spirit which will walk bravely upon the waters.[850]

(See also Appendix III for the entire oration).

The British Press acknowledged Collins' part in Ireland's freedom.

The *Daily Telegraph* wrote:

---

848 *The Irish Times*, 24 August 1922. **849** Gogarty confirmed that there were 'two wounds caused by the fatal bullet, entry and exit'. Connolly, Colm. *Michael Collins*, 1996, p. 94. **850** *Irish Independent*, 29 August 1922.

He was a bitter and implacable enemy of England while the British garrison remained in Ireland and Ireland was not free to govern herself in her own way....The dead man, beyond all doubt, was of the stuff of which great men are made.[851]

The *Daily Chronicle* called him a 'young and brilliant leader'.[852] The *Evening Post* described his death as a 'staggering blow'.[853]

The London *Daily Sketch* editorialised so:

The hand that struck down Michael Collins, guided by a blinded patriotism, has aimed a blow at the unity of Ireland for which every one of her sons is fighting. Collins was probably the most skilled artisan of the fabric of a happier Ireland. Certainly he was the most picturesque figure in the struggle; and in the rearing of a new State a popular ideal serves as the rallying point to draw the contending elements. The death of Collins leaves the ship of the Free State without a helmsman.[854]

The London Times printed the following

After the Treaty was signed Mr Collins showed himself quickly to be something more than a fighting man. The debates in the Dáil proved him to be a shrewd man of affairs, with a firm grasp of details, and, what was very valuable in that hot-bed of sentimentalism, a saving sense of humour. He was frank, mild, courteous in his dealings with men of all parties, and even a brief conversation with him left one with the impression that here was a man who, conscious of his burden of responsibility, was conscious also of his limitations and would not be too proud to learn. It is difficult to make any estimate of the effect of Mr Collins's death in the immediate course of affairs in Ireland. One thing however is certain. There can be no further talk, or even whisper, of compromise with the Republican extremists. This murder will dissipate the last fragment of sympathy with their cause, will inspire the Army with new resolution, and will rally the whole force of national opinion solidly behind the Government. In one sense it is a stricken Government; in another sense it has been reinforced, for now more than ever the people's strength will be at its service. Michael Collins's blood will help to cement the foundation of the Free State.[855]

In a message to William Cosgrave, General Sir Neville Macready, former GOC

---

851 *Daily Telegraph*, 23 August 1922. **852** *Daily Chronicle*, 23 August 1922. **853** *Evening Post*, 23 August 1922. **854** *Daily Sketch*, 24 August 1922. **855** *The London Times*, 24 August 1922.

British troops in Ireland, and the man who turned over Dublin Castle to Collins earlier in 1922 wrote:

> On the many occasions during the last year when we met on official business I always found him ready and willing to help in all matters that were brought to his notice in connection with the forces under my command. I deeply regret that he should not have been spared to see in a prosperous and peaceful Ireland the accomplishment of his work.[856]

Collins died intestate, leaving an estate of £1,950.9s.11d, which passed to his brother Johnny.

Shane Leslie wrote the following lines:

> What is that curling flower of wonder
> As white as snow, as red as blood?
> When Death goes by in flame and thunder
> And rips the beauty from the bud.
>
> They left his blossom white and slender
> Beneath Glasnevin's shaking sod;
> His spirit passed like sunset splendour
> Unto the dead Fianna's God.
>
> Good luck be with you, Michael Collins,
> Or stay or go you far away;
> Or stay you with the folk of fairy,
> Or come with ghosts another day.

Bloody Sunday, Dublin (21 November 1920)
Baggot Street Lower, Croke Park, Earlsfort Terrace, Jones Road, Morehampton Road, Lower Mount Street, Pembroke Road, Sackville Street Upper:

In 1920 'The Cairo Gang' had been recruited and formed by Col. Ormonde Winter, KBE, CB, CMG, DSO, Chief of the British Combined Intelligence Services in Ireland from the spring of 1920 until the Truce. The IRA/Volunteers knew him as the 'Holy Terror'. The Cairo Gang was ruthless and efficient, and set out specifically to eliminate Michael Collins and his Intelligence Department. It had been primarily responsible for tracking down Dan Breen and Seán Treacy, and had killed Treacy in Talbot Street, Dublin, 14 October 1920.

Collins, Cathal Brugha and others sentenced over twenty British officers at their 35 Lower Gardiner Street meeting on 20 November. (The publicised and 'official'

[856] Macready quoted in the *Daily Sketch*, 24 August 1922.

figures stated that 11 officers were killed and 4 escaped, but Frank Thornton's unpublished memoirs listed 19 killed, at 8 different addresses in Dublin. Joe Leonard stated that there were 'fourteen engagements that morning', but he does not list any.[857] In addition to those locations at which British agents were killed, the IRA/Volunteers set out to attack agents at two others: the Shelbourne Hotel where a squad entered and tried to kill some British officers but the officers all escaped — the squad climbed a staircase, turned a corner and fired at armed men, only to find they had fired at their reflection in a large mirror; at 7 Ranelagh Road, Cpt. Noble, a British intelligence agent, had rooms — IRA/Volunteers were assigned to kill him, but he wasn't home.) In fact 11 British officers, 2 Auxiliary Cadets and 2 civilians (T.H. Smith and L.E. Wilde) were killed in 8 locations as follows:

> 92 Lower Baggot Street: Cpt. W.F. Newbury
> 119 Lower Baggot Street: Cpt. George T. Baggallay
> 28 Earlsfort Terrace: Cpt. John Fitzgerald
> 117 Morehampton Road: Cpt. Donald L. MacClean, T.H. Smith
> 22 Lower Mount Street: Lt H.R. Angliss (alias Patrick 'Paddy' McMahon), Auxiliary Cadets Garner and Morris
> 38 Upper Mount Street: Lt Peter Ames, Cpt. George Bennett
> 28 Upper Pembroke Road: Maj. C.M.G. Dowling, Col. Hugh F. Montgomery, Cpt. Leonard Price
> Upper Sackville Street, Gresham Hotel: Cpt. Patrick MacCormack, L.E. Wilde

Dave Neligan stated that the incident: 'caused complete panic in Dublin Castle'.[858]

Prime Minister David Lloyd George: 'They got what they deserved — beaten by counter-jumpers!' 'Ask Griffith for God's sake to keep his head and not to break off the slender link that had been established. Tragic as the events in Dublin were, they were of no importance. These men were soldiers, and took a soldier's risk.'[859]

Collins said:

> My one intention was the destruction of the undesirables who continued to make miserable the lives of ordinary decent citizens. I have proof enough to assure myself of the atrocities, which this gang of spies and informers have committed. Perjury and torture are words too easily known to them. If I had a second motive it was no more than a feeling I would have for a dangerous reptile. By their destruction the very air is made sweeter. For myself, my conscience is clear. There is no crime in

857 Leonard, Joseph. *Witness Statement* 547. 858 Neligan, David. *The Spy in the Castle*, 1968, p. 123. 859 Gleeson, James. *Bloody Sunday*, 1962, p. 181.

detecting and destroying, in wartime, the spy and the informer. They have destroyed without trial. I have paid them back in their own coin. [860] [861]

Services for six of the Protestant officers were held at Westminster Abbey and services for the Catholic men, Peter Ames, George Bennett and H.R. Angliss, were held at Westminster Cathedral.

Following the morning raids, sixteen Irish were killed at 2 locations:

Jones Road/Croke Park: Mick Hogan (Tipperary football player, for whom the Hogan Stand is named), Jane Boyle (26), James Burke, Daniel Carroll, Michael Feery, Thomas Hogan, James Matthews, Patrick O'Dowd, Jeremiah (Jerry) O'Leary (10), William (Willie) Robinson (11), Thomas Ryan (he was shot dead while whispering the Act of Contrition in Mick Hogan's ear), John Scott (14), Joseph Traynor, and James Teehan
Lincoln Place: 7 civilians shot, 2 died.

Sixty-two people were injured in Croke Park in the raid by a mixed force of Black and Tans, RIC, Auxies and British Army troops, and another 12 were injured in the stampede out.

Maj. Mills commanded the Regular Army back-up troops at Croke Park and reported adversely on the actions of the Black and Tans, Auxies and RIC.

Dick McKee and Peadar Clancy, along with Conor Clune, were killed in Dublin Castle on Sunday night. McKee and Clancy were captured on Saturday night in Seán Fitzpatrick's house in Lower Gloucester Street – supposedly a 'safe house'. (James [Shankers] Ryan, the tout who turned them in, was later killed outside Shanahan's Pub in Foley Street.) Conor Clune, a Gaelic Leaguer from Co. Clare, was taken in Vaughan's Hotel on Saturday night. Clune had nothing to do with the Volunteers and only had come to Dublin to confer with journalist Piaras Béaslaí. Clune was staying in Vaughan's, which was a noted IRA/Volunteer meeting place, and so was killed in Dublin Castle with McKee and Clancy on Sunday.

1 Brendan Road, Donnybrook Batt and Maire O'Connor's home. Collins often lunched here, stayed here, and used it for meetings. 'Jameson' (John Charles Byrne) was lured here to see if he was a spy. (See also Ballymun Road, Harcourt Street, Nutley Lane, Sackville Stret Upper, and Winthrop Street, Cork, County Cork [Appendix I].) Collins hid £25,000 in gold in a baby's coffin under the floor.

23 Brendan Road, Donnybrook Susan (Sinead) Mason and her aunt, Mrs Donovan, owned this house. Collins often stayed here. She was Collins' personal and private secretary, and endured an enormous workload as well as dangerously carrying

860 Ibid, p. 191. **861** Townshend, Charles. 'Bloody Sunday: Michael Collins Speaks', *European Studies Review*, Vol. IX, (1979).

dispatches from location to location. For a while their friends, the Batt O'Connors and Collins' sister, Margaret Mary, thought they'd marry.

5 Cabra Road Michael Foley's home, where Collins first met Éamon (Ned) Broy.
Camden Street Nora O'Keefe's restaurant. Collins often lunched here and used it as an 'office' between 76 Harcourt Street and 22 Mary Street.
15 Cadogan Gardens, London House used by Collins and his personal bodyguards and staff during the Treaty negotiations from 11 October to 6 December 1921.

Upon his return here on the morning of 6 December, he wrote his prophetic letter to John O'Kane:

> Think — what have I got for Ireland? Something which she has wanted these past seven hundred years. Will anyone be satisfied with the bargain? Will anyone? I tell you this — early this morning I signed my own death warrant. I thought at the time how odd, how ridiculous — a bullet might just as well have done the job five years ago.[862]

147 North Circular Road home of Patrick and Margaret Collins O'Driscoll, Michael's eldest sister. Michael often visited here. Margaret was elected to the Dáil in 1923, and served as a TD until 1933.
3 Crow Street The Department of Intelligence office was on the second floor, above J.F. Fowler's, printers. Though it was technically the head office of his Ministry, Collins infrequently came here. Under the name of Irish Products Company, Liam Tobin, Collins' Chief of Intelligence, had his office here[863], assisted by Tom Cullen and Frank Thornton. Principal Staff: Charlie Dalton, Joe Dolan, Joe Guilfoyle, and Frank Saurin.
1 Dame Street Craig Gardiner & Co, Chartered Accountants; Collins worked here before the Rising. His co-workers included Frank Henderson and Joe McGrath, also Volunteers.
21 Dawson Street Eileen McGrane's home where Collins kept many papers; it was raided on 31 December 1920. Éamon (Ned) Broy's papers were found here leading to his arrest as well as hers.[864]
Denzille Lane Batty Hyland owned a garage here; Batty was Collins' regular driver, and his brother, Joe, also drove for Collins.
Dublin Castle The Castle was handed over to Collins on 16 January 1922 by Edmund Bernard FitzAlan-Howard, 1st Viscount FitzAlan of Derwent, KG, PC, Lord Lieutenant of Ireland.
Dun Laoghaire, Co. Dublin Royal Marine Hotel. Collins and Kitty Kiernan were dancing here when Joe O'Reilly came to tell them of the truce in July 1921.

John and Hazel Lavery stayed here when they came to Ireland so that John

---

862 Costello, Frank, editor, *Michael Collins: In His Own Words*, 1997, p. 79.   **863** Tobin, Liam. Witness Statement 1753.   **864** Neligan, David. Witness Statement 380.

could work on his painting on the subject of the Civil War in August 1922. They were in residence when Collins was killed.

10 Exchequer Street First 'real' Irish National Aid and Volunteers' Dependents' Fund office where Collins worked for Kathleen Clarke after his release from Frongoch. The office moved to 32 Bachelor's Walk later in 1917.

Frongoch Prison Camp, North Wales Collins was Irish Prisoner 1320 here. Collins smoked 30 cigarettes a day in Frongoch – he gave them up in 1920, after the Tans arrived, saying he would not be a slave to anything.

Furry Park, Raheny Home of Crompton and Moya Llewelyn (O'Connor) Davies. Her father, James O'Connor, was a Centre of the IRB in Dublin.

When she was 11, her mother and three sisters died of food poisoning after eating tainted mussels taken from a contaminated pool at the rear of their house in Blackrock. James Joyce used the story in *Finnegan's Wake*.[865] [866]

One of Collins' most effective couriers and sources, she was imprisoned during the War of Independence.

Collins often stayed here. He ate dinner here on 17 August 1922 with the Laverys, Sir Horace and Lady Plunkett, Piaras Béaslaí, Joe O'Reilly and others. A man named Dixon (formerly a marksman with the Connaught Rangers) was apprehended with a rifle. When he claimed he wanted to kill Collins he was taken by Collins' guards and shot.

Gardiner Row Linda Kearns' home; Collins used the house for meetings and stayed here occasionally.

35 Gardiner Street, Lower Typographical Society's Rooms/HQ of the Dublin Printer's Union. On 20 November 1920 Collins met Cathal Brugha, Peadar Clancy, Paddy Daly, Dick McKee, Richard Mulcahy and Seán Russell here to finalise plans for Bloody Sunday.

65 Great Britain Street Home of Mr and Mrs Maurice Collins (no relation), where Michael Collins often stayed overnight.[867] It was raided 31 January 1920.

68–69 Great Britain Street Liam Devlin's Pub, just off Rutland Square. It was 'Joint No 2' – the 'unofficial HQ' of Collins. He waited here for Bloody Sunday reports.

1-8 Great Brunswick Street (now Pearse Street) (corner of Townsend Street): DMP G-Division HQ. Éamon (Ned) Broy let Collins in on the night of 7 April 1919 to look over the G-Division files on the Volunteers. (Collins met Seán Nunan on the way to meet Broy and took him along, so Nunan also saw the files). It was on this foray that Collins read his own file; the contents indicated that he 'belongs to a family of "brainy" people and of advanced Sinn Féin sympathies'. That gave Collins such a hearty laugh that Broy heard him from his office down the hall and was concerned they would be discovered.

865 Lowth, Cormac F. 'The O'Connor tragedy', *The Dun Laoghaire Borough Historical Society Journal*, No. 10, 2001. **866** Lowth, Cormac F. 'James O'Connor, Fenian and the tragedy of 1890', *Dublin Historical Record*, Vol. IV, No. 2, Autumn 2002. **867** Collins, Maurice. Witness Statement 550.

8 Haddon Road, Clontarf Thomas Gay's home. Gay was the librarian in Capel Street Municipal Library. Weekly conferences were held here with Éamon Broy, James McNamara and David Neligan.[868]

*6 Harcourt Street Ministry of Finance office, raided on 12 September 1919.[869]

8 Harcourt Street Ivanhoe Hotel. Collins hid on the roof here when 6 Harcourt Street was raided.

*76 Harcourt Street Raided in November 1919.

*17 Harcourt Terrace Used from the end of May to June 1921.

*21, 22 Harry Street Used as a primary office and also a Department of Intelligence office. It was not in use for long.

1 Island View, Howth Home of Mrs Quick. She rented rooms to many young women and Collins often enquired after them in letters. Susan Killeen, a London 'girlfriend' lived here following the start of World War I.

King's Cross, London On 25 April 1914 Collins was enrolled in the 'German' Gymnasium into Company No 1 of the London Branch of the Irish Volunteers. His cousin, Seán Hurley, enrolled him. P.S. O'Hegarty signed his membership card.

London On 21 January 1922 Sir James Craig, Prime Minister of Northern Ireland, met Collins in London in order to resolve the impasse between north and south and to promote some kind of co-operation between the two governments.[870] The result was the first Craig-Collins Pact. The parties agreed on a mechanism that would be more suitable than the Council of Ireland proposal from the British Government. Collins promised that the 'Belfast Boycott' on Ulster goods, which was in operation in the South, would be discontinued. For his part, Craig promised to help stop attacks on Northern Catholics, especially those working in shipyards, and to see to it that some of the 10,000 'redundant' Catholic shipyard workers would be reinstated. The pact's language appeared to recognise there were now two governments in Ireland. Craig certainly believed this to be the case. Collins did not — or maybe changed his mind — and the agreement fell apart within a few weeks in a welter of renewed violence.[871]

In March 1922, a second 'formal' pact was agreed between the British, Northern Ireland and Provisional governments. It reiterated earlier promises made in January but additionally called for a cessation of IRA/Republican activity in Northern Ireland, promised to sort out the border issues through the Boundary Commission. It made detailed provision for policing by a mixed Catholic-Protestant police force.[872] This pact, too, was shortly ignored.[873]

*5 Mary Street Collins used this as an office for a short while in 1919.

---

868 Gay, Thomas B. Witness Statement 780. **869** The eight addresses marked here with an asterisk * indicate Collins' primary offices during the period. **870** Macardle. *The Irish Republic*, p. 966 ff. **871** Taylor. Op. cit., p. 318 ff. **872** Hopkinson, Michael A. 'The Craig-Collins pacts of 1922: two attempted reforms of the Northern Ireland government', *Irish Historical Studies*, Vol. XXVII, No. 106, November 1990. **873** Boyle, K. 'The Tallents Report on the Craig-Collins Pact of 30 March 1922', *The Irish Jurist*, Vol. XII, 1977.

*22 Mary Street Collins' primary Department of Finance office at the time, it was raided 26 May 1921 (the day after the Custom House fire). This raid was one of Collins' closest calls. Alice Lyons, a typist, and Bob Conlan, the office messenger, were in the office when it was raided, but Collins had had a premonition and stayed away after his lunch with Gearóid O'Sullivan. Collins always said there was a traitor in the camp, always claimed he knew who it was, and knew of the details of the raid – including the fact that the tout had been paid £500 on the condition that there would be no bloodshed.

*28-29 Mary Street Raided in June 1921. Batt O'Connor built a secret compartment in the draper's shop here.

5 Mespil Road, Ballsbridge The home of Collins' secretary Patricia Hoey and her mother. It was raided on 1 April 1921 and Ms Hoey was arrested when a revolver was found. She was released when she stuck to her story that the revolver must have been left by a former lodger. When she was taken home the RIC hid in her house, waiting for Collins to appear. She had her mother fake a heart attack, and passed the word to Collins through a friendly female doctor. Still the RIC found a cache of documents and then sent Ms Hoey to prison for several months; she was not released until after the Truce.

*5 Mespil Road, Ballsbridge Close to Leeson Street Bridge it was used as a primary office and also a Department of Intelligence office. It was raided on 1 April 1921. Jenny Mason was the secretary here.

77 Mespil Road, Ballsbridge Julia O'Donovan's Dairy; she was Gearóid O'Sullivan's aunt. Collins lived here after the Munster Hotel period and had meetings here every Sunday at noon.[874]

9 Morehampton Road: Home of Mrs Andrew Woods. Collins often stayed here.

Mountjoy Street: Seán McGarry's home. Collins stayed here on the night the Volunteer Cabinet was arrested for the purported 'German Plot', and after McGarry had been arrested (17-18 May 1918).

30 Mountjoy Street Across from Áras na nGael. This was the home of Madeline 'Dilly' Dicker, a 'girlfriend' of Collins before Kitty Kiernan.

1 Mountjoy Square Home of Alderman Walter Cole. The Dáil met here in 1919 and 1920. Collins sometimes stayed here.

44 Mountjoy Square Munster Private Hotel, known as Áras na nGael. Myra T. McCarthy was the owner. It was Collins' first residence after Frongoch and his primary residence until it was raided in December 1919. He stayed here infrequently thereafter, but he still left his laundry here and collected it on Saturday mornings.

21 Oakley Road, Rathfarnham/Ranelagh Cullenswood House; the first location of St Enda's. Collins had a basement office here ('The Dug-Out') and Richard Mulcahy and his wife (née Mary Josephine Ryan)[875] had the top-floor flat. Raided 20 January 1920.

874 O'Donovan, Julia. Witness Statement 475. 875 Mulcahy, Mary Josephine. Witness Statement 399.

Portobello Road Portobello Barracks (renamed Cathal Brugha Barracks). It was Collins' office during the Civil War. He left Dublin from here on his fatal journey. (See Béal na mBláth, above.)

16 Rathdown Road The Belton family home. Seán Hurley found Collins a room here on his return from London in January 1916. This was the address he gave to the British after the Rising and when sent to Frongoch.

29–30 Rutland Square Vaughan's Hotel. 'Joint No 1'– it was unsafe after mid-1920.

39 Rutland Square The home of Dr Paddy Browne of Maynooth College; Collins watched the raid on Vaughan's from here on the night of 20 November 1920.

46 Rutland Square The Squad was 'officially' established on 19 September 1919 at this address (though by that time it had been in operation for two months and had already carried out two killings). Members were paid £4.10s per week.

The first four members were: Ben Barrett, Paddy Daly (Paddy Ó Dalaigh, sometimes said to have succeeded Mick McDonnell as leader, but usually considered the leader [876]; he became a major general in the national army. See also Ballyseedy Cross, Appendix I), Seán Doyle and Joe Leonard (came right behind Daly in the chain of command). Other 'original' members were Mick McDonnell (described by some as the first leader), James Conroy, Jim McGuinness, Jimmy Slattery (a Clareman with only one hand, after being injured in the Custom House fire) and William 'Billy' Stapleton (a Dubliner)[877]. Added to the 'original' nine after a few months to form 'The Twelve Apostles' (a name first applied, derisively, by Austin Stack) were Vinnie Byrne, Tom Keogh (from Wicklow, later killed in the Civil War) and Mick O'Reilly.[878]

Others were added in January 1920 and thereafter, and were chosen for 'jobs' as needed. Not all did many 'jobs' for Collins, and many were members of various Dublin units who were picked by Collins to assist the 'regular' Squad members; this was particularly true on Bloody Sunday. In 1921 several more were added and when men from the Dublin 'Active Service Unit' were included the unit was then known as 'The Guard'. Those sometimes chosen were: Frank Bolster, J. Brennan, Ned Breslin, Ben Byrne, Charlie Byrne (a Dubliner called 'The Count' because of his cheerful mien in all situations), Eddie Byrne, Seán (John Anthony) Caffrey, Patrick (Paddy) Colgan (from Maynooth, Co. Kildare, he married Delia Larkin), James Connolly, Herbie Conroy, Jim Conway (the 'one-man column'), Andy Cooney, Seán Culhane, Tom Cullen (a teetotaler), Charlie Dalton (he was the brother of Emmet Dalton and wrote *With the Dublin Brigade* about his experiences as a member), Jim Dempsey (a Dubliner and an old IRB man who fought in the Rising), Joe Dolan (another Dubliner, always armed with a .45 and wore a British

876 Leonard, Joseph. Witness Statement 547.   **877** Stapleton, William J. (Bill). 'Michael Collins' Squad', *Capuchin Annual*, 1969.   **878** Leornard indicates the 'original' twelve were O'Daly, Leonard, Barrett, Doyle, Kehoe, Slattery, O'Reilly, Eddie Byrne, Vinnie Byrne, Ben Byrne, Eddie Byrne and Frank Bolster. Leonard, Joseph. Witness Statement 547.

Army badge in his lapel), Joe Dowling, Pat Drury, Tom Duffy, John Dunne, Leo Dunne, Tom Ennis, Mick Flanagan, Paddy Flanagan (the oldest member of The Squad), Paddy Griffin, Jack Hanlon, Seán Kavanagh (a Dubliner and later a prison governor), Ned Kelliher (a Dubliner), Mick Kennedy, Paddy Kennedy (from Tipperary), Martin Lavan, Paddy Lawson, Seán Lemass (the future Taoiseach), Billy McClean, Pat McCrae (a great driver), Pat McKeon, Peadar McMahon (later Chief of Staff of the Free State Army), Mick O'Hanlon, Diarmuid O'Hegarty (a Corkman and Director of Organisation of the IRA/Volunteers), Bob O'Neill (a Clareman), Albert Rutherford, Frank Saurin (a Dubliner, known as the best-dressed Volunteer), Frank Teeling, Liam Tobin (became assistant in the Department of Intelligence), George White and Johnny Wilson.

Sam's Cross, Clonakilty, Co. Cork the birthplace of Michael Collins, there is a memorial to Collins here. 'Woodfield' was the name given by Collins' mother to the new house she built in 1908. The Essex Division, under the command of Maj. Arthur Emmett Percival, burned it in 1920.

3 St Andrew Street owned by Batt O'Connor; Collins hid some gold and also conducted some financial business here.

21 St Stephen's Green (north) school run by Louise Gavan-Duffy; Collins used the school for meetings.

Stafford Detention Barracks Collins arrived here on 1 May 1916, Irish Prisoner 48F.

Appendix III

Statements and Documents 1913-1923

CONTENTS

1   **Padraig Pearse Oration at the Wolfe Tone Commemoration, Bodenstown, Co. Kildare, 22 June 1913**[879]

We have come to the holiest place in Ireland; holier to us even than the place where Patrick sleeps in Down. Patrick brought us life, but this man died for us. And though many before him and some since have died in testimony of the truth of Ireland's claim to nationhood, Wolfe Tone was the greatest of all that have made that testimony, the greatest of all that have died for Ireland whether in old time or in new. He was the greatest of Irish Nationalists; I believe he was the greatest of Irish men. And if I am right in this I am right in saying that we stand in the holiest place in Ireland, for it must be that the holiest sod of a nation's soul is the sod where the greatest of her dead lies buried.

I feel it difficult to speak to you today; difficult to speak in this place. It is as if one had to speak by the graveside of some dear friend, a brother in blood or a well-tried comrade in arms, and to say aloud the things one would rather keep to oneself. But I am helped by the knowledge that you who listen to me partake in my emotion: we are none of us strangers, being all in a sense own brothers to Tone, sharing in his love. I have then, only to find expression for the thoughts and emotions common to us all and you will understand even if the expression be a halting one.

We have come here not merely to salute this noble dust and to pay our homage to the noble spirit of Tone. We have come to renew our adhesion to the faith of Tone; to express once more our full acceptance of the gospel of Irish Nationalism which he was the first to formulate in worthy terms, giving clear definition and plenary meaning to all that had been thought and taught before him by Irish-speaking and English-speaking men; uttered half articulately by a Shane O'Neill in some defiance flung at the English, expressed under some passionate metaphor by a Geoffrey Keating, hinted at by Swift in some biting gibe, that clearly and greatly stated by Wolfe Tone, and not needing now ever to be stated anew for any generation.

He has spoken for all time, and his voice resounds throughout Ireland, calling to us from this grave, when we wander astray following other voices that ring less true.

This, then, is the first part of Wolfe Tone's achievement – he made articulate dumb voices of the centuries. He gave Ireland a clear and precise and worthy concept of Nationality. But he did more than this: not only did he define Irish Nationalism, but he armed his generation in defence of it. Thinker and doer, dreamer of the immortal dream and doer of the immortal deed – we owe to this dead man more than we can ever repay him by making pilgrimages to his grave or by raising to him the stateliest monument in the streets of his city. To his teaching we owe it that there is such a thing as Irish Nationalism, and to the memory of the deed he nerved his generation to do, to the memory of '98, we owe it that there is any manhood left in Ireland.

---

879 Patrick Pearse Papers, National Library of Ireland.

I have called him the greatest of our dead. In mind he was great above all the men of his time or of the after time; and he was greater still in spirit. It was to that nobly-dowered mind of his that Kickham, himself the most nobly-dowered of a later generation, paid reverence when he said:

> 'Oh, knowledge is a wondrous power;
> Tis stronger than the wind ...
> And would to the kind heavens
> That Wolfe Tone were here today.'

But greater than that full-orbed intelligence, that wide, graciously, richly sorted mind, was the mighty spirit of Tone. This man's soul was a burning flame, so ardent, so generous, so pure, that to come into communion with it is to come into a new baptism, into a new regeneration and cleansing. If we who stand by this graveside could make ourselves at one with the heroic spirit that once inbreathed this clay, could in some way come into loving contact with it, possessing ourselves of something of its ardour, its valour, its purity, its tenderness, its gaiety, how good a thing it would be for us, how good a thing for Ireland with what joyousness and strength should we set our faces towards the path that lies before us, knowing with us a fresh life from this place of death, a new resurrection of patriotic grace in our souls!

Try to get nearer the spirit of Tone, the gallant soldier spirit, the spirit that dared and soared, the spirit that loved and served, the spirit that laughed and sang with the gladness of a boy. I do not ask you to venerate him as a saint; I ask you to love him as a man. For myself, I would rather have known this man than any man of whom I have ever heard or ever read. I have not read or heard of any who had more of heroic stuff in him than he, any that went so gaily and so gallantly about a great deed, any who loved so well, any who was so beloved. To have been this man's friend, what a privilege that would have been! To have known him as Thomas Russell knew him! I have always loved the very name of Thomas Russell because Tone so loved him.

I do not think there has ever been a more true and loyal man than Tone. He had for his friends an immense tenderness and charity, and now and then there breaks into what he is writing or saying a gust of passionate love for his wife, or for his children. 'O my babies. my babies,' he exclaims. Yes, this man could love well, and it was from such love as this he exiled himself, with such love as this crushed in his faithful heart that he became a weary but indomitable ambassador to courts and camps, with the memory of such love as this, with the little hands of his children plucking at his heartstrings, that he lay down to die in that cell on Arbour Hill.

Such is the high and sorrowful destiny of the heroes: to turn their backs to the pleasant paths and their faces to the hard paths, to blind their eyes to the fair things of love, to stifle all sweet music in the heat, the low voices of women and the laughter of little children, and to follow only the far, faint call that leads them into the battle, or to the harder death at the foot of a gibbet.

Think of Tone. Think of his boyhood and young manhood in Dublin and Kildare, his adventurous spirit and plans, his early love and marriage, his glorious failure at the bar, his healthy contempt for what he called 'a foolish wig and gown', and then – the call of Ireland. Think of how he put virility into the Catholic movement, how this heretic toiled to make free men of Catholic ghosts, how, as he worked among them, he grew to know and love the real, the historic Irish people, and the great, clear, sane conception came to him that in Ireland there must be not two nations or three nations, but one nation, that Protestant and Dissenter must be brought into amity with Catholic, and that Catholic, Protestant and Dissenter must unite to achieve freedom for all.

Then came the United Irishmen, and those journeys through Ireland – to Ulster and to Connacht – which, as described by him, read like epics infused with a kindly human humour. Soon the government realised that this is the most dangerous man in Ireland – this man who preaches peace among brother Irishmen. It does not suit the government that peace and goodwill between Catholic and Protestant should be preached in Ireland. So Tone goes into exile, having first pledged himself to the cause of Irish freedom on the Cave Hill above Belfast. From America to France: one of the great implacable exiles of Irish history, a second and a greater Fitzmaurice, one might say to him as the poet said to Sarsfield:

> 'Ag Déanamh do ghearáin leis na ríghthibh
> Is gut fhag nú Eiré Gaedhil bhocht'
> claoidhte,
> Och, Ochón.'

But it was no 'complaint' that Tone made to foreign rulers and foreign senates, but wise and bold counsel that he gave them; wise because bold. A French fleet ploughs the waves and enters Bantry Bay – Tone on board. We know the sequel: how the fleet tossed about for days on the broad bosom of the Bay, how the craven in command refused to make a landing because his commander-in-chief had not come up, how Tone's heart was torn with impatience and yearning – he saw his beloved Ireland, could see the houses and the people on shore – how the fleet set sail, that deed not done that would have freed Ireland.

It is the supreme tribute to the greatness of this man that after that cruel disappointment he set to work again, indomitable. Two more expeditions, a French and a Dutch, were fitted out for Ireland, but never reached Ireland. Then at last came Tone himself; he had said he would come, if need be, with only a corporal's guard: he came with very little more.

Three small ships enter Lough Swilly. The English follow them. Tone's vessel fights: Tone commands one of the guns. For six hours she stood alone against the whole English fleet. What a glorious six hours for Tone! A battered hulk, the vessel struck. Tone, betrayed by a friend, was dragged to Dublin and condemned to a traitor's death. Then the last scene in the Provost Prison, and Tone is dead, the greatest of the men of '98. To this spot they bore him, and here he awaits the judgment and we stand at his graveside and remember that his work is still unaccomplished after more than a hundred years.

When men come to a graveside they pray, and each of us prays here in his heart. But we do not pray for Tone – men who died that their people may be free have no need of prayer. We pray for Ireland that she may be free, and for ourselves that we may free her. My brothers, were it not an unspeakable privilege if to our generation it should be granted to accomplish that which Tone's generation, so much worthier than ours, failed to accomplish! To complete the work of Tone!

And let us make no mistake as to what Tone sought to do, what it remains for us to do.

We need not re-state our programme, Tone has stated it for us:

To break the connection with England, the never-failing source of all our political evils, and to assert the independence of my country – these were my objects. To unite the whole people of Ireland, to abolish the memory of all past dissensions, and to substitute the common name of Irishmen in place of the denomination of Protestant, Catholic and Dissenter – these were my means.

I find here implicit all the philosophy of Irish Nationalism, all the teaching of the Gaelic League and the later prophets. Ireland one and Ireland free – is not this the definition of Ireland a Nation? To that definition and to that programme we declare our adhesion anew; pledging ourselves as Tone pledged himself – and in this sacred place, by his graveside, let us not pledge ourselves unless we mean to keep our pledge – we pledge ourselves to follow in the steps of Tone, never to rest, either by day or by night until his work be accomplished, deeming it the proudest of all privileges to fight for freedom, to fight, not in despondency, but in great joy, hoping for the victory near or far, never lowering our ideal, never bartering one jot or tittle of our birthright, holding faith to the memory and the inspiration of Tone, and accounting ourselves base as long as we endure the evil thing against which he testified with his blood.

2 Manifesto of The Irish Volunteers, 25 November 1913[880]

Ulster

At a time when legislative proposals universally confessed to be of vital concern for the future of Ireland have been put forward, and are awaiting decision, a plan has

---

880 *Volunteer Gazette*, December 1913. The manifesto was read at the first turn-out in Dublin on 25 November 1913, and re-issued in June 1914. It was written by Eoin MacNeill and adopted by the first Provisional Committee. A copy is in the Irish Volunteer papers, University College, Dublin.

been deliberately adopted by one of the great English political parties, advocated by the leaders of that party and by its numerous organs in the Press, and brought systematically to bear on English public opinion, to make the display of military force and the menace of armed violence the determining factor in the future relations between this country and Great Britain.

The Tories
The party which has thus substituted open force for the semblance of civil government is seeking by this means not merely to decide an immediate political issue of grave concern to this nation, but also to obtain for itself the future control of all our national affairs. It is plain to every man that the people of Ireland, if they acquiesce in this new policy by their inaction, will consent to the surrender, not only of their rights as a nation, but of their civic rights as men.

Act of Union
The Act of Union deprived the Irish nation of the power to direct its own course and to develop and use its own resources for its own benefit. It gave us, instead, the meager and seldom effective right of throwing our votes into the vast and complicated movement of British politics. Since the Act of Union a long series of repressive statutes has endeavored to deal with the incessant discontent of the Irish people by depriving them of various rights common to all who live under the British Constitution. The new policy goes farther than the Act of Union, and farther than all subsequent Coercion Acts taken together. It proposes to leave us the political franchise in name, and to annihilate it in fact. If we fail to take such measures as will eventually defeat this policy, we become politically the most degraded population in Europe, and no longer worthy of the name Nation.

Our Rights
Are we to rest inactive, in the hope that the course of politics in Great Britain may save us from the degradation openly threatened against us? British politics are controlled by British interests, and are complicated by problems of great importance to the people of Great Britain. In a crisis of this kind, the duty of safeguarding our own rights is our duty first and foremost. They have rights who dare maintain them. If we remain quiescent, by what title can we expect the people of Great Britain to turn aside from their own pressing concerns to defend us? Will not such an attitude of itself mark us out as a people unworthy of defence?

Our Opportunity
Such is the occasion, not altogether unfortunate, which has brought about the inception of the Irish Volunteer movement. But the Volunteers, once they have been enrolled, will form a prominent element in the national life under a National Government. The Nation will maintain its Volunteer organisation as a guarantee

of the liberties which the Irish people shall have secured.

If ever in history a people could say that an opportunity was given to them by God's will to make an honest and manly stand for their rights, that opportunity is given us to-day. The stress of industrial effort, the relative peace and prosperity of recent years, may have dulled the sense of the demands of civic duty. We may forget that the powers of the platform, the Press, and the polling booth are derived from the conscious resolve of the people to maintain their rights and liberties. From time immemorial, it has been held by every race of mankind to be the right and duty of a freeman to defend his freedom with all his resources and with his life itself. The exercise of that right distinguishes the freeman from the serf, the discharge of that duty distinguishes him from the coward.

Citizen Army

To drill, to learn the use of arms, to acquire the habit of disciplined and concerted action, to form a citizen army from a population now at the mercy of almost any organised aggression – this, beyond all doubt, is the program that appeals to all Ireland, but especially to young Ireland. We begin at once in Dublin, and we are confident that the movement will be taken up without delay all over the country. Public opinion has already and quite spontaneously formed itself into an eager desire for the establishment of the Irish Volunteers.

Our Object

The object proposed for the Irish Volunteers is to secure and maintain the rights and liberties common to all the people of Ireland. Their duties will be defensive and protective, and they will not contemplate either aggression or domination. Their ranks are open to all able-bodied Irishmen without distinction of creed, politics, or social grade. Means will be found whereby Irishmen unable to serve as ordinary Volunteers will be enabled to aid the Volunteer forces in various capacities. There will also be work for women to do, and there are signs that the women of Ireland, true to their record, are especially enthusiastic for the success of the Irish Volunteers.

Widest Basis

We propose for the Volunteers' organisation the widest possible basis. Without any other association or classification, the Volunteers will be enrolled according to the district in which they live. As soon as it is found feasible, the district sections will be called upon to join in making provision for the general administration and discipline, and for the united cooperation. The provisional Committee which has acted up to the present will continue to offer its service until an elective body is formed to replace it.

Freemen

A proportion of time spared, not from work, but from pleasure and recreation, a voluntary adoption of discipline, a purpose firmly and steadily carried through, will renew the vitality of the Nation. Even that degree of self-discipline will bring back to every town, village, and countryside a consciousness that has long been forbidden them – the sense of freemen who have fitted themselves to defend the cause of freedom.

Unity: Liberty

In the name of National Unity, of National Dignity, of National and Individual Liberty, of Manly Citizenship, we appeal to our countrymen to recognise and accept without hesitation the opportunity that has been granted to them to join the ranks of the Irish Volunteers, and to make the movement now begun not unworthy of the historic title which it has adopted.

3   Address of Padraig Pearse at the grave of Jeremiah O'Donovan Rossa, 1 August 1915[881]

It has seemed right, before we turn away from this place in which we have laid the mortal remains of O'Donovan Rossa, that one among us should, in the name of all, speak the praise of that valiant man, and endeavor to formulate the thought and the hope that are in us as we stand around his grave. And if there is anything that makes it fitting that I, rather than some other, I rather than one of the grey-haired men who were young with him and shared in his labour and in his suffering, should speak here, it is perhaps that I may be taken as speaking on behalf of a new generation that has been re-baptised in the Fenian faith, and that has accepted the responsibility of carrying out the Fenian programme. I propose to you then that, here by the grave of this unrepentant Fenian, we renew our baptismal vows; that, here by the grave of this unconquered and unconquerable man, we ask of God, each one for himself, such unshakable purpose, such high and gallant courage, such unbreakable strength of soul as belonged to O'Donovan Rossa.

Deliberately here we avow ourselves, as he avowed himself in the dock, Irishmen of one allegiance only. We of the Irish Volunteers, and you others who are associated with us in to-day's task and duty, are bound together and must stand together henceforth in brotherly union for the achievement of the freedom of Ireland. And we know only one definition of freedom: it is Tone's definition, it is Mitchel's definition, it is Rossa's definition. Let no man blaspheme the cause that the dead generations of Ireland served by giving it any other name and definition than their name and their definition.

---

881 Many newspapers carried copies of the address, most notably the *Irish Volunteer*. The original handwritten script is on display in the Pearse Museum, St. Enda's, Rathfarnham, Dublin. 16.

We stand at Rossa's grave not in sadness but rather in exaltation of spirit that it has been given to us to come thus into so close a communion with that brave and splendid Gael. Splendid and holy causes are served by men who are themselves splendid and holy. O'Donovan Rossa was splendid in the proud manhood of him, splendid in the heroic grace of him, splendid in the Gaelic strength and clarity and truth of him. And all that splendour and pride and strength was compatible with a humility and a simplicity of devotion to Ireland, to all that was olden and beautiful and Gaelic in Ireland, the holiness and simplicity of patriotism of a Michael O'Clery or of an Eoghan O'Growney. The clear true eyes of this man almost alone in his day visioned Ireland as we of to-day would surely have her: not free merely, but Gaelic as well; not Gaelic merely, but free as well.

In a closer spiritual communion with him now than ever before or perhaps ever again, in a spiritual communion with those of his day, living and dead, who suffered with him in English prisons, in communion of spirit too with our own dear comrades who suffer in English prisons to-day, and speaking on their behalf as well as our own, we pledge to Ireland our love, and we pledge to English rule in Ireland our hate. This is a place of peace, sacred to the dead, where men should speak with all charity and with all restraint; but I hold it a Christian thing, as O'Donovan Rossa held it, to hate evil, to hate untruth, to hate oppression, and, hating them, to strive to overthrow them. Our foes are strong and wise and wary; but, strong and wise and wary as they are, they cannot undo the miracles of God who ripens in the hearts of young men the seeds sown by the young men of a former generation. And the seeds sown by the young men of '65 and '67 are coming to their miraculous ripening to-day. Rulers and Defenders of Realms had need to be wary if they would guard against such processes. Life springs from death; and from the graves of patriot men and women spring living nations. The Defenders of this Realm have worked well in secret and in the open. They think that they have pacified Ireland. They think that they have purchased half of us and intimidated the other half. They think that they have foreseen everything, think that they have provided against everything; but the fools, the fools, the fools! – they have left us our Fenian dead, and while Ireland holds these graves, Ireland unfree shall never be at peace.

4 Eoin MacNeill Memorandum to the Irish Volunteers, February 1916[882]

In the first place, we must avow ourselves clearly and courageously, without heeding either sneers or jeers or even the most honest reproaches, that if we can win our rights by being ready to fight for them but without fighting, then it is our duty to do so and we shall not be ashamed of it. I am aware that this is a difficult position to assert to the general body of men organised as a military force, carrying military

---

882 A copy is in the Irish Volunteer papers, University College, Dublin.

arms, and trained in military exercises. It might be misunderstood by them, and might lead them to think that in the minds of their leaders their military character was a sham. Even in regular armies, under states which have no casus belli, the courageous military man does not like the notion of going through his military career without ever fighting a battle or engagement. But it must be remembered that the Irish Volunteers, if they are a military force, are not a militarist force, and that their object is to secure Ireland's rights and liberties and nothing else but that. The reproach of the former Irish Volunteers is not that they did not fight but that they did not maintain their organisation till their objects had been secured.

Secondly, we must clearly recognise the position in which we stand and which we have already gained. Until a short time ago, England ruled Ireland normally by what are called peaceful means. The country was controlled, even politically, by the police. Except rarely in the case of a formidable street riot, the military were not called into action; in fact, Ireland was – to outward appearance at least, and in substance – governed as England itself is governed.

We have now reached this position, that the ordinary citizen in Ireland is no longer dominated by England's peace establishment. The Irish Volunteers no longer stand in danger of the police. The only question with them for a long time past has been on what occasions they ought to resist wrongful police actions by force of arms. Moreover there is good ground for believing that among the police there is, to say the least, a considerable leaven of men who feel strongly that they should not be used in hostility to the Irish Volunteers.

It is not perhaps generally realised what a great change this means in the whole Irish situation, and what a substantial gain it is for the Irish Volunteers and by them. It is in fact a substantial military gain for them, being due to their own sturdiness, discipline and courage – as much a gain as if they had marched against and occupied a military position of the first importance. Its importance is this – not that it makes the Irish Volunteers a match in any sense for the military force at the disposal of the government but that it makes it impossible for the government to suppress the Volunteers without adopting military measures. Now the government wants and has always wanted to suppress the Irish Volunteers. It could at any time have used sufficient military force to suppress them if opposed by them in military fashion. Why then has the government not employed military force against us? Because the government is convinced that it would lose more than it could gain by moving its military forces against us, unless we create a special opportunity for it.

Moreover, the position we have gained is such that it enables us to strengthen our general position still further and indefinitely, by increasing our numbers of armed men and developing their training and organisation, and by getting the country more and more on our side. Our policy in these circumstances is to use these advantages, not to throw them away or bring them to a standstill. At present we are far from being at a standstill. We are gaining steadily in numbers, in armament and in training – also in organisation. But it is incomprehensible to me that any of us should be as childish as to think that the comparative state of efficiency that has been reached in Dublin is at all representative of the condition of the Volunteers elsewhere. Some of us are plainly obsessed by the efficiency of Dublin. No doubt it could not be helped that our H.Q. staff should have worked so much in Dublin and so little out of it. In general, outside of Dublin, our training of officers is only as yet begun.

There is plenty of scope for courage and enterprise and intelligence in the work of arming the Volunteers. On that point, this is to be said, that whereas, in my conscientious judgment, an armed revolt at present would be wrong and unpatriotic and criminal, it is quite a different case with regard to the provision and retention of our arms. I have not the slightest doubt on the point that we are morally and in every way justified in keeping by all necessary force such arms as we have or can get. I hold myself entitled to resist to death any attempt to deprive me of any arms or ammunition or other military articles that I have or can protect for myself or for the Irish Volunteers. If in such resistance any man meets his death through my act or counsel or command, I shall have no guilt on my conscience.

We have to remember that what we call our country is not a poetical abstraction, as some of us, perhaps all of us, in the exercise of our highly developed capacity for figurative thought, are sometimes apt to imagine – with the help of our patriotic literature. There is no such person as Caitlin Ni Uallachain or Roisin Dubh or Sean-bhean Bhocht, who is calling upon us to serve her. What we call our country is the Irish nation, which is a concrete and visible reality. Now we believe that we think rightly on national matters, and if possibly we do not all agree on every point we believe that the consensus we hold among us is right as far as it goes. We are all agreed that, in worldly matters, our country's good has first claim on us, and can claim the greatest sacrifices from us. We feel it is our duty to realise this and to act on this principle. Very well, if so, it is also our duty to so act that our country itself, i.e. the Irish nation, shall learn, so far as may be secured, to think in the same way and be ready to act on the same principle. In other words, if we are right nationally, it is our duty to get our country on our side, and not be content with the vanity of thinking ourselves to be right and other Irish people to be wrong. As a matter of patriotic principle, we should never tire of endeavoring to get our country on our side.

In a much more narrow sense, as a matter of ordinary military policy, it is imperative that we, who are engaged in national military organisation, should most earnestly endeavor to get our country on our side. In the event of actual fighting, it is a military factor of the highest importance to be able to fight in a friendly country.

Now it is universal testimony – I can quote unionist and Redmonites as well as our own least sanguine and most sanguine friends for it – that the country is steadily coming over to our side. Are we entitled to stop that process, is it wise or excusable for us to stop it? It is really only beginning. The government itself is daily helping to create a deep and solid conviction that we are right. The unionists, even in Ulster, are damping off. The new taxation may be confidently expected to make them discontented.

That applies to all the rest. I do not know at this moment whether the time and circumstances will yet justify distinct revolutionary action, but on this I am certain, that the only possible basis for successful revolutionary action is deep and wide-spread popular discontent. We have only to look around us in the streets to realise that no such condition exists in Ireland. A few of us, a small proportion, who think about the evils of English government in Ireland, are always discontented. We should be downright fools if we were to measure many others by the standard of our own thoughts.

I wish it then to be clearly understood that under present conditions I am definitely opposed to any proposal that may come forward involving insurrection. I have no doubt at all that my consent to any such proposal at this time and under these circumstances would make me false to my country, besides involving me in the guilt of murder. No reproach from any quarter will have the least effect on me as regards this decision. I will oppose any such proposal with all the force I can, actively and not passively. I will not give way or resign or shirk any trouble in opposing it.

If any feasible proposal is brought forward to increase the arming of the Volunteers, I will support it – and those who are impatient of inaction should find scope enough for their activity in that direction.

5   Manifesto of The Irish Volunteers, March 1916[883]

With regard to the recent proceedings of the Government towards the Irish Volunteers, the council of the Irish Volunteers, which met on the 26th inst., wish to warn the public that the general tendency of the Government's action is to force a highly dangerous situation. The Government is well aware that the possession of arms is essential to the Irish Volunteer organisation, and the Volunteers cannot submit to being disarmed either in numbers or detail without surrendering and abandoning the position they have held at all times since their first formation. The Volunteer organisation also cannot maintain its efficiency without organisers. The raiding for arms and attempted disarming of men, therefore, in the natural course of things can only be met by resistance and bloodshed. None of the Irish Volunteers recognise, or will ever recognise, the right of the Government to disarm them or to imprison their officers and men in any fashion. The council also draws attention to the repeated instances in which the Government's arbitrary action has been

883 A copy is in the Irish Volunteer papers, University College, Dublin.

associated with the movements of hostile crowds, which are led to believe they act under the Government's approval. In this council's belief, this feature of the case is based on a deliberate policy of creating factious hostility between sections of the Irish people. Nothing need be hoped from remonstrance with the Government, but we appeal to the Irish people to look closely into the facts in every instance and keep a watch on the conduct and policy of the authorities, and to fix the responsibility for any grave consequence that may arise.

6   Cancellation Order of Eoin MacNeill, 22 April 1916[884]

Owing to the very critical position, all orders given to Irish Volunteers for tomorrow, Easter Sunday, are hereby rescinded, and no parades, marches, or other movements of Irish Volunteers will take place. Each individual Volunteer will obey this order strictly in every particular.

Eoin MacNeill
Holy Saturday, 22 April 1916

7   MacDonagh and Pearse Order to Parade, 24 April 1916[885]

24 April
1   The four City Battalions will parade for inspection and route march at 10 a.m. today. Commandants will arrange centres.
2   Full arms and equipment and one day's rations to be carried.

Thomas MacDonagh
Brigade Commandant

Coy E 3 will parade at Beresford Place at 10 a.m.
PH Pearse
Comdt.

---

884 *Sunday Independent*, 23 April 1916. **885** Printed in the *Sinn Féin Rebellion Handbook* published by *The Irish Times*, 1916, p. 45. A copy is in the Irish Volunteer papers, University College, Dublin.

8 Proclamation of the Irish Republic, 24 April 1916

Poblacht na hÉireann
The Provisional Government of the Irish Republic
To the People of Ireland

Irishmen and Irishwomen: In the name of God and of the dead generations from which she receives her old tradition of nationhood, Ireland, through us, summons her children to her flag and strikes for her freedom.

Having organised and trained her manhood through her secret revolutionary organisation, the Irish Republican Brotherhood, and through her open military organisations, the Irish Volunteers and the Irish Citizen Army, having patiently perfected her discipline, having resolutely waited for the right moment to reveal itself, she now seizes that moment, and supported by her exiled children in America and by gallant allies in Europe, but relying in the first on her own strength, she strikes in full confidence of victory.

We declare the right of the people of Ireland to the ownership of Ireland and to the unfettered control of Irish destinies, to be sovereign and indefeasible. The long usurpation of that right by a foreign people and government has not extinguished the right, nor can it ever be extinguished except by the destruction of the Irish people. In every generation the Irish people have asserted their right to national freedom and sovereignty; six times during the past three hundred years they have asserted it in arms. Standing on that fundamental right and again asserting it in arms in the face of the world, we hereby proclaim the Irish Republic as a Sovereign Independent State, and we pledge our lives and the lives of our comrades in arms to the cause of its freedom, of its welfare, and of its exaltation among the nations.

The Irish Republic is entitled to, and hereby claims, the allegiance of every Irishman and Irishwoman. The Republic guarantees religious and civil liberty, equal rights and equal opportunities to all its citizens, and declares its resolve to pursue the happiness and prosperity of the whole nation and of all its parts, cherishing all of the children of the nation equally, and oblivious of the differences carefully fostered by an alien Government, which have divided a minority from the majority in the past.

Until our arms have brought the opportune moment for the establishment of a permanent National Government, representative of the whole people of Ireland and elected by the suffrages of all her men and women, the Provisional Government, hereby constituted, will administer the civil and military affairs of the Republic in trust for the people.

We place the cause of the Irish Republic under the protection of the Most High God, Whose blessing we invoke upon our arms, and we pray that no one who serves that cause will dishonour it by cowardice, inhumanity, or rapine. In this supreme hour the Irish nation must, by its valour and discipline, and by the readiness of its children to sacrifice themselves for the common good, prove itself worthy of the august destiny to which it is called.

Signed on Behalf of the Provisional Government,
Thomas J. Clarke, Seán Mac Diarmada,
Thomas Mac Donagh, P.H. Pearse, Éamonn Ceannt
James Connolly, Joseph Plunkett

9 Pearse Statement from the GPO, Thursday 28 April 1916[886]

The Forces of the Irish Republic, which was proclaimed in Dublin, on Easter Monday, 24th April, have been in possession of the central part of the Capital, since 12 noon on that day. Up to yesterday headquarters was in touch with all the main outlying positions, and, despite furious, and almost continuous assaults by British Forces all those positions were then still being held, and the commandants in charge were confident of their ability to hold them for a long time.

During the course of yesterday afternoon, and evening, the enemy succeeded in cutting our communications, with our other positions in the City, and Headquarters is today isolated.

The enemy has burnt down whole blocks of houses, apparently with the object of giving themselves a clear field for the play of Artillery and Field guns against us. We have been bombarded during the evening and night, by Shrapnel and Machine Gun fire, but without material damage to our position, which is of great strength.

We are busy completing arrangements for the final defence of Headquarters, and are determined to hold it while buildings last. I desire now, lest I may not have an opportunity later, to pay homage to the gallantry of the soldiers of Irish freedom who have during the past four days been writing with fire and steel the most glorious chapter in the later history of Ireland. Justice can never be done to their heroism, to their discipline, to their gay and unconquerable spirit in the midst of peril and death.

Let me, who have led them into this, speak in my own, and in my fellow-commanders' names, and in the name of Ireland present and to come, their praise, and ask those who come after them to remember them.

For four days they have fought and toiled, almost without cessation, almost without sleep, and in the intervals of fighting they have sung songs of the freedom of Ireland. No man has complained, no man has asked 'why?' Each individual has

---

[886] Original's whereabouts are unknown. Printed by the *Irish War News* from O'Keefe's Printers on Halston Street by Joe Stanley at Pearse's direction. Later printed in the *Sinn Féin Rebellion Handbook* published by *The Irish Times*, 1916, p. 47. A copy is in the Irish Volunteer papers, University College, Dublin.

spent himself, happy to pour out his strength for Ireland and for Freedom. If they do not win this fight, they will at least have deserved to win it. But win it they will although they win in death.

Already they have won a great thing. They have redeemed Dublin from many shames, and made her name splendid among cities.

If I were to mention names, my list would be long.

I will name only that of Commandant General James Connolly, Commanding the Dublin Division. He lies wounded, but is still the guiding brain of our resistance.

If we accomplish no more than we have accomplished, I am satisfied. I am satisfied that we have saved Ireland's honour. I am satisfied that we should have accomplished more, that we should have accomplished the task of enthroning as well as proclaiming the Irish Republic as a Sovereign State, had our arrangements for a simultaneous Rising of the whole country, with a combined plan as sound as the Dublin plan has proved to be, been allowed to go through on Easter Sunday. Of the fatal countermanding order which prevented those plans being carried out, I shall not speak further. Both Eoin MacNeill and we have acted in the best interests of Ireland.

For my part, as to anything I have done in this, I am not afraid to face the judgment of God, or the judgment of posterity.

Padraig H. Pearse
Commandant General
Commander in Chief of the Army
President of the Provisional Government
April 1916   9.30 a.m.

10 Brig. Gen. Lowe Note to Padraig Pearse requiring Unconditional Surrender, 29 April 1916 [887]

From Commander of Dublin Forces

To P.H. Pearse

29 April/16
1.40 p.m.

A woman has come in and tells me you wish to negotiate with me.
I am prepared to receive you in BRITAIN ST at the North End of MOORE ST provided that you surrender unconditionally –

[887] National Library of Ireland.

You will proceed up MOORE ST accompanied only by the woman who brings you this note under a white flag –
W.M. Lowe
B. Gen.

11 Pearse Surrender Order, 29 April 1916[888]

In order to prevent the further slaughter of Dublin citizens, and in the hope of saving the lives of our followers, now surrounded and hopelessly outnumbered, the members of the Provisional Government at present at Headquarters have agreed to an unconditional surrender, and the Commandants of the various districts in the City and County will order their commands to lay down arms

Padraig H. Pearse
29 April 1916
3.45 pm

12 Connolly Surrender Order, 29 April 1916[889]

I agree to these conditions for the men only under my command in the Moore Street District and for the men in the Stephen's Green Command.

James Connolly
April 29/16

13 MacDonagh Surrender Order, 29 April 1916[890]

On consultation with Commandant Ceannt and other officers I have decided to agree to unconditional surrender also.

Thomas MacDonagh
30.iv.16
3.15 p.m.

---

888 Pearse signed several typed copies to be sent to the various garrisons. A copy is in the National Library of Ireland. **889** Connolly signed copies to be sent to Michael Mallin in St Stephen's Green. A copy is in the National Library of Ireland. **890** National Library of Ireland.

14 Pearse Statement to Court Martial, 2 May 1916 [891]

The following is the substance of what I said when asked today by the President of the Court Martial at Richmond Barracks whether I had anything to say in defence:

I desire in the first place to repeat what I have already said in letters to General Sir John Maxwell and Brigadier General Lowe. My object in agreeing to unconditional surrender was to prevent further slaughter of the civilian population of Dublin and to save the lives of our gallant fellows, who, having made for six days a stand unparalleled in military history, were now surrounded and (in the case of those under the immediate command of headquarters) without food. I fully understand now, as then, that my own life is forfeit to British law, and I shall die very cheerfully if I can think the British Government, as it has already shown itself strong, will now show itself magnanimous enough to accept my single life in forfeiture and to give a general amnesty to the brave men and boys who have fought at my bidding. In the second place, I wish it to be understood that any admissions I make here are to be taken as involving myself alone. They do not involve and must not be used against anyone who acted with me, not even those who have set their names to documents with me. [The Court assented to this.]

I admit I was Commandant-General Commander-in-Chief of the forces of The Irish Republic which have been acting against you for the past week, and that I was President of the Provisional Government. I stand over all my acts and words done or spoken in these capacities. When I was a child of ten I went down on my knees by my bedside one night and promised God that I should devote my life to an effort to free my country. I have kept that promise.

First among all earthly things, as a boy and a man, I have worked for Irish Freedom. I have helped organise, to arm, to train, and to discipline my fellow-countrymen to the sole end that, when the time came, they might fight for Irish Freedom. The time, as it seemed to me, did come and we went into the fight. I am glad that we did, we seem to have lost, we have not lost. To refuse to fight would have been to lose, to fight is to win, we have kept the faith with the past, and handed a tradition to the future.

I repudiate the assertion of the prosecutor that I sought to aid and abet England's enemy. Germany is no more to me than England is. I asked for and accepted German aid in the shape of arms and expeditionary force, we neither asked nor accepted German gold, nor had any traffic with Germany but what I state: my aim was to win Irish Freedom; we struck the first blow ourselves but I should have been glad of an ally's aid.

I assume I am speaking to Englishmen who value their own freedom, and who profess to be fighting for the freedom of Belgium and Serbia. Believe that we too

891 Patrick Pearse papers, National Library of Ireland.

love freedom and desire it. To us it is more desirable than anything else in the world. If you strike us down now we will rise again and renew the fight. You cannot conquer Ireland. You cannot extinguish the Irish passion for freedom. If our deed has not been sufficient to win freedom, then our children will win it by a better deed.

Padraig Pearse
Address to his Court Martial
Written in Kilmainham Gaol
2 May 1916

15 Brig. Gen. Blackadder Statement after Pearse Court Martial, 2 May 1916 [892]

I have just done one of the hardest tasks I have ever had to do. I have had to condemn one of the finest characters I have ever come across. There must be something very wrong in the state of things, that makes a man like that a rebel.

16 Pearse Letter to his Mother, 3 May 1916 [893]

My Dearest Mother,

I have been hoping up to now it would be possible to see you again, but it does not seem possible. Good-bye, dear mother. Through you I say good-bye to 'Wow? Wow!', Mary Brigid, Willie, Miss B., Michael, cousin Maggine, and everyone at St. Enda's. I hope and believe Willie and the St. Enda's boys will all be safe.

I have written two papers about financial affairs and one about books which I want you to get. With them are a few poems I want added to the poems in MS. in my bookcase. You asked me to write a little poem which would seem to be said by you to me. I have written it, and a copy is in Arbour Hill barracks with other papers. ['The Mother']

I have just received Holy Communion. I am happy, except for the great grief of parting from you. This is the death I should have asked for if God had given me the choice of all deaths – to die a soldier's death for Ireland and for freedom. We have done right. People will say hard things of us now, but later on will praise us. Do not grieve for all of this but think of it as a sacrifice God asked of me and you.

Good-bye, dear mother, may God bless you for your great love for me and for your great faith and may He remember all you have so bravely suffered. I hope soon to see papa, and in a little while we shall all be together again. I have not words to tell you of my love for you and how my heart yearns for you all. I will call to you in my heart at the last moment.

Your son,
Pat

17 MacDonagh Statement to Court Martial, 2 May 1916[894]

Gentlemen of the Court Martial

I choose to think that you have done your duty, according to your lights, in sentencing me to death. I thank you for your courtesy. It would not be seemly for me to go to my doom without trying to express, however inadequately, my sense of the high honour I enjoy in being of those predestined in this generation to die for Irish Freedom. You will, perhaps, understand this sentiment, for it is one to which an Imperial poet of a bygone age bore immortal testimony: ''Tis sweet and glorious to die for one's country.' You would all be proud to die for Britain, your Imperial patron, and I am proud and happy to die for Ireland, my glorious Fatherland.

There is not much left to say. The Proclamation of the Irish Republic has been adduced in evidence against me as one of the signatories; you think it is already a dead and buried letter, but it lives, it lives. From minds alight with Ireland's vivid intellect, it sprang; in hearts aflame with Ireland's mighty love it was conceived. Such documents do not die.

The British occupation of Ireland has never for more than one hundred years been compelled to confront in the field a Rising so formidable as that which overwhelming forces have for the moment succeeded in quelling. This Rising did not result from accidental circumstances. It came in due recurrent season as the necessary outcome of forces that are ever at work. The fierce pulsation of resurgent pride that disclaims servitude may one day cease to throb in the heart of Ireland – but the heart of Ireland will that day be dead. While Ireland lives, the brain and brawn of her manhood will strive to destroy the last vestige of British rule in her territory.

In this ceaseless struggle, there will be, as there has been, and must be an eternal ebb and flow. But, let England make no mistake. The generous high-bred youth of Ireland will never fail to answer the call of war to win their country's freedom.

---

894 The source of this statement is unknown. It was first printed in Dublin in June 1916 and the printers were prosecuted under the Defence of the Realm Act. The speech's authenticity was questioned but Donagh MacDonagh and the MacDonagh family have always asserted its authenticity. In suport of its authenticity, it is accepted MacDonagh did make a statement to his Court Martial, as he refers to it in his last statement below.

Other and tamer methods they will leave to other and tamer men; but they must do it or die.

It will be said that our movement was foredoomed to failure. It had proved so. Yet it might have been otherwise. There is always a chance for brave men who challenge fortune. That we had such a chance none knows so well as your statesmen and military experts. The mass of the people of Ireland will doubtless salve their consciences to sleep for another generation by the now exploded fable that Ireland cannot successfully fight England. We do not profess to represent the mass of the people of Ireland. We stand for the intellect and the soul of Ireland. To Ireland's intellect and soul the inert mass, drugged and degenerate by ages of servitude, must, in the distant day of resurrection, render homage and free service – receiving in return the vivifying impress of a free people.

Gentlemen, you have sentenced me to death and I accept your sentence with joy and pride, since it is for Ireland I am to die. I go to join the goodly company of men who died for Ireland, the least of whom was worthier than I can claim to be; and that noble band are, themselves, but a small section of that great unnumbered army of martyrs, whose Captain is the Christ Who died on Calvary. Of every white-robed knight in all that goodly company, we are the spiritual kin. The forms of heroes flit before my vision; and there is one, the star of whose destiny sways my own; there is one, the key-note of whose nature chimes harmoniously with the swan-song of my soul. It is the great Florentine, Savonarola, whose weapon was not the sword but prayer and teaching. The seed he sowed fructifies to this day in God's Church.

Take me away, and let my blood bedew the sacred soil of Ireland. I die in the certainty that once more the seed will fructify.

Thomas MacDonagh
Address to his Court Martial
2 May 1916

18 Final Statement of Thomas MacDonagh, 2 May 1916 [895]

I, Thomas MacDonagh, having now heard the sentence of the court martial held on me today, declare that in all my acts – all the acts for which I have been arraigned – I have been actuated by one motive only, the love of my country, the desire to make a sovereign independent state. I still hope and pray that my acts will have for consummation her lasting freedom and happiness.

I am to die at dawn, 3.30 a.m. 3rd May. I am ready to die, and I thank God that I die in so holy a cause. My country will reward my deed richly.

---

[895] The original is in the possession of the MacDonagh family. MacLochlainn, Piaras F. *Last Words*, p. 63.

On April 30th I was astonished to receive by a message from P.H. Pearse, Commandant General of the Army of the Irish Republic, an order to surrender unconditionally to the British General. I did not obey the order as it came from a prisoner. I was then in supreme command of the Irish Army, consulted with my second in command and decided to confirm the order. I knew that it would involve my death and the deaths of other leaders. I hoped it would save many true men among our followers, good lives for Ireland. God grant it has done so, and God approve our deed. For myself, I have no regret. The one bitterness that death has for me is the separation it brings from my beloved wife, Muriel, and my beloved children Donagh and Barbara. My country will take them as wards, I hope.

I have devoted myself too much to national work, and too little to the making of money to leave them a competence. God help them and support them and give them a happy and prosperous life. Never was there a better, truer, purer woman than my wife, Muriel, or more adorable children than Don and Barbara. It breaks my heart to think that I shall never see my children again, but I have not wept or mourned. I counted the cost of this and I am ready to pay it.

Muriel has been sent for here. I do not know if she can come. She may have no one to take the children while she is coming. If she does.

My money affairs are in a bad way. I am insured for £200 in the New York Life Co. but have borrowed £101. I am insured for £100 in the Alliance Co, but have a bank debt for £80. That leaves me less than £120 from these sources if they produce nothing. In addition I have insured my two children for £100 each in the Mutual Co. of Australasia, payments of premiums to cease at my death the money to be paid to the children at the age of twenty-one. I ask my brother, Joseph MacDonagh, and my good and constant friend, David Houston, to help my poor wife in these matters. My brother John, who came with me and stood by me all last week has been sent away from here, I do not know where to. He, if he can, will help my family too. God bless him and my other sisters and brothers. Assistance has been guaranteed from funds in the hands of Cumann na mBan and other funds to be collected in America by our fellow countrymen there in provision for the dependants of those who fall in this fight. I appeal without shame to the persons who control these funds to assist my family. My wife and I have given all for Ireland.

I ask my friend David Houston to see Mr W.G. Lyon, publisher of my latest book, *Literature in Ireland*, and see that its publication may be useful to my wife and family. If Joseph Plunkett survives me and is a free man I make him with my wife my literary executor. Otherwise my wife and David Houston will take charge of my writings. For the first time I pray that they may bring in some profit at last. My wife will want money from every source.

Yesterday at my court martial in rebutting some trifling evidence, I made a statement as to my negotiations for surrender to General Lowe. On hearing it read after it struck me that it might sound like an appeal. It was not such. I made no appeal, no recantation, no apology for my acts. In what I said I merely claimed that

I had acted honourably in all that I set myself to do. My enemies, in return, treated me in an unworthy manner. But that can pass. It is a great and glorious thing to die for Ireland and I can well forget all petty annoyances in the splendour of this. When my son, Don, was born I thought that to him and not to me would this be given. God has been kinder to me than I hoped.

To my son Don. My darling little boy, remember me kindly. Take my hope and purpose with my deed. For your sake and for the sake of your beloved mother and sister I wish to live long, but you will recognize the thing I have done, and see this as a consequence. I think still I have done a great thing for Ireland, and, with the defeat of her army, won the first step of her freedom. God bless you my son.

My darling daughter, Barbara, God bless you. I loved you more than ever a child has been loved.

My dearest love, Muriel, thank you a million times for all you have been to me. I have only one trouble in leaving life – leaving you so soon. Be brave, darling, God will assist and bless you. Goodbye, kiss my darlings for me. I send you the few things I have saved out of this war. Goodbye, my love, till we meet again in Heaven. I have a sure faith of our union there. I kiss this paper that goes to you. I have just heard that they have not been able to reach you. Perhaps it is better so. Yet Fr Aloysius is going to make another effort to do something. God help and sustain you, my love. But for your suffering this would all be joy and glory. Goodbye.

Your loving husband,

Thomas MacDonagh

I return the darlings' photographs. Goodbye, my love.

Thomas MacDonagh
Written at midnight, 2 May 1916
Kilmainham Gaol
Executed 3 May 1916

19 Clarke Statement[896]

This is the beginning, our fight has saved Ireland. The soldiers of tomorrow will finish the task.

Thomas J. Clarke
Executed 3 May 1916

---

896 In possession of the Clarke family. MacLochlainn. Op. cit., p. 42.

20 Clarke Letter to Kathleen, 30 April 1916[897]

Dear K,

I am in better health and more satisfied than for many a day – all will be well eventually – but this is my good-bye for now – you are ever before me to cheer me – God bless you and the boys. Let them be proud to follow the same path – Seán is with me and McG, all well – they are all heroes. I'm full of pride my love.

Your
Tom

Love to John & Madge Etc.

Written to Kathleen from Richmond Barracks
30 April 1916
Executed 3 May 1916

21 MacDermott Letter to Kathleen Clarke, 30 April 1916[898]
Written on the back of Tom Clarke's letter to his wife

Dear Cait,

I never felt so proud of the boys. 'Tis worth a life of suffering to be with them for one hour.
God bless you all,
Seán.

Executed 12 May 1916

897 In possession of the Clarke family. MacLochlainn. Op. cit., p. 42. 898 In possession of the Clarke family. MacLochlainn. Op. cit., p. 165.

22 Clarke Statement, 3 May 1916[899]

I and my fellow signatories believe we have struck the first successful blow for Freedom. The next blow, which we have no doubt Ireland will strike, will win through. In this belief we die happy.

Thomas J. Clarke
3 May 1916
Kilmainham Gaol
Executed 3 May 1916

23 Plunkett Will, 23 April 1916[900]

Will of Joseph Mary (Patrick) Plunkett made this day April 23rd 1916.
I give and bequeath everything of which I am possessed or may become possessed to Grace Evelyn (Mary Vandeleur) Gifford.

Signed Joseph Mary Plunkett
Witnessed George Oliver Plunkett

24 Plunkett Letter to Grace Gifford, 29 April 1916[901]

To Miss Grace Gifford, 8 Temple Villas
Palmerston Rd.

6th Day of the Irish Republic
Saturday April 29th 1916. About noon.
Somewhere in Moore St.

My Darling Grace,

This is just a little note to say I love you and to tell you that I did everything I could to arrange for us to meet and get married but that it was impossible.
    Except for that I have no regrets. We will meet soon.
    My other actions have been as right as I could see and make them, and I cannot wish them undone. You at any rate will not misjudge them.

899 In possession of the Clarke family. MacLochlainn. Op. cit., p. 42. **900** Originally in possession of Maeve Donnelly, now in Grace Gifford Plunkett Papers, National Library of Ireland. **901** Originally in possession of Maeve Donnelly, now in Grace Gifford Plunkett Papers, National Library of Ireland.

Give my love to my people and friends. Darling, darling child, I wish we were together. Love me always as I love you. For the rest all you do will please me. I told a few people that I wish you to have everything that belongs to me. This is my last wish so please see to it. Love xxxx

Joe

25 Will of Michael O'Hanrahan, 4 May 1916[902]

I, Micheal O hAnnrachain, give and bequeath all my rights in 'A Swordsman of the Brigade' to my mother & after her to my sisters.

Micheal O hAnnrachain
Kilmainham
4/5/16

May 4th 16

T.Wright, S.M
MPSC
B.L. Barnett, Lieut.
59th Sig Co. RE

Will of Michael O'Hanrahan
Kilmainham Gaol
Executed 4 May 1916

26 Brig. Gen. Blackadder Statement after MacBride Court Martial, 4 May 1916[903]

All the men behaved well, but the one who stands out and the most soldierly was John MacBride. He, on entering, stood to attention facing us and in his eyes I could read: 'You are soldiers. I am one. You have won. I have lost. Do your worst.'

Brigadier General Charles Blackadder

---

902 Given to Fr Augustine, O.F.M, Cap. A copy is now in the National Library. **903** Charles Wyse-Power heard Brig. Gen. Blackadder say this at a luncheon and told Victor Collins who wrote to John Devoy. William O'Brien, editor, *John Devoy's Post Bag*, Vol. I-II. MacLochlainn. Op. cit., p. 105.

27 General Lowe Letter about Elizabeth O'Farrell, 4 May 1916[904]

4.5.16

Miss Elizabeth O'Farrell was of great assistance & voluntarily accompanyied a staff officer to various Rebel Commandants. I trust that this will be taken into consideration at a future date.

Gen. Lowe
G.O.C. Dublin Forces

28 MacDermott Letter to his Sister, 7 May 1916[905]

Let there be no talk of 'foolish enterprises'. I have no vain regrets. If you really love me, teach the children the history of their own land and teach them that the cause of Caitlin ni h-Uallachain never dies. Ireland shall be free from the centre to the sea as soon as the people of Ireland believe in the necessity for Ireland's freedom and are prepared to make the necessary sacrifices to obtain it.

Seán MacDermott's letter to his sister, a Dominican nun
Written in Kilmainham Gaol
7 May 1916

Executed 12 May 1916

29 Mallin Letter To his Wife, 7 May 1916[906]

My Darling Wife, Pulse of my heart,

This is the end of all earthly things; sentence of Death has been passed, and a quarter to four tomorrow the sentence will be carried out by shooting and so must Irishmen pay for trying to make Ireland a free nation. God's will be done.
 I am prepared, but oh my darling, if only you and the little ones were coming too, if we could all reach heaven together. My heart-strings are torn to pieces when I think of you and them, of our manly Seámus, happy-go-lucky Seán, shy warm Una, Daddy's little girl, and oh, little Joseph, my little man, my little man.

904 National Library of Ireland. **905** In possession of the MacDermott family. MacLochlainn. Op. cit., p. 168. **906** In possession of the Mallin family. MacLochlainn. Op. cit., p. 121-123.

Wife, dear Wife, I cannot keep the tears back when I think of him. He will rest in my arms no more. To think that I have to leave you to battle through the world with them without my help.

We have been married thirteen years or so and in all that time you have been a true loving wife, too good for me.

You love me, my own true darling. Think only of the happy times we spent together, forgive and forget all else.

I do not believe our blood has been shed in vain. I believe Ireland will come out greater and grander but she must not forget she is Catholic, she must keep her faith.

I find no fault with the soldiers or police. I forgive them all from the bottom of my heart. Pray for all the souls who fell in this fight, Irish and English.

God and his Blessed Mother take you and my dear ones under their care. A husband's blessing on your dear head, my loving wife.

A father's blessing on the heads of my dear children Seámus, Seán, Una, Joseph, my little man, my little man. His name unnerves me again. All your dear faces arise before me.

God bless you, God bless you, my darlings. Your loving Husband, Michael Mallin, Commandant, Stephen's Green Command.

I enclose the buttons off my sleeve. Keep them as a memory of me.
Mike XXXXXX

Written in Kilmainham Gaol
7 May 1916
Executed 8 May 1916

30 Mallin Letter to his Parents, 7 May 1916[907]

Forgive your poor son who is set to meet his death. Dear Father, forgive me all, and you, dear Mother, the pain I give you now.

I tried, with others, to make Ireland a free nation and failed. Others failed before us and paid the price and so must we. Goodbye until I meet you in heaven.

Goodbye again. A kiss for you, dear Mother. God bless you all.

Your loving son, Michael

Written in Kilmainham Gaol
7 May 1916
Executed 8 May 1916

907 In possession of the Mallin family. MacLochlainn. Op. cit., p. 123-124.

31 Ceannt Statement, 7 May 1916[908]

I leave for the guidance of other revolutionaries, who may tread the path which I have trod, this advice, never to treat with the enemy, never to surrender to his mercy, but to fight to a finish. I see nothing gained but grave disaster caused, by the surrender which has marked the end of the Irish Insurrection of 1916 – so far at least as Dublin is concerned. The enemy has not cherished one generous thought for those who, with little hope, with poor equipment, and weak in numbers, withstood his forces for one glorious week. Ireland has shown she is a Nation. This generation can claim to have raised sons as brave as any that went before. And in the years to come, Ireland will honour those who risked all for her honour at Easter in 1916. I bear no ill will against whom I have fought. I have found the common soldiers and the higher officers human and companionable, even the English who were actually in the fight against us. Thank God soldiering for Ireland has opened my heart and made me see poor humanity where I expected to see only scorn and reproach. I have met the man who escaped from me by a ruse under the Red Cross. But I do not regret having withheld my fire. He gave me cakes!

I wish to record the magnificent gallantry and fearless, calm determination of the men who fought with me. All, all were simply splendid. Even I knew no fear nor panic and shrank from no risk as I shrink not now from the death which faces me at daybreak. I hope to see God's face even for a moment in the morning. His will be done. All here are very kind. My poor wife saw me yesterday and bore up – so my warden told me –even after she left my presence. Poor Áine, poor Ronan. God is their only shield now that I am removed. And God is a better shield than I.

I have just seen Áine, Nell, Richard and Mick and bade them a conditional good-bye. Even now they have hope.

Éamonn Ceannt
7 May 1916
Kilmainham Gaol – Cell 88 before he was moved to Cell 20
Executed 8 May 1916

32 Ceannt Letter to his Wife, Áine, 8 May 1916[909]

My Dearest Wife Áine,

Not wife, but widow before these lines reach you. I am here without hope of this world, and without fear, calmly awaiting the end. I have had Holy Communion,

908 National Library of Ireland. MacLochlainn. Op. cit., p. 136-137. **909** National Library of Ireland. MacLochlainn. Op. cit., p. 140-141.

and Fr Augustine has been with me, and will be back again.

Dearest silly little Fanny! My poor little sweetheart of how many years now? Ever my comforter, God comfort you now.

What can I say? I die a noble death for Ireland's freedom. Men and women will vie with one another to shake your dear hand.

Be proud of me, as I am and ever was of you. My cold exterior was a mask. It served me in these last days. You have a duty to me and to Ronan – that is to live.

My dying wishes are that you remember your state of health. Work only as much as may be necessary, and freely accept the little attentions which in due course will be showered upon you.

You will be, you are, the wife of one of the leaders of the Revolution. Sweeter still, you are my little child, my dearest pet, my sweetheart, of the hawthorn hedges, and summer eves. I remember all, and I banish all, so that I may die bravely. I have but one hour to live; then God's judgment, and through His infinite mercy, a place near your poor Grannie and my mother and father and Jem, and all the fine Irish who went through the scourge of similar misfortune from this vale of tears into the Promised Land.

Biodh misneach agat a stóirín mo chroide. Tog do cheann agus mo chroide. Tog do cheann agus biodh foighde agat go bhfeicfimid a chéile arís i bhFlaithis Dé —Tusa, agus mise agus Ronan beag beag bocht.

Adieu

Éamonn

Have courage the love of my heart. Take your head and my heart and have hope that we will be together again in the vision [kingdom or joy] of God. Poor you, and me and poor little Ronan.

Éamonn Ceannt
Letter to his wife – 8 May 1916
Kilmainham Gaol
Executed 8 May 1916

33 Connolly Written Statement to Court Martial, 9 May 1916[910]

The evidence went mainly to establish the fact that the accused, James Connolly was in command at the General Post Office, and was also Commandant-General of the Dublin division.

---

910 Given to Nora Connolly on the morning of 12 May 1916. Connolly, Nora, *The Unbroken Tradition*, 1918, p. 185.

Two of the witnesses, however, tried to bring in alleged instances of wantonly risking the lives of prisoners. The court held that this charge was irrelevant, and could not be placed against the prisoner.

I do not wish to make any defence except against the charges of wanton cruelty to prisoners. These trifling allegations that have been made, if they record facts that really happened, deal with the almost unavoidable incidents of a hurried uprising against long established authority, and nowhere show evidence of set purpose to wantonly injure unarmed persons.

We went out to break the connection between this country and the British Empire, and to establish an Irish Republic. We believe the call that we then issued to the people of Ireland was a nobler call, in a holier cause, than any call issued to them during this war, having any connection with the war. We succeeded in proving that Irishmen are ready to die endeavoring to win for Ireland those national rights which the British Government has been asking them to die for in Belgium. As long as that remains the case, the cause of Irish Freedom is safe.

Believing that the British Government has no right in Ireland, never had any right in Ireland, and never can have any right in Ireland, the presence of any one generation of Irishmen of even a respectable minority, ready to die to affirm that truth, makes that government forever a usurpation and crime against human progress.

I personally thank God that I have lived to see the day when thousands of Irish men and boys, and hundreds of Irish women and girls were ready to affirm that truth and attest it with their lives, if need be.

James Connolly
Commandant-General, Dublin Division
Army of the Irish Republic

Written Statement to Court Martial
9 May 1916
Executed 12 May 1916

34 MacDermott Letter to his Brothers and Sisters, 11 May 1916[911]

My Dear Brothers and Sisters

I sincerely hope that this letter will not come as a surprise to any of you, and above all that none of you will worry over what I have to say. It is just a wee note to say that I have been tried by Courtmartial and sentenced to be shot—to die the death

---

911 In possession of the MacDermott family. MacLochlainn. Op. cit., p. 168.

of a soldier. By the time this reaches you, I will, with God's mercy, have joined in heaven my poor father and mother as well as my dear friends who have been shot during the week. They died like heroes and with God's help I will act throughout as heroic as they did. I only wish you could see me now. I am just as calm and collected as if I were talking to you all or taking a walk to see Mick Wrynn or some of the old friends or neighbors around home. I have priests with me almost constantly for the past twenty four hours. One dear old friend of mine, Revd Dr Brown of Maynooth, stayed with me up to a very late hour last night. I feel a happiness the like of which I never experienced in my life before, and a feeling I could not describe. Surely when you know my state of mind none of you will worry or lament my fate. No, you ought to envy me. The cause for which I die has been re-baptised during the past week by the blood of as good men as ever trod God's earth and should I not feel justly proud to be numbered among them. Before God let me again assure you of how proud and happy I feel. It is not alone for myself so much I feel happy but for the fact that Ireland has produced such men.

Enough of the personal note. I had hoped Pat to be able to help you in placing the children in positions to earn their livelihood, but God will help you provide for them. Tell them how I struck out for myself and counsel them to always practice truth honesty straightforwardness in all things and sobriety. If they do this and remember their country they will be all right. Insist on their learning the language and history. I have a lot of books and I am making arrangements with one of the priests to have them turned in to a library, but I can arrange that you get some of them for the children. You might like to keep these clothes that I am wearing to have them in memory of me, so I will arrange if possible to have them sent to my old lodgings and you ought to come there and take them and any other things belonging to me that you'd like to have – of course for Dan & Maggie also. There are a few copies of a recent photo that you can take, and you might like to order more copies for friends who might like to have one. Of course you got the letter I sent you a few days before Easter. By the way, when you are in Dublin find if I owe any money to my landlady, and if so pay her. I do not think I do but at the moment I am not certain. One word more about the children. Put some of them to learn trades if you can at all. You will see if they show any promise of mechanical or technical skill, they were too small when I saw them to advise. Tell Maggie she ought to try & get Mary Anne to go for teaching. I don't know what Caty Bee ought to do. As for Dan, I suppose he will decide for himself. God direct him. He need not regret having stayed at home for so long.

Make a copy of this and send it to the others as soon as you can. A lot of my friends will want to hear about me from James, Rose & Kate. They can tell them all that in my last hours I am the same Seán they always knew and that even now I enjoy a laugh and a joke as good as ever. I don't know if you will require a pass to get to Dublin, but you better find out before you start. Perhaps martial law will have been withdrawn before you can come, it was passed for one month only and

I don't think it will be renewed. If I think of any other things to say I will tell them to Miss [Mary] Ryan, she who in all probability, had I lived, would have been my wife. I will send instructions to my landlady, but she knows you all right.

Good Bye, Dear Brothers & Sisters make no lament for me. Pray for my soul and feel a lasting pride at my death. I die that the Irish nation might live. God bless and guard you all & may He have mercy on my soul.

yours as ever

Seán

P.S. I find I have not mentioned Patrick or his mother but they know they are included for very old times sake, yes, long before there was a thought of Maggie marrying Patk. Also Mary and Bessie. I'd love to clasp the hand of each of you and many other dear friends but I will meet you all soon in a better place. Remember me to all my friends and give some money to Fathers Foy & McLoughlin for mass for me.

Good Bye

Seán

Written in Kilmainham Gaol
11 May 1916
Executed 12 May 1916

35 MacDermott Letter to John Daly, 11 May 1916[912]

My dear Daly,

Just a wee note to bid you Good Bye. I expect in a few hours to join Tom and the others in a better world. I have been sentenced to a soldier's death – to be shot tomorrow morning. I have nothing to say about this only that I look on it as a part of the day's work. We die that the Irish nation will live. Our blood will re-baptise and reinvigorate the old land. Knowing this it is superfluous to say how happy I feel. I know now what I have always felt – that the Irish nation can never die. Let present-day place-hunters condemn our actions as they will, posterity will judge us aright from the effects of our action.

I know I will meet you soon; until then Good Bye. God guard and protect you and all in No. 15. You have had a sore trial, but I know quite well that Mrs Daly

912 In possession of the MacDermott family. MacLochlainn. Op. cit., p. 170-171.

and all the girls feel proud in spite of a little temporary and natural grief that her son and the girls their brother as well as Tom are included in the list of honours. Kindly remember me specially to Mrs Clarke and tell her I am the same Seán she always knew.

God bless you all.
As ever.
Sincerely yours
Seán MacDiarmada

Letter from Seán MacDiarmada to John Daly
Written in Kilmainham Gaol
11 May 1916
Executed 12 May 1916

36 Connolly Quotation at Execution, 12 May 1916[913]

Fr Aloysius: 'Will you pray for the men who are about to shoot you?'

James Connolly: 'I will say a prayer for all brave men who do their duty. Forgive them for they know not what they do.'

James Connolly to Fr Aloysius
Kilmainham Gaol – Stonebreaker's Yard
Executed 12 May 1916

37 MacDermott Final Statement, 12 May 1916[914]

Kilmainham Prison
12 May 1916
3.30 a.m

I, Seán Mac Diarmada, before paying the penalty of death for my love of Ireland, and abhorrence of her slavery, desire to make known to all my fellow-countrymen that I die, as I have lived, bearing no malice to any man, and in perfect peace with Almighty God. The principles for which I give my life are so sacred that I now walk to my death in the most calm and collected manner. I meet death for Ireland's

---

913 MacLochlainn. Op. cit., p. 193. 914 The authenticity of this statement has not been proven. There are no original copies extant, but a copy is in the National Library. MacLochlainn. Op. cit., p. 173.

cause as I have worked for the same cause all my life. I have asked the Revd E. McCarthy who has prepared me to meet my God and who had given me courage to face the ordeal I am about to undergo, to convey this message to my fellow-countrymen.

God Save Ireland
Seán MacDiarmada
Executed 12 May 1916

38 George Bernard Shaw Letter to the *Daily News*, 10 May 1916[915]

Sir,
You say that 'so far as the leaders are concerned no voice has been raised against the infliction of punishment which has so speedily overtaken them'. As the Government shot the prisoners first and told the public about it later, there was no opportunity for effective protest. But it must not be assumed that those who merely shrugged their shoulders when it was useless to remonstrate accept for one moment the view that what happened was the execution of a gang of criminals.

My own view – which I should not intrude on you had you not concluded that it does not exist – is that the men who were shot in cold blood after their capture or surrender were prisoners of war, and it was, therefore, entirely incorrect to slaughter them. The relation of Ireland to Dublin Castle is in this respect precisely that of the Balkan States to Turkey, of Belgium or the city of Lille to the Kaiser, and of the United States to Great Britain.

Until Dublin Castle is superseded by a National Parliament and Ireland voluntarily incorporated with the British Empire, as Canada, Australasia, and South Africa have been incorporated, an Irishman resorting to arms to achieve the independence of his country is doing only what Englishmen will do, if it be their misfortune to be invaded and conquered by the Germans in the course of the present war. Further, such an Irishman is as much in order morally in accepting assistance from the Germans in his struggle with England, as England is in accepting the assistance of Russia in her struggle with Germany. The fact that he knows his enemies will not respect his rights if they catch him, and that he must, therefore, fight with a rope around his neck, increases his risk, but adds in the same measure to his glory in the eyes of his compatriots and of the disinterested admirers of patriotism throughout the world. It is absolutely impossible to slaughter a man in this position without making him a martyr and a hero, even though the day before the rising he may have been only a minor poet. The shot Irishmen will now take

915 *Daily News*, 10 May 1916.

their places beside Emmet and the Manchester Martyrs in Ireland, and beside the heroes of Poland and Serbia and Belgium in Europe; and nothing in heaven or earth can prevent it...

The Military authorities and the English Government must have known that they were canonising their prisoners...

I remain an Irishman, and am bound to contradict any implication that I can regard as a traitor any Irishman taken in a fair fight for Irish Independence against the British Government, which was a fair fight in everything except the enormous odds my countrymen had to face.

39 Irish Declaration of Independence, 21 January 1919[916]

Irish Declaration of Independence
21st January 1919
First Dáil Éireann

Enacted by the Parliament of the Republic of Ireland

Whereas the Irish People is by right a free people:

And whereas for seven hundred years the Irish People has never ceased to repudiate and has repeatedly protested in arms against foreign usurpation:

And whereas English rule in this country is, and always has been, based upon force and fraud and maintained by military occupation against the declared will of the people:

And whereas the Irish Republic was proclaimed in Dublin on Easter Monday, 1916, by the Irish Republican Army, acting on behalf of the Irish People:

And whereas the Irish People is resolved to secure and maintain its complete independence in order to promote the common weal, to re-establish justice, to provide for future defence, to ensure peace at home and good will with all nations, and to constitute a national policy based upon the people's will with equal right and equal opportunity for every citizen:

And whereas at the threshold of a new era in history the Irish electorate has in the General Election of December, 1918, seized the first occasion to declare by an overwhelming majority its firm allegiance to the Irish Republic:

Now, therefore, we, the elected Representatives of the ancient Irish People in National Parliament assembled, do, in the name of the Irish Nation, ratify the establishment of the Irish Republic and pledge ourselves and our people to make this declaration effective by every means at our command:

916 Dáil Éireann, *Minutes of the Proceedings of the First Parliament of the Republic of Ireland*, 21 January 1919.

We ordain that the elected Representatives of the Irish People alone have power to make laws binding on the people of Ireland, and that the Irish Parliament is the only Parliament to which that people will give its allegiance:

We solemnly declare foreign government in Ireland to be an invasion of our national right which we will never tolerate, and we demand the evacuation of our country by the English Garrison:

We claim for our national independence the recognition and support of every free nation in the world, and we proclaim that independence to be a condition precedent to international peace hereafter:

In the name of the Irish People we humbly commit our destiny to Almighty God Who gave our fathers the courage and determination to persevere through long centuries of a ruthless tyranny, and strong in the justice of the cause which they have handed down to us, we ask His Divine blessing on this the last stage of the struggle we have pledged ourselves to carry through to freedom.

40 Irish Constitution, 21 January 1919[917]

Irish Constitution
21st January 1919
First Dáil Éireann

Article 1
All legislative powers shall be vested in Dail Éireann, composing of Deputies, elected by the Irish people from the existing Irish Parliamentary constituencies.

Article 2
(a) All executive powers shall be vested in the members, for the time being, of the Ministry.
(b) The Ministry shall consist of a President of the Ministry, elected by Dail Éireann, and four Executive Officers, viz.;
A Secretary of Finance
A Secretary of Home Affairs
A Secretary of Foreign Affairs
A Secretary of National Defence
each of whom the President shall nominate and have power to dismiss.
(c) Every member of the Ministry shall be a member of Dail Éireann, and shall at all times be responsible to the Dail.
(d) At the first meeting of Dail Éireann after their nomination by the President, the

---

917 Dáil Éireann, *Minutes of the Proceedings of the First Parliament of the Republic of Ireland*, 21 January 1919.

names of the Executive Officers shall be separately submitted to Dail Éireann for approval.

(e) The appointment of the President shall date from his election, and the appointment of each Executive Officer from the date of the approval by the Dail of his nomination.

(f) The Ministry or any member thereof may at any time be removed by vote of the Dail upon motion for that specific purpose, provided that at least seven days notice in writing of that motion shall have been given.

Article 3

A Chairman elected annually by the Dail, and in his absence a Deputy Chairman so elected, shall preside at all meetings of Dail Éireann. Only members of the Dail shall be eligible for these offices. In case of the absence of the Chairman and Deputy Chairman the Dail shall fill the vacancies or elect a temporary Chairman.

Article 4

All monies required by the Ministry shall be obtained on vote of the Dail. The Ministry shall be responsible to the Dail for all monies so obtained, and shall present properly audited accounts for the expenditure of the same -twice yearly- in the months of May and November. The audit shall be conducted by an Auditor or Auditors appointed by the Dail. No member of the Dail shall be eligible for such appointment.

Article 5

This Constitution is provisional and is liable to alteration upon seven days written notice of motion for that specific purpose.

41 Dáil Message to the Free Nations of the World, 21 January 1919[918]

To the Nations of the World – Greeting
The Nation of Ireland having proclaimed her national independence, calls, through her elected representatives in Parliament assembled in the Irish Capital on January 21st, 1919, upon every free nation to support the Irish Republic by recognising Ireland's national status and her right to its vindication at the Peace Congress.

Naturally, the race, the language, the customs and traditions of Ireland are radically distinct from the English. Ireland is one of the most ancient nations in Europe, and she has preserved her national integrity, vigorous and intact, through seven centuries of foreign oppression; she has never relinquished her national rights, and throughout the long era of English usurpation she has in every generation

---

918 Dáil Éireann, *Minutes of the Proceedings of the First Parliament of the Republic of Ireland,* 21 January 1919.

defiantly proclaimed her inalienable right of nationhood down to her last glorious resort to arms in 1916.

Internationally, Ireland is the gateway to the Atlantic; Ireland is the last outpost of Europe towards the West; Ireland is the point upon which great trade routes between East and West converge; her independence is demanded by the Freedom of the Seas; her great harbours must be open to all nations, instead of being the monopoly of England. To-day these harbours are empty and idle solely because English policy is determined to retain Ireland as a barren bulwark for English aggrandisement, and the unique geographical position of this island, far from being a benefit and safeguard to Europe and America, is subjected to the purposes of England's policy of world domination.

Ireland to-day reasserts her historic nationhood the more confidently before the new world emerging from the war, because she believes in freedom and justice as the fundamental principles of international law; because she believes in a frank co-operation between the peoples for equal rights against the vested privileges of ancient tyrannies; because the permanent peace of Europe can never be secured by perpetuating military dominion for the profit of empire but only by establishing the control of government in every land upon the basis of the free will of a free people, and the existing state of war, between Ireland and England, can never be ended until Ireland is definitely evacuated by the armed forces of England.

For these among other reasons, Ireland – resolutely and irrevocably determined at the dawn of the promised era of self-determination and liberty that she will suffer foreign dominion no longer – calls upon every free nation to uphold her national claim to complete independence as an Irish Republic against the arrogant pretensions of England founded in fraud and sustained only by an overwhelming military occupation, and demands to be confronted publicly with England at the Congress of the Nations, that the civilised world having judged between English wrong and Irish right may guarantee to Ireland its permanent support for the maintenance of her national independence.

42 Dáil Democratic Programme, 21 January 1919[919]

We declare in the words of the Irish Republican Proclamation the right of the people of Ireland to the ownership of Ireland and to the unfettered control of Irish destinies to be indefeasible, and in the language of our first President, Padraic Pearse, we declare that the nation's sovereignty extends not only to all men and women of the nation, but to all its material possessions; the nation's soil and all its resources, all the wealth and all the wealth-producing processes within the nation and with him we re-affirm that all the rights to private property must be subordinated to the public right and welfare.

919 Dáil Éireann, *Minutes of the Proceedings of the First Parliament of the Republic of Ireland*, 21 January 1919.

We declare that we desire our country to be ruled in accordance with the principles of Liberty, Equality and Justice for all, which alone can secure permanence of government in the willing adhesion of the people.

We affirm the duty of every man and woman to give allegiance and service to the commonwealth, and declare it is the duty of the nation to assure that every citizen shall have opportunity to spend his or her strength and faculties in the service of the people. In return for willing service, we, in the name of the Republic, declare the right of every citizen to an adequate share of the produce of the nation's labour.

It shall be the first duty of the government of the Republic to make provision for the physical, mental and spiritual well-being of the children, to secure that no child shall suffer hunger or cold from lack of food or clothing or shelter, but that all shall be provided with the means and faculties requisite for their proper education and training as citizens of a free and Gaelic Ireland.

The Irish Republic fully realises the necessity of abolishing the present odious, degrading, and foreign poor-law system, substituting therefore a sympathetic native scheme for the care of the nation's aged and infirm, who shall no longer be regarded as a burden, but rather entitled to the nation's gratitude and consideration. Likewise it shall be the duty of the Republic to take measures that will safeguard the health of the people and ensure the physical as well as the moral well-being of the nation.

It shall be our duty to promote the development of the nation's resources, to increase the productivity of the soil, to exploit its mineral deposits, peat bogs, and fisheries, its waterways and harbours, in the interest and for the benefit of the Irish people.

It shall be the duty of the Republic to adopt all measures necessary for the re-creation and invigoration of our industries, and to ensure their being developed on the most beneficial and progressive co-operative industrial lines. With the adoption of an extensive Irish consular service trade with foreign nations shall be revived on terms of mutual advantage and good will; while undertaking the organisation of the nation's trade, import and export, it shall be the duty of the Republic to prevent the shipment from Ireland of food and other necessaries until the wants of the Irish people are fully satisfied and provided for.

It shall devolve upon the national government to seek the co-operation of the governments of other countries in determining a standard of social and industrial legislation with a view to general and lasting improvements in the conditions under which the working classes live and labour.

43 Articles of Agreement for a Treaty between Great Britain and Ireland, 6 December 1921[920]

1.   Ireland shall have the same constitutional status in the Community of Nations known as the British Empire as the Dominion of Canada, the Commonwealth of Australia, the Dominion of New Zealand, and the Union of South Africa with a Parliament having powers to make laws for the peace order and good government of Ireland and an Executive responsible to that Parliament, and shall be styled and known as the Irish Free State.

2.   Subject to the provisions hereinafter set out the position of the Irish Free State in relation to the Imperial Parliament and Government and otherwise shall be that of the Dominion of Canada, and the law, practice and constitutional usage governing the relationship of the Crown or the representative of the Crown and of the Imperial Parliament to the Dominion of Canada shall govern their relationship to the Irish Free State.

3.   The representative of the Crown in Ireland shall be appointed in like manner as the Governor-General of Canada and in accordance with the practice observed in the making of such appointments.

4.   The oath to be taken by Members of the Parliament of the Irish Free State shall be in the following form:-

I .... do solemnly swear true faith and allegiance to the Constitution of the Irish Free State as by law established and that I will be faithful to H.M. King George V., his heirs and successors by law, in virtue of the common citizenship of Ireland with Great Britain and her adherence to and membership of the group of nations forming the British Commonwealth of Nations.

5.   The Irish Free State shall assume liability for the service of the Public Debt of the United Kingdom as existing as the date hereof and towards the payment of War Pensions as existing at that date in such proportion as may be fair and equitable, having regard to any just claim on the part of Ireland by way of set-off or counter claim, the amount of such sums being determined in default of agreement by the arbitration of one or more independent persons being citizens of the British Empire

6.   Until an arrangement has been made between the British and Irish Governments whereby the Irish Free State undertakes her own coastal defence, the defence by sea of Great Britain and Ireland shall be undertaken by His Majesty's Imperial Forces, but this shall not prevent the construction or maintenance by the Government of the Irish Free State of such vessels as are necessary for the protection of the Revenue or the Fisheries. The foregoing provisions of this article shall be reviewed at a conference of Representatives of the British and Irish governments, to be held at the expiration of five years from the date hereof with a view to the undertaking by Ireland of a share in her own coastal defence

920 National Library of Ireland.

7.   The Government of the Irish Free State shall afford to His Majesty's Imperial Forces (a) In the time of peace such harbour and other facilities as are indicated in the Annex hereto, or such other facilities as may from time to time be agreed between the British Government and the Government of the Irish Free State; and (b) In time of war or of strained relations with a Foreign Power such harbour and other facilities as the British Government may require for the purposes of such defence as aforesaid.

8.   With a view to securing the observance of the principle of international limitation of armaments, if the Government of the Irish Free State establishes and maintains a military defence force, the establishments thereof shall not exceed in size such proportion of the military establishes maintained in Great Britain as that which the population of Ireland bears to the population of Great Britain.

9.   The ports of Great Britain and the Irish Free State shall be freely open to the ships of the other country on payment of the customary port and other dues.

10. The Government of the Irish Free State agrees to pay fair compensation on terms not less favourable than those accorded by the Act of 1920 to judges, officials, members of Police Forces and other Public Servants who are discharged by it or who retire in consequence of the change of government effected in pursuance hereof. Provided that this agreement shall not apply to members of the Auxiliary Police Force or to persons recruited in Great Britain for the Royal Irish Constabulary during the two years next preceding the date hereof. The British Government will assume responsibility for such compensation or pensions as may be payable to any of these excepted persons.

11. Until the expiration of one month from the passing of the Act of Parliament for the ratification of this instrument, the powers of the Parliament and the Government of the Irish Free State shall not be exercisable as respects Northern Ireland, and the provisions of the Government of Ireland Act 1920, shall, so far as they relate to Northern Ireland remain of full force and effect, and no election shall be held for the return of members to serve in the Parliament of the Irish Free State for constituencies in Northern Ireland, unless a resolution is passed by both Houses of the Parliament of Northern Ireland in favour of the holding of such elections before the end of the said month.

12. If before the expiration of the said month, an address is presented to His Majesty by both Houses of the Parliament of Northern Ireland to that effect, the powers of the Parliament and the Government of the Irish Free State shall no longer extend to Northern Ireland, and the provisions of the Government of Ireland Act, 1920, (including those relating to the Council of Ireland) shall so far as they relate to Northern Ireland, continue to be of full force and effect, and this instrument shall have effect subject to the necessary modifications. Provided that if such an address is so presented a Commission consisting of three persons, one to be appointed by the Government of the Irish Free State, one to be appointed by the Government of Northern Ireland, and one who shall be Chairman to be appointed by the British Government shall determine in accordance with the wishes of the

inhabitants, so far as may be compatible with economic and geographic conditions the boundaries between Northern Ireland and the rest of Ireland, and for the purposes of the Government of Ireland Act, 1920, and of this instrument, the boundary of Northern Ireland shall be such as may be determined by such Commission.

13. For the purpose of the last foregoing article, the powers of the Parliament of Southern Ireland under the Government of Ireland Act, 1920, to elect members of the Council of Ireland shall after the Parliament of the Irish Free State is constituted be exercised by that Parliament.

14. After the expiration of the said month, if no such address as is mentioned in Article 12 hereof is presented, the Parliament and Government of Northern Ireland shall continue to exercise as respects Northern Ireland the powers conferred on them by the Government of Ireland Act, 1920, but the Parliament and Government of the Irish Free State shall in Northern Ireland have in relation to matters in respect of which the Parliament of Northern Ireland has not the power to make laws under the Act (including matters which under the said Act are within the jurisdiction of the Council of Ireland) the same powers as in the rest of Ireland, subject to such other provisions as may be agreed in manner hereinafter appearing.

15. At any time after the date hereof the Government of Northern Ireland and the provisional Government of Southern Ireland hereinafter constituted may meet for the purpose of discussing the provisions subject to which the last foregoing Article is to operate in the event of no such address as is therein mentioned being presented and those provisions may include:-

(a) Safeguards with regard to patronage in Northern Ireland.

(b) Safeguards with regard to the collection of revenue in Northern Ireland.

(c) Safeguards with regard to import and export duties affecting the trade or industry of Northern Ireland.

(d) Safeguards for minorities in Northern Ireland.

(e) The settlement of the financial relations between Northern Ireland and the Irish Free State.

(f) The establishment and powers of a local militia in Northern Ireland and the relation of the Defence Forces of the Irish Free State and of Northern Ireland respectively, and if at any such meeting provisions are agreed to, the same shall have effect as if they were included amongst the provisions subject to which the powers of the Parliament and the Government of the Irish Free State are to be exercisable in Northern Ireland under Article 14 hereof.

16. Neither the Parliament of the Irish Free State nor the Parliament of Northern Ireland shall make any law so as either directly or indirectly to endow any religion or prohibit or restrict the free exercise thereof or give any preference or impose any disability on account of religious belief or religious status or affect prejudicially the right of any child to attend a school receiving public money without attending the religious instruction at the school or make any discrimination as respects State aid between schools under the management of different religious denominations or

divert from any religious denomination or any educational institution any of its property except for public utility purposes and on payment of compensation.

17. By way of provisional arrangement for the administration of Southern Ireland during the interval which must elapse between the date hereof and the constitution of a Parliament and Government of the Irish Free State in accordance therewith, steps shall be taken forthwith for summoning a meeting of members of Parliament elected for constituencies in Southern Ireland since the passing of the Government of Ireland Act, 1920, and for constituting a provisional Government, and the British Government shall take the steps necessary to transfer to such provisional Government the powers and machinery requisite for the discharge of its duties, provided that every member of such provisional Government shall have signified in writing his or her acceptance of this instrument. But this arrangement shall not continue in force beyond the expiration of twelve months from the date hereof.

18. This instrument shall be submitted forthwith by His Majesty's Government for the approval of Parliament and by the Irish signatories to a meeting summoned for the purpose of the members elected to sit in the House of Commons of Southern Ireland and if approved shall be ratified by the necessary legislation.

(Signed)

On behalf of the British Delegation,   On behalf of the Irish Delegation.

D. Lloyd George   Art Ó Griobhtha
Austen Chamberlain   Micheál Ó Coileain
Birkenhead   Riobárd Bartún
Winston S. Churchill   E.S. Ó Dugain
L. Worthington-Evans   Seórsa Ghabháin Uí Dhubhthaigh
Hamar Greenwood
Gordon Hewart
6th December, 1921.

44 George Bernard Shaw Letter to Hannie Collins, 24 August 1922[921]

My Dear Miss Collins

Don't let them make you miserable about it: how could a born soldier die better than at the victorious end of a good fight, falling to the shot of another Irishman – a damned fool but all the same an Irishman who thought he was fighting for Ireland – 'a Roman to a Roman'?

I met Michael for the first and last time on Saturday last, and I am very glad I did. I rejoice in his memory and will not be so disloyal to it as to snivel over his valiant death.

---

921 Lavery, Sir John, *The Life of a Painter*, 1940, p. 127.

So tear up your mourning and hang up your brightest colours in his honour; and let us all praise God that he had not to die in a snuffy bed of a trumpery cough, weakened by age, and saddened by the disappointments that would have attended his work had he lived.

Sincerely,
Bernard Shaw
August 24th, 1922

George Bernard Shaw letter to Hannie Collins.

45 Oration of Gen. Richard Mulcahy at the graveside of Micheal Collins, 28 August 1922[922]

Our country is today bent under a sorrow such as it has not been bent for many a year. Our minds are cold, empty, wordless, and without sound. But it is only our weaknesses that are bent under this great sorrow that we meet with today. All that is good in us, all that is strong in us, is strengthened by the memory of that great hero and that great legend who is now laid to rest.

We bend today over the grave of a man not more than thirty years of age, who took to himself the gospel of toil for Ireland, the gospel of working for the people of Ireland, and of sacrifice for their good, and who had made himself a hero and a legend that will stand in the pages of our history with any bright page that was ever written there.

Pages have been written by him in the hearts of our people that will never find a place in print. But we lived, some of us, with these intimate pages; and those pages that will reach history, meagre though they be, will do good to our country and will inspire us through many a dark hour. Our weaknesses cry out to us, 'Michael Collins was too brave.'

Michael Collins was not too brave. Every day and every hour he lived he lived it to the full extent of that bravery which God gave to him, and it is for us to be brave as he was – brave before danger, brave before those who lie, brave even to that very great bravery that our weakness complained of in him.

When we look over the pages of his diary for 22nd August, 'Started 6.15 am. Macroom to Ballineen, Bandon, Skibbereen, Roscarberry, Clonakilty', our weakness says he tried to put too much into the day. Michael Collins did not try to put too much into the day. Standing on the little mantelpiece of his office was a bronze plaque of President Roosevelt of the United States, and the inscription on it ran, 'I wish to preach, not the doctrine of ignoble ease, but the doctrine of strenuous

922 Nelson, Justin, *Michael Collins, The Final Days*, 1997, p. 85-88.

life, the life of toil and effort, of labour and strife; to preach that highest form of success that comes, to the man who does not shrink from danger, hardship or bitter toil, and who, out of these, wins the splendid triumph.'

Unless the grain of corn that falls to the ground dies, there is nothing but itself in it, but if it dies it gives forth great fruit. Michael Collins' passing will give us forth great fruit, and Michael Collins' dying will give us forth great fruit. Every bit of his small grain of corn died, and it died night and day during the last four or five years. We have seen him lying on a bed of sickness and struggling with infirmities, running from his bed to his work.

On Saturday, the day before he went on his last journey to Cork, he sat with me at breakfast writhing with pain from a cold all through his body, and yet he was facing his day's work for that Saturday, and facing his Sunday's journey and Monday's journey and his journey on Tuesday. So let us be brave, and let us not be afraid to do too much in the day. In all that great work, strenuous it was, comparatively it was intemperate, but it was the only thing that Michael Collins was intemperate in.

How often with a shout he used to get out of bed in the morning at 5 or 6 o'clock crying, 'All the time that is wasted in sleep', and would dash around the room, or into some neighbouring room where some of us lay in the hope of an hour or two's sleep, and he would clear all the blankets off us, or would pound vigorously at the door which prudence had locked.

Crossing the square of the barracks on the Saturday morning that I mention, he told of his visit to one of the barracks in the South on his first trip there, and of finding most of the garrison in bed at 10 o'clock; and thinking of all the lack of order, lack of cleanliness, lack of moral strength and efficiency that goes with this particular type of sloth, and of all the demoralisation following on the dissatisfaction that one has with one's self all the day that starts with an hour's disadvantage. 'Oh', he said, 'if our fellows would only get up at 6 o'clock in the morning'.

Yes, get up to read, to write, to think, to plan, to work, or like Ard Riogh Éireann long ago, simply to greet the sun. The God-given long day fully felt and fully seen would bring its own work and its own construction. Let us be brave, then, and let us work.

'Prophecy', said Peter, who was the great rock, 'is a light shining in the darkness till the day dawn.' And surely 'our great rock' was our prophet and our prophecy, a light held aloft along the road of 'danger of hardship or bitter toil'. And if our light is gone out it is only as the paling of a candle in the dawn of its own prophecy.

The act of his, the word of his, the look of his was day by day a prophecy to us that loose lying in us lay capabilities for toil, for bravery, for regularity, for joy in life; and slowness and in hesitancy and in weariness half yielded to, his prophecies came true in us.

And just as he as a person was a light and a prophecy to us individually, he looked to it and wished that this band of brothers, which is the Army, will be a prophecy to our own people. Our Army had been the people, is the people, and will be the people. Our green uniform does not make us less the people. It is a cloak of service, a curtailer of our weakness, and an amplifier of our strength.

We are jealous for his greatness. Words have been quoted as being his last words; Michael Collins is supposed to have said the fragile words, 'Forgive them'. Michael Collins never said these words, 'Forgive them', because his great big mind could not have entertained the obverse thought, and he knew those around and worked with him that they, too, were too big to harbour in their minds the obverse thought.

When Michael Collins met difficulties, met people who obstructed him, and worked against him, he did not turn aside to blame them, but facing steadily ahead, he worked bravely forward to the goal he intended. He had that faith in the intensity of his own work that in its development and in its construction he would absorb into one homogeneous whole in the nation, without the necessity for blame or for forgiveness, all those who differed from and those who fought against him.

He is supposed to have said, 'Let the Dublin Brigade bury me.' Michael Collins knows that we will never bury him. He lies here among the men of the Dublin Brigade. Around him there lie forty-eight comrades of his from our Dublin battalions. But Michael Collins never separated the men of Dublin from the men of Kerry, nor the men of Dublin from the men of Donegal, nor the men of Dublin from the men of Cork.

His great love embraced our whole people and our whole Army, and he was as close in spirit with our men in Kerry and Donegal as he was with our men in Dublin. Yes, even those men in different districts in the country who sent us home here our dead Dublin men – we are sure he felt nothing but pity and sorrow for them for the tragic circumstances in which they find themselves, knowing that in fundamentals and in ideals they were the same.

Michael Collins had only a few minutes to live and to speak after he received his death wound, and the only word he spoke in these few minutes was 'Emmet'. He called to the comrade alongside, the comrade of many fights and many plans, and I am sure that he felt in calling that one name that he was calling around him the whole men of Ireland that he might speak the last word of comradeship and love.

We last looked at him in the City Hall and in the small church in Vincent's Hospital. And, studying his face with an eager gaze, we found there the same old smile that met us always in our work. And seeing it there in the first dark hour of our blow, the mind could not help travelling back to the dark storm-tossed Sea of Galilee and the frail barque tossed upon the Waters there, and the strong, calm smile of the Great Sleeper in the stern of the boat.

Tom Ashe, Tomas MacCurtain, Traolach MacSuibhne, Dick McKee, Micheal O'Coileain, and all you who lie buried here, disciples of our great chief, those of us you leave behind are all, too, grain from the same handfull, scattered by the hand of the Great Sower over the fruitful Soil of Ireland. We, too, will bring forth our own fruit.

Men and women of Ireland, we are all mariners on the deep, bound for a port still seen only through storm and spray, sailing still on a sea full 'of dangers and hardships, and bitter toil'. But the Great Sleeper lies smiling in the stern of the boat, and we shall be filled with that spirit which will walk bravely upon the waters.

Appendix IV

**Organizations, Uniforms, Flags and Emblems of the Period
War of Independence: Black and Tans and the Auxiliaries
Political Parties Following the 1921 Treaty**

CONTENTS

1   A Soldier's Song/*Amhrán na bhFiann*

Peadar Kearney (Peadar Ó Cearnaigh) wrote the lyrics and is usually given 'credit' (1907). Paddy Heaney wrote the music. (There is some evidence Seán Rogan may have assisted with the music). By 1907 Kearney wanted to write something more rousing and original and produced the words of 'A Soldier's Song'. According to Seámus de Burca, Kearney's nephew, Heaney 'worked on the melody for a week and gave up in despair when half way through the chorus – his inspiration had failed. When Kearney called round to see him on a Sunday morning, Heaney was dejected. Kearney asked him anxiously how the music was coming along and for a reply Heaney threw the manuscript in the fire. Kearney snatched it out, smoothed it on the table. The tune was all right, but the chorus was all wrong. They went over the words and Kearney suggested they go back on the melody of the verse. So Heaney toned out the tune and Kearney lilted the words. And thus "A Soldier's Song" was born.' Bulmer Hobson published the song lyrics in *Irish Freedom* in 1912. It was first published in sheet form in 1916 with the image of a rifle entwined with Celtic designed lettering: Words by Peadar Kearney, Music by Patrick Heaney, arranged by Cathal MacDubhghaill and published by Whelan & Son, 17 Upper Ormond Quay, Dublin. Following the Rising the music was arranged and published by Victor Herbert in New York in December 1916, with the proceeds going to Ireland. The song was written in English and translated into Irish by Liam O'Rinn.[923] [924]

Though written in 1907, the song was not widely known until it was sung both at the GPO during the Rising and later at various camps where Volunters/ICA were interned. Soon after, it was adopted as the unofficial national anthem, replacing 'God Save Ireland'.

It was officially recognised as the Irish National Anthem in 1926.

---

[923] De Burca, Seámus. *The Soldier's Song: The Story of Peadar Kearney* (pamphlet, Dublin, 1958).   [924] Hearn, Vincent. *Origin of the Irish National Anthem* http://www.from-ireland.net/history/origin.htm

2 ORGANIZATIONS

The Irish Republican Brotherhood

In Peter Lanigan's timber yard, Lombard Street, Dublin, on St Patrick's Day, 1858, James Stephens formally established the Irish Republican Brotherhood. It was originally named the Irish *Revolutionary* Brotherhood, but soon came to be known as the Irish *Republican* Brotherhood (IRB).

(Stephens was a Young Irelander, and was a lieutenant to William Smith O'Brien at the 'Battle of Widow McCormack's cabbage patch' in Ballingary, Co. Tipperary, in August 1848. He was wounded three times and was left in a ditch half conscious. He climbed out after the police left. The authorities made a determined effort to arrest all the leaders, but there was a fake 'funeral' for Stephens in which a coffin full of rocks was buried in the graveyard of St Canice's Cathedral in Kilkenny. Stephens was smuggled onto a ship to England and then to France where he spent the next eight years. Upon his return to Dublin in 1856, he determined to organise the revolutionary movement and that led to the founding of the IRB.

John O'Mahony and Michael Doheny sent Owen Considine to Ireland on behalf of the exiled Young Irelanders in America to help establish the IRB. The IRB was a small, secret, revolutionary body whose sole object was to 'establish and maintain a free and independent Republican Government in Ireland'. It became known as the Fenian movement in the 1850's and 1860's, and was committed to the use of force to establish an independent Irish republic. After organising an abortive rising in March 1867, it suffered deep internal divisions over leadership and strategy in both the US and Ireland – whether it was best to strike at England, in Ireland or in Canada. The issue was resolved after a series of failed interventions in Canada in 1866, 1867 and 1871, and bombings in England which did not lead Ireland closer to independence.

In the US, the IRB's reorganisation was begun after the release from prison in 1871 of two of its most effective leaders – Jeremiah O'Donovan Rossa and John Devoy.

Riven by continuing internal squabbles, in Ireland the IRB was unable to exploit the weaknesses and divisions in the constitutional movement following Parnell's divorce scandal, 1890-1891.

The IRB's unit of organisation was the 'Circle' which could be sub-divided into groups of not more than ten. Each Circle was under the command of an elected 'Centre'.

Circles were grouped to form Districts under District Centres, and these were grouped into County Circles under a County Centre. The whole organisation was divided into eleven Districts, eight in Ireland, two in England and one in Scotland.

It was eventually rejuvenated in Ireland about 1907, led by Bulmer Hobson and Tom Clarke, thus preparing the way for all that followed.

One of the leaders of the resurgent IRB was Belfast's Denis McCullough, who later became President. Imbued with the idealism of Irish separatism, he recruited several other young men of his own spirit into the IRB, and within two years after his initiation in 1901 he was elected a Centre in Belfast. Straightaway, he required that all members be 'sober, disciplined and active' or get out. This became the credo of the entire IRB. When these warnings were not taken seriously the veteran IRB members found themselves eliminated one by one from membership. One of the members dismissed this way was McCullough's own father.[925]

The governing body was the Supreme Council. Before 1916, this consisted of eleven members, and after the 1917 reorganisation it contained fifteen members. Constitutionally, this body met at least once every four months. When not in session, all powers of the Supreme Council, except for declaring war, devolved onto an executive of three: the President, Secretary and Treasurer. The Constitution provided for the establishment of a Military Council, subordinate to the Supreme Council. (The seven signatories of the *1916 Proclamation* constituted the entire Military Council at that time.)

Its members spoke of it as 'The Organisation' according to Bulmer Hobson. The organisation's oath was as follows:

I, _____, in the presence of Almighty God, do solemnly swear allegiance to the Irish Republic, now virtually established; and that I will do my very utmost, at every risk, while life lasts, to defend its independence and integrity; that I will bear true allegiance to the Supreme Council of the Irish Republican Brotherhood and Government of the Irish Republic and implicitly obey the Constitution of the Irish Republican Brotherhood and, finally, that I will yield implicit independence in all things, not contrary to the laws of God, to the commands of my superior officers and will preserve inviolable the secrets of the organisation. So help me God! Amen.

Its Constitution was dedicated to force against England at any favorable opportunity, but this was to be a democratic decision: 'The IRB shall await the decision of the Irish Nation as expressed by a majority of the Irish people as to the fit hour of inaugurating a war against England and shall, pending such an emergency, lend its support to every movement calculated to advance the cause of Irish independence, consistent with the preservation of its own integrity.' (IRB Constitution, 1873).[926] This clause was adopted following controversies arising out of the 1867 Rising.[927]

The IRB planned the Rising. The Irish Volunteers and the Irish Citizen Army made it possible. The establishment of the Irish Volunteers gave the IRB the great

925 Martin, F.X., OSA. 'McCullough, Hobson and Republican Ulster', in Martin, F.X., OSA. *Leaders and Men*, p. 97. 926 Nowlan, Kevin B. 'Tom Clarke, McDermott, and the IRB', in Martin, F.X., OSA. *Leaders and Men*, p. 110. 927 Ryan, Desmond. *The Rising*, p. 9.

opportunity to 'train and equip its members as a military body for the purpose of securing independence for Ireland by force of arms' and securing 'the cooperation of all Irish military bodies in the accomplishment of its objects'. (IRB Constitution, 1920).

Numerically, the IRB probably never exceeded two thousand members. However, they were all extremely loyal and well trained, and there was very tight security.

The executions of 1916 just about wiped out the Supreme Council, and after the prisoners were released the IRB had to reconstitute itself. In 1917, Seán McGarry was elected President, Michael Collins was elected Secretary, and Diarmuid Lynch was elected Treasurer.

According to the IRB Constitution, the President, 'in fact, as well as by right', was regarded as the head of the government of the Irish Republic. However, the Constitution subsequent to 1920 was amended to take into account the oath required by Dáil Deputies and officials committing them to support and defend the Irish Republic and its government.

Provisional Presidents of the IRB were:

James Stephens (1858-1866)
Thomas J. Kelly (1866-1867)
James Francis Xavier O'Brien (1869?-1872?)
Charles Joseph Kickham (1873-1882)
John O'Connor (1882?-1891?)
John O'Leary (1891?-1907)
Neal O'Boyle (1907-1910)
John Mulholland (1910-1912)
James (Seámas) Deakin (1913-1914)
Denis McCullough (1915-1916)
Thomas Ashe (1916-1917)
Seán McGarry (1917-1919)
Michael Collins (1919-1922)

Cumann Luthcleas Gael/Gaelic Athletic Association (GAA)

In the 1880's, many, including Dr Thomas W. Croke (Archbishop of Cashel), maintained that 'ball-playing, hurling, football kicking according to Irish rules ... may now be said to be not only dead and buried, but in several localities to be entirely forgotten. What the country needed was an Irish organisation to bring order and unity to sport on a nation-wide basis'.

In August 1884 Michael Cusack, at a meeting in Loughrea, Co. Galway, outlined his plans to a group of local athletic enthusiasts to establish a national organisation for Irish athletes and to revive hurling. On 1 November 1884 the Gaelic Athletic Association was founded at Miss Hayes' Commercial Hotel, Thurles, Co. Tipperary by Michael Cusack (Clareman, teacher, sportsman and nationalist) and Maurice Davin (Tipperary man who at the time was Ireland's most famous athlete). Other founding members present were John Wyse-Power, John McKay, J.K. Bracken, Joseph O'Ryan and Thomas St George McCarthy. Many of the seven men who attended the meeting were Fenians. Not present at the Thurles meeting was Patrick W. Nally, a keen athlete and leading IRB organiser who also played a prominent role in bringing about the birth of this new Association: he was the one who suggested the organisation to Cusack. Maurice Davin was elected president of the new organisation. Three secretaries were elected: Cusack, Wyse-Power and McKay. In a brief speech Davin called for a body to draft rules to help revive Irish games and to open athletics to the man in the street. The meeting also agreed to invite Archbishop Croke of Cashel, Charles Stewart Parnell and Michael Davitt to become patrons. All three accepted, although Dr Croke resigned after conflicts with Cusack. The GAA drew up its first set of rules in 1885. The essential objectives of the Association were:

1)   to bring about the organisation of Irish sport by Irish men;

2)   to draft new rules for Irish games;

3)   to devise schemes of recreation for Irish people.

Patrick W. Nally was the first to organise a national athletic sport meeting on his father's farm in Balla, Co. Mayo.

Connradh na Gaeilge/the Gaelic League

Founded by Douglas Hyde (first President of Ireland), Fr Michael Hickey, Fr Eugene O'Growey, and Eoin MacNeill on 31 July 1893. Douglas Hyde became its first President and Eoin MacNeill was Vice-President and Hon. Secretary. Its original purpose was not revival but to help Irish speakers where Irish was still spoken. Its first official newspaper was *Fainne an Lae* (Dawn) which was edited by Eoin MacNeill. By 1906 Connradh na Gaeilge had 900 branches with 100,000 members. Its membership shrank after it achieved in getting Irish as a recognized degree subject in the National University in 1909.

An Claidheamh Soluis ('The Organ of Militant Freedom')
This was the official newspaper of the Gaelic League. It was also known by the one word *Claidheamh*. Padraig Pearse was the editor from 1903 to 1909, then Seán Forde. (It is noted in some books that 'Forde' was an alias, and he was really named Tomas Ó Maoileoin [Malone]. Tomas Ó Maoileoin and his brother, Seámas, were originally from Mullingar, Co. Westmeath and both worked for

Michael Collins in the War of Independence, primarily in Co. Cork, Galway and Clare. Seámas often went by the alias 'Liam Forde'.[928] [929] [930]) The O'Rahilly was the manager. Eoin MacNeill's article *'The North Began'*, on 1 November 1913, suggested that the rest of Ireland would do well to imitate the Ulster Volunteers and form citizen forces. Afterward MacNeill was approached by Bulmer Hobson to 'head' the Irish Volunteers.

*Inghinidhe na hÉireann/*Daughters of Ireland

Founded by Maud Gonne MacBride in 1900; she became the first President with Jennie Wyse-Power, Anna Johnston (better known by her pen name Ethna Carberry), Annie Egan and Alice Furlong, elected Vice-Presidents, and Maire T. Quinn as Hon. Secretary. The organisation eventually merged with Cumann na mBan in May 1914. Ironically the organisational meeting took place at Easter 1900.

The first meeting determined to give Arthur Griffith a new blackthorn stick for the one he supposedly broke over the head of the editor of the society paper *Figaro* because the editor claimed Maud Gonne was an English spy. It was also at this meeting that it was determined to give sweets to all children who did *not* go to the Phoenix Park to see Queen Victoria. In July 1900, it organised a treat for 30,000 school-children as a counter-attraction to the official celebration of Queen Victoria's visit.

The objectives of Inghinidhe na hÉireann were: the re-establishment of the complete independence of Ireland; to encourage the study of Gaelic, of Irish literature, history, music, and art especially among the young (by organising and teaching classes dedicated to the above aims); to support and popularise Irish manufacture; to discourage the reading and circulation of low English literature, the singing of English songs, the attending of vulgar English entertainments at the theatres and music halls, and to combat in every way English influence, which was seen to be doing so much injury to the artistic taste and refinement of the Irish people; and to form a fund called the National Purposes Fund, for the furtherance of the above objectives.[931]

In 1908, the organisation initiated *Bean na hÉireann*, the first nationalist-feminist journal to be produced in Ireland. ('The women's paper that men buy!') *Bean na hÉireann* was edited by Helena Molony.[932] The staff comprised: Madeline ffrench-Mullen, Sydney Gifford, Bulmer Hobson, Maud Gonne MacBride, Dr Pat

---

928 Twohig, Patrick J. *Blood on the Flag, Autobiography of a Freedom Fighter*, 1996, p. vii. Translation of *B'fhiu an Braon Fola*, written by James Malone (Seámas Ó Maoileoin), 1958. The title, *B'fhiu an Braon Fola*, means 'the drop of blood was worth it', a reference to Daniel O'Connell's famous statement: 'The freedom of Ireland isn't worth the shedding of one drop of blood.' Though 'Seán Forde' may have been the editor's alias, since Tomas was born in 1893 it is highly unlikely the editor and Collins' agent were the same man. Tomas Malone ('Alias Seán Forde, Commandant IRA, Limerick, 1921') makes no mention of the editorship in his Witness Statement 845. **929** Ebenzer, Lyn. *Fron-Goch and the Birth of the IRA*, 2006, p. 206. **930** Malone, Tom. *Alias Seán Forde*. Danesfort, 2000. **931** *United Irishman*, 13 October 1900. **932** Molony, Helena. Witness Statement 391.

MacCartan, Seán McGarry, Countess Markievicz. The contributors included Sir Roger Casement, Maeve Cavanagh, Padraic Colum, Madeline ffrench-Mullen (as 'M O'Callaghan' or 'Dectora'), Sydney Gifford (as 'John Brennan' or 'Sorcha Ni Hanlon'), Arthur Griffith, Maude Gonne MacBride (as 'Maidbh'), Terence MacSwiney, Helena Malony (as 'Emer', 'E', or 'A Worker'), Count Markievicz, Countess Markievicz (as 'Armid' or 'Macha'), Susan Mitchell, Padraic Ó Conaire, Seámus O'Sullivan, Joseph Plunkett, George Russell (Æ), James Stephens, and Katherine Tynan.[933]

Cumann na nGaedheal

Arthur Griffith founded this organisation in 1900, with the Celtic Literary Society as its nucleus. It was in fact a federation of literary societies aimed at the sovereign independence of Ireland. Its purpose was to promote a 'Buy Irish' campaign. It combined with the Dungannon Clubs in April 1907 to create the Sinn Féin League.

Not to be confused with the party founded by William T. Cosgrave in 1923 (See below).

Fianna na hÉireann (also sometimes referred to as Na Fianna Éireann)

Founded by Bulmer Hobson on 26 June 1902 at the Catholic Boys' Hall, Falls Road, Belfast. It held its inaugural Dublin meeting on 16 August 1909, and elected officers: Bulmer Hobson, President; Countess Markievicz, Vice-President; Padraig Ó Riain, Secretary; Liam Mellowes, National Organiser (1914).

'The Fianna were clearly under the aegis of the IRB Supreme Council, which had gotten the idea from Bulmer Hobson…and which appointed Hobson to join the founders of the Fianna in order to keep it under IRB control… For some time things worked satisfactorily, but in 1912 Seán MacDermott was for a change of personnel, and so were others. MacDermott advised the Supreme Council to get Liam Mellowes as national organiser, and Mellowes was nominated… Henceforth, the secretaries and instructors of the Fianna were sworn IRB men.'[934]

Pearse said in February 1914: 'We believe that Fianna na hÉireann has kept the Military Spirit alive in Ireland over the past four years, and that if the Fianna had not been founded in 1909 [in Dublin], the Volunteers of 1913 would never have arisen.'

Most members wore kilts with double-breasted dark green tunics, but senior officers wore breeches and leggings. Their headdress was the Baden-Powell Scout hat. They shared a motto with St Enda's: 'Strength in our arms, Truth on our lips, Purity in our hearts.'

933 Czira, Sydney Gifford. *The Years Flew By*, 1974, p. 48-53. **934** LeRoux, Louis N. *Tom Clarke and the Irish Freedom Movement*, 1936, p. 78-83.

Dungannon Clubs

In March 1905, Bulmer Hobson and Denis McCullough founded the Dungannon Clubs (named after the meeting place of the Volunteers in 1783) and engaged Seán MacDermott as their full-time organiser in 1907. They were established as open debating and literary societies.

Their object was 'the regaining of the Political Independence of Ireland by a passive resistance to the government of this country by any other than the people of Ireland'.

Their newspaper was *The Republic*, and its first editorial stated their aim:

> We stand for an Irish Republic because we see that no compromise with England, no repeal of the Union, no concession of Home Rule, or Devolution will satisfy the national aspirations of the Irish people nor allow the unrestricted mental, moral or material development of our country. National independence is our right; we ask no more and will accept no less.

Irish Women's Franchise League

Founded in 1908 by Hanna and Francis Sheehy-Skeffington and Margaret Cousins. The officers were Hanna Sheehy-Skeffington, Chairwoman, and Meg Connery, Vice-Chairwoman; Grace Gifford, Kathleen Keevey and Maude Gonne MacBride were very active members. The IWFL was the most outspoken and public manifestation of women's discontent and radical feminism in Ireland. Its primary aim was to secure women's suffrage within Home Rule. Its journal was *Irish Citizen*.[935]

Clan na nGaedheal/Girl Scouts of Ireland

Founded by Countess Markievicz and sisters Liz and May Kelly in 1910. Their rules were strict:

1. No person shall have power to start a Branch of Clan na nGaedheal without first getting permission from Headquarters.
2. Clan na nGaedheal shall be organised and divided into companies as laid down by the Executive.
3. A Company shall contain at least 12 members controlled by a Captain, Adjutant, and Quartermaster.

---

935 Ryan, Louise. *Irish Feminism and The Vote: An Anthology of The Irish Citizen Newspaper, 1912-1920.* Dublin, 1996.

4. The Adjutant shall call a roll at each meeting and shall keep a written report of all work done. Monthly reports must be forwarded regularly to Headquarters.

5. No member of Clan na nGaedheal can wear her uniform at any meeting or function without permission from her Company Captain.

6. No member of Clan na nGaedheal is permitted to dance any but Irish dancing when in uniform.

7. The Constitution must be observed by all members of the Organisation

8. The following Declaration must be taken by all members of Clan na nGaedheal:

   (Added in 1917)

   I pledge my allegiance to the Irish Republic proclaimed in 1916 and promise to do all in my power to protect it from all enemies, foreign and domestic, and not to relax in my efforts until the Irish Republic is universally recognised. I also promise to obey my superior officers.

Its 1917 Purpose was:

Clan na nGaedheal is an independent national organisation for girls, pledged to uphold the Republic proclaimed in 1916. The aims of the Organisation are: to organise the girls of Ireland and train them mentally and physically that their services may be utilised in the best interests of the Republic.

MEANS:	The training of the youth of Ireland on the following lines:
	Educational: Citizenship, Irish language, Irish history, Music and Drama
	Physical: Scouting, Signalling, Drill, Physical Exercises, First Aid and Gaelic Games
MEMBERSHIP:	Membership will be open to all girls of good character. No member of Clan na Gaedheal can be a member of any political organisation.

Irish Women's Workers' Union

Founded in 1911. As many as 2000 workers at the Jacob's Biscuit Factory went on strike and this led to the foundation of the union. The leading spirits were Delia Larkin (James' sister), Hanna Sheehy-Skeffington, and Countess Markievicz; Helena Molony was the Secretary.

The Irish National Guard

In 1911 Augustin (Gussy) Finlay, a member of Na Fianna Éireann, founded the Irish National Guard as a youth organisation for the sons and daughters of the working class. Later it became an adjunct of the Irish Citizen Army. Their motto was: 'The Guard Dies but Never Surrenders!' In line with the equality views of the Citizen Army, there was a female section of the Guard. Most members had pistols or shotguns. The Guard did not fight as a unit in the Rising, but many of its members merged with various companies of the Citizen Army.

The Irish Citizen Army

The Irish Citizen Army (ICA) was proposed in August 1913, giving equal rights to men and women. In November 1913, Connolly announced the organisation of an 'Irish Citizen Army' 'to protect workers' meetings' and 'to prevent the brutalities of armed thugs occurring in the future'. In March 1914, a constitution was drafted which included explicitly nationalist aims.

> *Article One*: The first and last principle of the Irish Citizen Army is the avowal that the ownership of Ireland, moral and material, is vested of right in the people of Ireland.
> *Article Two*: That its principal objects should be (a) To arm and train all Irishmen capable of bearing arms to enforce and defend its first principle, and (b) To sink all differences of birth, privilege and creed under the common name of the Irish people.
> *Article Three*: The Irish Citizen Army shall stand for the absolute unity of Irish nationhood, and recognition of the rights and liberties of the democracies of all nations.
> *Article Four*: That the Citizen Army shall be open to all who are prepared to accept the principles of equal rights and opportunities for the People of Ireland and to work in harmony with organized labour towards that end.
> *Article Five*: Every enrolled member must be, if possible, a member of a Trades Union recognized by the Irish Trades Union Congress.

The Dublin Trades Council approved the Army on 6 April 1914.

The Irish Volunteers

On 25 November 1913, Eoin MacNeill and Laurence Kettle (son of A.J. Kettle, aide to Charles Stewart Parnell) held the first meeting to enrol Irish Volunteers. Seán T. O'Kelly chaired the meeting. Over 4000 signed up on that night. Padraig Pearse was one of the principal speakers. Others were Seán MacDermott, James McMahon,

Michael Judge, and Councillor Richard Carroll. Batt O'Connor and Bulmer Hobson addressed the crowd outside. The band that started off the night was the St James' Brass and Reed Band.

The IRB pushed many nationalists to join the Volunteers, but it had not backed the ITGWU during the Lockout. Kettle was a well-known opponent of the Union. When he spoke, fights broke out between Union protestors and the disturbance was drowned out by the song 'God Save Ireland'. This was the start of the disagreements between Union members and other Volunteers and led to Connolly's reluctance to join with the Volunteers.

The Manifesto of the Irish Volunteers was issued at the first turn-out in Dublin on 25 November 1913; it was re-issued in June 1914. It was written by Eoin MacNeill and adopted by the first Provisional Committee (see Kildare Street for the members of the Committee and Appendix III for the Manifesto).

In February 1914, the Committee issued a provisional constitution, embodying the objects of the Volunteers:

1.   To secure and maintain the rights and liberties common to all the people of Ireland;

2.   To train, discipline, arm and equip a body of Irish Volunteers for the above purpose;

3.   To unite for this purpose Irishmen of every creed and of every party and class.

Volunteers were required to read aloud and sign the following statement:

The Objects of the Irish Volunteers are:

1.   To secure and maintain the rights and liberties common to all the people of Ireland.

2.   To train, discipline and equip for this purpose an Irish Volunteer Force.

3.   To unite in the service of Ireland, Irishmen of every creed and of party and class.

I, the undersigned, desire to be enrolled for service in Ireland as a member of the Irish Volunteer Force. I subscribe to the Constitution of the Irish Volunteers, and pledge my willing obedience to my superior officers. I declare that in joining the Irish Volunteer Force I set before myself the stated objects of the Irish Volunteers and no others.

Following August 1919, the Volunteers were required to take an Oath to the Dáil:

I _____ do solemnly swear (or affirm) that I do not, and shall not, yield a voluntary support to any pretended Government, Authority, or Power inside Ireland hostile or inimical thereto; and I do further swear (or affirm) that to the best of my knowledge and ability I shall support and defend the Irish Republic, which is Dáil Éireann, against all enemies foreign and domestic, and that I will bear true faith and allegiance to the same and that I take this obligation freely without any mental reservation or purpose of evasion. So help me God.

Cumann na mBan/Irishwomen's Council

The first meeting to discuss its founding was held on 25 November 1913, the same night as the first meeting of the Volunteers. Its first 'official' meeting was at Wynn's Hotel on 2 April 1914. Agnes O'Farrelly was its first President and Mary Colum was one of its first organisers.

The first Provisional Committee consisted of Agnes O'Farrelly, Agnes MacNeill, Nancy O'Rahilly, Mary Colum, Jennie Wyse-Power, Louise Gavan-Duffy, Maire Tuohy, and Maureen MacDonagh O'Mahoney.

Its initial appeal was to women who could give time to the establishment of the organisation, women who did not need to work, but soon most were women who worked for a living – influenced by suffrage and labour issues.

The Cumann na mBan convention of November 1914 voted to support the minority Irish Volunteers led by Eoin MacNeill. Cumann na mBan issued a statement in the *Irish Volunteer*:

> We came into being to advance the cause of Irish liberty…We feel bound
> to make the pronouncement that to urge or encourage Irish Volunteers
> to enlist in the British Army cannot, under any circumstances, be regarded
> as consistent with the work we have set ourselves to do.

There were forty-three affiliated branches before the Rising. In April 1916 Countess Markievicz was President and Sorcha MacMahon was Secretary. Leaders included: Elizabeth Bloxham, Winifred Carney, Áine Ceannt, Kathleen Clarke (President of the Central Branch), Nora Connolly (O'Brien), Margaret Dobbs, Louise Gavan-Duffy, Mrs Duffy Edwards, Agnes MacNeill, Una O'Brien, Nancy O'Rahilly, Niamh Plunkett, Jennie Wyse-Power, Maire Tuohy. Its objects were:

- to advance the cause of Irish liberty
- to organise Irishwomen in the furtherance of this object
- to assist in arming and equipping a body of Irishmen for the defence of Ireland
- to form a fund for these purposes, to be called 'The Defence of Ireland Fund'[936]
- to continue collecting for the 'Defence of Ireland Fund' and any other fund to be devoted to the arming and equipping of the men and women of Ireland

936 *Cumann na mBan Convention Report, 1917*, National Library of Ireland.

- to assist in the movement to secure representation of Ireland at the Peace Conference by the election of Republican candidates, etc.
- to follow the policy of the Republican Proclamation by seeing that women take up their proper position in the life of the nation.[937]
- to develop the suggested military activities in conjunction with the Irish Volunteers
- to organise opposition to conscription along the lines laid down in the two anti-conscription pledges

In 1916, there were three branches of Cumann na mBan in Dublin: Central, with headquarters at 25 Parnell Square; Inghinidhe na nÉireann, based at 6 Harcourt Street; and Columcill in Blackhall Place.

In August 1916 Cumann na mBan held a convention in Dublin presided over by Louise Gavan-Duffy. Countess Markievicz was re-elected President, though she was still in prison.

In June 1918, Cumann na mBan organised an 'Ireland Womens' Day' (Lá na mBan), as part of the effort to resist conscription. Approximately 40,000 signed the 'pledge' in Dublin's City Hall

> Because the enforcement of conscription on any people without their consent is tyranny, we are resolved to resist the conscription of Irishmen.
>
> We will not fill the places of men deprived of their work through enforced military service.
>
> We will do all in our power to help the families of men who suffer through enforced military service.

Cumann na mBan played a larger role in the Civil War than in the Rising. The members held their own Convention on the Treaty on 5 February 1922, and voted 419 to 63 against the Treaty. Countess Markievicz was elected president. Pro-Treaty members were asked to resign, and they formed their own group, called Cumann na Saoirse (Society of Freedom), which was not militarily active during the Civil War.

1922 CONSTITUTION (CORUGHADH)

Cumann na mBan is an independent body of Irishwomen pledged to maintain the Irish Republic established on January 21st, 1919, and to organise and train the women of Ireland to work unceasingly for its international recognition. All Irish women of birth or descent are eligible for membership, except that no woman who is a member of the enemy organisation or who does not recognise the Government of the Republic as the lawfully constituted Government of the people can become a member.

---

937 *Cumann na mBan Convention Report, 1918*, National Library of Ireland.

Objects: (Cuspora)

1. (a) The complete separation of Ireland from all foreign powers.
   (b) The Unity of Ireland
   (c) The Gaelicisation of Ireland

Means (Slighthe)

1. To maintain the Republic by every means in our power against all enemies, foreign and domestic.
2. To assist Oglaigh na h-Éireann, the Irish Volunteers, in its fight to maintain the Republic.
3. That at elections, Cumann na mBan, as such, give no assistance to any Organisation which does not give allegiance to the Government of the Republic.
4. To become perfect citizens of a perfect Irish Nation by
   (a) Taking Honour, Truth, Courage and Temperance as the watchwords of Cumann na mBan;
   (b) By fostering an Irish atmosphere, politically, economically, and socially;
   (c) Discouraging Emigration by brightening the social life of the district;
   (d) Supporting Irish industries.
5. At all times and in all places to uphold the spirit and the letter of the Cumann na mBan Constitution.
6. The Constitution of Cumann na mBan may not be altered except by a two-thirds majority vote of the Convention.

Cumann na dTeachaire/League of Women Delegates

Founded in April 1917 as the League of Women Delegates. At a meeting on 16 October the name was Gaelicised and a constitution was drawn up with the following aims: to safeguard the political rights of Irishwomen; to ensure adequate representation for them in the Republican Government; to urge and facilitate the appointment of women to Public Boards throughout the country; and to educate Irishwomen in the rights and duties of citizenship.[938] Their primary focus was to promote the representation and participation of women in the reorganisation of Sinn Féin.[939]

Women's Prisoners' Defence League

Founded by Maud Gonne MacBride and Charlotte Despard (sister of the Viceroy, Lord French) in 1922 to organise in support of the prisoners during the Civil War. Known as 'The Mothers', its members gathered at prison gates and helped inmates

---

938 *Minutes of Cumann na d'Teachtaire*, 16 October 1917, Sheehy-Skeffington Papers, MS 21,194 National Library of Ireland. **939** Ward, Margaret. 'The League of Women Delegates and Sinn Féin, 1917', *History Ireland*, Vol. IV, No. 3, 1996.

and relatives in various ways. Operated throughout the Civil War and afterwards. Mrs MacBride stated their Republican aims clearly:

> The women of the Defence League swore that the traitors and murderers who had stained Ireland's name with such foul crimes should never be allowed to appear publicly in the city they have disgraced. We kept our word. Our men were in jail or fighting in the country, but we women drove Cosgrave, Mulcahy, and Blythe off the streets; each time they tried to hold public meetings we were there in the name of the men they had murdered.[940]

3   UNIFORMS AND FLAGS

Volunteers' uniforms
Messers Morrogh Brothers of Douglas Woollen Mills, Cork, were the official suppliers of 'high-class uniform serge of a gray-green cloth of a very suitable colour for field work in Ireland … The uniform consists of tunic, two-buttoned knickers and puttees.' The first contract to supply the uniforms was awarded to the Limerick Clothing Factory that was located in Lower Bridge Street, Dublin.

Volunteers' cap badge
Designed by Eoin MacNeill: 'The letters FF represent Fianna Fáil, the legendary first standing army of Ireland. Neither sunburst nor any other symbolic theme underlay the choice of an 8-pointed star with its flamiform accompaniment.'

Volunteer badge colours
A golden sunrise of 9 rays on a field of blue. Represents the coming of Lugh, the sun god out of the Kingdom of Mananan to rescue Ireland from the grip of Formor. Known as the Deilgreine, it was the standard of Finn McCool (Fionn MacCumhaill).

Irish Citizen Army uniforms
Messers Arnott were the official suppliers. Cpt. Jack White made the original order for fifty uniforms. They were of a darker green than the Volunteers' uniforms, and their Cronje hat usually had the left side fastened up with a Red Hand badge of the Union movement.

Tricolour of Green, White and Orange
Designed by Thomas Francis Meagher, of Young Ireland, in 1848, and presented to the citizens of Dublin. (William Smith O'Brien brought back a tricolour from France in 1848. He was arrested and deported to Van Dieman's Land, now Tasmania.) John Mitchel of Young Ireland said 'I hope to see that flag one day waving as our

---

[940] Maud Gonne MacBride. 'Must We Fight Again for Ireland's Honour?', *An Phoblacht*, 9 December 1933.

national emblem.' It was seldom flown before the Rising. Confirmed by Article 7 of the 1937 Irish Constitution as the official flag of the Republic of Ireland.

The Plough and the Stars

Flag of the Irish Citizen Army; George Russell (Æ) suggested the emblem. The flag was a green background (changed to blue in 1943) with a plough and seven stars imposed on it: the plough and the stars symbolising the present and the future of the working class respectively. R.M. Fox wrote: 'In the interests of historical accuracy it should be noted that the original Starry Plough banner – now in the National Museum – is of green poplin with a design of a plough in yellow outlined in black. There are seven eight pointed stars. This banner was missing for years and – in the meantime – the accepted version of the flag was that of a blue background formed of silver stars.'[941]

Golden Harp of Ireland

Had 9 Silver Strings. Clairseach, the curved Harp. 'The Oak of the Two Greens'. Used in all Volunteer emblems, banners and flags. Represents the Harp of Dagda which, when he played it, it caused the four seasons to pass over the earth; a symbol of life that joyously renews itself.

4   WAR OF INDEPENDENCE

Black and Tans (The Tans) first appeared in Ireland on 25 March 1920

They were established as a section of the RIC and first appeared in the village of Upperchurch, Co. Tipperary. Their uniform was a khaki tunic and dark green or black trousers, some with civilian hats, but most with green caps and black leather belts of the RIC. Christopher O'Sullivan, editor of the *Limerick Echo*, gave the name: 'Judging by their attire, they resembled something one would associate with the Scarteen Hunt.' The Scarteen Black and Tans were well known for their savagery.

They were paid 10 shillings per day (£3.10s per week, rising to £4.15s per week.)

Ultimately there were 7000, though most came to Ireland after November 1920. About 4400 were recruited in England, Scotland and Wales, with about 2600 coming from northeast Ulster.

The Irish often referred to them as the 'roughs'.

The Auxiliary Cadets (Auxies) were authorized 23 July 1920, and arrived in September 1920.

They were to be 'Auxiliary' to the RIC. Originally called the Temporary Cadets, they wore the initials TC on their shoulder straps; they were ranked as 'cadets' but were 'graded as RIC sergeants for the purpose of discipline'. Gen. Frank P. Crozier was

---

941 R.M. Fox quoted in O'Dubhghaill, M. *Insurrection Fires at Eastertide*, p. 109.

their first O/C. He disapproved of many of their actions and tried to instill discipline or dismiss wrongdoers, but on 1 November 1920 higher authority took his powers of dismissal away from him. Ultimately, he resigned on 19 February 1921, calling them 'insubordinate, dishonest, sadistic and drunken'. 'Up to November 1st, 1920, I had "dismissed" or "dispensed with the services of" over fifty Auxiliary policemen (ex-officers) for various acts of indiscipline, but after that date a heavy and hidden hand came down. My powers of dismissal and dispensal were taken from me. Why? I had to wait a few months to find out. "They" feared a kick-back from England caused by "talk" on the part of the "kicked-out." Later "they" got the "kick" in return.'[942]

Originally, they were issued tunics, breeches and puttees of khaki, and their accouterments, consisting of a bandolier across the chest, a belt with a bayonet and scabbard, and an open holster for a revolver on the right thigh, were of black leather. They were later equipped with dark blue uniforms (sometimes khaki tunics) and a dark green Balmoral/Glengarry Cap, and they wore all their military decorations

In August 1920 Gen. Sir Neville Macready, Commander-in-Chief of the Army in Ireland, urged Dublin Castle to provide the Auxies with a uniform which could not be mistaken for a soldier's uniform and that is how the famous 'Tam O'Shanter' hat came into being. He was not so much concerned with what the Auxies or Tans did, but he did not want the Army blamed.

They had to be former officers in the English Army to be employed, and they were paid £1 per day, and given uniforms. Their employment was guaranteed for 12 months.

Their HQ in Dublin in Beggar's Bush Barracks, but only the 'F' Division took its orders from Dublin Castle.

Ultimately there were 1500 in Ireland, divided into companies of about 100, they were much more mobile than the Tans or RIC. (The first of these mobile companies commandeered Macroom Castle in October 1920.)

They were thoroughly dangerous and far more intelligent than the Tans. All had considerable combat experience, were men of reckless courage, knew no fear, but gave obedience to no one – neither to their own officers nor to the Government that paid them. Their brief was to eliminate the IRA by any means available.

Usually each was armed with two Webley .45 revolvers, a rifle, and two bandoliers of rifle ammunition.

Their transport was usually a Crossley tender, with Rolls Royce Whippet armoured cars with one or two Vickers' guns.

The Irish often referred to them as the 'toughs'.

Though photos of the time are often confusing, the 'Tans' could be distinguished from the 'Auxies' by the fact that the Tans were 'other ranks' and wore puttees, while the Auxies were all demobilized officers and wore dark tunics and

---

942 Crozier, General Frank P. *Ireland Forever*, 1932.

trousers with tall boots or leather leggings. At times, both units wore the Balmoral cap, but that was always worn by the Auxies.

5 POLITICAL PARTIES FOLLOWING THE TREATY, 6 DECEMBER 1921

Fine Gaedheal
Founded at the Convention of the Irish Race in Paris on 27 January 1922; Éamon de Valera was President.

Cumann na Poblachta/The Republican League
Anti-Treaty Party. Founded by Éamon de Valera on 15 March 1922. The Republican League comprised TDs who were anti-Treaty.

Cumann na nGaedheal
Treaty Party.
Founded by William T. Cosgrave in March 1923.[943] It was the Free State Party to be succeeded by Fine Gael. (Fine Gael was formed by a 1933 merger of the pro-Treaty Cumann na nGaedheal, the National Guard [a quasi-fascist group popularly called 'The Blueshirts'] and the small National Centre Party.)

Fianna Fáil
'Soldiers of Destiny' Founded by Éamon de Valera on 16 May 1926. Incorporated most of the Republicans who were to sit in the Dáil.

(In Tralee in 1925 he spoke to concerns about the oath and said: 'I know you are all wondering if we will enter the Free State parliament. As long as water flows, we will never go in. Our business is to stand fast and firm. And fast and firm we shall stand, even if we are reduced to the last man.' On 9 March 1926 de Valera proposed a motion at the Sinn Féin Ard Fheis that it would be a matter of principle for Republicans to enter the parliaments in Dublin and Northern Ireland if the Oath of Allegiance was removed. This motion was defeated 223-218, and de Valera resigned from Sinn Féin in 1927.)

On 10 August 1927 de Valera was contacted by Labour Party leader Thomas Johnson, and was told that in return for Fianna Fáil's support of him as President, if he were elected Johnson would take immediate steps to have a constitutional referendum held to try to abolish the oath.[944] Fianna Fáil in convention decided to subscribe to the book containing the oath, but first issued a statement that they proposed 'to regard the declaration as an empty formality and repeat that their only allegiance is to the Irish nation, and that it will be given to no other power or authority'.[945] This was de Valera's famous 'empty formula' solution.

943 Cosgrave, William. Witness Statements 268, **449**.   944 Johnson, Thomas. Witness Statement 1755.
945 *Gaelic American*, 27 August 1927.

On 12 August 1927 the 44 elected Fianna Fáil Deputies, led by de Valera, signed the book containing the oath, and took their seats in the Dáil.

On entering the Dáil the Fianna Fáil TDs signed the book containing the oath, but covered the words while signing, placed the Bible face down in the furthest corner of the room, and insisted they were not taking any oath. De Valera, himself, moved the Bible as far from the table as possible, and upon returning to the table stressed 'I am taking no oath.' He then placed some paper over the oath at the top of the page and signed his name 'as if it were a blank piece of paper'. 'I signed it in the same way as I would sign an autograph in a newspaper.'[946]

Later, de Valera described this entry into the Dáil as 'painful and humiliating'.[947]

Clann na Poblachta
Radical Republican Political Party founded in 1946 and headed by Seán MacBride. Became part of a coalition government in 1948.

946 Kathleen O'Connell, de Valera's secretary, said he told her all the Fianna Fáil TDs signed the book in this manner. Quoted in Pakenham, Frank (Lord Longford) and Thomas P. O'Neill. *Éamon de Valera, A Biography*, 1970, p. 269. **947** Coleman, Shane. 'The Day We Decided to Sit Down and Fight', *Sunday Tribune*, 12 August 2007.

Appendix V

CONTENTS

Flags flown during the 1916 Easter Rising

Boland's Mill: Green Flag with Harp
City Hall: Tricolour
College of Surgeons: Tricolour
Four Courts: a professionally made green flag with a plain gold harp
GPO: Tricolour (flown on the Henry Street corner) and Green Flag with Gold
    'Irish Republic' (flown on the Prince's Street corner)
    The flags were raised over the GPO by Gearóid O'Sullivan (The Tricolor), the
    youngest officer in the GPO and Michael Collins' cousin, and Edward (Éamon)
    Bulfin ('Irish Republic'). [948]
    The British returned the 'Irish Republic' flag to Ireland in 1966 after Padraig Ó
    Snodaigh, Curator of the National Museum, identified it. Robert Walpole
    claimed this flag had been made at Fry's Poplin Factory, Cork Street, and was
    painted at Countess Markievicz's house by Theo Fitzgerald. [949]
Imperial Hotel: Tricolour and Plough and Stars
Jacob's: Tricolour
Marrowbone Lane: Green Flag with Harp
Mendicity Institute: Tricolour with *horizontal* bands of colour
South Dublin Union: Tricolour.

Easter Rising Garrisons in Dublin

Garrison	Men	Women	Total	Executed	Killed
General Post Office Headquarters Sackville Street Area Cabra Bridge Area Fairview Area	425	75	500	6	17
1st Battalion Four Courts Magazine Fort Mendicity Institute North Dublin Union	345	49	394	2	9
2nd Battalion Jacob's Biscuit Factory	187	10	197	3	3

948 Bulfin, Éamon. Witness Statement 497. **949** Walpole, Robert. Witness Statement 218.

Garrison	Men	Women	Total	Executed	Killed
3rd Battalion Boland's Mills Mount Street Bridge	180	0	180	0	9
4th Battalion Jameson's Distillery Marrowbone Lane Roe's Distillery South Dublin Union	199	31	230	2	7
5th Battalion Ashbourne, County Meath North County Dublin	73	4	77	0	3
City Hall	43	13	56	0	5
St Stephen's Green	116	28	144	1	7
Non-Assigned Volunteers	60	40	100	(2[950])	(4[951])
Totals	1628	250	1878	14(16)	64

1   GARRISON LISTS OF THE RISING

Army of the Irish Republic

This was an amalgamation of the Irish Volunteers, the Irish Citizen Army, along with the auxiliary organizations, Cumann na mBan and the Fianna. Padraig Pearse was appointed Commandant-General and James Connolly was appointed Commandant-General of the Dublin Division.[952]

There has always been disagreement on how many were 'out' during the Rising

---

950 Thomas Kent was executed by firing squad on 9 May at Cork Detention Barracks. Sir Roger Casement was hung in Pentonville Prison on 3 August. **951** Official lists indicate 64 'rebels' killed. Con Keating, Charles Monaghan and Donal Sheehan drowned in Co. Kerry. Richard Kent was killed in Co. Cork. **952** According to Éamon de Valera, the plan outlined to the Dublin commandants was for Padraig Pearse to be in command of all the Volunteers throughout the country, and James Connolly was to be in command of the five Dublin battalions. Ó Neill, Tomas and Padraig Ó Fiannachta. *De Valera*, Vol. I, 1968-1970, p. 41.

in Dublin. Charles Dalton claimed it was a total of 687 men, including the Citizen Army, for the duration of the Rising.[953] However, it was surely more than that. In the 1949 edition of *The Rising: The Complete Story of Easter Week*, Desmond Ryan wrote 'there were little more than 700 volunteers...nor were they to gain more than another 200 at most before the end.'[954] However, in the Appendix to later editions, he wrote 'The figures...excluded the Citizen Army, but are an underestimate...These vary from 1200 to 1500.'[955] On mobilisation, total strength did not exceed about 1000 men and women, but this was considerably augmented as the week wore on. It is reliably estimated the total number of rebels in Dublin was ultimately about 1878–1655 Volunteers and Cumann na mBan and 220 ICA men and women. (R.M. Fox lists 162 names of ICA men and women, but the total is probably nearer 220.[956]) (G.A. Hayes-McCoy wrote that 'less than 1000 mustered on Monday and about 800 more joined them during the next day or so'.[957])

A 'Roll of Honour' was compiled and presented to the government on 24 May 1936 that listed the total of all insurgent forces in Dublin to be 1358, including 1104 surviving, and 254 names of those executed, killed in action or since deceased. However, there is no official record of prisoners in the British Records Office, so there was no complete record of the number of prisoners taken. There were some obvious omissions from the Roll, mostly for political reasons. For example, Richard Mulcahy was notably absent from the Ashbourne garrison in the original Roll. Over the years, provisions were made to add to the Roll, and it currently lists 1596 individuals in the Dublin garrisons, and an additional 59 in Louth and Meath. Yet, on the 25th Anniversary in 1941, 2477 individuals received medals for service in the Rising.[958]

The same uncertainty must be said of the numbers attached to the individual garrisons because they, too, increased during the week. For example, while some claim the strength of the GPO garrison was 400, that is probably the number who passed through the GPO during the week. It is accepted that only about 180 Volunteers and ICA troops 'charged' the GPO on Easter Monday at noon, so it is unlikely the garrison was ever at 400 at any one time.[959] (However, G.A. Hayes-McCoy wrote that about '400 men, including those from other nearby garrisons, were driven out by the flames and that their exit onto Henry Street was hasty'.[960] In contrast, Desmond Ryan, who was in the GPO at the escape and surrender, wrote 'out into Moore Street marched the Volunteers, less than 200 of them, sleepless, weary, hungry, defeated, yet with a curious pride and sense of freedom stirring in them all'.[961]) To a greater degree than any other location, many Volunteers occupied

953 Dalton, Charles. *With the Dublin Brigade*, London, 1929, p. 19. **954** Ryan, Desmond. *The Rising*, p. 129. **955** Ibid, 1957 edition, Appendix IV. **956** Fox, R.M. *History of the Irish Citizen Army*, 1944. **957** Hayes-McCoy, G.A. *A Military History History of the 1916 Rising*, *in* Nowlan, Kevin. *The Making of 1916*, p. 266. **958** Joye, Labhras and Brenda Malone. 'The Roll of Honour of 1916', *History Ireland*, Vol. XIV, No. 2, 2006. **959** Steinmeyer, Charles. 'The Evacuation of the GPO', *An tÓglach*, 27 February 1926. **960** Hayes-McCoy, G.A. *A Military History History of the 1916 Rising*, in Nowlan, Kevin. *The Making of 1916*, p. 295. **961** Ryan, Desmond. *The Rising*, p. 256.

the GPO from other positions, having fled to it as their earlier positions were over-run, and then they remained or were re-posted to other sites. As a result, there are many more Volunteers or ICA members who are listed as serving in the GPO than were ever there at any one time during the Rising. (See, for example, Richard [Dick] Coleman who mobilised with the Fingal Brigade at Saucers Town, went to the GPO, then was sent to the Mendicity Institute but is counted with the 5th Battalion at Ashbourne).

The following conversation between Padraig Pearse, Desmond Fitzgerald and Peggy Downey (an experienced caterer and a member of Cumann na mBan) which took place in the GPO on Tuesday, 25 April, illustrates the point that the totals were weekly, not necessarily at any single time:

> Pearse: 'How long will the food supply last?'
> Fitzgerald: 'For how many men?'
> Pearse: 'A little over 200.'
> Fitzgerald checked with Peggy Downey who told him: 'With rigid economy, we have enough for three weeks.'
> Fitzgerald to Pearse: 'With rigid economy, we have enough for three weeks'.
> Pearse: 'Then exercise rigid economy, we may be here that long.'[962]

(As a result of this movement between garrisons, and the confusion it entailed, some Volunteers, ICA and Cumann na mBan members might be listed as serving at more than one garrison, particularly in the GPO, but only counted once for the total. Generally, a person is listed where he/she reported, unless otherwise indicated. Also, many names are the same. When more than one like-named participant served in a location, both names are listed.)

In addition, many lists are inaccurate because the Volunteers or ICA members refused to give their correct names when captured or imprisoned. For example, when he was captured Cmdt William (W.J.) Brennan-Whitmore (who was in the GPO) gave his name as 'William Whitmore' and it was under that name he was always listed.[963]

Finally, in 1916, very few participants used the Irish form of their names. However, shortly thereafter that became common. For example, Michael Collins was listed as a prisoner under the name Michael Collins, but signed the Dáil Loan documents and the Treaty as Micheal Ó Coileain. These changes of names caused further confusion when lists of participants were recorded after several years, as it was unclear if a participant listed as 'John Kelly' was the same person as Seán Kelly, or 'Seán O'Kelly', or 'Seán Ó Ceallaigh'. In further example, by the time the Treaty was voted upon, on 7 January 1922, all 121 voting TDs were listed in the Dáil minutes

---

962 Coffey. *Thomas M. Agony at Easter*, London, 1969, p. 95. **963** See the *Weekly Irish Times, Sinn Féin Rebellion Handbook*, 1916, p. 75 (1998 Mourne River Press Edition, p. 74).

by their Irish names. For that reason, whenever an individual used or was known by both the Irish and English versions an attempt is made to list both names in these rosters.

For women, the first name listed is that by which the woman was called at the time of the Rising as far as could be determined. Likewise for women participants, some became known by the Irish version of their name and these are listed whenever known. Also a maiden name and a married name are listed whenever known, with the married name in parentheses if she was married after the Rising.

When only one version is listed it is because only that version was found in a list or roster (at a prison camp like Frongoch for example).

For alphabetical purposes, the individuals are categorized according to the English versions.

Allowing for some omissions and some who claimed to be 'out' who were not, the 1878 figure appears most accurate.

The geographical areas for the residences of the Volunteer Brigades prior to the Rising were generally as follows:

> 1st Battalion: North of the Liffey and West of Sackville Street
> 2nd Battalion: North of the Liffey and East of Sackville Street
> 3rd Battalion: South of the Liffey
> 4th Battalion: South townships, Rathmines etc
> 5th Battalion: Engineers only
> 6th Battalion: South Co. Dublin, Kingstown

Dublin Brigade

Thomas MacDonagh (Tomás MacDonnchada, executed 3 May 1916, aged 38).* Commandant. In Kilmainham, he was seen by Fr Aloysius. His sister, Sister Mary Francesca, also visited him, and gave him their Mother's rosary. He put it around his neck, and she received it back the next day from Fr Aloysius, though it had had six beads shot off.[964]

Cpt. Michael W. O'Reilly (Vice-Commandant, Camp O/C at Frongoch and subsequently director of Training for the IRA)

Cmdt Éamon de Valera (Adjutant)

Names followed by an asterisk *signify those executed and names preceded by two asterisks ** signify those who died during the Rising. Officially, sixty-four Volunteers and ICA members died in addition to those executed. **964** MacDonagh, Sr Francesca. Witness Statement 717.

GPO Headquarters Battalion, Men

They mustered at Liberty Hall; garrison totals approximately 250–300 at any one time; killed 13; executed 6.

Padraig Pearse (Pádraic MacPiarais, executed 3 May 1916, aged 36).* In Kilmainham, he was attended by Fr Aloysius.[965]

Tom Clarke (Tomás Ó Clerigh, executed 3 May 1916, aged 59).* In Kilmainham, he was seen by Fr Columbus who told him he had to 'admit that he had done a great wrong' in order to get absolution. Clarke threw him out: 'I'm not a bit sorry for what I did. I glory in it. And if that means I'm not entitled to absolution, then I'll have to go to the next world without it. To say I'm sorry would be a lie and I am not going to face my God with a lie on my tongue.' To Kathleen, he said of MacNeill: 'I want you to see to it that our people know of his treachery to us. He must never be allowed back into the national life of the country, for sure as he is, so sure he will act treacherously in a crisis. He is a weak man, but I know every effort will be made to whitewash him.' He summed up his position in his pamphlet *Glimpses of an Irish Felon's Life* years before: 'I was then what I had been, and what I still am, an Irish Nationalist. I asked no favours, I got none, and I am proud of it.'[966]

James Connolly (Seámus Ó Conghile, executed 12 May 1916, aged 46).* In Dublin Castle, he recounted the story of the escape to Nora and said: 'We can't fail now. Such lads will never forget.' In Dublin Castle and at Kilmainham, Fr Aloysius attended him. Connolly was shot in a chair as he was too badly wounded to stand. [967] [968] The doctor in Dublin Castle was Surgeon Richard Tobin.

Seán MacDermott (Seán MacDiarmada, executed 12 May 1916, aged 32; crippled by polio in June 1911).* In Kilmainham, he was visited by the Ryan sisters, Mary and Phyllis. Fr McCarthy and Fr Augustine attended him.[969] He was shot sitting on a soapbox according to Fr Augustine's statement.

Joseph Mary Plunkett (Seosamh Ópluingcéad, executed 4 May 1916, aged 29).* He carried a sword that belonged to Robert Emmet. In Kilmainham, Fr Sebastian saw him. Fr McCarthy, who also brought Grace back to see him, married him to Grace Gifford.

Willie Pearse (Liam MacPiarais, executed 4 May 1916).* In Kilmainham, he was attended by Fr Augustine,[970] and saw his mother and his sister, Margaret. He was the only one to plead guilty to all the charges at his Court Martial.

---

965 Aloysius, Revd OFM. Witness Statements 200, 207. **966** Clarke, Thomas J. *Glimpses of an Irish Felon's Life*, pamphlet, p. 62. **967** Aloysius, Revd OFM. Witness Statements 200, 207. **968** But J.L. Hyland notes that Connolly 'was not strapped to a chair, but placed seated on a rough wooden box…and then executed.' Hyland, J.L. *Life and Times of James Connolly*, p. 54. **969** Augustine, Revd OFM. Witness Statement 920.

Arthur Agnew; from Liverpool, he was part of the Kimmage garrison; he had originally been assigned to O'Connell Bridge at the outset of the Rising, imprisoned at Frongoch.

James Bannon (Seámus Ó Bhaonain)

Michael Behan

Andrew Bermingham; imprisoned at Frongoch.

John Bermingham; imprisoned at Frongoch.

Joseph Billings; imprisoned at Frongoch.

Patrick Bird; an ICA member, imprisoned at Frongoch.

Thomas Patrick Blanchfield; mustered at Cabra Bridge, then moved to the GPO after his position was overrun.

Edmund (Ned) Boland, Harry's brother; he was in the Imperial Hotel and escaped to Cathedral Street. The priests of the Pro-Cathedral told some Volunteers that if they wanted to leave their guns in the vaults they could do so – some did and escaped capture.

Harry Boland; he had come in from Fairview with the group led by Cpt. Frank Henderson. He and Dairmuid Lynch were underground making the ammunition safe, unknown to Pearse and the others, so Boland was the penultimate person to leave the GPO. He was imprisoned in Mountjoy Prison, then Dartmoor, then Lewes in Sussex, and finally in Maidstone Prison.

Lt Michael Boland; in command on the roof, imprisoned at Frongoch. He had been in the Boer War and thought it 'madness' to take and hold buildings. 'Shut in here with our leaders, and the flags over our heads to tell the enemy just where to find us when they want us. We should have taken to the hills like the Boers.'

Peadar Bracken; one of the Kimmage garrison. He had originally been in charge of three others at O'Connell Bridge at the outset of the Rising, then he led the men in 'Kelly's Fort'.

Michael Brady

Cpt. Liam Breen; detailed to the Reis & Co Building. He was in the O'Rahilly's party, and as he was an engineer he was designated to supervise the establishment of the defences when they reached the Williams and Woods factory. He was imprisoned at Frongoch.

Maurice Brennan; mustered at Cabra Bridge, then moved to the GPO after his position was overrun.

970 Ibid.

Seámus Brennan; from Tullamore, he was posted at the Tower Bar directly across Henry Street from the GPO. He came in from Kimmage with George Plunkett.

Cmdt W.J. Brennan-Whitmore; aide to Joseph Plunkett. He helped Michael Collins get Plunkett to the GPO, and led some Volunteers in North King Street. He was wounded escaping from the Imperial Hotel. When he was captured he gave his name as 'William Whitmore' and it was under that name he was always listed.[971] He wrote *Is Dublin Burning?* and *With the Irish in Frongoch*.

[972] Daniel (Dan) Brophy

Donal Buckley (Domhnall Ó Buachalla); was elected a TD in the First Dáil from Kildare North.

Edward (Éamon) Bulfin; a member of the Rathfarnham Company, he was posted on the roof of the GPO, and raised the 'Irish Republic' flag.

Frank Burke; a teacher at St Enda's. He was imprisoned at Frongoch. He became a second lieutenant in E Company during the War of Independence.

Nicholas Burke

**Andrew Byrne

Christopher Byrne

Edward Byrne

James Byrne; imprisoned at Frongoch.

Joe Byrne; an IRB member, he was *not* a Volunteer, but reported to the GPO on Tuesday.

John Byrne; imprisoned at Frongoch.

Louis Byrne

Peter Byrne

Tom Byrne; a member of the Kildare Volunteers, he travelled from Kildare, joined with the Maynooth Volunteers and came to the GPO. He fought in the Boer War and was thereafter known as 'The Boer'.

#Patrick Caddell; imprisoned at Frongoch.

Patrick Caldwell

Joseph Callen

971 See the *Weekly Irish Times, Sinn Féin Rebellion Handbook*, 1916, p. 75 (1998 Mourne River Press Edition, p. 74). **972** Those indicated by # reported to the 5th Battalion at Ashbourne but were sent to the GPO on Tuesday, 25 April. They are counted in the Ashbourne garrison. Lawless, Joseph. Witness Statement 1043.

Ignatius Callender; when he went off to fight, his mother pinned a badge of the Little Flower of Jesus on his chest with the remark 'You're all right now – the Little Flower will protect you.' A courier, he made ten trips between the GPO and the Four Courts garrison.[973] [974]

Daniel Canny

Bernard Carmichael

Peter Carpenter

Walter Carpenter

**Charles Carrigan

Peter Carroll (Peadar Ó Cearbhail); imprisoned at Frongoch.

James Cassells

Joseph Cassidy

#John Clarke

Lt Liam Clarke; badly wounded when a homemade bomb exploded prematurely. When he got to the hospital, one Volunteer remarked: 'So much for those bloody canisters. If it didn't blow Liam's head off, the divil use it is to us.' Went to work for Kathleen Clarke and the Irish National Aid and Volunteers' Dependents' Fund.

Patrick J. Clinch; imprisoned at Frongoch.

John Coate

Seán Cole

#Richard (Dick) Coleman; mobilised with the Fingal Brigade at Saucers Town, went to the GPO, then was sent to the Mendicity Institute. (See 5th Battalion at Ashbourne, and 1st Battalion, Mendidity Institute).

Patrick Colgan (Padraic Colgain); he married Delia Larkin.

Harry Colley; on Sunday he had taken his 3 rifles to Fr Mathew Park, expecting the Rising to start then. Imprisoned at Frongoch. He became a TD, as did his son, George, born in 1922.

Maurice Collins; imprisoned at Frongoch.

Cpt. Michael Collins (Micheal Ó Coileain); aide to Joseph Plunkett. He led the final party out of the GPO to Moore Street.

Patrick Colwell

Patrick Connaughton

---

973 Callender, Ignatius. Witness Statement 923. **974** Callender, Ignatius. 'A Diary of Easter Week', *Dublin Brigade Review*, 1939.

Rory (Rauri, Roddy) Connolly; James' son, he was sent to William O'Brien's home later during the week.

Andy Conroy; ICA sharpshooter, sent to Hopkins and Hopkins where his sharp-shooting from the roof slowed the fire from TCD.

Seán Conway

Laurence Corbally

Richard Corbally; imprisoned at Frongoch.

Thomas Corbally; imprisoned at Frongoch.

Charles Corrigan

**Edward Cosgrave

**Edward Costello

Daniel Courtney

Michael Cowley

**Henry (Harry) Coyle (28); killed in the escape down Henry Street when he was trying to break open a door with a rifle and shot himself.

Thomas Craven; came with the Fairview garrison.

#James Crenegan

Joseph Cripps; a druggist, he made many forays to find medical supplies and was on Red Cross duty.

Lt Gerald Crofts; a famous singer, he was with the men in the Imperial Hotel who 'escaped' towards Marlborough Street but were captured.

Gerard Croke

Michael Croke

Thomas Croke

**John Cromien

Liam Cullen; became one of Michael Collins' most trusted lieutenants. Imprisoned at Frongoch.

Tom Cummins; he was wounded in Moore Street on their attempted escape with The O'Rahilly.

Patrick Dalton

Denis (Dinny) Daly

Liam Daly; a telephone operator, he installed a telephone to the roof of the GPO, and was wounded in the arm when escaping with the leaders. Imprisoned at Frongoch.

Paddy Daly; was in Frongoch, and went on hunger strike as a result of being punished for a minor infraction of the camp rules. The strike was successful and he was released to the general prisoner population. Became the leader of 'The Squad'. Later he became a major general in the Irish Army. (See also Ballyseedy Cross, Appendix I.)

Seámus Daly

**Peter Darcy

James Dempsey; mustered at Cabra Bridge, then moved to the GPO after his position was overrun.

Patrick Dennahy

Joseph Derham; imprisoned at Frongoch.

Patrick Devereux

Francis Devine

Thomas Devine

Seámus Devoy; one of the Volunteers who carried Connolly's stretcher.

Frank Donaghy; a Dublin journalist.

Charles Donnelly

Paddy Donnelly; greenkeeper at the Grange Golf Club. He became the QM of E Company, 4th Battalion, in the War of Independence – the 'Rathfarnham Company'.

Éamon Dore; Seán MacDermott's 'bodyguard'. He was from Limerick and married Nora Daly, Kathleen Clarke's sister, in May 1918.

Michael Dowling

John Doyle; imprisoned at Frongoch.

Peter Doyle; imprisoned at Frongoch.

Cpt. Seán (J.J.) Doyle; acted as medical officer until James Ryan arrived.

#William Doyle

Edward Duffy; imprisoned at Frongoch.

Joseph Duffy

Francis Dunne; imprisoned at Frongoch.

John Dunne; imprisoned at Frongoch.

Joseph Dunne; imprisoned at Frongoch.

Patrick Dunne; mustered at Cabra Bridge, then moved to the GPO after his position was overrun. Imprisoned at Frongoch.

Thomas Dunne; imprisoned at Frongoch.

Michael Dwyer; an ICA member, imprisoned at Frongoch.

Albert Dyas

John Early

Frank English (Frainnc Inglis)

Patrick English

Tom Ennis; on Wednesday afternoon he entered Henry Street with a party led by Connolly and went down to Liffey Street, returning by way of Abbey Street the next morning. Imprisoned at Frongoch. He led the Custom House attack in 1921.

John Faulkiner; mustered at Cabra Bridge, then moved to the GPO after his position was overrun.

Michael Finegan

Desmond Fitzgerald; Quartermaster in the GPO. He led the party of Cumann na mBan and wounded to Jervis Street Hospital. He became editor of *The Irish Bulletin* and subsequently Irish Free State Minister for Foreign Affairs and then Minister for Defence.

John J. Fitzharris

Andrew Fitzpatrick

Fr John (O') Flanagan; a priest who came to the GPO from the Pro-Cathedral. Almost from the beginning a secluded corner was set aside for him to hear confessions and he gave conditional absolution to the Volunteers.

Matthew Flanagan

Ignatius Flynn

Thomas Fogarty; imprisoned at Frongoch.

Michael Fox

Bernard Frick

Andrew Furlong

James Gahan

Patrick Gallagher

Paul Galligan

Seán Gallogly; came from Glasgow to fight for Irish Independence.

Henry Gannon

Patrick Garland

John Gavan; imprisoned at Frongoch.

Richard Gibson; imprisoned at Frongoch.

Michael Giffney; imprisoned at Frongoch.

Joseph Gleeson

Martin Gleeson; imprisoned at Frongoch.

Richard P. (Dick) Gogan; one of James Connolly's stretcher-bearers on the escape. He became a TD.

Alfred (Joe) Good (21); from London, he was part of the Kimmage garrison. He had originally been assigned to O'Connell Bridge at the outset of the Rising, then he was in Kelly's Fort. Imprisoned at Frongoch. Wrote *Enchanted by Dreams, The Journal of a Revolutionary*.

Tom Harris; a member of the Kildare Volunteers, he travelled from Kildare, joined the Maynooth Volunteers and came to the GPO. He was slightly wounded in the foot and was imprisoned in Frongoch. He commanded a flying column in Co. Kildare during the War of Independence and later would become a TD.

J.J. Hayes

Seámus Hayes; imprisoned at Frongoch.

**John Healy (14); killed carrying messages to Phibsboro. He was the youngest Fianna/Volunteer to be killed.

Richard Healy

Michael Heffernan

Seán Hegarty

Cpt. Frank Henderson; led the garrison recalled from Fairview. Imprisoned at Frongoch.

Cpt. Leo Henderson; imprisoned at Frongoch and became O/C in charge of the 1st Dormitory. Organized the 'Belfast Boycott', and was arrested in a raid on Ferguson's Garage at the start of the Civil War.

Frederick Higgins

Peter Higgins

Hugh Holohan; a friend of the Lemass brothers, he told them to come into the GPO on Tuesday even though their unit, the 3rd Battalion, was at the Four Courts. Imprisoned at Frongoch.

Patrick Hughes; imprisoned at Frongoch.

T. Hughes

Richard (Dick) Humphreys (Risteard MacAmblaoibh); The O'Rahilly's nephew.

James Hunter; a friend of the Ring brothers and also a carpenter. Imprisoned at Frongoch.

Tom Hunter

**Seán (Jack) Hurley (29); killed in one of the last hand-to-hand fights as the Volunteers broke-out from the GPO. A great friend of Michael Collins from West Cork.

Joseph Hutchison

#John (Jack) Hynes

Peter Jackson; imprisoned at Frongoch.

Thomas Jones

Brian Joyce; imprisoned at Frongoch.

Seámus Kavanagh; he was lame in one leg, and was given clerical duties as a result. Imprisoned at Frongoch.

John Kealy

Thomas Kearney

Hubert Kearns

Christopher Keeling

Edward Kelly (Éamon Ó Ceallaigh)

Fergus Kelly; seized the Wireless School with Johnny (Blimey) O'Connor.

Frank Kelly

#John (Jack) Kelly; imprisoned at Frongoch.

Joseph Kelly; imprisoned at Frongoch.

#Richard (Dick) Kelly

Austin Kennan

Luke Kennedy; escaped after the surrender and was not imprisoned.

Henry Kenny

James Kenny; shot by an over-enthusiastic Dutchman but survived. He was recruited to fight the English on the day of the Rising and was not a Volunteer.

Joe Kenny; seriously wounded in his leg, he never properly recovered.

John Kenny

Michael Kenny

Bernard Keogh; imprisoned at Frongoch.

**Gerald Keogh (20); a Fianna member. He was killed in front of Trinity College while summoning Volunteers from Larkfield, and then buried in Trinity until after the Rising.

Michael Keogh

Seán Kerr; on Wednesday afternoon he went into Henry Street with a party led by Connolly, down to Liffey Street, and they returned by way of Abbey Street the next morning.

P. Kerwan

John Kiely; taught Irish with Francis Macken at St Enda's.

Tom Kilgallon

Robert Killeen; an ICA member, imprisoned at Frongoch.

P. Kilmartin

King brothers (Arthur, George, Michael and Sam); taken from Frongoch and handed over to the English military for desertion, and eventually discharged as 'persons not likely to give loyal and faithful service to His Majesty'.

Michael Knightly; a journalist, imprisoned at Frongoch.

#Edward Lawless; imprisoned at Frongoch.

Thomas Leahy; a shipyard worker, moved to England, then moved back to Dublin in 1914 after World War I was declared. Imprisoned at Frongoch.

Joseph Ledwith

Hugh Lee

Joseph Lee; imprisoned at Frongoch.

Noel Lemass (19); was with Brennan-Whitmore in the Imperial Hotel and was wounded while escaping.

Seán Lemass (17); future Taoiseach, he took up a position on the roof on Tuesday.

Seámus Lundy; was in the Hopkins and Hopkins garrison.

Cpt. Dermot (Dairmuid) Lynch; he was a member of the Supreme Council of the IRB. He and Harry Boland were underground making the ammunition safe, unknown to Pearse and the others, so Lynch was the very last person to leave the GPO. He organised Sinn Féin's blockade of food exports in 1918 and was deported for doing so. While deported, he was elected TD for Cork South East.

John Lynch; imprisoned at Frongoch.

Martin Lynch; imprisoned at Frongoch.

Patrick Lynch; on Wednesday afternoon, he went into Henry Street with a party led by Connolly, down to Liffey Street, and they returned by way of Abbey Street the next morning.

Garrett (Gearóid) MacAuliffe

Michael MacCraic

Rory MacDermott

John MacDonnell

John (Seán) MacEntee; sent to Ardee to rouse his unit, he returned to the GPO on Wednesday. He was a Belfast engineer, and led a Volunteer unit at Castlebellingham in Co. Louth where he lined up Constable McGee and an English Grenadier officer named Dunville against some railings with other prisoners and shot them (McGee died and Dunville survived). Only a year before he had been an enthusiastic John Redmond supporter and tried to get a commission in the British army. Became Tánaiste (deputy Prime Minister) of the Republic.[975]

Thomas MacEvoy (17)

Leo MacKey

Michael MacKey

D. MacLaughlin

Patrick MacMahon

Brian MacMullen

John McArdle; mustered at Cabra Bridge, then moved to the GPO after his position was overrun.

Kevin McCabe; imprisoned at Frongoch.

William McCleane

---

975 MacEntee, Seán. Witness Statement 1052.

Pat McCrea; went with Michael W. O'Reilly to an arms depot in Rutland Square to get more weapons.

Joseph McDonagh; an ICA member, imprisoned at Frongoch.

J.J. McElligott; led some men to the GPO from the Imperial Hotel.

John McEntagart

Dominick McEvoy

Thomas McEvoy

James McGallogly

John McGallogly

Seán McGarry; a great friend and confidant of Tom Clarke. Of Clarke he wrote: 'To him the Irish nation was very real. He spoke of fighting for Ireland as casually as he did about any item of the days news. To fight England was to him the most natural thing in the world for an Irishman…He was slow to condemn, always ready to hear the other side, and was perhaps over-tolerant to his friends…He was always content to do the work and get it done; the credit could go anywhere…It is not for us who were the contemporaries of these seven gallant men who signed the proclamation of 1916 to apportion greatness nor indeed to say if any of the seven signatories were great. But, if one may hazard a guess, it is that history will write Tom Clarke as a great Irishman – Great in his love for Ireland, great in his faith in her destiny, great in his purpose, great in his achievement, and great in his death.'[976]

C. McGinley

Liam McGinley

Patrick McGinley

Conway McGinn

Seámus McGowan; an ICA member, he supervised the removal of the war stores from Liberty Hall on Monday afternoon.[977]

Christopher McGrane

Patrick McGrath Jnr

Patrick McGrath Snr

Tom McGrath

Dan McLaughlin; attended medical school for ten years but did not earn a degree. He assisted James Ryan.

---

976 McGarry, Seán. Witness Statement 368. 977 McGowan, Seámus. Witness Statement 542.

John (Seán) McLoughlin (16); he was a messenger, often shuttling between the Mendidity Institute and the GPO. He was appointed a Commandant by Connolly and was in command of a group of thirty assigned to take the *Irish Independent* offices on Thursday afternoon.[978] Connolly led them to the *Independent*. It was on this foray that Connolly was wounded in the ankle. (Some report McLoughlin was later promoted to 'Commandant-General' by Connolly, and thus it was he, not de Valera, who was the highest-ranking survivor of 1916.[979]) Imprisoned at Knutsford and then Frongoch. In 1921, he helped Roddy Connolly found the Communist Party of Ireland. He fought on the anti-Treaty side during the Civil War, and was imprisoned in Mountjoy Prison. His father, Patrick 'Ruggie' McLoughlin, was a leader in the Lockout of 1913, and helped organise the ITGWU.

Donal McMahon; imprisoned at Frongoch.

Seán McMahon; imprisoned at Frongoch.

Patrick McManus; imprisoned at Frongoch.

#John McNally; imprisoned at Frongoch.

William (Liam) McNeive; IRB member from Liverpool, he led a company of Volunteers from Liverpool in the GPO. Imprisoned at Frongoch.

Frank McPartland

Peter McPartlin; imprisoned at Frongoch.

John McQuaid

**Francis Macken; taught Irish at St Enda's.

John (Seán) Madden; imprisoned at Frongoch.

J. Maguire

Matthew Maguire

P.J. Mahon

Patrick J. Mahon, Jnr; imprisoned at Frongoch.

Thomas Mahon

Louis Maire

J.J. Malone

Thomas Mangan

Henry Manning

978 McLoughlin, Seán. Witness Statement 290.   **979** McGuire, Charlie. 'Seán McLoughlin: the boy commandant of 1916', *History Ireland*, Vol. XIV, No. 2, March/April, 2006.

#James Marks

Thomas Mason; imprisoned at Frongoch.

Caffrey Matthew

Patrick Meagher

#William Meehan

Seán Milroy; a Sinn Féin journalist. TD for Co. Cavan from 1921 to 1924.

James Mooney; he had been at the Fairyhouse Races, and when he reported to the GPO he was sent to St Stephen's Green then back to the GPO. Imprisoned at Frongoch.

Patrick Mooney; imprisoned at Frongoch.

Edward Moore

Patrick Moore (Padraig Ó Mordha); imprisoned at Frongoch.

P.J. (Paddy) Moran; from Glasgow, he was part of the Kimmage garrison. He had originally been assigned to O'Connell Bridge at the outset of the Rising. Imprisoned at Frongoch.

Ned Morgan

William P. 'Steenie' Mulvey; a Volunteer from Bray, imprisoned at Frongoch.

**Michael Mulvihill

Barney Murphy; he was employed at the Abbey Theatre as a line prompter.

Charles Murphy

Fintan Murphy

Michael Murphy (Miceal Ó Murchu); married Martha Kelly. He was imprisoned in Frongoch.

Peter Murphy (Peadar Ó Murchadha)

R.J. Murphy

Cpt. Seámus Murphy

Stephen Murphy

Paddy Murray; from Galway, imprisoned in Frongoch.

Thomas Murray; imprisoned at Frongoch.

Francis Murtagh; imprisoned at Frongoch.

John Neale; cockney member of the ICA, often used the term 'comrade'. He took 'potshots' at Lord Nelson's nose on the Pillar until Connolly ordered him to desist.

Henry (Harry) Nicholls; imprisoned at Frongoch.

T. Nolan

James Norton; imprisoned at Frongoch.

#Joe Norton

Michael Nugent; imprisoned at Frongoch.

Patrick Nugent; imprisoned at Frongoch.

Ernest (Ernan Ó Nunain) and Seán Nunan (Seán Ó Nunain) (brothers); had been sent by their father from London to join the Rising. They were taken from Frongoch and handed over to the English military for desertion, and eventually discharged as 'persons not likely to give loyal and faithful service to His Majesty'. Seán later accompanied Michael Collins when Ned Broy let them in to see the G-Division files.

John O'Brien; imprisoned at Frongoch.

Eoghan O'Brien (Ó Briain)

Matt O'Brien; imprisoned at Frongoch.

Michael O'Brien

Thomas O'Brien (Tomas Ó Briain)

James O'Byrne; imprisoned at Frongoch.

Kevin O'Carroll; was next to The O'Rahilly when he was killed, and was himself badly wounded in the stomach. Imprisoned at Frongoch.

James O'Connor; imprisoned at Frongoch.

Lt Johnny 'Blimey' O'Connor; originally from London, he had been at Kimmage. An electrician, he installed many communications throughout the GPO; he and others had attempted to restore wireless equipment from the Telephone Company School opposite the GPO. They broadcast 'Ireland Proclaims Republic' from Monday night until later in the week when they were driven out by fire. Imprisoned at Frongoch. He fought on the Republican side during the Civil War.

Patrick O'Connor; imprisoned at Frongoch.

Peter O'Connor

Rory O'Connor; he was an assistant to Joe Plunkett before the Rising. He would be the Information Officer for the anti-Treaty IRA. He was executed in reprisal for Seán Hales' assassination.

Paddy O'Donoghue; he was taken from Frongoch and handed over to the British military for desertion, and eventually discharged as 'a person not likely to give loyal and faithful service to His Majesty'.

Thomas O'Donoghue (Tomas Ó Donnchadha)

Liam O'Gorman

Brian O'Higgins; one of the party who moved the explosives into the GPO basement. He was imprisoned in Frongoch, became a TD and fought on side of IRA/Republicans in the Civil War. He wrote *The Soldier's Story of Easter Week*.

James O'Higgins; mustered at Cabra Bridge, then moved to the GPO after his position was overrun.

Padraig (Paudeen) O'Keefe; led some men to the GPO from the Imperial Hotel. Imprisoned at Frongoch. From 1918 he was Assistant Secretary of Sinn Féin. TD for Co. Cork, North East. He supported the Treaty and was the Deputy Governor of Mountjoy Prison during the Civil War executions.

Fergus O'Kelly; in command of the detail in the wireless school and then the Dublin Bread Company.

Joseph O'Kelly

Seán T. O'Kelly (Seán T. Ó Cellaigh), future President of the Republic of Ireland; he was Pearse's adjutant during the Rising. He was sent to release Hobson on Monday evening from Seán Harling's home in Cabra Park.

Lt Ted O'Kelly; a member of the Kildare Volunteers, he travelled from Kildare, joined the Maynooth Volunteers and came to the GPO where he was slightly wounded.

— O'Laughlin; wounded in the breakout and taken to the McKane house in Moore Street.

Diarmuid O'Leary (Ó Laoghaire)

Edward (Éamon) O'Mahoney

Matthew O'Mahoney

George Oman

Donough O'Moore

Jim O'Neill; ICA officer who acted as QM during the Rising. He was primarily responsible for the issuance of 'bombs'.

John O'Neill; imprisoned at Frongoch.

John O'Neill

Seámus O'Neill

**The O'Rahilly (Michael Joseph, aged 41); munitions officer. He said to Countess Markievicz at Liberty Hall just before marching off: 'It is madness, but it is glorious madness.' Left the GPO about 8.00 pm on Friday night to find a way to Williams and Woods: 'It will either be a glorious victory or a glorious death.' Another Volunteer in the GPO reported: 'I heard the burst of fire, then the sound of feet running, then the sound of one's man feet, then silence.' The O'Rahilly wrote this note to his wife: 'Written after I was shot – Darling Nancy I was shot leading a rush up Moore Street, took refuge in a doorway. While I was there I heard the men pointing out where I was & I made a bolt for the lane I am in now. I got more than one bullet I think. Tons & tons of love dearie to you & to the boys & to Nell & Anna. It was a good fight anyhow. Please deliver this to Nannie O'Rahilly 40 Herbert Park, Dublin. Good bye darling.' He wrote this note on a note he'd received from his son, Aodghan; it had a bullet hole through it. (Some commentators have his party as comprising 12, some about 30, others 40 men.[980] [981] [982] Jack Plunkett's unpublished memoir indicated there were a dozen men in the party.[983])

Des O'Reilly

J.K. O'Reilly

Joe O'Reilly; became Michael Collins' 'assistant' after Frongoch.

Cpt. Martin O'Reilly; led the party of wounded and women to Jervis Street Hospital. The party consisted of Fr Flanagan, Cpt. Mahoney, sixteen wounded men and twelve women.

Cpt. Michael W. (M.W.) O'Reilly; QM on the Brigade Staff; became O/C at Frongoch.

Samuel P. O'Reilly; mustered at Cabra Bridge, then moved to the GPO after his position was overrun. Imprisoned at Frongoch.

**Thomas O'Reilly

Gearóid O'Sullivan; cousin of Michael Collins. He was a few months younger than Collins, and moved to Dublin in 1909 to attend St Patrick's Training College on his way to becoming a teacher, then he attended the Royal University. He was the second youngest officer in the GPO. He raised the Irish Tricolor flag on the roof between 1 and 2 pm on 24 April. Later, he ran with a mattress around himself from Clery's to the GPO, fell, got up and made it across unscathed. He was sent to Frongoch and was released in the general amnesty on 21 December 1916. On 19 October 1922 he married Maud Kiernan, Kitty's sister, in what was to be a double

980 40— Hayes-McCoy, G.A. *A Military History of the 1916 Rising*, in Nowlan, Kevin. *The Making of 1916*, p. 295. **981** 12—Caulfield, Max. *The Easter Rising*, p. 257. O'Higgins, Brian. *The Soldier's Story of Easter Week*, p. 35. **982** 25—MacEntee, Seán. *Episode at Easter*, 1966, p. 160. **983** Plunkett, John (Jack). Witness Statements 488, 865.

wedding with Kitty and Michael Collins. Kitty was a bridesmaid, but dressed all in black. He became Adjutant General of the Free State Army. He died on Good Friday 1948 and was buried in Glasnevin on Easter Monday.

James O'Sullivan

William O'Toole; imprisoned in Frongoch.

Matthew Parnell

Liam Pedlar

#Thomas Peppard

Cpt. George Plunkett; brother of Joseph and Jack. He was Chief of Staff of the IRA during the 1940's.

Jack Plunkett; brother of Joseph and George.

Cpt. Vincent Poole; an ICA member. Connolly promoted Oscar Traynor over his head, much to Poole's chagrin.

Seán Price

Charles Purcell; imprisoned in Frongoch.

Patrick Rankin

Seámus Reader; member of the Glasgow Volunteers. He left Glasgow on 15 January and carried explosives to Ireland.

Willie Reagan (Liam Ó Raogain)

Andy Redmond

John Reid; one of the party who moved the explosives into the GPO basement. Imprisoned at Frongoch.

Matthew Reilly

Sam Reilly; he was a sniper on the roof with Joseph Sweeney. He became a caretaker at Columbia University in New York.

John R. Reynolds

Peter Reynolds

Henry Ridgeway; wore a Red Cross armlet, which was ripped off by British soldiers.

Ring; five brothers, four of whom were carpenters, Joseph, Leo, Liam, Patrick and Tim. They were used well in 'burrowing' passages through buildings, especially in the Moore Street area under the command of Frank Henderson.

Seámus Robinson; one of the Kimmage garrison, led the men in Hopkins and Hopkins. He later commanded the South Tipperary Brigade, and led the Soloheadbeg ambush. He was an anti-Treaty TD in the Second Dáil.

Thomas Roche; imprisoned at Frongoch.

William Roche /

Charles Rossiter; imprisoned at Frongoch.

Thomas Roth

Seán Russell; was in the Hotel Metropole.

Desmond Ryan; lived at St Enda's and was a prolific writer about Pearse and St Enda's.

James Ryan; medical student at UCD nearing his final exam, and bandaged Connolly's arm. He was a friend of Connolly, but had been sent to Cork to relay MacNeill's cancellation order to the Cork Brigade. Imprisoned at Frongoch. TD for Wexford from 1918. Later he became a Senator. Served in de Valera Cabinets after 1932.[984]

Oliver Ryan

Thomas Ryan

William Ryan (Liam Ó Riain)

Maj. Charles Saurin; he was in the Metropole Hotel, then the GPO. Imprisoned at Frongoch.

Martin Savage; he was killed during the Ashtown ambush of Lord French in 1919.

Joseph Scollan; O/C of the Hibernian Rifles, his command was in the Exchange Hotel, and held off assaults by the Irish Fusiliers. They retreated to the GPO on Thursday afternoon.

Francis Scullin

Patrick Scullin; imprisoned at Frongoch.

James Seville

James Sexton; imprisoned at Frongoch.

Frank Sheridan

James Sheridan

Arthur Shields; went to the wireless school with Fergus O'Kelly. A Protestant, he was imprisoned in Frongoch.

**Patrick (Paddy) Shortis (23); on Wednesday afternoon he went into Henry Street with a party led by Connolly, down to Liffey Street, and they returned by way of Abbey Street the next morning. He was shot dead in Moore Street with The O'Rahilly on their attempted escape. He was originally from Ballybunion.

Tom Slator

Peadar Slattery

Charles Smith

Michael Staines (Miceal Ó Stainear); QM of the Volunteers. He took the telegraphy room upstairs in the GPO. He was one of James Connolly's stretcher-bearers during the escape. He became QM of the Dublin Brigade after returning from Frongoch, and was a TD in the first three Dáils. He was the first Commissioner of the Garda Siochana, then retired from politics. Subsequently he became director of the New Ireland Insurance Company, with offices on Bachelor's Walk formerly occupied by the Kapp and Peterson and 'Kelly's Fort' premises.

Joe Stanley; an IRB member, he was *not* a Volunteer, yet nevertheless reported to the GPO. Imprisoned at Frongoch. He was the one who printed the *Irish War News* from the GPO at the direction of Pearse and Connolly. Later he was the owner of the *Drogheda Argus* and other regional newspapers.

Charles Steinmayer; was in the breakout party with The O'Rahilly.

Paddy J. Stephenson; he and Seán McLaughlin were the dispatch carriers, especially to and from the Mendicity Institute. Imprisoned at Frongoch.

Jim Strich

Padraig Stupple; imprisoned at Frongoch.

Tony Swann; he was with The O'Rahilly when the latter was shot. He was to be deported, but was deemed to be too young. His brother was at King Street.

Paddy Swanzy; imprisoned at Frongoch.

James Sweeney; imprisoned at Frongoch.

Joseph Sweeney; lived at St Enda's and was a student at Trinity. He was a sniper on the roof of the GPO. He was imprisoned at Frongoch and later fought for the Free State in the Civil War.[985] He was a TD from Co. Donegal in the first three Dáils. He retired as a major general in the Republic of Ireland Army.

Lt Patrick E. Sweeney

Charles Tallon; brother, imprisoned at Frongoch

---

985 Griffith and O'Grady. *Ireland's Unfinished Revolution*, pp 264. ff.

Christopher Tallon; imprisoned at Frongoch.

James Tallon; brother, imprisoned at Frongoch.

Joe Tallon; brother, known as 'the chef' because he cooked in The Metropole Hotel. Imprisoned at Frongoch.

Liam Tannam; one of James Connolly's stretcher-bearers during the escape. When the Lancers charged down Sackville Street, he was the one who gave the order to fire.[986] Imprisoned at Frongoch.

Cpt. Frank Thornton; brought the armory from Citizen Hall, then led the garrison in the Imperial Hotel and Clery's. He was the leader of the Liverpool Volunteers before the Rising.

Hugh Thornton

Patrick Thornton

Liam Tobin (19); became Michael Collins' Assistant Director of Intelligence.

John Toomey (brother); imprisoned at Frongoch.

Joe Toomey (brother); their sister, Statia, was also in the GPO. Imprisoned at Frongoch. Their brother, Eddie, was sent home because he was only 16.

Lt Oscar Traynor (30); after Fairview Strand fell, he led the seventy Fairview Volunteers to the GPO, then was sent to the Metropole Hotel, and after its fall, he returned to the GPO. Imprisoned at Frongoch. He fought for the IRA/Republicans in the Civil War, and became the Chief of Staff. Still later he became a Minister in the Dáil.

Joseph Trimble

J.J. Tuohy

Patrick Tuohy; imprisoned at Frongoch.

Cormac Turner; one of the Hopkins and Hopkins garrison.

Francis Turner

Joseph Turner

John Twamley; a lineman in the engineering office of the Post Office and prior to the Rising he was detailed to determine how to 'cut' all lines of communication with England. On Sunday, he was sent to Bray, then returned to Dublin via Lamb Doyle's where he had a pint!

P. Twamley

986 Tannam, Liam. Witness Statement 242.

Timothy Tyrell

Michael Wade

Charles Walker; he helped print the Irish War News.

Harry (Henry) Walpole; Connolly's 'bodyguard' since he was 'kidnapped' in January 1916. Imprisoned at Frongoch.

Christopher Walsh

**Edward Walsh

James J. Walsh; originally from Cork, he marched in from Fairview with a section of thirty Hibernian Rifles. He knew Morse Code and sent out queries from the GPO hoping for replies. He would be Ireland's first Minister for Posts and Telegraphs after the Treaty.

Mark Walsh

John Ward

James Wardock

**Cpt. Tom Weafer (26)[987] He was killed in the fire at Dublin Bread Company.

Thomas Wheatley

A. Weeks

Joseph Whelan

Cpt. Jack White DSO; an ICA officer and trainer, he left the ICA in 1914.

Michael White

Henry Willis

#James Wilson

#Peter Wilson

#William (Beck) Wilson

#William (Cody) Wilson

James Wren

GPO Headquarters Battalion, Women

There was a total of about seventy-five women from the ICA and Cumann na mBan in the GPO, but only a fraction of that number at any one time. Only three

---

987 *Who's Who* has the name as 'Patrick' Weafer. O'Farrell, Padraic. *Who's Who,* p. 100.

of them – Winifred Carney, Julia Grenan and Elizabeth More O'Farrell – remained after the other women and the wounded were evacuated early on Friday.

Mary Adrian

Catherine Byrne; she was sent by Pearse with a message for the Four Courts, and rolled his messages in her hair bun.

L. Burke (McGinty)

Ellen Bushel; an usher at the Abbey Theater, she carried many messages to and from the GPO. She was imprisoned after the Rising.

Winifred Carney; an ICA member, she was James Connolly's secretary. She changed her opinion of Joseph Plunkett when at his capture Plunkett gave her his ring to pass on to Grace Gifford.

May Chadwick

Gerta Colley; she was detained for a short time at Broadstone Railway Station.

Maire Comerford; she reported to St Stephen's Green, but was turned away because she was deemed too young and spent the week carrying dispatches from here.

Brigid Connolly

Winifred Conway

Mary Cullen; sent with Brigid Grace to the Northumberland Road garrison to warn it of the arriving troops.

Laura Daly (O'Sullivan)

Nora Daly (Dore)

Aoife de Burca

Eileen Dempsey; employed at McCrad Collar Manufacturers, she lost her job after the Rising.

Brid Dixon; a great friend of Leslie Price, she and Price spent much of the week under fire as couriers.

Peggy Downey; from Liverpool, she was the chief cook.

Louise Gavan-Duffy (Luise Ni Dhubhthaigh); chief assistant to QM Fitzgerald.

Maire English

M. Fagan (MacSherry)

Nora Foley (Ni Fogludha)

May Gahan (O'Carroll); from Dublin, she remembered people pelting her with bottles and horse dung as she walked to imprisonment in Kilmainham Gaol. During the War of Independence, she and her husband opened a pub and she often bought weapons from British soldiers. She even bought a machine gun and had it lowered out of Ship Street Barracks.

Lucie Gethings

May Gibney

Brigid Grace; sent with Mary Cullen to the Northumberland Road garrison to warn it of the arriving troops. Her brother, James, was killed there at 25 Northumberland Road.

Julia Grenan (sometimes named as 'Shelia Grennan'); *Who's Who* claims 'Sheila' was the one who conveyed the instructions for the surrender with Elizabeth More O'Farrell, but most commentators agree that the woman's name was Julia Grenan, although Brian O'Higgins has it spelled 'Grennan'.[988] [989] For example *Last Words* by Piaras MacLochlainn names her as Julia Grenan.[990] See, also, her own articles published shortly after the Rising.[991]

Mary Hanley (Maire Ni Ainle)

Annie Higgins

Patricia Hoey

Mary Ellen (Nell) Humphreys; a sister of The O'Rahilly. Although she came to the GPO several times during the week, she was not involved in the fighting. She was captured in the vicinity of her home at 54 Northumberland Road, and was imprisoned.

Kathleen Kelly (Barber)

Martha Kelly; married Michael Murphy. She was imprisoned in Kilmainham.

Bridget Lambert

Ellen Lambert (Stynes)

Mary Lawless

Maeve MacDowell

Sorcha MacMahon; with Kathleen Clarke, she was primarily responsible for establishing and operating the Irish National Aid and Volunteers' Dependents' Fund.

Mabel McConnell (Fitzgerald)

Mary McLoughlin; she was Seán's school-girl sister.

---

988 O'Farrell, Padraic. *Who's Who*, p. 39. **989** O'Higgins, Brian. *The Soldier's Story of Easter Week*, p. 88. **990** MacLochlainn, Piaras. *Last Words*, p. 183. **991** Grenan, Julia. 'After the Surrender', *Wolfe Tone Annual*, Special 1916 Edition. 'Events of Easter Week', *Catholic Bulletin*, June 1917.

Maire Mapotar

Mary Mulcahy

Gertie Murphy

Kathleen Murphy; imprisoned.

Martha Murphy

Rose Ann Murphy; she was from Liverpool.

Eileen Murray

Mae Murray

Ellen Noone

Elizabeth More O'Farrell; she went out the door of 15 Moore Street at about 12.45 pm on Saturday, in order to find the British commander, Gen. Lowe, to convey the leaders' wish to surrender. Subsequently, he asked her to go to the other garrison commanders and convey the terms of surrender. She went on to become a nurse and midwife at Holles Street Hospital.

Mary O'Hanrahan

Annie O'Higgins

Maire O'Neill

Cathleen O'Reilly

Molly O'Reilly (Corcoran); became one of Michael Collins' best 'sources'.

Leslie Price; she married Tom Barry. Tom Clarke sent her to the Pro-Cathedral to fetch a priest on Thursday – she brought Fr Flanagan back.[992]

Margaret Quinn

Annie Redmond

Mollie Reynolds; was very active in the later anti-conscription campaign.

Bridie Richards

Anne (Áine Ni Rian) Ryan

Phyllis (Eilis Ni Rian) Ryan; she was a sister of Jim, later Mrs Seán T. O'Kelly.

Mary Josephine (Min) Ryan; sister of Jim. She was Seán MacDermott's fiancée and later married Richard Mulcahy. She and her sister, Phyllis, were the last two to see Seán MacDermott in Kilmainham Gaol: 'He preferred to talk of casual matters,

992 Barry, Mrs Tom. Witness Statement 1754.

asking about different people we knew, enjoying little jokes almost as though we were in Bewley's. He had worked and planned for Irish Independence since boyhood. His last words save for his prayers, were "God Save Ireland". At four o'clock, when the shooting was done, a gentle rain began to fall – the tears of Dark Rosaleen.'[993]

Veronica (Ni Rian) Ryan (Ui Glasam)

Tillie Simpson

Lucy Smith (Byrne)

Christine Stafford-Brooks

M.J. Stapleton (Slevin)

Annie Tobin (Soalfield)

Statia Toomey (Byrne)

Aoife (Effie) Taaffe

Catherine Treston; imprisoned

Brigid Bean Ui Faoithe

Bridie Walsh

Martha Walsh (Murphy)

Esther Wisley (O'Moore)

British prisoners in the GPO

2Lt A.D. Chalmers; a British officer from the 14th Royal Fusiliers who was using the postal facilities in the GPO at the time the Rising began. He was 'trussed up' with telephone cord by Michael Collins and remained captive all week. The O'Rahilly 'appointed' him to keep a watch to note that nothing had been 'stolen' by the Volunteers. 'I want this officer to watch the safe to see that nothing is touched. You will see that no harm comes to him.' He was shot in the thigh when the prisoners were let go in advance of The O'Rahilly's escape bid.

Pvt. James Doyle, Royal Irish Regiment; escaped and hid in the Coliseum Theatre, and was discovered only on 3 May.

Sgt Henry, School of Musketry; with Pvt. Doyle, he escaped and hid in the Coliseum Theatre, and also was discovered only on 3 May.

2Lt King, Royal Irish Fusiliers

---

993 Mulcahy, Mary Josephine. Witness Statement 399.

Lt George O'Mahoney, a doctor in the English Indian Army Medical Corps. He was on convalescent leave after injuring his leg in a fall in the Himalayas. He was originally from Cork. As a prisoner he helped take care of the wounded, and treated Connolly's leg wound. Connolly told him: 'You are the most valuable thing we've captured!'

1st Battalion, Men

A, B and C Companies mustered in Blackhall Place under Cmdt Daly and proceeded to Brunswick Street. D Company mustered in Temple Street under Cpt. Heuston and proceeded to Liberty Hall.

Garrison totals about 355 men and women; killed 10; executed 2. North Brunswick Street, Church Street, Constitution Hill, Four Courts, Fr Mathew Hall, North Dublin Union, North King Street ('Reilly's Fort'), Magazine Fort.

Mendicity Institute: garrison: about 45. Most of the Volunteers were Fianna, and most were between 12 and 25 years old (Heuston was only 25 years old). He was instructed to hold this position for two hours to delay English deployment; they held for three days. They started with two weapons and one box of ammunition. They were reinforced with 13 reinforcements from North County and there were 2 killed. The Fianna only surrendered when they ran out of ammunition on Wednesday, infuriating the British that so few youngsters held them off for so long. Heuston was the youngest executed.

Commandant Edward (Ned) Daly (Éamonn Ó Dalaigh, executed 4 May 1916, aged 25):* 'I am the commander. At all events I was in charge.' In Kilmainham, he was in cell number 66 and was attended by Fr Columbus. In addition, he was seen by his sisters, Madge, Laurie (his favorite), and Kathleen (Kattie) Clarke. Madge felt Laurie falter and told her: 'Remember, you're a Daly.' He was the second youngest to be executed.

**Lt Thomas Allen; ordered a policeman to turn over the keys to the Chancery Place entrance to the Four Courts and they entered at that point.
Liam Archer; became Chief of Staff of the Free State Army.
Richard (Dick) Balfe; he was badly wounded, imprisoned at Frongoch and became O/C of E Co. of the North Camp.
Tom Bannon
Piaras Béaslaí, Vice-Commandant; became editor of *An tÓglach* (The Soldier). Born and educated in Liverpool, he moved to Dublin at age 23. TD for Kerry East in the first three Dáils. Published one of the first biographies of Michael Collins.
Robert Beggs; Four Courts.
Daniel Begley; Four Courts, imprisoned at Frongoch.
John Bent; Four Courts, imprisoned at Frongoch.

Charles Bevan; Four Courts

James Bevan; Four Courts

Joseph Bevan; Four Courts

Thomas Bevan; Four Courts

James Bird; Four Courts, imprisoned at Frongoch

Michael Blanchfield; imprisoned at Frongoch.

Peter Blanchfield; Four Courts, imprisoned at Frongoch.

Patrick (Paddy) Boland; Fianna, was at the Magazine Fort, imprisoned at Frongoch.

Joseph Brabazon; Four Courts. Wounded at the Church Street Bridge barricade.

Edward Brennan (Éamon Ó Braonain); Four Courts, imprisoned at Frongoch.

James J. Brennan; Mendicity Institute

James Breslin; Four Courts

Peadar Breslin; Four Courts

Thomas Breslin; Four Courts

Edward Bridgeman; Four Courts, imprisoned at Frongoch.

Fred Brooks; Mendicity Institute

James Burns; Four Courts

George Butler; Four Courts

Ambrose Byrne; Four Courts, imprisoned at Frongoch.

Charles Byrne; Four Courts

John Joseph Byrne; imprisoned at Frongoch.

Laurence Byrne; Four Courts

Patrick Byrne; Four Courts, imprisoned at Frongoch.

Seámus Byrne; Four Courts

Seán Byrne; Four Courts

William Byrne; Four Courts

Arthur Cahill; imprisoned at Frongoch.

James Cahill; Four Courts

M.J. Campbell; Four Courts

Peter Carroll (Peadar Ó Cearbhaill); Four Courts

Lt William Carroll (Liam Ó Cearbhaill); Four Courts

Thomas Cassidy; Four Courts

John Patrick Catlin; Four Courts

Lt Peadar Clancy; he led a group of Volunteers to 5 Church Street. He became
   Vice-Brigadier of the Dublin Brigade and was murdered on Bloody Sunday.

James Clarke; imprisoned at Frongoch.

John Clarke; Four Courts

Seán Cody; Mendicity Institute

Joseph Coffey; Four Courts

#Richard (Dick) Coleman; mobilised with the Fingal Brigade at Saucers Town,
   went to the GPO, then was sent to the Mendicity Institute. (See 5th Battalion at
   Ashbourne).

Maurice Collins; he took up his post in Lamb's public house after he was released from guarding Bulmer Hobson on Monday evening, then went to the Four Courts. He was imprisoned in Wandsworth. After his release he opened a tobacconist and confectioner shop, with a billiard room.

Luke Condron; Four Courts, imprisoned at Frongoch.

Martin Conlan; he was in charge at Fr Mathew Hall, after guarding Bulmer Hobson until Monday evening.

James Conroy Snr; Four Courts

Lt Michael Cosgrave

F.X. Coughlan; Four Courts

Redmond Cox; Four Courts

William Coyle; Four Courts, imprisoned at Frongoch.

James Crenigan; Mendicity Institute

John F. Cullen; Mendicity Institute, imprisoned at Frongoch.

Joseph Cullen; Four Courts

Thomas Cullen; Four Courts, imprisoned at Frongoch.

Paddy Daly; a Fianna member. Some months before the Rising he got a job with a building firm making repairs at the Magazine Fort and he knew the Fort's lay out. He was the engineer for the whole Brigade. Wounded in an attack on the Lancers in the Medical Mission. Imprisoned at Frongoch.

Michael Darker; Four Courts

Edward Delemere; Four Courts, imprisoned at Frongoch.

James Dempsey; Four Courts

Michael Derham; Four Courts, imprisoned at Frongoch.

Liam Derrington; Four Courts

Christopher Doggett; Four Courts

John Domican; Four Courts; imprisoned at Frongoch.

Sylvester Donohoe; Four Courts

Andrew Dowling; Four Courts

John Dowling; Four Courts

Thomas Dowling; Four Courts

John Doyle; Four Courts

Thomas Doyle; Four Courts

Christopher Duffy; Four Courts, imprisoned at Frongoch.

Éamonn J. Duggan; Four Courts. Became a Plenipotentiary in the Treaty negotiations of December 1921.

Thomas Dunn (Dunne?); Four Courts, imprisoned at Frongoch.

**John Dwan (25); killed in North King Street. He lived on Lower Gardiner Street.

Michael Edwards; Four Courts, imprisoned at Frongoch.

John (Seán) Ellis; Four Courts, imprisoned at Frongoch.

John Fagan; Four Courts

Michael Fagan; Four Courts

Cpt. Frank Fahy; later Ceann Comhairle (Speaker) of the Dáil.
John Farrell; Four Courts
**Patrick Farrell (19)
Thomas Farrell; Four Courts
Christopher Farrelly; Four Courts
Seán Farrelly; Four Courts
Stephen Farren; Four Courts
Gerald Feeny; Four Courts
Denis Fitzpatrick; Four Courts
M. Fitzsimons; imprisoned at Frongoch.
Maurice Flanagan; imprisoned at Frongoch.
Seán Flood; Four Courts, imprisoned at Frongoch.
John Fogarty; Four Courts
Patrick Fogarty; Four Courts
Michael Foley (Micheal Ó Foghludha); Four Courts
Seán Forde; Four Courts
Frederick Foy; Four Courts, imprisoned at Frongoch.
Denis Frawley; Four Courts
Mathew Gahan; Four Courts
Frank Gaskin; Magazine Fort
Arthur Gaynor; Four Courts, imprisoned at Frongoch.
John (Seán) Geraghty; Four Courts, imprisoned at Frongoch.
Bob Gilligan; a member of the Fianna, he was in the Magazine Fort.
Patrick Gilsenan
James Graham; Four Courts, imprisoned at Frongoch.
Patrick Green; Four Courts
John Griffin; imprisoned at Frongoch.
William Griffith; Four Courts
Michael Grimley; Four Courts
John Halpin; Four Courts
Peter (Peadar) Halpin; Four Courts, imprisoned at Frongoch.
Thomas Hamill; Four Courts, imprisoned at Frongoch.
Frank Harding; Four Courts
Seán Harling (14); he was in the North Dublin Union. At the beginning of the
    Rising he was selling racecards for the Fairyhouse Race Meeting outside
    Broadstone Station.[994] He became aide to de Valera, witnessed the dictation of
    letters appointing the Plenipotentiaries to the Treaty negotiations, and delivered
    the letters to them.[995] He fought for the IRA/Republicans in the Civil War.[996]
James Harmon; imprisoned at Frongoch.
John Harpur; imprisoned at Frongoch.

---

994 Griffith and O'Grady. *Ireland's Unfinished Revolution*, pp. 56 ff. **995** Ibid, p. 252 ff. **996** Harling, Seán.
Witness Statement 935.

Alf Harnett; Four Courts, imprisoned at Frongoch.

Seán Harrington; Mendicity Institute

Diarmuid Healy; imprisoned at Frongoch.

Peadar Healy; a ticket collector at the Broadstone Railway Station, he was taken by surprise and reported to his battalion position late.

John O'Kelly Hegarty; imprisoned at Frongoch.

Lt Diarmuid O'Hegarty (Diarmuid Ó hEigeartaigh); Four Courts

Thomas Henderson; Four Courts, imprisoned at Frongoch.

Edward Hendrick; Four Courts, imprisoned at Frongoch.

James Joseph Hendrick; Four Courts

Seán ('Jack') Heuston (Seán MacAodha, executed 8 May 1916, aged 25);* Mendicity Institute, held by Fianna Volunteers, D Company, all aged between 12 and 25. This was the first garrison to capitulate. In Kilmainham, he was in cell number 19. Fr Albert [997] [998] and also Seán's brother, Michael, who was studying to be a Dominican priest, as well as Fr Browne, the Dominican novice master, saw him. His mother, sister, aunt and a first cousin also saw him.

James Higgins; imprisoned at Frongoch.

P.J. Hogan; Four Courts

William Hogan; he was in North King Street.

William Conor Hogan; Four Courts

Gerry Holohan (Gearóid Ó hUallachain); a Fianna member. It was his assignment to buy a football for the game at Phoenix Park in the area known as the Fifteen Acres. He bought it at a shop on Ormond Quay on his way to the Park, where he was one of the Fianna assigned to destroy the Magazine Fort. With Denis O'Callahan he set Linenhall Barracks alight.

Cmdt Paddy Holohan; a Fianna member, he was O/C in the North Dublin Union, imprisoned at Frongoch.

Con Howard; Four Courts

**Seán Bernard Howard (17); Four Courts. A friend of Seán Harling, and member of the Fianna Pipers Band, he and a few members of the Fianna blew up a rail road bridge in north Dublin to impede the British.

Michael Howlett; Four Courts

Thomas Hunter

Thomas Hyland; Four Courts, imprisoned at Frongoch.

Seán Hynes; Four Courts

Thomas Kane (Tomas Ó Canain); Four Courts

J. Kavanaugh; imprisoned at Frongoch.

James Kavanaugh; Four Courts, imprisoned at Frongoch.

James Kavanaugh; Four Courts

Patrick Kearns; Four Courts, imprisoned at Frongoch.

---

997 Fr Albert, OFM. Cap. 'Seán Heuston's Last Moments', *Fianna*, May 1926. **998** Fr Albert, OFM. Cap. 'Seán Heuston: How Seán Heuston Died', *Capuchin Annual,* 1942.

Joseph Kelly; Four Courts, imprisoned at Frongoch.

Michael Kelly; Four Courts, imprisoned at Frongoch.

Patrick Kelly; Four Courts, imprisoned at Frongoch.

Patrick Kelly (Padraig Ó Ceallaigh); Mendicity Institute

J. Kennedy; imprisoned at Frongoch.

Seán Kennedy; Four Courts

James J. Kennedy; Four Courts

John Kennedy; Four Courts

Luke Kennedy

John Kenny; Four Courts

Cyril Keogh; imprisoned at Frongoch.

Cpt. Nicholas Laffan

John Larkin; imprisoned at Frongoch.

Frank Lawlor (brother); imprisoned at Frongoch.

Laurence Lawlor (brother); imprisoned at Frongoch.

Seán Lawlor; Four Courts

Peter Ledwith; Four Courts

Robert Leggett; Four Courts, imprisoned at Frongoch.

Michael Lennon; Four Courts. His house at 5 Church Street Upper was taken over by Volunteers led by Peadar Clancy. Lennon was wounded, but survived, after having his wound dressed by Brigid Lyons. Imprisoned at Frongoch.

Nicholas Lennon; Four Courts

George Levins; Mendicity Institute

Arnold Lowe; Four Courts

Cpt. Fionan Lynch (Fionan Ó Loinsigh); Four Courts. He was a prisoner in Mountjoy Prison when Tom Ashe was carried out of his cell to be force-fed. Lynch cried out 'Stick it, Tom.' Ashe replied, 'I'll stick it, Fin.' TD for Kerry South from 1918, he was the Minister for Education in the first Irish Free State Government, and then Minister for Fisheries.

Charles Lynch; Four Courts

Gilbert Lynch; Four Courts

Michael Lynch (Miceal Ó Loinsigh); Four Courts

Charlie Lyons; Four Courts

Edward Lyons; Four Courts, imprisoned at Frongoch.

John E. Lyons; Four Courts, imprisoned at Frongoch.

Andy MacDonald; a member of the Fianna.

Joseph MacDonough; Four Courts

Edward (Eunan) MacGinley; a member of the Fianna, imprisoned at Frongoch.

Maighnas MacMearigh; Four Courts

Patrick MacNamara; Four Courts

M. McAntee (MacMeachtaigh); Four Courts

Frank McCabe; he was in North King Street.

Thomas McCann; Four Courts

Tommy McCarthy; he brought in a load of ammunition.

Christopher McCormack; Four Courts

**James McCormack; Four Courts

Thomas McDonnell; Four Courts

Louis McEvatt; Four Courts

Joseph McGill; Four Courts

Frank McGuinness; Four Courts. He was an uncle of Brigid Lyons (Thornton). Wounded in Gardiner Place.

Lt Joseph McGuinness; uncle of Brigid Lyons (Thornton). He was in command of the first twenty Volunteers sent to take the Four Courts. He won the South Longford election on 9 May 1917: 'Put him *in* to get him *out*' was the election slogan. He was imprisoned in Lewes Gaol at the time of the election.

Owen McKeon; Four Courts, imprisoned at Frongoch.

William McKeon; Four Courts

Peter McLaughlin; Four Courts

Peter McMahon; imprisoned at Frongoch.

Joseph McMenarigh; Four Courts

Francis (Frank) McNally; Four Courts, imprisoned at Frongoch.

James McNamara; Four Courts

Patrick McNestry; Four Courts

Michael McNulty; Four Courts, imprisoned at Frongoch.

Peadar McNulty; Four Courts

Patrick Macken; Four Courts

Michael Magee; Four Courts

Thomas Maguire; Four Courts

**Peter (Peadar) Paul Manning (25); Four Courts

L. Marie; a Fianna member, Four Courts.

James Marks; Mendicity Institute

Christopher Martin; a member of the Fianna, he was in the Magazine Fort.

Éamonn Martin; a Fianna member, he was wounded with a bullet through his lung. He helped to set the Linenhall Barracks on fire.

Frank Mason; Four Courts

George Mason; Four Courts

Henry Meade; Four Courts

Walter Meade; imprisoned at Frongoch.

William Meade; imprisoned at Frongoch.

William Meehan; Mendicity Institute

Herbert (Barney) Mellows; a Fianna member. He went in the group to 5 Church Street. Imprisoned at Frongoch.

Michael Merrigan; Four Courts

Thomas Merrigan; Four Courts

Philip Monaghan; imprisoned at Frongoch.

Patrick Mooney; Four Courts, imprisoned at Frongoch.

Éamon (Ned) Morkan; Four Courts, imprisoned at Frongoch.

Michael Mullen; imprisoned at Frongoch.

Peter Mullen

James Mullkearns; Four Courts, imprisoned at Frongoch.

William (Liam) Murname; Four Courts, imprisoned at Frongoch.

Brian Murphy (Ó Murchadha); Four Courts

Colm Murphy; imprisoned at Frongoch.

Christopher Murphy (Cristoir Ó Murchadha); Four Courts

Francis (Frank) C. Murphy; Four Courts, imprisoned at Frongoch.

Hubert J. Murphy; Four Courts, imprisoned at Frongoch.

John Murphy; a member of the Fianna, he was in the Magazine Fort. Imprisoned at Frongoch.

Martin Murphy; Four Courts, imprisoned at Frongoch.

Michael Murphy (Michael Ó Murchadha); Four Courts

William Murphy; he was in North King Street.

Joseph M. Murray; Four Courts

Joseph Murtagh; a Fianna member.

Laurence Murtagh; Four Courts, imprisoned at Frongoch.

Patrick Murtagh; Four Courts

Denis Musgrave; Four Courts

Joe Musgrave; imprisoned at Frongoch.

Denis Neary; Four Courts

Joseph Neary; imprisoned at Frongoch.

Arthur Neilan; Four Courts

Patrick Nevin; Four Courts, imprisoned at Frongoch.

Thomas Nolan (Tomas Ó Nuallain); Four Courts

Joseph Norton; Mendicity Institute

Thomas Ó Briain; Four Courts, imprisoned at Frongoch.

John O'Brian (Seán Ó Briain); a member of the Fianna, he was in the Magazine Fort and then the Four Courts.

Joseph O'Brien (Seosamh Ó Broin); Mendicity Institute

Michael O'Brien; Four Courts

Patrick O'Brien; Four Courts

Charles (Cathal) O'Byrne; imprisoned at Frongoch.

William O'Byrne; imprisoned at Frongoch.

Cpt. Denis O'Callaghan; a Fianna member and deputy to Daly, he was sent to capture Broadstone Station, but the mission was aborted. With Gerry Holohan and Éamonn Martin he set Linenhall Barracks on fire.

Duncan O'Callaghan (Donnchadh Ó Ceallachain); Four Courts

Michael O'Carroll; Four Courts

Robert O'Carroll; Four Courts, imprisoned at Frongoch.

Seán O'Carroll; Four Courts, imprisoned at Frongoch

William O'Carroll; imprisoned at Frongoch

M. Ó Conallan; Four Courts

Mortimer O'Connell; he became Chief Clerk of Dáil Éireann.

James S. O'Connor (brother); Four Courts, imprisoned at Frongoch.

John O'Connor; Four Courts, imprisoned at Frongoch.

Patrick O'Connor (brother); Four Courts, imprisoned at Frongoch.

Tommy O' Connor (brother); Four Courts, imprisoned at Frongoch.

Michael O'Dea; Four Courts

William O'Dea

Fionan O'Doherty; Four Courts

Liam O'Doherty; Four Courts

Con O'Donovan (Ó Donnaghain); Four Courts. On Holy Saturday he had been one of those detailed to guard Bulmer Hobson.

Seán O'Duffy; Four Courts, imprisoned at Frongoch.

Francis (Frank) O'Flanagan; Four Courts, imprisoned at Frongoch.

George O'Flanagan; Four Courts, imprisoned at Frongoch.

Maurice O'Flanagan; Four Courts

Michael O'Flanagan; Four Courts

**Patrick O'Flanagan; he was killed entering 'Reilly's Fort'.

Liam O'Gorman

Bernard O'Hanlon; Four Courts

Patrick O'Hanlon; Four Courts, imprisoned at Frongoch.

Fergus O'Kelly; imprisoned at Frongoch.

Michael O'Kelly; Four Courts, imprisoned at Frongoch.

Patrick Joseph O'Leary; Four Courts, imprisoned at Frongoch.

Robert Oman; Four Courts, imprisoned at Frongoch.

Seán O'Mahoney; imprisoned at Frongoch.

Chris O'Malley; imprisoned at Frongoch.

Seán O'Moore; Four Courts

Joseph O'Neill; Four Courts, imprisoned at Frongoch.

Michael O'Neill; Four Courts, imprisoned at Frongoch.

Patrick Francis O'Neill; Four Courts, imprisoned at Frongoch.

William O'Neill; Four Courts, imprisoned at Frongoch.

Michael O'Reardon; Four Courts

Desmond O'Reilly; imprisoned at Frongoch.

Luke O'Reilly; Four Courts

Peter O'Reilly; Four Courts

Sam O'Reilly; on Monday night he was in charge of a detail to blow up the Midland Railway lines near Broadstone Station; they destroyed the signal system and cut telegraph lines. He went to the GPO on Tuesday. Imprisoned at Frongoch.

Thomas O'Reilly; Four Courts, imprisoned at Frongoch.

Cpt. James O'Sullivan; Battalion Adjutant, he occupied positions on the Cabra Road and South Circular Road, then went to the GPO.

Bernard Parker; a member of the Fianna, he was in the Magazine Fort

T. Peppard; Mendicity Institute

Frank Pollard; Four Courts, imprisoned at Frongoch.

Stephen Pollard; Four Courts

Stephen Prendergast; Four Courts

Seán Price

Albert Sylvester Rawley; Four Courts

Joseph Redmond; imprisoned at Frongoch.

Laurence Regan; Four Courts

Seán Reid; Four Courts

John Richmond; Four Courts, imprisoned at Frongoch.

Joseph Roache; Four Courts

E. Roche (de Roiste); Mendicity Institute

Michael Joseph Roche; Four Courts, imprisoned at Frongoch.

Timothy (Tom) Roche; he commandeered the jaunting car for the Fianna escape from Phoenix Park.

William Ross; imprisoned at Frongoch.

William Ryan (Liam S. Ó Riain); Four Courts

Michael Sanders; Four Courts

F.K. Scullan; imprisoned at Frongoch.

Michael Scully (Micheal Ó Scollaighe); Four Courts

William Scully; Four Courts

Charles Sheehy; Four Courts

James Sheridan; Four Courts

John Sheridan; imprisoned at Frongoch.

Thomas Sherrin; he was in North King Street.

Frank Shouldice; he was in Fr Mathew Hall: 'It was a terrible slaughter.' He was a very effective sniper, firing from a perch on the Jameson's Tower. Imprisoned at Frongoch

Lt Jack Shouldice

Liam Siuptal; Four Courts

Thomas Smart; Four Courts

Liam Staines; Mendicity Institute, he was badly wounded.

Paddy Stephenson

Paddy Swann; deported after the Rising. His brother was in the GPO.

Joseph Sweeney; Four Courts

Éamonn Tierney; from London, he 'Fetched the flag' on the retreat from North King Street, and was unscathed.

Liam Tobin; Four Courts.

Michael Tobin; Four Courts
Edward Travers; Four Courts
James Walsh; Four Courts, imprisoned at Frongoch.
**Philip Walshe (28)
George Ward; Four Courts
Gilbert Ward (Gilbert Mac an Bhaird); Four Courts
Seán Ward; Four Courts
James Weldon; imprisoned at Frongoch.
George Whelan; Four Courts, imprisoned at Frongoch.
John Williams; Four Courts
John Williamson; he served in North King Street.
James Wilson; Mendicity Institute
Mark Wilson; Four Courts, imprisoned at Frongoch.
Peter Wilson
**Peter Wilson; a Swords Volunteer, he was killed by a British sniper at the Mendicity Institute when the Volunteers were being formed up to leave after their surrender.
William Wilson

1st Battalion, Women

Margaret Byrne (Copeland); Four Courts
Mary Byrne; Four Courts
Maire (Meg) Carron (Maire McCarron); imprisoned.
Áine ui Chonail
Mrs Martin Conlon
Marcella Cosgrave
Katie Derham; she and Brigid Lyons went from the Four Courts to set up a canteen and first-aid station at 5 Church Street Upper.
Eilis Elliott (Ni Birain); sister, Four Courts
Emily Elliott (Ledwith); sister, Four Courts
M. Elliott
Ellen (Nellie) Ennis (Costigan); Four Courts. Imprisoned.
Anna (Mrs Frank) Fahy; Four Courts
Dora Hartford
Mary Christina Hayes (O'Gorman); Four Courts
Cathleen Healy; Four Courts
Teresa Healy (Byrne); Four Courts
Áine Heron
May Kavanaugh (Duggan); Four Courts
Kathleen Kenny (Blackhead); Four Courts
Bessie Lynch (Kelly)

Brigid Lyons (Thornton); went with Katie Derham from the Four Courts to set up a canteen and first aid station at 5 Church Street Upper.[999] Imprisoned in Kilmainham Gaol.

Lt Catherine (Katy) McGuinness; Four Courts. Wife of Joe, and aunt of Brigid Lyons.

Rose McGuinness; wounded by flying glass, she was a cousin of Brigid Lyons.

Rose McManners; Vice Commandant of the Inghinidhe branch of Cumann na mBan and chief cook of the garrison.

Brigid (Brid) S. Martin; imprisoned.

Kathleen (Kate) Martin

Margaret Martin (Murname); Four Courts

Florence (Flossie) Mead

Caroline (Carrie) Mitchell

May Moloney (McQuiale); Four Courts

Pauline Morkan (Keating); Four Courts

Phyllis Morkan; Four Courts

Elizabeth (Lily) Murnane (Coleton); Four Courts

Mrs E. (Seámus) Murphy

Brigid Murrane (McKeon); Four Courts

Mary Murray (Allen); Four Courts

Áine Ní Rian

Mary O'Carroll (Lawlor); Four Courts

Eilis (Ni Riain) O'Connell (Bean Ui Chonaill); Four Courts

Ellen O'Flanagan (Parker); Four Courts

Annie O'Keefe (O'Carroll); Four Courts

Maura O'Neill (Mackay)

Louise (Dolly) O'Sullivan (Pollard); Four Courts, imprisoned.

Mary (Mollie) O'Sullivan (O'Carroll); Four Courts

Eileen Parker

Mary Stephenson; Four Courts

Peig Bean Ui Channallan; Four Courts

Eileen Walsh (Murphy); Four Courts

2nd Battalion, Men

Most mustered at St Stephen's Green and occupied Jacob's Biscuit Factory on Peter Street and Bishop Street, but about half the battalion went to the GPO after mustering at Fr Mathew Park in Fairview; garrison total about 190 men and women; killed, 3; executed, 3.

Commandant Thomas MacDonagh (Tomás MacDonnchada, executed 3 May 1916, aged 38).*

---

[999] Griffith and O'Grady. *Ireland's Unfinished Revolution*, pp. 53 ff.

Michael O'Hanrahan (Micheal Ó hAnnrachain, executed 4 May 1916) Vice-Commandant.* In Kilmainham, he was in cell Number 67 and was seen by his sisters, Áine (Ciss), Maire and Eily,[1000] and he was attended by Fr Albert.

James Barrett

William Barrett

Joseph Begley

John Bermingham; imprisoned at Frongoch.

William Berry

William J. Blake

Gerald Boland (Gearóid Ó Beolain); Harry's brother. Gerald was imprisoned in Frongoch with Michael Collins, where his dislike for Collins increased.

Francis Brady

John Brady

Patrick Brady; imprisoned at Frongoch.

Laurence Brennan

Patrick Breslin; imprisoned at Frongoch.

John Brian

William J. Buckley

Thomas Burke; imprisoned at Frongoch, and became a Vice-President of the General Council.

**James Byrne (19)

Joseph Byrne (Seosamh de Brun)

Vincent Byrne (14); became a member of 'The Squad'.

William Byrne

John Callaghan (Seán Ó Ceallachain)

James Carberry

Francis Joseph Carney

James Casey (Seámus Ó Casaigh); imprisoned at Frongoch.

James Cassells; imprisoned at Frongoch.

Daniel Chambers

Peter Christie; imprisoned at Frongoch.

Seán Colbert

Andrew Comerford; imprisoned at Frongoch.

James (Jimmy) Conroy, Jnr; from Dublin, he bought the paraffin to burn the Custom House in 1921.

James Conroy; quite aged, he was Jimmy's father.

Joseph Cotter

Richard Cotter

Thomas Cotter

Peter Cullen

James Cunningham; imprisoned at Frongoch.

1000 O'Reilly, Eily O'Hanrahan. Witness Statements 270, 415.

Michael Curtain (Micheal Ó Cortain)

William Daly (Liam Ó Dáilaigh); imprisoned at Frongoch.

Patrick Leo Darcy; imprisoned at Frongoch.

Seán Deegan

Patrick Dolan

Peter Dolan

Thomas Doyle; imprisoned at Frongoch.

Thomas Drumm

Samuel Ellis; imprisoned at Frongoch.

Christopher Ennis; imprisoned at Frongoch.

Michael Ennis; imprisoned at Frongoch.

James Fairhill (Seámus Ó Maoilfinn)

James Farrell

Christopher Farrelly

Michael Fitzpatrick

Michael Fleming; imprisoned at Frongoch. He later hid Seán Treacy after Treacy's escape from Professor Carolan's house.

John Furlong

Joseph Furlong; from Wexford and an IRB member. Prior to the Rising he was engaged in undercover work for the IRB.

Matthew Furlong

Tadhg Gahan

D.P. Gleeson

Charles Goulding; imprisoned at Frongoch. His son, Cathal, born in 1922, became Chief of Staff of the IRA from 1962 until the split between the Official and Provisional IRA in December 1969, when he became a founding member of Official Sinn Féin.

James Goulding; imprisoned at Frongoch.

Richard Grattan

John (Seán) Gregory; imprisoned at Frongoch.

Michael Hayes (Ó hAodha); a founder member of the Irish Volunteers in 1913, he managed to avoid arrest after the Rising. He sheltered Sinn Féin colleagues during the War of Independence in Ballykinlar camp. While in prison he was elected as a Sinn Féin TD in the 1921 General Election for the National University of Ireland. He was released after the Truce of August 1921, supported the Treaty and served as Minister for Education from January to September 1922. He was Ceann Comhairle from 1923 to 1932. Of the Rising, he felt that 'this was the only course but that the venture was a hopeless one'.

James Hayes (Seámus Ó hAodha); imprisoned at Frongoch.

Robert Humphreys; imprisoned at Frongoch.

Thomas (Tom) Hunter; Battalion Vice-Commandant, he tearfully informed rank and file of their surrender. He broke his sword in two on the stairway before he informed his men. He was de Valera's ADC in Lewes Prison. TD for Cork North East in the first two Dáils.

John Joyce; imprisoned at Frongoch.

Joseph James Joyce

Daniel Kavanaugh

Patrick Keane (Padraig Ó Cathalain)

Peadar Kearney (Peadar Ó Cearnaigh); one of a group which seized Barmack's Malthouse in New Row (Fumbally Lane). Upon being informed of the surrender, he was one of those who argued for a mass breakout to the hills. He wrote 'A Soldier's Song'.

Frank Kearns; imprisoned at Frongoch.

John Kearns; brother, imprisoned at Frongoch.

Joseph Kearns; brother, imprisoned at Frongoch.

Thomas Kearns; brother, imprisoned at Frongoch.

Henry Kelly

John Kelly

Joseph Kelly (Seosamh S. Ó Cellaigh)

Patrick Kelly (Padraig Ó Cellaigh); he went to the Fairyhouse Races on Easter Monday, and while there heard about the Rising. He arrived at the GPO that night and was told to go to Jacob's. He was imprisoned at Frongoch.

James Kenny; imprisoned at Frongoch.

Thomas Keogh; became a member of 'The Squad'.

Seán King

John Watson Lake

Edward (Ned) Lane

Patrick Lanigan; imprisoned at Frongoch.

M. Lawless

Patrick Long

Thomas Losty; imprisoned at Frongoch.

Michael Love

Seán Lynch

William Lynch; imprisoned at Frongoch.

Edward Lyons; imprisoned at Frongoch.

Maj. John MacBride (Seán MacBhríde, executed 5 May 1916, aged 51).* 'Liberty is a priceless thing and anyone of you that sees a chance, take it. I'd do so myself but my liberty days are over. Good luck, boys. Many of you may live to fight another day. Take my advice, never allow yourselves to be cooped inside the walls of a building again.' In Kilmainham, Fr Augustine, to whom he said 'It's not the first time I looked down their guns, Father', attended him.[1001] 'Mind the Flag' reportedly were his last words before the firing squad. He was witness at the New York wedding of Tom and Kathleen Clarke.

1001 Augustine, Revd OFM. Witness Statement 920.

John MacDonagh, brother of Thomas. Interned at Frongoch. He was a theatre manager and directed Michael Collins' 1919 film promoting the Dáil Loan.

Bernard J. MacMahon

Richard McDavitt (Risteard MacDaibhis)

Owen McDermott

Matthew McDonnell; imprisoned at Frongoch.

Michael (Mick) McDonnell; imprisoned at Knutsford and Frongoch, became a member of 'The Squad'.

Patrick McDonnell; imprisoned at Frongoch.

Patrick McEvoy

John McGlure

Thomas McGrane

Daniel McGrane

Daniel McGrath

Dick McKee; became O/C of the Dublin Brigade and was murdered on Bloody Sunday. Imprisoned at Frongoch.

James McParland

William Maher

Patrick Manning

Peter Martin; imprisoned at Frongoch.

Michael Meade

Owen Meade

John Meldon

Thomas Meldon

Michael Molloy; one of the printers of the *Proclamation*, he was chosen by James Connolly to oversee the printing, as he was an experienced compositor. He was detailed to Fumbally Lane, one of the Jacob's outposts, at the start of the Rising, and later did duty on one of the Jacob's towers. He carried with him the piece of paper signed by the signatories to the *Proclamation* until he found himself in Richmond Barracks after the surrender, when he chewed it up and spat it out to prevent its discovery. He was sent to Knutsford Prison, and thence to Frongoch.[1002] He was released in August 1916.

Richard Molloy; imprisoned at Frongoch.

James Moran (Seámus O Murain)

Patrick (Paddy) Moran; imprisoned at Frongoch. He was hanged at Mountjoy Prison for the Bloody Sunday killings even though he hadn't taken part in the killings for which he was charged. (See Kilmainham Gaol, Mountjoy Prison.)

Martin Mullen; imprisoned at Frongoch.

John J. (Seán) Murphy; imprisoned at Frongoch.

Patrick Nolan; imprisoned at Frongoch.

Patrick O'Byrne; imprisoned at Frongoch.

1002 Molloy, Michael. Witness Statement 716.

Art Ó Cahill
James Joseph O'Carroll
James O'Carroll
Richard O'Carroll
Patrick O'Connell
**Patrick O'Connor
Christopher O'Donnell
James O'Donnell
**John O'Grady (27); one of fifteen cyclists who set off to relieve some of de Valera's
men in Boland's. They were unable to force their way in, and he was killed on
the return journey: 'I fear they got me.' He had been married only eight months.
Hugh O'Hagan
Edward O'Hanrahan; imprisoned at Frongoch.
Henry O'Hanrahan; he was a brother of Michael, 2nd Battalion Vice Commandant.
Joseph O'Hanrahan
Christopher O'Malley
Patrick O'Reilly; imprisoned at Frongoch.
Thomas O'Reilly; imprisoned at Frongoch.
Lt Danny O'Riordan
Fred O'Rourke; later with the St Stephen's Green garrison.
John O'Rourke (Seán Ó Ruairc)
Michael O'Rourke; imprisoned at Frongoch.
Thomas O'Rourke (Tomas Ó Ruairc)
Dermot O'Shea
James O'Shea; imprisoned at Frongoch.
Michael Phelan; imprisoned at Frongoch.
James S. (Seámus) Pounch; a member of Fianna Éireann, of the so-called 'Surrey
House Clique', a number of Fianna boys who used to meet regularly at Countess
Markievicz's house in Leinster Road, Rathmines.[1003] In Jacob's, he was responsible
for provisions, and describes raiding surrounding shops for bread, potatoes and
other food. He also describes a 'miniature céilí' in the factory and the construction
of an improvised Tricolour from materials to hand.
Éamon (Bob) Price; Cpt. of C Company, imprisoned at Frongoch and became
O/C of J Company of the North Camp. He married Maire nic Shiubhlaigh.
Thomas Pugh; a member of the Socialist Party of Ireland, but joined the Volunteers
rather than the Citizen Army because Richard Mulcahy persuaded him. When
the order for the Rising was countermanded, he went to an exhibition of paint-
ings in the Royal Hibernian Academy, and mobilised the next day. He later met
his wife in Knutsford Prison, where he was sent after the surrender.
Patrick Redmond; imprisoned at Frongoch.
William J. Redmond

1003 Pounch, Seámus. Witness Statements 267, 294.

John A. Reynolds

Seán Roche

Richard Roe

Patrick Rooney

Dennis Ross

John Ryder

William Ryder

Frederick Schweppe; imprisoned at Frongoch.

Philip Shanahan; imprisoned at Frongoch. He was originally from Tipperary and
his pub on Foley Street was 'home' to Volunteers from 'the country'.

Denis Shelly

Thomas Shelley; imprisoned at Frongoch.

Michael Sheppard; imprisoned at Frongoch.

James Shiels; imprisoned at Frongoch.

Terence Simpson; imprisoned at Frongoch.

Michael Slater

Thomas Slater; a member of the IRB since 1905.

William Slater

James Slattery (14); imprisoned at Frongoch. He became a member of 'The Squad'
and lost an arm in the Custom House fire, May 1921.

Michael Smyth; imprisoned at Frongoch.

Daniel Charles Somers

William (Bill) Stapleton; he was the guard commander. Imprisoned at Frongoch.
He became a member of 'The Squad'.

Dick Stokes

P. Emmett Sweeney

Joseph Tormey (Seosamh Ó Torma)

John Turner

Andrew Tyrell

John Walker (brother)

Michael Walker (brother)

John Walsh

Patrick Walsh; imprisoned at Frongoch.

Martin Walton (15); his parents did not want him to fight so they took the valves
from his bicycle tyres, and he was unable to get to Jacob's until Tuesday morning.
He fought for the Free State in the Civil War. A great friend of Michael Collins.

George Ward; imprisoned at Frongoch.

Nicholas Ward

Christopher Whelehan

Henry J. Williams

Peter Williams; imprisoned at Frongoch.

2nd Battalion, Women

Cecelia Conroy (O'Neill)
Maire Deegan
Saoirse Hayes (MacAodha)
Sara Kealy
Kathleen McCarthy (Lane)
Teresa Magee
Maire Nic Shiubhlaigh (née Molly Walker) (Mrs Éamon [Bob] Price); in command of the women, she was a famous actress in the early days of the Abbey Theatre.
Annie O'Hagan (McQuade)
Eileen (Eily) O'Hanrahan (O'Reilly); sister of Michael O'Hanrahan, who was executed. On the Wednesday before the Rising she undertook to go to Enniscorthy, Co. Wexford, to deliver a dispatch (sewn into the lining of her red fox fur) to the leader of the Volunteers there. She assumed this dispatch to be an order to rise. On her way back, she met Min Ryan, whom, she later concluded, had delivered a countermanding order.[1004] This was confirmed years later by the recipient of both, Seámus Doyle.
Josie Pollard (Daly)
Kathleen Pollard (McDonald) (sister of Josie)

3rd Battalion

Boland's Bakery/Mill; A, B and D Companies mustered in Great Brunswick Street. C Company mustered in Earlsfort Terrace; garrison totals about 180; killed, 10. Boland's Mill, Grand Canal Street, Westland Row Station, and Mount Street Bridge.

Commandant Éamon de Valera; In Kilmainham, he was in cell number 59. While on penal servitude at Princetown in Dartmoor, Devonshire, though, his number was Convict 95, and there was a song written with that number in the title:

> 'Twas in Kilmainham prison yard our fifteen [*sic*] martyrs died
> And cold and still in Arbour Hill they are lying side by side,
> But we will yet pay back the debt for the spirit is still alive
> In men who stood through fire and blood with Prisoner 95.

Patrick Baird (Padraig Mac an Bhaird)
Henry Banks; imprisoned at Frongoch.
Seán Banks
P. Begley; Vice-Commandant at Boland's and left his post on Thursday.
Stephen Boylan
John Bracken; imprisoned at Frongoch.

1004 O'Reilly, Eily O'Hanrahan. Witness Statements 270, 415.

John Bracken Jnr; imprisoned at Frongoch.

John (Seán) Breen; imprisoned at Frongoch.

Patrick Brennan

Toby Breslin

William Brown; imprisoned at Frongoch.

James Browne

William Browne

Frederick Burton

C. Byrne

Dermot Byrne

Henry Byrne; imprisoned at Frongoch.

John Byrne; imprisoned at Frongoch.

**Joseph Byrne (32)

Michael Byrne; imprisoned at Frongoch.

Paddy Byrne; 1, 2 Clanwilliam Place/25 Northumberland Road detachment, sent home because of his youth.

Patrick Byrne; imprisoned at Frongoch.

Peter Byrne

Thomas Byrne

Dudley Carroll

Christopher Carbury (Christoir Ó Cuirbre); tortured in Dublin Castle during the War of Independence.

Leo Casey; imprisoned at Frongoch.

Thomas Cassidy; imprisoned at Frongoch.

William Christian; 1, 2 Clanwilliam Place/25 Northumberland Road detachment. Imprisoned at Frongoch.

Joe Clarke; 1, 2 Clanwilliam Place/25 Northumberland Road detachment. Imprisoned at Frongoch.

Peter Coates; imprisoned at Frongoch.

Daniel Colgan

William Conroy

Robert Cooper

John Cosgrove; imprisoned at Frongoch.

**2Lt John Costello

Thomas Coyne

Cpt. Michael Cullen; erected the decoy flag on the Ringsend Distillery tower. He 'watched over' de Valera when de Valera went to sleep and then cried 'set the Railway on fire'. Imprisoned at Frongoch.

Seán Cullen

James Daly

Cpt. Simon Donnelly; O/C of C Company. He joined the IRB in 1914 and was part of the Howth gunrunning project. He was one of the Volunteers who bought his own rifle and bought his Martini in 1914. Imprisoned at Frongoch and became O/C of H Company of the North Camp.

Michael Donovan

James (Seámus) Doyle; 1, 2 Clanwilliam Place/25 Northumberland Road detachment. Imprisoned at Frongoch.

James H. Doyle; imprisoned at Frongoch.

**Patrick Doyle (36); 1, 2 Clanwilliam Place/25 Northumberland Road detachment. He was a Volunteer musketry instructor.

Patrick J. Doyle; O/C at St Stephen's Parochial Hall, 1, 2 Clanwilliam Place/25 Northumberland Road detachment. Imprisoned at Frongoch.

Thomas Drennan; imprisoned at Frongoch.

John Dunne (Seán O Duinn); imprisoned at Frongoch.

**Edward Ennis (33)

Timothy Finn; imprisoned at Frongoch.

Lt James Fitzgerald; imprisoned at Frongoch.

Leo Fitzgerald

Thomas Fitzgerald; imprisoned at Frongoch.

Willie Fitzgerald (15); imprisoned at Frongoch.

John Fitzpaul (Seán Mac Giollaphol)

Paddy Flanagan

Michael Fleming; imprisoned at Frongoch.

John Flynn

Thomas Fullam

Patrick Gilbride (Padraig MacGiolla Bhridge)

James Gill; imprisoned at Frongoch.

Edward Gordon

James Grace; 1, 2 Clanwilliam Place/25 Northumberland Road detachment.

Martin Griffin; imprisoned at Frongoch.

Lt John (Seán) Guilfoyle; wanted to escape to the mountains and continue fighting. He tunnelled into a shop across from Beggar's Bush Barracks and harrassed the Barracks with rifle-fire. Imprisoned at Frongoch and became O/C of F Company of the North Camp.

Joseph Guilfoyle; brother of John, he had been guarding a bridge on the line to Harcourt Street Station. Imprisoned at Frongoch.

Augustine Hayes (Ó hAodha); imprisoned at Frongoch.

James Henry; imprisoned at Frongoch.

Michael Hickey; imprisoned at Frongoch.

Sam Irwin

Francis Jackson

Joseph Jackson; imprisoned at Frongoch.

James Kavanaugh; imprisoned at Frongoch.

Peter (Peadar) Kavanaugh; imprisoned at Frongoch.

William (Liam) Kavanaugh; imprisoned at Frongoch.

Michael Kearney (Michael Ó Caomhanaigh)

Patrick Kelly; imprisoned at Frongoch.

Thomas Kelly; imprisoned at Frongoch.

Charles Kenny; imprisoned at Frongoch.

John Kinsella; imprisoned at Frongoch.

Edward Kirwan

Edward (Éamon) Lawlor

Edward Leonard

Michael Lennon (Miceal Ó Leannain); imprisoned at Frongoch.

Leo Lifforoi

George A. Lyons; he was a B Company officer, and was in the Westland Row Railway Station detatchment.[1005]

Patrick MacCormack; originally from Belfast, imprisoned at Frongoch.

Joe MacDermott

Cathal MacDowell; imprisoned at Frongoch.

Seán (John) MacMahon

Owen McArdle

Patrick McBride; imprisoned at Frongoch.

William (Liam) McCabe; imprisoned at Frongoch.

Patrick McCabe; imprisoned at Frongoch.

Bernard McCarthy; imprisoned at Frongoch.

Michael McCarthy; imprisoned at Frongoch.

Joseph McCurran

Joseph McDermott

Seán McDermott

Andrew McDonnell; armed only with a pike, he was ordered to stop a tram outside de Valera's HQ.

Patrick McDowell

Seán McEffoy

Patrick McGill (Padraig MacGhaill); imprisoned at Frongoch.

P.B. McGrath; 1, 2 Clanwilliam Place/25 Northumberland Road detachment. Imprisoned at Frongoch.

Cpt. John (Seán) McMahon; he was O/C of B Company, and imprisoned at Frongoch.

**Peadar Macken; an officer, he reprimanded a Volunteer who kept ignoring the order for silence. The truculent Volunteer shot him through the heart.

James Mallon; imprisoned at Frongoch.

**Lt Michael Malone (28); O/C of the 25 Northumberland Road detachment. He was the best marksman in his company. De Valera ended up with his Mauser and kept it for the rest of his life.

Robert Malone; imprisoned at Frongoch.

1005 Lyons, George A. 'Occupation of Ringsend Area in 1916', *An tOglach*, 10-24 April 1926.

Joe Martin

Michael Meagher

Patrick Meagher

Michael Merriman

Joseph Molloy; imprisoned at Frongoch.

Cpt. Frank Mullen; halted his company on Mount Street Bridge and told them: 'Any Volunteer who wishes may hand over his rifle and leave our ranks.' Only one did.

Patrick Mullen; imprisoned at Frongoch.

Christopher Murphy

John Murphy; imprisoned at Frongoch.

**Richard Murphy; 1, 2 Clanwilliam Place/25 Northumberland Road detachment.

William (Liam) Murphy; imprisoned at Frongoch.

Frank Murray

Michael Murray

Seámus Murray

Arthur Nolan; he was a baker at Boland's.

Patrick Nolan

Peter Nolan; ripped out rails on the line to Harcourt Street Station.

John Nugent

Joseph Nugent

William O'Brien; imprisoned at Frongoch, and became O/C of Company of the North Camp.

William (Liam) Ó Broin

Lt Joseph O'Byrne; Red Cross officer, served as a doctor. Imprisoned at Frongoch.
   Thomas O'Byrne; imprisoned at Frongoch.

Cpt. Joseph O'Connor; he was Vice-Commandant and O/C of A Company. Michael Malone said to him on Good Friday: 'Well, Joe, it's pretty close to hand. I know you'll come through, but I won't.' Imprisoned at Frongoch and became O/C in charge of the 5th Dormitory.

Denis O'Donoghue; 1, 2 Clanwilliam Place/25 Northumberland Road detachment.

Anthony O'Grady

John O'Hanlon; imprisoned at Frongoch.

John (Seán) O'Keefe; an ICA member, imprisoned at Frongoch.

Peter O'Meara (Peadar Ó Meadra); imprisoned at Frongoch.

Andrew O'Neill

Christopher O'Reilly

Patrick O'Reilly; imprisoned at Frongoch.

Thomas O'Rourke

Seán O'Shea

Seámus O'Treacy

Richard Parle (16) 'Go home mother, this is no place for a woman.' Imprisoned at Frongoch.

Thomas Peate; imprisoned at Frongoch.

Denis Peelo

James Pender; imprisoned at Frongoch.

Owen Porter; imprisoned at Frongoch.

Patrick Power; imprisoned at Frongoch.

James Purfield

Lt John Quinn; he commanded B Company at Westland Row Station.

Seán Quinn

Thomas Quinn; imprisoned at Frongoch.

Liam Raftis

James Redican; imprisoned at Frongoch.

John Reid; imprisoned at Frongoch.

Patrick Reid

**George Reynolds; a silversmith by trade, he was O/C in Clanwilliam House, 1, 2 Clanwilliam Place.

Patrick Roe

William Roe

William (Willie) Ronan (Rownan?); 1, 2 Clanwilliam Place/25 Northumberland Road detachment.

Michael Rowe; 1, 2 Clanwilliam Place/25 Northumberland Road detachment, sent home because of his youth.

Cornelius Ryan

Thomas Shelly (Tomas Ó Scolaige)

Liam Stanley

John Stokes; imprisoned at Frongoch.

Michael A. (Miceal) Tannam; imprisoned at Frongoch.

Alexander Thompson

Thomas Traynor; imprisoned at Frongoch. A bootmaker from Tullow, Co. Carlow and father of 10 children, he was executed in Mountjoy Prison on 25 April 1921.

John Vincent (Seán Mac UinSeánn)

John Walker; imprisoned at Frongoch.

James Walsh; 1, 2 Clanwilliam Place/25 Northumberland Road detachment. Imprisoned at Frongoch.

Thomas Walsh; 1, 2 Clanwilliam Place/25 Northumberland Road detachment.

Patrick Ward; he'd had pneumonia earlier in the year and moved to Sandyford. He did not receive notice of the Rising and so reported only on Tuesday morning. Imprisoned at Frongoch.

James Watters; imprisoned at Frongoch.

**Patrick Whelan (23); he had been dispatched to Tralee, but returned with the discouraging news of Casement's capture, and that Robert Monteith denounced the Germans bitterly.

Patrick Williams; imprisoned at Frongoch.

William Woodcock; imprisoned at Frongoch.

De Valera was the only battalion commandant who did not allow women in the garrison.

4th Battalion, Men

South Dublin Union Workhouse, mustered in Emerald Square, Dolphin's Barn; garrison total about 230 men and women; killed, 8; executed, 2. Fairbrother's Field, James's Street, Jameson's Distillery, Marrowbone Lane, Mount Brown, Roe's Distillery, Watkins Brewery, Ardee Street. Ceannt surrendered 42 (actually 43 were still active as Brugha was still there and alive).

Commandant Éamonn (Edmund) Ceannt (executed 8 May 1916, aged 34);* In Kilmainham, he was in cell number 88 (upper floor) and was moved to cell number 20. He was seen by his wife Áine, Lily O'Brennan (Áine's sister), and attended by Fr Augustine.[1006] Ceannt hoped for 1000 men, but only about 100 showed up on Monday.

John Adams; Marrowbone Lane
James Arnold; South Dublin Union, imprisoned at Frongoch.
Patrick Bailey; Marrowbone Lane
William Bowles; Roe's Distillery
Joseph Bowman; Marrowbone Lane, imprisoned at Frongoch.
William Bowman; Marrowbone Lane
Thomas Boylan; South Dublin Union
Seámus Breathnach; Marrowbone Lane
Cathal Brugha, Vice-Commandant; South Dublin Union. First President Pro Tem of Dáil Éireann, then Minister for Defence.
James Burke; South Dublin Union
Matthew Burke; Marrowbone Lane, imprisoned at Frongoch.
**William F. (Frank) Burke; South Dublin Union
Con Butler; Marrowbone Lane
James Butler; Marrowbone Lane
Mick Butler
Alphonsus Byrne; Marrowbone Lane
Christopher Byrne; Marrowbone Lane
Frank Byrne; Marrowbone Lane, imprisoned at Frongoch.
George Byrne; Roe's Distillery
James Byrne; Marrowbone Lane, imprisoned at Frongoch.
Joseph Byrne; South Dublin Union, imprisoned at Frongoch.
Liam Byrne; South Dublin Union

1006 Augustine, Revd OFM. Witness Statement 920.

Michael Byrne; Marrowbone Lane

Patrick Byrne; Marrowbone Lane

Leo Carroll; South Dublin Union

Thomas Carty; Marrowbone Lane, imprisoned at Frongoch.

Joseph Clarke; Marrowbone Lane, imprisoned at Frongoch.

William Coady; South Dublin Union, imprisoned at Frongoch.

Con Colbert (Conchubhair Ó Colbaird, exected 8 May 1916, aged 28);* Watkin's Brewery/Ardee Street Brewery. In Kilmainham he was in cell number 17, and was seen by the wife of prisoner Seámus Ó Murchadha. Fr Augustine attended him: 'Perhaps I'll never again get the chance of knowing when I was to die, and so I'll try and die well.'[1007]

William (Liam) Condron; South Dublin Union, imprisoned at Frongoch.

Joseph Corcoran, OFM; Marrowbone Lane

James Corrigan; Marrowbone Lane

Philip Cosgrave

Lt William Cosgrave; Adjutant and Brugha's deputy. A Sinn Féin Councillor on the Dublin Corporation. He was the first Irish Minister for Local Government, then succeeded Griffith, then Collins as the head of the Free State Government.

James Coughlan; a member of C Company, imprisoned at Frongoch.

John Cullen; Marrowbone Lane, imprisoned at Frongoch.

Thomas Cullen; South Dublin Union. Became one of Michael Collins' most trusted lieutenants. Imprisoned at Frongoch.

Michael Cunningham; Roe's Distillery

John Darcy; Marrowbone Lane

William Dempsey; Marrowbone Lane

**Brendan Donnelan (18); a Fianna member, he was killed on the very first day of the Rising.

John Downey; South Dublin Union

Joseph Downey; Marrowbone Lane

Christopher Doyle; Marrowbone Lane, imprisoned at Frongoch.

Gerald Doyle; South Dublin Union

Alderman Peadar Doyle; Ceannt's orderly. Imprisoned at Frongoch. Later a TD and Lord Mayor of Dublin. His son, Seán, died fighting the English in 1920.

Thomas Doyle; Marrowbone Lane, imprisoned at Frongoch.

Seán Dowling

Dennis K. Dunne; Marrowbone Lane, imprisoned at Frongoch.

Patrick J. Dunne; Marrowbone Lane, imprisoned at Frongoch.

Peter Dunne (Peadar Ó Duinn); Marrowbone Lane; imprisoned at Frongoch.

Michael Dwyer; Marrowbone Lane, imprisoned at Frongoch.

John Edwards; Marrowbone Lane, imprisoned at Frongoch.

Patrick Egan; Roe's Distillery

1007 Augustine, Revd OFM. Witness Statement 920.

Robert Evans; South Dublin Union

William Fagan; Roe's Distillery

Michael Farrell; South Dublin Union

James Fitzpatrick; Marrowbone Lane, imprisoned at Frongoch.

James Flaherty (Seámus Ó Florbheartaigh); South Dublin Union

William Flaherty (Liam Ó Florbheartaigh); South Dublin Union. Imprisoned at Frongoch.

William Foley; Marrowbone Lane

James Foran; Ceannt gave him charge of the front gate of the Union. He and Cosgrave met Thomas MacDonagh to get the terms of surrender. Imprisoned in Knutsford Prison.

Cpt. Douglas ffrench-Mullen; a talented musician, wounded at the South Dublin Union.

Henry Gaskin

Edward Gibson; South Dublin Union, imprisoned at Frongoch.

Michael Gibson; South Dublin Union, imprisoned at Frongoch.

James Glynn; South Dublin Union, imprisoned at Frongoch.

John G. Gogan; Roe's Distillery

James Gregan; Marrowbone Lane, imprisoned at Frongoch.

D. Haran; Roe's Distillery

Patrick Harbone; Marrowbone Lane

Seán Harborne; Marrowbone Lane

Patrick Harman

Dan Holland; brother of Frank, Robert and Walter, imprisoned at Frongoch.

Frank Holland; brother, South Dublin Union, imprisoned at Frongoch.

Robert Holland; brother, shot an English sniper who appeared at a window dressed as a woman. His birthday was 25 April and Walter brought him a cake. Imprisoned in Frongoch.

Walter (Watty) Holland (15); brother, imprisoned at Frongoch.

George Irvine; South Dublin Union

John Joyce; a section-commander, he led an ambush of troops of the 3rd Royal Irish Regiment.

John Patrick Judge; Marrowbone Lane.

James Kavanaugh, brother; Marrowbone Lane, imprisoned at Frongoch.

Martin Kavanaugh, brother; Marrowbone Lane

Tom Kavanaugh; he was a brother of Martin and James.

Thomas Kearney (Tomas Ó Caomhanaighe); Marrowbone Lane, imprisoned at Frongoch.

Edward Keegan; South Dublin Union

Seán Keely; Roe's Distillery

William (Bill) Kelly; imprisoned at Frongoch.

Joseph F. Kelly; South Dublin Union

Joseph Kennedy; Marrowbone Lane

James Kenny; Marrowbone Lane, imprisoned at Frongoch.

James Kenny; South Dublin Union

Kieran Kenny; Marrowbone Lane, imprisoned at Frongoch.

John Keogh; Marrowbone Lane, imprisoned at Frongoch.

Martin Keogh; Roe's Distillery

Michael Kerr; South Dublin Union, imprisoned at Frongoch.

Sgt Owen Kerrigan; Marrowbone Lane, imprisoned at Frongoch.

John Keys; Marrowbone Lane

Patrick Lamb; Marrowbone Lane

James Leigh; Marrowbone Lane

Michael (Mick) Liston; known as 'Supersniper', he was the best shot in the battalion and was wounded.

**William MacDowell (44)

Dan MacCarthy; South Dublin Union, imprisoned at Frongoch.

Diarmuid MacNeill; Marrowbone Lane

Edward McCabe; Marrowbone Lane, imprisoned at Frongoch.

Michael McCabe; Marrowbone Lane

Peter McCabe; Marrowbone Lane, imprisoned at Frongoch.

William McCabe; Marrowbone Lane, imprisoned at Frongoch.

Patrick McCarthy; Marrowbone Lane

Cpt. Thomas McCarthy; he was in Roe's Distillery and left his post on Thursday.

Lughaidh McDermott (MacDuirmuid); Marrowbone Lane

William McDowell; South Dublin Union

Christopher McEvoy; Marrowbone Lane

John (Seán) McGlynn; South Dublin Union, imprisoned at Frongoch.

Joe McGrath; he escaped after the surrender: 'Toor-a-loo, boys, I'm off.' First Secretary of the National Aid and Volunteers' Dependents' Fund. He became a TD and a Minister, and later started the Irish Sweepstakes.

Patrick McGrath; Marrowbone Lane, imprisoned at Frongoch.

Seán McGrath; Marrowbone Lane

Bernard McKenna; Marrowbone Lane, imprisoned at Frongoch.

John McKenna; South Dublin Union

Daniel McMahon; South Dublin Union, imprisoned at Frongoch.

James Maguire; South Dublin Union, imprisoned at Frongoch.

Edward Marrinan; Marrowbone Lane

D.H. Mason; Marrowbone Lane

Patrick Moloney; South Dublin Union

John Morgan; Marrowbone Lane, imprisoned at Frongoch.

James Morrissey; South Dublin Union

Patrick Morrissey; South Dublin Union

Martin Mullen; Marrowbone Lane, imprisoned at Frongoch.

Patrick Mullen; Marrowbone Lane, imprisoned at Frongoch.

Francis (Frank) Murphy; Marrowbone Lane, imprisoned at Frongoch.

Cpt. James Murphy (Seámus Ó Murchadha); he was in Jameson's Distillery in Marrowbone Lane and in Roe's Distillery. Imprisoned at Frongoch.

John Murphy; South Dublin Union, imprisoned at Frongoch.

Gabriel Murray; Marrowbone Lane

Lt Henry (Harry) Murray; imprisoned at Frongoch.

Revd Eugene Nevin; acted as chaplain to the Volunteers.

John Nugent; Roe's Distillery

Denis O'Brien; Marrowbone Lane. He married Anne Cooney.

Denis O'Brien; South Dublin Union, imprisoned at Frongoch.

Lt Larry O'Brien; Marrowbone Lane

Laurence (Lorcan) O'Brien; Marrowbone Lane, imprisoned at Frongoch.

Liam O'Brien; South Dublin Union

Patrick O'Brien (Padraig Ó Broin); Marrowbone Lane

Peter (Peadar) O'Brien; Marrowbone Lane, imprisoned at Frongoch.

Stephen O'Brien; South Dublin Union, imprisoned at Frongoch.

Hugh O'Byrne; Marrowbone Lane, imprisoned at Frongoch.

John (Seán) O'Byrne; Marrowbone Lane, imprisoned at Frongoch.

'Big' Jim O'Callaghan

Michael (Mick) O'Callaghan; imprisoned at Frongoch.

Joseph O'Carroll; Marrowbone Lane

James O'Connell; Marrowbone Lane, imprisoned at Frongoch.

William O'Corrigan; South Dublin Union

John O'Doherty; South Dublin Union

John J. O'Gorman; Marrowbone Lane

Joseph O'Gorman; Marrowbone Lane, imprisoned at Frongoch.

Charles O'Grady; Roe's Distillery

James O'Hagen; Marrowbone Lane

Patrick O'Laughlin; South Dublin Union, imprisoned at Frongoch.

Edward O'Neill; Marrowbone Lane

Joseph O'Neill; Marrowbone Lane, imprisoned at Frongoch.

Michael O'Neill; Marrowbone Lane, imprisoned at Frongoch.

John O'Reilly

Patrick O'Reilly; South Dublin Union, imprisoned at Frongoch.

**Richard O'Reilly; South Dublin Union; a brother of John. Two other brothers were in the British Army and one of them was killed in France.

Michael O'Riordan; Marrowbone Lane

Patrick O'Rourke; Marrowbone Lane

Seán O'Shaughnessy; South Dublin Union

John O'Toole; Marrowbone Lane

**John (Seán) Owens; South Dublin Union

Henry Pender; Marrowbone Lane

George Plunkett

Arthur Power; brother of Liam.

Joseph Power (Seosamh Peiceir); Marrowbone Lane

Liam (Billy) Power; brother of Arthur.

George Quinn; imprisoned at Frongoch.

**James Quinn; South Dublin Union

Paddy Rigney; South Dublin Union

Mick Riordan

William Roche; Marrowbone Lane, imprisoned at Frongoch.

James Russell; South Dublin Union, imprisoned at Frongoch.

Frank Saul; Marrowbone Lane with his brother Jack.

Jack Saul; Marrowbone Lane, imprisoned at Frongoch.

David Sears; he was the youngest in the garrison. He and his father, William, were journalists, and William became a TD in the first four Dáils.

Michael Sweeney; South Dublin Union

James Teehan; Marrowbone Lane

Seán Tracey; South Dublin Union

**John (Seán) J. Traynor (17); South Dublin Union; he was the best shot in his company.

Dan Troy; Marrowbone Lane, imprisoned at Frongoch.

Paddy Troy; Marrowbone Lane. He was a brother of Dan and imprisoned at Frongoch.

Thomas Venables; Marrowbone Lane, imprisoned at Frongoch.

James Walsh; Marrowbone Lane, imprisoned at Frongoch.

Patrick Walsh; Marrowbone Lane, imprisoned at Frongoch.

Bernard Ward; Roe's Distillery

Patrick Ward; Roe's Distillery, imprisoned at Frongoch.

Peter Ward; South Dublin Union, imprisoned at Frongoch.

Richard Whelan; South Dublin Union, imprisoned at Frongoch.

Mick White

E.C. Young; Marrowbone Lane

Patrick Young; Marrowbone Lane

Robert Young; Marrowbone Lane, imprisoned at Frongoch.

Tom Young; brother of Robert. He led a patrol to scout the Ardee Street Brewery for Con Colbert. Imprisoned at Frongoch.

4th Battalion, Women

The women's HQ was in Marrowbone Lane where they guarded the rear of the South Dublin Union.

Katie Byrne; imprisoned.

Mary (May) Byrne (Doyle)

Winnie Byrne

Áine (Annie) Cooney (O'Brien) (20) (sister); imprisoned. From a very nationalist family, her first job was selling souvenir programmes at the funeral of Jeremiah O'Donovan Rossa. She recalled that when being marched to Kilmainham Gaol she and the other women prisoners were taunted by women who had men serving in France. These women had been deprived of their 'separation allowance' when the GPO was occupied, and as a result many families faced hunger and hardship until things were sorted out. Before he was executed, the sisters saw Con Colbert for the last time in Kilmainham Gaol. He wrote to Áine and Lily and left them his gloves and rosary beads.[1008]

Eileen Cooney (Harbourne) (16) (sister); imprisoned.

Lily Cooney (Curran) (18) (sister); imprisoned.

Alice Corcoran

Marcella Cosgrave; Quartermaster and Second in Command. Imprisoned.

Miss Cumiskey

Brigid Hegarty (Harmon)

Margaret Hennessey; later she was elected a Senator.

Josephine Kelly (Greene); imprisoned

Margaret L. Kennedy

Agnes MacNamee; imprisoned.

Josephine (Josie) McGowan; she loaded two rifles in turn for Robert Holland, and from their position in one of the grain storerooms they commanded the view to the west for four days of fighting. Imprisoned.

Rose (McNamara) (Mrs Seámus) Murphy (Ó Murchadha); her husband was Cpt. Murphy. She was the women's commander. She cooked for the Marrowbone Lane garrison. At Kilmainham Gaol, she met John MacBride who told her 'You'll be all right, you'll be out tomorrow.' Of himself, he said 'Ah no, we won't be out, we'll be shot.'[1009] Imprisoned.

Two Monaghan sisters

Lizzie Mulhall; imprisoned.

Rose Mullally (Farrelly); imprisoned

Kathleen Murphy

Lily O'Brennan; she was Éamonn Ceannt's sister-in-law, Áine's sister, and was imprisoned in Kilmainham after the Rising when he was there. She and Áine saw him before his execution.

Cissie O'Flaherty

Margaret O'Flaherty (Simmons); imprisoned

Mollie O'Hanlon

Sheila (Sighle) O'Hanlon (Lynch); imprisoned

1008 O'Brien, Annie (née Cooney). Statement 805. Jointly with her sisters: Eileen (Cooney) Harbourne and Lily (Cooney) Curran. **1009** McNamara, Rose. Witness Statement 482.

Josephine (Josie) O'Keefe; imprisoned
Emily O'Keefe (Hendley); imprisoned
Maria Quigley (Clince); imprisoned
Priscilla (Cilla) Quigley (Kavanaugh); imprisoned
Josephine Spencer (Spicer?); imprisoned

5th Battalion, Men

North Co. Dublin, Rath (Rathbeal, Ratoath) Cross Roads, RIC Barracks at Ashbourne, Co. Meath; garrison total about 75 men and women (including approximately 20 Volunteers who were sent to the GPO on Tuesday, 25 April); 2 killed (plus one died afterward from his wounds); 8 RIC killed. Known after the Rising as the Fingal Brigade, it foreshadowed the flying columns and barracks' attacks of the 1920 campaigns.

Commandant Thomas Ashe; a native of Dingle, Co. Kerry, previously he was a schoolteacher at Corduff, Co. Dublin. He was known as an inspirational, but somewhat impractical, leader, and was the great uncle of actor Gregory Peck.
Dick Aungier
Peadar Blanchfield (brother); he became the 'official grenadier' as he was the only one with experience with bombs.
Tom Blanchfield (brother)
Paddy Brogan; a member of the Lusk Company.
#[1010] Dan Brophy
#Patrick Caddell; Lusk Company.
#John Clarke; Lusk Company.
#Dick Coleman (25); Captain of the Swords Company. He died of flu in Usk Prison, Wales, on 9 December 1918 while a candidate for parliament. (See also GPO and 1st Battalion at Mendicity Institute).
Jimmy Connor; a member of the Lusk Company.
#James Crenegan; from the Roganstown Company.
**John (Jack) Crenigan (21); he worked for the Dublin Tramways Company and was a member of the Swords Company.
Johnny Devine; a member of the Lusk Company.
Francis (Frank) Daly; imprisoned at Frongoch.
Paddy Doyle
#William Doyle; Swords Company.
Richard Duke
Thomas Duke
Walter Farrelly

1010 Those indicated by # reported to the 5th Battalion but were sent to the GPO on Tuesday, 25 April. They are counted in the Ashbourne garrison. Lawless, Joseph. Witness Statement 1043.

Mick Fleming

Jerry Golden

Jack Gowan; sent home on Thursday because he was too young.

Paddy Grant

Dr Richard Hayes; medical officer and an intelligence officer. He had formerly been the O/C, but resigned in favor of Ashe due to the pressures of his medical practice. Became a TD.

Paddy Houlihan (Holohan); imprisoned at Frongoch.

#Jack Hynes; Lusk Company.

**John Keely (15); killed in Phibsborough while carrying dispatches.

#Jack Kelly; Swords Company.

Jimmy Kelly

#Richard (Dick) Kelly; Corduff Company.

Matthew Kelly; a member of the Corduff Company, he was wounded and imprisoned at Frongoch.

#Patrick Kelly

Edmund Kent

Colm Lawless; sent home on Thursday becausee he was too young.

#Edward Lawless

Frank Lawless Sr; Battalion QM. Became a TD.

Jim Lawless; Captain of the St Margaret's Company; imprisoned at Frongoch.

Joseph Lawless; one of the section leaders, as well as assisting his father, Frank, as QM. Imprisoned at Frongoch.[1011]

Bennie McAllister; brother, imprisoned at Frongoch.

John McAllister; brother.

Michael (Mick) McAllister; brother.

John McCann

James McArdle; (brother), imprisoned at Frongach.

Patrick McArdle; (brother), imprisoned at Frongach.

#John McNally; Swords Company.

#James Marks; Swords Company.

Tom Maxwell

#William Meehan; Lusk Company.

Richard Mulcahy, Vice-Commandant. On Sunday evening, he was sent by Connolly to Howth to cut the undersea telephone wires between Dublin and London. It was impossible to return to Dublin so he went to Ashbourne and Ashe appointed him Vice-Commandant for the Rising. Imprisoned at Frongoch and became O/C of D Company of the North Camp. He succeeded Michael Collins as Commander in Chief of the Free State Army.

1011 His Witness Statement, Number 1043, runs to 418 pages and provides a remarkably complete and detailed account of the Finglas Volunteers in the Ashbourne engagement and the north Dublin area from 1913 through the entire revolutionary period.

Éamonn Murphy

Bill Norton; sent home on Thursday because he was too old.

#Joe Norton

Christy Nugent

James O'Connor; a member of the St Margaret's Company of the Volunteers. He
was imprisoned in Wakefield Prison.

Arthur O'Reilly

#Thomas Peppard; Lusk Company.

Jack Rafferty; a member of the Lusk Company, he was wounded and imprisoned
at Frongoch.

**Thomas (Tommy) Rafferty (22); died of wounds after the Rising.

Thomas Reilly

Edward N. (Ned) Rooney; Captain of the Lusk Company, he was wounded in the
eye and imprisoned at Frongoch.

James Rooney

Paddy Sheehan (Sherwin?)

Ned Stafford

Joe Taylor; a member of the Swords Company, he was wounded.

Nicholas Teehan (Teeling?); a member of the St Margaret's Company.

Joe Thornton; Captain of the Skerries Company, imprisoned at Frongoch.

Willie Walsh; wounded in his hand, he was a member of the Volunteers from
Liverpool.

Bartle Weston

Charles Weston; one of the section leaders. He was detailed to blow up the bridge
at Rogerstown Viaduct.[1012] Imprisoned at Frongoch.

#James Wilson

#Peter Wilson

#William (Beck) Wilson

#William (Cooty) Wilson; Swords Company.

5th Battalion, Women

Molly Adrian; a redoubtable messenger, she was in and out of Dublin all week.

Monica (Dot) Fleming; she married Joseph Lawless.

Eileen Lawless; she became one of Michael Collins' secretaries.[1013]

Kathleen Lawless

Irish Citizen Army/City Hall, Men

Mustered at Liberty Hall; Dublin Castle/City Hall; garrison total: 10 in City Hall

---

1012 Weston, Charles. Witness Statement 149. 1013 Lawless, Sister Eithne. Witness Statement 414.

and about 40 others spread over the other posts; 9 women accompanied the men from Liberty Hall; killed, 5; executed, 1.

Commandant James Connolly (Seámus Ó Conghile, executed 12 May 1916, aged 46).* In Dublin Castle 'hospital', he was seen by Fr Aloysius.

Christopher Brady; he was in the detachment that seized the guardroom, and went into the Upper Yard of Dublin Castle. He had helped print the *Proclamation*.

John Byrne; a member of the 123 Parliament Street squad, imprisoned at Frongoch.

**Louis Byrne

Patrick Byrne; garrisoned the Synod Hall in High Street, imprisoned at Frongoch.

**Cpt. Seán Connolly (33, a brother of Éamonn, George and Matt, his sister Katie was also in the garrsion); first to fire a killing shot (Constable James O'Brien) and first Volunteer/ICA to die in the Rising. He was employed in the motor tax office of Dublin Castle. James Connolly: 'Good luck, Seán, we won't meet again.' He was killed on the roof about 3.15 pm. Dr Kathleen Lynn wrapped him in the green flag from the play *Under Which Flag* in which he starred only a week before. As she did, she recalled his final speech from the play: 'Under this flag only will I serve. Under this flag, if need be, I will die.'[1014]

Éamonn (Edward) Connolly; a member of the 123 Parliament Street squad.

George Connolly; he was in the detachment that seized the guardroom, and went into the Upper Yard of Dublin Castle.

Matt Connolly (14); brother of Seán.[1015]

John (Thomas) Coyle; he was severely wounded and imprisoned at Frongoch.

Tom Daly; he was in the detachment that seized the guardroom, and went into the Upper Yard of Dublin Castle. Imprisoned at Frongoch.

**Charles Darcy (Darcey) (15); 'I'm ready, lads, where do you need me?' He was shot on the roof by a sniper. A member of the 123 Parliament Street squad.

Michael Delaney; held the Nicholas Street graveyard.

James Donnelly; a member of the 123 Parliament Street squad.

Elliot (Ellett) Elmes; a member of the 123 Parliament Street squad. A Protestant, he was imprisoned in Frongoch.

Dennis Farrell; imprisoned at Frongoch.

John Finlay; imprisoned at Frongoch.

Francis Fitzpatrick; a member of the Dublin Evening Mail, 38-40 Parliament Street squad.

**George Geoghegan (35); he was in the City Hall garrison, and was killed in the grounds of Dublin Castle while escaping.[1016]

William Halpin; a member of the 123 Parliament Street squad, imprisoned at Frongoch.

Thomas Healy; garrisoned the Synod Hall in High Street.

1014 Lynn, Dr Kathleen. Witness Statement 357. **1015** Connolly, Matthew. Witness Statement 1746.
1016 MacThomais, Éamonn. *Down Dublin Streets*, 1965, p. 15.

Tom Kain; he led the men into the guard room, and went into the Upper Yard of Dublin Castle. Imprisoned at Frongoch.

Martin Kelly; a member of the Dublin Evening Mail, 38-40 Parliament Street squad.

Arthur King

George King

Michael King; he led the contingent to take the Telephone Exchange in Crown Alley.

Samuel King; a member of the 123 Parliament Street squad

James Lambert

James McDonnell; a member of the Dublin Evening Mail, 38-40 Parliament Street, squad, imprisoned at Frongoch.

Michael Mullaley; a member of the Volunteers.

Thomas Nelson

John Nolan

George Norgrove

James O'Dwyer

John O'Keefe; garrisoned the Synod Hall in High Street. Imprisoned at Frongoch.

Philip O'Leary; he was in the detachment that seized the guardroom, and went into the Upper Yard of Dublin Castle. Imprisoned at Frongoch.

**Lt Seán (Jack) O'Reilly; he succeeded Seán Collins in command.

John Poole; brother, imprisoned at Frongoch.

Pat Poole; brother, imprisoned at Frongoch

James Seerey; he was in the detachment that seized the guardroom, and went into the Upper Yard of Dublin Castle. Imprisoned at Frongoch.

Michael Sexton; imprisoned at Frongoch.

Thomas Walsh; imprisoned at Frongoch.

Patrick Joseph Williams; held the Nicholas Street graveyard and imprisoned at Frongoch.

Henry Winstanley; a member of the Volunteers

Irish Citizen Army/City Hall, Women

Kitty Barrett

Brigid Brady

Katie Connolly (Barrett); she was Seán's sister.

Mattie Connolly

Brigid Davis (O'Duffy)

Bessie Lynch Kelly

Dr Kathleen Lynn; an ICA captain, she was at St Stephen's Green before she was called to the City Hall to treat Seán Connolly. After both Connolly and O'Reilly were killed, as the Medical Officer she took command and she was the officer who surrendered the garrison.[1017]

1017 Lynn, Dr Kathleen. Witness Statement 357.

Helena Molony; in 1907 when she was in America, she encouraged James Connolly to return to Ireland as a union organizer. She was one of the founders of the Fianna, an ICA officer and Abbey actress, and was the Secretary of the Irish Womens' Workers' Union at this time.

Annie Norgrove (16); she was a daughter of George and Mrs Norgrove.

Emily Norgrove (Hanratty); she was a daughter of George and Mrs Norgrove.

Mrs George Norgrove

Molly O'Reilly

Jenny Shanahan; she was not in uniform, and when passed by the English as she was walking away from City Hall it was assumed she had been a prisoner. When asked 'How many rebels are on the roof?' she answered 'There must be hundreds of them still on the roof.' So the British left it for the morning. However, when she was taken to 'identify' some 'rebels', she was recognized instead and welcomed by her friends, and the British then confined her.

Liberty Hall

Peter Ennis; he was the caretaker.

Seámus McGowan; he commanded the rear party after the Volunteers had marched to the GPO. He was on the first Army Council of the ICA, and would serve on the last in 1935.[1018]

William (Willie) Oman; bugler, he sounded the bugle to fall in at 11.45 am on 24 April. He also played 'The Last Post' at the Glasnevin Cemetery funeral of O'Donovan Rossa on Sunday, 1 August 1915.

Irish Citizen's Army/St Stephen's Green/College of Surgeons, Men

Mustered at Liberty Hall: garrison totals about 115 men and women; killed 6; executed 1; 100 men and 11 women surrendered.

Michael Mallin (executed 8 May 1916) Commandant.* He was ICA Chief of Staff under Connolly. He had served twelve years as a drummer in the Royal Fusiliers. In Kilmainham he was in cell number 18, and was seen by his two brothers Tom and Bart, his sister Kate, his wife, and his children – Seámus (12), Seán, Una and Joseph (2 years and 6 months). The Dominican novice master, Fr Browne, and Fr Albert also attended him.

**John Adams (38)

Nicholas Alexander; imprisoned at Frongoch.

John Bannon; imprisoned at Frongoch.

James Brougham; imprisoned at Frongoch.

Thomas Bryan; imprisoned at Frongoch.

1018 McGowan, Seámus. Witness Statement 542.

Edward Burke; imprisoned at Frongoch.

Paddy Buttner (15)

Christopher Byrne

James Byrne; imprisoned at Frongoch.

Joseph Byrne; imprisoned at Frongoch.

Owen Carton; imprisoned at Frongoch.

P. Chaney

William Chaney

Michael Charlton; imprisoned at Frongoch.

**Philip Clarke (41); he sent a message with a little girl, Alice Mac Thomais, on a bicycle to his wife in Cork Street. When she returned with some cigarettes from his wife, he was already dead, leaving his widow and eight children.

Tom Clifford

Joseph Connolly; a brother of Seán, he had a wonderful voice and led rebel songs at night. He and Margaret Skinnider pushed to lob a bomb through the Russell Hotel windows. One ICA soldier, Freddie Ryan, was killed and Skinnider was wounded three times. Connolly dragged Mick Doherty off the roof after Doherty had been hit. He became Chief of the Dublin Fire Brigade.

John (Seán) Conroy; imprisoned at Frongoch.

**James Corcoran (33)

Bernard Courtnay; imprisoned at Frongoch.

Barney Craven

Christopher Crothers

Pat Cullen; imprisoned at Frongoch.

Henry (Harry) Daniel; imprisoned at Frongoch.

Lt Bob de Coeur; he called out 'If you are any bloody good, come in and fight for Ireland' and Liam Ó Briain and Harry Nichols jumped the fence into St Stephen's Green. Imprisoned at Frongoch.

Peter Devereaux; imprisoned at Frongoch.

Pvt. Michael (Mick) Doherty; he was wounded fifteen times on the roof of the College of Surgeons. ('I'm afraid you're a goner, Mick, may the Lord have mercy on your soul.') But he survived, only to die in the 1918 influenza epidemic.

Michael Donnelly; imprisoned at Frongoch.

Dennis Doyle

Edward Doyle; imprisoned at Frongoch.

Joseph Doyle; he led one detachment of sixteen men at J. & T. Davy's Pub. Imprisoned at Frongoch.

Patrick K. Duffy; imprisoned at Frongoch.

Andy Dunn; imprisoned at Frongoch.

James Dwyer; imprisoned at Frongoch.

Christopher Dynan

M. Fay

Gerard Fitzmorris

James (Seámus) Fox; imprisoned at Frongoch.

**James (Jimmy) Fox (16); a member of the Fianna, he was an only child of Paddy Fox, a former activist in the Land Wars whose age precluded him from joining in the Rising. Early on Tuesday morning he was shot in a trench opposite the United Services Club.

Martin Foy; imprisoned at Frongoch.

George Fullerton; imprisoned at Frongoch.

Eugene Geraghty

Thomas Gleeson; imprisoned at Frongoch.

William Gleeson; imprisoned at Frongoch.

Jim Gough; imprisoned at Frongoch.

William Halpin; imprisoned at Frongoch.

James Hampton; imprisoned at Frongoch.

John Joseph Hendrick; he came from London specifically to participate in the Rising.

Fred Henry; imprisoned at Frongoch.

James Heron; imprisoned at Frongoch. He married Ina Connelly.

Patrick Holden

Peter Jackson; imprisoned at Frongoch.

Edward Joyce; imprisoned at Frongoch.

James Joyce (35); he came from J. & T. Davy's Pub.

Seámus Kavanagh; he was leader of the reinforcements sent from Jacob's by Thomas MacDonagh. As a 'mobilizer' he was to contact 7 or 8 men prior to mobilizing. Imprisoned at Frongoch.

Tommy Keenan (12); after Jimmy Fox was killed, Mallin sent him home and his parents locked him in his room, but he 'escaped' and returned to the Green.

Lt Michael Kelly; just promoted to the rank of lieutenant on the morning of 24 April, he led the second detachment of sixteen men on the railway bridge crossing the Grand Canal at J. & T. Davy's Pub. Imprisoned at Frongoch.

James Keogh; imprisoned at Frongoch.

Martin King

J. Lambert

Patrick Lawlor

Peter Leddy

James (Jem) Little; imprisoned at Frongoch.

Edward Luke (Juke?)

Cpt. Richard McCormick; sent by MacDonagh with a section of the Citizen Army to take Harcourt Street Station. He was the one who lowered the Tricolour and raised the white flag. Imprisoned at Frongoch.

Peter MacGrath

J. MacMahon

Daniel McArt

John McDonald; imprisoned at Frongoch.

Michael McGinn; imprisoned at Frongoch.

James McGowan; imprisoned at Frongoch.

James Maguire (McGuire?); imprisoned at Frongoch.

John Mahon; imprisoned at Frongoch.

Edward Mannering; imprisoned at Frongoch.

Patrick Mitchell; imprisoned at Frongoch.

Andrew Monks; imprisoned at Frongoch.

Fred Murphy; imprisoned at Frongoch.

Patrick Murphy; imprisoned at Frongoch.

** Daniel Murray (27)

James Nelson; imprisoned at Frongoch.

Cpt. Harry Nicholls; 4th Battalion, Volunteers, jumped the St Stephen's Green fence with Liam Ó Briain. He was an Ulsterman and a Protestant, and was imprisoned in Frongoch.

Alfred Norgrove; imprisoned at Frongoch.

Liam Ó Briain; a Volunteer in the 1st Dublin Battalion. He was first at J. & T. Davy's Pub at Portobello Bridge on his way to St Stephen's Green, and then just stayed at St Stephen's Green. Professor of Romance languages at the National University. He cycled around Dublin trying to get information for Eoin MacNeill, and carried cancellation messages from MacNeill in the days before the Rising. Imprisoned at Frongoch. Arrested as a Dáil/Republican judge early in 1920, he remained in prison for the remainder of the War of Independence. He took the Treaty side in 1922, and became a well-known writer and professor.[1019]

Frank O'Brien

Christopher O'Byrne; imprisoned at Frongoch.

John O'Byrne; imprisoned at Frongoch.

Joseph L. O'Byrne; imprisoned at Frongoch.

John O'Callaghan; 'I stuck my sandwiches in one pocket of my coat, the bullets in the other, and my rifle down my pants, got on my bicycle and went off to declare war on the British Empire. And you know what? In the end we beat 'em.' Imprisoned at Frongoch.

Michael O'Doherty; imprisoned at Frongoch.

Michael O'Kelly; imprisoned at Frongoch.

David O'Leary

William (Willie) Oman; he was the ICA bugler. He played the bugle to fall in the ICA and Volunteers outside Liberty Hall, and at the funeral of Jeremiah O'Donovan Rossa in 1915. Oman preceded his involvement with the Rising with an operation for appendicitis, carried out under the auspices of Dr Kathleen Lynn. On Easter Monday, he was posted to Castle St, just beside City Hall, but came under fire from troops, and escaped, just ahead of a hostile mob, to his home in High Street. Next day, he joined the Jacob's garrison, but was sent later that week to bring supplies to the College of Surgeons, and stayed there with his Citizen

1019 Ó Briain, Liam. Witness Statements 3, 6, 7.

Army comrades. He recalled that the Citizen Army nickname for Countess Markievicz was 'Lizzie'.[1020] Imprisoned at Frongoch.

Cpt. John O'Neill; his men supported Michael Kelly's men, and they were assigned to the railway bridge overlooking Harcourt Road. Imprisoned at Frongoch.

Timothy O'Neill; imprisoned at Frongoch.

Joseph O'Reilly; imprisoned at Frongoch.

Patrick O'Reilly; imprisoned at Frongoch.

Fred O'Rourke (16); imprisoned at Frongoch.

Albert O'Shea; imprisoned at Frongoch.

Sgt James O'Shea; he had been a member of the ICA since its inception. Imprisoned at Frongoch.

Robert O'Shea; imprisoned at Frongoch.

Councillor William (Bill) Partridge; led the rosary each night in his sonorous voice. He was wounded in the head. Sentenced to fifteen years penal servitude, but was released in 1917 because he had Bright's disease. He died in 1917. The handling of the vacancy caused by his early death caused a split in the Dublin Labour Party and eventually in Irish Labour as a whole.

Cpt. Christopher Poole

John Purfield

Augustus Percy Reynolds; imprisoned at Frongoch.

Sgt Frank Robbins; his twenty men were to operate in Hatch Street and he led a group that seized the College of Surgeons. There were only three men and three women (including Countess Markievicz) to take the College. He sought greater cooperation between the ICA and the Volunteers.[1021] Imprisoned at Frongoch.

Seán Rogan; imprisoned at Frongoch.

** Freddie Ryan (17); killed in the party in which Margaret Skinnider was wounded trying to set fire to the Russell Hotel.

Patrick Seery

Martin Shannon

**Patrick Sheehy

Tom Shiels; imprisoned at Frongoch.

Mr Sullivan; jumped the railings with Liam Ó Briain, and Ó Briain was 'saddled' with him for the duration. From Tralee, Sullivan seemed to be fighting Denis Coffee, President of UCD, not the British.

Edward Tuke; imprisoned at Frongoch.

Arthur Abraham Weekes

John Whelan; imprisoned at Frongoch.

Irish Citizen's Army/St Stephen's Green/College of Surgeons, Women

Chris Caffrey; captured while taking a message to the GPO disguised as a war widow.

1020 Oman, William. Witness Statement 421. **1021** Robbins, Frank. Witness Statement 585.

She was strip searched but ultimately released.

Kathleen Cleary

Eileen Conroy

Mary Devereaux

Mary Donnelly

Madeleine ffrench-Mullen; an ICA Officer. She commanded the medical detachment. She was imprisoned at Richmond Barracks and Kilmainham Gaol.

Brigid Foley; imprisoned and interned until July 1916.

Mary Gahan; imprisoned.

Helen (Nellie) Gifford (Donnelly); she was in charge of the commissary. Imprisoned.

Nora Gillies (O'Daly); she was a medical officer.

Brigid Goff; was remembered for entertaining the garrison with her jokes as they worked. Imprisoned.

Roseanne (Rosie) Hackett; imprisoned. An employee at Jacob's Biscuit Factory she was one of the most militant in the 1911 strike, was locked out in 1913 and was not able to get employment thereafter. One of the founders of the Irish Women's Worker's Union and worked full time as the Clerk of the ITGWU. Helped with the printing of the *Proclamation*. Fought at St Stephen's Green and later was in charge of a Red Cross station in the College of Surgeons and was imprisoned. Devoted the rest of her life to labour causes. She died in 1976.[1022]

Mary (Molly) Hyland; a noted actress, she commandeered food and brought it into the garrison.

Maggie Joyce; imprisoned.

Annie Kelly

Kate (Kitty) Kelly; imprisoned.

Elizabeth Ann 'Lily' Kempson; after the Rising she escaped to America with just the clothes on her back. 'Tell Mom I'm off to Amerikay.'

Bessie Lynch

Maj. Countess Markievicz (48); Vice-Commandant. Originally she was to liaise between the GPO and St Stephen's Green, but Mallin told her he needed her as second in command. She was said to have shot RIC Constable Michael Lahiff who approached the Grafton Street gate around noon and told the party to clear out, and then to have shouted, 'I shot him! I shot him.' However, she was delivering supplies with Dr Kathleen Lynn at the time and only arrived at the Green some time later on Monday afternoon. She did take part in the subsequent fighting that day when a party of Royal Irish Rifles came along Camden Street, and also took part in the sniping from the roof of the College of Surgeons.

Brigid Murtagh (O'Daly)

Christine Maire Ni Dhubhgaill

Mary (May) O'Moore; imprisoned.

Molly Reynolds

1022 Hackett, Rose. Witness Statement 546.

Margaret Ryan

Kathleen Seary; imprisoned.

Margaret Skinnider (23); a mathematics teacher from Glasgow, she was wounded on Wednesday when in a party sent to set fire to the Russell Hotel. Wounded three times (once in the right arm, right side and back), she was carried back to the College by William (Bill) Partridge. At Christmas 1915 she had brought detonators to Ireland on the boat from Glasgow. She wrote *Doing My Bit for Ireland*, describing her role as a sniper on the roof of the College of Surgeons: 'It was dark there, full of smoke, a din of firing, but it was good to be in the action; more than once I saw a man I aimed at fall.'

Maeve Ward

Amee (May) Wisley

Unassigned men in Co. Dublin
denotes imprisoned at Frongoch

#Pat Callen	#Patrick Halpin	#Joseph Murray	#G. Purcell
Michael Campbell	#Thomas Hilton	#Nicholas Murray	#Joseph Redmond
#Hugh Casey	#Stephen Jordan	#John Newman	#Pat Reilly
#John Cody	Tom Keogh (The Squad)	#Thomas O'Breslin	#Patrick Ronan
#Walter Cole	#Robert Leggitt	#Joseph P. O'Byrne	#John Rooney
#Herbert Conroy	#Joe Leonard (The Squad)	#Batt O'Connor	#William Ross
#T.S. Cuffe	#Charles Lyons	#John F. O'Connor	#Philip Sargent
Seámus Dempsey	#Hugh McCrory	#Thomas O'Connor	#Tom Sinnott
#Dan Devitt	#Patrick McDonald	Michael O'Cuill	#James Stritch
#Henry Dixon	#Michael McInerney +	#Robert O'Donoghue	#Harry Turner
#James Doherty	#Laurence Mackay	Michael O'Hehir	# _____ Tully (brother)
#Thomas Drennan	Seámus Melin	Garrett O'Holohan	#William Tully (brother)
#John Ellis	Michael Mervyn	# Seán O'Mahoney	#Thomas Ward
#Christy Geraghty	#Éamon Moran	Chris O'Malley	# _____ Weldon
#George Geraghty	#M.J. Moriarty	#Kevin O'Reilly	#William Whelan

+ McInerney was the driver of the car that went off Ballykissane Pier in Co. Kerry, killing Con Keating, Charles Monoghan and Donal Sheehan.

Unassigned Women in Co. Dublin

Kate Brown, imprisoned

Martha Brown, imprisoned

Eileen Byrne, imprisoned

Maeve Cavanagh

Agnes Daly, took messages to Co. Kerry.

Helen Donnelly
Kathy Doran
Frances Downey
Kathleen Fleming, imprisoned
Eilis (Betsy) Gray
Kathleen Kearney; later Mrs Behan, mother of Brendan Behan.
Linda Kearns; she set up a first aid station in North Great Georges Street, and
   worked as a courier for the Volunteers, but escaped capture after the Rising.
Bridie Kennedy, imprisoned
K. Kennedy
Catherine Liston, imprisoned
Mary Liston, imprisoned
May MacLaughlin
Julia McCauley (McAley), imprisoned
Maggie McLaughlin, imprisoned
Anastasia McLaughlin
Agnes McNamara, imprisoned
Agnes McNanice, imprisoned
Kathleen Maher, imprisoned
Kathleen Mahon
Pauline Markham, imprisoned
J. Milner
Pauline Morecombe
Katie O'Connor
Florence O'Doherty
Grace O'Sullivan, imprisoned
Mary Partridge, imprisoned
Marie Perolz; though not involved in the fighting in Dublin, she carried many
   messages on dangerous missions between garrisons, and down to Cork and Tralee,
   where she was arrested on 1 May, and was later imprisoned in Mountjoy Prison.
S. Quigley
Barbara Retz, imprisoned
Agnes Ryan
K. Ryan
Mary Shannon
Nora Thornton
A. Tobin
Mary Jo Walsh

Belfast

Joseph Connolly; imprisoned at Frongoch. A Free State Senator and Minister under de Valera after 1932.[1023]

Dr Pat McCartan; the O/C in Tyrone. He was a TD in the first three Dáils.[1024]

Denis McCullough; President of the IRB; imprisoned in Frongoch and became O/C in charge of the 2nd Dormitory.[1025]

Cathal O'Shannon; he had been Connolly's representative in Belfast and was imprisoned at Frongoch. He served as Deputy Leader of the Labour Party in the Third Dáil.

Ina Connolly (Heron); daughter of James, she relayed messages from Belfast to Dublin.[1026]

Nora Connolly (O'Brien); daughter of James, she relayed messages between Belfast and Dublin, and from Dublin to Co. Tyrone. A founder of the Young Republicans and the Belfast branch of Cumann na mBan. She married Seámus O'Brien in 1922, and became Paymaster-General of the IRA in 1923 after Margaret Skinnider was arrested. She was imprisoned by the Free State in the Civil War. In 1926 she became a member of the Seánad and sat three terms.[1027]

Co. Cork

Thomas MacCurtain, O/C; followed MacNeill's order to stand down, after he stopped the English from seizing the Cork HQ. He often said of 2000 Volunteers in the County only 80 would report for the Rising after MacNeill's order, so he stood the unit down. (One count on Sunday, before MacNeill's order reached them, had the Battalion muster at 221.) He was arrested on 3 May and later sent to Frongoch where he was the O/C Dormitory No 2, then to Reading Gaol. He was elected Lord Mayor of Cork in 1920, and was murdered by the Black and Tans on 20 March 1920.

Terence MacSwiney; second in command. Arrested on 3 May and imprisoned in Wakefield Prison, then in Frongoch where he was the O/C Dormitory No 4, then to Reading Gaol. His sister Annie said later: 'The torment of that week to Terry was appeased only by the sacrifice [his death on hunger strike] in Brixton.'[1028] Elected to the First Dáil, he succeeded MacCurtain as Lord Mayor of Cork. He was arrested by the English and died after a 74-day hunger strike in Brixton Prison on 25 October 1920. 'If only a few are faithful found, they must be the more steadfast for being but a few.'

Thomas Kent (Tomas Ceannt, executed 9 May 1916, Cork)*; Fermoy, Co. Cork, Bawnard House, Castlelyons, owned by Mrs Kent. Executed at Victoria Barracks, Cork, for the killing of Head Constable Rowe. Thomas was a veteran of the Land Wars. On the night of 2 May, an RIC party went to the house on a 'clearing-up operation'. The fight took place between 2.45 am and 6.00 am. Constable Rowe

1023 Connolly, Joseph. Witness Statement 124. **1024** McCartan, Dr Pat. Witness Statements 99, 100, 766. **1025** McCullough, Denis. Witness Statements 111, 636, 914, 915, 916. **1026** Heron, Ina. Witness Statement 919. **1027** O'Brien, Nora. Witness Statement 286. **1028** McSwiney Eithne (Ni Suibhne). Witness Statement 119.

was killed at the outset of the fighting according to RIC reports, though at his trial Kent said he never fired a shot. The Kents had been armed with one rifle and three shotguns. The aged Mrs Kent re-loaded the weapons for her sons during the fighting.[1029] While Thomas was in Victoria Barracks, now Cork Detention Barracks, Fr John Sexton attended him. Rowe was killed after the rebels in Dublin had surrendered. Many thought Kent was executed not just because Rowe died, after all it was in a firefight, but as a warning to all that the 'Rising was over, and no more fighting would be accepted'.

David Kent (brother); he was severely wounded in the side and lost two fingers. He was elected to the First Dáil and was re-elected subsequently.

** Richard Kent (brother); he was shot while 'trying to escape'. He had been a famous athlete in the area.

William Kent (brother);[1030] He was elected a TD on his brother's retirement.

2   ADDITIONAL PERSONS ON THE LIST OF DEAD IN DUBLIN
Con Keating (Ballykissane Pier, Co. Kerry)
Charles Monaghan (Ballykissane Pier, Co. Kerry)
Domhall (Donal) Sheehan (Ballykissane Pier, Co. Kerry)

3   CASUALTIES OF SOLDIERS, POLICE AND CIVILIANS IN DUBLIN
Official estimates have 126 English soldiers killed, and 322 wounded.
Officially there were 13 RIC constables and 3 DMP police killed.
Official estimates have 254 civilians killed and over 2200 wounded.

4   EXECUTIONS AFTER THE RISING
3 May, Tomas Clarke, Padraig Pearse, Thomas MacDonagh
4 May, Edward (Ned) Daly, Willie Pearse, Joseph Plunkett, Michael O'Hanrahan
5 May, John MacBride
8 May, Seán Heuston, Michael Mallin, Con Colbert, Éamonn Ceannt
9 May, Thomas Kent (Cork)
12 May, Seán MacDermott, James Connolly
3 August, Roger Casement (Pentonville Prison, England).

5   SENTENCES OF MEN IMPRISONED
Ninety-seven Volunteers were sentenced to death but had the sentences reduced to some years of penal servitude.

1029 King, RIC Constable Frank. Witness Statement 635. **1030** Kent, William. Witness Statement 75.

Sentenced to death but commuted to penal servitude for life

Thomas Ashe
Robert Brennan
William T. Cosgrave
Éamon de Valera

Thomas Hunter
Countess Markievicz
Henry O'Hanrahan
John (Jack) Shouldice.

Sentenced to death but commuted to ten years penal servitude

Thomas Bevan
Peter Clancy
Richard Davys
John Doherty
Peter Doyle
Francis Fahy
James T. Hughes
George Irvine
Frank Lawless
James Lawless
Finian Lynch
Jeremiah C. Lynch
Patrick McNestry

James (Seámus) Melinn
Michael Mervyn
Bryan Molloy
Denis O'Callaghan
George Plunkett
John Plunkett
J.J. Reid
P.E. Sweeney
William Tobin
James J. Walsh
Thomas Walsh
John Williams.

Sentenced to death but commuted to penal servitude

Charles Bevan, 3 years
Henry Boland, 5 years
Michael Brady, 3 years
J. Brennan, 3 years
Maurice Brennan, 3 years
Robert Brennan, 5 years
F. Brooks, 3 years
James Burke, 3 years
John Joseph Byrne, 3 years
J. Clarke, 3 years
R. Coleman, 3 years
William P. Corrigan, 5 years
Philip Cosgrave, 5 years
Gerald Crofts, 5 years
John F. Cullen, 3 years
Michael de Lacy, 5 years
James Dempsey, 3 years

J. Dorrington, 3 years
James Downey, 3 years
Gerald Doyle, 3 years
James Doyle, 5 years
John Etchingham, 5 years
John Faulkner, 3 years
Patrick Fogarty, 3 years
Peter Galligan, 5 years
Richard Hayes, 20 years
James Joyce, 5 years
P. Kelly, 3 years
R. Kelly, 3 years
Richard King, 5 years
George Levins, 3 years
Philip MacMahon, 3 years
John McArdle, 3 years
Seán McGarry, 8 years

J. Marks, 3 years
W. Meehan, 3 years
James Morrissey, 3 years
J. Norton, 3 years
John O'Brien, 3 years
Fergus O'Connor, 3 years
W. O'Dea, 3 years
C. O'Donovan, 5 years
T. O'Kelly, 3 years
James O'Sullivan, 8 years

T. Peppard, 3 years
Vincent Poole, 5 years
John Quin, 3 years
James Rafter, 5 years
Michael Reynolds, 3 years
Michael Scully, 3 years
J. Wilson, 2 years
P. Wilson, 3 years
W. Wilson, 3 years.

Sentenced to penal servitude

Thomas Barrett, 1 year
Thomas Bennett, 1 year
Harry Boland, 10 years, 5 remitted
Timothy Brosnan, 20 years, 15 remitted
Joseph Burke, 3 years
Christopher Carrick, 3 years
John Carrick, 3 years
Eddy Corcoran, 3 years
John Corcoran, 3 years
William Corcoran, 3 years
J. Crenigan, 1 year
Gerald Crofts, 10 years, 5 remitted
William Darrington, 2 years, 1 remitted
Michael Donohue, 1 year
Frank Drennan, 20 years, 10 remitted
Murtagh Fahy, 1 year
Patrick Fahy, 10 years
Thomas Desmond Fitzgerald, 10 years
Patrick Flanagan, 3 years
Michael Fleming, 3 years
Michael Fleming Jnr, 1 year
Thomas Fury, 3 years
Thomas (Fred) Fury, 3 years
Patrick Fury, 3 years
John Grady, 1 year

Michael Grady, 1 year
John Greaves, 6 months
J. Grenigan, 2 years, 1 remitted
John Haniffy, 1 year
Martin Hansbury, 1 year
Michael Hehir, 3 years
Michael Higgins, 1 year
Michael Higgins (Oranmore), 3 years
Joseph Howley, 3 years
William Hussey, 3 years
Patrick Kennedy, 1 year
Thomas Kennedy, 1 year
Joseph Ledwick, 6 months
James Loughlin, 3 years
Eoin MacNeill, life
Conor McGinley, 3 years
James Murray, 1 year
Charles O'Neill, 1 year
William Partridge, 15 years, 5 remitted
E. Roach, 1 year
Michael Scully, 10 years, 7 remitted
Michael Toole, 3 years
Patrick Weafer, 6 months
Charles White, 1 year.

6 WOMEN IMPRISONED

Though seventy-seven women were taken prisoner after the Rising, most were soon released. However the following marked with ^ were imprisoned for some time:

Kitty Barrett
Bridget Brady
Kate Brown
Martha Brown
Margaret Buckley
Ellen Bushel
Eileen Byrne
Katie Byrne
Mary Byrne
^Winifred Carney
Maire (Mary, Meg) Carron
Kathleen Clarke
^Annie Cooney
Eileen Cooney
Lily Cooney
Marcella Cosgrave
Bridget Davis
Ellen Ennis
^Madeleine ffrench Mullen
Kathleen Fleming
^Brigid Foley
^Mary (May) Gahan
Helen (Nellie) Gifford
Bridget Goff
Julia Grenan
Roseanne Hackett
Brigid Hegarty
Annie Higgins
Mary Ellen (Nell) Humphreys
Maggie Joyce
Josephine Kelly
Kate (Kitty) Kelly
Martha Kelly
Margaret Kennedy
Bridie Kenny
Catherine Liston
Mary Liston

Bessie Lynch
^Dr Kathleen Lynn
Brigid Lyons
Sorcha MacMahon
Rose MacNamara
Agnes MacNamee
Julia McCauley
Josephine McGowan
Maggie McLaughlin
Agnes McNamara
Agnes McNanice
Kathleen Maher
^Helena Malony
Pauline Markham
^Countess Markievicz
^Brigid Martin
Kate Martin
Florence Mead
Caroline Mitchell
Lizzie Mulhall
Rose Mullally
Kathleen Murphy
Rose Murphy
Margaret O'Flaherty
Sheila O'Hanlon
Emily O'Keefe
Josephine O'Keefe
Mary (May) O'Moore
Grace O'Sullivan
Louise O'Sullivan
Mary Partridge
^Marie Perolz
Countess Plunkett
Maria Quigley
Priscilla Quigley
Barbara Retz
^Mary Kate Ryan

^Nell Ryan   Josephine Spencer (Spicer?)
Kathleen Seary   Catherine Treston.

7   ENGLISH UNITS SERVING IN DUBLIN DURING THE RISING

Army Service Corps
Connaught Rangers
Duke of Lancaster's Own Yeomen
Grenadier Guards
176th Infantry Division, the 2/5th and 2/6th South Staffordshire and 2/5th and
    2/6th North Staffordshire Regiments
177th Infantry Division, 2/4th and 2/5th Lincolnshire Regiments
178th Infantry Division, the 2/5th, 2/6th, 2/7th, 2/8th Sherwood Forester Regiments
2nd King Edward's Horse Regiment
Kingstown Volunteer Corps
6th Reserve Cavalry Regiment
Royal Army Medical Corps
4th Battalion Royal Dublin Fusiliers
10th Battalion Royal Dublin Fusiliers
Royal Engineers
Royal Field Artillery
Royal 8th Hussars
Royal Iniskilling Fusiliers
Royal Irish Fusiliers
3rd Battalion Royal Irish Rifles
3rd Battalion Royal Irish Regiment
18th Royal Irish Rifle Regiment
5th and 12th Royal Lancers
Royal Leicestershire Regiment
Royal Leinster Regiment, relieved the OTC at Trinity
Royal Navy, HMS *Helga*
Royal Scots
Volunteer Training Corps (Trinity)

Sources and Bibliography

MANUSCRIPT, NEWSPAPERS AND PRINTED PRIMARY SOURCES

Fr Aloysius, OFM, Cap. 'Memories of Easter Week', Allen Library, North Richmond Street, Dublin.
An Barr Buadh.
An Claidheamh Soluis.
An Cosantoir.
An Macaomh.
An tÓglach.
An Phoblacht.
An Saorstat (The Free State).
Arrangements governing the Cessation of Active Operations in Ireland which came into force on 11 July 1921, 1921, HM Stationery Office, CMD 1534 XXIX 785.
Cpt. George F.H. Berkeley Papers, National Library of Ireland, Kildare Street, Dublin, 2.
Kevin Barry Papers, University College Library, Belfield, Dublin, 4.
Robert Barton Papers, Trinity College Dublin, 2.
Robert Barton scrapbooks, National Library of Ireland.
Bean na hÉireann.
Augustine Birrell Papers, Manuscripts 49372, 49382, British Museum, London.
Augustine Birrell Papers, National Library of Ireland.
Blackwood's Magazine.
Bloody Sunday File, British Public Record Office (PRO), WO35/88, Kew, London.
Ernest Blythe Papers, University College Library.
British Parliamentary Archive Papers, 'The Irish Uprising, 1914–1921'.
Cathal Brugha Papers, University College Library.
Máire Ni Shuibhne Brugha Papers, University College Library.
Capuchin Annual.
Roger Casement Papers, National Library of Ireland.
Catholic Bulletin.
Clann na Poblachta Party Papers, University College Library.
Clare Champion.
R. Erskine Childers Papers, National Library of Ireland.
R. Erskine Childers Papers, Trinity College Dublin.
Brig. Gen. Sir George Kynaston Cockerill Papers, National Library of Ireland.
Daniel Cohalan Papers, National Library of Ireland.
Michael Collins Papers, National Library of Ireland.
Maire Comerford Papers, University College Library.
Command Papers relating to the Articles of Agreement for a Treaty between Great Britain and Ireland, HM Stationery Office, CMD 1560, 1921.
Command Papers relating to the Draft Constitution of the Irish Free State, HM Stationery Office, CMD 1688, 1922.

Commander of the Imperial General Staff to Secretary of State for War, 'Mobilisation arrangements in the event of disturbances in Ireland', 4 July 1914, British Public Record Office (PRO), WO 329569.
Commonweal.
The Constabulary Gazette.
Contemporary Review.
Cork Constitution.
Cork Examiner.
Cork People.
Correspondence relating to the proposals of HM Government for an Irish Settlement, HM Stationery Office, CMD 1502, 1921.
Further Correspondence relating to the proposals of HM Government for an Irish Settlement, HM Stationery Office, CMD 1539, 1921.
Correspondence between HM Government and the Prime Minister for Northern Ireland relating to proposals for an Irish Settlement, HM Stationery Office, CMD 1561, 1921.
Cumann Na mBan Convention Reports: 1917, 1918, 1919, 1920, 1921.
Cumann Na mBan Executive: 'The Present Duty of Irishwomen'. (1918).
Cumann Na nGaedheal Party Papers, University College Library.
Current History.
Dáil Éireann:
    Correspondence Relating to Peace Negotiations, June-September 1921.
    Minutes of the Proceedings of the First and Second Parliaments of Ireland, 1919-1921.
    Minutes of the Treaty Debates, 1921-1922.
Daily Mail.
Daily Telegraph.
Éamonn de Barra Papers, National Library of Ireland.
Department of the Taoiseach.
Éamon de Valera Papers, University College Dublin.
John Devoy Papers, National Library of Ireland.
Documents relative to the Sinn Féin movement, HM Stationery Office, CMD 1108, 1921.
Peadar Doyle, 'Reminiscences of Five Years Service of an Irish Volunteer', Allen Library.
Dublin Brigade Review.
Dublin Chamber of Commerce, Annual Reports and Minutes, National Archives of Ireland, Bishop Street, Dublin 8.
Dublin Corporation, minutes and reports, Dublin City Archives, Pearse Street, Dublin 2.
Dublin Gazette.
Dublin, Leinster and Connaught Trades' Directory, accompanied with a gazetteer of Ireland, 1912.
Dublin Trade Council minutes, National Library of Ireland.
Easter Commemoration Digest, 1964.
Éire.
Éire-Ireland, A Journal of Irish Studies.
Éire Og.
Evening Herald.
Evening Press.
Evening Standard.
Thomas Farren Papers, National Library of Ireland.
Fianna Fáil Party Papers, University College Library.
Fine Gael Party Papers, University College Library.
Foreign Affairs.
Fortnightly Review.
Forward.
Freeman's Journal.
Gaelic American.
Gaelic League Annual Reports: 1898-1909.

Frank Gallagher Papers, National Library of Ireland.

George Gavan-Duffy Papers, National Library of Ireland.

Jerry Golden, 'The Story of the Fight at Rath Crossroads', Allen Library.

Arthur Griffith Papers, National Library of Ireland.

The Harp.

Mary Hayden Diaries, National Library of Ireland.

T.M. Healy Papers, University College Library.

Mrs Augustine Henry Diary, National Library of Ireland.

History Ireland.

Bulmer Hobson Papers, National Library of Ireland.

Robert Holland, 'An account of action at Marrowbone Lane', Allen Library.

Paddy Holohan, 'The Battle of Ashbourne', National Library of Ireland, MS 18098.

Joseph Holloway Diaries, National Library of Ireland.

Hue and Cry (Dublin Castle).

Richard (Dick) Humphreys, a diary of the GPO reconstructed during his internment, notes written on toilet paper in Wakefield Prison, May 1916, National Library of Ireland, MS 18829.

Sighle Humphreys Papers, University College Library.

Douglas Hyde Memoirs manuscript, University College Library.

Douglas Hyde Papers, National Library of Ireland.

Ireland at Berne. Reports presented to the International Labour and Socialist Conference held at Berne, Switzerland, February 1919.

Irish Bulletin.

Irish Catholic.

Irish Citizen.

Irish Department of External Affairs, *Cuimhneachan 1916-1966: A Record of Ireland's Commemoration of the 1916 Rising* (Dublin, 1966).

Irish Freedom.

Irish Historical Studies.

Irish Independent/Sunday Independent.

Irish Jurist.

Irish Opinion.

Irish Press/Sunday Press.

Irish Republican Brotherhood Papers, University College Library.

Irish Review.

Irish Sword.

The Irish Times.

Irish Transport and General Workers' Union: Annual reports, 1911 to 1925.

Irish Volunteer.

Irish Volunteers, 'General Instructions for forming Companies, 1914', Hobson MSS, National Library of Ireland, MS 13174.

Irish Volunteers, 'Military Instructions for Units, 1914', Hobson MSS, National Library of Ireland, MS 13174.

Irish Volunteers Papers, University College Library.

Irish Worker.

Pte J. Jameson. 2635/Sherwood Foresters. 'My Experiences whilst in Ireland', Document Reference No. 999/519, National Archives of Ireland.

Lt Gen. Sir Hugh Jeudwine Papers, Imperial War Museum, Box 72/82/2. 'Record of the Rebellion in Ireland in 1920-1921 and the Part Played by the Army in Dealing with it.'

Thomas Johnson Papers, National Library of Ireland.

The Journal of British Studies.

Journal of Contemporary History.

Journal of the Donegal Historical Society.

Journal of the Irish Labour History Society.

Journal of the Irish Military Society.

Journal of the Old Athlone Society.
Journal of the Westport Historical Society.
The Kerryman.
Kilmainham Gaol Museum and Document Collection.
Labour Party Report of the Labour Commission to Ireland, London, 1921.
The Leader.
Seán Lemass Papers, University College Library.
Limerick Echo.
Limerick Leader.
'List of persons killed or wounded brought to Dublin hospitals', compiled by Sgt Michael Mannion,
     29 May 1916, British Public Record Office (PRO), WO 35/69.
Literary Digest.
Patrick Little Papers, University College Library.
Living Age.
(London) *Daily Sketch.*
(London) *The Times.*
Diarmuid Lynch Papers, National Library of Ireland.
Seán MacEntee Papers, University College Library.
Gen. Seán MacEoin Papers, University College Library.
Edward MacLysaght Papers, National Library of Ireland.
Eoin MacNeill Papers, National Library of Ireland.
Mary MacSwiney Papers, Trinity College Dublin.
Mary MacSwiney Papers, University College Dublin.
Terence MacSwiney Papers, University College Dublin.
Patrick McCartan Papers, National Library of Ireland.
Denis McCullough Papers, University College Library.
Joseph McGarrity Papers, National Library of Ireland.
Macready Committee Report, Cabinet Paper 1317, 19 May 1919, 'Formation of a special force for
     service in Ireland', British Public Record Office (PRO), WO 32/9517.
Midland Reporter.
Military Archives of Ireland, Cathal Brugha Barracks, Rathmines, Dublin 6.
     'British Over-sea Commitments, 1919, 1920, 1921', Liaison Papers 1921-1922, Box 4.
     'Introduction to The Bureau of Military History 1913-1921', Military Archives,
         Defence Forces Printing Press, 2003.
     Michael Collins Papers, 1919-1921.
     Gen. Maxwell Report to Field Marshal, Commanding-in-Chief, Home Forces, 25 May 1916.
     Ernie O'Malley Notebooks.

Bureau of Military History Witness Statements

Aghlas (Ashe), Nora. Statement 645.
Aherne, Maurice. Statement 483.
Aloysius, Revd OFM. Statements 207, 220.
Archer, Liam. Statement 819.
Augustine, Revd OFM. Statement 920.
Austin, John. Statement 904.
Balfe, Richard. Statement 251.
Barry, Tom. Statement 1743.
Barry, Mrs Tom (née Leslie Price). Statement 1754.
Barton, Dulcibella. Statement 936.
Barton, Robert. Statement 979.
Béaslaí, Piaras. Statements 261, 675.
Beaumont, Seán. Statement 709.
Beaumont, Mrs Seán (Maureen McGavock).

Statement 385.
Begley, Florence. Statements 32, 1771.
Berry, Patrick J. Statement 942.
Bevan, Seámus. Statements 1058, 1059.
Bloxam, Elizabeth. Statement 632.
Blythe, Ernest. Statement 939.
Bolger, John C. Statement 1745.
Boylan, Peter. Statement 269.
Boylan, Seán. Statements 212, 1715.
Brady, Christopher J. Statement 705.
Brady, Margaret (née Sweeney). Statement 1267.
Bratton, RIC Constable Eugene. Statement 467.
Breen, Daniel. Statements 1739, 1763.
Brennan, Patrick J . Statement 1773.

Brennan, Robert. Statements 125, 779, 790.
Broderick, John. Statement 344.
Browne, Revd Michael. Statement 538.
Browne, Msgr Patrick. Statement 729.
Broy, Éamon. Statements 1280, 1284, 1285.
Brunswick, Seán. Statement 898.
Buckley, Tim. Statement 43.
Bucknill, Sir Alfred. Statement 1019.
Bulfin, Éamon. Statement 497.
Burgess, Alfred. Statement 1634.
Burke, Fergus (Frank). Statement 694.
Byrne, Bernard C. Statement 631.
Byrne, Christopher. Statements 167, 642.
Byrne, Gerald. Statement 143.
Byrne, Joseph. Statement 461.
Byrne, Seán. (F Co, 1 BN, 1916) Statement 422.
Byrne, Seán. (C Co, 3Bn, 1916) Statement 579.
Byrne, Tom. Statement 564.
Byrne, Vincent. Statement 423.
Caffrey, John Anthony. Statement 569.
Cahill, Bessie (née Harrington). Statement 1143.
Cahill, James. Statement 503.
Calahane, John. Statement 72.
Caldwell, Patrick. Statement 638.
Callender, Ignatius. Statement 923.
Carpenter, Walter. Statement 583.
Carrigan, James. Statement 613.
Cavanaugh, Maeve. Statement 258.
Ceannt, Áine. Statement 264.
Christian, William. Statement 646.
Clarke, Josephine. Statement 699.
Cody, Seán. Statement 1035.
Coffey, Diarmuid. Statement 1248.
Coghlan, Francis X. Statement 1760.
Colbert, Elizabeth. Statement 856.
Colley, Harry. Statement 1687.
Collins, Con (Conor, Cornelius). Statement 90.
Collins, Maurice. Statement 550.
Collins, Patrick. Statement 506.
Conlon, Martin. Statement 798.
Conlon, Mrs Martin. Statement 419.
Connolly, Joseph. Statement 124.
Connolly, Matthew. Statement 1746.
Corkery, Dan. Statements 93, 1719.
Corrigan, William. Statement 250.
Cosgrave, William T. Statements 266, 449.
Costello, John D. Statement 1330.
Cotton, Alfred. Statement 184.
Coughlan, James. Statement 304.
Cregan, Mairin. Statement 416.
Cremin, Mary A. (née Sheehan). Statement 924.
Crenegan, James. Statements 148, 1395.
Crothers, Christopher. Statement 1759.

Culhane, Seán. Statement 746.
Cullen, James. Statement 1342.
Curran, Lily (née Cooney). Statement 805.
Cusack, Brian. Statement 736.
Czira, Sidney Gifford. Statement 909.
Dalton, Charles. Statement 434.
Dalton, Gen. Emmet. Statement 641.
Daly, Francis. Statement 278.
Daly, Madge. Statements 209, 855.
Daly, Seámus. Statement 360.
Daly, Una. Statement 610.
Davitt, Cahir. Statements 993, 1751.
De Barra, Leslie Price Bean. Statement 1754.
De Brun, Seosamh. Statement 312.
De Burca, Aoife. Statement 359.
De Burca, F. Statement 105.
De Roiste (Roche), Liam. Statement 1698.
Dillon, Geraldine Plunkett. Statements 29, 358, 424.
Dolan, Edward. Statement 1078.
Dolan, Joseph (Joe). Statements 663, 900.
Donnelly, Nellie (née Gifford). Statement 256.
Dore, Éamon. Statement 392.
Dore, Nora (née Daly). Statement 154.
Doyle, Gerald. Statement 1511.
Doyle, Revd James. Statement 311.
Doyle, James. Statements 127, 309.
Doyle, James. (Gresham Hotel). Statement 771.
Doyle, Seumus. Statement 166.
Duffy, Thomas. Statement 1409.
Egan, Patrick. Statement 327.
Fahy, Anna. Statement 202.
Fahy, Frank. Statement 442.
Farrelly, Seán. Statements 1648, 1734.
Farrington, Annie. Statement 749.
Fay, Bridget (née Diskin). Statement 484.
Feeley, Michael. Statement 68.
Fitzgerald, George. Statement 684.
Fitzgibbon, Seán. Statement 130.
Fitzsimmons, Christopher. Statement 581.
Flood, James. Statement 606.
Fogarty, Revd Dr Michael. Statement 271.
Foley, Mrs Michael. Statement 539.
Foran, James. Statement 243.
Fox, Thomas. Statement 365.
Fulham, James. Statement 630.
Garvey, John. Statement 178.
Gaskin, Frank. Statement 386.
Gavan-Duffy, George. Statement 381.
Gavan-Duffy, Louise. Statement 216.
Gay, Thomas B. Statement 780.
Ginnell, Alice. Statement 982.
Gogan, Liam. Statement 799.
Gogarty, Oliver St John. Statement 700.

Golden, Jerry. Statements 177, 206, 521, 522.
Good, Joe. Statement 388.
Grace, Seumus. Statement 310.
Griffith, Maud. Statement 205.
Hackett, Rose. Statement 546.
Hales, Tom. Statement 20.
Harling, Seán. Statement 935.
Harpur, James. Statement 536.
Harte, Christopher. Statement 2.
Hayes, Michael. Statement 215.
Hayes, Dr Richard. Statements 97, 876.
Healy, Seán. Statements 686, 1479, 1643.
Hehir, Hugh. Statement 683.
Henderson, Frank. Statement 821.
Heron, Áine. Statement 293.
Heron, Ina (née Connolly). Statement 919.
Hilliard, Michael. Statement 1622.
Hobson, Bulmer. Statements 30, 31, 50, 51, 52, 53, 81, 82, 83, 84, 85, 86, 87, 652, 1089, 1365.
Hobson, Claire (née Gregan). Statement 685.
Holland, Robert. Statements 280, 371.
Holohan, Garry. Statements 328, 336.
Hughes, Julia. Statement 880.
Hynes, James. Statement 867.
Hyland, Joseph (Joe). Statement 644.
Hynes, Frank. Statement 446.
Hynes, Thomas. Statement 714.
Jackson, Valentine. Statement 409.
Johnson, Thomas. Statement 1755.
Joyce, Col. J.V. Statement 1762.
Kavanagh, Cpt. Seámus. Statement 493, 1670.
Kavanagh, Seámus. Statements 208, 998.
Kavanagh, Seán. Statement 524.
Keady, Margaret. Statement 455.
Kearney, Dr Joseph. Statement 704.
Keating, Pauline. Statement 432.
Keegan, John. Statement 217.
Kelliher, Edward J. Statement 477.
Kelly, Edward. Statement 1094.
Kelly, Paddy. Statement 726.
Kelly, Thomas. Statement 378.
Kenna, Mark. Statement 1167.
Kennedy, Senator Margaret. Statement 185.
Kennedy, Patrick (Paddy). Statement 499.
Kennedy, Seán. Statements 842, 885.
Kennedy, Tadgh. Statements 135, 1413.
Kenny, James. Statement 174.
Kent, William. Statement 75.
Keiran, Peter. Statement 494.
Kenny, James. Statement 141.
Kenny, Lt James. Statement 174.
Kent, William. Statement 75.
Keogh, Margaret. Statement 273.

Keogh, Seán. Statement 1615.
Kerney, Leopold H. Statement 825.
King, RIC Constable Frank. Statement 635.
King, Martin. Statement 543.
Knightly, Michael (Mike). Statement 833.
Laffan, Nicholas. Statements 201, 703.
Lalor, Mary (née Hyland). Statement 295.
Langley, Liam. Statement 816.
Larkin, James. Statement 906.
Laurence, Revd. Statement 899.
Lavelle, Patricia. Statement 837.
Lavin, Revd Thomas. Statement 1407.
Lawless, Sr Eitne (Evelyn, Eibhlin). Statement 414.
Lawless, Col. Joseph V. Statement 1043.
Lawson, Patrick. Statement 667.
Leahy, Thomas. Statement 660.
Leonard, Joseph (Joe). Statement 547.
Lynch, Diarmuid. Statements 4, 120, 121, 364, 651.
Lynch, Fionan. Statement 192.
Lynch, Michael. Statement 511.
Lynn, Dr Kathleen. Statement 357.
Lynskey, William. Statement 1749.
MacAuley, Charles J. Statement 735.
MacCarvill, Eileen. Statement 1752.
MacDonagh, Sr Francesca. Statement 717.
MacDonagh, John. Statements 219, 532.
MacEntee, Margaret (née Browne). Statement 322.
MacEntee, Seán. Statement 1052.
MacGarry, Maeve. Statement 826.
MacNeill, Agnes. Statement 213.
MacNeill, Hugo. Statement 1377.
MacNeill, Niall. Statement 69.
McAleese, Daniel. Statement 1411.
McAllister, Michael. Statement 1494.
McBride, Maud Gonne. Statement 317.
McCartan, Patrick. Statements 99, 100, 766.
McCarthy, Dan. Statement 722.
McCorley, Roger. Statement 389.
McCrave, Thomas. Statement 695.
McCrea, Patrick. Statement 413.
McCullough, Denis. Statements 111, 636, 914, 915, 916.
McDonnell, Andrew. Statement 1768.
McDonnell, Daniel. Statement 486.
McDonnell, Kathleen. Statement 88.
McDonnell, Michael (Mick). Statement 225.
McDonnell, Vera. Statement 1050.
McDonough, Joseph. Statement 1119.
McDowell, Cathal. Statement 173.
McDowell, Maeve (née Cavanagh). Statement 258.
McElligott, T.J. Statement 472.
McEoin, Cpt. James. Statement 436.
McGarry, Seán. Statement 368.

McGowan, Seámus. Statement 542.
McGuinness, Joseph. Statement 607.
McKenna, Kathleen (née Napoli). Statement 643.
McLoughlin, John (Seán). Statement 290.
McMahon, Revd J.T. Statement 362.
McMahon, Leo. Statement 274.
McManners, Rose. Statement 482.
McNamara, Rose. Statement 482.
McNeill, Josephine. Statement 303.
McSwiney, Eithne (Ni Suibhne). Statement 119.
McSwiney, Muriel. Statement 637.
McWhinney, Linda (née Kearns). Statement 404.
Macardle, Dorothy. Statement 457.
Maguire, Conor A. Statement 708.
Mallin, Thomas. Statement 382.
Malone, Bridget (née Walsh). Statement 617.
Malone, Tomas ('Seán Forde'). Statement 845.
Mannix, Patrick. Statement 502.
Martin, Brigid (née Foley). Statement 398.
Mee, RIC Constable Jeremiah. Statement 379.
Mernin, Lily. Statement 441.
Mitchell, Albert. Statement 196.
Molloy, Brian. Statement 345.
Molloy, Michael. Statement 716.
Moloney, Katherine (née Barry). Statement 731.
Molony, Helena. Statement 391.
Moriarty, Maurice. Statement 117.
Morkan, Phyllis. Statement 210.
Moylan, Seán. Statements 505, 838.
Moylett, Patrick. Statement 767.
Mulcahy, Mary Josephine (née Ryan). Statement 399.
Mullen, Patrick. Statement 621.
Murphy, Eileen (née Walsh). Statement 480.
Murphy, Fintan. Statement 370.
Murphy, Gregory. Statement 150.
Murphy, John J. (Seán). Statement 204.
Murphy, Seámus. Statement 1756.
Murphy, Stephen. Statement 545.
Murphy, William. Statement 352.
Murray, Joseph. Statement 254.
Neilan, John Joe. Statement 1042.
Neligan, David. Statement 380.
Nevin, Revd Eugene. Statement 1605.
Newell, Thomas (Sweeney). Statements 572, 698.
Ni Bhriain, Maire. Statement 363.
Nicholls, Harry. Statement 296.
Nolan, George. Statement 596.
Noyk, Michael. Statement 717.
Nugent, Laurence. Statement 907.
Nunan, Seán. Statement 1744.
O'Boyle, Manus. Statement 289.
Ó Briain, Liam. Statements 3, 6, 7, 565, 784.
O'Brian, Laurence. Statement 252.

O'Brien, Annie (née Cooney). Statement 805.
Jointly with her sisters:
Eileen (Cooney) Harbourne
Lily (Cooney) Curran
O'Brien, John Joe. Statement 1647.
O'Brien, Laurence. Statement 252.
O'Brien, Liam. Statement 323.
O'Brien, Nora (née Connolly). Statement 286.
O'Brien, William. Statement 1766.
Ó Brolchain, Maire. Statements 302, 321.
Ó Buachalla, Domhnall. Statement 194.
O'Byrne, Maire (née Kennedy). Statement 1029.
O'Callaghan, Cait. Statement 688.
O'Callaghan, Margaret (née Flanagan). Statement 747.
Ó Ceallaigh, Padraig. Statement 376.
O'Connell, Mortimer. Statement 804.
O'Connor, Éamon. Statement 114.
O'Connor, James. Statement 142.
O'Connor, Joseph. Statements 157, 487, 544.
O'Connor, Maire (Mrs Batt). Statement 330.
O'Connor, Patrick J. ('Ninepence'). Statement 608.
O'Carroll, Joseph. Statement 728.
O'Daly, Patrick. Statements 220, 387.
O'Doherty, Kitty. Statement 355.
O'Donel, Geraldine. Statement 861.
O'Donnell, Mrs Bernard (née Eithne Coyle). Statement 750.
O'Donoghue, Daithi. Statement 548.
O'Donoghue, Florence. Statement 554.
O'Donoghue, Patrick. Statement 847.
O'Donovan, Daniel. Statement 1480.
O'Donovan, James L. Statement 1713.
O'Donovan, Julia. Statement 475.
O'Duffy, Seán M. Statements 313, 618, 619.
O'Flahery, Liam. Statement 248.
O'Flanagan, George. Statement 131.
O'Flanagan, Michael. Statements 800, 908.
O'Grady, Charles. Statement 282.
O'Hanigan, Donal. Statement 161.
O'Hegarty, P.S. Statements 26, 27, 28, 259, 839, 840, 841, 897.
O'Hegarty, Seán. Statement 54.
O'Keefe, Patrick (Paudeen). Statement 1725.
O'Keefe, Seán. Statement 188.
O'Kelly, Fergus. Statement 351.
O'Kelly, J.J. (Sceilg). Statements 384, 427.
O'Kelly, Kathleen Murphy. Statement 180.
O'Kelly, Seámus. Statement 471.
O'Kelly, Seán T. Statements 611, 1765.
O'Leary, Mortimer. Statement 107.
Ó Lochlainn, Colm. Statement 751.
Oman, William. Statement 421.

O'Mara, Mrs M.A. Statement 690.
O'Mara, Peadar. Statement 377.
Ó Monachain, Ailbhe. Statement 298.
O'Mullane, Brigid (Bridie). Statements 450, 485.
O'Neill, Edward. Statement 203.
O'Rahilly, Áine. Statement 333.
O'Reilly, Bridie. Statement 454.
O'Reilly, Eily (née O'Hanrahan). Statement 270.
O'Reilly, Michael W. Statement 886.
O'Riain, Padraig. Statement 98.
O'Rourke, Joseph. Statement 1244.
O'Shea, James. Statement 733.
O'Shiel, Kevin. Statement 1770.
O'Sullivan, Dermot. Statement 508.
O'Sullivan, Patrick. Statement 34.
O'Sullivan, Seumas. Statement 393.
Peppard, Thomas. Statement 1399.
Perolz, Marie (née Flanagan). Statement 246.
Plunkett, Grace Gifford. Statement 257.
Plunkett, John (Jack). Statements 488, 865.
Pounch, Seámus. Statements 267, 294.
Prendergast, Seán. Statements 755, 820.
Price, Gen. Éamon. Statement 995.
Price, Seán. Statement 769.
Pugh, Thomas. Statement 397.
Quilty, John J. Statement 516.
Rankin, Patrick. Statement 163.
Reynolds, Molly. Statement 195.
Reynolds, Peter. Statement 350.
Rigney, Mary. Statement 752.
Robbins, Frank. Statement 585.
Rooney, Catherine (née Byrne). Statement 648.
Rosney, Joseph. Statement 112.
Ryan, Desmond. Statements 724, 725.
Ryan, Dr James. Statement 70.
Ryan, Mairin (née Cregan). Statement 416.
Ryan, Molly. Statement 403.
Saunders, Seán. Statements 817, 854.
Saurin, Charles. Statement 288.
Saurin, Frank. Statement 715.
Scully, Thomas. Statement 491.

Shelly, Charles. Statement 870.
Shields, Jack. Statement 224.
Shouldice, Jack (John F.). Statement 162.
Slater, Thomas (Tom). Statement 263.
Slattery, James (Jim). Statement 445.
Smart, Thomas. Statement 255.
Smith, Eugene. Statement 334.
Smyth, Patrick. Statement 305.
Soughley, Michael T. Statement 189.
Stack, Una. Statements 214, 418.
Stafford, Jack. Statement 818.
Staines, Michael. Statements 284, 943, 944.
Stapleton, William James (Bill). Statement 822.
Styles, John J. Statement 175.
Tannam, Liam. Statement 242.
Thornton, Dr Brigid (née Lyons). Statement 259.
Thornton, Frank. Statements 510, 615.
Thornton, Nora. Statement 655.
Tobin, Liam. Statement 1753.
Traynor, Oscar. Statement 340.
Treacy, Thomas. Statements 590, 1093.
Tully, James. Statement 628.
Twamley, John. Statement 629.
Ui Chonnaill, Eilis Bean (née Ryan). Statement 568.
Walker, Charles. Statements 241, 266.
Walker, Michael. Statement 139.
Wall, Charles. Statement 164.
Walpole, R.H. (Harry). Statement 218.
Walsh, J.J. Statement 91.
Walsh, James and Thomas. Statement 198.
Walsh, Michael. Statement 144.
Walsh, Richard. Statement 400.
Ward, Patrick. Statement 1140.
Weston, Charles. Statement 149.
Whelan, William. Statement 369.
White, George. Statement 956.
Woods, Mary(née Flannery). Statement 624.
Wylie, W.E. Statement 864.
Wyse-Power, Charles. Statement 420.
Wyse-Power, Nancy. Statements 541, 587, 732.
Young, Thomas. Statement 531.

Bureau of Military History Contemporary Documents

Augustine, Fr OFM. Document 159.
Barton, Robert. Documents 239, 264.
Bulfin, Éamon. Document 99.
Ceannt, Áine. Documents 94, 295.
Colivet, Michael. Document 145.
Collins, Seán. Document 1.
Collins, Mrs Seán. Document 2.
Colum, Mary. Document 30.

Comerford, Maire. Document 59.
Cosgrave, William. Documents 18, 125.
Dillon, Geraldine Plunkett. Documents 5, 33, 60, 80, 191.
Fogarty, Most Rev Dr Michael. Document 150.
Heron, Áine. Document 130.
Heuston, Revd John, OP. Document 309.
Hobson, Bulmer. Documents 8, 38, 41.

Lynch, Diarmuid. Document 16.
Lyons, George. Documents 54, 300.
Macardle, Dorothy. Documents 9, 118, 137.
McCartan Dr Patrick. Document 231.
Mee, RIC Constable Jeremiah. Document 255.
Molony, Helena. Document 119.
Mulcahy, Richard. Document 139.

Ó Buachalla, Domhnall. Document 114.
O'Connor, John ('Blimey'). Document 152.
O'Donoghue, Florence. Documents 27, 43.
O'Reilly, Michael W. Document 302.
Plunkett, John (Jack). Documents 179, 320.
Wyse-Power, Nancy. Documents 193, 194, 200.

Kathleen Barry Moloney Papers, University College Library.
Col. Maurice Moore Papers, National Library of Ireland.
Munster Express.
Gen. Richard Mulcahy Papers, University College Dublin.
1916 Papers, Box 5608, No. 5688, National Archives of Ireland.
Kathleen McKenna Napoli Papers, National Library of Ireland.
The Nation.
National Observer.
National Student.
New Ireland.
Nineteenth Century.
North Dublin Inner City Folklore Project, Amiens Street, Dublin 1.
North King Street Atrocities Files, British Public Record Office (PRO), WO 141.21, 141.27.
William O'Brien Papers, National Library of Ireland.
J.J. (Ginger) O'Connell Papers, National Library of Ireland.
Batt O'Connor Papers, University College Library.
Rory O'Connor Papers, University College Library.
Florence O'Donoghue Papers, National Library of Ireland.
Agnes O'Farrelly Papers, University College Library.
Official reports on the court martial proceedings of rebel leaders, British Public Record Office (PRO), WO 71.
Duirmuid O'Hegarty Papers, University College Library.
Seán T. O'Kelly (Ó Ceallaigh) Papers, National Library of Ireland.
Ernie O'Malley Papers, University College Dublin.
Brigid (Bridie) O'Mullane Papers, National Archives of Ireland.
The O'Rahilly (Michael Joseph) Papers, University College Library.
James Pearse Papers, National Library of Ireland.
Patrick Pearse Papers, National Library of Ireland.
William (Willie) Pearse Papers, National Library of Ireland.
Lt Gen. A.E. Percival Papers, Imperial War Museum, Folder 411. 'Guerrilla Warfare in Ireland, 1919-1921, Folder 411, pp. 19-23.
Count George Noble Plunkett Papers, National Library of Ireland.
Sir Horace Plunkett Papers, University College Library.
Poblacht na hÉireann
'Report on the Intelligence Branch of the Chief of Police from May 1920 to July 1921', Col. Ormonde de l'Epée Winter, British Public Records Office (PRO), WO 35/214.
'Report of the Proceedings of the Sinn Féin Convention, 25-26 October 1917', British Public Records Office (PRO), CO 904/23.
The Republic, published by the Irish Institute.
Return showing the number of serious outrages in Ireland reported by the Royal Irish Constabulary and the Dublin Metropolitan Police during the months of October, November, and December 1920, 1922 CMD 1165 XVII 807, 815.
Diarmuid Ó Donnabhain Rossa, 1831-1915: Souvenir of Public Funeral (Dublin, 1915).
Royal Commission on the Landing of Arms at Howth on 26th July 1914, Report, (1914), Cd. 7631.
Royal Commission on the Rebellion in Ireland, Report (1916), Cd. 8279, Minutes of Evidence, Cd. 8311, 1916. Commission appointed 10 May 1916.

Royal Commission on the Arrest and Subsequent Treatment of Mr Francis Sheehy Skeffington, Mr Thomas Dickson, Mr Patrick James McIntyre, Report (29 September 1916), Cd. 8376.

Royal Irish Constabulary, Auxiliary Division: Outline of Terms on which Cadets of the Auxiliary Division were engaged, HM Stationery Office, CMD 1618, XVII 785, 1922.

The Royal Irish Constabulary Magazine.

Desmond Ryan Papers, University College Library.

Dr James Ryan Papers, University College Library.

St Enda's School Papers, University College Library.

Saothar.

Sinn Féin.

Hanna Sheehy-Skeffington Papers, National Library of Ireland, MS 21 194.

Sinn Féin Convention Reports: 1917, 1918, 1919, 1920, 1921. National Library of Ireland.

Sinn Féin Party Papers, University College Library.

Sligo Champion.

Austin Stack Papers, National Library of Ireland.

Studies, *The Irish Jesuit Quarterly Review.*

The Spark.

Gen. Sir E.P. Strickland Papers, Imperial War Museum, P. 362, pp. 97-98. 'The Irish Rebellion in the 6th Divisional Area: From after the 1916 Rebellion to December 1921'.

Mark Sturgis' Diaries, British Public Record Office (PRO), WO 30/59.

Sunday Express.

Sunday Tribune.

Thom, Alexander, *Thom's Irish Almanac and Official Directory.*

Tipperary Historical Review.

Trinity College Library.

    Manuscript Department

    Fogarty, M. 'Letter on the Death of Thomas Ashe from the Bishop of Killaloe', 30 September 1914.

    Peadar Kearney, 'Reminiscences of Easter Week', TCDMS 3560.

    Lt A.A. Luce, '12th Royal Irish Rifles, Recollections of Easter 1916', TCDMS 4874.

    Mahaffy, Elise. 'Ireland in 1916: An Account of the Rising in Dublin'. TCDMS 2073.

    Ó Cearnaigh, Peadar. 'Founding of the Irish Republican Brotherhood'. TCDMS 2560/2.

    Ó Cearnaigh, Peadar. 'Reminiscences of the Irish Republican Brotherhood and Easter Week 1916'. TCDMS 3560/1.

    Plunkett, G.N. 'Letter to the People of North Roscommon upon Election to Office'. 17 March 1917. TCDMS 2074

    Posters warning against the evils of the British army, TCDMS 2074.

    Prayer cards for the repose of the souls of the following Irishmen who were executed by English law, 1916, TCDMS 2074.

Volunteer Gazette.

The Voice of Labour.

The Watchword of Labour.

The Weekly Summary (Dublin Castle).

Westmeath Examiner.

Sir Henry Wilson Papers, Imperial War Museum, DS/MISC/80, HHW/2/2B.

Wolfe Tone Annual.

The Worker.

Workers Republic.

BOOKS

Aalen, F.H.A. and K. Whelan. *Dublin City and County from Pre-History to Present* (Dublin, 1992).

aan de Wiel, Jerome. *The Catholic Church in Ireland 1914-1918* (Dublin, 2003).

aan de Wiel, Jerome. *The Irish Factor, 1899-1919. Ireland's Strategic and Diplomatic Importance for Foreign Powers* (Dublin, 2008).

Abbott, Richard. *Police Casualties in Ireland,* 1919-1922 (Cork, 2000).

Adams, Gerry. *Who Fears to Speak? The Story of Belfast and the 1916 Rising* (Belfast, 2001).

Adams, Michael. *Censorship, The Irish Experience* (Montgomery, Alabama, 1968).

Adams, R.J.Q. and Sidney Poirier. *The Conscription Controversy in Great Britain, 1900-1918* (Basingstoke, 1978).

Adas, Michael. *Prophets of Rebellion* (Chapel Hill, North Carolina, 1979).

Aitken, William Maxwell (Lord Beaverbrook). *Politicians and the War, 1914-1916* (London, 1928).

Aitken, William Maxwell (Lord Beaverbrook). *The Decline and Fall of Lloyd George* (London and New York, 1963).

Akenson, Donald K. *Small Differences: Irish Catholics and Irish Protestants. 1815-1922. An International Perspective* (Dublin, 1988).

Alberti, Johanna. *Beyond Suffrage: Feminists in War and Peace, 1914-1928* (Basingstoke, 1998).

Alderman, Clifford Lindsey. *The Wearing of the Green, The Irish Rebellion, 1916–1921* (1972).

Alexander, Yonah and Alan O'Day, editors. *Ireland's Terrorist Dilemma* (Dartrecht, 1986).

Alexander, Yonah and Alan O'Day, editors. *The Irish Terrorist Experience* (Aldershot, 1991).

Allen, Gregory. *The Garda Siochana* (Dublin, 1999).

Allen, Kieran. *The Politics of James Connolly* (London, 1990).

Ambrose, Joe. *Dan Breen and the I.R.A.* (Cork, 2007).

Anonymous. *Arthur Griffith, A Study of the Founder of Sinn Féin* (Dublin, *c.* 1917).

Anderson, Benedict. *Imagined Communities: Reflections on the Origins and Spread of Nationalism* (London, 1983).

Anderson, William. *James Connolly and the Irish Left* (Dublin, 1994).

Andrew, Christopher and David Dilks, editors. *The Missing Dimension. Governments and Intelligence Communities in the Twentieth Century* (London, 1984).

Andrews, C.S. *Dublin Made Me* (Cork, 1979; Dublin, 2001).

Andrews, C.S. *Man of No Property* (Cork, 1982; Dublin, 2001).

Angell, Norman. *The Public Mind* (London, 1926).

Arnstein, Walter. *The Bradlaugh Case: Atheism, Sex, and Politics among the Late Victorians* (Columbia, Missouri, 1983).

Arthur, Christopher, editor. *Engels Today: A Centenary Appreciation* (London, 1996).

Arthur, Sir George. *General Sir John Maxwell* (London, 1932).

Ash, B. *The Last Dictator: A Biography of Field Marshal Sir Henry Wilson* (London, 1968).

Ashe, Julian. *The Irish Book of Lists* (Cork, 2008).

Asquith, Lady Cynthia. *Diaries, 1915-1918* (London, 1968).

Asquith, H.H. (Earl of Oxford and Asquith). *The Paisley Policy* (London, 1920).

Augusteijn, Joost. *From Public Defiance to Guerrilla Warfare* (Dublin, 1996).

Augusteijn, Joost, editor. *The Irish Revolution* (Basingstoke, 2002).

Ayling, Ronald, editor. *Seán O'Casey, Modern Judgments* (London, 1969).

Baganal, Philip H. *The American-Irish and their Influence on Irish Politics* (London, 1882).

Baker, J. *My Stand for Freedom: Autobiography of an Irish Republican Soldier* (1988).

Bailey, Thomas A. *Woodrow Wilson and the Great Betrayal* (New York, 1945).

Balfour, Arthur. *Nationality and Home Rule* (London, 1914).

Ballinger, W.A. *The Men that God Made Mad* (New York, 1969).

Bambury, Chris. *Ireland's Permanent Revolution* (London, 1986).

Bardon, Jonathan. *A History of Ulster* (Belfast, 1992).

Barrett, J.J. *In the Name of the Game.* (Bray, 1997).

Barry, Tom. *The Reality of the Anglo-Irish 1920-21 in West Cork: Refutations, Corrections and Comments on Liam Deasy's Towards Ireland Free* (Dublin, 1974).

Barry, Tom. *Guerilla Days in Ireland: A Personal Account of the Anglo-Irish War* (Dublin, 1981).

Bartlett, T. and Keith Jeffery, editors. *A Military History of Ireland* (Cambridge, 1996).

Barton, Brian. *From Behind a Closed Door: Secret Court Martial Documents of the 1916 Rising* (Belfast, 2002).

Bayley, Sir Admiral Lewis. *Pull Together!* (London, 1939).

Béaslaí, Piaras. *With the I.R.A. in the fight for Freedom: The Red Path of Glory* (The Kerryman, undated, about 1922).

Béaslaí, Piaras. *How It Was Done: I.R.A. Intelligence: Dublin's Fighting Story* (1926).

Béaslaí, Piaras. *Michael Collins and the Making of the New Ireland.* 2 Vols (London, 1926).

Béaslaí, Piaras. *Michael Collins: Soldier and Statesman* (Dublin, 1937).

Beckett, I.F.W., editor. *The Army and the Curragh Incident, 1914* (London, 1986).

Beckett, James Camlin. *The Making of Modern Ireland, 1603-1923* (London and New York, 1966).

Beckett, James Camlin. *A Short History of Ireland* (London, 1973).

Beckett, James Camlin. *The Anglo-Irish Tradition* (London, 1976).

Begley, Diarmuid. *The Road to Crossbarry: The Decisive Battle in the War of Independence* (Cork, 1999).

Behan, Brian. *Mother of All the Behans: the autobiography of Kathleen Behan as told to Brian Behan* (London, 1984).

Bell, J. Bowyer. *The Gun in Politics: An Analysis of Irish Political Conflict, 1916-1986* (New Brunswick, New Jersey, 1991).

Bell, J. Bowyer. *The Secret Army, The I.R.A.* (Dublin, 1997).

Bence-Jones, Mark. *Twilight of the Ascendancy* (London, 1967).

Bennett, D. *The Encyclopaedia of Dublin* (Dublin, 1991).

Bennett, George. *The History of Bandon* (Cork, 1862, 1869).

Bennett, Richard. *The Black and Tans* (London 1964, 2001).

Bergin, James J. *History of the Ancient Order of Hibernians* (Dublin, 1910).

Bew, Paul, Peter Gibbon and Henry Patterson. *The State in Northern Ireland, 1921-1972: Political Forces and Social Classes* (Manchester, 1979)

Bew, Paul and Henry Patterson. *Seán Lemass and the Making of Modern Ireland* (Dublin, 1982).

Bew, Paul, Ellen Hazelkorn and Henry Patterson. *The Dynamics of Irish Politics* (London, 1989).

Bew, Paul. *Ideology and the Irish Question* (Oxford, 1994).

Bew, Paul. *John Redmond* (Dublin, 1996).

Bew, Paul. *Ireland: The Politics of Enmity, 1789-2006* (Oxford, 2007).

Bewley, Charles. *Memoirs of a Wild Goose* (Dublin, 1989).

Birmingham, George A. *An Irishman Looks at His World* (London, 1919)

Birrell, Augustine. *Things Past Redress* (London, 1937).

Black, R.D. *Economic Thought and the Irish Question* (Cambridge, 1960).

Blake, Robert. *The Unknown Prime Minister* (London, 1955).

Blake, Robert. *Unrepentant Tory* (New York, 1956).

Bodkin, M. McD. *Recollections of an Irish Judge: Press, Bar and Parliament* (London, 1914).

Boland, Kevin. *Up Dev.* (Dublin, 1977).

Bolger, Dermot, editor. *16 On 16* (Dublin, 1989).

Bonham Carter, Violet. *Winston Churchill as I knew him* (London, 1965).

Bonsall, Penny. *The Irish RMs: the resident magistrates in the British administration in Ireland* (Dublin, 1997).

Borgonovo, John. *Florence and Josephine O'Donoghue's War of Independence: A Destiny that Shapes our Ends* (Dublin, 2006).

Borgonovo, John. *Spies, Informers & the Anti-Sinn Féin Society* (Dublin, 2007).

Bourke, Marcus. *John O'Leary* (Tralee, 1967).

Bourke, Marcus. *The O'Rahilly* (Tralee, 1967).

Bowden, Tom. *The Breakdown of Public Security: The Case of Ireland 1916-1921 and Palestine 1936-1939* (London, 1977).

Bowen, Elizabeth. *The Shelbourne. A Centre in Dublin Life for More than a Century* (London, 1951).

Bowers, Claude G. *Ireland's Orators. A History of Ireland's Fight for Freedom* (New York, 1916).

Bowman, John. *De Valera and the Ulster Question, 1917-1973* (Oxford, 1982).

Bowman, Timothy. *Carson's Army: The Ulster Volunteer Force 1910-1922* (Manchester, 2008).

Boyce, D. George. *Englishmen and Irish Troubles: British Public Opinion and the Making of Irish Policy, 1918-1922* (London, 1972; Aldershot, 1994).

Boyce, D. George. *Nationalism in Ireland* (London, 1982).

Boyce, D. George, editor. *The Revolution in Ireland, 1879-1903* (London, 1988).

Boyce, D. George. *Nineteenth-Century Ireland: The Search for Stability* (Dublin, 1990).

Boyce, D. George, Robert Eccleshall and Vincent Geoghegan, editors. *Political Thought in Ireland since the Seventeenth Century* (London, 1993).

Boyce, D. George and Alan O'Day, editors. *The Ulster Crisis* (Basingstoke, 2006).

Boyd, E.A. *Ireland's Literary Renaissance* (New York, 1916).

Boylan, Henry. *A Dictionary of Irish Biography* (Niwot, Colorado, 1998; Dublin, 1999).

Boyle, Andrew. *The Riddle of Erskine Childers* (London, 1977).

Boyle, John F. *The Irish Rebellion of 1916* (London, 1916).

Boyle, John William. *Leaders and Workers* (Cork, 1986).

Boyle, John William. *The Irish Labor Movement in the Nineteenth Century* (Washington DC, 1988).

Bradbridge, Lt Col. E.U. *Fifty Ninth Division, 1915-1918, A Compilation* (Chesterfield, 1928).

Brady, Ciaran, editor. *Interpreting Irish History: the Debate on Historical Revisionism* (Dublin, 1994).

Brady, Conor. *Guardians of the Peace* (Dublin, 1974).

Brady, Edward M. *Ireland's Secret Service in England* (Dublin, 1924).

Brasier, Andrew and John Kelly. *Harry Boland, A Man Divided* (Dublin, 2000).

Brayden, W.H. *Republican Courts in Ireland* (Chicago, Illinois, 1920).

Breathnach, M. *A Basic History of Ireland* (Dublin, undated).

Breathnach, Séamus. *The Irish Police* (Dublin, 1974).

Breen, Dan. *My Fight for Irish Freedom* (Dublin, 1924; Tralee, 1964).

Brennan, Michael. *The War in Clare 1911-1921* (Dublin, 1980).

Brennan, Nial. *Dr Mannix* (Sydney, 1965).

Brennan, Robert, editor. *Ireland's Case Against Conscription* (Dublin and London, 1918).

Brennan, Robert. *Allegiance* (Dublin, 1950).

Brennan-Whitmore, W.J. *With the Irish in Frongoch* (Dublin, 1917).

Brennan-Whitmore, W.J. *Dublin Burning: The Easter Rising from Behind the Barricades* (Dublin, 1996).

Brewer, John D. *The Royal Irish Constabulary: An Oral History* (Belfast, 1990).

Briollay, Sylvain, writing under the pseudonym of Roger Chauvire. *Ireland in Rebellion* (Dublin, 1922).

Briscoe, R., with A. Hatch. *For the Life of Me* (London, 1958).

Broderick, Marian. *Wild Irish Women* (Dublin, 2001).

Brodie, Malcolm. *100 Years of Irish Football* (Belfast, 1980).

Bromage, Mary C. *De Valera and the March of a Nation* (New York, 1956).

Bromage, Mary C. *Churchill and Ireland* (Notre Dame, Indiana, 1964).

Brooke, Rupert. *Letters from America* (London, 1916).

Brooks, Sydney. *The New Ireland* (Dublin, 1907).

Brophy, Brigid. *Black Ship to Hell* (New York, 1962).

Brown, Malcom. *The Politics of Irish Literature* (Seattle, Washington, 1972).

Brown, T.N. *Irish-American Nationalism* (New York, 1966).

Browne, C. *The Story of the 7th. A Concise History of the 7th Battalion Cork No. 1 Brigade I.R.A. from 1915-1921* (undated).

Browne, Noel. *Against the Tide* (Dublin, 1986).

Browne, Revd Paddy, editor. *Aftermath of Easter Week* (1917).

Bruce, Steve. *The Red Hand: Protestant Paramilitaries in Ireland* (Oxford, 1992).

Brugha, Maire MacSwiney. *History's Daughter* (Dublin, 2005).

Buckland, Patrick. *Irish Unionism, The Anglo-Irish and the New Ireland* (Dublin, 1972).

Buckland, Patrick. *Irish Unionism, Ulster Unionism and the Origins of Northern Ireland* (Dublin, 1973).

Buckland, Patrick. *James Craig* (Dublin, 1980).

Buckland, Patrick. *A History of Northern Ireland* (Dublin, 1981).

Buckley, Donal. *The Battle of Tourmakeady: a study of the IRA ambush and its aftermath* (Dublin, 2008).

Buckley, Margaret. *The Jangle of the Keys* (Dublin, 1938).

Bull, Philip. *Land, Politics and Nationalism* (Dublin, 1996).

Bussy, F.M. *Irish Conspiracies: Recollections of John Mallon* (London, 1910).

Butler, David and Jennie Freeman. *British Political Facts, 1900-1960* (New York, 1961).

Butler, Ewan. *Barry's Flying Column: The Story of the I.R.A.'s Cork No. 3 Brigade, 1919–1921* (London, 1971).

Byrne, Anne and Madeleine Leonard, editors. *Women and Irish Society: A Sociological Reader* (Belfast, 1997).

Byron, Lesley. *Opportunist Sinn Féiners* (London, 1921).

Bywater, H.C. and H.C. Ferraby. *Strange Intelligence* (London, 1931).

Cahill, Liam. *Forgotten Revolution: Limerick Soviet, 1919* (undated).

Callanan, Frank. *The Parnell Split: 1890-91* (Cork, 1992).

Callanan, Frank. *T.M. Healy* (Cork, 1996).

Callwell, Maj. Gen. Sir C.E. *Field Marshal Sir Henry Wilson* (London, 1927).

Cameron, Sir Charles. *An Autobiography* (Dublin, 1920).

Campbell, Colm. *Emergency Law in Ireland, 1918–1925* (Oxford, 1994).

Campbell, F. *Land and Revolution: Nationalist Politics in the West of Ireland, 1891-1921* (Oxford, 2005).

Campbell, P. *Thirty-Five Years on the Job* (London, 1958).

Cannadine, David. *The Decline and Fall of the British Aristocracy* (New Haven, Connecticut, 1990).

Canning, Paul. *British Policy towards Ireland, 1921-1941* (Oxford, 1985).

Caprani, Vincent. *A Walk Around Dublin* (Belfast, 1992).

Carbery, Ethna, writing under the pseudonym of A.J. MacManus. *The Four Winds of Eirinn* (1902).

Cardoza, Nancy. *Maud Gonne* (London, 1979).

Carey, Tim. *Hanged for Ireland.* (Dublin, 2001).

Carroll, D. *They Have Fooled You Again: Michael Flanagan, 1872-1942* (Dublin, 1993).

Carroll, Francis M. *American Opinion and the Irish Question, 1910–1923* (Dublin, 1978).

Carroll, Francis M., editor. *The American Commission on Irish Independence 1919. The Diary, Correspondence and Report.* Irish Manuscripts Commission (Dublin, 1985).

Carson, William A. *Ulster and the Irish Republic* (Belfast, 1956).

Carty, James. *Bibliography of Irish History, 1912-1921* (Dublin, 1936).

Carty, James. *Ireland—From the Great Famine to the Treaty of 1921* (Dublin, 1951).

Carty, Xavier. *In Bloody Protest, The Tragedy of Patrick Pearse* (Dublin, 1978).

Casement, Sir Roger. *Ireland, Germany and the Freedom of the Seas* (New York, 1914).

Casement, Sir Roger. Edited by H.O. Mackey. *The Crime against Europe* (Dublin, 1958).

Cashman, Denis B. Edited by C.W. Sullivan III. *Fenian Diary* (Dublin, 2001).

Caulfield, Max. *The Easter Rebellion, Dublin 1916* (Dublin, 1963, 1995).

Ceannt, Áine. *The Story of the Irish White Cross, 1920-1947* (Dublin, undated).

Cecil, Lord Robert. *The New Outlook* (London, 1919).

Cett, Jim. *Not While I have Ammo: a history of Captain Connie Mackey, defender of the Strand* (Dublin, 2008).

Chamberlain, Austen. *Down the Years* (London, 1935).

Chatterton, Edward Keble. *Danger Zone* (London, 1934).

Chevasse, Moirin. *Terence MacSwiney* (Dublin and London, 1961).

Childers, Robert Erskine. *The Framework of Home Rule* (London, 1911).

Choille, Breandan MacGiolla, editor. *Intelligence Notes 1913-1916. Preserved in the State Paper Office* (Baile Átha Cliath, 1966).

Chorley, Katherine. *Armies and the Art of Revolution* (London, 1943).

Chubb, B. *The Government and Politics of Ireland* (Stanford, 1982).

Churchill, Randolph S. *Lord Derby: King of Lancashire* (London, 1959).

Churchill, Sir Winston S. *The Aftermath* (London, 1929).

Churchill, Sir Winston S. *The World Crisis, 1911-1918* (London, 1931).

Clark, Wallace. *Guns in Ulster* (Belfast, 1967).

Clarke, Austin. *A Penny in the Clouds: More Memories of Ireland and England* (London, 1968).

Clarke, Gordon. *Tourist Trail: A Signposted Walking Tour of Dublin* (Dublin, undated).

Clarke, Kathleen. Edited by Helen Litton. *Revolutionary Woman, My Fight for Ireland's Freedom* (Dublin, 1997).

Clarkson, Jesse Dunsmore. *Labour and Nationalism in Ireland* (New York, 1925, 1978).

Clerkin, Paul. *Dublin Street Names* (Dublin, 2001).

Clifford, Angela. *The Constitutional History of Éire/Ireland* (Belfast, 1987).

Clifford, Brendan. *The Irish Civil War: The Conflict that Formed the State* (Aubane, 1993).

Clifford, Brendan. *Casement as Traitor Patriot* (London, 2002).

Coalter, Mark. *Rebel With a Cause. Dan Breen and the I.R.A.* (Cork, 2006).

Coates, Ken and Tony Topham. *The Making of the Transport and General Workers' Union: The Emergence of the Labour Movement, 1870-1922* (Oxford, 1991).

Coates, Tim, editor. *The Irish Uprising, 1914-1921: Papers from the British Parliamentary Archive* (London, 2000).

Cockerill, Brig. Gen. Sir George. *What Fools We Were* (London, 1944).

Cody, Seámus, John O'Dowd and Peter Rigney. *The Parliament of Labour, 100 Years of the Dublin Council of Trade Unions* (Dublin, 1986).

Coffey, Diarmuid. *Douglas Hyde* (Dublin, 1938).

Coffey, Thomas M. *Agony at Easter* (London, 1969).

Coldrey, Barry. *Faith and Fatherland: The Christian Brothers and the Development of Irish Nationalism, 1838-1921* (Dublin, 1988).

Coleman, Marie. *County Longford and the Irish Revolution* (Dublin, 2003).

Collier, Basil. *Brass Hat: A Biography of Field Marshal Sir Henry Wilson* (London, 1961).

Collins, Michael. Edited by Tim Pat Coogan. *The Path to Freedom* (Dublin and London, 1922; Cork, 1996).

Collins, Peter, editor. *Nationalism and Unionism: Conflict in Ireland, 1885-1921* (Belfast, 1994).

Collins, Tom. *The Irish Hunger Strike* (Dublin, 1986).

Colls, Robert. *Identity of England* (Oxford, 2002).

Colum, Mary M. *Life and the Dream* (Dublin, 1928, New York, 1947).

Colum, Padraic. *Poems of the Irish Revolutionary Brotherhood* (Boston, Massachusetts, 1916).

Colum, Padraic. *An Anthology of Irish Verse* (1922; New York, 1948).

Colum, Padraic. *The Road Round Ireland* (New York, 1926).

Colum, Padraic. *Arthur Griffith* (Dublin, 1959).

Colvin, Ian D. *Life of Lord Carson.* Vols II and III (London, 1934). (See Marjoribanks, Edward, for Vol. I).

Colvin, Ian D. *Carson the Statesman* (New York, 1935).

Comerford, Anthony. *The Easter Rising, Dublin 1916* (New York, 1969).

Comerford, James. *My Kilkenny I.R.A. Days, 1916-1922* (Kilkenny, 1978).

Comerford, Maire. *The First Dáil, January 21st 1919* (Dublin, 1969).

Comerford, R.V. *The Fenians in Context: Irish Politics and Society 1848-82* (Dublin, 1985).

Comerford, R.V. *Inventing the Nation: Ireland* (London, 2003).

Conlon, Lil. *Cumann na mBan and the Women of Ireland, 1913-1972* (Kilkenny, 1969).

Connell, Joseph E.A., Jnr *Where's Where in Dublin, A Directory of Historic Locations 1913-1923* (Dublin, 2006).

Connolly, Colm. *The Illustrated Life of Michael Collins* (Boulder, Colorado, 1996).

Connolly, Cyril. *Enemies of Promise* (New York, 1983).

Connolly, James. *Socialism and Nationalism* (undated).

Connolly, James. *Socialism Made Easy* (undated).

Connolly, James. *Workshop Talks* (Cork, undated).

Connolly, James. *Erin's Care: The End & The Means* (Dublin, 1897).

Connolly, James. *The Worker's Republic* (Dublin, 1898).

Connolly, James. *The New Evangel* (Dublin, 1898).

Connolly, James. *Labour in Irish History* (Dublin, 1910, 1983).

Connolly, James. *The Axe to the Root* (Dublin, 1914).

Connolly, James. Edited by Desmond Ryan. *Labour and Easter Week; A Selection from the Writings of James Connolly* (Dublin, 1949).

Connolly, James. *Revolutionary Warfare* (Dublin, 1968).

Connolly, Linda. *The Irish Women's Movement* (New York, 2002; Dublin, 2003).

Connolly, Nora. *The Irish Rebellion of 1916* or *The Unbroken Tradition* (New York, 1918).

Connolly, Nora (O'Brien). *Portrait of a Rebel Father* (Dublin and London, 1975).
Connolly, Nora (O'Brien). *We Shall Rise Again* (London, 1981).
Connolly, S.J., editor. *The Oxford Companion to Irish History* (Oxford, 1998, 2001).
Coogan, Oliver. *Politics and War in Meath, 1913-1923* (Dublin, 1983).
Coogan, Tim Pat. *Ireland Since the Rising* (London, 1966).
Coogan, Tim Pat. *The IRA* (London, 1973).
Coogan, Tim Pat. *The Irish, A Personal View* (London, 1975).
Coogan, Tim Pat. *Michael Collins, The Man Who Made Ireland* (London, 1992).
Coogan, Tim Pat. *De Valera: Long Fellow, Long Shadow* (London, 1993).
Coogan, Tim Pat and George Morrison. *The Irish Civil War* (London, 1998).
Coogan, Tim Pat. *1916: The Easter Rising* (London, 2001).
Cooke, Pat. *Scéal Scoil Éanna* (Dublin, 1986).
Cooper, Duff. *Old Men Forget* (London, 1953).
'Coilin'. *Patrick H. Pearse: A Sketch of his Life* (Dublin, 1917).
Corish, P.J., editor. *A History of Irish Catholicism* (Dublin, 1967).
Corkery, Daniel. *The Hounds of Banba* (1920).
Corlett, Christiaan. *Darkest Dublin: The Story of the Church Street disaster and a pictoral account of the slums of Dublin in 1913* (Dublin, 2008).
Corlett, Christiaan and Robert L. Chapman. *Robert L. Chapman's Photographs from the Chapman Collection 1907-1957* (Dublin, 2008).
Corry, Eoghan. *An Illustrated History of the GAA* (Dublin, 2005).
Costello, Francis. *Enduring the Most: The Life and Death of Terence MacSwiney* (Dingle, 1995).
Costello, Francis, editor. *Michael Collins In His Own Words* (Dublin, 1997).
Costello, Francis. *The Irish Revolution and its Aftermath, 1916–1923* (Dublin, 2003).
Costello, Peter. *The Heart Grown Brutal: The Irish Revolution in Literature from Parnell to the Death of Yeats, 1891-1939* (Dublin, 1977).
Côté, Jane. *Fanny and Anna Parnell: Ireland's patriot sisters* (Dublin, 1991).
Cottrell, Peter. *The Anglo-Irish War: The Troubles of 1913-1922* (Oxford, 2006).
Coulter, Carol. *The Hidden Tradition: Feminism, Women, and Nationalism in Ireland* (Cork, 1993).
Courtney, D.A. *Reminiscences of the Easter Rising* (Nenagh, 1916, 1980).
Cousins, James and Margaret Cousins. *We Two Together* (Madras, 1950).
Cowell, John. *Where They Lived in Ireland* (Dublin, 1980).
Cowell, John. *Dublin's Famous People and Where They Lived* (Dublin, 1996).
Cowell, John. *A Noontide Blazing. Brigid Lyons Thornton. Rebel, Soldier, Doctor* (Dublin, 2005).
Cowling, Maurice. *The Impact of Labour 1920-1924: The Beginnings of Modern British Politics* (Cambridge, 1971).
Coxhead, Elizabeth. *Lady Gregory* (London, 1961).
Coxhead, Elizabeth. *Daughters of Erin* (London, 1965).
Crane, C.P. *Memories of A Resident Magistrate, 1880-1920* (Edinburgh, 1938).
Crawford, F.H. *Guns for Ulster* (Belfast, 1947).
Creel, George. *Ireland's Fight for Freedom* (New York, 1919).
Cronin, Mike. *Sport and Nationalism in Ireland: Gaelic Games, Soccer, and Irish Identity since 1884* (Dublin, 1999).
Cronin, Seán. *Our Own Red Blood, the Story of the 1916 Rising* (Dublin, 1966).
Cronin, Seán. *The Story of Kevin Barry* (Cork, 1971).
Cronin, Seán. *Ideology of the I.R.A.* (Ann Arbor, Michigan, 1972).
Cronin, Seán. *The McGarrity Papers* (Tralee, 1972).
Cronin, Seán. *Young Connolly* (Dublin, 1978).
Cronin, Seán. *Frank Ryan: The Search for the Republic* (Dublin, 1980).
Cronin, Seán. *Irish Nationalism: Its Roots and Ideology* (Dublin, 1980).
Cronin, Seán. *Washington's Irish Policy, 1916-1986. Independence, Partition, Neutrality* (Tralee, 1987).
Cronin, Seán and Richard Roche. *Freedom the Wolfe Tone Way* (Tralee, 1973).
Crossman, Virginia. *Politics, Law and Order in 19th Century Ireland* (Dublin, 1996).

Crowley, Flor. *In West Cork Long Ago* (Dublin, 1979).

Crowley, Tony. *The Politics of Language in Ireland 1366-1922* (London, 2000).

Crozier, Gen. Frank P. *Impressions and Recollections* (London, 1930).

Crozier, Gen. Frank P. *A Brass Hat in No Man's Land* (London, 1930).

Crozier, Gen. Frank P. *A Word to Ghandi: The Lesson of Ireland* (London, 1931).

Crozier, Gen. Frank P. *Ireland Forever* (London and Toronto, 1932).

Crozier, Gen. Frank P. *The Men I Killed* (London, 1937).

Cuimhni na bPiarsach: Memories of the Brothers Pearse. Edited by the Pearse Brothers Commemorative Committee (Dublin, 1966).

Cullen, L.M. *Eason & Son, A History* (Dublin, 1989).

Cullen, Mary and Maria Luddy, editors. *Women, Power and Consciousness* (Dublin, 1995).

Cullen, Mary and Maria Luddy. *Female Activists, Irish Women and the Change. 1900-1960* (Dublin, 2001).

Curran, C.P. *Under the Receding Wave* (Dublin, 1970).

Curran, Joseph M. *The Birth of the Irish Free State, 1921–1923* (Birmingham, Alabama, 1980).

Curry, Charles E. *Sir Roger Casement's Diaries* (Munich, 1922).

Curtin, Nancy. *The Revolution in Ireland, 1879–1923* (Oxford, 1994).

Curtis, Edmund. *A History of Ireland* (London, 1936).

Curtis, Edmund and R.B. McDowell, editors. *Irish Historical Documents, 1172-1922* (London, 1943; New York, 1968).

Curtis, L.P., Jnr. *Coercion and Conciliation in Ireland, 1880-1892* (Princeton, New Jersey, 1963).

Curtis, Liz. *The Cause of Ireland: From the United Irishmen to Partition* (Belfast, 1994).

Czira, Sydney Gifford. *The Years Flew By* (Dublin, 1974).

Dalton, Charles. *With the Dublin Brigade* (London, 1929).

Daly, Dominic. *The Young Douglas Hyde* (Dublin, 1974).

Daly, Mary E. *Dublin, The Deposed Capital: A Social and Economic History 1860-1914* (Cork, 1985).

Daly, Mary E., editor. *Roger Casement in Irish and world history* (Dublin, 2006).

Daly, Mary E. and Margaret O'Callaghan, editors. *1916 in 1966: Commemorating the Easter Rising* (Dublin, 2007).

Daly, Paul. *Creating Ireland: The Words and Events that Shaped Us* (Dublin, 2008).

Dangerfield, George. *The Damnable Question: A Study in Anglo-Irish Relations* (Boston, Massachusetts, 1976).

Dangerfield, George. *The Strange Death of Liberal England* (New York, 1980).

D'Arcy, William. *The Fenian Movement in the United States* (Washington DC, 1947).

David, E., editor. *Inside Asquith's Cabinet. From the Diaries of Charles Hothouse* (London, 1977).

Davis, Richard P. *Arthur Griffith and Non-Violent Sinn Féin* (Dublin, 1974).

Dawson, Richard. *Red Terror and Green* (First published in Great Britain by John Murray in 1920; London, 1972).

Deasy, Liam. *Towards Ireland Free, The West Cork Brigade in the War of Independence, 1917–1921* (Dublin, 1973).

Deasy, Liam. *Brother Against Brother* (Cork, 1998).

De Blacam, Aodh. *Towards the Republic* (Dublin, 1918).

De Burca, Marcus. *The G.A.A.: A History of the Gaelic Athletic Association* (Dublin, 1980).

De Burca, Marcus. *Michael Cusack and the GAA* (Dublin, 1989).

De Burca, Padraig and John Boyle. *Free State or Republic?* (Dublin, 1922, 2002).

Denieffe, Joseph. *A Personal Narrative of the Fenian Brotherhood (Irish Republican Brotherhood).* (New York, 1906; Dublin, 1969).

Denman, Terence. *Ireland's Unknown Soldiers* (Dublin, 1992).

Denman, Terence. *A Lonely Grave* (Dublin, 1995).

De Paor, Liam. *Divided Ulster* (London, 1970).

De Paor, Liam. *On the Easter Proclamation and Other Declarations* (Dublin, 1997).

De Rosa, Peter. *Rebels: The Irish Rising of 1916* (London, 1990).

Desmond, Shaw. *The Drama of Sinn Féin* (London, 1923).

De Valera, Éamon. *Ireland's Request to the Government of the United States for Recognition as a Sovereign Independent State* (Washington DC, 1920).

Devine, Francis, editor. *Essays in Irish Labour History: a festschrift for Elizabeth and John W. Boyle* (Dublin, 2008).

Devine, K., editor. *Modern Irish Writers and the Wars* (Gerrards Cross, 1999).

Devoy, John. *Recollections of an Irish Rebel* (New York, 1929).

Dicey, Albert Venn. *England's Case Against Home Rule* (London, 1886).

Dickson, David, D. Keogh and K. Whelan, editors. *The United Irishmen: Republicanism, Radicalism, and Rebellion* (Dublin, 1993).

Digby, Margaret. *Horace Plunkett* (Oxford, 1949).

Dillon, Geraldine Plunkett. *All in the Blood* (Dublin, 2007).

Dillon, John. *The Irish Electors* (Dublin, 1921).

Diner, Hasia. *Erin's Daughters in America* (Baltimore, Maryland, 1983).

Doerries, Reinhard. *Prelude to the Easter Rising. Sir Roger Casement in Imperial Germany* (London, 2000).

Doheny, Michael. Edited by Arthur Griffith. *The Felon's Track* (Dublin, 1914).

Doherty, Gabriel and Dermot Keogh, editors. *Michael Collins and the Making of the Irish State* (Cork, 1998).

Doherty, Gabriel and Dermot Keogh. *De Valera's Ireland* (Cork, 2003).

Doherty, Gabriel and Dermot Keogh, editors. *1916. The Long Revolution* (Cork, 2007).

Doherty, J.E. and D.J. Hickey. *A Chronology of Irish History Since 1500* (Dublin, 1989).

Dolan, Anne. *Commemorating the Irish Civil War: history and memory, 1923-2000* (Cambridge, 2003).

Dolan, Anne, editor. *Reinterpreting Robert Emmet: Essays on the Life and Legacy of Robert Emmet* (Dublin, 2007).

Donnelly, Mary. *The Last Post: Glasnevin Cemetery* (Dublin, 1994).

Dooley, Brian. *Choosing the Green, Second Generation Irish and the Cause of Ireland* (Belfast, 2004).

Dooley, Terence. *John Devoy, The Greatest of the Fenians* (Dublin, 2003).

Dooley, Thomas P. *Irishmen or English Soldiers?* (Liverpool, 1995).

Doorley, Michael. *Irish-American Diaspora Nationalism: The Friends of Irish Freedom, 1916-1935* (Dublin, 2005).

Doyle, Jennifer, Francis Clarke, Eibhlis Connaughton and Orna Somerville. *An Introduction to the Bureau of Military History, 1913-1921* (Dublin, 2002).

Doyle, Tom. *The Civil War in Kerry: Defending the Republic* (Cork, 2008).

Drisceoil, Donal. *Peadar O'Donnell* (Dublin, 2001).

Drury, Martin, editor. *The Page and the Stage: The Plough and the Stars* (Dublin, 2003).

Dublin, 1913: A Divided City. Curriculum Development Unit (Dublin, 1982).

Duff, Charles. *Six Days to Shake an Empire* (London, 1966).

Duff, Douglas V. *Sword for Hire* (London, 1934).

Duff, Douglas V. *The Rough with The Smooth* (London, 1940).

Duff, Douglas V. *The Way the Wind Blows* (London, 1948).

Duffy, Séan and Patrick Power. *Timetables of Irish History* (London, 2001).

Duggan. John P. *A History of the Irish Army* (Dublin, 1991).

Dungan, Myles. *Irish Voices from the Great War* (Dublin, 1995).

Dungan, Myles. *They Shall Not Grow Old: Irish Soldiers and the Great War* (Dublin, 1997).

Dungan, Myles. *Speaking Ill of the Dead* (Dublin, 2008).

Dunleavy, Janet Egelson and Gareth Dunleavy. *Douglas Hyde: A Maker of Modern Ireland* (Berkeley, California, 1991).

Dunne, Tom. *Theobald Wolfe Tone: Colonial Outsider* (Cork, 1982).

Durant, Will and Ariel Durant. *Lessons of History* (New York, 1968).

Durney, James. *Far From the Short Grass* (Naas, 1999).

Durney, James. *On the One Road: Political Unrest in Kildare, 1913-1994* (Naas, 2001).

Durney, James. *The Volunteer: Uniforms, Weapons, and History of the Irish Republican Army, 1913-1917* (Naas, 2004).

Dwane, David T. *The Early Life of Éamon de Valera* (Dublin, 1922).

Dwyer, T. Ryle. *Éamon de Valera* (Dublin, 1980).

Dwyer, T. Ryle. *Michael Collins and the Treaty* (Dublin, 1981).

Dwyer, T. Ryle. *De Valera's Darkest Hour, 1919–1932* (Dublin, 1982).

Dwyer, T. Ryle. *Michael Collins: The Man Who Won the War* (Cork, 1990).

Dwyer, T. Ryle. *De Valera: the Man and Myth* (Swords, 1992).

Dwyer, T. Ryle. *Tans, Terror and Troubles: Kerry's Real Fighting Story, 1913–1923* (Cork, 2001).

Dwyer, T. Ryle. *The Squad and the Intelligence Operations of Michael Collins* (Cork, 2005).

Dwyer, T. Ryle. *I Signed my Death Warrant: Michael Collins and the Treaty* (Cork, 2007).

Ebenezer, Lyn. *Fron-Goch and the Birth of the I.R.A.* (Llanrwst, Wales, 2006).

Ecksteins, Modris. *Rites of Spring: The Great War and the Birth of the Modern Age* (New York, 1989).

Edmonds, Seán. *The Gun, The Law and the Irish People* (London, 1971).

Edmunds, Cpt. G.J. *The 2/6th Battalion: The Sherwood Foresters, 1914-1918: its part in the defeat of the Irish Rebellion, 1916* (Chesterfield, 1960).

Edwards, Owen Dudley and Fergus Pyle, editors. *1916, The Easter Rising* (London, 1968).

Edwards, Owen Dudley and Bernard Ransom, editors. *James Connolly: Selected Political Writings* (London, 1973).

Edwards, Owen Dudley. *Éamon de Valera* (Cardiff, 1987).

Edwards, Ruth Dudley. *Patrick Pearse: The Triumph of Failure* (London, 1977).

Edwards, Ruth Dudley. *James Connolly* (Dublin, 1981).

Eglington, John. *A Memoir of Æ* (London, 1937).

Eichacker, Joanne Mooney. *Irish Republican Women in America. Lecture Tours, 1916-1925* (Dublin, 2003).

Elliott, Marianne. *The Catholics of Ulster: A History* (New York, 2001).

Ellis, Peter Beresford. *A History of the Irish Working Class* (London, 1972).

Ellis, Peter Beresford, editor. *James Connolly, Selected Writings* (Harmondsworth, Middlesex, 1973).

English, Richard and Cormac O'Malley, editors. *Prisoners: The Civil War Letters of Ernie O'Malley* (Dublin, 1991).

English, Richard. *Ernie O'Malley. I.R.A. Intellectual* (Oxford, 1998).

English, Richard. *Armed Struggle: a History of the I.R.A.* (London, 2003).

Ensor, R.C.K. *England, 1870-1914* (Oxford, 1936).

Everett, Katherine. *Brick and Flowers* (London, 1949).

Ervine, St John. *Sir Edward Carson and the Ulster Movement* (London and Dublin, 1913).

Ervine, St John. *Parnell* (London, 1936).

Ervine, St John. *Craigavon, Ulsterman* (London, 1949).

Ervine, St John. *Bernard Shaw* (London, 1956).

Ewart, Wilfred. *A Journey in Ireland, 1921* (New York, 1922).

Fallis, Richard. *The Irish Renaissance* (Syracuse, New York, 1977).

Fallon, Charlotte H. *Soul of Fire: A Biography of Mary MacSwiney* (Dublin, 1986).

Falls, C. *History of the First Seven Battalions, The Royal Irish Rifles in the Great War* (London, 1925).

Fanning, Ronan. *The Irish Department of Finance, 1922-1958* (Dublin, 1978).

Fanning, Ronan. *Independent Ireland* (Dublin, 1983).

Fanning, Ronan, Michael Kennedy, Dermot Keogh and Eunan O'Halpin. *Documents on Irish Foreign Policy, 1919-1922* (Dublin, 1998).

Farragher, Seán P. *Dev and His Alma Mater* (Dublin, 1984).

Farrell, Brian. *The Founding of Dáil Éireann* (Dublin, 1971).

Farrell, Brian. *Chairman or Chief? The Role of the Taoiseach in Irish Government* (Dublin, 1971).

Farrell, Brian, editor. *The Irish Parliamentary Tradition* (New York, 1973).

Farrell, Brian. *Seán Lemass* (Dublin, 1983).

Farrell, Brian, editor. *De Valera's Constitution and Ours* (Dublin, 1988).

Farrell, Brian, editor. *The Creation of the Dáil* (Dublin, 1994).

Farrell, J.G. *Troubles* (New York, 2002).

Farry, Michael. *Sligo, 1914-1921* (Trim, 1992).

Farry, Michael. *The Aftermath of Revolution: Sligo, 1921-1923* (Dublin, 2000).

Fay, Gerald. *The Abbey Theatre: Cradle of Genius* (London, 1958).

Feehan, John M. *The Shooting of Michael Collins: Murder or Accident?* (Cork, 1991).

Feeney, Brian. *Sinn Féin, A Hundred Turbulent Years* (Dublin, 2002).

Feeney, Tom. *Seán MacEntee: A Political Life* (Dublin, 2008).

Fennell, Desmond. *The Revision of Irish Nationalism* (Dublin, 1989).

Fennell, Desmond. *Heresy: The Battle of Ideas in Modern Ireland* (Dublin, 1993).

Ferguson, Stephen. *'Self Respect and a little extra leave': GPO staff in 1916* (An Post, Dublin, 2006).

Fergusson, Sir James. *The Curragh Incident* (London, 1964).

Ferriter, Diarmuid. *Lovers of Liberty? Local Government in Twentieth Century Ireland* (Dublin, 2001).

Ferriter, Diarmuid. *The Transformation of Ireland, 1900-2000* (London, 2004).

Ferriter, Diarmuid. *Judging Dev: A Reassessment of the Life and Legacy of Éamon de Valera* (Dublin, 2007).

Figgis, Darrell. *A Chronicle of Jails* (Dublin, 1917).

Figgis, Darrell. *The Irish Constitution Explained* (Dublin, 1922).

Figgis, Darrell, writing under the pseudonym of Michael Ireland *The Return of the Hero.* (London, 1923).

Figgis, Darrell. *Recollections of the Irish War* (London, 1927).

Fingall, Countess Elizabeth. *Seventy Years Young* (1937; Dublin, 1991).

Finnan, Joseph P. *John Redmond and Irish Unity, 1912–1918* (Syracuse, New York, 2004).

FitzGerald, Desmond. *Prelude to Statescraft* (London, 1939).

FitzGerald, Desmond. *Desmond's Rising* (Dublin, 1968).

FitzGerald, Garrett. *Towards a New Ireland* (Dublin, 1972).

FitzGerald, Garrett. Edited by Fergus Fitzgerald. *Reflections on the Irish State* (Dublin, 2003).

Fitzgerald, Redmond. *Cry Blood, Cry Erin: The Fight for Irish Freedom* (London, 1966).

Fitzgerald, William G., editor. *The Voice of Ireland* (Dublin and London, 1924).

FitzGibbon, Constantine. *Out of the Lion's Paw: Ireland Wins Her Freedom* (New York, 1969).

FitzGibbon, Constantine. *The Life and Times of Éamon de Valera* (New York, 1973).

Fitzhenry, Edna C. *Nineteen-Sixteen – An Anthology* (1935).

Fitzpatrick, David. *Politics and Irish Life, 1913–1921: Provincial Experience of War and Revolution* (Dublin, 1977).

Fitzpatrick, David. *Ireland and the First World War* (Dublin, 1986).

Fitzpatrick, David, editor. *Revolution: Ireland, 1917–1923* (Dublin, 1990).

Fitzpatrick, David. *The Two Irelands* (Oxford, 1998).

Fitzpatrick, David. *Harry Boland's Irish Revolution* (Cork, 2003).

Flanagan, Thomas. *The End of the Hunt* (London, 1994).

Fogerty, L. *James Fintan Lalor* (Dublin, 1921).

Foley, Conor. *Legion of the Rearguard: The I.R.A. and the Modern Irish State* (London, 1992).

Follis, Bryan A. *A State Under Siege: The Establishment of Northern Ireland* (Oxford, 1995).

Forester, Margery. *Michael Collins: The Lost Leader* (Dublin, 1989).

Foster, Roy F. *Modern Ireland, 1600-1972* (London, 1988).

Foster, Roy F. *The Oxford History of Ireland* (Oxford, 1992).

Foster, Roy F. *Paddy and Mr Punch: Connections in Irish and English History* (London, 1993).

Foster, Roy F. *The Irish Story* (London, 2001).

Foster, Roy F. *W.B. Yeats: A Life* (Oxford, 2003).

Fox, R.M. *Rebel Irishwomen* (Dublin and Cork, 1935).

Fox, R.M. *Green Banners: The Story of the Irish Struggle* (London, 1938).

Fox, R.M. *History of the Irish Citizen Army* (Dublin, 1944).

Fox, R.M. *James Connolly, The Forerunner* (Tralee, 1946).

Fox, R.M. *Louie Bennett: Her Life and Times* (Dublin, 1957).

Foxton, David. *Revolutionary Lawyers. Sinn Féin and the crown courts in Ireland and Britain, 1916-1923* (Dublin, 2008).

Foy, Michael T. and Brian Barton. *The Easter Rising* (Stroud, 1999).

Foy, Michael T. *Michael Collins' Intelligence War* (Stroud, 2006; Dublin, 2007).

Fraser, T.G. *Partition in Ireland, India and Palestine, Theory and Practice* (London, 1984).

Fraser, T.G. and Keith Jeffery, editors. *Men, Women and War* (Dublin, 1993).

French, Hon. E.G.F. *The Life of Field Marshal Sir John French* (London, 1931).

Fussell, Paul. *The Great War and Modern Memory* (New York, 1975).

GAA Golden Jubilee Supplement (Dublin, 1934).

Gaffney, T. St John. *Breaking the Silence* (New York, 1930).

Gallagher, Frank. *Days of Fear, A Diary of A Hunger Strike* (London, 1928).

Gallagher, Frank, writing under the pseudonym of David Hogan. *The Four Glorious Years* (Dublin, 1953).

Gallagher, Frank. *The Indivisible Island, The Story of the Partition of Ireland* (London, 1957).

Gallagher, Frank. Edited with Introduction by T.P. O'Neill. *The Anglo-Irish Treaty* (London, 1965).

Gallivan, G.P. *Decision at Easter* (Dublin, 1960).

Gallivan, G.P. *Dev.* Career of de Valera, 1919-1932, a two act play (1977).

Gallivan, G.P. *Selected Plays* (Dublin, 1999).

Garnham, Neal. *Association Football and Society in Pre-Partition Ireland* (Belfast, 2004).

Garnier, Charles M. *A Popular History of Ireland* (Cork, 1961).

Gavan-Duffy, George. *A Short History of Thomas Davis* (London, 1895).

Garvin, Tom. *The Evolution of Irish Nationalist Politics* (Dublin, 1981).

Garvin, Tom. *Nationalist Revolutionaries in Ireland, 1858-1928* (Oxford, 1987).

Garvin, Tom, editor. *The Revolution in Ireland* (Basingstoke, 1988).

Garvin, Tom. *1922: The Birth of Irish Democracy* (Dublin, 1996).

Gaughan, J. Anthony, editor. *Memoirs of Constable J. Mee, R.I.C.* (Dublin, 1975).

Gaughan, J. Anthony. *Austin Stack. Portrait of a Separatist* (Dublin, 1977).

Gaughan, J. Anthony. *Thomas Johnson, 1872-1963* (Mount Merrion, 1980).

Gavin, Joseph and Stephen O'Donnell. *Military Barracks Dundalk* (Dundalk, 1999).

Gibbon, Monk, editor. *The Living Torch: Æ* (London, 1937).

Gibbon, Monk. *Inglorious Soldier* (London, 1968).

Gibbs, A.M. *Bernard Shaw Chronology* (New York, 2001).

Gibbs, A.M. *Bernard Shaw. A Life* (Gainesville, Florida, 2006)

Gilmore, George. *The Relevance of James Connolly in Ireland Today* (Dublin, undated).

Gilmore, George. *Labour and the Republican Movement* (Dublin, 1966).

Gilmore, George. *The Irish Republican Congress* (Cork, 1978).

Ginnell, Laurence. *Land and Liberty* (undated).

Ginnell, Laurence. *D.O.R.A. at Westminster* (Dublin, 1918).

Ginnell, Laurence. *The Irish Republic: Why? Official Statement prepared for submission to the Peace Conference* (Dublin, 1919; New York, 2007).

Girvin, Kevin. *Seán O'Hegarty: Officer Commanding First Cork Brigade, I.R.A.* (Cork, 2007).

Githens-Mazer, Jonathan. *Myths and Memories of the Easter Rising: Cultural and Political Nationalism in Ireland* (Dublin, 2006).

Glandon, Virginia E. *Arthur Griffith and the Advanced Nationalist Press in Ireland, 1900-1922* (New York, 1985).

Gleeson, James. *Bloody Sunday* (London, 1962).

Glenavy, Lady Beatrice. *Today We Will Only Gossip* (London, 1964).

Godley, Gen. Sir Alexander. *Life of an Irish Soldier: reminiscences of General Sir Alexander Godley, GCB, KCMG* (London, 1939).

Gogarty, Oliver St John. *An Offering of Swans* (London, 1924).

Gogarty, Oliver St John. *As I Was Walking Down Sackville Street* (London, 1937).

Gogarty, Oliver St John. *It Isn't This Time of Year At All* (London, 1954).

Golding, G.M. *George Gavan Duffy, 1882-1951* (Dublin, 1982).

Goldring, Douglas, writing under the pseudonym 'An Englishman'. *Dublin Explorations and Reflections* (Dublin, 1917).

Goldring, Douglas, writing under the pseudonym 'An Englishman'. *A Stranger in Ireland* (Dublin, 1918).

Goldring, Douglas. *Odd Man Out* (London, 1935).

Goldring, Maurice. *Faith of Our Fathers* (Dublin, 1982).

Goldring, Maurice. *Pleasant the Scholar's Life, Irish Intellectuals and the Construction of the Nation State* (London, 1993).

Golway, Terry. *For the Cause of Liberty: A Thousand Years of Ireland's Heroes* (New York, 2000).

Good, Joe. Edited by Maurice Good. *Enchanted by Dreams, The Journal of a Revolutionary* (Tralee, 1996).

Goodfellow, Kathleen, writing under the pseudonym of Michael Scott. *Three Tales of the Times* (Dublin, 1921).

Grant, Neil. *The Easter Rising* (New York, 1972).

Gray, J. *City in Revolt: James Larkin and the Belfast Dock Strike of 1907* (Belfast, 1985).

Gray, Tony. *Ireland this Century* (New York, 1994).

Greaves, C. Desmond. *The Life and Times of James Connolly* (London, 1961).

Greaves, C. Desmond. *Liam Mellows and the Irish Revolution* (London, 1971, 1987).

Greaves, C. Desmond. *The Irish Transport and General Workers Union: The Formative Years: 1909–1923* (Dublin, 1982).

Greaves, C. Desmond. *1916 as History: The Myth of the Blood Sacrifice* (Dublin, 1991).

Green, Alice Stopford. *Irish Nationality* (London, undated).

Gregory, Aidan and Senia Paseta, editors. *Ireland and the Great War* (Manchester, 2002).

Gregory, Padraic, editor. *The Poems of John Francis MacEntee* (Dublin, undated).

Griffin, Gerald. *The Dead March Past* (London, 1937).

Griffin, Padraig. *The Politics of Irish Athletics, 1850-1990* (Ballinamore, 1990).

Griffith, Kenneth. *Hang Out Your Brightest Colours* (London, 1972*).*

Griffith, Kenneth and Timothy O'Grady, editors. *Ireland's Unfinished Revolution, An Oral History.* Originally published as *Curious Journey, An Oral History of Ireland's Unfinished Revolution* (London, 1982; Cork, 1998).

Grob-Fitzgibbon, Benjamin. *Turning Points of the Irish Revolution: the British Government, intelligence and the cost of indifference, 1912-1921* (Dublin, 2008).

Gunther, John. *Inside Europe* (London, 1938).

Gwynn, Denis. *The Irish Free State* (London, 1928).

Gwynn, Denis. *The Life and Death of Roger Casement* (London, 1931).

Gwynn, Denis. *The Life of John Redmond* (London, 1932).

Gwynn, Denis. *De Valera* (London, 1933).

Gwynn, Denis. *Young Ireland* (Cork, 1948).

Gwynn, Denis. *The History of Partition, 1912-1925* (Dublin, 1950).

Gwynn, Stephen. *John Redmond's Last Years* (London, 1919).

Gwynn, Stephen. *Scattering Branches* (London, 1940).

Hachey, Thomas and Lawrence McCaffrey, editors. *Perspectives on Irish Nationalism* (Lexington, Kentucky, 1989).

Haicead, Padraig. *In Bloody Protest: North Tipperary's I.R.A. Role of Honour, 1916-1926* (Nenagh, 1966).

Hammond, Bill. *Soldier of the Rearguard* (Fermoy, 1977).

Hancock, W.K. *Survey of British Commonwealth Affairs: Problems of Nationality, 1918-1936* (London, 1937).

Handbook of the Ulster Question. Free State Stationery Office (Dublin, 1923).

Hanley, Brian. *A Guide to Irish Military Heritage* (Dublin, 2004).

Hannigan, Dave. *The Garrison Game: The State of Irish Football* (Edinburgh, 1998).

Hannigan, Dave. *De Valera in America: The Remarkable 1919 Campaign* (Dublin, 2008).

Harkness, David W. *The Restless Dominion: The Irish Free State and the British Commonwealth of Nations, 1921-1931* (London, 1969; New York, 1970).

Harkness, David W. *Northern Ireland Since 1920* (Dublin, 1983).

Harnett, Mossie. *Victory and Woe* (Dublin, 2002).

Harrington, Niall. *The Kerry Landing, August 1922* (Dublin, 1992).

Harrison, Henry. *Parnell Vindicated* (London, 1931).

Harrison, Henry. *The Neutrality of Ireland* (London, 1932).

Harrison, Henry. *Ulster and the British Empire* (London, 1939).

Hart, Peter, P. O'Cuanachain, D.R. O'Connor Lysaght, B. Murphy and Meda Ryan. *Kilmichael: The False Surrender* (Aubane, 1999).

Hart, Peter. *The IRA and its Enemies: Violence and Community in Cork, 1916-1923* (Oxford, 1999).

Hart, Peter, editor. *British Intelligence in Ireland, 1920–21: The Final Reports* (Cork, 2002).

Hart, Peter. *The I.R.A. at War, 1916–1923* (Oxford, 2003).

Hart, Peter. *Mick: The Real Michael Collins* (London, 2006).

Harte, Paddy, TD. *Young Tigers and Mongrel Foxes* (Dublin, 2005).

Hartley, Stephen. *The Irish Question as a Problem in British Foreign Policy, 1914-1918* (London, 1987).

Haslip, J. *Parnell* (London, 1936).

Hassell, Christopher. *Rupert Brooke* (New York, 1964).

Haswell, Jock. *Citizen Armies* (London, 1973).

Haverty, Anne. *Countess Markievicz, An Independent Life* (London, 1988).

Hayden, Mary and G.A. Moonan. *A Short History of the Irish People* (Dublin, 1926).

Haydon, Anthony. *Sir Matthew Nathan* (Queensland, 1976).

Hayes, Alan, editor. *The Years Flew By: Recollections of Madame Sydney Gifford Czira* (Galway, 2000).

Hayes, James. *Patrick H. Pearse: Storyteller* (Dublin, 1919).

Hayes-McCoy, G.A., editor. *The Irish at War* (Cork, 1964).

Hazelhurst, Cameron. *Politicians at War, July 1914 to May 1915* (London, 1971).

Headlam, Maurice. *Irish Reminiscences* (London, 1947).

Healy, T.M. *Letters and Leaders of My Day.* Vol. II (London, 1928; Dublin, undated).

Heaney, Paddy. *At the Foot of the Slieve Bloom: History and Folklore of Cadamstown* (Dublin, 2000).

Hegarty, Shane and Fintan O'Toole. *The Irish Times Book of the 1916 Rising* (Dublin, 2006).

Hennessey, Thomas. *Dividing Ireland: World War I and Partition* (London, 1998).

Henry, Robert Mitchell. *The Evolution of Sinn Féin* (Dublin, 1920).

Henry, William. *Supreme Sacrifice: The Story of Éamonn Ceannt, 1881-1916* (Cork, 2005).

Hepburn, A.C. *The Conflict of Nationality in Modern Ireland* (Belfast, 1980).

Hepburn, A.C. *A Past Apart: Studies in the History of Catholic Belfast, 1850-1950* (Belfast, 1996).

Hepburn, A.C. *Ireland, 1905-1925.* Vol. II (Newtownards, 1998).

Herlihy, Jim. *The Royal Irish Constabulary* (Dublin, 1997).

Herlihy, Jim. *The Royal Irish Constabulary: A Complete Alphabetical List of Officers and Men, 1816-1922* (Dublin, 1999).

Herlihy, Jim. *The Dublin Metropolitan Police: A Complete Alphabetical List of Officers and Men, 1836-1925* (Dublin, 2001).

Heuston, John M., OP. *HQ Battalion, Army of the Irish Republic, Easter Week* (Tallaght, 1966).

Hickey, D.J., and J.E. Doherty. *A New Dictionary of Irish History from 1800* (Dublin, 2004).

Hiden, J. *Germany and Europe: 1919-1939* (London, 1977).

Hill, J.R. and M. Marsh, editors. *Modern Irish Democracy* (Dublin, 1993).

Hill, J.R. *A New History of Ireland, 1921-1984* (Oxford, 2004).

Hill, Myrtle and Vivienne Pollock. *Image and Experience: Photographs of Irishwomen, 1880-1929* (Belfast, 1993).

Hill, Myrtle. *Women in Ireland: A century of change* (Belfast, 2003).

Hobsbawm, Eric. *Labouring Men* (London, 1971).

Hobsbawm, Eric and Terence Ranger, editors. *The Invention of Tradition* (Cambridge, 1983).

Hobsbawm, Eric. *Nations and Nationalism Since 1780: Programme, Myth, Reality* (Cambridge, 1990).

Hobson, Bulmer. *The Creed of the Republic* (Belfast, 1907).

Hobson, Bulmer. *Defensive Warfare. A Handbook for Irish Nationalists* (Belfast, 1909).

Hobson, Bulmer. *A Short History of the Irish Volunteers, 1913–1916* (Dublin, 1918).

Hobson, Bulmer. *Ireland, Yesterday and Tomorrow* (Tralee, 1968).

Holmes, Richard. *The Little Field Marshal, Sir John French* (London, 1981).

Holt, Edgar. *Protest in Arms: the Irish Troubles, 1916–1923* (London, 1960).

Hone, Joseph M. *Ireland Since 1922* (London, 1932).

Hone, Joseph M. *W.B. Yeats, 1865-1939* (London, 1962).

Hopkinson, Michael. *Green Against Green: a History of the Irish Civil War* (Dublin, 1988).

Hopkinson, Michael, editor. *Frank Henderson's Easter Rising, Recollections of a Dublin Volunteer* (Cork, 1998).

Hopkinson, Michael. *The Irish War of Independence* (Dublin, 2004).

Hoppen, K. Theodore. *Ireland Since 1800: Conflict and Conformity* (London, 1989).

Horgan, J.J. *Parnell to Pearse* (Dublin, 1948).

Horgan, J.J. *Lemass* (Dublin, 1997).

Horne, John, editor. *Our War: Ireland and the Great War* (Dublin, 2008).

Hoy, Hugh Cleland. *40 O. B. or How the War was Won* (London, 1932).

Hutchinson, John. *The Dynamics of Cultural Nationalism: The Gaelic Revival and the Creation of the Irish State* (Boston, Massachusetts, 1987).

Hyde, H. Montgomery. *Carson* (London, 1953).

Hyde, H. Montgomery. *The Trial of Roger Casement* (London, 1960).

Hyland, James L. *Democratic Theory: The Philosophical Foundations* (Manchester, 1995).

Hynes, Samuel. *A War Imagined* (Princeton, New Jersey, 1990).

Inglis, Brian. *West Briton* (London, 1962).

Inglis, Brian. *The Story of Ireland: Roger Casement* (London, 1973).

Innes, C.L. *Woman and Nation in Irish Literature and Society: 1880-1935* (London, 1993).

Ireland, Denis. *Patriot Adventurer* (London, 1936).

Ireland, John de Courcy. *The Sea and the Easter Rising* (booklet, Dublin, 1966, 1996).

Ireland, John de Courcy. *Ireland's Revolutionary Tradition* (booklet, Dublin, 1972).

Irish Boundary Commission, Report and Documents (Shannon, 1969).

Irish Free State Official Handbook. Saorstát Éireann (Dublin, 1932).

The Irish Times. *1916 Rebellion Handbook* (Dublin, 1917; Mourne Press Edition, Dublin, 1998).

Irwin, Wilmot. *Betrayal in Ireland* (Northern Whig, 1968, 1998).

Jackson, Alvin. *Sir Edward Carson* (Dublin, 1993).

Jackson, Alvin. *Ireland: 1798-1998* (Oxford, 1999).

Jackson, T.A. *Ireland Her Own* (London, 1946; New York, 1970).

Jalland, Patricia. *The Liberals and Ireland: The Ulster Question in Irish Politics to 1914* (Brighton, 1980).

Jamie, Lt Col. J.P.W. *The 177th Brigade, 1914-1918* (Leicester, 1931).

Jeffares, A. Norman, editor. *Yeats's Poems* (Dublin, 1989).

Jeffery, Keith and Peter Hennessey. *States of Emergency: British Governments and Strikebreaking since 1919* (London, 1983).

Jeffery, Keith. *The British Army and the Crisis of Empire, 1918–1922* (Manchester, 1984).

Jeffery, Keith. *The Military Correspondence of Sir Henry Wilson* (London, 1985).

Jeffery, Keith, editor. *An Irish Empire? Aspects of Ireland and the British Empire* (Manchester, 1996).

Jeffery, Keith, editor. *A Military History of Ireland* (Cambridge, 1996).

Jeffery, Keith, editor. *The Sinn Féin Rising as They Saw It* (incorporating *The Sinn Féin Rising as I Saw It* by Mary Norway and *Experiences in War* by Arthur Hamilton Norway) (Dublin, 1999).

Jeffery, Keith. *Ireland and the Great War* (Cambridge, 2000).

Jeffery, Keith. *The GPO and the Easter Rising* (Dublin, 2006).

Jeffery, Keith. *Field Marshal Henry Wilson, A Political Soldier* (Oxford, 2008).

Jenkins, Roy. *Asquith* (London, 1964).

Johnson, Thomas. *A Handbook for Rebels. A Guide to Successful Defiance of the British Government* (Dublin, 1918).

Johnston, Andy, James Larragy and Edward McWilliams. *Connolly, A Marxist Analysis* (Dublin, 1990).

Johnston, Joe. *Civil War in Ulster* (1913; Dublin, 1999).

Johnston, Roy. *A Century of Endeavour* (Dublin, 2007).

Johnston, Sheila Turner. *Alice: A Life of Alice Milligan* (Omagh, 1994).

Johnstone, Tom. *Orange, Green and Khaki. The Story of the Irish Regiments in the Great War* (Dublin, 1992).

Jones, Francis P. *History of the Sinn Féin Movement and the Irish Rebellion of 1916* (New York, 1917, 1920).

Jones, Mary. *These Obstreperous Lassies, A History of the Irish Women's Worker's Union* (Dublin, 1988).

Jones, Stephen and Jo Fletcher, editors. *Gaslight and Ghosts* (London, 1988).

Jones, Thomas. *Lloyd George* (London, 1951).

Jones, Thomas. *Whitehall Diary, Vol. III, Ireland, 1918-1925* (Oxford, 1971).

Jordan, Anthony. *Major John MacBride: MacDonagh and MacBride, Connolly and Pearse* (Westport, 1991).

Jordan, Anthony J. *W.T. Cosgrave: Founder of Modern Ireland* (Westport, 2007).

Joy, Maurice, Siobhan Lankford and James Reidy, editors. *The Hope and the Sadness* (1980)

Joy, Maurice, editor. *The Irish Rebellion of 1916 and its Martyrs: Erin's Tragic Easter* (1916; New York, 2007).

Joy, Sinead. *The I.R.A. in Kerry: 1916-1921* (Cork, 2007).

Kamenka, Eugene, editor. *Nationalism: the Nature and Evolution of an Idea* (London, 1973).

Kautt, William H. *The Anglo-Irish War, 1916–1921* (Westport, Connecticut, and London, 1999).

Keane, Elizabeth. *Seán MacBride: A Life* (Dublin, 2007).

Keane, Maureen. *Ishbel, Lady Aberdeen in Ireland* (Dublin, 1999).

Kearns, Kevin. *Dublin Tenement Life: An Oral History* (Dublin, 1994).

Kearns, Kevin. *Dublin Street Life and Lore* (Dublin, 1997).

Kearns, Linda. Edited by Annie P. Smithson. *In Times of Peril* (Dublin, 1922).

Keatinge, Patrick. *The Formulation of Irish Foreign Policy* (Dublin, 1973).

Keatinge, Patrick. *A Place Among the Nations* (Dublin, 1978).

Kee, Robert. *The Green Flag* (a single volume combining three books entitled *The Most Distressful Country, The Bold Fenian Men* and *Ourselves Alone*) (London, 1972, 2000).

Kee, Robert. *Ireland: A History* (London, 1981).

Kehoe, Elisabeth. *Ireland's Misfortune: The Turbulent Life of Kitty O'Shea* (New York, 2008)

Kelly, J. and R. Schuchard, editors. *The Collected Letters of W.B. Yeats. Vol. III, 1901-1904* (Oxford, 1994).

Kelly, Matthew. *The Fenian Ideal and Irish Nationalism, 1882-1916* (Dublin, 2006).

Kelly, Seámus. (Published anonymously). *Pictorial Review of 1916* (Dublin, 1916).

Kendle, John. *Walter Long, Ireland and the Union, 1905-1920* (Montreal, 1992).

Kenna, G.B. *Facts and Figures of the Belfast Pogrom. 1920-1922* (Dublin, 1992).

Kenneally, Ian. *Paper Wall: Newspapers and Propaganda in Ireland, 1919-1921* (Cork, 2008).

Kennedy, Dennis. *The Widening Gulf: Northern Attitudes to the Independent Irish State, 1919-1949* (Belfast, 1988).

Kenny, K. *The American Irish: a history* (Harlow, 2000).

Kenny, Michael. *The Road to Freedom: Photographs and Memorabilia from the 1916 Rising and Afterwards* (Dublin, 1993).

Kenny, Michael. *The Fenians* (Dublin, 1994).

Keogh, Dermot. *The Rise of the Irish Working Class* (Belfast, 1982).

Keogh, Dermot. *The Vatican, the Bishops and Irish Politics* (Dublin, 1986).

Keogh, Dermot. *Twentieth Century Ireland: Unequal Achievement* (Dublin, 1988).

Keogh, Dermot. *Ireland and Europe, 1919-1948* (Dublin, 1988).

Keogh, Dermot. *Twentieth Century Ireland: Nation and State* (Dublin, 1994).

Keogh, Dermot. *Twentieth-Century Ireland: Revolution and State Building* (Dublin, 2005).

Keogh, Dermot and Andrew McCarthy. *The Making of the Irish Constitution 1937: Bunreacht na hÉireann* (Cork, 2007).

The Kerryman. *Dublin's Fighting Story, 1916–1921, Told by the Men Who Made It* (Tralee, 1947).

The Kerryman. *Kerry's Fighting Story, 1916-1921* (Tralee, 1947).

The Kerryman. *Limerick's Fighting Story, 1916-1921* (Tralee, 1948).

The Kerryman. *With the I.R.A. in the Fight for Freedom, 1919 to the Truce, The Red Path of Glory* (Tralee, 1955).

The Kerryman. *Rebel Cork's Fighting Story, 1916-1921* (Tralee, 1961).

The Kerryman. *Sworn to be Free: The Complete Book of I.R.A. Jailbreaks, 1918-1921* (Tralee, 1971).

Kettle, T.M. *The Open Secret of Ireland* (London, 1912).

Kettle, T.M. *The Ways of War* (New York, 1918).

Kettle, Tom. *The Day's Burden* (Dublin, 1937).

Kiberd, D. *Inventing Ireland* (London, 1995).

Kiely, Benedict. *Counties of Contention* (Cork, 1945).

Killeen, Richard. *The Easter Rising* (Hove, 1995).

Killeen, Richard. *Short History of Modern Ireland* (Dublin, 2003).

Killeen, Richard. *A Short History of the Irish Revolution. 1912-1927* (Dublin, 2007).

Killeen, Richard. *A Short History of the 1916 Rising* (Dublin, 2008).

King, Carla and W.J. McCormack, editors. *Michael Davitt: from the Gaelic American* (Cork, 2008).

King, Clifford. *The Orange and the Green* (London, 1965).

Kissane, Bill. *Politics of the Irish Civil War* (Oxford, 2005).

Kleinrichart, Denise. *Republican Internment and the Prison Ship Argenta* (Dublin, 2004).

Knightley, Philip. *The First Casualty* (London, 1975).

Knirk, Jason. *Ghosts and Realities: Female TD's and the Treaty Debate* (New Jersey, 1997).

Knirk, Jason. *Women of the Dáil* (Dublin, 2006).

Knott, George H., editor. *The Trial of Roger Casement* (London, 1926).

Kohfeldt, Mary Lou. *Lady Gregory: The Woman behind the Irish Renaissance* (London, 1984).

Kohn, Leo. *The Constitution of the Irish Free State* (London, 1932).

Kostick, Conor. *Revolution in Ireland, Popular Militancy, 1917 to 1923* (London, 1996).

Kostick, Conor and Lorcan Collins. *The Easter Rising: A Guide to Dublin in 1916* (Dublin, 2000).

Kotsonouris, Mary. *Retreat from Revolution, The Dáil Courts, 1920-1924* (Dublin, 1994).

Laffan, Michael. *The Partition of Ireland, 1911–1925* (Dundalk, 1983).

Laffan, Michael. *The Resurrection of Ireland: The Sinn Féin Party, 1916–1923* (Cambridge, 1999).

Lalor, Brian, editor. *The Encyclopaedia of Ireland* (Dublin, 2003).

Landreth, Helen. *The Mind and Heart of Mary Childers* (Boston, Massachusetts, 1965).

Lane, Jack, editor. *The 'Boys' of the Millstreet Battalion Area* (Aubane, 2003).

Larkin, Emmet. *James Larkin, Irish Labour, 1876-1947* (London, 1965).

Larkin, James Jnr. *In the Footsteps of Big Jim: A Family Biography* (Undated).

Lavelle, Patricia. *James O'Mara: A Staunch Sinn Féiner* (Dublin, 1961).

Lavery, Sir John. *The Life of a Painter* (London, 1941).

Lawlor, B. *The Ultimate Dublin Guide* (Dublin, 1991).

Lawlor, Sheila. *Britain and Ireland, 1914–1923* (Dublin, 1983).

Lawrenson-Swanton, Daisy. *Emerging from the Shadow* (Dublin, 1994).

Lazenby, Elizabeth. *Ireland—A Catspaw* (London, 1928).

Lee, Joseph J. *The Modernisation of Irish Society 1848-1918* (Dublin, 1973).

Lee, Joseph J, editor. *Towards a Sense of Place* (Cork, 1985).

Lee, Joseph J. *Ireland, 1912-1985: Politics and Society* (Cambridge, 1989).

Lee, Joseph and Gearoid Ó Tuathaigh. *The Age of de Valera* (Dublin, 1982).

Leiberson, Goddard, editor. *The Irish Uprising, 1916-1922* (New York, 1966).

Lenihan, Eddie. *Defiant Irish Women* (Cork, 1991).

Lenin, V.I. *Lenin on Ireland* (Dublin, 1970).

Lerner, Gerda. *Why History Matters* (New York and Oxford, 1997).

LeRoux, Louis N. Translated by Desmond Ryan. *Patrick H. Pearse* (Dublin, 1932).

LeRoux, Louis N. *Tom Clarke and the Irish Freedom Movement* (Dublin, 1936).

Leslie, John. *The Irish Question 1894: The Land League, The Church and the Working Class* (Cork, 1986).

Leslie, Shane, editor. *Memoirs of Brigadier-General Gordon Shephard* (privately printed, 1924).

Leslie, Shane. *The Irish Tangle for English Readers* (London, 1946)

Levenson, Leah. *With Wooden Sword: A Portrait of Francis Sheehy-Skeffington* (Boston, Massachusetts, 1983).

Levenson, Leah and Jerry Natterstad. *Hanna Sheehy-Skeffington: Irish Feminist* (Syracuse, New York, 1986).

Levenson, Samuel. *James Connolly: A Biography* (London, 1973).

Levenson, Samuel. *Maud Gonne* (London, 1977).

Lewis, Gifford. *Eva Gore-Booth and Esther Roper: a biography* (London, 1988).

Liam, Cathal. *Forever Green. Ireland Now & Again* (Cincinnati, Ohio, 2003).

Linklater, Andro. *An Unhusbanded Life: Charlotte Despard, Suffragette, Socialist, and Sinn Féiner* (London, 1980).

Litton, Helen. *The Irish Civil War: An Illustrated History* (Dublin, 1995).

Litton, Helen. *Irish Rebellions: An Illustrated History* (Dublin, 1998).

Lloyd George, David. *Is It Peace?* (London, 1923).

Lloyd George, David. *Memoirs of the War,* Vol. I (London, 1938).

Lloyd George, Richard. *Lloyd George* (London, 1960).

Llywelyn, Morgan. *A Pocket History of Irish Rebels* (Dublin, 2000).

Long, Viscount. *Memories* (London, 1923).

Longford, C. *The Story of Dublin* (Dublin, 1936).

Lowe, W.J. *Disbandment and After: The Old R.I.C. in the New Free State* (undated).

Lucy, Gordon. *The Ulster Covenant: A Pictorial History of the 1912 Home Rule Crisis* (Belfast, 1989).

Luddy, Maria and Cliona Murphy. *Women Surviving: Studies in Irish Women's History in the 19th and 20th Centuries* (Dublin, 1990).

Luddy, Maria. *Hanna Sheehy-Skeffington* (Dundalk, 1995).

Luddy, Maria. *Women in Ireland 1800-1918, A Documentary History* (Cork, 1999).

Lynch, Arthur. *Ireland—Vital Hour* (London, 1915).

Lynch, Diarmuid. Edited by Florence O'Donoghue. *The I.R.B. and the 1916 Insurrection* (Cork, 1957).

Lynch, Mary C. and Seámus O'Donoghue. *O'Sullivan Burke, Fenian* (Carrigadrohid, 1999).

Lynch-Robinson, Sir Christopher. *The Last of the Irish R.M.s* (London, 1951).

Lynd, Robert. *Ireland, a Nation* (London, 1919).

Lyons, F.S.L. *The Irish Parliamentary Party, 1890-1910* (London, 1951).

Lyons, F.S.L. *John Dillon* (London, 1968).

Lyons, F.S.L. *Ireland Since the Famine* (London, 1971).

Lyons, F.S.L. *Parnell.* (London, 1977).

Lyons, F.S.L. *Culture and Anarchy in Ireland, 1890-1939* (Oxford, 1979).

Lyons, George. *Some Recollections of Griffith and his Times* (Dublin, 1923).

Lyons, J.B. *Oliver St John Gogarty* (Dublin, 1980).

Lyons, J.B. *The Enigma of Tom Kettle* (Dublin, 1983).

Lyons, J.B. *What Did I Die Of?* (Dublin, 1991).

MacAnBheatha, Proinsias. *James Connolly and the Worker's Republic* (Dublin, 1981).

MacAonghusa, Proinsias and Liam Ó Reagain, editors. *The Best of Pearse* (Cork, 1967).

MacAonghusa, Proinsias, editor. *Quotations from P.H. Pearse* (Cork, 1979).

MacAonghusa, Proinsias, editor. *Quotations from Éamon de Valera* (Dublin, 1983).

MacAonghusa, Proinsias, editor. *What Connolly Said* (Dublin, 1995).

MacAtasney, Gerard. *Seán MacDiarmada, The Mind of the Revolution* (Dublin, 2005).

MacBride, Maud Gonne. *Servant of the Queen* (Dublin, 1950).

MacBride, Maud Gonne. Edited by Anna MacBride White and A. Norman Jeffaries. *The Gonne-Yeats Letters, 1893-1938* (London, 1992).

MacBride, Seán. *That Day's Struggle* (Dublin, 2005).

MacCarthy, Col. J.M., editor. *Limerick's Fighting Story, 1916-1921* (Tralee, 1949).

MacCiarnain, Seámus, editor. *The Last Post.* National Graves Association (New York, 1986).

MacColl, Rene. *Roger Casement: A New Judgement* (London, 1956).

MacCurtain, Fionnuala. *Remember, It's for Ireland* (Cork, 2006).

MacCurtain, Margaret and D. O'Corrain, editors. *Women, the Vote and Revolution, Women in Irish Society, The Historical Dimension* (Dublin, 1978).

MacDonagh, Michael. *The Irish at the Front* (London, 1916).

MacDonagh, Oliver. *Ireland: The Union and its Aftermath* (Englewood Cliffs, New Jersey, 1968).

MacDonagh, Oliver. *States of Mind: A Study of Anglo-Irish Conflict, 1780-1980* (London, 1983).

MacDonagh, Oliver, W.F. Mandle and Pauric Travers, editors. *Irish Culture and Nationalism, 1750-1950* (London, 1983).

MacDonagh, Thomas. *When Dawn is Come* (Dublin, 1908).

MacDonagh, Thomas. *Literature in Ireland* (Dublin, 1916, 1920).

MacDonagh, Thomas. *Poetical Works* (Dublin, 1916).

MacDonald, Malcolm. *Titans and Others* (London, 1972).

MacDonnell, J.M. *The Story of Irish Labour* (undated).

MacDowell, R.B. *The Irish Convention, 1917-1918* (London, 1970).

MacDowell, Vincent. *Michael Collins and the Irish Republican Brotherhood* (Dublin, 1997).

MacEntee, Seán. *Episode at Easter* (Dublin, 1966).

MacEoin, Gary. *Northern Ireland: Captive of History* (New York, 1974).

MacEoin, Uinseann. *The IRA in the Twilight Years, 1923-1948* (Dublin, 1997).

MacEoin, Uinseann, editor. *Survivors* (Dublin, 1980).

MacEoin, Uinseann. *Harry* (Dublin, 1985).

MacGuinness, C.J. *Nomad* (London, 1934).

MacKenna, Stephen, writing under the pseudonym of Martin Daly. *Memories of the Dead* (Dublin, 1917).

MacLochlainn, Alf and Andrée Sheehy-Skeffington. *Writers, Raconteurs and Notable Feminists, Monographs* (Dublin, 1993).

MacLochlainn, Piaras. *Last Words, Letters and Statements of the Leaders Executed After the Rising at Easter, 1916* (Dublin, 1971).

Mac Lua, Brendan. *The Steadfast Rule: A History of the GAA Ban* (Dublin, 1967).

MacLysaght, E. *East Clare 1916-1921* (Ennis, 1954).

MacMahon, Deirdre. *Republicans and Imperialists* (London and New Haven Connecticut, 1984)

MacManus, L. *White Light and Flame* (Dublin, 1929).

MacManus, M.J. *Éamon de Valera* (Dublin, 1944)

MacManus, Seumas. *The Story of the Irish Race* (Dublin, 1921; Old Greenwich, Connecticut, 1978).

MacNeill, Eoin. *Phases of Irish History* (Dublin, 1937).

MacSuain, Seámus. *County Wexford's Civil War* (Wexford, 1985).

MacSwiney, Muriel. Introduction by Angela Clifford. *Letters to Angela Clifford* (Belfast, 1996).

MacSwiney, Terence. *Principles of Freedom* (Dublin, 1921, 1936).

McBride, Ian, editor. *History and Memory in Modern Ireland* (Cambridge, 2001).

McBride, Lawrence W. *The Greening of Dublin Castle* (Washington DC, 1991).

McBride, Lawrence W., editor. *Images, Icons and the Irish Nationalist Imagination* (Dublin, 1999).

McCaffrey, Lawrence. *The Irish Question, 1800-1922* (Lexington, Kentucky, 1968).

McCaffrey, Lawrence. *The Irish Diaspora in America* (Bloomington, Indiana, 1976).

McCaffrey, Lawrence. *Ireland: From Colony to Nation State* (Englewood Cliffs, New Jersey, 1979).

McCann, Éamonn. *War and an Irish Town* (London, 1974).

McCann, John. *War by the Irish* (Tralee, 1946).

McCartan, Patrick. *With de Valera in America* (Dublin, 1932).

McCarthy, Cal. *Cumann na mBan and the Irish Revolution* (Cork, 2008).

McCarthy, Charles. *Trade Unions in Ireland, 1894-1960* (Dublin, 1977).

McCarthy, J. *Irish Recollections* (London, 1911).

McCarthy, John R. *Kevin O'Higgins* (Dublin, 2006).

McCartney, Donal. *The National University of Ireland and Éamon de Valera* (Dublin, 1983).

McCay, Hedley. *Padraic Pearse: A New Biography* (Cork, 1966).

McColgan, John. *British Policy and the Irish Administration, 1920-1922* (London, 1983).

McConville, Seán. *Irish Political Prisoners, 1848-1922* (London, 2003).

McCoole, Sinéad. *Hazel, A Life of Lady Lavery* (Dublin, 1996).

McCoole, Sinéad. *Guns and Chiffon* (Dublin, 1997).

McCoole, Sinéad. *No Ordinary Women, Irish Female Activists in the Revolutionary Years* (Dublin, 2003).

McCormack, John. *A Story of Dublin* (Dublin, 2000).

McCormack, John. *A Story of Ireland* (Dublin, 2002).

McCracken, J.P. *Representative Government in Ireland, 1919-1948* (London, 1958).

McDermott, Jim. *Northern Divisions: The Old I.R.A. and the Belfast Pogroms, 1920-1922* (Belfast, 2001).

McDiarmid, Lucy. *The Irish Art of Controversy* (Dublin, 2005).

McDonagh, T., editor. *Was Ireland a Colony? Economics, Politics and Culture in Nineteenth-Century Ireland* (Dublin, 2005)

McDonald, Walter. *Some Ethical Questions of Peace and War* (Dublin, 1998).

McDonnell, Kathleen Keyes. *There is a Bridge at Bandon* (Cork, 1972).

McDonnell, Vincent. *Michael Collins: Most Wanted Man* (Cork, 2008).

McDowell, R.B. *Alice Stopford Green: a passionate historian* (Dublin, 1967).

McDowell, R.B. *The Irish Convention of 1917–1918* (London, 1970).

McDowell, R.B. *The Irish Administration, 1801-1914* (London and Toronto, 1964).

McEneany, Kevin T., editor. *Pearse and Rossa* (New York, 1982).

McGahern, John. *Amongst Women* (New York, 1991).

McGarry, Fearghal. *Eoin O'Duffy: A Self Made Man* (Oxford, 2005, 2008).

McGee, Owen. *The I.R.B.: The Irish Republican Brotherhood from the Land League to Sinn Féin* (Dublin, 2005).

McGuffin, John. *Internment* (New York, 1973).

McGuire, Charlie. *Roddy Connolly and the Struggle for Socialism in Ireland* (Cork, 2008).

McHugh, Roger, editor. *Dublin, 1916* (London, 1966).

McInerney, Michael. *The Riddle of Erskine Childers* (Dublin, 1971).

McInerney, Michael. *Peadar O'Donnell: Irish Social Rebel* (Dublin, 1974).

McKenna, G.B. *Facts and Figures of the Belfast Pogrom, 1920-1922* (Dublin, 1922).

McKenna, Lambert. *The Social Teachings of James Connolly*. Originally published by the Catholic Truth Society, Dublin, 1920 (Dublin, 1991).

McKenzie, F.A. *The Irish Rebellion. What Happened and Why* (London, 1916).

McMahon, Paul and Boydell Brewer. *British Spies and Irish Rebels: British Intelligence and Ireland, 1916-45* (Dublin, 2008).

McMahon, Seán. *A Short History of Ireland* (Cork, 1996).

McMahon, Seán. *Charles Stewart Parnell* (Cork, 2000).

McMahon, Seán. *Rebel Ireland: Easter Rising to Civil War* (Cork, 2006).

McMahon, Timothy. *Padraig S. Fathaigh's War of Independence: Recollections of a Galway Gaelic Leaguer* (Cork, 2000).

McManus, Ruth. *Dublin 1910-1940, Shaping the City and Suburbs* (Dublin, 2002).

McNamara, Maedhbh and Paschal Mooney. *Women in Parliament: Ireland 1918-2000* (Dublin, 2000).

McNeill, Ronald (Lord Cushendun). *Ulster's Stand for Union* (London, 1922).

McNiffe, Liam. *A History of the Garda Siochána* (Dublin, 1997).

McRedmond, Louis, editor. *Ireland: The Revolutionary Years: Photographs from the Cashman Collection, Ireland, 1910-1930* (Dublin, 1992).

Macardle, Dorothy, writing under the pseudonym of Margaret Callan. *Earthbound, Nine Stories of Ireland* (New York, 1924).

Macardle, Dorothy. *Tragedies of Kerry, 1922-1923* (1924; Dublin, 1998).

Macardle, Dorothy. *The Irish Republic* (New York, 1937, 1965).

Mackay, James. *Michael Collins: A Life* (Edinburgh, 1996).

Mackey, Herbert O. *Roger Casement* (Dublin, 1962).

Macready, Gen. Sir Nevil. *Annals of an Active Life*. 2 Vols (London, 1925, 1942).

Madden, Richard R. *The United Irishmen* (London, undated).

Maguire, Michael. *The Civil Service and the Revolution in Ireland, 1912-1923: 'shaking the blood-stained hand of Mr Collins'* (Manchester, 2008).

Maher, Jim. *The Flying Column: West Kilkenny 1916-1921* (Dublin, 1987).

Maher, Jim. *Harry Boland, A Biography* (Cork, 1998).

Mahon, Thomas and James J. Gillogly. *Decoding the IRA* (Cork, 2008).

Mair, Peter. *The Irish Party System* (London, 1987).

Malins, Edward. *Yeats and the Easter Rising* (Dublin, 1965).

Malone, A.E. *The Irish Drama* (London, 1929).

Malone, James. Translated by Patrick J. Twohig. *Blood on the Flag, An Autobiography of a Freedom Fighter* (Ballincollig, 1996).

Malone, Tom. *Alias Seán Forde* (Danesfort, 2000).

Maloney, William J. *The Forged Casement Diaries* (Cork, 1936).

Mandle, William. *The Gaelic Athletic Association and Irish Nationalist Politics, 1884-1924* (Dublin, 1987).

Mansergh, Nicholas. *The Irish Question, 1840-1921* (London, 1965; Toronto, 1966).

Mansergh, Nicholas. *The Unresolved Question: The Anglo-Irish Settlement and its Undoing, 1912-1972* (London, 1991).

Mansergh, Nicholas. *Nationalism and Independence: Selected Irish Papers* (Cork, 1997).

Maritain, Jacques and R. O'Sullivan, editors. *Man and the State* (London, 1954).

Marjoribanks, Edward. *Life of Lord Carson. Vol. I.* (London, 1932) (See Colvin, I.D. for Vols II and III.)

Markievicz, Countess Constance. *A Call to the Women of Ireland* (Dublin, 1918, reprinted 1918)

Marley, Laurence. *Michael Davitt: Freelance Radical and Frondeur* (Dublin, 2007).

Marreco, Anne. *The Rebel Countess, The Life and Times of Constance Markievicz* (London, 1967).

Martin, Francis X., OSA, editor. *The Irish Volunteers, 1913-1915* (Dublin, 1963).

Martin, Francis X., OSA. *The Howth Gun-Running and the Kilcoole Gun-Running* (Dublin, 1964).

Martin, Francis X., OSA, editor. *The Irish Volunteers, Recollections and Documents* (Dublin, 1966).

Martin, Francis X., OSA, editor. *The Easter Rising, 1916, and University College, Dublin* (Dublin, 1966).

Martin, Francis X., OSA, editor. *Leaders and Men of the Easter Rising* (London, 1967).

Martin, Francis X., OSA, and J.F. Byrne, editors. *The Scholar Revolutionary: Eoin MacNeill* (Shannon, 1973).

Martin, Hugh. *Ireland in Insurrection* (London, 1921).

Matthews, Kevin. *Fatal Influences: The Impact of Ireland on British Politics, 1920-1925* (Dublin, 2004).

Maume, Patrick. *D. P. Moran* (Dundalk, 1995).

Maume, Patrick. *The Long Gestation, Irish Nationalist Life, 1892-1921* (Dublin, 1999).

Maye, Brian. *Arthur Griffith* (Dublin, 1997).

Meacham, Standish. *A Life Apart: The English Working Class, 1890-1914* (Cambridge, Massachusetts, 1977).

Meaghre, T.J. *Inventing Irish America* (Notre Dame, Indiana, 2001).

Meakin, Lt W. *The 5th North Staffords and the North Midland Territorials, 1914-1919* (Longton, 1920).

Meleady, Dermot. *Redmond: The Parnellite* (Cork, 2007).

Metschler, Priscilla. *Republicanism and Socialism in Ireland: a Study in the Relationship of Politics and Ideology from the United Irishmen to James Connolly* (Frankfurt am Main, 1986).

Earl of Midleton. *Ireland – Dupe or Heroine?* (London, 1932).

Earl of Midleton. *Records and Recollections, 1856-1939* (London, 1939).

Mikhail, E.H. and John O'Riordan. *The Sting and the Twinkle: Conversations with Seán O'Casey* (London, 1974).

Miller, David W. *Queen's Rebels* (Dublin, 1971).

Miller, David W. *Church, State, and Nation in Ireland, 1898-1921* (Dublin, 1973).

Milotte, Mike. *Communism in Modern Ireland: The Pursuit of the Workers' Republic since 1916* (Dublin, 1984).

Mitchel, John. *Jail Journal* (Dublin, 1921).

Mitchell, Arthur and Padraig Ó Snodaigh. *Irish Political Documents, 1916-1949* (Dublin, 1985).

Mitchell, Arthur. *Labour in Irish Politics, 1890-1930* (Dublin, 1974).

Mitchell, Arthur. *Revolutionary Government in Ireland: Dáil Éireann, 1919-1922* (Dublin, 1995).

Mitchell, David. *Women on the Warpath* (London, 1966).

Mitchell, Maud. *The Man with the Long Hair* (Aubane, 1993).

Molony, John. *A Soul Came into Ireland: Thomas Davis, 1814-1845* (Dublin, 1995).

Mommsen, Wolfgang and Gerhard Hirschfield, editors. *Social Protest, Violence and Terror in Nineteenth and Twentieth Century Europe* (New York, 1982).

Montague, H. Patrick. *The Saints and Martyrs of Ireland* (Gerrards Cross, 1981).

Monteith, Robert. *Casement's Last Adventure* (Dublin, 1953).

Moody, T.W. *Thomas Davis* (Dublin, 1945).

Moody, T.W., editor. *The Fenian Movement* (Cork, 1968).

Moody, T.W., editor. *Nationality and the Pursuit of National Independence* (Belfast, 1978).

Moran, James. *Staging the Easter Rising: 1916 as theatre* (Cork, 2006).

Moran, James, editor. *Four Irish Rebel Plays* (Dublin, 2008).

Moran, Seán Farrell. *Patrick Pearse and the Politics of Redemption* (Washington DC, 1994).

Morgan, Austen and Bob Purdie, editors. *Ireland: Divided Nation, Divided Class* (London, 1983).

Morgan, Austen. *James Connolly: A Political Biography* (Manchester, 1988).

Morgan, K.O. *Consensus and Disunity: The Lloyd George Coalition Government, 1918-1922* (Oxford, 1979).

Morris, Catherine. *From the Margins: Alice Milligan and the Irish Cultural Revival* (Aberdeen, 1999).

Morrissey, Thomas J. s.j. *William Martin Murphy* (Dundalk, 1997).

Morrissey, Thomas J. s.j. *William O'Brien, 1881-1968* (Dublin, 2007).

Morrogh, Michael McCarthy. *The Irish Century: A Photographic History of the Last Hundred Years* (Niwot, Colorado, 1998).

Mowatt, C.L. *Britain Between the Wars* (London, 1955).

Moylan, Seán. *Seán Moylan: In His Own Words* (Millstreet, 2003).

Moynihan, Maurice, editor. *The Speeches and Statements by Éamon de Valera, 1917–1973* (Dublin, 1980).

Muenger, Elizabeth. *The British Military Dilemma in Ireland. Occupation Politics, 1886-1914* (Lawrence, Kansas, 1991).

Mulcahy, Risteard. *Richard Mulcahy (1886–1971), A Family Memoir* (Dublin, 1999).

Mulholland, Marie. *The Politics and Relationships of Kathleen Lynn* (Dublin, 2002).

Mullins, Billy. *The Memoirs of Billy Mullins, Veteran of the War of Independence* (Tralee, 1983).

Mulqueen, John and Jimmy Wren. *De Valera: An Illustrated Life* (Dublin, 1989).

Mulvihill, Margaret. *Charlotte Despard* (London, 1989).

Munck, Ronaldo. *Ireland: Nation, State and Class Struggle* (Boulder, Colorado, 1985).

Munck, Ronaldo. *The Difficult Dialogue: Marxism and Nationalism* (London, 1986).

Murdoch, Iris. *The Red and the Green* (New York, 1965).

Murphy, Brian P. *Patrick Pearse and the Lost Republican Ideal* (Dublin, 1991).

Murphy, Brian P. *John Chartres: Mystery Man of the Treaty* (Dublin, 1995).

Murphy, Brian P. and Niall Meehan. *Troubled History: a 10th anniversary critique of Peter Hart's 'The IRA and its Enemies'* (Aubane, 2008).

Murphy, Cliona. *The Women's Suffrage Movement and Irish Society in the Early Twentieth Century* (London, 1989).

Murphy, Jeremiah. *When Youth was Mine: A Memoir of Kerry, 1902-1925* (Dublin, 1998).

Murphy, John A. *Ireland in the Twentieth Century* (Dublin, 1975).

Neeson, Eoin. *The Civil War in Ireland* (Cork, 1966).

Neeson, Eoin. *The Life and Death of Michael Collins* (Cork, 1968).

Neeson, Eoin. *Birth of a Republic* (Dublin, 1998).

Neeson, Eoin. *Myths From Easter 1916* (Aubane, 2007).

Neeson, Eoin. *The Battle of Crossbarry* (Aubane, 2008).

Neill, Kenneth. *The Irish People* (Dublin, 1979).

Neligan, David. *The Spy in the Castle* (London, 1968, 1999).

Nelson, Justin. *Michael Collins, The Final Days* (Dublin, 1997).

Neville, Peter. *A Traveller's History of Ireland* (London, 2002).

Nevin, Donal, editor. *1913: Jim Larkin and the 1913 Lockout* (Dublin, 1964).

Nevin, Donal. *Connolly Bibliography* (Dublin, 1968).

Nevin, Donal. *Trade Unions and Change in Irish Society* (Cork, 1980).

Nevin, Donal. *Trade Union Century* (Dublin, 1994).

Nevin, Donal, editor. *Tribute to James Larkin, Orator, Agitator, Revolutionary, Trade Union Leader on the 50th Anniversary of his death*. Services, Industrial, Professional, and Technical Union (SIPTU) publication (Dublin, 1997).

Nevin, Donal, editor. *James Larkin: Lion of the Fold* (Dublin, 1998).

Nevin, Donal. *James Connolly: A Full Life* (Dublin, 2006).

Nevin, Donal, editor. *Between Friends: James Connolly Letters and Correspondence, 1889-1916* (Dublin, 2008).

Nevinson, Henry. *Last Changes, Last Chances* (London, 1928).

Newman, Jeremiah. *Studies in Political Morality* (Dublin, 1962).

Nicholson, Sir Harold. *George V.* (London, 1952).

Ní Chuilleanáin, Eiléan, editor. *Joseph Campbell's Prison Diary, 1922-1923* (Cork, 2001).

Ní Dheirg, Isold. *The Story of Michael Collins* (Dublin, 1978; Cork 2008).
Ní Dhonnchadha, Máirín and Theo Durgan, editors. *Revising the Rising* (Derry, 1991).
Nic Shiubhlaigh, Máire, as told to Edward Kenny. *The Splendid Years* (Dublin, 1955).
Nixon, W. and Cpt. Eric Healy. *Asgard* (Dublin, 2000).
Norman, Diana. *Terrible Beauty: A Life of Constance Markievicz* (London, 1988).
Norman, E.R. *The Catholic Church and Ireland in the Age of Rebellion* (Ithaca, New York, 1965).
Norstedt, Johann A. *Thomas MacDonagh. A Critical Biography* (Charlottesville, Virginia, 1980).
Norway, Mary. *The Sinn Féin Rebellion as I Saw It* (London, 1916).
Novick, Ben. *Conceiving Revolution, Irish Nationalist Propaganda during the First World War* (Dublin, 2001).
Nowlan, Kevin, editor. *The Making of 1916, Studies in the History of the Rising* (Dublin, 1969).
Noyes, Alfred. *The Accusing Ghost or Justice for Casement* (London, 1957).

Oates, Lt Col. W.C. *The Sherwood Foresters in the Great War, 1914-1919* (Nottingham, 1920).
O'Balance, Edgar. *Terror In Ireland* (Novato, California, 1981).
O'Brien, Barry. *Munster at War* (Cork, 1971).
O'Brien, Brendan. *History of the I.R.A.* (Dublin, 1997).
O'Brien, Conor Cruise. *Parnell and His Party, 1880-1890* (London, 1957).
O'Brien, Conor Cruise, editor. *The Shaping of Modern Ireland* (London, 1960).
O'Brien, Conor Cruise. *States of Ireland* (London, 1972).
O'Brien, Conor Cruise. *Ancestral Voices: Religion and Nationalism in Ireland* (Dublin, 1994).
O'Brien, George. *Four Green Fields* (Dublin, 1936).
O'Brien, Joseph V. *Dear, Dirty Dublin* (Berkeley, California, 1982).
O'Brien, Mark. *The Irish Times: A History* (Dublin, 2008).
O'Brien, Paul. *Blood on the Streets: 1916 & the Battle of Mount Street Bridge* (Cork, 2007).
O'Brien, R. Barry. *Dublin Castle and the Irish People* (London, 1909, 1912).
O'Brien, R. Barry. *A Hundred Years of Irish History* (London, 1911).
O'Brien, Séamus. *The Irish Rebellion of 1916 and its Martyrs* (1916).
O'Brien, William. *'The Party': Who they are and what they have done* (Dublin and London, 1917).
O'Brien, William. *The Downfall of Parliamentarianism* (Dublin and London, 1918).
O'Brien, William. *The Irish Revolution and How It Came About* (London, 1923).
O'Brien, William and Desmond Ryan, editors. *Devoy's Postbag, 1871-1928* (Dublin, 1953).
O'Brien, William. Edited by Edward MacLysaght. *Forth the Banners Go* (Dublin, 1969).
Ó Broin, Leon. *Cuimhní Cinn* (Dublin, 1951).
Ó Broin, Leon. *Dublin Castle and the 1916 Rising* (London, 1966).
Ó Broin, Leon. *Charles Gavan-Duffy: Patriot and Statesman* (Dublin, 1967).
Ó Broin, Leon. *The Chief Secretary. Augustine Birrell in Ireland* (London, 1969).
Ó Broin, Leon. *Fenian Fever: An Anglo-American Dilemma* (New York, 1971; London, 1979).
Ó Broin, Leon. *Revolutionary Underground: The Story of the I.R.B., 1858–1924* (Dublin, 1976).
Ó Broin, Leon. *Michael Collins* (Dublin, 1980).
Ó Broin, Leon. *In Great Haste: Letters of Michael Collins and Kitty Kiernan* (Dublin, 1983).
Ó Broin, Leon. *Protestant Nationalism in Revolutionary Ireland* (Dublin, 1985).
Ó Broin, Leon. *W.E. Wylie and the Irish Revolution, 1916-1921* (Dublin, 1989).
Ó Buachalla, Séamus, editor. *The Literary Writings of Patrick Pearse* (London, 1979).
Ó Buachalla, Séamus, editor. *The Letters of P.H. Pearse* (London, 1980).
Ó Buachalla, Séamus, editor. *A Significant Educationalist: The Educational Writings of P.H. Pearse* (Dublin, 1980).
O'Callaghan, Michael. *For Ireland and Freedom* (New York, 1964).
O'Callaghan, Seán. *The Easter Lily* (London, 1956).
O'Callaghan, Seán. *Execution* (London, 1974).
O'Carroll, Derval and Seán Fitzpatrick, editors. *A History of the Custom House Docks Dublin* (Dublin, 1996).
O'Carroll, J.P. and John A. Murphy, editors. *De Valera and His Times* (Cork, 1983).

O'Casey, Seán. *I Knock at the Door* (London, 1939).

O'Casey, Seán. *Pictures in the Hallway* (London, 1942).

O'Casey, Seán. *Drums Under the Windows* (London, 1945).

Ó Cathasaigh, Aindrias, editor. *James Connolly, The Lost Writings* (Harmonsworth, 1997).

Ó Ceallaigh, Seán T. *Seán T.* Proinsias Ó Conluain, editor (Dublin, 1963, 1973).

Ó Ceallaigh, Seán T. *A Trinity of Martyrs* (Dublin, undated).

O'Ceirin, Kit and Cyril O'Ceirin. *Women of Ireland* (Galway, 1996).

O'Connor, Anne V. and Susan M. Parker. *Gladly Learn and Gladly Teach: A History of Alexandra College and School, 1866-1966* (Dublin, 1986).

O'Connor, Batt. *With Michael Collins in the Fight for Independence* (London, 1929).

O'Connor, Emmet. *Syndicalism in Ireland, 1917-1923* (Cork, 1988).

O'Connor, Emmet. *A Labour History of Ireland, 1824-1960* (Dublin, 1992).

O'Connor, Frank. *The Big Fellow: Michael Collins and the Irish Rebellion* (London, 1937; Swords, 1979).

O'Connor, Frank. *A Book of Ireland* (London, 1959).

O'Connor, Frank. *An Only Child* (London, 1961, 1970).

O'Connor, Frank. *My Father's Son* (London, 1968).

O'Connor, E. *Reds and the Green* (Dublin, 2004).

O'Connor, Sir James. *History of Ireland: 1798–1924* (London, 1929).

O'Connor, John. *The 1916 Proclamation* (Dublin, 1986).

O'Connor, Kevin. *Ironing the Land* (Dublin, 1999).

O'Connor, Seámus. *Tomorrow Was Another Day* (Dublin, 1970).

O'Connor, Ulick. *Oliver St John Gogarty* (London, 1964).

O'Connor, Ulick. *Michael Collins and the Troubles: The Struggle for Irish Freedom, 1912-1922* (Edinburgh, 1975, 1996).

O'Connor, Ulick. *A Terrible Beauty is Born: The Irish Troubles, 1912–1922* (Hamish Hamilton Edition, London, 1975) (pagination is different).

O'Connor, Ulick. *A Terrible Beauty is Born: The Irish Troubles, 1912–1922* (Panther Books Edition, London, 1981, 1985) (pagination is different).

O'Connor Lysaght, D.R. *Early History of Irish Trotskyism* (London, undated).

O'Connor Lysaght, D.R., editor. *The Communists and the Irish Revolution* (undated).

O'Connor Lysaght, D.R. *The Making of Northern Ireland* (Dublin, undated).

O'Connor Lysaght, D.R. *The Republic of Ireland* (Cork, 1970).

O'Connor Lysaght, D.R. *The Literary Politics of Conor Cruise O'Brien* (1976).

Ó Cruadhlaoich, D. *Step by Step: From the Republic back into the Empire* (unknown place or date).

Ó Cuinneagain, Micheál. *On the Arm of Time* (Donegal, 1992).

Ó Cuive, Brian, editor. *A View of the Irish Language* (Dublin, 1969).

O'Day, Alan, editor. *Reactions to Irish Nationalism* (London, 1987).

O'Day, Alan. *Irish Home Rule, 1867-1921* (Manchester, 1998).

O'Doherty, Katherine. *Assignment America* (New York, 1957).

O'Doherty, Michael Kevin. *My Parents and Other Rebels* (Dublin, 1999).

O'Donnell, Charles J. and Brendan Clifford. *Ireland in the Great War* (Belfast, 1992).

O'Donnell, E.E. *The Annals of Dublin: Fair City* (Dublin, 1987, 2008).

O'Donnell, Peadar. *There Will Be Another Day* (Dublin, 1963).

O'Donnell, Peadar. *The Gates Flew Open* (Cork, 1965).

O'Donnell, Ruán. *The Impact of the 1916 Rising Among the Nations* (Dublin, 2008).

O'Donoghue, Florence. *No Other Law* (Dublin, 1954, 1986).

O'Donoghue, Florence. *Tomás MacCurtain, Soldier and Patriot* (Tralee, 1971).

O'Donovan, Donal. *Kevin Barry and His Time* (Glendale, 1989).

O'Driscoll, Donal. *Peadar O'Donnell* (Cork, 2001).

O'Driscoll, Robert and Lorna Reynolds. *The Untold Story, the Irish in Canada* (Toronto, 1988).

Ó Dubghaill, M. *Insurrection Fires at Eastertide* (Cork, 1966).

O'Duffy, Eimar. *The Wasted Island* (London, 1929).

Ó Duigneain, Proinnsios. *Linda Kearns, A Revolutionary Irish Woman* (Manorhamilton, 2002).

Ó Dulaing, Donncha. *Voices of Ireland* (Dublin, 1984).

O'Dwyer, Frederick. *Lost Dublin* (Dublin, 1985).

O'Dwyer, Martin. *A Pictorial History of Tipperary, 1916-1923* (Cashel, 2004).

Ó Faolain, Seán. *The Life of de Valera* (Dublin, 1933).

Ó Faolain, Seán. *Constance Markievicz* (London, 1934).

Ó Faolain, Seán. *King of the Beggars* (London, 1938).

Ó Faolain, Seán. *De Valera* (London, 1939).

Ó Faolain, Seán. *Vive Moi! An Autobiography* (London, 1965, 1993).

O'Farrell, B. *The Founding of Dáil Éireann* (Dublin, 1971).

O'Farrell, Mick. *A Walk Through Rebel Dublin, 1916* (Cork, 1999).

O'Farrell, Mick. *Things you don't know about 1916* (Cork, 2008)

O'Farrell, Padraic. *Ireland's English Question* (London, 1971).

O'Farrell, Padraic. *England and Ireland since 1800* (Oxford, 1975).

O'Farrell, Padraic. *The Seán MacEoin Story* (Dublin, 1981).

O'Farrell, Padraic. *The Ernie O'Malley Story* (Dublin, 1983).

O'Farrell, Padraic. *Seán MacEoin: The Blacksmith of Ballinalee* (Mullingar, 1993).

O'Farrell, Padraic. *Who's Who in the Irish War of Independence and Civil War* (Dublin, 1997).

O'Farrell, Patrick. *Ireland's English Question: Anglo-Irish Relations, 1534-1970* (London, 1971).

O'Farrell, Peter. *Memoirs of Irish Volunteer Activity, 1917–1924* (New York, 1978).

Ó Flaimghaile, Tomas. *For the Tongue of the Gael* (London, 1896).

Ó Gadhra, Nollaig. *Civil War in Connacht, 1922-1923* (Cork, 1999).

Ó Grada, Cormac. *Ireland and New Economic History, 1780-1939* (Oxford, 1994).

Ó hAodha, Micheal. *The O'Casey Enigma* (Dublin, 1998).

O'Halloran, Clare. *Partition and the Limits of Irish Nationalism* (Dublin, 1987).

O'Halpin, Eunan. *The Decline of the Union* (Dublin, 1987).

O'Halpin, Eunan. *Defending Ireland* (New York, 1999).

O'Halpin, Eunan, editor. *Intelligence, Statecraft and International Power* (Dublin, 2008).

O'Hanrahan, Michael. *The Swordsman of the Brigade* (1914).

O'Hanrahan, Michael. *When the Normans Came* (1919).

O'Hara, Bernard. *Davitt* (Mayo County Council, 2007).

O'Hegarty, P.S. *John Mitchel, with some appreciation of Young Ireland* (Dublin, 1917).

O'Hegarty, P.S. *An Indestructible Nation* (Dublin, 1918).

O'Hegarty, P.S. *Sinn Féin: An Illumination* (Dublin and London, 1919).

O'Hegarty, P.S. *A Short Memoir of Terence MacSwiney* (Dublin, 1922).

O'Hegarty, P.S. *The Victory of Sinn Féin* (Dublin, 1924, 1998).

O'Hegarty, P.S. *A History of Ireland under the Act of Union* (London, 1952).

O'Hegarty, Peter. *Peadar O'Donnell* (Cork, 1999).

O'Higgins, Brian. *The Soldier's Story of Easter Week* (Dublin, 1925).

O'Leary, Daniel and J.L. Wisenthal, editors. *What Shaw Really Wrote About the War* (Gainesville, Florida, 2006).

O'Leary, John. *Recollections of Fenians and Fenianism* (London, 1896).

O'Leary, Paul, editor. *Irish Migrants in Modern Wales* (Liverpool, 2004).

Ó Luing, Seán. *Art Ó Griofa*. Biography in Irish (Dublin, 1953).

Ó Luing, Seán. *I Die in a Good Cause. A Study of Thomas Ashe, Idealist and Revolutionary* (Tralee, 1970).

O'Mahony, David. *The Irish Economy* (Cork, 1962).

O'Mahony, Seán. *Frongoch, University of Revolution* (Killiney, 1987, 1995).

O'Mahony, Seán. *The First Hunger Strike – Thomas Ashe, 1917* (Dublin, 2001).

Ó Maitiu, Seámas. *W&R Jacob: Celebrating 150 Years of Irish Biscuit Making* (Dublin, 2001).

O'Malley, Cormac H.K. and Anne Dolan, editors. *No Surrender Here! The Civil War Papers of Ernie O'Malley* (Dublin, 2007).

O'Malley, Edward. *Memories of a Mayoman* (Westport, 1981).

O'Malley, Ernie. *On Another Man's Wound* (Originally published as *An Army Without Banners, Adventures of an Irish Volunteer*, Dublin, 1937; published as *On Another Man's Wound*, London, 1961; Dublin, 1979).

O'Malley, Ernie. *The Singing Flame* (Dublin, 1978).

O'Malley, Ernie. *Raids and Rallies* (Dublin, 1982).

O'Malley, Ernie. *Rising Out: Seán Connolly of Longford* (Dublin, 2007).

O'Malley, Kate. *Ireland, India and Empire: Indo-Irish Radical Relations, 1919-1964* (Manchester, 2008).

O'Malley, Padraig. *Biting at the Grave* (Belfast, 1990).

O'Neill, Brian. *Easter Week* (New York, 1939).

O'Neill, Máire. *From Parnell to de Valera, A Biography of Jennie Wyse Power, 1858-1941* (Dublin, 1991).

O'Neill, Marie. *Grace Gifford Plunkett and Irish Freedom, Tragic Bride of 1916* (Dublin, 2000).

O'Neill, Tom. *The Battle of Clonmel* (Dublin, 2006).

Ó Neill, Tomas and Padraig Ó Fiannachta. *De Valera*. 2 Vols (Dublin, 1968-1970).

Oppenheimer, A.R. *IRA: The Bombs and Bullets: a history of deadly ingenuity* (Dublin, 2008).

Oram, Hugh. *The Newspaper Book* (Dublin, 1983).

O'Rahilly, The (Michael Joseph). *The Secret History of the Irish Volunteers* (Dublin, 1915).

O'Rahilly, Aodogan. *Winding the Clock: The O'Rahilly and the 1916 Rising* (Dublin, 1991).

O'Reilly, Terence. *Our Struggle for Independence* (Cork, 2008).

Ó Riain, Seámus. *Maurice Davin, First President of the GAA* (Dublin, undated).

O'Riordan, Michael. *The Connolly Column* (Dublin, 1979).

Orpen, William. *Stories of Old Ireland and Myself* (London, 1924).

Orr, Philip. *The Road to the Somme* (Belfast, 1987).

O'Shannon, Cathal, editor. *Fifty Years of Liberty Hall, 1909-1959* (Dublin, 1959).

O'Shiel, Kevin. *The Rise of the Irish Nation League* (1916).

Ó Siochain, Seámus. *Roger Casement: Imperialist, Rebel, Revolutionary* (Dublin, 2007).

Ó Suilleabhain, Micheal. *Where Mountainy Men Have Sown* (Tralee, 1965).

O'Sullivan, Donal. *The Irish Free State and its Senate* (London, 1940).

O'Sullivan, Michael. *Seán Lemass* (Dublin, 1994).

O'Sullivan, Michael and Bernadine O'Neill. *The Shelbourne and its People* (Dublin, 1999).

O'Sullivan, Naimh. *Every Dark Hour: A History of Kilmainham Gaol* (Dublin, 2007).

O'Sullivan, Seumas. *Essays and Recollections* (Dublin, 1944).

O'Sullivan, T.F. *The Story of the G.A.A.* (Dublin, 1916).

Osborne, Chrissy. *Michael Collins, Himself* (Douglas, Co. Cork, 2003).

Osborne, Chrissy. *The Michael Collins Album: A Life in Pictures* (Cork, 2007).

O'Toole, Fintan. *The Irish Times Book of the Century* (Dublin, 1999).

Ó Tuile, Padraig. *Life and Times of Brian O'Higgins* (Navan, undated).

Owen, Frank. *Tempestous Journey: Lloyd George, his Life and Times* (London, 1954).

Owens, Rosemary Cullen. *Smashing Times, A History of the Irish Women's Suffrage Movement, 1889-1922* (Dublin, 1984).

Owens, Rosemary Cullen. *Did Your Granny Have a Hammer?* (Dublin, 1984).

Owens, Rosemary Cullen. *Louie Bennett* (Cork, 2001).

Pakenham, Frank (Lord Longford). *Peace by Ordeal* (London, 1935, 1972).

Pakenham, Frank (Lord Longford) and Thomas P. O'Neill. *Éamon de Valera, A Biography* (Dublin, 1970).

Pakenham, Thomas. *The Year of Liberty* (London, 1969).

Pankhurst, Emmeline. *My Own Story* (London, 1914).

Pankhurst, Sylvia. *The Life of Emmeline Pankhurst* (London, 1935).

Parks, Edd W. and Aileen W. Parks. *Thomas MacDonagh: the Man, the Patriot, the Writer* (Athens, Georgia, 1967).

Parmiter, Geoffrey de C. *Roger Casement* (London, 1936).

Parnell, Anna. Edited by Dana Hearne. *Tale of a Great Sham* (Dublin, 1986).

Paseta, Senia. *Before the Revolution. Nationalism, Social Change and Ireland's Catholic Elite, 1879-1922* (Cork, 1999).

Paseta, Gregory and Senia Paseta, editors. *Ireland and the Great War; 'A War to Unite Us All?'* (Manchester, 2002).

Patterson, Henry. *Class Conflict and Sectarianism* (Belfast, 1980).

Patterson, Henry. *The Politics of Illusion: Republicanism and Socialism in Modern Ireland* (London, 1989).

Paul-Dubois, Louis. *Contemporary Ireland* (Dublin, 1907).
Paul-Dubois, Louis. *The Irish Struggle and its Results* (London, 1934).
Pearl, Cyril. *The Three Lives of Gavan-Duffy* (Kensington, New South Wales, 1979).
Pearce, Edward. *Lines of Most Resistance: The Lords, Tories, and Ireland: 1886-1914* (London, 1999).
Pearse, Mary Brigid, editor. *The Home Life of Padraig Pearse* (Dublin, 1934).
Pearse, Padraig. *The Singer and Other Plays* (Dublin, 1918).
Pearse, Padraig. *Poets of the Insurrection* (Dublin, 1918).
Pearse, Padraig H. *Collected Works of Padraig H. Pearse. Political Writings and Speeches* (5th Edition, Dublin, 1922; 1952).
Pearson, Peter. *The Heart of Dublin* (Dublin, 2000).
Phillips, W. Alison. *The Revolution in Ireland, 1906–1923* (London, 1923).
Phoenix, Éamon. *Northern Nationalism: Nationalist Politics, Partition, and the Catholic Minority in Northern Ireland, 1890-1940* (Belfast, 1994).
Pilkington, Lionel. *Theatre and State in Twentieth Century Ireland: Cultivating the People* (London, 2001).
Pinkman, John A. Edited by Francis E. Maguire. *In the Legion of the Vanguard* (Cork, 1970, 1998).
Piper, Leonard. *The Tragedy of Erskine Childers* (London, 2003).
Plunkett, Sir Horace. *Ireland in the New Century* (London, 1905).
Pollard, Cpt. H.B.C. *The Secret Societies of Ireland: Their Rise and Progress* (London, 1922).
Pomfret, J.E. *The Struggle for Land in Ireland, 1880-1923* (Princeton, New Jersey, 1930).
Porter, Norman, editor. *The Republican Ideal: Current Perspectives* (Belfast, 1998).
Porter, Raymond J. *P.H. Pearse* (New York, 1973).
Power, P.C. *Carrick-on-Suir and its People* (Dun Laoghaire, 1976).
Prager, Jeffrey. *Building Democracy in Ireland* (Cambridge, 1986).
Prunty, Jacinta. *Dublin Slums, 1800-1925* (Dublin, 1998).
Puirsell, Niamh. *The Irish Labour Party 1922-1973* (Dublin, 2007).
Purdon, Edward. *The 1916 Rising* (Cork, 1999).
Purdon, Edward. *The Civil War, 1922–23* (Cork, 2000).
Purdon, Edward. *The War of Independence* (Cork, 2001).
Pyle, Hilary. *Susan Mitchell, Red-Headed Rebel* (Dublin, 1998).

Qualter, T.H. *Propaganda and Psychological Warfare* (New York, 1962).
Quigley, Aidan. *Green is My Sky* (Dublin, 1974).
Quigley, Martin. *Great Gaels in Peace and War* (New York, 1944).

Rafferty, Oliver. *The Catholic Church and the Protestant State: Nineteenth-Century Irish Realities* (Dublin, 2007).
Ramon, Marta. *A Provisional Dictator: James Stephens and the Fenian Movement* (Dublin, 2007).
Ranelagh, John. *Ireland: An Illustrated History* (London, 1981).
Ransom, Bernard. *Connolly's Marxism* (Dublin, 1980).
Redican, Noel. *Shadows of Doubt: the story of a republican 'gone wrong'* (Cork, 2008).
Redmond, John. *The Rising* (London, 1916).
Redmond, Maj. William, MP. *Trench Pictures from France* (London, 1917).
Redmond-Howard, L.G. *Six Days of the Irish Republic* (Dublin, 1916).
Rees, Russell. *Ireland, 1905-1925. Volume I* (Newtownards, 1998).
Regan, J. *The Irish Counter Revolution, 1921-1936* (Dublin, 1999).
Reeve, Carl and Ann Barton. *James Connolly and the United States: The Road to the 1916 Irish Rebellion* (Atlantic Highlands, New Jersey, 1978).
Reid, B.L. *The Man from New York* (Oxford, 1968).
Reid, B.L. *The Lives of Roger Casement* (New Haven, Connecticut, 1976).
Reynolds, John J. *A Fragment of 1916 History* (Dublin, 1919).
Riddell, Lord George Allardice. *Intimate Diary of the Peace Conference and After* (London, 1933).
Riddell, Patrick. *Fire over Ulster* (London, 1970).
Ring, Jim. *Erskine Childers* (London, 1996).

Robins, J. *Custom House People* (Dublin, 1993).

Robbins, Frank. *Under the Starry Plough. Recollections of the Irish Citizen Army* (Dublin, 1977).

Robertson, K.G., editor. *British and American approaches to intelligence* (Basingstoke, 1994).

Robertson, Nora. *Crowned Harp: Memories of the Last Years of the Crown in Ireland* (Dublin, 1960).

Robinson, Sir Henry. *Memories, Wise and Otherwise* (London, 1923).

Roche, Anthony J., editor. *A Family in Revolution* (Dublin, 2000).

Roche, R. *Here's Their Memory. A Tribute to the Fallen Republicans of Wexford* (1966).

Roper, Esther, editor. *Prison Letters of Countess Markievicz* (London, 1934, 1987).

Rose, Paul. *The Manchester Martyrs: The Story of a Fenian Tragedy* (London, 1970).

Rose, Richard. *Governing Without Consensus* (Boston, Massachusetts, 1971).

Roskill, Stephen. *Hankey: Man of Secrets Vol. II, 1919-1931* (London, 1972).

Rossa, Jeremiah O'Donovan. *Irish Rebels in English Prisons* (New York, *1872*; Dublin, 1991).

Rossa, Jeremiah O'Donovan. Introduction by Seán Ó Luing. *O'Donovan Rossa's Recollections* (New York, 1898; Shannon, 1972).

Rowbotham, Sheila. *A Century of Women* (New York and London, 1997).

Ruane, Medb. *Ten Dublin Women* (Dublin, 1991).

Rumpf, Erhard and A.C. Hepburn. *Nationalism and Socialism in Twentieth Century Ireland* (Liverpool, 1977).

Russell, George William. (Æ). *The National Being* (Dublin, 1916).

Lord Russell of Liverpool. *That Reminds Me* (London, 1959).

Ryan, A.P. *Mutiny at the Curragh* (London, 1956).

Ryan, Annie. *Witnesses: Inside the Easter Rising* (Dublin, 2005).

Ryan, Annie. *Comrades: Inside the War of Independence* (Dublin, 2006).

Ryan, B. *A Full Private Remembers the Troubled Times* (Hollyfield, 1969).

Ryan, Desmond, editor. *Collected Works of Padraic H. Pearse: St. Enda's and Its Founder* (Dublin, undated).

Ryan, Desmond, editor. *The Story of a Success by P.H. Pearse, Being a Record of St. Enda's College, September 1908 to Easter 1916* (Dublin, 1917).

Ryan, Desmond. *The Man Called Pearse* (Dublin, 1919).

Ryan, Desmond. *James Connolly and His Life* (Dublin, 1924).

Ryan, Desmond. *Remembering Sion: A Chronicle of Storm and Quiet* (London, 1934).

Ryan, Desmond. *Unique Dictator: A Study of Éamon de Valera* (London, 1936).

Ryan, Desmond. *The Phoenix Flame* (London, 1937).

Ryan, Desmond. *Seán Treacy and the Third Tipperary Brigade, I.R.A.* (Tralee, 1945).

Ryan, Desmond. *Socialism and Nationalism: A Collection of the Writings of James Connolly* (Dublin 1948).

Ryan, Desmond. *The Rising: The Complete Story of Easter Week* (Dublin, 1949, 1957).

Ryan, Desmond, editor. *The 1916 Poets* (Dublin, 1963, 1995)

Ryan, Desmond, editor. *Political Writings and Speeches* (Dublin, 1966).

Ryan, Desmond. *The Fenian Chief: A Biography of James Stephens* (Dublin, 1967).

Ryan, Desmond. *Michael Collins: The Invisible Army* (Tralee, 1968).

Ryan, Frederick. *Sinn Féin and Reaction* (Dublin, 1984).

Ryan, Louise. *Irish Feminism and The Vote: An Anthology of The Irish Citizen Newspaper, 1912-1920* (Dublin, 1996).

Ryan, Louise and Margaret Ward, editors. *Irish Women and Nationalism: Soldiers, New Women and Wicked Hags* (Dublin, 2004).

Ryan, Louise and Margaret Ward, editors. *Irish Women and the Vote* (Dublin, 2007).

Ryan, Mark. *Fenian Memories* (Dublin, 1945).

Ryan, Mary, Seán Browne and Kevin Gilmour, editors. *No Shoes in Summer: Days to Remember* (Dublin, 1995).

Ryan, Meda. *The Tom Barry Story* (Dublin, 1982).

Ryan, Meda. *The Day Michael Collins Was Shot* (Dublin, 1989).

Ryan, Meda. *Michael Collins and the Women in His Life* (Dublin, 1996). Republished as *Michael Collins and the Women Who Spied for Ireland* (Cork, 2007).

Ryan, Meda. *Tom Barry: I.R.A. Freedom Fighter* (Cork, 2003).

Ryan, Meda. *The Real Chief, The Story of Liam Lynch* (Dublin, 2005).
Ryan, W.P. *The Pope's Green Ireland* (London, 1912).
Ryan, W.P. *The Irish Labour Movement From the 'Twenties to Our Own Day* (Dublin, 1919).
Ryder, Chris. *The R.U.C., 1922-1997. A Force Under Fire* (London, 1997).

Salmon, L.M. *The Newspaper and the Historian* (New York, 1923).
Stanford, W.B. and R.B. McDowell. *Mahaffy, A Biography of an Anglo-Irishman* (London, 1971).
Sawyer, Roger. *Casement, the Flawed Hero* (London, 1984).
Sawyer, Roger. *'We are but Women': Women in Ireland's History* (London, 1993).
Schmitt, P. *The Irony of Irish Democracy: The Impact of Political Culture on Administrative and Democratic Development in Ireland* (Lexington, Kentucky, 1973).
Schuller, G. *James Connolly and Irish Freedom: A Marxist Analysis* (Cork, 1986).
Sellwood, A.V. *The Red-Gold Flame* (London, 1966).
Severn, Bill. *Irish Statesman and Rebel: The Two Lives of Éamon de Valera* (Folkstone, 1971).
Seward, Barbara. *The Symbolic Rose* (New York, 1960).
Sexton, Seán. *Ireland: Photographs, 1840-1930* (London, 1994).
Shakespeare, Sir Geoffrey. *Let Candles be Brought In* (London, 1949).
Shannon, Catherine. *Arthur J. Balfour and Ireland, 1874-1922* (Washington, DC 1988).
Shaw, George Bernard. Edited by Dan H. Lawrence and David H. Greene. *The Matter with Ireland* (London and New York, 1962).
Shearman, Hugh. *Not an Inch: A Study of Northern Ireland and Lord Craigavon* (London, 1942).
Shearman, Hugh. *Anglo-Irish Relations* (London, 1948).
Sheehan, Tim. *Mrs Lindsay, Lady Hostage* (Dripsey, 1990).
Sheehan, Tim. *Execute Hostage Compton-Smith* (Dripsey, 1993).
Sheehan, William. *British Voices from the Irish War of Independence: 1918-1921* (Cork, 2005, 2007).
Sheehan, William. *Fighting for Dublin: The British Battle for Dublin, 1919-1921* (Cork, 2007).
Sheehy, Jeanne. *The Rediscovery of Ireland's Past: The Celtic Revival, 1830–1930* (London, 1980).
Sheehy-Skeffington, Andrée and Rosemary Owens, editors. *Votes for Women: Irish Women's Struggle for the Vote* (Dublin, 1975).
Sheehy-Skeffington, Frank. *War and Feminism* (Dublin, 1914).
Sheehy-Skeffington, Hanna. *Impressions of Sinn Féin in America* (Dublin, 1919).
Sheridan, Owen. *Propaganda as Anti-History: Peter Hart's 'The IRA and its Enemies' Examined* (Aubane, 2008).
Short, K. *The Dynamite War* (Atlantic Highlands, New Jersey, 1979).
Shute, Nevil. *Slide Rule* (London, 1954).
Singleton-Gates, Peter and M. Girodias. *The Black Diaries* (London, 1959).
Sinn Féin, A Century of Struggle (Dublin, 2005).
Sissen, Elaine. *Pearse's Patriots* (Cork, 2004).
Skinnider, Margaret. *Doing My Bit for Ireland* (New York, 1917).
Small, Stephen. *An Irish Century, 1845-1945* (Dublin, 1998).
Smith, Anthony. *National Identity* (London, 1991)
Smith, Nadia Clare. *Dorothy Macardle: A Life* (Dublin, 2007).
Smith, Nadia Clare. *A 'manly study'? Irish Women Historians, 1868-1949* (Dublin, 2008).
Smith, W.G. *Report of work done by St John's Ambulance Brigade during the Sinn Féin Rebellion, April-May 1916* (booklet, Dublin, 1916).
Smithson, Annie. *Myself and Others* (Dublin, 1944).
Smuts, Jan Christian. *Jan Christian Smuts* (London, 1952).
Smuts, Jan Christian. *Collections from the Smuts Papers* (London, 1973).
Smythe, Ailbhe, editor. *A Dozen Lips* (Dublin, 1994).
Somerville-Large, Peter. *Dublin* (London, 1979).
Somerville-Large, Peter. *Dublin the Fair City* (London, 1996).
Somerville-Large, Peter. *Irish Voices: Fifty Years of Irish Life, 1916-1966* (London, 1999).
Spellissy, Seán and John O'Brien. *Limerick, The Rich Land* (Ennis, 1989).

Spellissy, Seán. *The History of Limerick City* (Limerick, 1998).

Spellissy, Seán. *A History of Clare* (Dublin, 2003).

Spellman, Cathy Cash. *An Excess of Love* (New York, 1986).

Spender, J.A. and Cyril Asquith. *Life of Herbert Henry Asquith, Lord Oxford and Asquith*. 2 Vols (London, 1932).

Spindler, Karl. *The Mystery of the Casement Ship* (Berlin, 1931).

Stanley, Derek. *Images of Ireland: Central Dublin* (Dublin, 1999).

Steele, Karen. *Women, Press and Politics During the Irish Revival* (Syracuse, New York, 2007).

Stephens, James. *The Insurrection in Dublin* (1916; Gerrards Cross, 1978).

Stephens, James. *Arthur Griffith, Journalist and Statesman* (Dublin, 1922).

Stephens, James. *The Charwoman's Daughter* (Dublin, 1923).

Stewart, A.T.Q. *The Ulster Crisis: Resistance to Home Rule, 1912-14* (London, 1967).

Stewart, A.T.Q. *Edward Carson* (Dublin, 1981).

Stewart, A.T.Q., editor. *Michael Collins: The Secret File* (Belfast, 1997).

Strauss, Eric. *Irish Nationalism and British Democracy* (New York, 1951).

Street, Maj. C.J.C., writing under the pseudonym of 'I.O.'. *The Administration of Ireland, 1920* (London, 1922).

Street, Maj. C.J.C., *Ireland in 1921* (London, 1922).

Stromberg, Roland. *Redemption by War: The Intellectuals and 1914* (Lawrence, Kansas, 1982).

Sturgis, Mark. Edited by Michael Hopkinson. *The Last Days of Dublin Castle: The Mark Sturgis Diaries* (Dublin, 1999).

Sugden, John and Alan Bairner. *Sport, Sectarianism, and Society in a Divided Ireland* (Leicester, 1995).

Taillon, Ruth. *When History Was Made: The Women of 1916* (Belfast, 1996).

Talbot, Hayden. *Michael Collins' Own Story* (London, 1923).

Tansill, Charles Callan. *America and the Fight for Irish Freedom, 1866-1922* (New York, 1957).

Taylor, A.J.P. *English History, 1914-1945* (Oxford, 1965).

Taylor, A.J.P., editor. *Lloyd George, Twelve Essays* (London, 1971).

Taylor, Rex. *Assassination* (London, 1961).

Taylor, Rex. *Michael Collins* (London, 1970).

Thompson, Sir Basil. *Queer People* (London, 1922).

Thompson, Sir Basil. *The Scene Changes* (London, 1939).

Thompson, William Irwin. *The Imagination of an Insurrection: Dublin, Easter 1916: A Study of an Ideological Movement* (London, 1967).

Thornley, Yseult, editor. *Radical, Republican, Socialist: essays in memory of David Thornley* (Dublin, 2008).

Tierney, Michael. *Bibliographical Memoir of Eoin MacNeill* (Dublin, 1964).

Tierney, Michael. *Eoin MacNeill, Scholar and Man of Action, 1867-1945* (Oxford, 1980).

Toby, Tyler. *Exemplary Violence Used in British Colonial Policy: One Explanation for General John Maxwell's Violent Reaction to the Easter Rising of 1916* (Boston, Massachusetts, 1997).

Tóibín, Colm. *Lady Gregory's Toothbrush* (Dublin, 2002).

Townshend, Charles. *The British Campaign in Ireland, 1919-1921* (Oxford, 1975).

Townshend, Charles. *Political Violence in Ireland. Government and Resistance since 1848* (Oxford, 1983).

Townshend, Charles. *Easter 1916, The Irish Rebellion* (London, 2005).

Travers, Revd Charles J. *Séan MacDiarmada (1883-1916)* (Dublin, 1966).

Travers, Pauric. *Settlements and Divisions: Ireland, 1870-1922* (Dublin, 1988).

Travers, Pauric. *Éamon de Valera* (Dublin, 1994).

Trimble, David. *The Easter Rebellion of 1916* (Belfast, 1992).

Tweedy, Hilda. *A Link in the Chain: The Story of the Irish Housewives' Association, 1942-1992* (Dublin, 1992)

Twohig, Patrick. J. *The Dark Secret of Béal na mBláth, The Michael Collins Story* (Ballincollig, 1990).

Twohig, Patrick. J. *Green Tears for Hecuba* (Cork, 1994).

Tynan, Patrick. *The Irish Invincibles and Their Times* (1894; Millwood, New York, 1983).

Urquart, Diane. *Women in Ulster Politics, 1890-1940* (Dublin, 2000).

Urquart, Diane. *Irish Women's History Reader* (Dublin, 2001).
Ussher, Arnold. *The Face and Mind of Ireland* (London, 1949).

Valiulis, Maryann G. *Almost a Rebellion: The Irish Army Mutiny of 1924* (Cork, 1985).
Valiulis, Maryann G. *Portrait of a Revolutionary: General Richard Mulcahy and the Founding of the Irish Free State* (Blackrock, 1992).
Valiulis, Maryann G. *Gender and Power in Irish History* (Dublin, 2008).
Van Voris, Jacqueline. *Constance de Markievicz: In the Cause of Ireland* (Amherst, Massachusetts, 1967).
Vane, Sir Francis. *Agin the Government* (London, 1929).
Vaughan, W.E., and A.J. Fitzpatrick, editors. *Irish Historical statistics: population, 1821-1971* (Dublin, 1978).
Vaughan, W.E., editor. *Ireland under the Union, 1870-1921* (Oxford, 1996).
Venturi, Franco. *Roots of Revolution* (London, 1960).
Vicary, Tim. *The Blood Upon the Rose* (London, 1992).

Wade, A., editor. *The Letters of W.B. Yeats* (London, 1954).
Walker, Brian. *Parliamentary Election Results in Ireland, 1918-1992* (Dublin, 1992).
Walker, Brian. *Past and Present: History, Identity and Politics in Ireland* (Belfast, 2000).
Waller, John. *Irish Flames* (Chiltenham, 2006).
Walsh, J.J. *Recollections of a Rebel: the Fenian Movement, Its Origins and Progress* (Tralee, 1949).
Walsh, Louis J. *On My Keeping and in Theirs* (Dublin and London, 1921).
Walsh, Louis J. *Old Friends: Being Memories of Men and Places* (Dundalk, 1934).
Walsh, Maurice. *The News from Ireland: Foreign Correspondents and the Irish Revolution* (Dublin, 2008).
Walsh, Oonagh. *Ireland's Independence, 1880-1923* (London, 2002).
Walsh, Pat. *Irish Republicanism and Socialism: The Politics of the Republican Movement, 1905-1994* (Belfast, 1994).
Walsh, Patrick. *William J. Walsh, Archbishop of Dublin* (London, 1928).
Walsh, Seán P. *Free and Gaelic: Pearse's Idea of a National Culture* (Dublin, 1979).
War History of the 6th Battalion South Staffordshire Regiment (London, 1921).
Ward, Alan J. *Ireland and Anglo-American Relations, 1899-1921* (London, 1969).
Ward, Alan J. *The Easter Rising: Revolution and Irish Nationalism* (Arlington Heights, Illinois, 1980).
Ward, Alan J. *The Irish Constitutional Tradition: Responsible Government and Modern Ireland, 1782-1992* (Washington, DC 1994).
Ward, Margaret. *Unmanageable Revolutionaries, Women and Irish Nationalism* (Dingle, 1983).
Ward, Margaret. *Maud Gonne. Ireland's Joan of Arc* (London, 1990).
Ward, Margaret, editor. *In Their Own Voice* (Dublin, 1995, 2001).
Ward, Margaret. *Hanna Sheehy-Skeffington, A Life* (Cork, 1997).
Warwick-Haller, Adrian and Sally Warwick-Haller, editors. *Letters from Dublin, Easter 1916: Alfred Fannin's Diary of The Rising* (Dublin, 1995).
Watson, G.J. *Irish Identity and the Literary Revival: Synge, Yeats, Joyce and O'Casey* (London, 1979).
Watts, J.F. and Sandra Stotsky, editors. *The Irish Americans, the Immigrant Experience* (New York, 1996).
Webb, Sidney and Beatrice Webb. *History of Trade Unionism* (London, 1911).
Weisser, Henry. *Ireland, An Illustrated History* (New York, 1999).
Welch, Robert, editor. *The Oxford Companion to Irish Literature* (Oxford, 1996).
Welch, Robert. *The Abbey Theatre, 1899-1999* (Oxford, 1999).
Weldon, John, writing under the pseudonym of Brinsley MacNamara. *The Clanking of Chains* (Dublin and London, 1920).
Wells, Warre B. and N. Marlowe. *A History of the Irish Rebellion of 1916* (Dublin, 1916).
Wells, Warre B. *An Irish Apologia. Some Thoughts on Anglo-Irish Relations and the War* (Dublin, 1917).
Wells, Warre B. *John Redmond: a biography* (London, 1919).
West, Nigel. *MI-5: British Secret Service Operations, 1900-1945* (London, 1981).
West, Trevor. *Horace Plunkett: Co-operation and Politics* (Gerrards Cross, 1986).
Wheare, K.C. *The Statute of Westminster and dominion status* (Oxford, 1938).
Wheatley, Michael. *Nationalism and the Irish Party, Provincial Ireland, 1910-1916* (Oxford, 2005).

Whelan, Gerard. *The Guns of Easter* (Dublin, 1996).
Wheller-Bennett, J.W. *Sir J. W. John Anderson, Viscount Waverly* (London, 1962).
White, Gerry and Brendan O'Shea. *Irish Volunteer Soldier, 1913-1923* (Northants, 2003).
White, Gerry and Brendan O'Shea. *Baptised in Blood* (Cork, 2005).
White, J.R. *The Significance of Sinn Féin* (Dublin, 1919)
White, Cpt. Jack. *Misfit, A Revolutionary Life* (Dublin, 1930, 2005).
White, Terence de Vere. *The Road of Excess* (London, 1946).
White, Terence de Vere. *Kevin O'Higgins* (London and Tralee, 1948, 1986).
White, Terence de Vere. *The Anglo-Irish* (London, 1972).
Whyte, J.H. *The Independent Irish Party* (Oxford, 1958).
Whyte, J.H. *Church and State in Modern Ireland: 1922-1979* (Dublin, 1980).
Wilkinson, Burke. *The Zeal of the Convert. The Life of Erskine Childers* (Washington DC, 1974).
Williams, Basil. *Erskine Childers* (privately printed, 1926).
Williams, T. Desmond, editor. *The Irish Struggle, 1916-1921* (London, 1966).
Williams, T. Desmond, editor. *Secret Societies in Ireland* (Dublin, 1973).
Wills, Clair. *Dublin 1916: The Seige of the GPO* (London, 2009)
Wilson, Philip. *The Beginnings of Modern Ireland* (Dublin and London, 1935).
Wilson, Thomas, editor. *Ulster under Home Rule* (Oxford, 1955).
Winter, Ormonde. *Winter's Tale* (London, 1955).
Woggan, Helga. *Silent Radical: Winifred Carney 1887-1943. A Reconstruction of her biography* (unpublished but compiled in Berlin, 1983; Dublin, 2000).
Wohl, Robert. *The Generation of 1914* (Cambridge, Massachusetts, 1979).
Wrench, John Evelyn. *Struggle, 1914-1920* (London, 1935).
Wright, Arnold. *Disturbed Dublin: The Story of the Great Strike of 1913-1914* (London, 1914).
Wright, Frank. *Northern Ireland: A Comparative Analysis* (Dublin, 1988).
Wright, Frank. *Two Lands on One Soil* (Dublin, 1996).

Yeates, Padraig and Jimmy Wren. *Michael Collins* (Dublin, 1989).
Yeates, Padraig. *Lockout: Dublin 1913* (Dublin, 2000).
Yeats, William Butler. *The Autobiography of William Butler Yeats* (New York, 1926).
Yeats, William Butler. *Letters from W.B. Yeats to John O'Leary and his Sisters*. Originals in the Berg Collection, New York City (New York, 1953).
Yeats, William Butler. *W.B. Yeats, The Major Works* (Oxford, 1997).
Young, Ella. *Flowering Dusk* (London, 1945).
Younger, Calton. *Ireland's Civil War* (London, 1968).
Younger, Calton. *A State of Disunion* (London, 1972).
Younger, Calton. *Arthur Griffith* (Dublin, 1981).

Zimmerman, G.D. *Songs of Irish Rebellion: Political Street Ballads and Rebel Songs, 1780-1900* (Hatsboro, Pennsylvania, 1967).

UNATTRIBUTED NEWSPAPER ARTICLES

'Liam Mellows in Galway', *An Phoblacht* (3-31 December 1927).
'Edward Daly', *An Phoblacht* (27 February 1997).
'The I.R.A. and the Treaty', *An Phoblacht* (17 April 1997).
'The Four Courts Attack', *An Phoblacht* (3 July 1997).
'The Toughest Leader', *An Phoblacht* (19 February 1998).
'Roger Casement: the internationalist', *An Phoblacht* (20 May 1998).
'Rebuilding the Republican Movement', *An Phoblacht* (29 July 1999).
'The East Clare Election', *An Phoblacht* (12 August 1999).
'Erskine Childers', *An Phoblacht* (29 November 1999).

'Thomas Kent', *An Phoblacht* (18 May 2000).
'The Kilcoole Gunrunning', *An Phoblacht* (3 August 2000).
'The Forgotten Ten', *An Phoblacht* (11 October 2001).
'The Missing Piece', *An Phoblacht* (27 March 2002).
'An Irish Hero', *An Phoblacht* (5 February 2005).
'The First Bloody Sunday', *An Phoblacht* (25 February 2007).
'The Last Days of Dublin Castle', *Blackwood's Magazine* (August 1922).
'Easter Week and After: Eyewitness Accounts and Biographies', *The Catholic Bulletin* (1916).
'Jacobs and Stephen's Green Area', *The Catholic Bulletin* (September 1918).
'Report of the Irish National Aid and Volunteers' Dependents' Fund', *The Catholic Bulletin* (August 1919).
'They were schoolboys – The Pearse Brothers at the "Row"', *Christian Brothers Westland Row Centenary Record, 1864-1964*.
'The McCartan Documents', *The Clogher Record* (1966).
'Quinlisk Killed', *Cork Examiner* (24 February 1920).
'Amazing Adventures', *Daily Sketch*, London (24 August 1922).
'Republican Women on Hunger Strike', *Éire* (10 November 1923).
'Interview with General Strickland', *The Evening Standard* (25 January 1921).
'The Meeting in the Rotunda Rink, 25 November 1913', *Freeman's Journal* (26 November 1913).
'Speech by P.H. Pearse', *Freeman's Journal* (26 November 1913).
'Inside Story of the Easter Week Rebellion', *Gaelic American* (29 July 1916).
'Graphic Story of Ashbourne', *Gaelic American* (23 September 1916).
'A Dublin Woman's Story of the Rebellion', *Gaelic American* (11-18 November 1916).
'CID Officers active, Captures in Dublin road', *Irish Independent* (2 March 1923).
Irish Independent, Golden Jubilee Supplement, 1966
'The Record of the Irish Rebellion of 1916'. Pamphlet published by *Irish Life* (1916).
'The Sinn Féin Rising. Scenes and Incidents in Dublin Streets. A Citizen's Diary', *The Irish Times* (2 May 1916).
'The Proclamation of the Republic', *The Irish Times* (6 May 1916).
'Inquiry into the Rebellion', *The Irish Times* (20 May 1916).
'Mr Michael Collins', *The Irish Times* (1 October 1917).
'Michael Collins' appearance', *The Irish Times* (17 August 1921).
'Collins in Armagh', *The Irish Times* (5 September 1921).
'Four Republicans Killed', *The Irish Times* (28 August 1922).
'Redmond's Double Refusal To Lord Kichener: No Oath of Allegiance; No Overseas Service', *The Irish Times* (16 May 1956).
'Gerry Boland's Story', *The Irish Times* (9 October 1968).
'De Valera 1882-1975', *The Irish Times*, 1976.
'Who was Kevin Barry?', *The Irish Times* (7 September 2001).
'Irish Volunteers – First Convention', *Irish Volunteer* (31 October 1914).
'The Volunteers Declare Their Policy', *Irish Volunteer* (31 October 1914).
'Programme of Military Training', Supplement to *Irish Volunteer* (13 January 1915).
'The State of the Irish Volunteers – October 1915', *Irish Volunteer* (6 November 1915).
Silver Jubilee 1916 Souvenir, *The Kerry Champion*, edited by Patrick Cahill (1941).
'The Late Miss Jo Power', *The Kerryman* (8 February 1969).
'The Death of the Honorable Mary Ellen Spring-Rice', *Limerick Chronicle* (4 December 1924).
'Rossa Buried in Dublin', *New York Times* (2 August 1915).
'Plunkett Married on the Eve of his Death', *New York Times* (7 May 1916).
'Sinn Féiners escape from English Prison; De Valera, Milroy, and McGarry Use Master Key Thrown to Them Over Wall', *New York Times* (5 February 1919).
'Countess Markievicz Released from Prison; Sinn Féin's Woman Leader Is Freed After Serving Seven Months of Sentence', *New York Times* (24 July 1921).
'Buckley, Margaret – President of Sinn Féin', *Saoirse – Irish Freedom* (July 1998).
'50 Years Ago', *Saoirse – Irish Freedom* (April 2003).
'It happened when two women met', *Sunday Express* (1953).

Sunday Independent, Easter Rising Commemorative Supplement, 1966.

'Crossfire baby recalls Barry ambush', *Sunday Independent* (14 October 2001).

'An interview with Alice Milligan', *Sunday Press* (21 October 1951).

'What Causes Reprisals', *The Weekly Summary*, No. 9 (8 October 1920).

'Cumann na mBan in Easter Week: Tribute from a Hostile Source', *Wolfe Tone Annual* (undated).

'Revolutionary Warfare', *Worker's Republic*. (This series of articles was unattributed but almost certainly written by James Connolly.) (29 May, 5, 12, 19 June, 3, 10, 17, 24 July 1915).

Editorial. 'The Helmsman Gone', *Daily Sketch*, London (24 August 1922).

Editorial. 'Arms and the Man', *National Student*, Vol. IV, No. 2 (December 1913).

Editorial. 'Rule Britannia', *National Student*, Vol. VI, No. 1 (December 1915).

ATTRIBUTED NEWSPAPER ARTICLES, BOOK CHAPTERS, LECTURES, PAMPHLETS, PAPERS/DISSERTATIONS/THESES, PERIODICALS, RADIO PROGRAMMES

aan de Weil, Dr Jerome. '*Austria-Hungary, France, Germany, the Vatican and the Irish Crisis from 1900 to 1917*', Lecture given at 'The Long Revolution: 1916 in Context', Conference in University College Cork (27 January 2006).

Ackerman, Carl. 'Ireland from a Scotland Yard Notebook', *Atlantic Monthly* (April 1922).

Ackerman, Carl. 'The Irish Education of Mr Lloyd George', *Atlantic Monthly* (May 1922).

Acland, Francis. *A Report of a Fortnight's Tour in Ireland* (pamphlet, 1920).

Acland, Francis. 'The Sinn Féin Fellowships', *Westminster Gazette* (29 April 1921).

Ainsworth, John. '*British Security Policy in Ireland, 1920-1921: A Desperate Attempt by the Crown to Maintain Anglo-Irish Unity by Force*', Ph.D. Dissertation, Queensland University of Technology, School of Humanities and Social Science (2001).

Akenson, D.H. and J.F. Fallon. 'The Irish Civil War and the Drafting of the Free State Constitution', *Éire-Ireland*, Vol. V (1970).

Fr Albert, OFM, Cap. 'Seán Heuston's Last Moments', *Fianna* (May 1926).

Fr Albert, OFM, Cap. 'Seán Heuston: How Seán Heuston Died', *Capuchin Annual* (1942).

Fr Aloysius, OFM, Cap. 'Personal Recollections', *Capuchin Annual* (1966).

Alter, Peter. 'Symbols of Irish Nationalism', *Studia Hibernica*, Vol. XIV (1974).

'An Rathach'. 'London Volunteers', *Irish Democrat* (April 1948).

'A Volunteer'. 'South Dublin Union Area', *Capuchin Annual* (1966).

Bacik, Ivana. 'Law in a Republic', *RTÉ 1 Thomas Davis Lecture* (19 May 2005).

Baldwin, Raper. 'The State of South Ireland', *The London Times* (9 March 1921).

Bartlett, Thomas. 'Theobald Wolfe Tone and Irish Republicanism and Separatism', *RTÉ 1 Thomas Davis Lecture* (21 April 2005).

Barton, Robert. *The Truth about the Treaty and Document Number 2* (pamphlet, Dublin, 1922).

Bastable, Charles F. 'A New Currency for the Free State', *Studies, The Irish Jesuit Quarterly Review*, Vol. XII (1923).

Béaslaí, Piaras. 'A Comrade's Tribute: The Message of a Hero's Death', *An Saorstat* (29 August 1922).

Béaslaí, Piaras. 'The Fixing of the Date of the 1916 Rising', *Irish Independent* (24 April 1952).

Béaslaí, Piaras. 'The National Army is Founded', *Irish Independent* (5 January 1953).

Béaslaí, Piaras. 'Moods and Memories', *Irish Independent* (October 1961-June 1965).

Beaumont, Catriona A. '*Women and the Politics of Equality, 1930-1943*', MA Thesis, University College Dublin, Dublin, 1989.

Bell, J. Bowyer. 'The Thompson Submachine Gun in Ireland', *Irish Sword*, Vol. VIII, No. 31 (1967).

Berman, David, Stephen Lalor, and Brian Torode. 'The Theology of the I.R.A.', *Studies, The Irish Jesuit Quarterly Review, Vol.* LXXIII (Summer 1983).

Bew, Paul. 'The Real Importance of Roger Casement', *History Ireland*, Vol. II, No. 2 (Summer 1994).

Bew, Paul. 'Moderate Nationalism and the Irish Revolution, 1916–1923', *The Historical Review*, Vol. XXVI (1999).

Bew, Paul. 'Why did Jimmie die?", *History Ireland,* Vol. XIV, No. 2 (March/April 2006).

Bielenberg, Andrew. *'Protestant emigration from the south of Ireland, 1911-1926',* Lecture given at 'Understanding our history: Protestants, the War of Independence, and the Civil War in Cork', Conference at University College Cork (13 December 2008).

Billigheimer, Rachel. 'The Rose of Ireland in the Early Poems of W.B. Yeats', *Studies, The Irish Jesuit Quarterly Review,* Vol. XC (2002).

Blackburn, G.A. 'Irish Free State: Five Years of Progress', *Current History,* Vol. XXV (March 1927).

Blythe, Ernest. 'Arthur Griffith', *Administration,* Vol. VIII (1960).

Bouch, J.J. 'Republican Proclamation of 1916', *Bibliographical Society of Ireland,* Vol. V, No. 3 (1933).

Bouchier-Hayes, Frank. 'An Irishman's Diary: Darrell Figgis', *The Irish Times* (21 April 2008).

Bouchier-Hayes, Frank. 'An Irishman's Diary: The Auxiliaries', *The Irish Times* (29 July 2008).

Bouchier-Hayes, Frank. 'An Irishman's Diary: The Irish Republican Brotherhood', *Irish Times* (4 August 2008).

Bouchier-Hayes, Frank. 'An Irishman's Diary: Cathal Brugha', *The Irish Times* (18 August 2008).

Bourke, Joanna. '"Irish Tommies": the Construction of a Martial Manhood, 1914-1918', *Historical Journal* (1999).

Bourke, Marcus. 'The G.A.A. and the Castle', *Irish Independent* (9, 10, 11 July 1964).

Bourke, Marcus. 'Thomas MacDonagh's Role in the Plans for the 1916 Rising', *The Irish Sword,* Vol. VIII (1968).

Bowden, Tom. 'Bloody Sunday, A Reappraisal', *European Studies Review,* Vol. II, No. 1 (1972).

Bowden, Tom. 'The Irish Underground and the War of Independence 1919–1921', *Journal of Contemporary History,* Vol. VIII, No. 2 (1973).

Bowden, Tom. 'The I.R.A. and the Changing Tactics of Terrorism', *Political Quarterly,* Vol. XLVII (1976).

Bowman, John. 'De Valera on Ulster, 1919-1920: What He Told America', *Irish Studies in International Affairs,* Vol. I (1979).

Bowman, John. 'Sinn Féin's Perspective of the Ulster Question: Autumn, 1921', *The Crane Bag,* Vol. IV, No. 2 (1980).

Bowman, Timothy. 'The Ulster Volunteers 1913–1914: Force or Farce?', *History Ireland,* Vol. X, No. 1 (Spring 2002).

Boyce, D. George. 'British conservative opinion, the Ulster question, and the partition of Ireland', *Irish Historical Studies,* Vol. XVII (1970-71).

Boyce, D. George. 'British Opinion, Ireland and the War, 1916-1918', *Historical Journal* Vol. XVII, No. 3 (1974).

Boyce, D. George and C. Hazelhurst. 'The Unknown Chief Secretary', *Irish Historical Studies,* Vol. XX, No. 79 (1977).

Boyle, John W. 'Irish Labour and the Rising, *Éire-Ireland,* Vol. II (1967).

Boyle, K. 'The Tallents Report on the Craig-Collins Pact of 30 March 1922', *The Irish Jurist,* Vol. XII (1977).

Bradshaw, B. 'Nationalism and Historical Scholarship in Modern Ireland', *Irish Historical Studies,* Vol. XXVI (1988-1989).

Brady, Tom. 'Man questioned on Pillar bomb 34 years later', *Irish Independent* (22 September 2000).

Branagan, W.J. 'Ireland and War Contracts', *Studies, The Irish Jesuit Quarterly Review,* Vol. IV (1915).

Brennan, Austin. 'Forcibly Fed at Five Bob a Head', *Limerick Leader* (16 December 1972).

Brennan, James J. 'Mendicity Institution Area', *Capuchin Annual* (1966).

Brennan, John. 'The Castle Document', *The Irish Times* (28 March 1958).

Brennan, Lily M. 'We Surrender', *An tÓglach* (12 June 1926).

Brennan, Robert. 'My War-Time Mission in Washington', *Irish Press* (28 April-17 May 1958).

Brennan-Whitmore, W.J. 'The Occupation of the North Earl Street Area', *An tÓglach* (30 January, 6 February 1926).

Brennan-Whitmore, W.J. 'The North Earl Street Area', *Irish Weekly Independent* (August-September 1953).

Brennan-Whitmore, W.J. 'How Long Could They Hold Out?', *Irish Independent* (11 April 1966).

Brooks, Sydney. 'The Irish Insurrection', *North American Review* (July 1966).

Brophy, Karl. 'Barry and comrades are laid to rest with honour and dignity', *Irish Independent* (15 October 2001).

Browne, Kevin J. 'A Man and a County', *Clare Champion* (October 1971-January 1972).

Buckland, P.J. 'The Southern Irish Unionists, the Irish Question and British Politics, 1906-14', *Irish Historical Studies*, Vol. XV, No. 59 (March 1967).

Buckland, P.J. '*Southern Unionism, 1885 – 1922* , MA Thesis, Queen's University, Belfast (1969).

Buckley, Anthony D. 'God's Chosen People', *The Irish Review*, Vol. II (1987).

Burke, Tom. 'Brotherhood Among Irishmen? The Battle of Wijtschate-Messines Ridge, June 1917', *History Ireland*, Vol. XV, No. 5 (September/October 2007).

Butler, R.M. 'The Reconstruction of O'Connell Street', *Studies, The Irish Jesuit Quarterly Review,* Vol. V (1916).

Byrne, Elaine. 'Hands that shaped Irish history', *The Irish Times* (29 July 2008).

Caffrey, P. 'Jacob's Women Workers during the 1913 Strike', *Saothar*, No. 16 (1991).

Cahill, Patrick. 'Who Blundered in Ireland?', *An Phoblacht* (13 September 1930).

Callan, Patrick. 'Recruiting for the British Army in Ireland during the First World War', *Irish Sword* (1987).

Callender, Ignatius. 'A Diary of Easter Week', *Dublin Brigade Review* (1939).

Campbell, Fergus. 'The Social Dynamics of Nationalist Politics in the West of Ireland, 1898-1918', *Past and Present*, No. 182 (2004).

Campbell, Fergus. 'The Easter Rising in Galway', *History Ireland,* Vol. XIV, No.2 (March/April 2006).

Campbell, Cmdt Liam. 'A Military Analysis of the Rising', *An Cosantoir* (April/May 2006).

Campbell, Cmdt Liam. 'A Tale of Two Soldiers', *An Cosantoir* (April/May 2006).

Canavan, Tony. 'Pearse Museum', *History Ireland,* Vol. XIV, No. 2 (March/April 2006).

Carey, Tim and Marcus de Burca. 'Bloody Sunday 1920: New Evidence', *History Ireland*, Vol. XI, No. 2 (Summer 2003).

Casey, James. 'Republican Courts in Ireland, 1919-1922', *Irish Jurist*, Vol. V (1970).

Casey, James. 'The Genesis of the Dáil Courts', *Irish Jurist*, Vol. IX (1974).

Ceannt, Áine. 'Looking Back to Easter Week, 1916', *The Leader* (20 April 1946).

Ceannt, Éamonn. 'The Founding of the Irish Volunteers', *Irish Volunteer* (20 June 1914).

Cecil, Lord Robert. *The New Outlook* (pamphlet, London, 1919).

Chartres, John, writing under the pseudonym of Edward Seaton. 'The Bloody English', *Irish Press* (Philadelphia), (7 January –15 April 1922).

Chartres, John, writing under the pseudonym of Fear Faire. 'The English Peril', *The Nation* (26 March, 2, 9 April 1927).

Chesterton, G.K. 'The Danger to England', *Manchester Guardian* (15 February 1921).

Chesterton, G.K. *The Delusion of a Double Policy* (pamphlet, undated).

Chesterton, G.K. *What are Reprisals?* (pamphlet, undated).

Childers, Robert Erskine. 'Military Rule in Ireland', *Daily News*, 8 Articles (March – May 1920).

Churchill, Ivor. 'Proclamation No. 1', *The Irish Times* (25 April, 1916).

Churchill, Ivor. 'Proclamation No. 2', *The Irish Times* (26 April 1916).

Clancy, Mary. '*Women's Contribution to Public Political Debate (with particular reference to Women's Issues) in the Irish Free State, 1922-37*', MA Thesis, University College, Galway, 1988.

Clarke, Thomas. Foreword by P.S. O'Hegarty. *Glimpses of an Irish Felon's Prison Life.* (pamphlet, Cork, 1970).

Clery, Arthur E. 'Thomas Kettle', *Studies, The Irish Jesuit Quarterly Review,* Vol. V (1916).

Clery, Arthur E. 'Pearse, MacDonagh and Plunkett: An Appreciation', *Studies, The Irish Jesuit Quarterly Review,* Vol. VI (June 1917).

Clery, Arthur E. 'The Gaelic League, 1893-1919', *Studies, The Irish Jesuit Quarterly Review,* Vol. VIII (1919).

Clery, Arthur E. 'A Review of Pearse's political writings and speeches', *Studies, The Irish Jesuit Quarterly Review,* Vol. XI (June 1922).

Clifford, Brendan. '*War, Insurrection & Election in Ireland, 1914-1921. A comment on the denunciation of the film Michael Collins by Professor Bew and others*' (pamphlet, Belfast, 1997).

Coady, Seán. 'Remembering St John's Convent', *Capuchin Annual* (1966).

Coakley, John. 'Patrick Pearse and the "Noble Lie" of Irish Nationalism', *Studies in Conflict and Violence*, Vol. LXII (1983).

Coleman, Shane. 'The Day We Decided to Sit Down and Fight', *Sunday Tribune* (12 August 2007).

Collins, Liam. 'Michael Collins had a Stalker', *Irish Independent* (9 October 2005).

Collins, Lorcan, Conor Kostick and Shane MacThomais. 'Tragedy in the Connolly Family', *History Ireland*, Vol. XII, No. 3 (Autumn 2004).

Collins, Michael. 'We Want', *Irish Independent* (18 April 1922).

Collins, Michael. *Arguments for the Treaty* (pamphlet, Dublin, 1922).

Collins, Michael. *Free State or Chaos* (pamphlet, Dublin, 1922).

Colum, Padraic. 'Effects of Dual Government in Ireland', *Current History*, Vol. XXXII, (July, 1930).

Colum, Padraic. 'The Career of Roger Casement', *Dublin Magazine* (October-December 1931).

Colum, Padraic. 'New Irish Constitution', *Commonweal*, Vol. XXVI (16 July 1937).

Comerford, Maire. 'Women in Struggle', *Éire Amach na Casca, Republican Publications* (1986).

Comerford, V. 'Patriotism as Pastime: The Appeal of Fenianism in Mid 1860's', *Irish Historical Studies*, Vol. XXII (1981).

Connolly, James ('Setanta'). 'The Mendicity and its Guests', *Workers' Republic* (27 August 1899).

Connolly, James. 'Socialism in Ireland', *The Harp* (March 1908).

Connolly, James. *Labour, Nationality and Religion* (pamphlet, Dublin, 1910).

Connolly, James. 'The Dublin Lock-Out: On the Eve', *Irish Worker* (30 August 1913).

Connolly, James. 'Arms and the Man', *Irish Worker* (13 December 1913).

Connolly, James.'Labour and the Proposed Partition of Ireland', *Irish Worker* (14 March 1914).

Connolly, James.'The Latest Massacre in Dublin', *Forward* (1 August 1914).

Connolly, James. 'Our Duty in this Crisis', *Irish Worker* (8 August 1914).

Connolly, James. 'Ruling by Fooling: Home Rule on the Statute Book', *Irish Worker* (19 September 1914).

Connolly, James. 'The Dublin Lock-out and its Sequel', *Worker's Republic* (29 May 1915).

Connolly, James. 'Conscription', *Worker's Republic* (27 November 1915).

Connolly, James. *The Re-Conquest of Ireland* (pamphlet, Dublin, 1915).

Connolly, James. 'The Programme of Labour', *Worker's Republic* (19 January 1916).

Connolly, James. 'Cannon Fodder for British Imperialism', *Worker's Republic* (12 February 1916).

Connolly, James. 'We Will Rise Again', *Worker's Republic* (25 March 1916).

Connolly, James. 'The Call to Arms', *Worker's Republic* (1 April 1916).

Connolly, James. 'The Irish Flag', *Worker's Republic* (8 April 1916).

Connolly, James. 'Labour and Ireland', *Worker's Republic* (22 April 1916).

Connolly, James and D. De Leon. *Connolly/De Leon Controversy on Wages, Marriage and the Church* (pamphlet, undated).

Connolly, James and William Walker. *The Connolly/Walker Controversy on Socialist Unity in Ireland* (pamphlet, Cork, undated).

Connolly, Matt. 'City Hall Area', *Capuchin Annual* (1966).

Connolly, Michael. 'James Connolly: socialist and patriot', *Studies, The Irish Jesuit Quarterly Review*, Vol. XLI (1952).

Connolly, Roddy. 'A Glimpse of Collins', *Michael Collins Memorial Foundation Supplement* (20 August 1966).

Connolly-Heron, Ina. 'James Connolly, The Search for Roots', *Liberty* (May 1966).

Connolly-Heron, Ina. 'James Connolly – A Biography', *Liberty* (August 1966).

Conroy, Joe. 'The Plough and Stars; Sixteen Characters in Search of Analysis', *Red Banner*, Issue 21 (March 2005).

Conway, An t-Athair Colmcille. 'The Third Tipperary Brigade (1921-1923)', *Tipperary Historical Journal* (1990, 9-26; 1991, 35-49; 1992, 23-30).

Coogan, Tim Pat. 'Collins was virtually airbrushed', *Cork Examiner* (26 February 1997).

Coogan, Tim Pat. 'Collins' Place in History Stands the Test of Time', *Irish Independent* (22 August 2002).

Coogan, Tim Pat. 'Memorial for 1916 Rising Leader O'Rahilly', *RTÉ 1* (April 2005).

Coogan, Tim Pat. 'Mick, the Real Michael Collins, by Peter Hart', *RTÉ 1 On The Shelf* (March 2006).

Coogan, Tim Pat. 'Reviewing the military parade marking 1916', *RTÉ 1* (April 2006).

Coogan, Tim Pat. 'What's so wrong with showing Nationalism in a favorable light?', *London Daily Mail* (31 May 2006).

Coogan, Tim Pat. 'What if... Michael Collins had survived the Civil War?' *RTÉ 1 'What If'* (March 2007).

Coogan, Tim Pat. 'The Big Book: Judging Dev: a reassessment of the life and legacy of Éamon de Valera', *History Ireland*, Vol. XVI, No. 3 (May/June 2008).

Cooney, Annie. 'The Marrowbone Lane Post', *An Phoblacht* (26 May 1930).

Corkery, Daniel. *What's this about the G.A.A.?* (pamphlet, undated.)

Corkery, Daniel. 'Terence MacSwiney', *Studies, The Irish Jesuit Quarterly Review*, Vol. IX (December 1920).

Corkery, Daniel. 'The Nation that was not a Nation', *Studies, The Irish Jesuit Quarterly Review*, Vol. XXIII (1934).

Cornish, Vaughan. 'The Strategic Geography of the British Empire', *Royal Colonial Institute Journal* (February 1916).

Costello, Con. 'The Curragh Camp: A Goodish Place, Sort of, in Dry Weather', *History Ireland*, Vol. VI, No. 3 (Autumn 1998).

Costello, Francis, 'The Republican Courts and the Decline of British Rule in Ireland', *Éire-Ireland*, Vol. XXV, No. 3 (1990).

Costigan, Giovanni. 'The Anglo-Irish Conflict, 1919-1921: A War of Independence or Systematic Murder?', *University Review*, Vol. V, No. 1 (1968).

Counahan, G. 'The People Backed the Movement, 1920', *Capuchin Annual* (1970).

Coyle, Eithne. 'The History of Cumann na mBan', *An Phoblacht* (8, 15 April 1933).

Cronin, Mike. 'Fighting for Ireland; playing for England? The nationalist history of the Gaelic Athletic Association and the English influence on Irish sport', *International Journal of the History of Sport*, Vol. XV, No. 3 (1998).

Cronin, Mike. 'Writing the history of the GAA', *High Ball, the official GAA Monthly Magazine*, Vol. XI, No. 6 (2003).

Crosbie, Judith. 'Executed men finally to receive a proper burial', *The Irish Times*, (7 September 2001).

'Cross Border Reflections on 1916', report of a conference organised by Drogheda-Shankill Partnership (pamphlet, 2001).

Crowley, Brian. '"His father's son": James and Patrick Pearse', *Folk Life*, Vol. XLIII (2004-5).

Crowley, Brian. '"The strange thing I am": his father's son?', *History Ireland*, Vol. XIV, No. 2 (March/April 2006).

Cunningham, John. 'Pádraic Ó Conaire's socialism', *Red Banner*, Issue 18 (December 2004).

Cunningham, John B. 'The Struggle for the Belleek-Pettigo Salient, 1922', *Donegal Annual*, No. 34 (1982).

Curran, C.P. 'Griffith, MacNeill and Pearse', *Studies, The Irish Jesuit Quarterly Review*, Vol. LV (Spring 1966).

Curran, Joseph. 'The Consolidation of the Irish Revolution, 1921-33', *University Review*, Vol. V (1968).

Curran, Joseph. 'Lloyd George and the Irish Settlement, 1921-1922', *Éire-Ireland*, Vol. VII (1972).

Curran, Joseph. 'The Decline and Fall of the I.R.B.', *Éire-Ireland*, Vol. X, No. 1 (1975).

Curtis, Lionel. 'The Anglo-Irish Predicament', *Twentieth Century Studies* (November 1970).

Curtis, Lionel. 'Moral and Physical Force: The Language of Violence in Irish Nationalism', *Journal of British Studies*, Vol. XXVII (April 1988).

Curtis, Lionel. *Ireland*, with introduction *'The Anglo Irish Treaty and the Lost World of Imperial Ireland'* by Pat Walsh (pamphlet, 1991).

Daly, Mary E. 'Women in the Irish Free State, 1922-1939, the Interaction between Economics and Ideology', *Journal of Women's History*, Vol. VI, No.4, Vol. VII, No. 1 (joint issue, Winter/Spring 1995).

Daly, Nora. 'Stephen's Green', *An tÓglach* (3 April 1926).

Daly, Terence Patrick. *'The early political career of Sir James Craig, 1906-14'*, Ph.D. Dissertation, University of Ulster (2002).

Davis, Richard P. 'Griffith and Ghandi: A Study in Non-violent Resistance', *Threshold* (Summer, 1959).

Davis, Richard P. 'Arthur Griffith', *Dublin Historical Society* (pamphlet, 1976).

Davis, Richard P. 'The Advocacy of Passive Resistance in Ireland, 1916-1922', *Anglo-Irish Studies*, Vol. III (1977).

Davis, Richard P. 'Ulster Protestants and the Sinn Féin Press, 1914-1922', *Éire-Ireland*, XV, Vol. 4 (1980).

Davis, Richard P. 'The IRB: a natural outcome of Young Irelandism?', *History Ireland*, Vol. XVI, No. 6 (November/December 2008).

Davis, T. 'The Irish Civil War and the "International Proposition" of 1922-1923', *Éire-Ireland* (Summer 1994).

Davison, Joe. 'Feature: Remembering James Connolly', *An Phoblacht* (9 May 2005).

Davitt, C. 'The Civil Jurisdiction of the Courts of Justice in the Irish Republic', *Irish Jurist*, Vol. III (1968).

Dawson, William. 'Tom Kettle: The Essayist, 1880-1916', *Studies, The Irish Jesuit Quarterly Review*, Vol. XX (1931).

Deasy, Liam. 'The Schull Peninsula in the War of Independence', *Éire-Ireland* (Summer 1966).

Deasy, Liam. 'The Beara Peninsula Campaign', *Éire-Ireland* (Fall 1966).

De Barra, Éamonn. 'A Valiant Woman: Margaret Mary Pearse', *Capuchin Annual* (1969).

De Blacam, Aodh. 'The Irish Question', *Nineteenth Century*, Vol. CXXIII (April 1938).

De Blaghd, Earnan. 'Ireland in 1915', *An tÓglach*, Vol. I, No. 5 (1962).

De Blaghd, Earnan. 'Organising the I.R.B. in Donegal', *Journal of the Donegal Historical Society*, Vol. VII, No. 1 (1966).

De Breadun, Deaglan. 'Free State account of controversial Kerry IRA deaths in 1923 contradicted by Garda report', *The Irish Times* (31 December 2008).

De Burca, Seámus. *The Soldier's Song: The Story of Peadar Kearney* (pamphlet, Dublin, 1958).

Dempsey, Jacqueline. '*Jennie Wyse Power, 1858-1941*', MA Thesis presented to St Patrick's College, Maynooth (1993).

Denman, Terence. 'The Catholic Irish Soldier in the First World War: the "Racial Environment"', *Irish Historical Studies*, Vol. XXVII, No. 108 (November 1991).

Denman, Terence. '"The red livery of shame": the campaign against army recruitment in Ireland, 1899-1914', *Irish Historical Studies*, Vol. XXIX, No. 114 (November 1994).

De Paor, Mairead and Siobhan De Paor (Cis and Jo Power). 'Blaze Away with your Little Gun', *The Kerryman* (21, 28 December 1968, 3 January 1969).

Derwin, Des. 'The taming of Jim Larkin', *Red Banner*, Issue 2 (December 2000).

De Valera, Éamon. *The alternative to the treaty: document no. 2* (pamphlet, Dublin, 1923)

De Valera, Éamon, et al. *The Anglo-Irish Treaty and de Valera's Alternative* (pamphlet, Dublin, Irish Nation Committee, 1924)

De Valera, Éamon. *National Discipline & Majority Rule* (Fianna Fail Pamphlet No. 1, 1936).

Dillon, Geraldine Plunkett. 'Casement and Easter Week', *Irish Press* (3 January 1936).

Dillon, Geraldine Plunkett. 'How Much did the Castle Know?', *Irish Press* (14 January 1936).

Dillon, Geraldine Plunkett. 'Joseph Plunkett: Origin and Background', *University* Review (1958).

Dillon, Geraldine Plunkett. 'The Irish Republican Brotherhood', *University Review*, Vol. II, No. 9 (1960).

Plunkett, Geraldine Plunkett. 'Joseph Plunkett's Diary of his Journey to Germany', *University Review* (1968).

Dillon, Thomas. 'Birth of the new Sinn Féin and the Ard-Fheis of 1917', *Capuchin Annual* (1967).

Doherty, Seán. 'Will the Real James Connolly Please Stand Up?', *International Socialism*, Issue 80 (September 1998).

Doherty, Shuna. '*Elizabeth O'Farrell and the Women of 1916*', unpublished MA Thesis, National University of Ireland (1995).

Dolan, Anne. 'Killing and Bloody Sunday, November 1920', *Historical Journal*, Vol. XLIX, Issue 3 (September 2006).

Dolan, Anne. 'The IRA, intelligence and Bloody Sunday, 1920' in O'Halpin, Eunan, Robert Armstrong and Jane Ohlmeyer, editors, *Intelligence, Statecraft and International Power* (Dublin, 2006).

Dolan, M. 'Galway in 1916', *Connacht Tribune* (2, 9, 16, 23 April 1966).

Donnelly, Brian, editor. 'The National Army Enters Cork, August 1922: A Diary Account by Mr Frank Bewitt', *Irish Archives* (Autumn 1994).

Donnelly, Mary. 'With the Citizen's Army in Stephen's Green', *An Phoblacht* (19 April 1930).

Donnelly, Rachel. 'Britain Offered Unity if Ireland Offered War', *The Irish Times* (15 February 2001).

Donnelly, Rachel. 'De Valera's Attitude to Churchill', *The Irish Times* (15 August 2001).

Donnelly, Simon. 'With the 3rd Battalion', *Poblacht na hÉireann* (20 April 1922).

Donnelly, Simon. *'Thou Shalt Not Pass—Ireland's Challenge to the British Forces at Mount Street Bridge, Easter 1916*, IMA CD 62/3/7. (pamphlet, undated).

Doolan, Joseph.'The South Dublin Union', *The Catholic Bulletin*, a 4 part account (March, April, May, June 1918).

Dooley, Pat. *Under the Banner of Connolly* (pamphlet, London, 1944).

Doorley, Michael. 'The Friends of Irish Freedom, a case study in Irish-American nationalism, 1916-1921', *History Ireland*, Vol. XVI, No. 2 (March/April 2008).

Dore, Éamonn. 'Seán MacDermott as I knew him', *Leitrim Guardian* (Christmas 1968).

Dowling, Michele. '"The Ireland That I Would Have": de Valera and the Creation of the Irish National Image', *History Ireland*, Vol. V, No. 2 (Autumn 1997).

Doyle, Kevin. 'A revolutionary misfit: Jack White', *Red Banner*, Issue 24 (June 2007).

Doyle, Paul and John O'Dowd, editors. *The Parliament of Labour: 100 Years of the Dublin Council of Trade Unions* (pamphlet, Dublin, 1986).

Doyle, Seámus. 'With Pearse in Arbour Hill', *Irish Press* (3 May 1932).

Duggan, G.C., writing under the pseudonym of 'Periscope'. 'The Last Days of Dublin Castle', *Blackwoods Magazine*, Vol. CCXII (August 1922).

Duggan, J.P. 'German Arms and the 1916 Rising', *An Cosantoir,* Vol. XXX (1970).

Duggan, J.P. 'Poltergeist Pistol', *History Ireland*, Vol. III (1995).

Lord Dunsany. 'Recollections of 1916', *Irish Digest* (April 1939).

Ervine, St John. 'The Story of the Irish Rebellion', *Century Magazine* (1917).

Fallon, Charlotte. 'Civil War Hungerstrikes: Women and Men', *Éire-Ireland,* Vol. XXII (1987).

Falls, C. 'Irish Free State's First Year', *Literary Digest*, Vol. LXXIV (3 February 1923).

Falls, C. 'Ireland Today', *Nineteenth Century*, Vol. XCIII (April 1923).

Fanning, Ronan. *'Leadership and transition from the politics of revolution to the politics of party: the example of Ireland 1914-1939'*, Lecture delivered at the XIV International Congress of Historical Sciences, San Francisco, California (August 1975).

Farrell, Brian. 'The Drafting of the Irish Constitution', *Irish Jurist* (1970).

Farrell, Brian. 'From First Dáil through Irish Free State', in Brian Farrell, editor, *De Valera's Constitution and Ours* (Dublin, 1988).

Fedorowitch, Kent. 'The problems of disbandment: the Royal Irish Constabulary and imperial migration, 1919-29', *Irish Historical Studies*, Vol. XXX, No. 117 (May 1996).

Fennell, Desmond. 'Against Revisionism', *Irish Review,* Vol. IV (Spring 1988).

Ferriter, Diarmuid. 'In Such Deadly Earnest', *Dublin Review*, No. 12 (Autumn 2003).

Figgis, Darrell. 'For Demand of Peace, or else not: A Forgotten Document in Irish History', *Studies, The Irish Jesuit Quarterly Review,* Vol. VII (1918).

Finch, Bruce-Andrew. 'Birth Pangs of a New Nation: Senator Thomas Westropp Bennett and the Irish Free State', *History Ireland*, Vol. XI, No. 4 (Winter 2003).

FitzGerald, Desmond. 'Mr Pakenham on the Anglo-Irish Treaty', *Studies, The Irish Jesuit Quarterly Review*, Vol. XXIV (1935).

FitzGerald, Desmond. 'Inside the GPO', *The Irish Times Supplement* (7 April 1966).

FitzGerald, Garret. 'The Significance of 1916', *Studies, The Irish Jesuit Quarterly Review,* Vol. LV (Spring 1966).

Fitzgerald, William G. 'The Historic Rising of Easter Week, 1916', in Fitzgerald, William G., editor. *The Voice of Ireland* (Dublin and London, 1924).

FitzGibbon, Constantine. 'Easter 1916, Part I', *An Phoblacht* (5 April 2004).

FitzGibbon, Constantine. 'Easter 1916, Part II', *An Phoblacht* (7 April 2004).

FitzGibbon, Seán. 'The Easter Rising from the Inside', *The Irish Times,* 5-Part Series (18-22 April 1949). (Dictated to and written by Michael J. Lennon).

Fitzpatrick, David. 'The Geography of Irish Nationalism: 1910-1922', *Past and Present*, No. 78 (1978).
  Fitzpatrick, David. 'The Logic of Collective Sacrifice: Ireland and the British Army, 1914-1918',
  Historical Journal, Vol. XXXVIII, No. 4 (1995).
Fitzpatrick, David. '"Decidedly a Personality": de Valera's Performance as a Convict, 1916–1917', *History
  Ireland*, Vol. X, No. 2 (Summer 2002).
Flanagan, Fr. 'The General Post Office Area', *Catholic Bulletin* (August 1918).
Flanagan, Thomas. 'Rebellion and Style: John Mitchel and the Jail Journal', *Irish University Review*,
  Vol. I (Autumn 1970).
Fleming, Diarmaid. 'Last Man Standing: Dan Keating,' *History Ireland*, Vol. XVI, No. 3 (May/June 2008).
Fleming, Noel C. 'Aristocratic Rule? Unionism and Northern Ireland', *History Ireland*, Vol. XV, No. 6
  (November/December 2007).
Foster, Roy. 'We are All Revisionists Now', *Irish Review*, Vol. I (1986).
Fox, R.M. 'How the Women Helped', in *Dublin's Fighting Story 1916-1921, Told by the Men Who Made
  It. The Kerryman* (1947).
Fox, R.M. 'Ireland, Retrospect and Prospect', *Nineteenth Century*, Vol. CII (August 1927).
Freeman, P.A. *'The Career of Michael Collins with Special Reference to the Treaty of 1921'*, MA Thesis,
  Bristol University (1963).
French, R.B.D. 'J.O. Hannay and the Gaelic League', *Hermanthene* (Spring 1966).

Gallagher, Frank. *King and Constitution* (pamphlet issued by Fianna Fáil, Dublin, 1926).
Gallagher, Frank. 'Literature of the Conflict', *Irish Book Lover*, Vol. XVIII (May – June 1930).
Gallagher, Frank, writing under the pseudonym of David Hogan. 'Tom Jones and the Welsh Wizard',
  Irish Press (21 October 1955).
Gallagher, Michael. 'The Pact Election of 1922', *Irish Historical Studies*, Vol. XXI (1979).
Gallen, Liza. 'Donegal Women in the Civil War', *An Phoblacht* (31 January 2002).
Gardiner, A.G. 'Stop the Terror', *Daily News* (6 November 1920).
Garnham, Neal. 'Accounting for the early success of the Gaelic Athletic Association', *Irish Historical
  Studies*, Vol. XXXIV, No. 133 (May 2004).
Garnham, Neal. 'Football and national identity in pre-great war Ireland', *Irish Economic and Social
  History*, Vol. XXVIII (2001).
Garvin, Tom. 'The Destiny of the Soldiers: Tradition and Modernity in the Politics of de Valera's
  Ireland', *Political Studies*, Vol. XXVI (1978).
Garvin, Tom. 'Priests and Patriots. Irish Separatism and Fear of the Modern, 1890-1914', *Irish Historical
  Studies*, Vol. XXV (May 1986).
Garvin, Tom. 'The Anatomy of a Nationalist Revolution: Ireland, 1858-1928', *Contemporary Studies in
  Society and History* (July 1986).
Garvin, Tom. 'The Politics of Language and Literature in Pre-Independence Ireland', *Irish Political
  Studies* (1987).
Gavan-Duffy, Margaret. 'Mick', *Free State* (30 August 1922).
Gearty, Conor. *'The Casement Treason Trial in its Legal Context'*, Lecture at the Royal Irish Academy
  Symposium: *'Roger Casement in Irish and World History'* (6 May 2000).
Gerson, Gal. 'Cultural Subversion and the background of the Irish "Easter Poets"', *Journal of Contemporary
  History*, Vol. XXX, No. 2 (April 1995).
Gibbon, Monk. 'Murder in Portobello Barracks', *Dublin Magazine*, Vol. V (1966).
Gibson, Norman. *Partition to-day* (pamphlet, undated).
Gilley, S. 'Pearse's Sacrifice: Christ and Cuchulainn Crucified and Risen in the Easter Rising, 1916', in
  Alexander, Yonah and Alan O'Day, editors, *Ireland's Terrorist Dilemma* (Dartrecht, 1986).
Gorry, David. *'The Gaelic Athletic Association in Dublin, 1884-2000'*, MA Thesis, University College
  Dublin (2001).
Gough, Gen. Hubert. 'The Situation in Ireland', *Review of Reviews*, Vol. LXIII (1921).
Gray, Betsy. 'A Memory of Easter Week', *Capuchin Annual* (1948).
Green, Alice Stopford. 'Arthur Griffith', *Studies, The Irish Jesuit Quarterly Review*, Vol. XI (1922).
Gregory, Padraic. 'Poets of the Insurrection: John F. MacEntee', *Studies, The Irish Jesuit Quarterly
  Review*, Vol. VI (1917).

Grenan, Julia. 'After the Surrender', *Wolfe Tone Annual*, Special 1916 Edition.

Grenan, Julia. 'Events of Easter Week', *Catholic Bulletin* (June 1917).

Grenan, Julia. 'Story of the Surrender', *Catholic Bulletin* (June 1917).

Grey, R.C. *The Auxiliary Police* (pamphlet, undated).

Griffith, Arthur. *The Resurrection of Hungary, A Parallel for Ireland* (pamphlet, Dublin, 1904).

Griffith, Arthur. *Arguments for the Treaty* (pamphlet, Dublin, 1922).

Gunther, John. 'Inside de Valera', *Harper's Magazine*, Vol. CMXXVI (August 1936).

Gwynn, Denis. 'Patrick Pearse', *Dublin Review* (January-March 1923).

Gwynn, Denis. 'Edward Martyn', *Studies, The Irish Jesuit Quarterly Review*, Vol. XIX (1930).

Gwynn, Denis. 'The Rising of 1848', *Studies, The Irish Jesuit Quarterly Review*, Vol. XXXVII (1948).

Gwynn, Denis. 'John Redmond', *Studies, The Irish Jesuit Quarterly Review*, Vol. XLV (1956).

Gwynn, Stephen. 'Ireland's Constitutiom', *The Nation*, Vol. CXV (26 July 1922).

Gwynn, Stephen. 'Dail Éireann and the Irish Constitution', *Fortnightly Review*, Vol. CXIII (December 1922).

Gwynn, Stephen. 'Free Ireland in Evolution', *Living Age*, Vol. CCCXXI (3 May 1924).

Gwynn, Stephen. 'Shift in Irish Leadership', *Current History*, Vol. XXXVI (April 1932).

Gwynn, Stephen. 'Ireland Since the Treaty', *Foreign Affairs*, Vol. XII (January 1934).

Hallinan, C.T. 'Ireland's Role in the British Empire', *New Republic*, Vol. XXIX (9 February 1922).

Hally, Gen. J.P., 'The Easter Rising in Dublin, the Military Aspects', *Irish Sword*, Part 1, Vol. VII (1966), Part 2, Vol. VIII (1967).

Hammond, J.L. 'A Tragedy of Errors', *The Nation and Athenaeum* (8 January 1921).

Hammond, J.L. 'The Terror in Action', *The Nation and Athenaeum* (30 April 1921).

Hanley, Brian. 'The myth of *Michael Collins*', *Red Banner*, Issue 1 (September 2000).

Hanley, Brian. 'Change and Continuity: Republican Thought Since 1922', *The Republic*, No. 2 (Spring/Summer 2001).

Hanley, Brian. 'James Connolly and the Workers' Republic', *RTÉ 1 Thomas Davis Lecture* (5 May 2005).

Hannay, J.O. 'Ireland and the War', *The Nineteenth Century and After*, Vol. LXXVII (August 1915).

Hardiman, Hon. Justice Adrian. '"*Shot in Cold Blood*": military law and Irish perceptions in the suppression of the 1916 Rising', Lecture given at 'The Long Revolution: 1916 in Context', Conference in University College Cork (27 January 2006).

Harkness, David. 'Mr de Valera's Dominion', *Journal of Commonwealth Political Studies*, 8:206-27.

Hart, Peter. 'Michael Collins and the Assassination of Sir Henry Wilson', *Irish Historical Studies*, Vol. XXVIII, No. 110 (November 1992).

Hart, Peter. 'The Geography of Revolution in Ireland, 1917-1923', *Past and Present*, No. 155 (May 1997).

Hart, Peter. 'Operations Abroad: The I.R.A. in Britain, 1919-1923', *English Historical Review*, Vol. CXV, No. 460 (2000).

Hart, Peter. 'Peter Hart and His Enemies', *History Ireland*, Vol. XIII, No. 4 (July/August 2005).

Hartnett, Sheila. 'Comradeship Kilmainham', *Irish Press* (30 December 1971).

Harvey, A.D. 'Who Were The Auxiliaries?' *Historical Journal*, Vol. XXXV, No. 3 (1992).

Hawkins, F.M.A. 'Defence and the Role of Erskine Childers in the Treaty Negotiations of 1921', *Irish Historical Studies*, Vol. XI (1970).

Hay, Marnie. '*Bulmer Hobson: the rise and fall of an Irish nationalist, 1900-16*', Ph.D. Dissertation, University College Dublin (2005).

Hayes, Michael. 'Dáil Éireann and the Irish Civil War', *Studies, The Irish Jesuit Quarterly Review*, Vol. XLVII (1958).

Hearn, Dana. 'The Irish Citizen, 1914-1916: Nationalism, Feminism, Militarism', *Canadian Journal of Irish Studies*, Vol. XVIII, No. 1 (July 1992).

Helferty, Seámus. '1916 in the de Valera Papers', *History Ireland*, Vol. XIV, No. 2 (March/April 2006).

Henderson, Frank. 'Irish Leaders of Our Time: Richard McKee', *An Cosantoir*, Vol. V (1945).

Henry, Robert M. 'Arthur Griffith', *Studies, The Irish Jesuit Quarterly Review*, Vol. XI (1922).

Henry, Robert M. 'Partition and a Policy of National Unity', *Studies, The Irish Jesuit Quarterly Review*, Vol. XXIV (1935).

Higgins, Roisin, Carole Holohan and Catherine O'Donnell. '1966 and all that', *History Ireland,* Vol. XIV, No. 2 (March/April 2006).

Hobson, Bulmer. 'The Origin of Óglaigh na hÉireann', *An tÓglach* (June 1931).

Hoff, Joan, and Moureen Coulter, editors. 'Irish Women's Voices: Past and Present', *Journal of Women's History*, Indiana University Press, Vol. VI, No. 4, Vol. VII, No. 1 (Winter, Spring 1995).

Hoff, Matthew. '*The Foundations of the Fenian Uprising*', Senior Thesis, United States Military Academy (2006).

Hoff, Matthew. '*A Succesful Failure: The Catalyst of the 1916 Easter Rising*', MA Thesis, United States Military Academy (2007).

Holohan, Paddy. 'The Four Courts Area', *Capuchin Annual* (1966).

Honohan, Iseult. 'Freedom as Citizenship: The Republican Tradition in Political Theory', *The Republic*, No. 2 (Spring/Summer 2001).

Honohan, Iseult. 'Reclaiming the Republican Tradition', *RTÉ 1 Thomas Davis Lecture* (14 April 2005).

Hopkinson, Michael. '*The Irish Question in American Politics from the End of the First World War to the Irish Civil War*', Ph.D. Dissertation, University of Cambridge (1971).

Hopkinson, Michael A. 'The Craig-Collins pacts of 1922: two attempted reforms of the Northern Ireland government', *Irish Historical Studies*, Vol. XXVII, No. 106 (November 1990).

Hopkinson, Michael. 'President Woodrow Wilson and the Irish Question', *Studia Hibernica*, No. 27 (1993).

Hopkinson, Michael. 'Review article: biography of the revolutionary period: Michael Collins and Kevin Barry', *Irish Historical Studies*, Vol. XXVIII, No. 111 (May 1993).

Horgan, John. 'Fianna Fáil and Arms Decommissioning, 1923–32', *History Ireland*, Vol. VI, No. 1 (Spring 1998).

Houlihan, Con. 'The Civil War was a joke, but it was an obscene and bloody joke', *Sunday Independent* (2 March 2008).

Houlihan, Con. 'Forget 1916, we need a revolution of the spirit', *Irish Independent*, (30 March 2008).

Houlihan, Barry. '*The Growth of Irish Theater and Cultural Nationalism*', MA Thesis, University of Limerick (2007).

Humphreys, Richard. 'A Rebel's Diary', *The Belvederian*, Vol. XXV, No. 2, Belvedere College Annual (1966).

Hutchison, John. 'Cultural Nationalism, Elite Mobility and Nation Building: Communitarian Politics in Modern Ireland', *The British Journal of Sociology*, Vol. XXXVIII, No. 4 (December 1987).

Hyland, James L. *Life and Times of James Connolly* (pamphlet, Dundalk, 1997).

Irish Republican Digest, Featuring the Rising of 1916, Book 1, *National Publication Committee* (pamphlet, Cork, 1965).

Irish Times, The. *Dáil Éireann - 90 Years of Parlimentary democracy* (21 January 2009).

Jackson, Alvin. 'Unionist Myths, 1912-1985,' *Past and Present*, No. 136 (1992).

Jackson, Alvin. 'Larne Gun Running, 1914', *History Ireland*, Vol. I, No. 1 (1993).

Jeffery, Keith. 'Irish Culture and the Great War', *Bullan* (1994).

Jeffery, Keith. '*The First World War and the Rising: moment, mode and memory*', Lecture given at 'The Long Revolution: 1916 in Context', Conference in University College Cork (27 January 2006).

Jones, Ernest. 'The Island of Ireland: A Psycho-Analytical Contribution to Political Psychology', *Psycho-Myth, Psycho-History: Essays in Applied Psychology* (1974)

Joyce, Mannix. 'The Story of Limerick and Kerry in 1916', *Capuchin Annual* (1966).

Joyce, Toby, 'The American Civil War and Irish Nationalism', *History Ireland*, Vol. IV, No. 2 (Summer 1996).

Joye, Labhras and Brenda Malone. 'The Roll of Honour of 1916', *History Ireland*, Vol. XIV, No. 2 (March/April 2006).

Judge, Michael J. 'The Inner History of the Volunteers', *Irish Nation*, Vol. I (22 July 1916-19 May 1917).

Kain, R. 'A Diary of Easter Week: One Dubliner's Experience', *Irish University Review*, Vol. X (Autumn 1980).

Kavanagh, Seán. 'The Irish Volunteers' Intelligence Organisation', *Capuchin Annual* (1969).

Kearney, Richard. 'The I.R.A.'s Strategy of Failure', *The Crane Bag* (1980).

Kearney, Richard. 'Faith and Fatherland Ireland. Dependence and Independence', *RTÉ/UCD Lecture, The Crane Bag* (1984).

Kearns, Martha. 'Mary (98) recalls her vigil the day Kevin Barry was hanged', *Irish Independent* (13 October 2001).

Kelly, James. 'We Were Framed', *Hibernia* (31 July 1980).

Kelly, Matthew. 'Dublin Fenianism in the 1880's: The Culture of the Future?', *The Historical Journal*, Vol. XLIII (2000).

Kelly, Matthew. 'Nationalism's pilot light?', *History Ireland*, Vol. XVI, No. 6 (November/December 2008).

Kennedy, Christopher Mark. '*Genesis of the rising, 1912-1916: a transformation of nationalist opinion?*', Ph.D. Dissertation, University College Cork (2003).

Keogh, Dermot. 'William Martin Murphy and the Origins of the 1913 Lockout', *Saothar*, No. 4 (1978).

Keogh, Dermot. 'The Treaty Split and the Paris-Irish Race Convention', *Etudes Irlandaises*, No. 12 (December 1987).

Kilcullen, James. 'Appreciation: Headmaster of St Enda's', *Éire-Ireland* (Summer 1967).

Kotsonouris, Mary. 'Revolutionary Justice: The Dáil Éireann Courts', *History Ireland*, Vol. II, No. 3 (Autumn 1994).

Kotsonouris, Mary. 'The George Gavan-Duffy Papers', *History Ireland*, Vol. VIII, No. 4 (Winter 2000).

Kotsonouris, Mary. 'Republic, A Hope Mislaid?', *RTÉ 1 Thomas Davis Lecture* (26 May 2005).

Laffan, Michael. 'The Sinn Féin Party', *Capuchin Annual* (1970).

Laffan, Michael. 'The Unification of Sinn Féin in 1917', *Irish Historical Studies*, Vol. XVII (1971).

Laffan, Michael. 'Violence and Terror in Twentieth Century Ireland: IRB and IRA', in Mommsen, Wolfgang and Gerhard Hirschfield, editors, *Social Protest, Violence and Terror in Nineteenth and Twentieth Century Europe* (New York, 1982).

Laing, Cmdt Victor, Sgt Christy Donovan and Pvt. Alan Manning. 'The Ashbourne Engagement', *An Cosantoir* (April/May 2006).

Larkin, Emmet. 'Church, State and Nation in Modern Ireland', *American Historical Review*, Vol. LXXX, No. 5 (1975).

Larkin, Felix M. 'A Great Daily Organ: The Freeman's Journal, 1763-1924', *History Ireland*, Vol. XIV, No. 3 (May/June 2006).

Lavery, Brian. 'Irish Rebury 10 Republicans Hanged by British in 1920's', *New York Times* (15 October 2001).

Law, H.A. 'Irish Free State in 1926', *Contemporary Review*, Vol. CXXXI (January 1927).

Law, H.A. 'Three Years of the Irish Free State', *Literary Digest*, Vol. LXXXIV (10 January 1928).

Law, H.A. 'Ireland in 1928', *Contemporary Review*, Vol. CXXXIII (May 1928).

Law, H.A. 'Ireland in 1930', *Contemporary Review*, Vol. CXXXVII (June 1930).

Law, H.A. 'Irish Free State in 1931', *Contemporary Review*, Vol. CXL (August 1931).

Law, H.A. 'Ireland in the Doldrums', *Fortnightly Review*, Vol. CXL (1 July 1933).

Law, H.A. 'Ireland in 1933: Retropect and Prospect', *Contemporary Review*, Vol. CXLIV (December 1933).

Law, H.A. 'Ireland After Twelve Years', *Fortnightly Review*, Vol. CXLI (1 January 1934).

Law, H.A. 'Ireland in 1934', *Contemporary Review*, Vol. CXLVII (January 1935).

Lawless, Cmdt Frank. 'Personal Recollections: Ashbourne', *An Cosantoir* (April/May 2006).

Lawless, Col. Joseph V. 'Ashbourne', *An tÓglach* (31 July 1926).

Lawless, Col. Joseph V. 'Ashbourne', *An Cosantoir* (April 1941).

Lawless, Col. Joseph V. 'Thomas Ashe', *An Cosantoir* (November 1946).

Lawless, Col. Joseph V. 'The Fight at Ashbourne', *Capuchin Annual* (1966).

Lawless, Col. Joseph V. 'From the Archives; A Contemporary View', *An Cosantoir* (April/May 2006).

Lawlor, Sheila. '*Civil-Military Relations in Ireland, 1921-1923*', Ph.D. Dissertation, University College Dublin (1976).

Lawlor, Sheila. 'Ireland From Truce to Treaty, War or Peace? July to October 1921', *Irish Historical Studies*, Vol. XXII (1980).

Lawson, Lt Gen. Sir Henry. *A Report on the Irish Situation* (pamphlet, London, 1921).

Lawson, Lt Gen. Sir Henry. *A Second Report on the Situation* (pamphlet, undated).

Lawson, Lt Gen. Sir Henry. *'A Soldier in Ireland'*, Address published by the Liberal Publication Department (undated).

Leary, William M. Jnr. 'Woodrow Wilson, Irish Americans, and the Election of 1916'. *Journal of American History*, Vol. LIV, No. 1 (1967).

Lee, Joseph J. 'De Valera's Use of Words: Three Case-Studies', *Radharc*, Vol. II (2001).

Lee, Joseph J. '1916 as Virtual History', *History Ireland*, Vol. XIV, No. 2 (March/April 2006).

Leeson, David. 'Death in the Afternoon: The Croke Park Massacre, 21 November 1920', *Canadian Journal of History*, Vol. XXXVIII, No. 1 (April 2003).

Lemass, Seán. 'I Remember 1916', *Studies, The Irish Jesuit Quarterly Review*, Vol. LV (Spring 1966).

Lennon, Michael J. 'A Retrospect', *Banba* (April 1922).

Lennon, Michael J. 'Easter Week Diary', *The Irish Times* (29 March-3 April 1948).

Lennon, Michael J. 'The Easter Rising from the Inside', The account of Seán Fitzgibbon. *The Irish Times* (18-22 April 1949).

Limond, David. 'A Work for Other Hands', *History Ireland*, Vol. XIV, No. 2 (March/April 2006).

Linge, John. 'The Royal Navy and the Irish Civil War', *Irish Historical Studies*, Vol. XXXI, No. 121 (May 1998).

Little, P.J. 'A 1916 Document', *Capuchin Annual* (1942).

Lord Longford and T.P. O'Neill. 'De Valera in the Easter Rising', *Sunday Telegraph* (27 March 1966).

Lowe, W.J. 'Sources: "Who were the Black and Tans?"', *History Ireland*, Vol. XII, No. 3 (Autumn 2004).

Lowth, Cormac F. 'The O'Connor tragedy', *The Dun Laoghaire Borough Historical Society Journal*, No. 10 (2001).

Lowth, Cormac F. 'James O'Connor, Fenian and the tragedy of 1890', *Dublin Historical Record*, Vol. IV, No. 2 (Autumn 2002).

Luddy, Maria. *'Hanna Sheehy Skeffington'*, Historical Association of Ireland. Pamphlet No. 5 (Dundalk, 1995).

Lynch, Brian. 'Through the Eyes of 1916', *History Ireland*, Vol. XIV, No. 2 (March/April 2006).

Lynch, Robert. 'The Clones Affray, 1922: Massacre or Invasion?', *History Ireland*, Vol. XII, No. 3 (Autumn 2004).

Lynd, Robert. *Who Began It?* (pamphlet, undated).

Lyons, George. 'Occupation of the Ringsend Area', *An tÓglach* (10, 17, 24 April 1926).

MacAonghusa, Miceal. *'A Comradship of Principle: Connolly and Pearse'*, Paper/Lecture presented to the James Connolly Education Trust, The Ireland Institute, Pearse House, Dublin (21 March 2006).

MacAodh, Seán. 'I.R.A. Wipe out "G" Division', *An Phoblacht* (6 September 2001).

MacAodh, Seán. 'Terence MacSwiney', *An Phoblacht* (25 October 2001).

MacAodh, Seán. 'Murder in the Castle', *An Phoblacht* (22 November 2001).

Mac An tSoir. 'Padraig MacPiaras', *Comhair*, Vol. XXI (1962).

MacBride, Maud Gonne. 'How We Beat the Terrorist Proclamations', *An Phoblacht* (12 November 1932).

MacBride, Maud Gonne. 'Must We Fight Again for Ireland's Honour?', *An Phoblacht* (9 December 1933).

MacBride, Maud Gonne. 'The Real Case Against Partition', *Capuchin Annual* (1943).

MacDonagh, Augustine. 'To Make a Right Rose Tree: Reflections on the Poetry of 1916', *Studies, The Irish Jesuit Quarterly Review*, Vol. LV (Spring 1966).

MacDonagh, Donagh. 'Patrick Pearse', *An Cosantair* (August 1945).

MacDonagh, Donagh. 'Joseph Plunkett', *An Cosantoir* (November 1945).

MacDonagh, Donagh. 'Éamonn Ceannt', *An Cosantoir* (October 1946).

MacDonnacha, Miceal. 'Civil War Executions Begin', *An Phoblacht* (28 November 2002).

MacDonnacha, Miceal. 'Partitionist States Established', *An Phoblacht* (5 December 2002).

MacDonnacha, Miceal. 'The Civil War – 80th Anniversary – Part 3', *An Phoblacht* (12 December 2002).

MacDonnacha, Miceal. 'The Civil War – 80th Anniversary – Part 4', *An Phoblacht* (19 December 2002).

MacDonnacha, Miceal. 'Deserting the Starry Plough', *An Phoblacht* (19 December 2002).

MacEvilly, M. 'Seán MacBride and the Republican Motor Launch St George', *Irish Sword* (1984).

MacGarry, Milo. 'Memories of Scoil Eanna', *Capuchin Annual* (1942).

MacLoughlin, Seán. 'Memories of the Easter Rising', *Camillian Post*, 13 (I) (1948).

MacLysaght, E. 'The East Clare By-Election, July 1917', *Irish Times* (28-9 June 1966).

MacLysaght, E. 'Some Memories of the Irish Convention of 1917-1918', *Capuchin Annual* (1968).

MacMahon, Paul. 'British Intelligence and the Anglo-Irish Truce, July-December 1921', *Irish Historical Studies*, Vol. XXV, No. 140 (November 2007).

MacNeill, Eoin. 'The North Began', *An Claidheamh Soluis* (1 November 1913).

MacNeill, Eoin. 'Ireland for the Irish Nation', *Irish Volunteer* (20 February 1915).

MacNeill, Eoin. 'Recollections of Pearse', *New Ireland* (14 June 1919).

MacNeill, Eoin. 'Ireland and World Contact in the Future', *Studies, The Irish Jesuit Quarterly Review*, Vol. VIII (1919).

MacNeill, Eoin. 'Ten Years of Irish Free State', *Foreign Affairs*, Vol. X (January 1932).

MacNeill, J.G. Swift. 'The Breakdown of the Dublin Castle Regime', *Contemporary Review*, Vol. CX (July 1916).

MacSwiney, Mary. 'Easter Number', *Poblacht na hÉireann* (20 April 1922).

MacThomais, Éamonn. *Down Dublin Streets, 1916* (pamphlet, Dublin, 1965).

MacThomais, Shane. 'The historical significance of 16 Moore Street', *An Phoblacht* (1 September 2005).

McAuliffe, Michael. '*From truce to civil war: reactions to the 1921 Anglo-Irish treaty in County Cork, July 1921-June 1922*', MA Thesis, Mary Immaculate College, University of Limerick (2003).

McCabe, Conor. '"*A situation of great novelty and difficulty*": the Irish railway munitions strike of 1920', M.Lit. Thesis, National University of Ireland Maynooth (2003).

McCaffrey, Lawrence. 'Irish Nationalism and Irish Catholicism: A Study in Cultural Identity', *Church History*, Vol. XVII (1972).

McCann, John. 'Burning of the Custom House', *The Kerryman* (17 March 1938).

McCartan, Padraig, editor. 'Extracts from the Papers of Dr Patrick McCartan', *Clogher Record* (1964 and 1965 editions).

McCarthy, Charles. '*Larkin and the Working Class, 1907-1913*', Paper read to the *Irish Labour History Society* (September 1980).

McCarthy, P.J. 'The R.A.F. and Ireland, 1920-1922', *Irish Sword*, Vol. XVII (1989).

McCartney, Donal. 'De Valera in the United States', *Studies in Irish History* (304-23).

McColgan, John. 'Partition and the Irish Administration, 1920-1922', *Administration*, Vol. XXVIII (1980).

McColgan, John. 'Implementing the 1921 Treaty, Lionel Curtis and the Constitutional Procedure,' *Irish Historical Studies*, Vol. XX, No. 79 (March 1997).

McConnell, James and Fearghal McGarry. 'Difficulties and opportunities: making sense of the Fenians', *History Ireland*, Vol. XVI, No. 6 (November/December 2008).

McCullough, Denis. 'The Events in Belfast', *Capuchin Annual* (1966).

McDermott, Noel. 'Jim Larkin: A man on a mission', *Red Banner*, Issue 20 (June 2005).

McDermott, Peter. 'Brothers in Arms', *The Irish Echo* (19-25 April 2006).

McDermott, Peter. 'One Family's Rising', *The Irish Echo* (3-9 May 2006).

McDonald, Marianne. 'Ancient Republics and other political dreams', *RTÉ 1 Thomas Davis Lecture* (7 April 2005).

McEwen, John. 'The Liberal Party and the Irish Question during the First World War', *Journal of British Studies*, Vol. XII (1972).

McGarrity, Joseph. 'Twenty Years Ago in America', *An Caman* (31 March 1934).

McGarry, Fearghal. 'Keeping an Eye on the Usual Suspects: Dublin Castle's "Personality Files", 1899-1921', *History Ireland*, Vol. XIV, No. 6 (November/December 2006).

McGee, Owen. '*Irish republicanism in the age of Parnell: the Irish Republican Brotherhood, 1879-1893*', Ph.D. Dissertation, University College Dublin (2003).

McGee, Owen. '*The politics of the IRB and its role in the Irish Revolution, 1916-1923*', Lecture given at 'The Long Revolution: 1916 in Context', Conference in University College Cork (27 January 2006).

McGill, P.J. 'Padraic Pearse in Donegal', *Donegal Annual*, Vol. III (1966).

McGuire, Charlie. 'Seán McLoughlin: the boy commandant of 1916'. *History Ireland*, Vol. XIV, No. 2 (March/April 2006).

McInerney, Michael. 'James Ryan', *The Irish Times* (15-17 March 1967).

McInerney, Michael. 'Gerald Boland's Story', *The Irish Times* (8-19 October 1968).

McInerney, Michael. 'Seán MacEntee', *The Irish Times* (22-25 July 1974).

McKay, Francis. 'Clann na nGaedheal Girl Scouts', *Irish Press* (3 May 1966).

McKearney, Tommy. 'The relevance of republicanism', *Red Banner*, Issue 8 (June 2002).

McKenna, Kathleen. 'The Irish Bulletin', *Capuchin Annual* (1970).

McKenna, Kathleen. 'In London with the Irish Treaty Delegates', *Capuchin Annual* (1971).

McKeown, Eithne. 'A Family in the Rising', *Electricity Supply Board Journal* (1966).

McKillen, Beth. 'Irish Feminism and National Separatism', *Éire-Ireland*, Vol. XVII (1982).

McKittrick, David. 'Rebels of 1916 Leave Mixed Legacy', *Irish Independent* (12 March 1991).

McLoughlin, Seán. 'Memories of the Easter Rising', *Camillian Post* (Spring 1948).

McLaughlin, Terry. 'The Aftermath', *An Cosantoir* (April/May 2006).

McMahon, Msgr John T. *The Cream of their Race: Irish Truce Negotiations, December 1920-January 1921* (pamphlet, 1970).

McMahon, Deirdre. '"A Worthy Monument to a Great Man": Piaras Béaslaí's Life of Michael Collins', *Bullan* (Winter/Spring 1996).

McMahon, Deirdre. 'Roger Casement: An Account from the Archives of his Reinterment in Ireland', *Journal of the Irish Society for Archives*, 3 (New Series), (1996).

McManagle, Dermot. 'Cavan's forgotten contribution to the War of Independence', *History Ireland*, Vol. XV, No. 6 (November/December 2007).

McNally, Frank. 'Thousands line streets for State funerals to Glasnevin', *The Irish Times* (15 October 2001).

McVeigh, Jim. 'Constance Markievicz: aiming for the stars', *An Phoblacht* (17 September 1998).

Macardle, Dorothy. 'Easter Week in Kilmainham 1923', *Éire-Ireland* (12 May 1923).

Macardle, Dorothy. 'Military prison, North Dublin Union, 1 May 1923', *Éire-Ireland* (26 May 1923).

Macken, Mary. 'W.B. Yeats, John O'Leary, and the Contemporary Club', *Studies, The Irish Jesuit Quarterly Review*, Vol. XXVIII (1939).

Maguire, Conor A. 'The Republican Courts', *Capuchin Annual* (1984).

Maguire, G. 'Mayo and Sligo, 1920', *Capuchin Annual* (1970).

Mair, Peter. 'de Valera and Democracy', in Garvin, Tom, Maurice Manning, and Richard Sinnott, editors, *Dissecting Irish Politics: Essays in Honour of Brian Farrell* (Dublin, 2004).

Malcolm, Ian. 'Home Rule All Round', *Nineteenth Century*, Vol. LXVIII (November 1910).

Mandle, William. 'Sport as Politics: The Gaelic Athletic Association 1884-1924', in Cashman, R. and M. McKernan, editors, *Sport in History* (Queensland, 1979).

Mandle, William. 'The IRB and the beginning of the Gaelic Athletic Association', *Irish Historical Studies*, Vol. XX, No. 80 (1977).

Manley, Therese. '*Sighle Humphreys, Her Republican Beliefs*', MA Thesis, National University of Ireland Maynooth (2002).

Malouf, Michael. 'With Dev in America: Sinn Féin and Recognition Politics, 1919-21', *Interventions: International Journal of Postcolonial Studies*, Vol. IV, No. 1 (1 April 2002).

Mangran, Henry C. 'John Chartres', *Irish Independent* (25 October 1935).

Mansergh, Martin. 'The Easter Proclamation of 1916 and the Democratic Programme', *RTÉ 1 Thomas Davis Lecture* (28 April 2005).

Manzor, Paul James. '*The impact of the American Civil War on the emergence of Irish-American nationalism*', MA Thesis, National University of Ireland Galway (2002).

Marcus, Louis. 'The G.A.A. and the Castle', *Irish Independent* (9-10 July 1964).

Markievicz, Countess Constance. '*Women, Ideals and the Nation*'. Lecture delivered to the Student's National Literary Society (pamphlet first issued 1909, reissued 1918).

Markievicz, Countess Constance. '*What Irish Republicans Stand For*' (pamphlet, 1923)

Markievicz, Countess Constance. 'Cumann na mBan', *Cumann na mBan*, Vol. XI, No. 10 (1926).

Martin, Augustine E. 'To Make a Right Rose Tree', *Studies, The Irish Jesuit Quarterly Review*, Vol. LV (Spring 1966).

Martin, Francis X., OSA. 'Eoin MacNeill on the 1916 Rising', *Irish Historical Studies*, Vol. XII, No. 47 (March 1961).

Martin, Francis X., OSA. 'Myth, Fact and Mystery', *Studia Hibernica*, Vol. VII (1966).

Martin, Francis X., OSA., editor. 'The McCartan Documents, 1916', *Clogher Record* (1966).

Martin, Francis X., OSA. 'The 1916 Rising—A Coup d'Etat or a "Bloody Protest"?', *Studia Hibernica*, Vol. VIII (1968).

Matthews, Ann. 'Citizen Army women in the GPO in 1916', *Red Banner*, Issue 28 (June 2007).

Matthews, Ann. 'Rebel women in prison in 1916', *Red Banner*, Issue 29 (September 2007).

Matthews, Mary Elizabeth. *'Women activists in Irish republican politics, 1900-1941'*, Ph.D. Dissertation, National University of Ireland Maynooth (2002).

Maume, Patrick. 'Lily Connolly's Conversion', *History Ireland*, Vol. II, No. 3 (Autumn 1994).

Maume, Patrick. 'Parnell and the I.R.B. oath', *Irish Historical Studies*, Vol. XXIX, No.115 (May 1995).

Maume, Patrick. 'From Deference to Citizenship: Irish Republicanism, 1870-1923', *The Republic*, No. 2 (Spring/Summer 2001).

Maume, Patrick. 'The man with thirty lives?', *History Ireland*, Vol. XIV, No. 2 (March/April 2006).

Maxwell, Kenneth R. 'Irish-Americans and the Fight for Treaty Ratification', *Public Opinion Quarterly*, Vol. XXXI, No. 4 (1967).

Mayhew, G. 'A Corrected Typescript of Yeat's "Easter 1916"', *Huntington Library Quarterly*, Vol. XXVII (November 1963).

Meehan, Helen. 'Ethna Carbery: Anna Johnston MacManus', *Donegal Annual* (1993).

Mellowes, Liam. 'An Account of the Irish Rebellion', reprinted in part in the *Wolfe Tone Annual* (1946).

Metscher, Priscilla. '"Ireland Her Own": Radical Movements in Nineteenth-Century Ireland', *The Republic* (Spring/Summer 2001).

Mills, Michael. 'Seán Lemass Looks Back', *Irish Press* (20 January–6 February 1969).

Mitchell, Angus. 'Casement's Black Diaries: Closed Books Reopened', *History Ireland*, Vol. V, No. 3 (Autumn 1997).

Mitchell, Angus. 'The Casement "Black Diaries" Debate: The Story So Far', *History Ireland*, Vol. IX, No. 2 (Summer 2001).

Mitchell, Angus. 'Robert Emmet and 1916', *History Ireland*, Vol. XI, No. 3 (Autumn 2003).

Mitchell, Arthur. 'Labour and the National Struggle, 1919-1921', *Capuchin Annual* (1971).

Molony, Helena. 'Women of the Rising', *RTÉ Archive* (16 April 1963).

Mooney, Joanne E. *'Varieties of Irish Republican Womanhood: San Francisco Lectures during their United States Tours: 1916-1925'*, MA Thesis, San José State University, San José, California, 1991.

Moore, Col. Maurice. 'The Rise of the Irish Volunteers', a serial in *Irish Press*, 4 January to 2 March 1938 (Apparently written in 1917. See National Library of Ireland ILB 94109).

Moran, B. 'Jim Larkin and the British Labour Movement', *Saothar*, No. 4 (1978).

Moran, Seán Farrell. 'Patrick Pearse and the European Revolt against Reason', *Journal of the History of Ideas*, Vol. L, No. 4 (1989).

Moran, Seán Farrell. 'Patrick Pearse, The Easter Rising and Irish History', *Graduate Review* (Summer 1989).

Morgan, J.H. 'How Ireland is Governed', *Nineteenth Century*, Vol. LXXIV (September 1913).

Moriarity, Theresa. *Work in Progress: Episodes from the history of Irish women's trade Unionism* (pamphlet, Dublin).

Morris, Catherine. 'In the enemy's camp, Alice Milligan and Fin de Siècle Belfast', in Nicholas Allen and Aaron Kelly, editors, *Cities of Belfast* (Dublin, 2003).

Morris, Ewan. '"God save the King" versus "The Soldier's Song": the 1929 Trinity College national anthem dispute and the politics of the Irish Free State', *Irish Historical Studies* Vol. XXXI, No.121 (May 1998).

Mortished, R.J.P. 'Trade Union Organisation in Ireland', *Journal of the Statistical and Social Inquiry Society of Ireland* (1925-1926).

Mulcahy, Gen. Richard. 'The Irish Volunteer Convention, 27 October 1917', *Capuchin Annual* (1967).

Mulcahy, Gen. Richard. 'Conscription and the General Headquarters Staff', *Capuchin Annual* (1968).

Mulcahy, Gen. Richard. 'Chief of Staff, 1919', *Capuchin Annual* (1970).

Mulcahy, Gen. Richard. *'The Development of the Irish Volunteers, 1916-1922'*, Address to *The Irish Military Society* (9 November 1978).

Mulcahy, Gen. Richard. 'The Development of the Irish Volunteers, 1916-1922, *An Cosantoir,* Vol. XL (1980).

Mulcahy, Risteárd. 'The Mulcahy Tapes and Papers', *History Ireland,* Vol. VIII, No. 1 (Spring 2003).

Mulcahy, Risteárd. 'Mulcahy and Collins – A Conjunction of Opposites', *History Ireland,* Vol. XVI, No. 2 (March/April 2008).

Murdoch, R. 'Robert Barton', *Sunday Press* (26 September-3 October 1971).

Murphy, Anne Barry. *The political philosophy of Michael Collins.* Unpublished MA Thesis, National University of Ireland, University College Cork (1988).

Murphy, Dr Brian P. 'The First Dáil Éireann', *History Ireland,* Vol. II, No. 1 (Spring 1994).

Murphy, Dr Brian P. *'Kate O'Callaghan, 1885-1962',* Lecture given at the Limerick City Library (14 January 2003).

Murphy, Dr Brian P. *'The Easter Rising in the context of censorship and propaganda with special reference to Maj. Ivor Price',* Lecture given at 'The Long Revolution: 1916 in Context', Conference in University College Cork (27 January 2006).

Murphy, Brian P. *The Origin and Organisation of British Propaganda in Ireland, 1920* (pamphlet, Cork, 2006).

Murphy, Dr Brian. 'The Gardener of Glenstal', *History Ireland,* Vol. XIV, No. 2 (March/April 2006).

Murphy, Maj. H.L. 'Countess Markievicz', *An Cosantoir* (June 1946).

Murray, May. 'A Girl's Experience in the GPO', *Poblacht na hÉireann* (20 April 1922).

Murray, Robert H. 'The Sinn Féin Rebellion'. *The Nineteenth Century and After* (June 1916).

Myers, Kevin. 'The Glory That Was Hijacked', *The Guardian,* (30 March 1991).

Neilan, Mattie. 'The Rising in Galway', *Capuchin Annual* (1966).

Nevin, Donal. 'Trade Unions and Changes in Irish Society', *RTÉ 1 Thomas Davis Lecture* (November 1980).

Nevinson, H. 'The Anglo-Irish War', *Contemporary Review,* No. 667 (July 1921).

Newsinger, John. 'I Bring Not Peace But a Sword: The Religious Motif in the Irish War of Independence', *Journal of Modern History,* Vol. XIII (July 1978).

Newsinger, John. 'Revolution and Catholicism in Ireland, 1848-1923', *European Studies Review,* Vol. IX (1979).

Newsinger, John. 'Canon and Martial Law: William O'Brien, Catholicism, and Irish Nationalism', *Éire-Ireland,* Vol. XVI (1981).

Newsinger, John. 'The Devil it was who sent Larkin to Ireland: the Liberator, Larkinism, and the Dublin Lockout of 1913', *Saothar,* No. 18 (1993)

Ní Chorra, Eilis. 'A Rebel Remembers', *Capuchin Annual* (1936).

Ní Chumnaill, Eithne. 'The History of Cumann na mBan', *An Phoblacht* (8 April 1933).

Novak, Rose. 'Keepers of Important Secrets: the Ladies Committee of the IRB', *History Ireland,* Vol. XVI, No. 6 (November/December 2008).

Novick, Ben. 'Postal Censorship in Ireland, 1914-1916', *Irish Historical Studies,* Vol. XXXI (1999).

Nunan, Ernie. 'The Irish Volunteers in London', *An tÓglach* (Autumn 1966).

Nunan, Ernie. 'The Kimmage Garrison', *An tÓglach* (Winter 1967).

Nunan, Seán. 'President de Valera's Mission to the U.S.A., 1919-20', *Capuchin Annual* (1970).

O'Beirne-Ranelagh, John. 'The I.R.B. from Treaty to 1924', *Irish Historical Studies,* Vol. XX, No. 77 (1976).

Ó Braonain, Cathaoir. 'Poets of the Insurrection II – Patrick H. Pearse', *Studies, The Irish Jesuit Quarterly Review,* Vol. V (September 1916).

O'Brennan, Lily. 'Letter to the Editor: An Appreciation of Erskine Childers', *Irish Independent* (21 November 1922).

O'Brennan, Lily M. 'The Dawning of the Day', *Capuchin Annual* (1936).

O'Brennan, Lily M. 'We Surrender', *An Cosantoir* (June 1947, reprinted *An Cosantoir,* April/May 2006).

Ó Briain, Liam. 'Saint Stephen's Green Area', *Capuchin Annual* (1966).

Ó Bric, D. 'Pierce McCann, MP, 1882-1919, Part 2', *Tipperary Historical Journal* (1990).

O'Brien, Gerard. 'The record of the first Dáil debates', *Irish Historical Studies,* Vol. XXVIII, No.III (May 1993).

O'Brien, Nora Connolly. 'Women in Ireland, Their Part in the Revolutionary Struggle', *An Phoblacht* (25 June 1932).

O'Brien, Nora Connolly. 'The Pearse I Knew', *Hibernia*, Vol. X (15 April 1977).

O'Brien, W. 'An Irish Soldier and the Rebellion', *The Irish Times* (9 May 1916).

O'Brien, William. 'Was the Date Changed?', *Irish Press* (25 January 1936).

O'Callaghan, Kate. 'The Limerick City Curfew Murders of March 7th, 1921', in *Limerick's Fighting Story, 1916-1921*, p. 115-139 (Kerry, 1948)

O'Casey, Seán, writing under the pseudonym of P. Ó Cathasaigh. *The Story of the Irish Citizen Army* (pamphlet, Dublin and London, 1919; re-issued London, 1980).

O'Casey, Seán. 'Inishfallen, Fare Thee Well', *Autobiographies* (1980).

Ó Cellaigh, Daltun. 'Republicanism and Nationalism: An Imagined Conflict', *The Republic* (Spring/ Summer 2001).

Ó Ceallaigh, Padraig. 'Jacob's Factory Area', *Capuchin Annual* (1966).

Ó Ceallaigh, Seán T. 'The Founding of the Irish Volunteers', *An Phoblacht* (30 April 1936).

Ó Ceallaigh, Seán T. 'Memoirs', *Irish Press* (3 July-9 August 1961).

Ó Ceallaigh, Seán T. 'The Founding of the Irish Volunteers', *Capuchin Annual* (1963).

Ó Clerigh, Gearoid. 'John Redmond and 1916', Letter to *The Irish Times* (7 April 2008).

Ó Clerigh, Nellie. 'A Political Prisoner in Kilmainham Jail – The Diary of Cecelia Saunders Gallagher', *Dublin Historical Record*, Vol. LVI, No. 1 (Spring 2003).

O'Connor, Joseph. 'Boland's Mill Area', *Capuchin Annual* (1966).

O'Connor, Sanchia Katherine. '*Public opinion and the Irish Civil War in Connaught, 1921-1923*', MA Thesis, National University of Ireland Galway (2001).

O'Connor Lysaght, D.R. 'The Rake's Progress of a Syndicalist: The Political Career of William O'Brien', *Saothar*, No. 9 (1983).

O'Connor Lysaght, D.R. 'The lockout in close-up', *Red Banner*, Issue 11 (March 2003).

O'Connor Lysaght, D.R. 'The Rhetoric of Redmondism, 1914–16', *History Ireland*, Vol. XI, No. 1 (Spring 2003).

O'Connor Lysaght, D.R. 'Talking about partition', *Red Banner*, Issue 13 (September 2003).

O'Connor Lysaght, D.R. 'In defence of Larkin: What would you have done?' *Red Banner*, Issue 15 (March 2004).

O'Connor Lysaght, D.R. 'The Irish Citizen Army, 1913-16', *History Ireland*, Vol. XIV, No. 2 (March/ April 2006).

O'Daly, Nora. 'The Women of Easter Week', *An tÓglach* (3 April 1926).

O'Daly, Nora. 'Cumann na mBan in Stephen's Green and the College of Surgeons', *An tÓglach* (3 April 1926).

O'Deirg, Iosold. '"Oh, Lord! The Unrest of the Soul": The Jail Journal of Michael Collins', *Studia Hibernia* (1994).

O'Doherty, L. 'Dublin, 1920', *Capuchin Annual* (1970).

O'Donnell, Jim. 'Recollections based on the diary of an Irish Volunteer', *Cathair na Mart* (10.1, 1990; 11 1991).

O'Donoghue, Florence. 'A Review of the 1916 Rising', *Irish Historical Studies* (September 1949).

O'Donoghue, Florence. 'A Review of Casement's Last Adventure', *Irish Historical Studies* (March 1955).

O'Donoghue, Florence. 'Plans for the 1916 Rising,' *University Review*, Vol. III (March 1963).

O'Donoghue, Florence. 'Guerrilla Warfare in Ireland', *An Cosantoir*, Vol. XXIII (1963).

O'Donoghue, Florence. 'The Failure of the German Arms Landing at Easter 1916', *Cork Historical and Archeological Society Journal*, Vol. LXXI (1966).

Ó Dubhighaill, Seumas. 'Activities in Enniscorthy', *Capuchin Annual* (1966).

Ó Duigneain, Proinnsias. 'Linda Kearns—The Sligo Nurse in the 1916 Rising', *Sligo Champion* (5 April 1991).

Ó nEochaidh, Éamonn. *Liam Mellowes* (booklet undated, and publisher unknown).

Ó Faolain, Seán. 'Michael Collins: The True Story of a Great Irishman', *Sunday Chronicle* (15 May 1932).

O'Farrell, Elizabeth. 'The Surrender', *Capuchin Annual* (1917).

O'Farrell, Elizabeth. 'Events of Easter Week', *Catholic Bulletin* (May 1917).

O'Farrell, Elizabeth. 'Recollections', *An Phoblacht* (26 April, 10 May 1930).

O'Ferrell, Fergus. 'Civic Republican Citizenship and Voluntary Action', *The Republic* (Spring/ Summer 2001).

O'Halpin, Eunan. 'H.E. Duke and the Irish Administration, 1916-1918', *Irish Historical Studies*, Vol. XX (1981).

O'Hanrahan, Michael. 'Irish Heroines', Lecture delivered to Cumann na mBan in 1915, subsequently released as a pamphlet (1917).

Ó hEidhin, Prionsias. 'Liam Mellows in Galway', *Sinn Féin* (26 April 1924).

O'Hegarty, P.S. 'P.H. Pearse', *Irish Commonwealth* (St Patrick's Day Issue 1919).

O'Hegarty, P.S. 'Arthur Griffith', *Studies, The Irish Jesuit Quarterly Review*, Vol. XI (1922).

O'Hegarty, P.S. 'The Significance of Woodrow Wilson', *Studies, The Irish Jesuit Quarterly Review*, Vol. XII (1924).

O'Hegarty, P.S. 'Patrick Pearse', *Dublin Magazine* (July-September 1931).

O'Hegarty, P.S. 'A bibliographical list of Arthur Griffith's writings and pamphlets' *Dublin Magazine*, (January-March 1937).

O'Higgins, Brian. 'The Soldier's Story of Easter Week', *Wolfe Tone Annual* (1935).

O'Higgins, Kevin. *The New De Valera* (pamphlet, Dublin, 1922).

O'Higgins, Kevin. *Civil War and the Events that Led to It* (pamphlet, Dublin, 1922).

O'Keefe, John. 'Easter Week and Connolly', *Workers' Voice* (14 May 1932).

O'Kelly, Seámus. *The Glorious Seven* (pamphlet, Dublin, 1996).

'Eyewitness Account of John J. O'Leary', *Dublin Saturday Post* (29 April, 6 May, 13 May 1916).

Oliver, F.S. 'Possibilities of a Federal Solution', *The London Times* (16 May 1918).

Ó Luing, Seán. 'Talking to Bulmer Hobson', *Irish Times* (6 May 1961).

Ó Luing, Seán. 'Arthur Griffith, 1871-1922: Thoughts on a Centenary', *Studies, The Irish Jesuit Quarterly Review*, Vol. LXI (Summer 1971).

O'Mahony, Seán. 'Three Murders in Dublin Castle' (pamphlet, Dublin, 2000).

O'Mahony, Seán. *The Burning of the Custom House in Dublin, 1921* (pamphlet, Dublin, 2000).

O'Malley, C.K.H. 'Ernie O'Malley Autobiographical Letter', *Cathair na Mart. Journal of the Westport Historical Society*, Vol. IX, No. 1 (1989).

O'Malley, Ernie. 'I.R.A. Raids', *Sunday Press* (23, 30 October and 6, 13 November 1955).

Ó Monachain, Ailbhe. 'Galway in Easter Week', *Irish Press* (5 April 1934).

O'Neill, Cmdt David. 'The Four Courts: Easter 1916', *An Cosantoir* (April/May 2006).

O'Neill, Col. E. 'The Battle of Dublin, 1916,' *An Cosantoir*, Vol. XXVI (1966).

O'Neill, Éamonn. 'Patrick Pearse, Some Other Memories', *Capuchin Annual* (1935).

O'Neill, Stephen. 'The Ambush at Kilmichael', *Christmas Number* (December 1937).

O'Neill, Thomas P. 'In Search of a Political Path: Irish Republicanism, 1922-1927', *Historical Studies*, 10:147-171.

O'Rahilly, Alfred. 'Some Theology about Tyranny', *Irish Theological Quarterly* (October, 1920).

O'Rahilly, Aodogan. 'The Civil War: A Teenager's Recollections 70 Years On', *Tipperary Historical Review* (1991).

The O'Rahilly. 'The History of the Irish Volunteers', *Gaelic American* (2 January 1915).

The O'Rahilly. 'The Volunteer Colours: Flags for the Regiments', *Irish Volunteer* (23 May 1915).

O'Regan, Danae. 'Anna and Fanny Parnell', *History Ireland*, Vol. VII, No. 1 (Spring 1999).

O'Reilly, Stephen. *Spirit Flowers: Poems and Essays* (booklet, Dublin, 1923).

Ó Riain, Michael. 'Nelson's Pillar: a Controversy that Ran and Ran', *History Ireland*, Vol. VI, No. 4 (Winter 1998).

Ó Riain, S. 'Dáil Éireann, 1919', *Capuchin Annual* (1969).

O'Riordan, Manus. *The Voice of a Thinking Intelligent Movement: James Larkin Junior and the Ideological Modernisation of the Irish Trade Unions* (First appeared as an article in *Saothar* No. 19, 1994.) *Journal of the Irish Labour History Society* (pamphlet, Dublin, 1995).

O'Rourke, Peter. 'Remembering the Past: Fitzgerald, Murphy and MacSwiney', *An Phoblacht* (2 November 1999).

O'Rourke, Peter. 'The Kilmichael Ambush', *An Phoblacht* (30 November 2000).

Ó Ruairc, Liam. 'Did the Black and Tans Run from the Rifles of the I.R.A.?', *History Ireland*, Vol. XII, No. 2 (Spring 2004).

O'Shea, Cmdt Brendan and CQMS Gerry White. 'The Road to Rebellion', *An Cosantoir* (April/May 2006).

O'Shea, Cmdt Brendan and CQMS Gerry White. 'The Volunteer Uniform', *An Cosantoir* (April/May 2006).

O'Shea, Cmdt Brendan and CQMS Gerry White. 'Events Outside Dublin, The Situation in Cork', *An Cosantoir* (April/May 2006).

O'Shiel, Kevin. *Handbook of the Ulster question* (pamphlet, Dublin, 1923).

O'Shiel, Kevin. 'Memories of my lifetime', *The Irish Times* (7-23 November 1966).

Ó Snodaigh, Aengus. 'General Amnesty – 1917', *An Phoblacht* (13 June 1997).

Ó Snodaigh, Aengus. 'Sir Henry Wilson Executed', *An Phoblacht* (19 June 1997).

Ó Snodaigh, Aengus. 'Arming the Volunteers', *An Phoblacht* (20 June 1997).

Ó Snodaigh, Aengus. 'The 1913 Lockout', *An Phoblacht* (27 August 1998).

Ó Snodaigh, Aengus. 'The Irish Volunteers Founded', *An Phoblacht* (26 November 1998).

Ó Snodaigh, Aengus. 'Gearing Up for War: Soloheadbeg, 1919', *An Phoblacht* (21 January 1999).

Ó Snodaigh, Aengus. 'The Lucky Four', *An Phoblacht* (28 January 1999).

Ó Snodaigh, Aengus. 'Daring Arms Raid', *An Phoblacht* (25 March 1999).

Ó Snodaigh, Aengus. 'The First 1916 Rising Casualty', *An Phoblacht* (1 April 1999).

Ó Snodaigh, Aengus. 'Electoral Success – The First Step', *An Phoblacht* (17 June 1999).

Ó Snodaigh, Aengus. 'Electoral Success – The Election of the Snows', *An Phoblacht* (24 June 1999).

Ó Snodaigh, Aengus. 'The Mansion House "Irish Assembly"', *An Phoblacht* (8 July 1999).

Ó Snodaigh, Aengus. 'South Longford By-Election', *An Phoblacht* (15 July 1999).

Ó Snodaigh, Aengus. 'Unbroken and Unbowed – The POW's Return Home', *An Phoblacht* (22 July 1999).

Ó Snodaigh, Aengus. 'Remembering the Past', *An Phoblacht* (5 August 1999).

Ó Snodaigh, Aengus. 'Sinn Féin and Sinn Féin', *An Phoblacht* (30 September 1999).

Ó Snodaigh, Aengus. 'Usk Jail Death, 1918', *An Phoblacht* (2 December 1999).

Ó Snodaigh, Aengus. 'The Declaration of Independence', *An Phoblacht* (13 January 2000).

Ó Snodaigh, Aengus. 'An Chead Dáil Éireann Opens', *An Phoblacht* (20 January 2000).

Ó Snodaigh, Aengus. 'Ireland's Independence Declared', *An Phoblacht* (27 January 2000).

Ó Snodaigh, Aengus. 'An Address to Free Nations', *An Phoblacht* (3 February 2000).

Ó Snodaigh, Aengus. 'The Democratic Programme', *An Phoblacht* (9 March 2000).

Ó Snodaigh, Aengus. 'The First Cabinet', *An Phoblacht* (16 March 2000).

Ó Snodaigh, Aengus. 'Press coverage for First Dáil', *An Phoblacht* (30 March 2000).

Ó Snodaigh, Aengus. 'Remembering the Past: The Rebirth of Sinn Féin', *An Phoblacht* (6 April 2000).

Ó Snodaigh, Aengus. 'Remembering the Past: The Battle of Mount Street Bridge', *An Phoblacht* (20 April 2000).

Ó Snodaigh, Aengus. 'Remembering the Past: The 1917 I.R.A. Convention', *An Phoblacht* (27 April 2000).

Ó Snodaigh, Padraig. 'Willie Pearse: Artist', *Leabhran Cuimhneachain* (undated).

O'Toole, Fintan. 'The Unreal Republic', *RTÉ 1 Thomas Davis Lecture* (12 May 2005).

Owens, Rosemary Cullen. '*Constance Markeivicz's "Three Great Movements" and the 1916 Rising*', Lecture given at 'The Long Revolution: 1916 in Context', Conference in University College Cork (27 January 2006).

Pearse, James. *'England's Duty to Ireland as Plain to a Loyal Irish Roman Catholic'* (pamphlet, Dublin, 1886).

Pearse, Sen. Margaret M. 'St Enda's', *Capuchin Annual* (1942).

Pearse, Sen. Margaret M. 'Patrick and Willie Pearse', *Capuchin Annual* (1943).

Pearse, P.H. 'Some Aspects of Irish Literature', *Studies, The Irish Jesuit Quarterly Review*, Vol. II (1913).

Pearse, Padraig. 'The Coming Revolution', *An Claidheamh Soluis* (8 November 1913).

Pearse, Padraig. 'At Last – An Irish Army!', *Irish Volunteer* (4 July 1914).

Pearse, Padraig. 'Why We Want Recruits', *Irish Volunteer* (22 May 1915).

Pearse, P.H. 'The Irish Flag', *Irish Volunteer* (20 March 1915).

Pearse, Patrick H. *The Murder Machine* (pamphlet, Dublin, 1916).

Petit, Philip. 'From Republican Theory to Public Policy', *RTÉ 1 Thomas Davis Lecture* (2 June 2005).

Pim, Herbert Moore. 'Sinn Féin: Past Present and Future', *Nineteenth Century*, Vol. LXXXV (1919).

Plunkett, Grace Gifford. 'The White Flag of 1916', *Phoblacht na h-Éireann*, Vol. I, No. 12 (15 March 1922)

Plunkett, Joseph Mary. 'I sought Him', (poem), *Studies, The Irish Jesuit Quarterly Review*, Vol. I (1912).

'Poets of the Insurrection', *Studies, The Irish Jesuit Quarterly Review*, Vol. VII (1918).

Pogatchnik, Shawn. 'Ireland Marks Rebels Hanged by Britain', *Irish Independent* (14 October 2001).

Porritt, Annie. 'The Irish Home Rule Bill', *Political Science Quarterly*, Vol. XXVII (1913).

Purcell, Bernard. 'Dev Tempted by Irish Unity Deal', *Irish Independent* (15 February 2001).

Putkowski, J.J. 'The Best Secret Service Man We Had: Jack Burns and the I.R.A.', *Lobster, The Journal of Parapolitics* (1994).

Qaulter, T.H. *'The Nature of Propaganda and its Function in Democratic Government: An Examination of the Principal Theories of Propaganda since 1880'*, Ph.D. Dissertation, University of London (1956).

Rafferty, Oliver P. 'The Catholic Church and Fenianism', *History Ireland*, Vol. XVI, No. 6 (November/ December 2008).

Raymond, R. James. 'Irish Nationalism in the Early Twentieth Century: A Reappraisal', *Canadian Review of Studies in Nationalism* (1987).

Reddin, Kenneth. 'A Man Called Pearse', *Studies, The Irish Jesuit Quarterly Review*, Vol. XXXIV (June 1943).

Reilly, Jerome. 'Mater Nuns Supported Rising, R.I.C. Files Claim', *Irish Independent* (2 April 2006).

Reynolds, H.J. 'Irishmen after Eight Years of Independence', *Current History*, Vol. XXXII (September 1930).

Reynolds, John J. 'The Four Courts and North King Street in 1916', *An tÓglach* (15 May, 22 May, 29 May 1926).

Reynolds, M. 'Cumann na mBan in the GPO', *An tÓglach* (27 March 1926).

Riordan, E.J. 'The War and Irish Industry', *Studies, The Irish Jesuit Quarterly Review*, Vol. IV (1915).

Riordan, E.J. 'Irish Industries after Twelve Months of War', *Studies, The Irish Jesuit Quarterly Review*, Vol. IV (1915).

Riordan, E.J. 'Restraint of Industry: Four Years of Irish Economy, 1914-1918', *Studies, The Irish Jesuit Quarterly Review*, Vol. VII (1918).

Robbins, Frank. 'The Citizen Army and Easter Week', *Irishman* (19 May 1928).

Roche, R. 'Events in Wexford — 1920', *Capuchin Annual* (1970).

Roth, Andreas. '"The German Soldier is not Tactful": Sir Roger Casement and the Irish Brigade in Germany during the First World War', *Irish Sword*, Vol. XIX (1995).

Rouse, Paul. 'The politics of culture and sport in Ireland: a history of the GAA ban on foreign games 1884-1971', *International Journal of the History of Sport*, Vol. X, No. 3 (1993).

Rouse, Paul. 'Why historians have ignored Irish sport', *The History Review*, Vol. XIV (2003).

Ruiseal, Liam. 'The Position in Cork', *Capuchin Annual* (1966).

Russell, George William (Æ). 'Four Years of Irish Economics: 1914-1918; Self Supporting Community', *Studies, The Irish Jesuit Quarterly Review*, Vol. VII (1918).

Russell, George William (Æ). 'Facts of Irish Freedom', *The Nation*, Vol. CXIV (4 January 1922).

Russell, George William (Æ). 'Castle Falls in Free Ireland', *Literary Digest*, Vol. LXXII (18 February 1922).

Russell, George William (Æ). 'Dublin's Rocky Road', *Literary Digest*, Vol. LXXIII (1 April 1922).

Russell, George William (Æ). 'Carrying on in the Irish Free State', *Literary Digest*, Vol. LXXIV (9 September 1922).

Russell, George William (Æ). 'Hunger Strike in Ireland', *The Nation*, Vol. CXVII (21 November 1923).

Russell, George William (Æ). 'Lessons of Revolution', *Studies, The Irish Jesuit Quarterly Review*, Vol. XII (1923).

Russell, George William (Æ). 'Ireland As It Is', *Living Age*, Vol. CCCXX (19 January 1924).

Ryan, Desmond. 'Pearse, St Enda's, and the Hound of Ulster', *Threshold* (1957).

Ryan, Desmond. 'St Enda's – Fifty Years After', *University Review* (1958).

Ryan, Desmond. 'The Easter Rising', *Irish Press* (24 April-29 April 1961).

Ryan, J.T. 'The Origin of the *Aud* Expedition', *An Phoblacht* (25 April 1931).

Ryan, Dr James. 'The General Post Office Area', *Capuchin Annual* (1966).

Ryan, Louise. 'The Irish Citizen, 1912-1920', *Saothar*, Vol. XVII (1992).

Ryan, Louise. 'Women without Votes: The Political Strategies of the Irish Suffrage Movement', *Irish Political Studies*, Vol. IX (1994).

Ryan, Meda. 'Tom Barry and the Kilmichael Ambush', *History Ireland*, Vol. XIII, No. 5 (September/ October 2005).

Ryan, Ray. 'The Man Who Stood Next to Collins' Killer', *Cork Examiner* (5 November 1985).

Ryan, Lt Col. Thomas. 'One Man's Flying Column', *Tipperary Historical Review* (1991).

Saurin, Charles. 'Hotel Metropole Garrison', *An tÓglach* (13, 20 March 1926).

Savage, David. *'The Irish Question and British Politics, 1914-1916'*, Ph.D. Dissertation, Princeton University (1963).

Savage, David. 'The Attempted Home Rule Settlement of 1916', *Éire-Ireland*, Vol. II (1967).

Sceilg (J.J. O'Kelly). *Stepping Stones* (pamphlet, Dublin, Irish Book Bureau, undated).

Sceilg (J.J. O'Kelly). *A Trinity of Martyrs* (pamphlet, Dublin, Irish Book Bureau, undated).

Sears, J.W. *'Naval Policy and Public Opinion in Great Britain, 1919 – 1922'*, B.Lit. Thesis, Oxford University (1957).

Sharkey, Neil. 'The Third Tipperary Brigade: A Photographic Record', *Tipperary Historical Journal* (1994, 9-25).

Shaw, Revd Francis S.J. 'The Canon of Irish History: A Challenge', *Studies, The Irish Jesuit Quarterly Review*, Vol. LXII (Summer 1972).

Shaw, George Bernard. 'Neglected Morals of the Irish Rising', *New Statesman* (6 May 1916).

Shaw, George Bernard. *How to settle the Irish question* (pamphlet, Dublin, 1917).

Sheehy-Skeffington, Andrée D. 'The Hatter and the Crank', *The Irish Times* (5 February 1982).

Sheehy-Skeffington, Hanna. 'Women and the University Question', *New Ireland Review*, Vol. XVII (March-August 1902).

Sheehy-Skeffington, Hanna. 'The Women's Movement – Ireland', *Irish Review* (July 1912).

Sheehy-Skeffington, Hanna. *British Militarism As I Have Known It* (New York, 1917. Pamphlet which was a printing of her lectures that she delivered in the US from 1916-1918).

Sheehy-Skeffington, Hanna. 'Constance Markievicz in 1916', *An Phoblacht* (14 April 1928).

Sheehy-Skeffington, Hanna. 'Women in Politics', *The Bell*, Vol. VII, No. 2 (November 1943).

Sheills, Derek. 'The Politics of Policing Ireland', in Emsley, Clive and Barbara Weinberger, editors, *Policing Western Europe Politics, Professionalism, and Public Order, 1850-1940* (Westport, Connecticut, 1991).

Simon, Sir John Allesbrook. 'Irish Reprisals: Auxiliary Division's Record', *The London Times* (25 April 1921).

Skinnider, Margaret. 'In Stephen's Green', *Irish Press Supplement* (9 April 1966).

Smith, Kevin. 'Fury over Irish state move on "forgotton patriots"', *Irish Independent* (10 October 2001).

Smith, Kevin. 'Ireland buries "forgotton patriots" with honors', *Irish Independent* (14 October 2001).

Smith, P.G. 'War at the Border', *The Beaver*, Vol. LXXXVII:5 (October/November 2007).

Smyth, Hazel P. 'Kathleen Lynn, MD, FRCSI, (1874-1955)', *Dublin Historical Record*, Vol. XXX (1997).

Somerville, Henry. 'Labour Disorders in Wartime', *Studies, The Irish Jesuit Quarterly Review*, Vol. IV (1915).

Somerville, Henry. 'The Economics of Nationalisation', *Studies, The Irish Jesuit Quarterly Review*, Vol. IX (1920).

Snoddy, Oliver. 'The Midland Volunteer Force 1913', *Journal of the Old Athlone Society* (1968).

Staines, Michael and M. O'Reilly. 'The Defence of the GPO', *An tÓglach* (23 January 1926).

Stapleton, William J. (Bill). 'A Volunteer's Story', *Irish Independent*, 1916 Golden Jubilee Supplement, (April 1966).

Stapleton, William J. (Bill). 'Michael Collins' Squad', *Capuchin Annual* (1969).

Steinmeyer, Charles. 'The Evacuation of the GPO', *An tÓglach*, (27 February 1926).

Stephens, James. 'Arthur Griffith', *Studies, The Irish Jesuit Quarterly Review*, Vol. XI (1922).

Stubbs, J.O. 'The Unionists and Ireland, 1914-1918', *Historical Journal*, Vol. XXXIII (1990).

Sugg, Wayne. 'British Intelligence Wiped Out', *An Phoblacht* (20 November 1997).

Sugg, Wayne. 'Bloody Sunday', *An Phoblacht* (27 November 1997).

Sugg, Wayne. 'State Executions', *An Phoblacht* (11 December 1997).

Sugg, Wayne. 'Death of Liam Lynch', *An Phoblacht* (30 April 1998).

Sugg, Wayne. 'Christmas Week Ambush', *An Phoblacht* (16 December 1999).

Tallant, Nicola. 'Dev Tricked Public into Investing in Irish Press, File Reveals', *Irish Independent* (31 October 2004).

Tarpey, Sr M.V. *'The Role of Joseph McGarrity in the Struggle for Irish Independence'*, MA thesis, University of Michigan (Ann Arbor, Michigan, 1970).

Thompson, Dorothy. 'The English Republic', *The Republic* (Spring/Summer 2001).

Thornly, David. 'Patrick Pearse', *Studies, The Irish Jesuit Quarterly Review*, Vol. LVI (Spring 1966).

Thornly, David. 'Patrick Pearse and the Pearse Family', *Studies, The Irish Jesuit Quarterly Review*, Vol. LXI (Autumn/Winter 1971).

Thornton, Cmdt Brigid Lyons. 'Women and the Army', *An Cosantoir* (November 1975).

Throne, John. 'Easter Rising – 1916. 60 Years After, What are the lessons', *Militant Irish Monthly*, No. 43 (May 1976).

Tierney, Michael. 'A Prophet of Mystic Nationalism: Æ', *Studies, The Irish Jesuit Quarterly Review*, Vol. XXVI (1937).

Tierney, Michael. 'The Problem of Partition', *Studies, The Irish Jesuit Quarterly Review*, Vol. XXVII (1938).

Tierney, Michael. 'Gladstone and Ireland', *Studies, The Irish Jesuit Quarterly Review*, Vol. XXVIII (1939).

Tierney, Michael. 'Nationalism and Revolution', *Studies, The Irish Jesuit Quarterly Review*, Vol. XXVIII (1939).

Tierney, Michael. 'Eoin MacNeill: a biographical study', *Saint Patrick* (1964).

Tóibín, Colm. 'Playboys of the GPO', *London Review of Books* (18 April 1966).

Towey, Thomas. 'The Reaction of the British Government to the 1922 Collins/de Valera Pact', *Irish Historical Studies*, 22:65 (1976).

Towey, Thomas. 'Hugh Kennedy and the Constitutional Development of the Irish Free State, 1922-1923', *Irish Jurist*, Vol. XII (1977).

Townshend, Charles. The Irish Railway Strike of 1920 – Industrial Action and Civil Resistance in the Struggle for Independence', *Irish Historical Studies*, Vol. XXI, (1978-79).

Townshend, Charles. 'Bloody Sunday: Michael Collins Speaks', *European Studies Review*, Vol. IX, (1979).

Townshend, Charles. 'The Irish Republican Army and the Development of Guerrilla Warfare, 1916–1921', *English Historical Review*, Vol. XCIV (1979).

Townshend, Charles. 'Martial Law: Legal and Administrative Problems of Civil Emergency in Britain and the Empire, 1800-1940', *Historical Journal*, Vol. XXV (1979).

Townshend, Charles. 'Military Force and Civil Authority in the United Kingdom, 1914-1921', *Journal of British Studies*, Vol. XXVIII (1989).

Townshend, Charles. 'Militarism and Modern Society.' *Wilson Quarterly* (Winter 1993).

Townshend, Charles. 'The Suppression of the Easter Rising,' *Bullan*, Vol. I (1) (1994).

Townshend, Charles. 'The Meaning of Irish Freedom; Constitutionalism in the Free State', *Transactions of the Royal Historical Society*, 6th Series, Vol. VIII (1998).

Townshend, Charles. 'Religion, War and Identity in Ireland', *Journal of Modern History*, Vol. LXXVI (2004).

Townshend, Charles. 'Making Sense of Easter 1916', *History Ireland*, Vol. XIV, No. 2 (March/April 2006).

Travers, Revd Charles. 'Seán MacDiarmada, 1883-1916', *Breifne* (1966).

Traynor, Oscar. 'The Burning of the Custom House – Dublin's Fighting Story', *The Kerryman* (1939).

Tremayne, Peter. 'A Reflection of Ghosts', in Stephen Jones and Jo Fletcher, editors, *Gaslight and Ghosts* (London, 1988).

Ui Cheallaigh, Phyllis Bean. 'The Story of Eight Women in 1916, Women of the Revolution', *RTÉ Archives* (8 April 1971).

Ui Chonaill, Eilis Bean. 'A Cumann na mBan Recalls Easter Week', *Capuchin Annual* (1966).
Ui Dhonnachadha, Sile Bean. 'Memories of Easter Week', *An Phoblacht* (27 March 1986).
'Ultach', 'The real case against partition', *Capuchin Annual,* (1943). (Subsequently published as a pamphlet, with the title *Orange Terror.*)

Valiulis, Maryann G. 'The army mutiny of 1924 and the assertion of civilian authority in independent Ireland', *Irish Historical Studies*, Vol. XXIII (1983).
Valiulis, Maryann G. 'Power, Gender and Identity in the Irish Free State', *Journal of Women's History*, Vol. VI, No. 4, Vol. VII, No. 1 (joint issue winter/spring 1995).

Walker, J. Crampton. 'Red Cross Work and Stretcher Bearing during the Irish Republic', *Irish Life* (26 May 1916).
Waller, B.C. 'First Seven Years of the Irish Free State', *Current History*, Vol. XXXI (February 1930).
Walsh, Paul V. *'The Irish Civil War, 1922–1923: A Military Study of the Conventional Phase, 28 June–11 August, 1922'*, Paper delivered at the CUNY Graduate Center (11 December 1998).
Walsh, Tom. 'The Epic of Mount Street Bridge', *Irish Press Supplement* (April 1966).
Ward, Alan. 'Lloyd George and the 1918 Irish Conscription Crisis', *Historical Journal*, Vol. XVII, No. 1 (1974).
Ward, Margaret. 'The Missing Sex: Putting Women into Irish History', in Smythe, Ailbhe, editor, *A Dozen Lips* (Dublin, 1994).
Ward, Margaret. 'The League of Women Delegates and Sinn Féin, 1917', *History Ireland*, Vol. IV, No. 3 (Autumn 1996).
Ward-Perkins, Sarah, editor. *Trade Union Records in Dublin* (pamphlet, Dublin).
Whelan, Diarmuid. *'Conor Cruise O'Brien and nationalism'*, Ph.D. Dissertation, University College Cork (1998).
Whelan, Kevin. 'The Recent Writing of Irish History', *UCD History Review* (1991).
White, Gerry and Brendan O'Shea. *'The Cork Brigade of Irish Volunteers, 1913-1916'*, Lecture given at 'The Long Revolution: 1916 in Context', Conference in University College Cork, (27 January 2006).
White, Terence de Vere. 'Lord Rugby Remembers', *The Irish Times* (3-5 July 1962).
White, Timothy J. 'Book Review: Pearse's Patriots: St Enda's and the Cult of Boyhood', *Celtic Studies Association Newsletter*, 22:2 (2005).
Wilkinson, Burke. 'Erskine Childers: Boston Connections', *Capuchin Annual* (1977).
Williams, Arthur Frederick Basil. "A Truce in Ireland', *Manchester Guardian* (9 December 1921).
Women POWs in Maghaberry. 'Women and the National Struggle', *The Captive Voice* (Autumn 1989).
Woodcock, Caroline. 'Experiences of an Officer's Wife in Ireland', *Blackwood's Magazine* (May 1921).
Wylie, John. *'Laurence Ginnell, 1852-1923: Westmeath's radical agrarian'*, MA Thesis, National University of Ireland, Maynooth (1999).

Yeates, Padraig. 'The Dublin Lockout, 1913', *History Ireland*, Vol. IX, No. 2 (Summer 2001).
Young, Cpt. Thomas. 'Fighting in South Dublin: With the Garrison in Marrowbone Lane during Easter Week, 1916', *An tÓglach* (6 March 1926).

TELEVISION AND VIDEO

Connolly, Colm. *The Shadow of Béal na mBláth*, RTÉ Television, 1989.
Eppel, Dr Isaac J. *Irish Destiny*, 1926. Video/DVD 2006.
Griffith, Kenneth. *Hang Up Your Brightest Colours*, Video, 1966.
Griffith, Kenneth. *Curious Journey: The Fight for Irish Freedom*, Video, 1972.
Hidden History: Founding Fathers: Frank Aitken, Mint Productions for RTÉ Television, 2006.
Hidden History: Founding Fathers: Eoin O'Duffy, RTÉ Television, 2006.
Hidden History: Rebel County: The Story of The Wind that Shakes the Barley, Produced and directed by Pat Collins for RTÉ Television, 2006.

Hidden History: The Burning of Cork, Produced by Seaview Pictures for RTÉ Television, 2006.
Hidden History: Figure of Hate, William Martin Murphy, RTÉ Televsion, 13 November 2007.
Hidden History: Get Collins, RTÉ Television, 2007.
Lentin, Louis and Michael Garvey. *Insurrection*, RTÉ Television, 10-17 April 1966.
Morrison, George. *Mise Éire*. 1959, Video/DVD 2005.

INTERNET RESOURCES

Answers, Irish Republican Army
    http://www.answers.com/topic/irish-republican-army-1922-1969
Béal na mBláth
    http://www.iol.ie/~obrienc/bnab.htm
Barrett, Suzanne. 'Madame: A Revolutionary Woman'
    http://www.irelandforvisitors.com/articles/madame.htm
BBC Easter Rising Sources
    http://www.bbc.co.uk/history/british/easterrising/
Census of Ireland — 1911
    http://www.census.nationalarchives.ie/
General Michael Collins
    http://generalmichaelcollins.com/
James Connolly Archive
    http://www.marxists.org/archive/connolly/
Chronology of James Connolly
    http://www.ucc.ie/celt/connolly.html
Chronology of Irish History, 1919-1923
    http://www.dcu.ie/~foxs/irhist/index.htm
The Curragh Mutiny
    http://www.curragh.info/articles/mutiny.htm
The Curragh Mutiny
    http://www.bbc.co.uk/history/british/easterrising/prelude/pro6.shtml
Dáil Éireann Debates
    http://historical-debates.oireachtas.ie/D/DT/D.T.192112140001.html
Dáil Éireann Treaty Debates Dáil Éireann – Volume 3 – 14 December, 1921
    http://historical-debates.oireachtas.ie/D/DT/D.T.192112140002.html
Dáil Éireann Treaty Debates Dáil Éireann – Volume 3 – 07 January, 1922
    http://historical-debates.oireachtas.ie/D/DT/D.T.192201070002.html
Dáil Elections since 1918
    http://www.ark.ac.uk/elections/gdala.htm
Dana, Jacqueline. 'Connolly Ain't Nothing but a Train Station In Dublin: The Exploitation of James
    Connolly's Revolutionary Legacy by Irish Republicanism'
    http://larkspirit.com/general/connolly.html
Department of the Taoiseach
    http://www.taoiseach.gov.ie/index.asp?locID=383&docID=511
Dublin Flames Kindled a Nation's Spirit
    http://www.iol.ie/~dluby/1916.htm
Grant, Ted and Alan Woods. 'Connolly and the 1916 Easter Uprising'
    http://www.marxist.com/james-connolly-easter-rising-6.htm
Vincent Hearn Origin of the Irish National Anthem
    http://www.from-ireland.net/history/origin.htm
'Insurrection' An RTE Drama 1966
    http://www.rte.ie/laweb/ll/ll_to6_strands_c.html
Irish Election of 1918
    http://www.ark.ac.uk/elections/h1918.htm

Irish Trade Union History: 1913-1988; 75 years since the Dublin Lock-out
    http://flag.blackened.net/revolt/ws88_89/ws29_1913.html
Irish Trade Union History: Rosie Hackett and the Union Women of Jacob's Biscuits
    http://flag.blackened.net/revolt/siptu/f5_history.html
Kelly, Jim Thomas. (Tom) Barry, Commandant, West Cork Flying Brigade, 1920-1921
    http://aohdiv1.org/tombarry.htm
Lantry, Margaret, compiler. Michael Collins: The Path to Freedom
    CELT: Corpus of Electronic Texts, University College, Cork
    http://www.ucc.ie/celt/online/E900001-001/header.html
Liam McCarthy Story
    http://www.rebelgaa.com/history/liammccarthy.asp
List of Members of the Irish Republican Army
    http://en.wikipedia.org/wiki/List_of_members_of_the_Irish_Republican_Army
Mahoney, Edward. Michael Collins His Life and Times
    http://www.generalmichaelcollins.com/pages/Michael_Collins.html#anchor
Liam Mellows
    http://www.taoiseach.gov.ie/index.asp?locID=200&docID=3087
National Library of Ireland 1916
    http://www.nli.ie/1916/
Neligan, David. A Man in a Million
    http://generalmichaelcollins.com/Ml.Collins_Growing_up/A_Man_in_a_million.html
North Kerry and the Irish Civil War
    http://www.rootsweb.com/~irlker/kercivwar.html
O'Connell, William P. Raising the First Dáil Loan
    http://generalmichaelcollins.com/Ml.Collins_Growing_up/Floating_first_Loan.html
O'Riordan, Tomas. John Redmond Cork MultiText Project
    http://multitext.ucc.ie/d/John_Redmond
Perry, Cieran. 'The Irish Citizen Army: Labour Clenches its Fist'
    http://flag.blackened.net/revolt/cc1913/ica.html
Poems of Joseph Plunkett
    http://poetry.elcore.net/CatholicPoets/Plunkett/
Searc's Web Guide to Irish Studies
    http://www.searcs-web.com/
    http://www.searcs-web.com/hist1916.html
    http://www.searcs-web.com/hist1917.html
    http://www.searcs-web.com/ashe.html Thomas Ashe
    http://www.searcs-web.com/barry3.html Tom Barry
    http://www.searcs-web.com/beas.html Pieras Béaslaí
    http://www.searcs-web.com/breen.html Dan Breen
    http://www.searcs-web.com/buckl.html Margaret Buckley
    http://www.searcs-web.com/despard.html Roger Casement
    http://www.searcs-web.com/ceannt.html Éamonn Ceannt
    http://www.searcs-web.com/childers.html Robert Erskine Childers
    http://www.searcs-web.com/clarke.html Thomas Clarke
    http://www.searcs-web.com/collins.html Michael Collins
    http://www.searcs-web.com/comer.html Maire Comerford
    http://www.searcs-web.com/conno.html James Connolly
    http://www.searcs-web.com/cousins.html Margaret Cousins
    http://www.searcs-web.com/czira.html Sidney Gifford Czira
    http://www.searcs-web.com/despard.html Charlotte Despard
    http://www.searcs-web.com/dev.html Éamon De Valera
    http://www.searcs-web.com/figgis.html Edward Darrell Figgis
    http://www.searcs-web.com/sjg.html Oliver St. John Gogarty

http://www.searcs-web.com/griff.html Arthur Griffith
http://www.searcs-web.com/larkin.html James Larkin
http://www.searcs-web.com/gonne.html Maud Gonne MacBride
http://www.searcs-web.com/mcdonagh.html Thomas MacDonagh
http://www.searcs-web.com/mcswin2.html Mary MacSwiney
http://www.searcs-web.com/mcswin1.html Terence MacSwiney
http://www.searcs-web.com/macwh.html Linda Kearns MacWhinney
http://www.searcs-web.com/maloney.html Helena Maloney
http://www.searcs-web.com/marki.html Constance Markievicz
http://www.searcs-web.com/mellows.html Liam Mellowes
http://www.searcs-web.com/obrenn.html Lily O'Brien
http://www.searcs-web.com/obrien.html Nora Connolly O'Brien
http://www.searcs-web.com/obrien2.html William O'Brien
http://www.searcs-web.com/oceall.html Seán T. Ó Cellaigh
http://www.searcs-web.com/ohan.html Michael O'Hanrahan
http://www.searcs-web.com/pearse.html Padraig Pearse
http://www.searcs-web.com/plunkett4.html Grace Gifford Plunkett
http://www.searcs-web.com/plunkett2.html Joseph Mary Plunkett
http://www.searcs-web.com/ssheff1.html Francis Sheehy-Skeffington
http://www.searcs-web.com/ssheff2.html Hanna Sheehy-Skeffington
http://www.searcs-web.com/skinn.html Margaret Skinnider
http://www.searcs-web.com/white.html James White
Senate of Ireland, 1921
http://www.ark.ac.uk/elections/h1921.htm
'Voices of the Easter Rising'
http://www.bbc.co.uk/history/british/easterrising/radio/index_js.shtml
Women's History Project
www.nationalarchives.ie/wh/whp.html

Index